The book is visual and full of illustrations, pictures and real life examples which support the students' learning process. In this new edition the authors have succeeded in making the book even better through new examples and relevant updating of the previous good examples from Europe, Asia and the US. Also new and relevant research has been implemented.
Carl Borge-Andersen, BI Norwegian School of Management

This text benefits from a clear writing style and an up to date and contemporary perspective. The well chosen case studies highlight current trends and challenges in the field of OB. The structure of the book comprising a careful intertwining of theoretical concepts with up to date examples, makes it a very useful text both for undergraduate and postgraduate students.
Dr Vivienne Byers, Dublin Institute of Technology

Organizational Behaviour
2nd Edition

Organizational Behaviour
2nd Edition

**Ray French · Charlotte Rayner ·
Gary Rees · Sally Rumbles**

John Schermerhorn Jr
James Hunt
Richard Osborn

John Wiley & Sons, Ltd

BRIEF CONTENTS

CONTENTS

PART 2   INDIVIDUAL DIFFERENCES AND THEIR RELEVANCE TO WORK   73

Source: Sharon K. Parker, Uta K. Bindl and Karoline Strauss, *Making Things Happen: A Model of Proactive Motivation*, *Journal of Management*, 2010 36: 827 Originally published online 14 May 2010, Reprinted by Permission of SAGE Publications.

PART 3   MANAGING THE ORGANIZATION   239

PART 4   PEOPLE, PROCESSES AND PERFORMANCE   389

PART 5   CASE STUDIES   629

ABOUT THE AUTHORS

The authors all work in the Department of Human Resource and Marketing Management in The University of Portsmouth.

(From left to right...)

Dr Ray French is a Principal Lecturer in Organizational Behaviour. He has a particular interest in cross-cultural aspects of work, organization and managing people. He is the author of *Cross-Cultural Management in Work Organisations*, 2nd edtion (2010), CIPD: London. He is co-editor with Gary Rees of *Leading, Managing and Developing People* (2010) CIPD: London and is author and co-author of four chapters in this book. Ray has occupied a number of management roles at the University of Portsmouth and is currently Course Director of undergraduate degrees taught in Singapore and Hong Kong.

Charlotte Rayner is Professor of Human Resource Management. She has a particular interest in the topic of bullying at work and has been involved in research in this area since the mid-1990s when she completed the first major UK survey for the BBC. Charlotte has recently published a book, *Workplace Bullying: what we know, who is to blame and what can we do?*, with Cary Cooper and Helge Hoel. Charlotte is particularly interested in strategies to prevent bullying and other forms of negative behaviour.

Gary Rees is a Principal Lecturer and Director of Postgraduate Human Resource Management Programmes at the Portsmouth Business School. His recent publications include co-editing *Leading, Managing and Developing People* (2010), CIPD: London with Ray French, in which he authored and co-authored five chapters. Gary has consultancy experience within both private and public sectors and is an active member of the Portsmouth Chartered Institute of Personnel Development (CIPD). He is also a member of the British Psychological Society.

Sally Rumbles is a Senior Lecturer in Human Resource Management and Course Leader for the Undergraduate Human Resource Management Programmes at the Portsmouth Business School. She has co-authored two chapters, on recruitment and selection and employee relations, in *Leading, Managing and Developing People* (2010), CIPD: London edited by Gary Rees and Ray French. Sally has also co-authored two chapters, on equality, diversity and dignity at work, and grievance, discipline and absence in *Human Resource Management* (2009), edited by Sarah Gilmore and Steve Williams, Oxford University Press: Oxford. She has worked as a human resource manager in both the private and public sectors and is a member of the Chartered Institute of Personnel and Development (CIPD) and Fellow of the Higher Education Academy.

HOW TO USE THIS BOOK

The book is divided into five **Parts,** each with a chapter list and part introduction to help navigate the text.

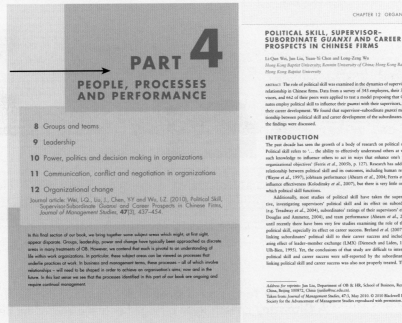

Each part ends with a full length **journal article** with associated questions.

Each chapter begins with an engaging **short vignette** that offers a snapshot of OB issues and trends in contemporary real-life situations.

The key **learning objectives** to be achieved are stated at the beginning of each chapter.

Figure 1.2: Organization and environment relationships.

Material resources are the technology, information, physical equipment and facilities, raw material and money that are necessary for an organization to produce some product or service.

Open systems transform human and physical resources received from their environment into goods and services that are then returned to the environment.

Of course, things can go wrong. An organization's survival depends on satisfying environmental demands. When the organization's goods and/or services are not well received by the environment, it will sooner or later have difficulty obtaining the resource inputs it needs to operate.

OB IN ACTION

Just as business outcomes have an impact on the business environment and society as a whole, world events can also influence business survival. The tourism industry was greatly affected by the 2004 Boxing Day tsunami and the October 2002 and 2005 terrorism attacks in Bali. Although initially the tourism industry in Indonesia and Malaysia slumped as a result of these events, the industry responded by applying survival strategies and some improved their performance as a direct result of refocusing the market. For example, after the 2002 bombings, the Indonesian tourism authorities and commercial providers actively promoted Bali to markets that, unlike Australia, did not have an emotional association with the Bali bombings. This resulted in a boost for Bali, where visitors from Singapore to Bali lifted from 17 666 in 2002 to 26 881 in 2003.[37]

Other tourism businesses in the Asia-Pacific region responded to the change in business environment.

After the Bali bombings, Australia promoted its destinations as 'safe' and the Philippines promoted its resorts as unaffected by the Boxing Day tsunami. Both countries seized upon the opportunity to attract tourists who might otherwise have travelled to Bali or the Malaysian coast.[28] Time will tell if these tourism businesses are able to sustain growth by attracting returning tourists in the future, or if loyal Bali and Malaysian coast patrons return to their previous preferred destinations.

MANAGERS IN ORGANIZATIONS

A manager is responsible for work that is accomplished through the performance contributions of one or more other people.

Now that we have examined some fundamental features of organizations, we can speak more precisely about what it means to be a manager. A manager is a person in an organization who is responsible for work that is accomplished through the performance contributions of one or more other people.

In many organizations the focus of both management research and practice is not so much on the manager as on the work team or unit. A work team or unit is a task-oriented group that includes a manager and his or her direct subordinates. Such groups are found in organizations of all types, whether small or large. Examples include departments in a retail store, divisions of a corporation, branches of a bank, wards in a hospital and teams in a manufacturing plant. Even university classes can be considered a work team; lecturers are their managers (they may prefer to use the term 'facilitators') and the students are team members. The study of such work teams has become a key area of OB research.

WHAT IS AN EFFECTIVE MANAGER?

Work teams or units are task-oriented groups that include a manager and his or her direct reports.

Task performance is the quality and quantity of work produced.

Human resource performance must be sustained if it is to have meaning; high performance should be sustainable. High levels of performance are affected by a manager's attention to a range of matters within the people management heading.

It is not easy to define what makes a manager an effective manager within a business context. The list of managerial competencies identified over the past few decades helps us understand more clearly the competencies required for effective management. However, such research also illustrates the difficulties in defining effective management because it is still hard to achieve expert consensus on what constitutes a basic core of competencies. It is even more difficult to find agreement on prioritized rankings of such competencies.[29] Many of the best-known writers in the management literature typically emphasize one managerial competence at the expense of all others. Fayol and Urwick have portrayed good managers as controllers.[30] This is a typical conclusion from the *classical school* of management in its assumption that managers should direct the work of others, in this case through formal mechanisms of control. The manager remains clearly in control while designing and monitoring structures within which employees carry out tasks and systems of work which are operated by workers. Later approaches to management (although the *human relations school* dates back as far as the 1930s), emphasize the important role of managing relationships.

Mintzberg[31] has drawn up a multifaceted concept of managers' work, identifying *interpersonal*, *informational* and *decisional* roles within the overall 'umbrella heading' of the term manager (Figure 1.3). Note that all *ten roles* set out by Mintzberg involve dealing with other people, even those that are not designated as interpersonal roles.

Fundamentally, any manager should seek two key results for a work unit or work team: task performance, which is defined by the quality and quantity of the work produced, or the services provided by the work unit and human resource performance, which involves the attraction and continuation of a capable workforce over time. This latter notion, while too often neglected, is extremely important. It is not enough for a work unit

---

OB in Action boxes provide thought-provoking examples drawn from wide-ranging work settings and international research.

All the **key terms** are defined in the margin of the text for easy reference. A **Glossary** collects them all together at the end of the book.

▶ COUNTERPOINT

Culture deteriorates in overcrowded prison[48]

An unannounced UK government inspection of Her Majesty's Prison at Leeds in Yorkshire in 2006 noted a deterioration in relationships between staff and prisoners since its last inspection. Specific problem areas highlighted by the visiting inspectors included:

* over a third of prisoners reported feeling unsafe; this figure rising to 43% for black and other minority ethnic prisoners;
* a high and mechanistic use of force;
* the segregation unit ran in a militaristic way, with insufficient support for prisoners at risk and an incident when an alleged assault on a prisoner had not been followed up;
* staff were heard referring to prisoners as 'bodies' or 'cons';
* black and ethnic minority prisoners continued to report 'undercover' racism and had no confidence in the race relations agenda. Fewer than half of those surveyed believed staff treated them with respect;
* there were only spaces for 60% of prisoners and prisoners without work could spend 23 hours in their cells.

Anne Owers, Her Majesty's Chief Inspector of Prisons, said:

'This inspection shows how difficult it is to sustain progress in a crowded inner-city local prison, where cultures are hard to change and governors are preoccupied with crisis management. Under such pressure, officers tend to revert to their comfort zone, and governors are preoccupied with crisis management. Managers were aware of the

task they faced, and conscious that some fundamental issues remained to be tackled However, achieving and sustaining lasting change will be difficult with current levels of overcrowding.'

Phil Wheatley, Director General of the Prison Service, said:

'The Chief Inspector makes it very clear that the main problems faced by HMP Leeds are exacerbated by the serious difficulties which overcrowding presents to busy local prisons. Leeds prison is working hard to address the feelings of insecurity experienced by prisoners and there is a very active safer prisons agenda currently in operation. The Governor is taking this agenda forward through projects such as the West Yorkshire Community Chaplains, which is working to deliver an inclusive approach to support prisoners and create a positive environment for black and ethnic minority prisoners.'

This 'Counterpoint' feature shows us that organizational culture is not only to be perceived in positive terms. Note also the impact of resource issues cited as having an impact both on the existing culture and attempts to change it. Consider the steps you would take if you were to embark on a further cultural change programme in this prison.

Figure 5.5: The management by objectives (MBO) process.

Employees must have freedom to carry out the required tasks; managers may have to carry out considerable coaching and counselling. As with other applied organizational behaviour programmes, managers should be aware of MBO's potential costs as well as its benefits.

EFFECTIVE MANAGER 5.2

Key issues for mutual goal setting in an MBO programme

* What must be done? Start with higher level goals, job descriptions stating tasks to be performed, outcomes expected, necessary supplies and equipment and so on.
* How will performance be measured? Time, money or physical units are often used to measure performance. If the job is more subjective, emphasize behaviours or actions believed to lead to success.
* What is the performance standard? Start with previous performance or the average performance of others doing this job. Where these

measures do not exist, use mutual supervisor–subordinate judgement and discussion.
* What are the deadlines for the goals? Discuss deadlines in terms of daily, weekly or longer terms.
* What is the relative importance of the goals? Not all goals are equally important. The manager and employee should decide the goal ranking together.
* How difficult are the goals? Watch especially for high task complexity and multiple goals. Come up with a clearly agreed decision.

Despite substantial research based on case studies of MBO success, such research has not always been rigorously controlled and it reports mixed results.[49] In general, and as an application of goal-setting theory, MBO has much to offer. But it is not easy to start and keep going. MBO may also need to be implemented organization-wide if it is to work well.[50]

KEY PERFORMANCE INDICATORS

The concept of individual goal setting has been further developed over the past few years to introduce the concept of key performance indicators (KPIs) – standards against which individual and organizational performance can be measured.

Such measurement is a step in the benchmarking process taken by companies wanting to achieve superior performance in a formal and structured way. High performance has

---

Counterpoint boxes encourage critical discussion of OB theories through consideration of negative work situations and alternative perspectives.

Effective Manager boxes include practical tips on managing in the real world.

Research in OB boxes link to a full journal article either at the end of the Part, or on the companion website at **www.wileyeurope.com/college/french**

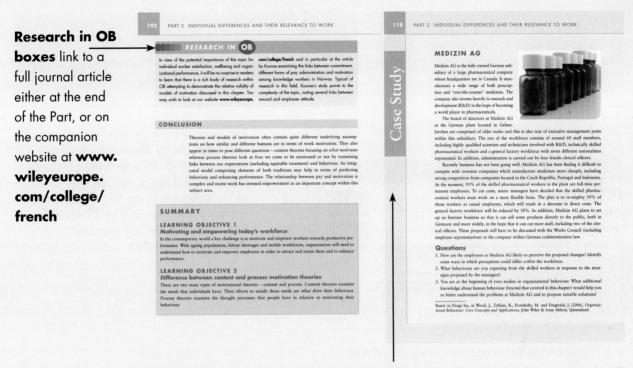

Case Studies at the end of each chapter and in Part 5 illustrate innovative and revealing aspects of OB from companies worldwide.

At the end of each chapter there is a **Summary** of the learning objectives that have been covered.

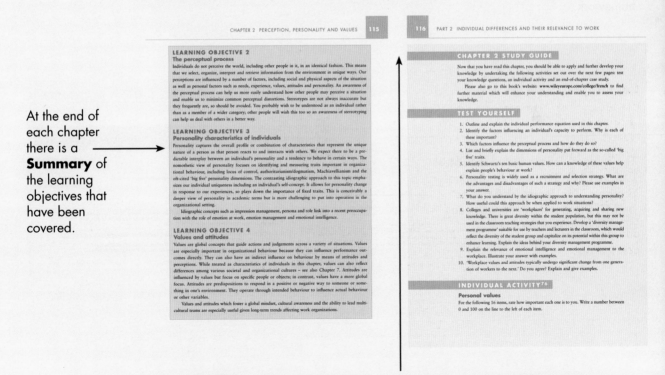

The **Study Guide** at the end of each chapter includes **Test Yourself questions** and an **Individual Activity**, which questions students' values and opinions.

Lecturer and student companion websites accompany this book at www.wileyeurope.com/college/french. All materials are available to lecturers in Blackboard and WebCT.

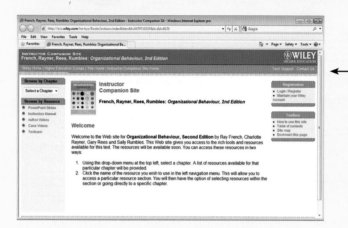

The instructor companion website includes an **Instructor's Manual** with visual overviews and discussion topics, class activities and suggested answers to all of the questions in the text. The site also contains a comprehensive **Electronic Test Bank** as well as editable **PowerPoint slides**.

A comprehensive video package, including **Case Study videos** and **Author Lecture videos**, is available for lecturers to use in the classroom or set as homework.

The student website includes Self-test Quizzes to test student's individual progress. The **Journal Articles** and **Glossary** from the text can also be found on the site.

PREFACE

We have been pleased to receive many positive comments on the first UK and European edition of this book, published in 2008, and have taken on board suggestions for improvement to this second edition. As before, this version draws on best-selling US editions written by Professors John Schermerhorn, James Hunt and Richard Osborn, and we have again adapted material from the Australasian edition authored by Professor Jack Wood, Dr Rachid Zeffane, Michele Fromholz, Dr Retha Wiesner and Dr Andrew Creed. The Australasian edition was the first to present subject content in a format which allowed for coverage within both one-semester and year-long teaching and learning patterns, and we have continued this approach in our own edition.

Previous versions of this book have been designed to introduce readers to new realities of work and knowledge-based organizations in the early 21st century. In particular, *Organizational Behaviour* has stressed the importance of a thorough understanding of OB frameworks and practices for existing and aspiring managers – and indeed all other workers – to help them to meet increasingly challenging performance targets. In highlighting challenges associated with the emergence of knowledge-based organizations and an increasingly 'globalized' business environment, previous editions of *Organizational Behaviour* have brought out the inherently relevant and topical nature of OB. The American and Australian authors have developed the themes of relevance and topicality most successfully, due in part to the lucidity of their writing style, considered use of case studies and other examples and by including an extensive and diverse range of learning resources, thereby encouraging readers to reflect on how OB models and concepts touch their own lives. We trust that these major strengths of the previous editions will also be apparent in this UK and European version.

There have been significant developments in business over the past three years, most notably the financial crisis which has affected much of the world. This dramatic development highlights how our subject area can be quickly and profoundly affected by external events and those who manage people often find themselves in the 'front line' of crises. In this edition we have included new *vignettes* and other learning activities which focus on OB in bad times – while hoping that the context of future editions will be sunnier.

What are the distinctive features of our contribution to what is already an extensive body of OB literature? In preparing this version, we have set out to marry academic rigour with relevance, within a perspective that stresses organizational success. We realize from talking to our own students that value for money will also guide readers in their choice of book. The following points summarize some of the themes underlying this book, which we hope you will find useful as you approach the study of OB.

Organizational Behaviour is a relatively new subject area but has already developed some central and enduring tenets. Equally, some theories and concepts have proven to be transitory, possessing a limited 'shelf life', while other seemingly radical departures from existing thought can, on closer examination, be revealed to be more akin to 'old wine in new bottles'. The challenging task for students is to appreciate what is changing and what is enduring within OB. Given the undoubtedly rapid and profound changes affecting work organizations, are some underlying themes in OB still valid? We will highlight the extent of deep and profound change, as opposed to more cosmetic modifications in the subject area, throughout this book. A historical perspective, outlining the developmental nature of much OB material can help us greatly in this regard.

A related theme centres on the *applicability* of knowledge derived from OB. We take the view that effective interventions, based on OB models and theories, can lead both to employees' needs and expectations being met and also to enhanced organizational performance in 'bottom line' terms. But equally a quizzical view of the relevance of some concepts is advisable, together with the need to maintain a balanced perspective on topics. This is, in any case, necessary as mutually-exclusive theories on aspects of people at work are a characteristic of Organizational Behaviour. A rounded approach, which we aim to provide in all subsequent chapters, should result in a deeper awareness of both the overall subject and individual topic areas. Our '*Counterpoint*' feature, included in all chapters, will alert you to negative occurrences within workplaces and alternative political perspectives: this should also help promote a balanced view. We also emphasize the critical importance of ethics in the subject area and this aspect is brought out in all chapters as it is embedded in OB topics.

All too often the study of OB can move swiftly from one topic to another, focusing on surface summaries of theories and models. Sometimes there is little attention given to the actual research from which such views emerge. In this book we seek to rectify this deficiency by including a number of research articles. Four are distributed throughout the text (one at the end of each of the first four parts of the book) and another eight can be found on our website: www.wileyeurope.com/college/french. You may wish to look at these articles in order to gain an in-depth view of how OB knowledge is arrived at. Note, for example, the research methods used in the studies referred to – are they valid in your view? Questions regarding how 'scientific' the study of OB is – and what we can, in any case, infer from that term when seeking to understand human attitudes and behaviour – are also addressed in Chapter 1.

We have sought to apply OB concepts squarely within a 21st century work and organizational context. Organizations have been subject to very significant changes within the last twenty years, and in some cases, working arrangements bear scant resemblance to those experienced by previous generations. We have already referred to the impact of the global financial crisis which took hold in 2008. There are other deep-rooted trends which are important. For example, remote or teleworking patterns mean that many of us spend as much, or more, time working from home – or on trains and planes – than we do in a conventional office. How do we apply theories of motivation and leadership (to take just two topics) in such a situation? Many organizations have also sought to outsource their operations, developing so-called network structures, far removed from the classical 20th century bureaucratic form. How do we understand these new organizational arrangements in terms of their structure and culture? We will address these contemporary issues consistently in relevant chapters.

A focus on contemporary trends may lead us to question the value of existing prescriptive models of human behaviour in the workplace and instead highlight *contingency* approaches – the overall conclusion that no one academic theory or practical method can always work well – rather it will all depend on the specific circumstances. Such approaches are not new – they emerged in the field of leadership in the 1950s for example. However, they may be judged to be especially applicable in such a rapidly changing context. One important area in this regard is national culture. We no longer need to migrate to encounter people from different cultural backgrounds at work. The multicultural make-up of workforces in cities such as London, Amsterdam and Berlin testifies to this fact. But most OB knowledge emerges from an Anglo-American context. There is, of course, nothing wrong with this *per se*. However, we might legitimately question whether motivation theories developed in the US can be applied to Chinese, Indian or Spanish workers. At the very least we should consider applying contingency – or flexible models – in new situations. We will argue, for example, that, increasingly, workers have changed *psychological contracts* – see Chapters 1 and 2 – meaning that they will need to be managed in new and imaginative ways at work. A flexible contingency approach is adopted throughout this book.

We have sought, finally, to put together a book which can be used in a one-semester course, but equally one in which the content can be stretched to encompass a longer period of study. As such, we trust that this book will not be too unwieldy and contain extraneous material. Please also refer to our website: www.wileyeurope.com/college/french which contains additional exercises and articles. Most importantly, please do not regard this book as the sum resource for your study of Organizational Behaviour. We hope that it will be the springboard to a lifetime's interest in a fascinating area which affects us all.

Dr Ray French
July 2010

ACKNOWLEDGEMENTS AND PHOTO CREDITS

The author team would like to acknowledge the contributions of the academics who have compiled the US and Australasian editions of this book: Professor John R. Schermerhorn, Professor James G. (Jerry) Hunt, Professor Richard N. Osborn, Professor Jack Wood, Dr Rachid Zeffane, Michele Fromholz, Dr Retha Wiesner and Dr Andrew Creed. We would also like to thank the academics who have contributed to the case studies contained in Part 5 of this book: Val Morrison of Southern Cross University; Tony Dawson of Liverpool John Moores University; Barry R. Armandi of SUNY-Old Westbary; Franklin Ramsoomair of Wilfred Laurier University. We would also like to acknowledge the work of the late Professor Iain Mangham who devised the scenario which formed the basis of our Channel 6 TV case study.

We have continued to benefit from an excellent working relationship with the editorial, development and production team at John Wiley in Chichester. For this second edition we would like to thank Steve Hardman, Ellie Wilson and Barbara Denuelle for their help throughout the writing process. Looking further back we acknowledge the contribution of Sarah Booth who first envisaged a European edition of the book and encouraged its development. Deborah Egleton, Anneli Mockett and Emma Cooper also helped greatly in steering the first edition towards completion. We are also grateful for the particularly constructive feedback from reviewers of the draft book and trust that we have responded to points made in the final version.

Finally, we would like to thank the following reviewers:

Dr Patrick Tissington, Aston University, UK;
Carl Borge-Andersen, BI Norwegian School of Management, Norway;
Ms Yoke Eng Tan, Canterbury Christ Church University, UK;
Dr Daniel King, Nottingham Trent University, UK;
Vivienne Byers, Dublin Institute of Technology, Republic of Ireland;
Professor Brian Terry, European Business School, Regents College London, UK;
Dr David Banner, University of Westminster, UK.

PHOTO CREDITS

All effort has been made to trace and acknowledge ownership of copyright. The publisher would be glad to hear from any copyright holders whom it has not been possible to contact. All images not listed below are provided by Shutterstock:

Chapter 1

The "Sunday Times 100 Best Companies 2010" logo. Used with permission.
The "Made with Passion" logo is reproduced with the kind permission of The Body Shop International, Plc

Chapter 5

London Marriott Hotel Lobby, Marble Arch. Reproduced by permission. www.marriott.co.uk

PART 1

INTRODUCTION

1 What is organizational behaviour?
Journal article: Baker-McClearn, D. Greasley, K. Dale, J. and Griffith, F. (2010),
    Absence management and presenteeism: the pressures on employees to
    attend work and the impact of attendance on performance, *Human Resource
    Management Journal,* **20**(3), 311–328.

Managing people in work organizations is frequently identified as a critically important element in terms of achieving an organization's aims and working towards its ultimate success. However, people can behave in unpredictable and seemingly contrary ways, so the management of people at work, while both interesting and rewarding, is also a challenging area. Organizational behaviour (OB) focuses on the behaviour of individuals and groups at work and seeks to provide explanations for such behaviour through a wide range of topics – which we will go on to explore in this book.

In this first part of our book we aim to underpin the subject matter set out in subsequent chapters by highlighting some broader issues relating to OB. We will explore the nature of this subject area by identifying differing definitions of OB and will also examine some of its underlying traditions and perspectives. In this context, one important issue is the extent to which findings from OB research can be regarded as valid in academic terms – how far can and/or should OB be regarded as 'scientific'? We furthermore aim to signal some key trends and issues affecting contemporary organizations and, in so doing, show how an understanding of OB can illuminate the reality of work organizations – to the benefit of everyone connected with them.

CHAPTER 1

What is organizational behaviour?

LEARNING OBJECTIVES

After studying this chapter you should be able to:

- understand the nature and scope of organizational behaviour (OB) as a subject area
- comprehend some of the theoretical traditions and political perspectives which inhabit the field of OB
- discuss the role of people management in fostering effective performance within organizations
- identify some of the key issues affecting organizations today
- explain why organizations' members, including managers, can benefit from a thorough understanding of OB principles and insights.

A GREAT PLACE TO WORK?

Since 2001 the London-based *Sunday Times* has produced an annual list of the '100 best companies to work for'. Each year the newspaper publishes the results of a large-scale survey highlighting examples of organizational policies and practices that, it is claimed, contribute to high levels of satisfaction among employees. The underlying question posed in the survey is what makes organizations great to work for? The survey has separate categories for 'small', 'mid-sized' and 'large' companies. Organizations are nominated for participation in the survey and data are mainly obtained via employee opinion questionnaires, although there is also input from the company itself. In 2010, 275 000 employees contributed to the survey. As we will see, the 2010 survey

also included 45 000 public sector workers and a new category – the best places to work in the public sector.

The key premise that underlies the survey, and resulting list of great places to work, is that employee satisfaction (at least in their working lives) is linked to specific areas. These are listed below and are, we propose, central to the academic field of OB. Another critically important proposal that we will discuss – and in some cases question – throughout this book is that worker satisfaction is an important factor influencing organizations' performance.

The *Sunday Times* survey methodology seeks to unravel workers' perceptions of eight factors (or key areas). Work organizations score strongly, and hence feature in the upper echelons of the list of best places to work, if employees 'exhibit strength'[1] in the following broad topic areas:

- *leadership* – under this heading workers are asked to give their views on the company head, senior managers and the quality of leadership provided by these individuals;
- *wellbeing* – this factor encompasses workers' perceived stress levels and in particular their work/home life balance;
- *my manager* – recognizing that senior managers may have little or no day-to-day contact with workers, this category records people's feelings about their 'immediate' supervisor(s) or manager(s);
- *my team* – this aspect explores employees' feelings concerning close work colleagues at a similar level in terms of role and seniority;
- *fair deal* – here workers express their feelings on their pay and other benefits within the broad area of remuneration and reward;
- *giving something back* – workers are asked to comment on how much they believe their company 'puts back' into society and more specifically the local community in which they are based;
- *my company* – the questioning in this case centres on feelings towards the employing organization, as opposed to co-workers;

- *personal growth* – employees record their views on the extent to which they feel challenged by their own job, whether their skills and other attributes are fully used and on their perceived scope for advancement.

Source: Rules of Engagement, *Sunday Times*, 14 March 2010.

The eight elements making up the *Sunday Times* survey and subsequent findings are intrinsic to the subject of OB. Questions on the nature of effective supervision (or empowerment), team working and what really motivates people at work lie at the very heart of much research in OB – although, as we will show in this book, OB is a broad area of study that often extends far beyond the workplace. Issues addressed within OB should be of personal interest to all of us in our possible roles as managers or other workers *within* organizations or as external stakeholders; for example as shareholders, customers, clients or neighbours of organizations. We are all affected by organizations throughout our lives: health providers play an important role in our birth, most of us are educated within institutions such as schools and universities, we can spend large parts of our lives as employees and our friends and relatives will be concerned with the service provided by funeral directors when we die. OB is highly relevant to all our lives, both at crucial life-changing points and on a day-to-day level.

We also frequently encounter the view that the study of OB is important in business terms, in that insights can be readily applied within organizations in order to help improve performance. As such, OB can routinely be found as part of a business and management studies curriculum. This *managerial focus* will be analysed, along with other perspectives on OB, later in the chapter.

As noted earlier, the 2010 *Sunday Times* survey was the first version to include data from the UK public sector. In overall terms, workers in the public sector sample gave positive ratings on the *fair deal* and *giving something back* headings. However in other areas, particularly *leadership* and *wellbeing*, the public sector was seen to be falling behind.[2] What was described as 'an ill wind of change' threatened public sector wellbeing, prompted by planned spending cuts formulated to deal with the UK's budget deficit. It appeared likely that managers in the public services would join their counterparts in the private sector in managing in difficult times; at the very least having to perform effectively with less resources. However the 2010 publication highlighted several examples of good practice in people management.

The top-rated public sector organization in the 2010 *Sunday Times* survey was the ACPO (Association of Chief Police Officers) Criminal Records Office, based in Fareham on England's South Coast. It should be noted firstly that this office had a culture of success. The Criminal Records Office had recently helped in securing convictions of global drug smugglers in addition to an already successful record in other murder and sexual offences cases. A sense of achievement underpinned morale in the office. High scores were recorded on all eight categories, with no other organization scoring higher for having senior managers who were perceived as listening rather than just telling people what to do. In the *my manager* category, Detective Superintendent Gary Linton came in for plenty of praise with 85% of respondents trusting him and 77% describing him as inspirational. Overall a youthful entrepreneurial culture pervaded the office.

It might be thought that the ACPO office described above had certain in-built advantages as a young and growing work unit where people felt a sense of excitement in their work due to its dramatic nature.

However, the value of good people management was also seen in the case of Sevenoaks District Council in Kent whose work involved the provision of more routine services over a longer time period.

A high proportion of Sevenoaks Council employees were aware of what is expected of them (which they valued), believed that they were set realistic deadlines and were happy with their work/home balance. Regular meetings had been set up by Chief Executive Robin Hales, where people were encouraged to give feedback on issues such as budget savings and communications. Most workers can do flexi-time, so combining work and home duties more easily. A diverse range of benefits included childcare vouchers and subsidized sports facilities. In overall terms this council scored well in the *leadership*, *good management* and *wellbeing* categories.

The picture of work organizations as essentially integrated and harmonious entities (as exemplified by these two examples from the UK public sector) should be viewed with some caution. Within the *Sunday Times* survey there is evidence of negative indicators, even amongst the '20 best big companies'. For example, there was a significant fall in employee perceptions of wellbeing across the nine-year period covered by the survey, with increasing levels of workplace stress evident, together with difficulty expressed in reconciling work, social and domestic commitments, in part due to a long-hours culture. The British psychologist Oliver James[3] has counselled against the negative effects of this phenomenon, which he interestingly characterizes as an Anglo-American problem. One commentator on an earlier *Sunday Times* survey noted furthermore that: 'the data did not reveal any information covering some very important workplace issues such as race, bullying and harassment, sickness policies, absenteeism rates, average salaries or trade union involvement.'[4] However, a preoccupation with fostering a sense of belonging does seem to work for both ACPO and Sevenoaks Council, reflecting many of the fundamental ingredients of a successful organization: its members are engaged and happy with their task; ideas are shared; workers are supported; and the organization is delivering worthwhile services. In the private sector this last focus may centre more on products that satisfy customers who in turn have an important role in making companies profitable.

Throughout this book you will learn about the complex field of OB – what people and groups do in organizations, and why. We will place a particular emphasis on identifying those management skills that extend beyond task-related competencies. Technical ability will not be sufficient if you wish to be a successful manager in the twenty-first century. The attributes needed to be at least a *potentially* effective manager in the organizations of today and tomorrow instead reflect the need to ensure that the work experiences of others are both productive and satisfying. According to Clegg *et al.*[5] 'managers today are expected to have some of the skills of a workplace psychologist, therapist, and counsellor and, as such, need a basic understanding of psychological principles and theories to help them in the complex task of managing people'.

Existing or aspiring managers also need to be aware of the profound changes taking place in the business environment. Bratton *et al.*[6] identify the following significant influences on organizations since 1985:

- political/economic changes, for example the implosion of Eastern European communist regimes, the expansion of the EU and NAFTA and the emergence of new major economic players such as China and India;

- technological advances in microelectronics and the rapid spread of the Internet;
- the advent of flexible and 'virtual' organizational arrangements;
- structural economic change resulting (at least in the European context) in increasing prevalence of knowledge-based organizations.

We might add the emergence of increasingly diverse workforces – in part a consequence of globalization – and some significant shifts in how employers and employees view each other. These types of changes require managers and other organizational members who are committed to learning about both classical and emerging themes in OB and who can then put them into effect. We hope this book will help you along that path.

Questions

1. Look again at the eight factors or key areas listed in the *Sunday Times* survey. Which are the three most important to you and why? Rank them.
2. Identify organizations that in your experience are not 'great places to work'. Give reasons for your conclusions.

These questions are intended to generate thought and discussion prior to you commencing your study of OB. We will refer to issues raised in greater detail throughout this book.

WHAT IS OB?

Although there is broad agreement on the subject matter covered by OB there are some illuminating differences in actual definitions or conceptions of the term. Consider, for example, the varying nuances of meaning contained in two remarks taken from leading OB textbooks. The first is this: 'Organizational behaviour is concerned with the study of people within an organizational setting. It involves the understanding, prediction and control of human behaviour.'[7] Contrast this with the statement that organizational behaviour should be viewed: 'first and foremost as practices of organizing and meaning-making, involving thinking, feeling and acting, that are not so dissimilar to everyday life.'[8] The differences can be related to the philosophical stances taken by the authors. The first statement is explicitly managerial; the second seems to point to shifting and constructed notions of reality, while focusing on the subjective experience of organizational actors.

Organizational behaviour *is the study of individuals and groups in organizations.*

For our purposes **organizational behaviour** is defined as *the study of individuals and groups in organizations*. This is a stripped-down definition that identifies the core elements of the subject while allowing readers to take insights and evidence from the OB 'knowledge bank' and to use these in a variety of contexts and from eclectic perspectives. While the overall tone of this book is moderately managerial (we welcome situations where the goals of employers and employees coincide and happy workers contribute to legitimate organizational success), we also acknowledge alternative critical perspectives. The experiences of many workers are in reality often repugnant and we will refer to negative occurrences, possibly caused by unethical business conduct, within our 'Counterpoint' features.

Organizational behaviour is a composite subject – often regarded as multidisciplinary – which draws on individual subject disciplines such as **psychology**, **sociology** and **anthropology**. There are also links to other social sciences such as economics and political science. Often the subjects are interrelated and it is necessary to draw on this variety of scholarly vantage points to build concepts, theories and understanding about human behaviour in organizations.

Psychology *is the study of mental life with a particular focus on the individual's thought processes and behaviour.*

Sociology *is the study of social structures and patterns, both in whole societies and subgroups.*

Anthropology *is the comparative study of different societies or tribes.*

OB *IN ACTION*

Immigrants have boosted UK growth

A report in the British newspaper, *The Independent*, in August 2006,[9] cast doubt on some popularly received 'commonsense' perceptions of the migration of eastern European workers into the UK and the effects of this phenomenon. The author concluded that, according to research from the Ernst & Young Item Club, 'the stereotypical image of Polish builders and plumbers has been blown apart by research showing that one in three immigrants from eastern Europe are taking up office managerial posts. The stereotype of the Polish plumber is well wide of the mark.' The research indicated that nearly one-third of eastern European entrants to the UK labour market in 2005 took up positions in administration, business and management services compared with 4% joining the construction industry. This research showed that approximately 300 000 citizens of the 10 countries that joined the European Union in 2004 have since taken new jobs in the UK. The item noted several positive aspects and consequences of the migration pattern, concluding that in 2006 interest rates were half a per cent lower than they would otherwise have been without the influx of new workers, suggesting also that this immigrant workforce would boost growth by 0.2% in 2006 and 0.4% in 2007.

The first point to note when considering this 'OB in Action' box is the topical nature of OB material. Global trends in the period from 1995 to 2008 led to much attention being focused on the phenomenon of migrant workers and the implications for managing people. However, the movement of workers from one culture to another has diminished somewhat since the onset of the global financial crisis and ensuing recession. The then UK Government Immigration Minister Phil Woolas claimed, in January 2010, for example, that half the incoming Polish workforce had left the UK since 2004.[10] We should recognize therefore that some OB preoccupations may change with time – although others, such as effective communication, are constant themes.

In academic terms the phenomenon of eastern European migration into the UK can be approached and understood from a variety of vantage points within OB, thereby supporting our conception of its eclectic and multidisciplinary nature. First, the issue is amenable to analysis from a *psychological perspective*, focusing, for example, on the perceptions of hosts and incoming workers and possible feelings of culture shock experienced by migrating eastern European workers. However, one could also approach the topic from a *sociological* viewpoint. Sociology takes as its focus for study societies and wider social groupings. Elements of the new migration pattern that could be studied from this viewpoint include cultural differences made real via globalization, power issues both at micro-organizational and macro-social level (see Chapter 10) and change issues (covered in Chapter 12). In all cases it would be entirely inadequate (and wrong) to focus on any one society by adopting an ethnocentric stance. For example, if significant migration has occurred from Poland to the UK, it is felt appropriate to focus on the impact in *both* societies.

Organizational behaviour is unique in its focus on applying diverse insights to create better understanding and management of human behaviour in organizations. Among the special characteristics of OB are its:

- *Applied focus.* The ultimate goals of the field are to help people and organizations achieve high performance levels and to help ensure that all members of organizations achieve satisfaction from their task contributions and work experiences. A concern to locate OB material within a practical orientation pervades this book. Nonetheless the effects of using OB with management interventions are by no means easy to quantify. Grey (2009) goes further in claiming that managerial analyses of organizations: 'for all their desire to speak effectively to the world of practice have consistently failed to come up with anything of much use to managers and others, a fact for which they are consistently criticized by others and over which they themselves persistently agonize.'[11] We hope that material presented in this book will not lend itself to this degree of suspicion, although we recognize some issues of credibility in this respect. Note, for example, the reaction of a manager who had commissioned a knowledge transfer project from the authors' own university. In acknowledging the success of the project in 'bottom-line' terms, he recorded that he 'imagined they'd be a bunch of theorists who couldn't run a hamburger stall, but the work they've done for us has given a major boost to our productivity.' The authors are academics – although one of us has run a candyfloss stall – however we are concerned to show the potential of OB in business terms and in some cases demonstrable actual benefits.

A contingency approach in OB identifies how situations can be understood and managed in ways that appropriately respond to their unique characteristics or circumstances.

- *Contingency orientation.* Rather than assume that there is a universal way in which to manage people and organizations, OB scholars have, from the 1960s onwards, tended to adopt a **contingency approach**.[12] That is, they recognize that behaviour may vary systematically depending on the circumstances and the people involved. For example, writers in the OB field increasingly recognize that 'cultural differences' among people may affect the way theories and concepts of management apply in different countries.[13] Management practices cannot simply be transferred from one part of the world to another without considering the cultural implications of the different settings in which they are to be applied.

- *Emphasis on rigorous study.* Organizational behaviour is highly relevant to all of us and is an accessible subject in that we have our own preformed views – not necessarily based on experience – on such questions as how workers can be effectively motivated or how to assess other people's personalities. This very relevance, which enhances many students' enjoyment of the subject, contains certain dangers. There is, for example, a tendency to regard the study of people in work organizations as akin to commonsense. The implication here is that knowledge in this area of study is obvious and unambiguous. Academics studying and researching in OB areas have felt a particular responsibility therefore to conduct their work in a rigorous and systematic way. So-called **commonsense thinking** is, of course, frequently flawed and based on misperceptions or even disinformation. Research on leadership and human resource management more generally in Germany[14] has revealed that the system of co-determination (or joint decision making) endemic within that country has led to a typically consultative style being adopted when managing people. This may be far removed from the preconceptions that many people may have concerning preferred German leadership styles, particularly if these views have been influenced by hostile and prejudiced media reporting – this is especially true in the UK. At any rate it is incumbent on researchers in OB to conduct open-minded studies that capture the *reality* of working life as opposed to relying on possibly inaccurate, stereotypical and outdated viewpoints as drivers of their work. As students of OB you are entitled to expect that knowledge in the field has been obtained via sound methods resulting from fair-minded enquiry.

> **Commonsense thinking** *is apparently obvious or assumed analysis of OB topics, without reference to rigorous study or evidence, which can result in false conclusions.*

There is a tradition within OB which uses – and believes one can legitimately use – natural scientific methods (as found in physics or chemistry) to develop and empirically test generalizations about behaviour in organizations. This idea is often referred to as **positivism**. The three key characteristics of positivist OB research and study are: the controlled and systematic process of data collection; careful testing of the proposed explanations; and acceptance of only explanations that can be scientifically verified.

One example of how this philosophical approach can work in reality is found in the work of Hendrick.[15] Hendrick conducted experimental-style research that compared samples of experienced and inexperienced aircraft pilots when normal control stick conditions were reversed. In other words when pilots would normally move the stick forward to ascend and back to descend, these controls were reversed from the norm and a similar change was made to the left/right turn instruments. The experiment was (prudently) carried out in a flight simulator and revealed clear statistically relevant

> **Positivism** *is the view that social sciences such as OB can, and should, be studied in the same way as natural sciences like physics, using similar methods with a view to predicting and controlling behaviour and performance.*

The **interpretivist** tradition within OB believes that research into human behaviour should incorporate the subject's understanding of their own and other people's behaviour and the meanings attached to actions. Research within this tradition typically uses qualitative methods specific to social sciences.

Participant observation is a method of study which involves the researcher becoming a member of the group – either overtly or via 'undercover' involvement – that they are studying.

Focus groups are a form of qualitative research method in which a group of people are asked about their attitudes towards particular items or issues.

Discourse involves ways of presenting and understanding any facet of the world via ideas, assumptions, vocabulary and actions. In this way reality is framed, thereby informing people's understanding and behaviour.

differences in performance. More experienced pilots made significantly more errors than their inexperienced counterparts. This finding was the result of entrenched learning and habit formation, which made experienced pilots less able on average to adapt to new conditions. The experiment can be firmly located within the positivist tradition. The research was predicated on a *hypothesis* – itself based on actual events (in this case air crashes). The hypothesis was tested using experimental conditions and the researchers were mindful of other variables (such as age of the pilots) confounding the results. Results were tested and verified through replication of the study. There is also a clear practical benefit to the study, for example in the design of training programmes when new aircraft types are introduced. The data also contribute to knowledge in OB – here in the topic of learning, which we address in Chapter 3.

It should be acknowledged though that positivist-style research such as that illustrated above is comparatively rare in OB. More common are qualitative methods that do not seek to lead to general theories or even laws, but instead attempt to capture the meanings that individuals give to their actions and experiences. This approach is known as the **interpretivist** school of thought. It has a long tradition within the social sciences and is particularly associated with the work of Max Weber (1864–1920). Weber used the term *verstehen* – translated from the German as intrinsic understanding – and believed that research into people's behaviour should address the subjects' understanding of their own behaviour and that of other people and should also address the meaning(s) that they attach to actions. This tradition necessarily promotes methods of study that do not attempt to emulate the natural sciences. Instead we find observation, **participant observation** and, most recently, **focus groups**. Proponents of these methods claim that they are well placed to capture a deep understanding of behaviour and indeed people's inner lives – those thoughts and feelings that do not demonstrably result in particular patterns of behaviour or indeed actions *per se*.

In 2006, Ward and Winstanley conducted a study exploring the experiences of sexual minorities in a unit and specific shifts or *watches* within the UK fire service.[16] The chief method employed in the study involved the formation of focus groups of workers from that organization. The focus groups were invited to discuss work-related stories and experiences presented by gay men and lesbians. In this way the study identified habitual ways of working in the fire service via an unravelling of the everyday vocabulary, signs and symbols – what social scientists term **discourse** – used in those workplaces, which determined or *framed* reality there. Such language and symbols impacted on the experiences of gay men and lesbians within the fire service. As sexual orientation is seen as invisible, unlike other areas of diversity, some gay workers had experienced feelings of isolation in a work setting that stressed and promoted a strong subculture at workplace or watch level. It is unlikely that the insightful and illuminating data that emerged from this study – which could plausibly inform management actions in future – would have been obtained via more quantitative or impersonal methods; the subject matter here is inherently linked to the methods used in the research study.

RESEARCH IN OB

Throughout this book we will stress that insights from OB can inform our understanding of work organizations and that concepts, theories and models deriving from the subject are superior to commonsense thinking. One reason for this conclusion lies in the rich tradition of research study in OB. At the end of each part of the book we have presented one research-based journal article in full, to give you a sense of the type of work carried out by academics working in this area. There are also additional journal articles on our website at **www.wileyeurope.com/college/french** that we will point you to throughout the text. At this point, you may wish to look at the article by Baker-McClearn et al. on absence management (at the end of Part 1, on pages 52–72) and the specific questions we have added to the article. Note, in particular, the combination of quantitative (survey) and qualitative (in-depth interviews) methods that these authors found necessary in order to research their chosen topic.

THE RELEVANCE OF OB

Organizational behaviour is not a static discipline. Managers are constantly seeking new insights and ideas to improve their effectiveness. Maybe you have already heard of some of these concepts – the learning organization, the virtual workplace and knowledge management, to name just a few. The study of OB is improving our understanding of old and new concepts alike, including such issues as stress, emotional intelligence and instinctive drive. You will learn about these as you progress through this book.

Organizational behaviour should help managers both deal with and learn from their workplace experiences. Managers who understand organizational behaviour are better prepared to know what to look for in work situations, to understand what they find and to take (or help others to take) the required action.

Effective managers need to understand the people they rely on for the performance of their unit. Each person, team/group and organization is complex and unique but the performance of an individual, team, group or organization depends on their capacity to work, willingness to work and opportunity to work. This concept can be summarized by the **performance equation** (Figure 1.1). The performance equation views performance as a combination of personal and/or group attributes, the work effort people make and the organizational support they receive.

Performance equation: *job performance = attributes × work effort × organizational support.*

| Job performance | = | attributes | × | work effort | × | organizational support |

Figure 1.1: The performance equation.

This equation can be applied to the three different units of analysis that form the structure of this book: individual, group/team and organization. The multiplication signs indicate that all three factors must be present for high performance to be achieved. This means that each factor should be maximized for each of the three units of analysis in work settings if the maximum level of accomplishment is to be realized. Every manager should be capable of understanding how these three factors, acting either alone or in combination, affect performance. We will use this equation as the theoretical guide for much of the material presented in this book. Part 2 looks at individual behaviour and performance. In Chapter 2 we will address individual attributes required to generate performance capacity; Chapters 3 and 4 deal with the topics of learning and motivation respectively showing how these can generate a willingness to perform. In Part 3 of the book, entitled *Managing the Organization,* we point to how organizations can provide individuals with the best opportunity to perform through innovative job design (Chapter 5), and go on to consider features of organizations that impact on people working there; namely organizational structure and design (Chapter 6) and organizational culture (Chapter 7). Part 4 of the book begins by examining the issue of organizational performance from a group/team perspective in Chapter 8. We then go on to explore a number of other very important organizational processes via an examination of the diverse topics of leadership, power, communication and change (Chapters 9–12). Even though these concepts are presented in different parts and chapters of this book, they are highly related. Remember that the multiplication sign in the performance equation indicates that all three factors (attributes, work effort and organizational support) must be present to gain a high level of performance.

For practitioners, the performance equation raises the question of whether performance is predictable. It is suggested that cognitive ability, or intelligence, is a reasonable predictor of job performance.[17] However, many human resource managers would argue that additional testing is required to ensure a good fit between capability and expected performance. Over the past few years the concept of **emotional intelligence** (EI or EQ) has surfaced, sparking hopes for creating another way to predict performance. Emotional intelligence is defined as a form of social intelligence that allows us to monitor and shape our emotions and those of others. Daniel Goleman, closely associated with the concept, suggests that *emotional competence* is a learned capability, based on emotional intelligence, which is associated with outstanding work performance. In these domains EI is considered to be a competency for performance. For example, people with a high level of emotional intelligence would be competent in recognizing their own strengths and weaknesses.

Emotional intelligence *is a form of social intelligence that allows us to monitor and shape our emotions and those of others.*

Reuven Bar-On developed a self-assessment instrument (emotional quotient inventory, or EQi)[18] measuring traits and abilities related to social knowledge. The EQi is a measure of psychological wellbeing and adaptation and can be a measure related to performance. Jack Meyer and Peter Salovey claim that EI is composed of mental abilities and skills.[19] They see EI as a form of intelligence that processes and benefits from emotions. They believe that other measures of intelligence fail to take into account individual differences in the ability to perceive, process and manage emotions. In Chapter 2 we expand on the notion of emotional intelligence as one of the individual attributes predicting capacity to perform at a high level.

IS OB JUST FOR MANAGERS?

The performance equation may be a useful model for managers to appreciate the intricacies of employee performance and ways to improve it, and an awareness of emotional competencies, as outlined earlier, can help managers to monitor and shape emotions with a view to enhancing performance. There are many other OB concepts – see, for example, Chapter 4 on motivation – which can aid managers in carrying out their varied jobs effectively through an understanding of people's attitudes and behaviour. Organizational behaviour is also of interest, however, to the bulk of the population who are not currently in managerial roles and may not necessarily aspire to occupy such positions. It provides us with an opportunity to reflect on our own experiences of work organizations and can lead to us becoming more self-aware. We can also gain a fuller understanding of events affecting us. For example, theories on sources of power within organizations (covered in Chapter 10) could help us become reconciled to losing out on a promotion if we can see clearly the games a successful rival colleague has played to manoeuvre into a winning position. It may even be the case that OB awareness is of benefit to those whose sympathies are not with managers and other members of an organization's dominant coalition but rather with so-called underdogs. For example, it is illuminating to read qualitative research documenting service sector workers' attempts to 'manage' difficult customers.[20] In an important sense OB can illuminate the realities of working life focusing on what *does,* as well as what *should,* routinely happen. A critical tradition within OB questions whether the subject should take as its primary focus managing people for performance and often adopts a stance which questions the dominant role of managers, both in actual and philosophical terms. Nonetheless as many of our readers are studying OB as part of business and management courses, we will adopt a largely managerial approach throughout this book – albeit a quizzical one in places.

WHY DO ORGANIZATIONS EXIST?

Simply stated, organizations exist because individuals are limited in their physical and mental capabilities. Organizations are mechanisms through which many people combine their efforts and work together to accomplish more than any one person could alone. The trend in Europe, North America and parts of Asia has been for increasingly large organizations following the 'industrialization' of societies in these regions. The sociologist Max Weber recorded the emergence of work organizations based on rational processes and legal authority (as opposed to authority based on either personal charisma or tradition) in the mid to late 19th century. Throughout much of the 20th century – at least in the Western world – there was a trend for increasing size of organizations, accompanied by greater *formality* and *complexity* – see Chapter 6 for a full treatment of the topic of organizational structure. However, as successful organizations cannot be static and must evolve and adapt to external trends and pressures, so the pattern of organizations is continually changing. In the early 21st century, for example, we can discern a trend for organizations to minimize their core activities and to outsource work or otherwise enter inter-organizational networking arrangements. Consider, for instance, the Ford Motor Company, which for much of the 20th century sought to bring its operations in-house, at one point buying up railway companies and forests in order to control supply and distribution infrastructure. In the 21st century, Ford contrastingly operates an elaborate system of **outsourcing** and supplier-production-dealer networks. *Inter-organizational networking* encompasses cooperative ventures including sharing of resources with a view to maintaining independence, while *collaboration* involves sharing of aspects of organizations' competence, including intellectual property. The proliferation of such arrangements has led to a renewed interest in trust and a concern among senior managers to avoid betrayal through opportunistic behaviour by prospective or actual partners. It should be recognized however, that despite the undoubted impact of outsourcing and widespread job reduction, resulting in many smaller 'core workforces', many people still routinely come into contact with, and have their lives shaped by, large organizations.

Outsourcing
involves organizations obtaining aspects of their work, for example production systems, from external suppliers for reasons of cost and/or quality rather than carrying out the work themselves.

A primary purpose of any organization is to produce a product or provide a service. Large and small businesses produce a diverse array of consumer products and services such as motor vehicles, appliances, telecommunications and accommodation. Not-for-profit organizations organize services with public benefits, such as healthcare and rehabilitation, public education and environmental management.

A clear statement of purpose, or 'goal statement', is seen as important in guiding the activities of an organization and its members. To illustrate, the following are goals of some prominent organizations:

- 'to be the world's mobile communications leader – enriching customers' lives, helping individuals, businesses and communities be more connected in a mobile world' (Vodafone Group);[21]
- 'to enhance our businesses and strengthen our position as a premier integrated communications services provider in the Asia Pacific region' (SingTel);[22]
- 'to become the most admired company in our industry as seen by our stakeholders' (Philips).[23]

In stressing the purposive nature of work organizations, one should not fall into the trap of thinking that there is likely to be unanimous ongoing agreement and compliance with organizational goals. Humans are thinking beings capable of taking a self-interested strategic view of their current situation and future intentions. It may also be that people within an organization are not always aware of its goals or may lose sight of them. In short managers cannot automatically assume that individuals, specifically workers, will commit to stated goals and may need to expend time and effort in re-emphasizing or promoting them.

The preceding analysis stressing the importance of *organizational goals* follows many other OB textbooks in using that term. However, to say that organizations have goals is not literally true; organizations are not living entities, except in the metaphorical sense. They are, of course, also legally recognized entities. When we refer to an organization's goals and purposes we should remember that these are designed by particular actors, typically the owners and senior managers of that organization. The term **dominant coalition** has been used to denote the people who are in a position of power and influence and who will, in all likelihood, have formulated or reformulated its goals. As new coalitions can emerge – in some cases replacing others – it follows that the stated goals of organizations are potentially transitory.

To achieve its purpose, any organization depends on human effort. The **division of labour** is the process of breaking the work to be done into specialized tasks that individuals or groups can perform: it is a way of organizing the efforts of many people to the best advantage of that employing organization and ideally the workers themselves.

The division of labour and task specialization will be quite clear in a typical fast-food restaurant; McDonald's, with outlets across large parts of the planet, will provide an evocative example for many readers. Certain people take your order and your money, others cook the food and still others clean after everyone else has gone home for the night. By dividing the labour and training of employees, orienting them to perform highly specialized tasks, such an organization strives for excellence in task accomplishment. In the fast-food sector, excellence is partly denoted by standardization.

The aim of effective division of labour is to help managers of organizations to mobilize the work of many people in order to achieve that organization's purpose.

A well-functioning organization with a clear purpose and appropriate division of labour, like those of fast-food restaurants, achieves **synergy**, which is the creation of a whole that is greater than the sum of its parts. Synergy in organizations occurs when people work well together while using available resources to pursue a common purpose. In psychology this is called a 'gestalt'.[24] Within an effective organization, this 'gestalt' is created by the organization's division of labour, task specialization and hierarchy of authority, as well as by effective managerial behaviour.

The aforementioned summary of organizational design involving coordination of the efforts of others is an essentially managerial analysis. Other writers taking a critical stance, most influentially Braverman, have stressed the *de-skilling* of work and its negative impact on workers.[25] The examples of fast-food restaurants and the contemporary phenomenon of call centres with their routinized work and scripted customer encounters, lend themselves relatively easily to explanations within a critical **de-skilling** perspective...should one wish to. It is also the case that the experience of work will vary enormously in different organizational settings, with some employees working within a framework of multi-skilling whereby they have to use a wide range of skills to fulfil their work roles. Other organizations employ terms like **empowerment**, and put structures and working practices in place that enable employees who are low down in the hierarchy to feel a sense of freedom or autonomy in their day-to-day working lives.

A **dominant coalition** denotes the people who are in a strong position of power and influence within organizations at any one time. Dominant coalitions are shifting and can be replaced by others.

Division of labour is the process of breaking the work to be done into specialized tasks that individuals or groups can perform.

Synergy is the creation of a whole that is greater than the sum of its parts.

De-skilling refers to a diminution of the attributes and proficiency required to perform work tasks. In Braverman's view, de-skilling is a deliberate strategy by owners and managers of organizations in order to reassert control over work.

Empowerment is the process by which managers delegate power to employees who therefore have an enhanced view of their work and role within the organization.

OB IN ACTION

Cité de l'Image

France needs more entrepreneurs like Stephane Ledoux, a fast-talking salesman in his early 30s who started work straight after leaving school at 18. Today he owns a specialist photo-processing company, Cité de l'Image, which employs 67 people at its labs on the south-western fringes of Paris. M. Ledoux borrowed money and bought the business from a larger group for which he had been working. He considered moving the labs to low-wage Poland or Romania but quickly realized that would be counter-productive.

Cité de l'Image is a photo-processing and pre-press production house for an international clientele that runs from Guerlain and Yves Rocher to Xerox, Henkel and Air France. The work requires expensive, sophisticated equipment and highly skilled staff. Some simple work has been passed to Poland and Romania for over-night processing, but the core of the business has stayed in Paris. To cut costs, M. Ledoux has outsourced func-tions such as IT and payroll processing. Last month a private-equity group, Green Recovery, recruited him to run a much bigger business: the collection of photo agencies and image-processing firms (including famous names such as Gamma, Keystone and Jacana) that it had bought from the Hachette Filipacchi publishing group.[26]

This extract from a 2007 article from *The Economist* deals with a number of issues facing 21st century managers. Note how it is possible that differential skill levels will be linked to specific countries in future. Consider, too, the outsourcing of parts of the business – a trend referred to earlier.

ORGANIZATIONS AS OPEN SYSTEMS

Human resources *are the individuals and groups whose contributions enable the organization to serve a particular purpose.*

Organizations ultimately depend for their success on the activities and collective efforts of many people. People are the essential **human resources** of an organization – the individuals and groups whose performance contributions enable the organization to serve particular purposes. But organizations need more than people if they are to survive and prosper. They also need **material resources**, which are the technology, information, physical equipment and facilities, raw materials and money necessary for an organization to produce some useful product or service.

Many OB scholars believe that organizations can be best understood as **open systems** that transform human and material resource 'inputs' received from their environment, into product 'outputs' in the form of finished goods and/or services. The outputs are then offered to the environment for consumption. If everything works, measured via feedback, the environment accepts these outputs and allows the organization to obtain the resource inputs it needs to continue operating in the future (Figure 1.2).

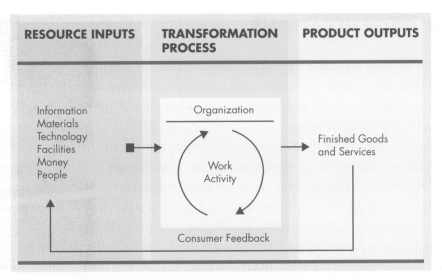

| RESOURCE INPUTS | TRANSFORMATION PROCESS | PRODUCT OUTPUTS |

Information
Materials
Technology
Facilities
Money
People

Organization

Work Activity

Consumer Feedback

Finished Goods and Services

Figure 1.2: Organization and environment relationships.

Material resources *are the technology, information, physical equipment and facilities, raw material and money that are necessary for an organization to produce some product or service.*

Open systems *transform human and physical resources received from their environment into goods and services that are then returned to the environment.*

Of course, things can go wrong. An organization's survival depends on satisfying environmental demands. When the organization's goods and/or services are not well received by the environment, it will sooner or later have difficulty obtaining the resource inputs it needs to operate.

OB IN ACTION

Just as business outcomes have an impact on the business environment and society as a whole, world events can also influence business survival. The tourism industry was greatly affected by the 2004 Boxing Day tsunami and the October 2002 and 2005 terrorism attacks in Bali. Although initially the tourism industry in Indonesia and Malaysia slumped as a result of these events, the industry responded by applying survival strategies and some improved their performance as a direct result of refocusing the market. For example, after the 2002 bombings, the Indonesian tourism authorities and commercial providers actively promoted Bali to markets that, unlike Australia, did not have an emotional association with the Bali bombings. This resulted in a boost for Bali, where visitors from Singapore to Bali lifted from 17 666 in 2002 to 26 881 in 2003.[27]

Other tourism businesses in the Asia-Pacific region responded to the change in business environment.

After the Bali bombings, Australia promoted its destinations as 'safe' and the Philippines promoted its resorts as unaffected by the Boxing Day tsunami. Both countries seized upon the opportunity to attract tourists who might otherwise have travelled to Bali or the Malaysian coast.[28] Time will tell if these tourism businesses are able to sustain growth by attracting returning tourists in the future, or if loyal Bali and Malaysian coast patrons return to their previous preferred destinations.

MANAGERS IN ORGANIZATIONS

*A **manager** is responsible for work that is accomplished through the performance contributions of others. A manager is concerned with making things happen and keeping work on schedule, engaging in routine interactions to fulfil planned actions.*

Now that we have examined some fundamental features of organizations, we can speak more precisely about what it means to be a manager. A **manager** is a person in an organization who is responsible for work that is accomplished through the performance contributions of one or more other people.

In many organizations the focus of both management research and practice is not so much on the manager as on the work team or unit. A **work team** or unit is a task-oriented group that includes a manager and his or her direct subordinates. Such groups are found in organizations of all types; whether small or large. Examples include departments in a retail store, divisions of a corporation, branches of a bank, wards in a hospital and teams in a manufacturing plant. Even university classes can be considered a work team; lecturers are their managers (they may prefer to use the term 'facilitators') and the students are team members. The study of such work teams has become a key area of OB research.

WHAT IS AN EFFECTIVE MANAGER?

***Work teams** or units are task-oriented groups that include a manager and his or her direct reports.*

Task performance is the quality and quantity of work produced.

Human resource performance must be sustained if it is to have meaning; high performance should be sustainable. High levels of performance are affected by a manager's attention to a range of matters within the people management heading.

It is not easy to define what makes a manager an effective manager within a business context. The list of managerial competencies identified over the past few decades helps us understand more clearly the competencies required for effective management. However, such research also illustrates the difficulties in defining effective management because it is still hard to achieve expert consensus on what constitutes a basic core of competencies. It is even more difficult to find agreement on prioritized rankings of such competencies.[29] Many of the best-known writers in the management literature typically emphasize one managerial competence at the expense of all others. Fayol and Urwick have portrayed good managers as controllers.[30] This is a typical conclusion from the *classical school* of management in its assumption that managers should direct the work of others, in this case through formal mechanisms of control. The manager remains clearly in control while designing and monitoring structures within which employees carry out tasks and systems of work which are operated by workers. Later approaches to management (although the *human relations school* dates back as far as the 1930s), emphasize the important role of managing relationships.

Mintzberg[31] has drawn up a multifaceted concept of managers' work, identifying *interpersonal*, *informational* and *decisional* roles within the overall 'umbrella heading' of the term manager (Figure 1.3). Note that *all ten roles* set out by Mintzberg involve dealing with other people, even those that are not designated as interpersonal roles.

Fundamentally, any manager should seek two key results for a work unit or work team: **task performance**, which is defined by the quality and quantity of the work produced, or the services provided by the work unit and **human resource performance**, which involves the attraction and continuation of a capable workforce over time. This latter notion, while too often neglected, is extremely important. It is not enough for a work unit

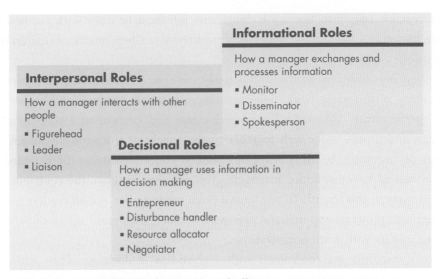

Figure 1.3: Ten roles of effective managers.

Source: Mintzberg, H. (1990), The Design School: Reconsidering the basic premises of strategic management. *Strategic Management Journal*, **11**, 176–195. Reproduced by permission of John Wiley & Sons, Ltd.

to achieve high performance on any given day; it must be able to achieve this level of input and outcome every day, both now and into the future. Good human resource performance is a major concern of OB. It directs a manager's attention to matters such as job satisfaction, job involvement, organizational commitment, absenteeism and turnover, as well as performance. Wendy Lenton, Vodafone director of people and brand, points out that 'The theory is that if you care for your people, your people will care for you, but if people feel unappreciated or unhappy at work, the anxiety manifests into ill health, low motivation, low productivity and absenteeism.'[32]

This book treats high task and human resource performance as results that any manager should seek. Indeed, the two results can be seen as twin criteria for an effective manager – that is, a manager whose work unit achieves high levels of task accomplishment and maintains itself as a capable workforce over time. This concept of the 'effective manager' offers an important framework for understanding OB and developing personal managerial skills. A special text feature, the 'effective manager' is used in this and later chapters to help remind us of these applications.

MANAGING TASK PERFORMANCE

Recall that task performance is determined by the quality and quantity of the work produced or the services provided. An effective manager must be concerned with the 'productivity' of work units and their members, although this can sometimes be difficult to evaluate. Formally defined, **productivity** is a summary measure of the quantity and quality of work performance achieved (task performance) that also accounts for resource use. It

Productivity *is a summary measure of the quantity and quality of work performance that also accounts for resource use.*

is not acceptable simply to 'get a job done'; any job must be done with the best use of available resources – human and material. Productivity is a benchmark of managerial and organizational success.

The best organizations want – and actively seek out – value-added managers whose efforts clearly enable their work units to achieve high productivity and improve 'bottomline' performance. Value-added managers create high-performance systems in which individuals and groups work well together to the benefit of the entire organization and its clients or customers. In many ways this book is about identifying the knowledge and attributes needed by value-added managers. You can thus evaluate the contribution that you could make in this regard. To reinforce a point made earlier, not all readers will aspire to management positions and material presented in this book should aid all of us when we come into contact with work organizations.

Today's managers are confronted with a considerable dilemma. They are asked to secure ever-increasing added value from their stock of human capital but measures to improve worker productivity also have the potential to increase worker stress, burnout and absenteeism and ultimately to result in a decline in worker productivity. The economic downturn that followed the 'credit crunch' of 2008 exacerbated these pressures and its effects were predicted to last for a considerable time. To maximize the potential benefits of new initiatives, we must balance their effect on productivity alongside a careful consideration of quality of work–life issues. In addition, as we note later in the chapter, effective people management should involve forward planning and not just focus on immediate problems. Workers will look back on how they were treated in bad times and they will want to feel that they were treated as well as could be reasonably expected during tough economic circumstances. The next section provides more detail on the broader issue of human resource performance.

HUMAN RESOURCE PERFORMANCE

The need to ensure long-term and sustainable high performance helps to focus a manager's attention on the need to *maintain* all of a work unit's resources (human and material resources alike). Just as managers should not allow a valuable machine to break down for lack of proper maintenance, they should never allow a valuable human contribution to be lost for lack of proper care.

Quality of work–life *refers to the overall quality of human experience in the workplace.*

Through their daily actions, the best managers in 21st century workplaces will be able to create conditions in which people achieve their highest performance potential while experiencing a high quality of work–life. The concept of **quality of work–life** (QWL) gained deserved prominence in OB study as an indicator of the overall quality of human experience in the workplace. It expresses a special way of thinking about people, their work and the organizations in which their careers are fulfilled. It establishes a clear objective that high productivity should be achieved along with job satisfaction for the people who do the required work. To take one example, Vodafone says it takes 'a holistic approach to work and lifestyle.'[33]

Quality of work–life activities represent special applications of the many OB concepts and theories discussed throughout this book. In particular, the following benchmarks of managerial excellence highlight true commitments to quality of work–life:[34]

* participation – involving people from all levels of responsibility in decision making;
* trust – redesigning jobs, systems and structures to give people more freedom at work;
* reinforcement – creating reward systems that are fair, relevant and contingent on work performance;
* responsiveness – making the work setting more pleasant and able to serve individual needs.

It is important to remember that a broader social value associated with work makes any manager's responsibilities more complex. Quality of work–life is an important component in the quality of life: negative work experiences can affect a person's nonworking life. Some common social problems – for example drug abuse – may be linked with the adjustment problems of people who are unable to find meaning and self-respect in their work.[35] The social importance of managers as major influences on the quality of work–life experienced by other people is well established. The study of OB recognizes that poor management can decrease overall quality of life, not just the quality of work–life. It also recognizes that good management can increase both.

MANAGING IN GOOD AND BAD TIMES

Managing human resource performance in an adverse economic climate can result in a renewed concentration on key issues. For example, one contribution to the literature, in evaluating the impact of economic recession on managing people, stressed the importance of *engagement*.[36] It was argued that managers have to continue to engage with employees because they are (hopefully) going to be with an organization when a recession ends. Engagement here is defined as an exchange of mutual value – one party does something for another and vice versa.

David Fairhurst, senior vice president at McDonald's northern Europe, has claimed that engagement could take a different form in a recession, with possible greater stress on so-called paternal concerns on the part of managers, for example making sure other employees do not dip out of pension schemes or become too short-term in their outlook. Fairhurst also draws attention to the need to approach staff reductions in a way that is regarded as fair and compassionate. He counsels against managers themselves losing their focus on people, noting that 'it's too easy to stop doing all these things like engagement, creativity and experimentation, and go right to the other end and say, now is the time to make sure that people have a desk and you don't bark at them – that's very short-sighted. If the [human resource management] profession as a whole can really hold together and focus and help them keep their nerve and remain creative in difficult times, then I think some good can be done in times of recession'.[37]

One can argue that the test of good and effective management of people is how managers adapt to tough circumstances. We hope that insights contained within this book are valid both in times of prosperity and hardship. The importance of maintaining human resource performance through worker engagement gives a particular impetus to understand human behaviour through analysis of OB concepts and practice.

THE PSYCHOLOGICAL CONTRACT

The **psychological contract** *specifies what an individual expects to give to and receive from an organization.*

You are probably familiar with the word 'contract' as it pertains to formal, written agreements such as a workplace agreement or an agreement between a union and an employer. Another, less formal contract deals with the 'relationship' between employees and their organization. We call this the **psychological contract** – specifically, what the individual and the organization expect to give to and receive from each other in the course of their working relationship. This contract represents the expected exchange of values that encourages the individual to work for the organization and motivates the organization to employ that person. When the individual is being recruited by the organization, this exchange is an anticipated one; later, during actual employment, expectations are either confirmed or denied. Part of the manager's job is to ensure that both the individual and the organization continue to receive a fair exchange of values under the psychological contract.

Contributions *are individual work efforts of value to the organization.*

Figure 1.4 depicts an exchange of values between the individual and the organization, as expressed in the psychological contract. The individual offers **contributions**, or work inputs of value, to the organization. These contributions – such as effort, skills, surrender of autonomy, loyalty and creativity – are extremely significant within the life of the individual worker, while one important measure of any organization's success is its ability to attract and maintain a high-quality workforce. The psychological contract is therefore a truly reciprocal exchange. In return for the worker's perceived inputs the organization gives the individual **inducements** – such as pay, benefits, status and job security – to encourage participation. These inducements are of value to the individual as ways of satisfying one or more important needs or expectations – see Chapter 4 for more detail on motivation theories.

Inducements *are what the organization gives to the individual on behalf of the group.*

When the exchange of values in the psychological contract is felt to be fair, a balance exists between inducements and contributions. This ideal condition creates a healthy psychological contract – one that fosters job satisfaction by allowing individuals to feel good about their work and relationship with the organization. When the exchange of values is perceived to be unfair, the psychological contract is unhealthy. Consequently, the individual may develop negative attitudes and lose the desire to work hard. These feelings correlate with absenteeism and job turnover rates, as otherwise good workers seek jobs elsewhere. As we will see in later chapters, the work of Adams is also relevant in his belief that our perceived inputs and outcomes are compared with those of others. Feelings of *equity* or inequity with others therefore also inform our psychological contract.

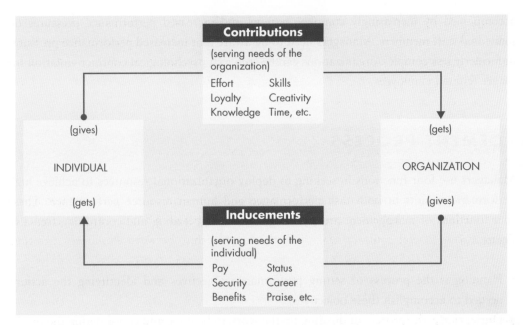

Figure 1.4: A healthy psychological contract means that inducements and contributions are in balance.

As we have already indicated, pressures in today's economic and business environment can make the management of psychological contracts a difficult task. Think about the sense of betrayed loyalty experienced by people who lose their jobs or who see others lose their jobs when an organization is 'downsized' or restructured to increase productivity.

Realigning the psychological contract

Most employees feel that their psychological contracts have been violated in some way by their employer at some time. Misunderstandings are often ignored. However, when a violation takes a serious form, such as a breach of promise and trust, feelings of betrayal can surface. According to Denise Rousseau[38] there are four main courses of action an individual may take in response to a perceived violation of psychological contract:

- *Voice* is a constructive effort to change and focus on restoring trust by discussing issues of concern with a manager or other appropriate colleague/supervisor.
- *Silence* reflects a willingness to accept unfavourable circumstances in the hope that they may improve.
- *Destruction/neglect* is most common when voice channels do not exist or if there is a history of conflict. This often causes counterproductive behaviour including theft, slowing or stopping work and intentions to destroy relationships.
- *Exit* is often the last resort when dealing with contract violations and refers to voluntary termination of the relationship.

One of the challenges faced by many managers is how to keep aligning psychological contracts in a rapidly changing business environment. Change is almost always accompanied by increasingly complex systems and increased performance pressures on individual staff members. Managers need to be aware that increased performance pressures in formerly less complex organizations can be seen as a psychological contract violation for longer tenured employees.

THE MANAGEMENT PROCESS

Managers use four functions in seeking to deploy organizational resources to achieve high performance results in both task performance and human resource performance. These four functions of management are planning, organizing, leading and controlling (see also Figure 1.5)

- Planning is the process of setting performance objectives and identifying the actions needed to accomplish these objectives.
- Organizing is the process of dividing up the work to be done and coordinating the results to achieve a desired purpose.
- Leading is the process of directing the work efforts of other people to help them to accomplish their assigned tasks.
- Controlling is the process of monitoring performance, comparing the results with the objectives and taking corrective action as necessary.

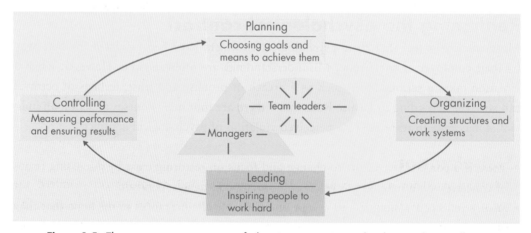

Figure 1.5: The management process of planning, organizing, leading and controlling.

There is no doubt that the task of managing both efficiently and effectively is becoming more complex. So far we have briefly discussed core and established OB themes. In addition to these well-established OB principles, today's business environment requires managers – and, of course, all other workers – to deal with emerging and fast-evolving challenges. The next part of this chapter will place the key concepts of OB into the real-world environment in which we are likely to work in future.

CONTEMPORARY THEMES IN OB

Among the biggest challenges that managers must deal with are globalization, the changing nature of work, the changing nature of the workforce and the changing nature of the relationships between employers and employees. These in turn create another challenge: that of managing change itself. One approach is **process re-engineering** – defined as 'the fundamental rethinking and radical redesign of business processes to achieve dramatic improvements in critical contemporary measures of performance such as cost, quality, service and speed'.[39] The result can involve a substantial shift in values, as shown in Effective Manager 1.1 below.

Process re-engineering *is the fundamental rethinking and radical redesign of business processes to achieve improvements in performance.*

EFFECTIVE MANAGER 1.1

Moving from traditional to re-engineered values

Traditional work values:

- the boss pays our salaries; keep the boss happy
- to keep your job, stay quiet and don't make waves
- when things go wrong, pass problems to others
- the more direct subordinates you control the better; a good manager builds an empire
- the future is predictable; past success means future success.

Re-engineered work values:

- customers pay our salaries; help keep them happy
- all of our jobs depend on the value we create
- accept ownership for problems; help solve them
- we are all part of a team; a good manager builds teams
- the future is uncertain; constant learning is the key to future success.

We will now briefly discuss some of the main contemporary issues in OB, already mentioned earlier in the chapter. We will revisit these themes throughout the book as your knowledge of OB builds.

Globalization

Globalization is not a new concept. The advantages and disadvantages – indeed the definition – of globalization have been the topic of much controversy for decades. We look at this debate in the 'Counterpoint' section later in this chapter. For our purposes we will define globalization as the process of becoming more international in scope, influence or application. In a business context, **globalization** is characterized by networks that bind countries, institutions and people in an interdependent global economy. In terms of relevance for OB, one specific aspect of globalization that stands out is its sense of greater interconnectedness between people from other cultures. This can manifest itself both in ever more frequent travel to new countries as a routine part of many job roles and increasing exposure to people from other cultures working within *any one* workplace – consider, for example, the inherently multicultural makeup of London's 21st century workforce. In both

Globalization *brings a greater sense of interconnectedness between people from diverse cultures. It has also been defined as the process of becoming more international in scope, influence or application.*

OB IN ACTION

Forty years after Britain's first race relations legislation, organizations are increasingly sending employees on race awareness courses. A BBC report on the topic[41] identifies a variety of (sometimes contentious) learning methods used by trainers in this field. Jane Elliott runs day-long courses in race awareness training. Her approach is described as uncompromising, brusque and authoritative. One of her techniques involves splitting her class into two groups, one formed of blue-eyed participants; the other composed of a brown-eyed group. The blue-eyed group is then verbally abused by the other group (on the instructions of the trainer). Posters denigrating the group are pinned up in the training room – for example asking 'would you want your child to marry a "bluey"?' While most diversity training does not seek to recreate emotional distress a number of methods do require participants to reflect on the impact of their language, possibly using less confrontational techniques. The levels of appropriate workplace behaviour are also explored – another diversity training programme asked whether cracking blonde jokes should be tolerated. Diversity training is increasing in popularity – there are over 100 specialist trainers listed in one directory – but this development is not universally welcomed with some people claiming that such courses reinforce a sense of difference between groups rather than bringing them closer. In the US, millions of dollars are spent on discrimination litigation costs, so if this trend is repeated elsewhere, there may be practical concerns indicating a further rise in diversity training, although the US is often characterized as a particularly litigious society.

cases globalization can impact on individuals' work patterns and roles and on the nature of relationships within organizations.[40]

Success in the increasingly global business environment will depend on a new breed of 'global manager' with global management skills and competencies. Global management skills and competencies include a strong and detailed understanding of international business strategy and cross-cultural management, including sensitivity to the existence and importance of cultural difference and an ability to manage a diverse workforce. The Effective Manager 1.2 section suggests ten important attributes of the successful global manager.

It is important for managers to study and learn about the management and organizational practices of their counterparts in other nations. What is being done well in other settings may be of great value at home, whether that 'home' is Britain, the Netherlands, Sweden or anywhere else in the world. So there could be important lessons from abroad. In addition, whereas the world at large once looked mainly to North America, Japan and Germany for management insights, today we recognize that no one culture possesses all of the 'right' answers to our management and organizational problems. It is also the case that cultural differences manifested at work can act as a brake on a manager's effectiveness – what works well in one culture may be ineffective elsewhere due to the values held by a local workforce or the institutional arrangements in place in another country.[42]

At this point we should re-emphasize that due to global labour migration, we do not have to travel abroad to come into contact with people from other cultures. While one can argue that people should adapt to the work environment of their new country – following the maxim of 'when in Rome do as the Romans do' – the reality is that workers will be influenced to some degree by their cultural upbringing. One good example of multicultural working can be found in the Elizabeth Garrett Anderson girls' school in London, which was visited by the US First Lady Michelle Obama in April 2009. Pupils at the school speak 55 different languages and 20% are the daughters of refugees or asylum-seekers. This school can be viewed as a testbed for cross-cultural management and teachers there are charged with fostering integration; even though the school only operates in one country.[43]

EFFECTIVE MANAGER 1.2

Ten attributes of the global manager

The global manager is able to:
- be culturally sensitive and adaptable;
- solve problems quickly and under different circumstances;
- motivate and communicate well with people from different cultures;
- understand different government and political systems;
- manage and create a sustainable environment;
- convey a positive attitude and enthusiasm when dealing with others;
- manage business in both traditional and virtual environments;
- view different economies as belonging to a single global market;
- negotiate effectively in different business environments;
- manage the 'triple bottom line' – society, economy and the environment.

OB IN ACTION

MADE WITH PASS!ON™

Dame Anita Roddick, the late co-founder of the Body Shop organization (purchased by L'Oreal in 2006), was well known for her distinctive views on the nature of business. Her vision of leadership – in her case of an environmentally aware, caring and successful organization – differed substantially from some conventional treatments of the topic. The external behaviour associated with leader-ship from her perspective involved 'going to every part of the organization, sitting in on meetings, going onto the factory floor, talking to everyone, educating and motivating staff, stretching their abilities and imagination. Communicating with customers, the community and the media. Developing a culture of being different.'[44] Strategies for implementing this vision which go beyond observable behaviour included: encouraging staff to question the status quo and encouraging dissonant feedback and devil's advocates.[45] This view of leadership – essentially personalized and interactive – differed from the command style that has been and continues to be prevalent in many work settings. However, the *contingency approach* referred to earlier in the chapter counsels us

against assuming that any one style of leadership will always be effective; the central message is that it all depends. Dame Anita's style apparently worked well in the context of the Body Shop; to what extent would it need to be re-evaluated in a more hierarchical setting, or in an organization with a very different *raison d'être* such as the armed forces? As we will see later in this chapter, one way of characterizing national cultures is *power distance*, which relates to people's perceptions of authority and hierarchy, so we might also question the acceptability of a participative management style in certain countries.

▶ COUNTERPOINT

Globalization for good or evil?

An article in the British magazine *Time Out*,[46] published in 2007, highlighted the downside of global migration patterns, in particular the 'churn' of people into and out of the UK, focusing on the experience of incoming workers who find themselves on the lowest rungs of the labour market. The article noted that 'we eat the food they have picked and wear the clothes they have sewn; they clean our homes and offices and even wipe our children's noses. Many things Londoners take for granted – fresh fruit and veg in the supermarket, cheap designer fashions and affordable childcare – rely on the work of foreign migrants who are employed here, legally and illegally, often in poorly paid and dangerous jobs'. The words of 'Ana', 34, from Brazil provide an eloquent case in point:

> I get up at 4.30 a.m. to go to work at two cleaning jobs. The first begins at 6.30 and is in a college in Westminster. I get there by bus from my flat. I clean for two hours a day for £34 a week. Then I take a bus to Docklands,

where I work in a business hotel cleaning rooms until 5 p.m. I'm paid £1.47 a room and we are expected to clean 18 rooms a day. On average I clean around 13 rooms as it's such hard work. We have to clean everything including the carpet, make the bed and clean the bathroom. There is no break and I usually don't eat as it would take up too much time. Occasionally I put some lunch in a bag and eat as I go along. There are about 15 cleaners but none of us say a word to each other during the day – we just don't have time.

> Sometimes the rooms are in a really bad state and everything is destroyed. People come

here to take drugs and I often find syringes, condoms, blood and vomit in the rooms. When I've finished I feel pretty depressed.

I arrived in London a year ago. I used to sell slimming products in Sao Paulo and I earned good money, but the company closed and I couldn't find another job. I also came here to send money home to my family. Sometimes I send as much as £50 a month. But usually it's difficult as it is so expensive to live here. I'm not happy, working so hard for so little money, and I'm looking for another job. Despite that my life is probably better here than it was in Brazil.

Questions

1. Summarize the issues surrounding globalization as presented above, identifying both positive and negative aspects.
2. How would you characterize 'Ana's' psychological contract. How could her current employers improve her working experience?

Source: London's twenty-first century slave trade. Time Out, March 21–27 2007, 1909 issue. Reproduced by permission of Time Out Magazine.

The changing nature of work

Work itself is changing rapidly due to globalization, advances in technology, the growth in the services sector and especially an increasing reliance on knowledge to generate new products and services. These changes require workers with different skills to the workers of the past, including the ability to continuously learn new skills and adapt to changing needs. Managing such workers presents a number of new challenges for managers. We will look at some of the biggest changes in the following sections.

Technology

Technology has emerged as an ever-present, dominant force in our lives. Just as 100 years ago people could not have accurately predicted the technology that is commonplace now, so we cannot foresee all the technological advances ahead of us. Our predictions of the future are bounded by what we know to be real right now: it is difficult to 'think the unthinkable'. What is almost certain is that continuing change in information and communications technology will have massive implications for workers, managers and organizations alike.

High technology allows machines to do many routine chores more cheaply and accurately than people can; it makes available more information for planning and control to more people at all levels of organizational responsibility and it is driving change in organizational structures and ways of working. For example, the use of e-mail has revolutionized office communication. It is a convenient medium among the more than 100 million e-mail users worldwide.[47] However, e-mail has potentially negative consequences in the workplace. The main problems are that written forms of communication are more official, less easy to withdraw and suffer from the absence of other additional communication modes, such as body language and intonation of voice. In addition, there is a growing body of research that suggests e-mail reduces a person's ability to build rapport and impairs the establishment of trust. These problems are exacerbated by cultural issues when e-mail users are in different countries.[48] Nevertheless, e-mail has proven to be a convenient communication medium that has changed work practices significantly. How many of us currently involved in white collar work begin our day by checking e-mails, either in the office, at home or even while travelling abroad?

Knowledge management

Another major driver of organizational change is the growth of the knowledge-based economy in which prosperity is built on 'intellectual capital' – the use of information in people's minds – rather than on physical resources. The OECD defines a **knowledge-based economy** as 'an economy in which the production, distribution and use of knowledge is the main driver of growth, wealth creation and employment across all industries – not only those industries classified as high tech or knowledge intensive.'[49]

Recognition of knowledge and the contribution that knowledge creation, distribution and use can make towards improved levels of performance and productivity is not new; economies have always relied on knowledge expansion and application through research and development to create new products and improvements in productivity. What is new is the speed at which knowledge is being created and the pace at which it is being transformed into new goods and services.

In a knowledge-based economy, the central questions for high-performing organizations are:

- What do we know and what is the currency of the knowledge we have?
- How do we organize to make best use of this knowledge?
- Who can add value to what we know?
- How quickly can we learn something new?
- How quickly can we deliver this new knowledge into the global marketplace?

Much knowledge resides within employees, including their skills, creativity and experience. It also exists in other areas such as the organization's systems, processes and structures, and in the relationships that organizations have with their customers, suppliers and other stakeholders. **Knowledge management** (KM) focuses on processes designed to improve an organization's ability to capture, share and diffuse knowledge in a manner that will improve business performance.

An important aspect of knowledge management is retaining people who possess the knowledge that the organization or the country needs. Such workers are increasingly mobile and are taking their knowledge with them to their new workplaces across the globe. Such movement across national boundaries is commonly referred to as **brain drain**.

A study by professional service firm Harvey Nash and the Centre for Economic and Business Research indicates that the UK is heavily dependent on the contribution of migrant workers in the professional and managerial spheres. The journal *Personnel Today*, reporting the results of this study, indicates that in Britain, many organizations such as the National Health Service (NHS) would not be able to function effectively without their migrant workforces.[50] In the case of the NHS, one striking statistic is that more than 30% of all nursing roles are taken by recent migrants to the UK.

A knowledge-based economy *is an economy in which the production, distribution and use of knowledge is the main driver of growth, wealth creation and employment across all industries – not only those classified as high-tech or knowledge intensive.*

Knowledge management *focuses on processes designed to improve an organization's ability to capture, share and diffuse knowledge in a manner that will improve business performance.*

Brain drain *refers to a characteristic of today's skilled workforce whose members are now more mobile and prepared to take their knowledge with them to their new workplaces as they pursue opportunities across the globe.*

The changing nature of the workforce

The composition of the workforce is changing. Managers must be aware of, and able to successfully manage in the context of, the following trends:[51]

- the size of the workforce is growing more slowly than in the past;
- the average age of the workforce is rising (the Conservative/Liberal Democrat Coalition Government in the UK plans a rise to statutory retirement ages from 2016);
- more women are entering the workforce;
- the proportion of ethnic minorities in the workforce is increasing;
- the proportion of immigrants in the workforce is increasing;
- workforce mobility is increasing;
- 'labour packaging' is growing through short-term migrant labour importation in many Asian and Middle Eastern countries;
- international careers and mobile managers are becoming commonplace;
- international experience is becoming a prerequisite for career progression to many top-level management positions.

Perhaps the most notable change in the workforce is that it is more diverse than at any time in history. The term **workforce diversity** refers to the presence of demographic differences among members of a given workforce.[52] These differences include gender, sexual orientation, race and ethnicity, culture, age and able-bodiedness.

In the sections below, we will look at the changing nature of the workforce in terms of culture, age and gender.

Workforce diversity *means a workforce consisting of a broad mix of workers from different racial and ethnic backgrounds, of different ages and genders and of different domestic and national cultures.*

Culture

The workforce is becoming more multicultural as a result of migration and as workforces increasingly span more than one country. To take two examples, Australia and New Zealand are among the more multicultural countries in the world. Almost one in three members of the workforce in major Australian cities such as Sydney and Melbourne was born outside Australia. About one in three people in the Auckland region of New Zealand was born overseas. Managers – whether or not they are directly involved in international business – must be able to manage people from different cultures effectively and make the most of the advantages that a diverse workforce can bring. For example, diversifying the workforce can be used as a strategic advantage. A diverse workforce can provide business with a competitive advantage by capitalizing on language skills, cultural knowledge, business networks and knowledge of business practices in overseas markets and intelligence about overseas markets, including intimate knowledge of consumer tastes and preferences. Businesses can use their skills to improve productivity and innovation in the workplace, developing domestic niche markets and entering new, or increasing market share in, overseas markets.[52]

Research has shown that styles of leadership, motivation and decision making and other management roles vary among different countries.[53] For example:

- Leadership. A study of international airlines found substantial differences in leadership styles despite the fact that the technology, types of jobs, skills required and basic operations are very similar from one company to another.[54]
- Motivation. Managers must avoid being parochial (where they fail to perceive difference due to limited horizons) or ethnocentric (in which case they believe that 'their way' is best). They cannot assume all people will be motivated by the same things and in the same ways as they are. Most of the popular theories of work motivation have been developed in the US. These theories may help explain the behaviour of North Americans but serious questions must be raised about how applicable they are to other cultures.[55] While North Americans, for example, value individual rewards, Japanese people prefer group rewards.
- Decision making. Latin American employees may feel uncomfortable with a boss who delegates too much authority to them. In France, research indicates that decisions tend to be made at the top of companies and passed down the hierarchy for implementation.[56] In other cultures, such as the Scandinavian countries contrastingly, employees prefer their managers to emphasize a participative, problem-solving approach. In Japan, many companies use the *ringi* system for making decisions. *Ringi* is a group decision approach whereby all affected company members affix their sign of approval to widely circulated written proposals. Culture may even play a role in determining whether a decision is necessary at all – that is, in whether the situation should be changed. Australians and New Zealanders tend to perceive situations as problems to be solved; others, such as Thai and Indonesian cultures, tend to accept situations as they are. Thus, an Australian is more likely to decide that a workplace problem exists and that something should be done about it.

The dimensions of culture

Geert Hofstede, a Dutch scholar and consultant, has identified five dimensions of national culture – power–distance, uncertainty avoidance, individualism–collectivism, masculinity–femininity and long-term–short-term orientation – which provide one way of understanding differences across national cultures.[57] Hofstede's five dimensions of national culture can be described as follows:

- Power–distance – the degree to which people in a country accept a hierarchical or unequal distribution of power in organizations. Indonesia, for example, is considered a high power–distance culture, whereas the Netherlands is considered a relatively low power–distance culture.
- Uncertainty avoidance – the degree to which people in a country prefer structured rather than unstructured situations. France, for example, is considered a high uncertainty avoidance culture, whereas Hong Kong is considered a low uncertainty avoidance culture.

- Individualism–collectivism – the degree to which people in a country focus on working as individuals more than on working together in groups, and the extent to which they are bonded into and identify with groups. The US, for example, is identified as one of the most strongly individualistic cultures, whereas China is considered a far more collectivist culture.
- Masculinity–femininity – the degree to which people in a country emphasize so-called masculine traits, such as assertiveness, independence and insensitivity to feelings, as dominant values (note the possibly stereotypical assumptions here). Japan, for example, is characterized as a highly masculine culture whereas Denmark is considered a more feminine culture. The Netherlands and the Scandinavian countries are, for Hofstede, the only societies that can be regarded as 'feminine'.
- A further so-called fifth dimension or long-term–short-term orientation was later developed by Hofstede in conjunction with Michael Bond.[58] Prompted by the success of many Asian economies from the 1980s onwards, this dimension identified a number of values including thrift and persistence, social obligations and tradition which together made up a long-term orientation. China, for example, is high on long-term orientation, whereas the US is, within this framework, more orientated towards the short term.

Continuing research on these cultural dimensions examines how countries can be grouped into clusters sharing generally similar cultures. Scholars are interested in such cluster maps as they try to determine how management practices can and do transfer across cultures. We will examine the validity of this approach, termed the *etic* or comparative view of culture, in Chapter 7, contrasting it with the *emic* view, which advocates deep understanding of individual cultures without recourse to comparison and categorization.

One such comparative grouping is shown in Figure 1.6. 'Anglo' countries tend to score quite low on the long-term–short-term dimension, whereas the Asian 'tigers' – Hong Kong, Singapore, South Korea and Taiwan – score quite high on this dimension. Hofstede and Bond argue that the long-term value and influence of Confucian dynamism may, at least in part, account for the surge of economic successes by these Asian nations. Chen (2004) suggests that cultural factors should also be considered when analysing economically difficult periods; for example the Asian recessions following 1997.[59]

Hofstede's work has been subject to some criticism in terms of whether his employee sample (based in large part on the IBM company) was nationally representative and also on his questionnaire-based research methodology.[60] We can usefully also bear in mind the regional cultural differences that can be found *within* nation states. However, his findings have formed the basis for an understanding of the role of culture in affecting workplace attitudes and behaviour and Hofstede's classifications remain a good guideline to the ways in which cultural differences play out in work organizations.

Age

Europe's rate of population growth is falling. Italy has a fertility rate of 1.2 children per parent, which is amongst the lowest in the world. The country has also experienced high levels of unemployment in recent years. Trends also indicate the increasing age of many

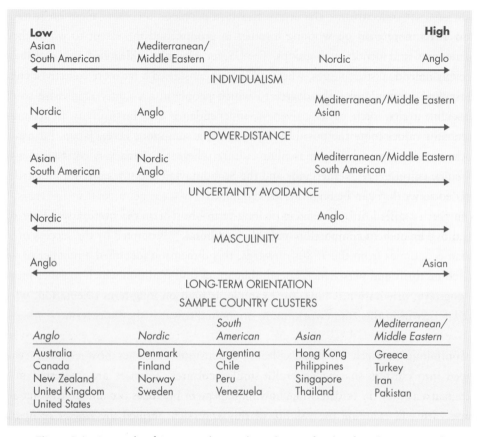

Figure 1.6: A sample of 'country clusters' based on Hofstede's five dimensions of national cultures.

populations. The percentage of over-65s was anticipated to rise from 15.4% of the EU population in 1995 to 22.4% by 2025.[61] Meanwhile Japan will have the most rapidly ageing population of any major power, and will experience an increasing shortage of labour. The ageing of the workforce has a number of important implications for organizations. These include:

- The possibility of a labour shortage – not enough workers with the right skills for the work that needs to be done.
- A loss of 'organizational memory' as the baby-boomer generation (born between 1946 and 1955) and the so-called shadow boomers (born between 1956 and 1964) reach retirement age and leave the workforce.
- An increasing representation of generations X (born after 1964) and Y (born after 1978) at senior levels within organizations as the baby boomer generation retires. The *modernization thesis* put forward by Ingelhart and Baker[62] suggests that the needs and preoccupations of these generations may move beyond a concern with material values to increasing 'quality of life' issues, coupled with a desire to engage with new forms of spirituality (in North America and western Europe), while in eastern Europe and other parts of the world we see a resurgence of traditional religious values.

- The need for new types of employment relationships to meet the needs of generations X and Y. For example, workers from generations X and Y are looking for different types of rewards for their work – they are less focused on just pay and job security. Vodafone, for example, meets this need by offering incentives such as giving workers the day off on their birthdays, allowing casual dress and giving them access to a health and wellbeing programme that includes such services as free massages.[63]
- Greater workforce mobility and less loyalty to the organization due to the different attitudes of members of generations X and Y. They expect to have a series of jobs and multiple careers over their working lives. This is in stark contrast to older generations who tended to work for one company, perhaps rising through the ranks over the years.
- The much higher levels of technical competence brought to the workplace by generation X and Y employees compared with their predecessors.

Gender

The past 40 years has been characterized by an increasing number of women entering the workforce, a breaking down of the traditional idea that some jobs are gender specific (for example, nurses are women, mechanics are men) and increasing – although for some still disappointing – numbers of women in senior positions within organizations. For example, research conducted by Grant Thornton in 2009 found that less than a quarter of senior management posts in privately-held businesses globally were occupied by women. The picture varied considerably across the world, with 42% of women holding such roles in Russia and 13% in Denmark.[64] The picture is very obviously imbalanced. Some implications of increased female participation in the workforce are for organizations to learn how to manage work–family relations such as parental leave (including paternity leave), reconsider what are deemed to be gender-specific roles and consider how work–life balance can be managed. This will be discussed later. We will consider gender as a factor influencing aspects of OB at various points throughout this book.

The changing nature of employer–employee relations

The relationship between employers and employees is changing. There are changes in the ways that organizations view their members and in how people view employers. In many 'new' workplaces, employment is often cut and streamlined for operational efficiency, businesses have flatter and more flexible structures and the workforce is more diverse and dispersed. This is especially true of countries coming under the Anglo-Saxon model of capitalism.[65]

Globalization has significantly altered the employment relationship, creating challenges for organizations, managers and employees. Wage earners find themselves working at home for foreign employers. More senior executives are arriving at their positions with the benefit of 'overseas experience'. And more junior executives are being asked and encouraged to take on such assignments. Consequently, today's managers must be able to both 'think globally' and 'act locally' in pursuing their opportunities.

Human rights and social justice are increasingly pursued in the new workplace, just as they are in the world at large. All managers must deal with growing pressures for self-determination from people at work. Workers may increasingly want input into major decisions that have a direct effect on their working lives.[66] Many workers want more freedom to determine how and when to do their jobs. They want the benefits of increased participation accrued through workplace initiatives such as industrial democracy, job enrichment, autonomous work groups, flexible working hours and family-friendly workplaces. All of these initiatives are changing the nature of day-to-day human resource management.

To create value-adding human capital, the 21st century manager must be well prepared to deal with not only the pressures outlined above but also pressures for:

- Employee rights. People in most cultural contexts expect their rights to be respected on the job as well as outside their work environment, including the rights of individual privacy, due process, free speech, free consent, freedom of conscience and freedom from sexual harassment.
- Job security. People expect their security to be protected in relative terms, including security of their physical wellbeing (in terms of occupational safety and health matters, as well as economic livelihood), guaranteed protection against layoffs and provisions for cost-of-living wage increases.
- Employment opportunity. People expect – and increasingly demand – the right to employment without discrimination on the basis of age, sex, ethnic background or disabilities. Among these demands are concerns to further the modest but important gains made in recent years by women and other groups that have been marginalized in the workplace. The concept of the 'glass ceiling' has been introduced into management vocabulary to describe the invisible discriminatory barriers that women may face as they seek to advance their careers in organizations (such as those arising from an organization's culture). Progress might be applauded, but it will not be accepted as a substitute for true equality of opportunity.
- Equity of earnings. People expect to be compensated to the same extent for the 'comparable worth' of their work contributions. The fact that certain occupations (such as nursing) have been traditionally dominated by women whereas others (such as carpentry) have been traditionally dominated by men is no longer accepted as justifying pay inequity. Equal pay for equal work, equity of rewards involving a comparison of inputs to output and other related issues such as money and motivation continue to be widely discussed topics.

We will now briefly examine a few of the major issues in the changing employment relationship.

WORK–LIFE BALANCE

Increasingly, workers are seeking balance between their work and the other aspects of their lives. Progressive organizations recognize the need to support their workforce to minimize stress levels and burnout, and to maximize work performance. Many companies recognize the increased pressures experienced in dual-income households, where both partners try to manage work and family commitments. Many companies are introducing initiatives to create a 'family-friendly workplace' to help employees better balance work and family commitments.

Workplace initiatives include work options such as job sharing, permanent part-time work and telecommuting, new leave provisions such as paid maternity and paid paternity leave, as well as supported childcare facilities.[67]

The website 'Where Women Want to Work' (**www.wherewomenwanttowork.com**)[68] identifies a number of specific initiatives that have been taken by business organizations in promoting work–life balance by focusing on parental responsibilities. The financial services provider HSBC offers its UK employees workplace nursery places and childcare vouchers for children up to 16 years old. This scheme is equivalent to a 6.5% pay increase for a typical clerical staff member and more for higher rate taxpayers. These vouchers can also be used to buy nursery care, nannies, au pairs, child-minders and for after-school schemes and school nursery cover. Around half of the 57 000-strong HSBC UK workforce has children under the age of 16 years. Staff can choose nursery places, childcare vouchers (or both) instead of salary. The company suggests that this improves employees' work–life balance, which benefits HSBC as well as the individual staff members.[69]

OB *IN ACTION*

But what about dad?

Most countries in the EU offer paid paternity leave, from two days in Spain to two weeks in France. Norway (which is not an EU member state), tops this particular European list though, staking a claim to be the most family-friendly country in Europe.

From July 1 2010, parents in Norway are entitled to 46 weeks of full governmental support (which may be less than full pay for people on a higher income level), provided both parents had been employed for the last six months before a child's birth. The mother has leave priority covering the last three weeks before birth and the six weeks following the birth. The father is entitled to ten weeks paternity leave.[70]

Interestingly, the remaining 27 weeks of parental leave are left for the parents to allocate between themselves. There is here an assumption of gender equality in decision-making within families – or at least consultation between the parents –

underlying the legislation. This is not surprising if we follow Hofstede's categorization of the Scandinavian societies as 'feminine' – see the discussion of Hofstede's work earlier in the chapter.

Questions

1. Summarize the business and ethical case for introducing or extending paternity leave in a country of your choice (research the actual legal position in that country first).

2. How could you explain Norway's preoccupation with this issue in the light of Hofstede's model of culture? See p. 32.

OUTSOURCING

As we have already seen, countries, cultures and peoples around the world are increasingly interconnected. One result is that it is increasingly possible to transfer jobs from one country to another. Job migration (the transfer of jobs from one country to another) and global outsourcing (the replacement of domestic jobs with contract workers in another country) has been an important phenomenon in recent years with a significant outflow of jobs to countries such as India, the Philippines and Russia, especially in IT-related jobs. With increasing use of virtual workspaces enabled by communications and information technology, it is easy to contract for many types of work anywhere in the world, at the lowest price. To remain competitive, organizations and workers themselves must continually change to achieve high performance.

 *IN ACTION*

Outsourcing to India

India places a high value on education and many workers have one or two degrees. Through successful global marketing of their knowledge-based workforces, many companies in a variety of industries (IT, aerospace, finance, telecommunications) are now outsourcing their work to India. Often the workers are shown video footage from the country they service; they watch local television shows via cable and partake in accent reduction courses, all in an effort to 'fit' with the culture they are servicing. One of the largest growth areas is finance. AXA Asia Pacific has its back-office functions and data entry work done in India, and part of the ANZ Bank's IT operations are also undertaken there. Organizations like GE Capital (which runs credit card operations for Coles Myer, Shell and Buyers Edge), HSBC Bank and American Express have relocated credit card fraud departments to India. This influx of new call centre jobs has proved to be very significant for India: in 1995 the Indian outsourcing sector turned over about US$100 million; by 2002 that figure had increased to US$2 billion.[71] Many companies outsource labour to developing countries, where skills are often high and labour costs are significantly cheaper. However, companies must carefully consider both internal (cost) and external (customer experience) factors when outsourcing services.

In the UK there has been a degree of negative publicity concerning call-centre operations in the Indian subcontinent and there is some evidence that the peak of the trend may be over. Powergen and Esure are returning their call centres to British locations, while a Natwest bank advertising campaign stresses that their call centres are in the UK. Some customers have failed to accept call centres that are not locally based (it is hoped this relates to actual quality of experience rather than xenophobic views), which could affect their trust in, and loyalty to, a certain brand, company or organization.

CASUALIZATION OF THE WORKFORCE

One of the key themes from the chapter so far has been that organizations and the environments in which they operate are rapidly changing. Organizations are seeking greater flexibility and adaptability to respond to these changes. Increasingly, organizations are seeking people who can adapt to changing needs. Another method of achieving this aim has been to change the composition of their workforce to consist of core workers and contingent (or peripheral) workers. The contingent workers are usually employed on a casual basis. **Casual work** is work where the number and schedule of work hours vary and there is little or no ongoing security of employment. Employing casual staff gives managers the ability to quickly increase or decrease the number of workers to meet demand but there are significant downsides for both employer and employees. For example, employees suffer a loss of job security and predictability of income; they may have less loyalty to their employer and they may be less likely to invest in new skills or knowledge that could benefit the employer. They may also not be well protected by health and safety measures. On 21 February 2004, 21 Chinese cockle pickers were drowned after being caught by the tide in Morecambe Bay in the north of England. Anyone who read transcripts of the mobile phone calls and text messages sent by some of these casualized workers as they awaited their death, cannot but be deeply moved and keen to avoid similar tragedies in future, in so far as anyone can realistically interfere with the workings of this part of the labour market.

> **Casual work** *is work where the number and schedule of work hours vary and there is little or no security of ongoing employment.*

TELEWORKING

Teleworking means working from a location other than the organization's offices. It often refers to working from home. **Teleworking** has become increasingly feasible due to technology (for example, mobile phones, e-mail) that allows easy communication with the office and co-workers. It is an increasingly widespread practice with a recent EU study[72] concluding that in Finland 16.8% of the workforce were classified as teleworkers – the highest figure in an EU state. There are benefits to employees in terms of work–life balance (for example, saved travelling time and being able to work in their home environment), but such employees can become socially isolated and may miss out on opportunities for promotion and workplace interaction more generally – see Chapter 4 for a discussion of workers' 'social needs'.

> **Telework** *principles relate to work conducted remotely from the central organization using information technology.*

Since the terrorist attack on the World Trade Center towers in New York on 11 September 2001, many companies have been reluctant to place all or most of their employees at one location. By having operations spread across different geographic locations – or even just different buildings – the risk of losing a large proportion of human, physical or intellectual resources in a terrorist attack or disaster such as an earthquake or fire is greatly reduced.

ETHICS AND VALUES

With an increasingly interconnected world, the growing representation of generation X and Y employees and employers, and a greater appreciation of the fragility of the natural environment, organizations, their members and the communities they exist within are placing more emphasis on ethical behaviour. The concepts of corporate social responsibility (that organizations have a responsibility to the societies that sustain them) and triple bottom-line reporting (that organizations need to consider society and the environment as well as their economic performance) are among the most prominent organizational responses to the increased emphasis placed on ethics and values.

Ethical behaviour is behaviour that is morally accepted as good and right, as opposed to that which is unethical (bad or wrong), in a particular setting. Business scandals resulting in the collapse of high-profile companies such as Enron and Worldcom highlighted the importance of ethics in managerial behaviour. Today a trend is clear: there are increasing demands that government officials, managers, workers in general and the organizations they represent all act in accordance with high ethical and moral standards.

Ethical managerial behaviour is behaviour that conforms not only to legal requirements but also to broader social moral codes. Exactly what moral code governs a person's choices is a subject of debate.

Corporate social responsibility includes such things as providing employment, caring for the environment, contributing to charities and operating in a way that meets the society's needs. Corporate social responsibility for some should remain the responsibility of individual companies, embedded in their own context, and not subject to regulation. The UK Confederation of British Industry (CBI), for example, states that corporate social responsibility should remain voluntary and market driven.[73]

An **ethical dilemma** occurs when a person must make a decision that requires a choice among competing sets of principles. Such a situation may arise when a member of an organization decides whether to do something that could be considered unethical, but that benefits the person or the organization or both. Is it ethical, for example, to pay to obtain a business contract in a foreign country? Is it ethical to allow your company to dispose of hazardous waste in an unsafe fashion? Is it ethical to withhold information in order to discourage a good worker from taking another job? Is it ethical to conduct personal business on company time? Ethical dilemmas are common in life and at work. Research suggests that managers encounter such dilemmas in their working relationships not only with superiors and employees but also with customers, competitors, suppliers and regulators. Common issues underlying the dilemmas involve honesty in communications and contracts, gifts and entertainment, outright bribery, pricing practices and ending workers' employment; either individually or collectively.[74]

People's approaches to ethics are influenced by the stance they adopt when confronting an ethical dilemma.

Ethical behaviour *is behaviour that is morally accepted as 'good' and 'right' as opposed to 'bad' and 'wrong' in a particular social context.*

Corporate social responsibility *refers to the notion that corporations have a responsibility to the society that sustains them; and the obligation of organizations to behave in ethical and moral ways.*

An **ethical dilemma** *occurs when a person must make a decision that requires a choice among competing sets of principles.*

- *Deontological* approaches view ethical behaviour in terms of the inherent goodness-or badness of an act. So they might decide that they would never kill another human being, steal or lie.
- *Consequential* approaches focus instead primarily on the consequences of an act; would it, for example, have been justifiable with hindsight to assassinate various political dictators?
- *Character virtue* links good behaviour with particular qualities residing in people. To take an extreme example, a Mafia member may threaten another person in order to demonstrate courage and their loyalty to the wider group.

OB IN ACTION

You are running late for a meeting in which staff redundancies are being discussed and you wish to protect your own department from this threat. The only car-parking space available near the meeting location is reserved for disabled access (you do not have a disabled sticker).

Confronted with this dilemma what would you do? Explain your thought process with reference to all three of the approaches to ethics listed above.

The increasingly topical area of ethics (was the credit crunch fuelled in part by unethical behaviour in the financial services sector?) will be addressed throughout our book and reinforced by ethical dilemma 'what would you do?' activities in subsequent chapters.

CONCLUSION

Organizational behaviour is relevant, topical and we trust will therefore be of interest to all readers. It should be possible to relate material from subsequent chapters to our own lives and our work experiences in particular. Knowledge within the field is drawn from a number of academic disciplines and researchers are very concerned to create a body of knowledge that is based on rigorous foundations, thereby rising above the commonsense level. By now you should also have an indication of why it is important for managers – and every other member of an organization – to have a good understanding of OB.

There is much evidence indicating that the successful 21st century manager will have to make the behavioural and attitudinal adjustments necessary to succeed in dynamic times.

Tomorrow's managers can come from any country or culture and may experience many placements and sample multiple locations in a wide-ranging career. They will also increasingly be highly educated – possibly to postgraduate level – with a global focus, able to manage in both regulated and deregulated economies in an environment typified by rapid change. They would be surprised by anything more than a limited-term, high-pressure appointment and their position will be results driven.

One important point to highlight at this stage is the inherent difficulty of managing people due to human beings' unique ability to engage in high-level reasoning and to adapt situations for their own advantage. This has led to the notion of *unintended consequences* when managers attempt to direct or mould behaviour. This concept is not new. When considering the effect of bureaucratic organizational structures which stress clear job descriptions and allocation of duties, some writers have noted the unintended consequence of over-adherence to these with a resultant 'jobsworth' mentality – or 'that's not my job' approach – which can have negative consequences.[75]

More recently a popular economics book pointed to unintended consequences of incentives.[76] In one example schoolteachers, faced with targets based on pupils' examination results, were statistically proven to have tampered with scripts before they were dispatched to the public examination board for marking. In another, staff at a crèche became tired of parents arriving late to pick up their children. In response they imposed a charge for late pick-ups. However, some parents regarded the charge as a fee for a service provided and lateness increased accordingly – precisely the opposite outcome of what was intended!

Unintended consequences are not inevitable. However, we counsel you against believing that people at work will behave in a predictable way if only you adopt particular policies and practices. Humans' ability to interpret cues in different ways, and in some cases to behave opportunistically, makes managing people more difficult but also more challenging and fun.

Your learning about OB may begin with this book and a module in a course as part of your formal education but it can and should continue in the future as you benefit from actual work experiences. Your most significant learning about OB may come with time as your career progresses but it will do so only if you prepare well and if you are ready to take maximum advantage of each learning opportunity that arises.

The terms 'lifelong learning' and 'recurrent learning' perhaps best conceptualize the learning and education of the future. The essence of these propositions is that education and learning should continue over the lifespan of the individual and should form part of actual work and life experiences. It is both a personal responsibility and a prerequisite for long-term career success. Day-to-day work experiences, conversations with colleagues and friends, counselling and advice from mentors, training seminars and workshops, professional reading and podcasts and the information available in the quality press and television (also the Internet used selectively and with caution) all provide frequent opportunities for continual learning about OB. In progressive organizations, supportive policies and a commitment to extensive training and development are among the criteria for organizational excellence. The opportunities for lifelong learning and recurrent education are there; you must make the commitment to take full advantage of them at all times.

SUMMARY

LEARNING OBJECTIVE 1
Organizational behaviour defined

Organizational behaviour is the study of individuals and groups in work organizations. This body of knowledge can assist managers to interact effectively with their employees and help improve organizational performance. Effective managers need to understand the people on whom they rely for the performance of their unit. However, people can behave unpredictably and unintended consequences are possible if and when we try to change their behaviour. The complexity of this area can be illuminated by the performance equation, which views performance as the result of the personal and/or group attributes, the work effort they make and the organizational support they receive.

Some scholars within OB focus more on people's own understandings and subjective experiences of life within organizations. This approach to OB uses more qualitative research methods when studying organizations and the people who are affected by them. It stresses important differences between natural and social science and locates OB firmly within the latter category.

LEARNING OBJECTIVE 2
Why organizations exist

Organizations are collections of individuals working together to achieve a common purpose or goal. But not all people will work towards organizational goals as they may have their own agendas such as their career development. Organizations exist because individuals are limited in their physical and mental capabilities. By working together in organizations, collections of individuals are able to achieve more than any individual could by working alone. The purpose of an organization is to produce a product or to provide a service. To produce such outputs, organizations divide work into required tasks to organize the efforts of people to their best advantage. This process is termed 'division of labour'. Organizations can be portrayed as 'open systems' in that they obtain human and material inputs from their external environment, then transform these inputs into product outputs in the form of finished goods or services, which they then offer back to the external environment for consumption. If the environment values these outputs then the organization will continue to survive; if not, then it may fail to obtain subsequent inputs for future production and it may ultimately cease to operate.

LEARNING OBJECTIVE 3
The role of people management

A manager is responsible for work that is accomplished through the performance contributions of one or more other people. The management process involves planning, organizing, leading and controlling. Managers should seek two key results for a work unit or work team: task performance, which is the quality and quantity of the work produced or the services provided by the work unit; and human resource performance, which is engendered through attraction, retention and development of a capable workforce over time. An effective manager's work unit achieves high levels of productivity and maintains itself as a capable workforce over time by keeping the psychological contract in balance. The psychological contract is based on individuals' expectations regarding what they and the organization expect to give and receive from each other as an exchange of values. In a 'healthy' psychological contract, the contributions made to the organization are believed to be in balance with the inducements received in return. The insights provided through the study of OB can help managers help others maintain healthy psychological contracts with their employers. They can also help managers to build and maintain work environments that offer their members a high quality of working life, which is marked by participation, independence, equity and responsiveness.

LEARNING OBJECTIVE 4
Key issues affecting organizations

Globalization is the process of becoming increasingly international in perspective and interconnected with others worldwide. A managerial career in today's work environment is highly likely to bring contact with international issues and considerations (even when managers remain in their home countries). Managing to perform effectively in a globalized marketplace requires many new skills and competencies.

Changes to the nature of work are largely due to globalization, advances in technology, the growth in the services sector and, especially, an increasing reliance on knowledge to generate new products and services. These changes to the nature of work require workers and managers with new skills and abilities.

The workforce is becoming diverse: more multicultural, older and there are more women working than ever before. Managing such a workforce requires new approaches.

Workers are seeking greater work–life balance. They are also seeking a greater variety of incentives for their work contribution. More workers expect to have a series of jobs or careers over their lifetime. Employers cannot and should not expect the same degree of loyalty as in the past. Employers are seeking a more flexible, adaptable workforce that can keep pace with the ever-increasing speed of change in the marketplace. Outsourcing and the use of casual workers are among the ways organizations are responding to these needs.

Organizations are under increasing pressure to conduct themselves ethically and to acknowledge that they have a responsibility to the society that sustains them.

LEARNING OBJECTIVE 5
The need to understand OB

Learning about OB is both a personal responsibility and a prerequisite for long-term career success. The field of OB helps managers to deal with and learn from their workplace experiences. Managers who understand OB are better prepared to know what to look for in work situations, to understand what they find and to take (or help others to take) the required action.

Even if you are not in a managerial role and/or have no desire to be in one, insights gleaned from OB – and we hope from reading this book – will help you to understand your own experiences of working in and otherwise dealing with organizations. It is virtually impossible to avoid organizations!

CHAPTER 1 STUDY GUIDE

Now that you have read this chapter, you should be able to apply and further develop your knowledge by undertaking the following activities set out over the next few pages: test your knowledge questions, an individual activity and an end-of-chapter case study.

Please also go to this book's website: **www.wileyeurope.com/college/french** to find further material which will enhance your understanding and enable you to assess your knowledge.

TEST YOURSELF

1. What is organizational behaviour and why do managers need to understand it?
2. Identify *four* factors that accelerate organizational change. Use contemporary examples to bring your answer to life.
3. What is an effective manager? What are the competencies needed by an effective global manager?
4. What do you understand by the term 'psychological contract'? Give examples from your own life – either current or past – to show how well this concept works in explaining attitudes and behaviour.
5. Why is human resource performance important to effective management? What negative effects on business performance may result from managers' neglect of people issues? Can managerial performance be measured using a single criterion? Explain your answer.
6. What is meant by the term 'global management'? What distinguishes it from other types of management?
7. How have developments in information technology changed the nature of the workplace and the practice of management? How do virtual organizations differ from more conventional forms?
8. Why is an understanding of cultural differences important to business? What are some steps that managers can take to develop greater cross-cultural awareness? How would you describe the culture into which you were born if you were attempting to attract foreign investment?
9. What do you understand by the *deontological*, *consequential* and *character virtues* approaches to understanding ethics? Provide one example of an ethical dilemma you have encountered at work (or imagine one) and show how each of the three approaches listed above could shape your response.
10. Why do attempts to mould human behaviour often founder due to unintended consequences? Account for the two unintended consequences cited by Levitt and Dubner in this chapter (schoolteachers and crèche users).

INDIVIDUAL ACTIVITY

Global awareness

As we noted in this chapter, the environment of business is becoming more global. The following assessment is designed to help you understand your readiness to respond to managing in a global context. You will agree with some of the following statements and disagree with others. In some cases, you may find it difficult to make a decision, but you should force a choice. Record your answers next to each statement using the following scale:

Strongly agree = 4

Somewhat disagree = 2

Somewhat agree = 3

Strongly disagree = 1

_____ 1. Although aspects of behaviour such as motivation and attitudes within organizational settings remain diverse across cultures, organizations themselves appear to be increasingly similar in terms of design and technology.

_____ 2. Spain, France, Japan, Singapore, Mexico, Brazil and Indonesia have cultures with a strong orientation towards authority.

_____ 3. Japan and Austria define male and female roles more rigidly and value qualities like forcefulness and achievement more than Norway, Sweden, Denmark and Finland.

_____ 4. Australia, the UK, the Netherlands, Canada and New Zealand have cultures that view people first as individuals and place a priority on their own interests and values, whereas Colombia, Pakistan, Taiwan, Peru, Singapore, Mexico, Greece and Hong Kong have cultures in which the good of the group or society is considered the priority.

_____ 5. The US, Israel, Austria, Denmark, Ireland, Norway, Germany and New Zealand have cultures with a low orientation towards authority.

_____ 6. The same manager may behave differently in different cultural settings.

_____ 7. Denmark, Canada, Norway, Singapore, Hong Kong and Australia have cultures in which employees tolerate a high degree of uncertainty but such levels of uncertainty are not well tolerated in Israel, Austria, Japan, Italy, Argentina, Peru, France and Belgium.

_____ 8. Societies while exhibiting national characteristics are composed of subcultures. Respond according to the 1–4 scale; also what do you understand by the term subculture and give *two* examples of subcultures.

For the interpretation of your results see page 51.

IS HE NOT CLEAR THEN? (THE WORLD'S WORST AIRCRAFT ACCIDENT)

On 27 March 1977 the world's worst aircraft accident to date occurred in Tenerife. By supreme irony, and as if to mock those who fear flying, the accident took place on the ground, with two Boeing 747 'jumbo jets' colliding on the runway at the Canary Island's airport. The disaster killed 583 people.

The crash took place when a KLM Royal Dutch Airlines plane taking off, in the captain's mistaken belief that he had clearance to depart, crashed into a Pan American plane taxiing on the same runway. The accident took place in thick fog and the Pan American crew missed its correct turn-off from the runway, leaving them in the direct path of the other flight.

There were several technical reasons for the crash including the obscuring of a simultaneous radio call from both planes through mutual interference on the radio frequency. If either message had been heard it should have alerted the other crew to the true sequence of events and offered an escape route from the impending collision. However the underlying reasons for the crash were human and rooted in the work environment, attitudes and behaviour.

The KLM Captain, Jacob van Zanten, was returning to route flying after six months of training duties on a simulator and possibly still attuned to training conditions. He may also have been keen to take off quickly to keep within crew duty hours. At any rate he *perceived* an air traffic controller's (ATC) instructions on departure route and what to do when airborne as actual clearance to take off. There was an element of miscommunication when the KLM crew gave an ambiguous message which crash investigators subsequently heard as either 'we are at take-off' or 'we are uh taking off' (they were unable to decipher which). The ATC responded to this message with a terse 'OK' (a nonstandard term in this context). His follow-up message; 'stand by for take-off, I will call you' was never heard due to the radio interference caused by a transmission from Pan Am at that precise second. And yet there was still one final chance to avoid the crash. The Flight Engineer on the KLM plane heard the Pan Am crew's radio message that they would report when they had cleared the runway. He was heard on the cockpit voice recorder to query his captain's decision to take off, asking 'Is he not clear then?' On receiving the response

---

This case study is adapted from a number of sources. Transcripts of cockpit voice recordings were taken from Stewart, S. (1986), *Air Disasters*, Ian Allan: Shepperton.

'what did you say?' from the captain, the Flight Engineer asked again 'Is he not clear, that Pan American?' However Captain Van Zanten responded decisively 'Oh yes!' and the Flight Engineer did not persist with his question as the plane continued to accelerate down the runway. Captain Van Zanten was one of the airline's most experienced pilots; he appeared on a magazine advertisement for the company and it was reported that when news of this disaster broke, KLM attempted to contact him to give public statements before learning that, tragically, he was the captain of the crashed plane.

The subsequent enquiry into the crash made several conclusions that reflected the human factors underlying the disaster. A new phrase 'line up and wait' was introduced for planes ready to take off but not yet cleared. Key instructions would henceforth have to be read back, not merely acknowledged with a phrase like 'OK'. Interestingly the report also focused on hierarchical relations among air crew with a greater emphasis proposed for mutual agreement on decision making.

Question

What OB topics do you consider relevant to an explanation of the events surrounding this real-life disaster? Refer to the chapter headings in the index of this book when formulating your response.

SUGGESTED READING

Thompson, P. & McHugh, D. (2009), *Work Organizations*, 4th edn, Palgrave Macmillan: Basingstoke. The authors provide an in-depth critical perspective on OB recommended for readers wishing to extend their study at advanced level.

Watson, T. J. (2006), *Organising and Managing Work*, 2nd edn, FT Prentice Hall: Harlow. The author's approach is to focus on task and practice at work and to use concepts and theories from OB and other academic areas in order to help make sense of them.

END NOTES

1. Rules of Engagement, *Sunday Times*, 14 March 2010.

2. Together for the Good of the UK, *Sunday Times*, 14 March 2010.

3. James, O. (2007), *Affluenza*, Vermilion: London.

4. Bolton, S. (2005), *The Sunday Times 100 Best Companies to Work For: Background, Methodology and Initial Findings for Dignity at Work*, Lancaster University, Management School Report: London.

5. Clegg, S., Kornberger, M. & Pitsis, M. (2008), *Managing and Organizations: An Introduction to Theory and Practice*, 2nd edn, Sage: London, p. 50.

6. Bratton, J., Sawchuk, P., Forshaw, C., Callinan, M. & Corbett, M. (2010), *Work and Organizational Behaviour*, 2nd edn, Palgrave Macmillan: Basingstoke.

7. Mullins, L.J. (2010), *Management and Organizational Behaviour*, 7th edn, FT Prentice Hall: Harlow, p. 3.

8. Knights, D. & Willmott, H. (2007), *Introducing Organizational Behaviour and Management,* Thomson: London, p. 36.

9. Mesure, S. (2006), Immigrants have boosted UK growth, *Independent,* 24 April.

10. Migrant Poles return claim denied, bbc.co.uk/news 22 January 2010 (accessed June 30 2010).

11. Grey, C. (2009), *A Very Short, Fairly Interesting and Reasonably Cheap Book About Studying Organizations,* 2nd edn, Sage: London, p. 8.

12. Lawrence, P.R. & Lorsch, J.W. (1967), *Organizations and Environment: Managing Differentiation and Integration,* Richard D. Irwin: Homewood, IL.

13. French, R. (2010), *Cross-Cultural Management in Work Organizations,* 2nd edn, CIPD: London.

14. Muller, M. (1998), Human resource and industrial relations practices of UK and US multinationals in Germany. *International Journal of Human Resource Management,* 9 (4), 732–744.

15. Hendrick, H. (1983), Pilot performance under reversed stick conditions. *Journal of Occupational Psychology,* **56**, 297–301.

16. Ward, J. & Winstanley, D. (2006), Watching the watch: the UK fire service and its impact on sexual minorities in the workplace. *Gender, Work and Organization,* **13** (2), 193–219.

17. Goleman, D. (2000), *Working with Emotional Intelligence,* Bantam: New York.

18. Bar-On, R. (1997), *The Emotional Intelligence Inventory (EQi),* Technical Manual, Multi Health System: Toronto.

19. Mayer, J.D. & Salovey, P. (1997), What is emotional intelligence? In *Emotional Development and Emotional Intelligence* (eds P. Salovey and D.J. Sluyter), Basic Books: New York.

20. See Watson (2006) [REF. Watson, T.J. (2006), *Organising and Managing Work,* 2nd edition, FT Prentice Hall: Harlow] for an account of air cabin crews' behaviour in this regard – which included deliberately overturning coffee cups into obnoxious passengers' laps and lacing their drinks with laxative.

21. Vodafone Group, 'Vision and values', www.voda-fone.com/article/0,3029,CATEGORY_ID%

253D30304%2526LANGUAGE_ID%253D0%2526CONTENT_ID%253D21016,00.html, (accessed 4 October 2005).

22. Singtel, 'Company profile', http://home.singtel.com/-about_singtel/company_profile/vision_n_mission/companypro_visionmission.asp, (accessed 9 March 2005).

23. Philips 'Our vision', www.philips.com/about/company/missionvisionvaluesstrategy/index.html, (accessed 1 April 2007).

24. Wertheimer, M. address to the Kant Society, Berlin, 7 December 1924, reprinted in Ellis, W.D. (1938), *Source Book of Gestalt Psychology,* Harcourt, Brace & Co: New York.

25. Braverman, H. (1974), *Labour and Monopoly Capital: The Degradation of Work in the Twentieth Century,* Monthly Review Press: New York.

26. A special report on European business. *The Economist,* 382, 10 February 2007.

27. Kurosawa, S. (2005), Vulture tourists, *The Australian,* 24 October, p. 10.

28. Ibid.

29. Fish, A. & Wood, J. (1996), Cross-cultural management competence in Australian business enterprises. *Asia Pacific Journal of Human Resources,* **35** (1), 274–301.

30. Fayol, H. (1949), *General and Industrial Management,* Pitman: London.

31. Mintzberg, H. (1990), The design school: reconsidering the basic premises of strategic management. *Strategic Management Journal,* **11**, 176–195.

32. From vodafone.com.

33. Ibid.

34. Champion-Hughes, R. (2001), Totally integrated employee benefits, *Public Personnel Management,* 30 (3); Joseph Sirgy, M., Efraty, D., Siegel, P. & Lee, D. (2001), A new measure of quality of work–life (QWL) based on need satisfaction and spill-over theories. *Social Indicators Research,* 55 (3), 241–302.

35. Ibid.

36. Rees, G. & French, R. (2010) (eds), *Leading, Managing and Developing People,* London: CIPD.

37. Ibid.

38. Rousseau, D. M. (2000), *Psychological Contract Inventory – Technical Report,* Carnegie Mellon University: Pittsburg.

39. Hammer, M. & Champy, J. (1993), *Re-engineering the Corporation*, HarperCollins: New York.

40. Broeways, M-J. & Price, R. (2008), *Understanding Cross-cultural Management*, FT Prentice Hall: Harlow.

41. Murza, M. (2005), *Ticking all the Boxes*, BBC News online, 12 December, see www.news.bbc.co.uk/1/hi/magazine/4521244.stm, (accessed 8 November 2007).

42. French, R. (2010), *Cross-Cultural Management in Work Organisations*, 2nd edn, London: CIPD.

43. Ibid.

44. *Belief Model for The Leadership of Anita Roddick*, www.mission-coach.co.uk/pages/belief, (accessed 2 April 2007).

45. Ibid.

46. London's twenty-first century slave trade. *Time Out*, March 21–27, 2007, 1909 issue. Reproduced by permission of Time Out Magazine.

47. Gottschalk, J. (2005), The risks associated with the business use of email. *Intellectual Property and Technology Law Journal*, **17** (7), 16–18.

48. Eason, N. (2005), Don't send the wrong message, when email crosses borders, a faux pas could be just a click away, *Business 2.0*, **6** (7), 102; Harris, S. Uh oh. *Government Executive*, **37** (1), 66–71.

49. Organisation for Economic Cooperation and Development (1996), *The Knowledge Based Economy*, OECD: Paris.

50. Skilled migrant workers add £54 bn to UK Economy. *Personnel Today*, 28 November 2006.

51. See also Workforce 2000 (1990), *Competing in a Seller's Market, Is Corporate America Prepared?* Tower Perrin/Hudson Institute: Indianapolis.

52. See Fernandez, J. P. (1991), Managing a diverse workforce. D.C Heath: Lexington, MA; O'Mara, J. (1991), *Managing Workplace 2000*, Jossey-Bass: San Francisco.

53. Department of Immigration and Multicultural and Indigenous Affairs, Productive diversity: Australia's competitive advantage, http://www.immi.gov.au/facts/07productive.htm, (accessed 25 October 2005).

54. House, R. J., Javidan, M. & Dorfman, P. (2001), The Globe Project. *Applied Psychology: An International Review*, **50** (4), 489–505.

55. Rieger, F. & Wong-Rieger, D. (1985), Strategies of international airlines as influenced by industry, societal and corporate culture. *Proceedings of the Administrative Sciences Association of Canada*, **6** (8), 129–150; Hofstede, G. (1980), Motivation, leadership, and organization: do American theories apply abroad? *Organizational Dynamics*, **9** (Summer), 42–63; Adler, N. (2002), *International Dimensions of Organizational Behaviour*, 4th edn, South-Western College Publishing: Thomson Learning.

56. Maurice, M., Sorge, A. & Warner, M. (1980), Societal differences in organizing manufacturing units: a comparison of France, West Germany and Great Britain. *British Journal of Industrial Relations*, **18** (3), 318–333.

57. Hofstede, G. (2001), *Culture's Consequences*, 2nd edn, Sage: Thousand Oaks, CA.

58. Hofstede, G. & Bond, M. (1988), The Confucius connection: from culture roots to economic growth. *Organizational Dynamics*, **16** (4), 4–21.

59. Chen, M. (2004), *Asian Management Systems*, 2nd edn, Thomson: London.

60. McSweeney, B. (2002), Hofstede's model of national cultural differences and their consequences: a triumph of faith – a failure of analysis. *Human Relations*, **55** (1), 89–118.

61. *Europe's Ageing Workforce*, BBC News Online, 20 June 2002, www.news.bbc.co.uk/1/world/europe/2053581.stm, (accessed 3 April 2007).

62. Ingelhart, R. & Baker, W. (2000), Modernization, cultural change and the persistence of traditional values. *American Sociological Review*, **65** (1), 19–51.

63. Vodafone Group, 'Working for Vodafone', www.vodafone.co.nz/aboutus/12.1.2.4_working.jsp?item=people&subitem=working, (accessed 29 September 2005).

64. Grant Thornton International Business report (2009).

65. Davis, E. & Lansbury, R. (1996), *Managing Together*, Longman: Sydney.

66. For a fuller analysis and some interesting cross-cultural comparisons see Needle, D. (2004), *Business in Context*, 4th edn, Thomson: London.

67. Albion, M. J. (2004), A measure of attitudes towards flexible work options. *Australian Journal of Management*, **29** (2), 275–294.

68. 'HSBC sets benchmark for staff childcare', www.wherewomenwanttowork.com/evidence/evidence2.asp?id, (accessed 5 April 2007).

69. *Engaging Employees: A Family Friendly Approach:* Employer of the Year Masterclass 2006, HSBC 20 June 2006.

70. www.nav.no/Familie/Svangerskap%2C+f%C3%B8dsel+adopsjon/Foreldrepenger+til+far+ved+f%C3%B8dsel+og+adopsjon (accessed 16 July 2010).

71. Lawson, M. (2003), Making the switch from Dubbo to Delhi, *Australian Financial Review,* March, http://afr.com/specialreports/report1/2003/03/20/FFXXYTV9DDD.html, (accessed 10 March 2005); Agence France Presse (2005), India set to emerge as a major outsourcing hub for global aerospace industry, www.independent-bangladesh.com/news/feb/14/14022005bs.htm#A13, (accessed 10 March 2005).

72. *Finland Leads Teleworking in Europe,* http://netti.sak.fi.sak/englanti/atricles/teleworking.htm, (accessed 5 April 2007).

73. Confederation of British Industry position on CSR (2007), http://www.cbi.org.uk/pdf/psdcsr1006.pdf, (accessed 8 November 2007).

74. Rayner, C. & Christy, R. (2010), Professionalism and Ethics in Managing People, in *Leading, Managing and Developing People* (eds G. Rees and R. French), CIPD: London.

75. Merton, R. K. (1940), Bureaucratic structure and personality, *Social Forces,* 18, 560–588, reprinted in Merton, R. K. (1957), *Social Theory and Social Structure,* New York: Free Press.

76. Levitt, S. D. & Dubner, S. J. (2005), *Freakonomics: A Rogue Economist Explores the Hidden Side of Everything,* William Morrow & Co: New York.

INTERPRETATION OF INDIVIDUAL ACTIVITY

All of the statements are true. Thus, your score should be close to 40. The closer your score is to 40, the more you understand the global context of organizational environments. The closer your score is to 10, the less you understand the global context. For development purposes you should note any particular items for which you had a low score and concentrate on improving your knowledge of those areas.

ABSENCE MANAGEMENT AND PRESENTEEISM: THE PRESSURES ON EMPLOYEES TO ATTEND WORK AND THE IMPACT OF ATTENDANCE ON PERFORMANCE

Denise Baker-McClearn, Kay Greasley, Jeremy Dale and Frances Griffith, Health Sciences Research Institute, Warwick Medical School, *University of Warwick*

Human Resource Management Journal, Vol 20, no. 3, 2010, pages 311–328

Absenteeism is an issue that has grown in importance over the past few years; however, little has been done to explore the impact of presenteeism on individual and organisational performance and well-being. This article is based on interviews collected in nine case study organisations in the UK. Two sector organisations (one private and one public) were studied to examine absence management and a conceptual model of presenteeism, with further illustration provided using data from the other seven case studies. This enabled a pattern of presenteeism to emerge, along with the contextual and individual factors which impact on it. In addition to previous research, we found that presenteeism is a complex 'problem' and that it is not a single one-dimensional construct, but is continually being shaped by individual and organisational factors. In addition, we found that performance and well-being are more closely related to the organisational reaction to presenteeism and absenteeism, rather than the act itself.

Contact: Dr Denise Baker-McClearn, Health Sciences Research Institute, Warwick Medical School, University of Warwick, Coventry CV4 7AL, UK. Email: denise.baker@warwick.ac.uk

INTRODUCTION

Optimising workforce health, the prevention of work- and lifestyle-related illness and managing absenteeism are issues that have grown significantly in importance over the past few years and are identified as public health and economic priorities. In the UK, Black's (2008) recent review of the health of Britain's working age population, 'Working for a healthier tomorrow', suggests that the development of a wellness, rather than a sickness, culture is essential to reduce absence and improve performance in the workplace. She suggests that such a culture requires good line management, support within the workplace and a change in the perception that work is damaging except for those who are totally fit. Waddell and Burton (2006) have similarly argued that the 'right' kind of work can be good for a person, but what is less frequently described is what the 'right' kind of working environment entails and how factors in the work environment, including policies, culture and perceptions of absence management impact on employee absence and presence (including presenteeism) at work.

As early as 1978, Steers and Rhodes voiced concerns about the impact of attending work when sick, suggesting that some absenteeism can be good for an organisation while over-reliance on absence figures as a measure of productivity can be counter-productive with unfavourable consequences for organisations and employees alike (Steers and Rhodes, 1978). The term presenteeism has been in usage for many years, although its definition is rather vague. For example, the trade union Unison (1999) used it to describe people 'who, despite complaints and ill health that should prompt rest and absence from work, are still turning up at their jobs' (Aronsson *et al.*, 2000: 503). Some studies define presenteeism as a reduction in productivity because of health-related conditions (Schultz and Edington, 2007); this is a different focus, not considered here.

This article briefly outlines current understanding of absence from the workplace as this forms part of the context of presenteeism. It then reviews the existing literature on presenteeism, drawing out the key themes into a model clarifying the multifaceted nature of this issue. This model is used as the framework for analysis of interview data collected during the course of a study on well-being at work. The nuances in the data in relation to the way presenteeism plays out across a number of diverse organisations suggest that, although presenteeism may be influenced by organisational policy, individual thresholds for presenteeism fluctuate. We step back from studies measuring the extent of the phenomenon (*e.g.* Caverley *et al.*, 2007) to look at its characteristics and to suggest how it reflects organisational and individual antecedents.

ABSENCE FROM THE WORKPLACE

Absenteeism has been described as the single largest source of lost productivity in business and industry in the UK, with minor illness causing the most short-term absence and stress, and mental health issues causing the most absence of over 4 weeks duration (CIPD Survey, 2005). The costs of absence are not only borne by organisations, in terms of health-related productivity losses resulting from staff absence, staff turnover, loss of skill base, recruitment and retraining, but also by the general population through costs to the health service (estimated at £5–11 billion a year), the government through supplying government benefits (£29 billion a year) and the loss of additional income through taxes of those off sick (£28–36 billion).

Monitoring absence and supporting health and well-being improves productivity and lowers absence levels, and may reduce the length of current and subsequent periods of absence (James *et al.*, 2002). Several large organisations, such as Mondial (Jenneh, 2006), Toshiba (Pollitt, 2006) and Cadbury Trebor Bassett (Pollitt, 2007), have implemented proactive health and absence management policies intended to 'empower' employees to take responsibility for their own health and well-being. Research from Scandinavia supports this idea arguing that by being proactive, economic benefits are realised in the form of increased performance and productivity and a reduction in absence levels (Van Amelsvoort *et al.*, 2006). How policies affect performance and employee well-being is not always evident. Grinyer and Singleton (2000) suggested that simply striving to reduce absence rates without focusing on those who attend work and under-perform produces artificially low absence figures and fails to improve organisational or individual efficiency. A balance, therefore, may be needed between managing absence and ensuring employees are able to perform adequately.

PRESENTEEISM

Presenteeism is increasingly being seen as a threat to employee efficiency and workplace safety. Although employers' groups have often been reluctant to address problems of presenteeism, individual employers are beginning to take the issue more seriously with the establishment of occupational health and flexible working. In this section, we review the international literature on presenteeism, drawing out the key themes to develop a model (see Figure 1) for use in further analysis.

A UK mixed method study by Grinyer and Singleton (2000) compared two public sector offices, one with higher long-term sickness than the other. Organisations were matched on key criteria such as size, employee profile and location, and employees were interviewed regarding two specific organisational factors related to the non-use of sick

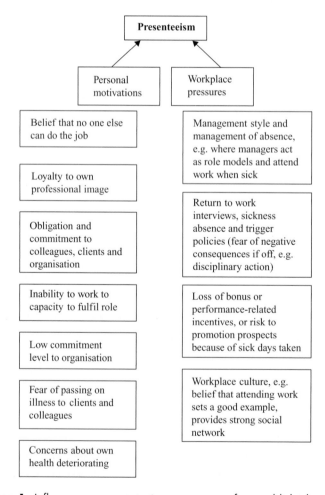

Figure 1: Influences on presenteeism: a summary from published studies

leave: obligation to colleagues (an internal pressure) and fear of reaching 'trigger' points (an external pressure). Work attendance was greater in those who felt strongly committed to serving others (clients or patients) or felt their absence would have negative consequences for themselves, colleagues or a third party. Organisational policies introduced to reduce 'casual sickness', such as increased monitoring of short-term sick leave, made staff fearful of being absent, which then left them feeling stressed and resentful. Policies were viewed as penalising the genuinely sick, as staff feared reaching a trigger point which would result in disciplinary action.

Chatterji and Tilley (2002), like Steers and Rhodes in the US, found in their mathematical modelling study that policies implemented to reduce absence, such as a reduction in sick pay, were more likely to increase presenteeism which in turn could lead to more illness and lower productivity. Taylor *et al.* (2003) concurred, suggesting that policies encouraging attendance at the cost of the employee adversely impact on employee morale and increase absence. Aronsson *et al.* (2000) and Hansson *et al.* (2006) in Scandinavia reported high presenteeism among organisations with a high 'attendance requirement' as employees felt they could not be replaced, often attending work when they were ill, in pain or before they were fully recovered.

In studies with public health-care workers in the US, New Zealand and Scandinavia, employees who worked directly with sick patients (Aronsson *et al.*, 2000; Shamansky, 2002; Pilette, 2005) suffered a great deal of internal conflict over whether to attend work while suffering from what they saw as a contagious illness. Dixon (2005), in a US survey, reported that 56 per cent of employers felt 'presenteeism' was a problem in their organisation; employee burnout and lost productivity were 7.5 times greater with 'presenteeism' than absenteeism. Samuel and Wilson (2007) suggested that employers who encouraged their staff to take sick leave and were sympathetic to their illness promoted higher staff morale and loyalty as staff felt that the importance of their well-being was recognised.

Dew *et al.* (2005) compared two hospitals and a manufacturing site in New Zealand. For health-care workers, presenteeism was related to commitment to colleagues, loyalty to professional image and the institution, and the clients/patients within it. In the manufacturing organisation, attendance was strongly linked to management style and the economic pressures that drive business.

In the US, Ramsey (2006) found that work attendance was influenced by management style. Widespread 'presenteeism' occurred when managers and supervisors failed to take days off when sick themselves. Managers felt that they had to be brave and set a good example, and that they needed to be in work as their job could not be done by anyone else. The researchers, however, suggested that the adverse effect of this may be to spread contagious illnesses to other employees, therefore contributing to a greater loss of productivity and increased absence.

Concerns have been voiced about the impact of attending work with long-term health problems. Kivimaki *et al.* (2002) found from the Whitehall II survey in the UK that male civil servants who felt unhealthy and stressed and who failed to take sick leave were at greater risk of coronary events than those who took moderate amounts of sick leave, suggesting therefore that there is some evidence linking presenteeism to long-term health conditions. Caverley *et al.* (2007) found that presenteeism tended to be inversely related to absence levels; they argued that job reductions in their case study organisation had led to high levels of presenteeism.

In this study, we have examined the key influences within the workplace which appear to contribute to presenteeism and devised a model of these factors based on this literature (see Figure 1). These key influences can be divided into two groups: *organisational pressures* and *personal motivations*. We also identify in the model other mediating factors which impact on an individual's decision to attend work. We aim to understand how ideas of presenteeism are embedded in organisational practices. What does the concept mean to people? How does it connect to the management of attendance?

THE STUDY

This article reports the findings from the secondary analysis of interview data collected as part of a wider study of health and well-being in the workplace. The aim of this study was to evaluate the impact of proactive intervention(s) on attendance management, employee well-being and the organisational climate, focusing on the contextual issues which influence the successful introduction of proactive interventions. Interviews were conducted as part of an in-depth, multi-method case study of organisational approaches to employee health and attendance management. A detailed pre- and post-intervention evaluation, which examined the organisational profile prior to and following the implementation of a number of tailored, corporate level interventions, was conducted. Interventions were aimed at helping nine diverse organisations develop a more pro-active approach to improving the health and well-being of their workforce. The study then assessed the impact of health management programmes on organisational and employee performance.

Presenteeism emerged as a significant sub-theme during data analysis. In this article, we explore employees' accounts of presenteeism to understand the subtle differences between organisational intent as laid down in policy and procedure, and the individual interpretation of this intent by employees. As described below, the nine organisations all had distinct interests in promoting health and well-being, and they might be expected to follow good practice and to have little presenteeism when compared with the mass of organisations. In fact, the concept proved to be important in all of them.

METHODS

Semi-structured interviews were conducted with 123 people from nine organisations. In addition, policy documents were examined and during data collection, observational notes were made to supplement the interviews.

Sampling

A two-stage process was used to sample for 8–10 organisations to give maximum variation of organisations and within these, a range of employees which included blue collar and white collar, skilled and unskilled workers (Patton, 1990: 182).

Sampling organisations The project team approached 86 organisations with which they had professional contact or had worked with in the past. Fifty-four of these expressed initial interest but subsequently withdrew because of internal pressures, or restructuring that might impact on the implementation of the wider project, or failed to respond to subsequent communication.

Following detailed explanation about the study, 14 organisations committed to participate in the study. Information about each organisation was gathered in a structured telephone interview with the nominated lead. This was then used to select organisations to provide maximum variation across the secondary sampling criteria in Table 1. The final sample consisted of two National Health Service (NHS) organisations, one police force, one local authority, two call centres, one manufacturing organisation, one power provider and one firm in heavy industry.

As the sample included an NHS organisation, we gained Multi-centre Research Ethics Committee approval and NHS Trust R&D approval.

Sampling employees for interview For each organisation, a 'reference group' comprising representatives from Human Resources, Occupational Health, Management and Employee representatives was established to identify key stakeholders and individuals from within the organisation who might be willing to be interviewed. Interviewees were purposively sampled to reflect as diverse an array of personnel as possible. Each interviewee was informed of the purpose of the study, given time to consider whether they wished to participate and completed a consent form. Interviewee roles and organisations are listed in Table 2. A total of 123 interviews were conducted with 47 employees, 26 line managers/supervisors, 21 middle managers, 4 senior managers, 13 Human Resource employees, 9 Occupational Health employees and 3 Trade Union representatives.

Primary criterion
   Commitment to participate in all aspects of the study at a senior (board) level
Secondary criteria
   Sector (public or private)
   Comparability
   Size (at least 100 employees to avoid sample bias and facilitate the conduct of the survey)
   Type of workforce
   Type of industry
   Current policies
   Location (Wales or Midlands)

Table 1: Criteria for organisation sampling

Case study organisation	No. of interviewees	Interviewee details
CS1: Insurance: private	15	8 Employees
		3 Supervisors
		3 Managers
		1 Human resources
CS2: Health: public sector	19	9 Employees
		3 Supervisors
		3 Managers
		1 Human resources
		1 Occupational health
CS3: Power: private	14	5 Employees
		3 Team leaders
		3 Managers
		2 Human resources
		1 Occupational health
CS4: Power: private	16	7 Employees
		4 Team leaders
		2 Managers
		2 Human resources
		1 Occupational health
CS5: Call centre: private	11	4 Employees
		1 Trade union employee
		3 Supervisors
		1 Manager
		1 Occupational health
		1 Human resources
CS6: Manufacturer: private	13	4 Employees
		1 Trade union employee
		3 Supervisors
		1 Manager
		1 Senior manager
		2 Occupational health
		1 Human resources
CS7: Local authority: public sector	14	4 Employees
		1 Trade union employee
		1 Occupational health employee
		2 Supervisors
		3 Managers
		1 Senior manager
		2 Human resources
CS8: Police force: public sector	12	4 Employees
		2 Supervisors
		2 Managers
		2 Senior managers
		1 Occupational health
		1 Human resources
CS9: Health: public sector	11	2 Employees
		3 Supervisors
		3 Managers
		2 Human resources
		1 Occupational health

Table 2: Interview sample by case study organisation

Interview process and data management

Semi-structured interviews followed a topic guide (summarised in Table 3) which had been piloted in one organisation. Interviews were audio recorded and transcribed.

Transcriptions were checked for accuracy then imported into NVivo (QSR International, Stockport, UK) to assist with data handling. For the wider study, a coding frame was developed by DB and KG working on different sets of data within the study. Their coding frames and definitions were compared, combined and discussed with the research team. Codes were derived from the research questions and questions included in the topic guide or were secondary themes which emerged from the data. Constant refinement of the coding frame took place as the study progressed with stand-alone codes being added. For this article, the secondary theme of presenteeism was examined. Each author read at least five full transcripts where presenteeism appeared as an important theme. They then read the data which was coded under presenteeism. This article reports this data, but draws on the rest of the interview along with observation notes and organisational policy documents for understanding the context.

Analysis process

The policies of each organisation relevant to sickness absence were examined as the interview data needs to be interpreted for the context in which each interviewee was working. Two of the case study organisations, one private (CS1) and one public (CS2) sector organisation, were found to have high rates of reported presenteeism, as identified by interviewees who consistently reported this theme during interviews. We therefore initially focused on the rich data from these two organisations and compared it with the model in Figure 1. We then used the data from the other organisations to support or refute our analysis.

FINDINGS
Policies relevant to sickness absence

Here we provide a summary of the organisation's policies relevant to sickness absence. When reporting the interview data, we provide additional detail as needed.

We had no prior knowledge of each organisation's sickness absence policies, so diversity on this issue was not controlled for. We found that sickness absence policies had distinct similarities; for example, they all had specific procedures for reporting absence, they all had stated periods of paid absence related to how long the employee had been working with the organisation; differences in the policies were generally related to how they were implemented and who was implementing them. All organisations had 'trigger' polices, where formal procedures were initiated if an employee had more than a certain number of absences (usually three) within a specific period of time (usually 12 months).

Sick pay entitlement was fairly standard for public sector organisations, but was more variable at private sector organisations. For example, at CS1, employees were only eligible for sick pay after 6 months of absence-free employment. They were also highly likely

Perceptions and experiences of attendance and health management policies and procedures

The role of departments, their functions and individuals, in attendance and health management

Inter-personal relationships within the organisation

Cultural influences on attendance and health management

Perceptions of absence in the workplace

Health-related issues that affect organisational performance

Rehabilitation in the workplace

Expectations of interventions and recommendations for improvement

Table 3: Topic guide summary

to have their sick pay suspended if they had more than three absences in a 12-month period. To have it reinstated, they had to have no absence for 6 months.

All organisations had procedures for rehabilitation which included phased return to work, or modified working, although employees often argued that some of the options were not offered to everyone.

Private sector organisations were more likely to offer financial or other incentives to those not taking any sickness absence; for example, one organisation entered employees with 100 per cent attendance records into a prize draw to win £500 while another offered employees the chance to win a car.

The model of presenteeism

The model of presenteeism derived from the previous literature (Figure 1) indicates a number of factors underlying an individual's decision to either attend or be absent from work when feeling unwell. Previous research has tended to focus on either workplace-related factors or the internal pressures individuals' experience when deliberating over whether to take time off for being sick. Often, these factors have been examined in isolation from one another, without an examination of how they might converge to produce different individual choices, in different situations. In testing the model, we aim to apply the findings of this study, which examined a wide range of causes of presenteeism in different workplaces, including those related to the *Institution* and those that emanate from the *Individual*, in the development of an understanding of how complex and multi-dimensional presenteeism is.

Institutionally mediated presenteeism (organisational pressures)

Institutionally mediated presenteeism was related to the organisational context or the working environment (including policies, procedures, management style and approach, and workplace culture).

Sickness absence and trigger policies Many interviewees perceived that their organisation's sickness absence policies and procedures compelled attendance at work, especially where sick pay was withdrawn, or there was a threat of disciplinary action or dismissal. This was very common at CS1, where this pressure was felt to contribute to low morale, lack of commitment to work, stress and anxiety. The most unpopular policy was the suspension of sick pay following a number of episodes of absence as it had the most wide-reaching implications, in and out of work, and was at the discretion of managers who were often perceived as being inconsistent in their approach.

> *I'm twenty and I've bought a house with my partner and obviously being that you've got to pay your bills it does get quite stressful because you think to yourself as much as you might not feel well enough to go into work you've got to because you won't get paid and it's fifty pounds, a lot of money to lose for a day. (Employee, private sector; CS1)*

Policies with 'trigger points' existed in all the case studies, but they appeared to create a great deal of pressure at CS1 where individuals approaching their third or fourth period of absence faced possible disciplinary procedures:

> *I do sympathise with people that are up to their second or third occasion of illness and they've had an interview with me and they've got absolutely desperate stomach ache, toothache whatever, they come into work and go home. (Manager, private sector: CS1)*

Another manager concurred suggesting that because sick pay is at the manager's discretion, employees drag themselves to work when they are sick, adding that germs then may get spread to others. The discomfort experienced by some managers was evident, especially where there was an expectation that policies should be strictly enforced as in both CS1 and CS2. Employees often felt they were in a 'lose–lose' situation; if they were absent they would be penalised, but if they attended work they would be unable to perform their duties effectively and would suffer too in terms of their health and general well-being. This was also in evidence at other case studies. At CS6, for example, interviewees reported that sick colleagues felt 'bullied' or 'pressured' back to work by organisational procedures which involved a representative from the organisation coming to their home if they were absent.

Absence management by HR Much of the interview data suggest that there is a perception that HR are primarily focused on getting people into the workplace and keeping them there, even when employees and managers felt that a period of absence was a better course of action. At CS2, for example, interviewees perceived a lack of flexibility and understanding on the part of HR when it came to understanding job roles; while some employees can return to work earlier in less physically demanding roles, this may not be appropriate for others. Managers felt pressure from HR departments and senior management to 'effectively manage' sickness absence, and reduce 'unofficial' absences. Many felt uncomfortable with that role as they did not feel supported by senior managers and they lacked an understanding of why they were required to carry out certain tasks, such as return-to-work interviews. Although it appeared from the interviews and discussions that HR departments were keen to devolve more responsibility for absence management to managers, in many cases there was little or inadequate training in 'people management' and a great deal of inconsistency in managers' approach to the role. This was demonstrated by the comments of a manager who described one type of management approach, explaining how policies might reduce absence, while also appearing unaware of how coercive her comments might sound:

> I think (if) the sickness and absence policies are being strictly worked and abided by then (staff will) be really worried about taking unofficial absence. I don't want people to come into work with germs and bugs and things. A genuine sickness, no problem. It's sporadic sickness, definitely, I want to stop because if you've got less people off sick, you're going to feel less pressurised and also not fear – shouldn't use the word fear – but they all know 'oh gosh I can't take this sporadic sickness because I'll have another interview, may be a first formal or second formal, I cannot risk losing my job or something' whereas in the past they got away with it. So hopefully they'll think there's more hard line management really. (Senior manager, public sector, CS8)

Employees often viewed HR departments as being for policy implementation and absence management.

> I feel that there's more of a push for people just to get them back into work, rather than supporting and it comes from an HR level and management level where it's a case of getting people back in and then we'll manage it afterwards. And that's where they see this penal side, where people think I'm being punished now for being ill. (Employee, private sector, CS6)

Occupational health (OH) departments, where they were available, were more often viewed as being for the benefit of the employee and in particular to look after their health. Where OH departments worked well, employees sought out help, advice, health checks and felt 'looked after '. In contrast, those with a less high profile or proactive role were viewed as being less supportive or the place that employees were sent if they had too many absences, or in the words of one employee 'the big stick'.

'Return-to-work' interviews Return-to-work interviews were often perceived as organisational 'tools' designed to get a person back to the workplace rather than a show of concern about the employee's well-being:

> Colleagues that have come in with broken legs that should really be covered by health and safety but are being told 'Oh, that's OK you can stay' and then later being told that no way should they be in the workplace. I know from my own experience... they lay quite heavily on you that if your sickness doesn't improve that they'll terminate, that your contract will be terminated. (Employee, public sector; CS2)

Employees who had experienced return-to-work interviews often reported that it felt like a 'telling off' rather than a means of receiving support. This often left employees feeling quite stressed on their return to work as they knew they would receive such an interview.

Management style and management of absence Just as employees disliked the way return-to-work interviews were conducted, some managers disliked their formality and the rigidity of policies:

> *I don't like our attendance policy, I don't like the pressure it puts on individuals to come into work when they're not feeling particularly well. I also don't like these back to work interviews because I think more of an informal chat is better, again it puts pressure on people to come back before they're ready maybe ... and then they go off sick again and I believe we don't believe them when they say they're sick. (Line manager, public sector; CS2)*

As this line manager suggests, the rigidity of procedures may not allow for a sensitive, supportive approach, and may support a general culture of not believing that employees are ill. Another senior manager at CS2 suggested that despite a reduction of 1 per cent in absence rates 'on paper' brought about by rigidly adhering to policies, there is evidence of some underlying problems with employees attending work sick, suffering stress and anxiety over their absence, not wanting to hit the trigger point and subsequently becoming more unwell.

How to manage absence was a major concern for managers. They demonstrated very different perceptions and views about this whole area, reflecting the issue of consistency of approach that emerged in all the case studies.

> *Probably like a lot of organisations, there are some people who have sickness who perhaps aren't entitled to it and it isn't challenged and that creates a culture where people feel the ability to ask for time off as a right. . . . The other side of the coin is, unfortunately, there are occasions where because of inept management some people don't get the support they need, and that to me is just poor management. (Senior manager, public sector; CS3)*

Expressions in the above quote such as 'aren't entitled to it' and 'time off as a right' are perhaps indicative of a culture of institutional presenteeism, where managers view sickness absence as discretionary rather than an employees' 'right'. In another extract illustrating the different management approaches to absence and sickness, a manager tries to downplay employees' feelings of being ill, suggesting it was her role to encourage her staff to think positively:

> *Somebody will say 'oh, I've got flu', and I say 'oh, you've only got a cold, just take an aspirin or something' and try and buck them up a bit really yes. . . . you've got to try and egg people on and say 'oh no, you're not as bad as you seem'. (Manager, private sector; CS1)*

This perception contrasted with those of other interviewees in the organisation, reflecting the diverse perspectives that underpin management style.

Bonuses, incentives and promotion prospects Bonuses and incentives were common at private sector companies for employees who did not take time off sick, or who met sales or other organisational targets. At the public sector sites, there were more concerns about promotion prospects and performance-related pay.

At CS1, for example, sales targets brought bonuses that enabled employees to increase their wages. Employees often relied on these to provide what they considered a reasonable living wage. If they were off sick, they were less likely to meet sales targets and, in addition, many were unlikely to receive sick pay.

> *I think not being paid for time off, that is obviously an incentive to come in – you can have time off, great, but you're not going to be paid for it. Again, not in our department but in (another) the fact that you're not coming in, you won't be making your policies, you won't be adding towards your bonus. . . . I think people do feel pressured to come back in just because of losing them. (Employee, CS1)*

Interviewees had mixed opinions regarding the offering of bonuses and incentives to discourage sickness absence. Some felt that staff that had 100 per cent attendance records should be rewarded by the organisation. However, many felt that the pursuit of incentives could make employees feel unduly pressured to attend work.

> *there's those who just don't go sick, unless they're really ill and there are those who do go sick. So, how do you differentiate between those? I just don't know. Looking at numbers, if you've not been sick for a year, that's good really, isn't it, because obviously, you have felt poorly at times? So perhaps acknowledging that in some way, recognising that you've not been off work all year, appreciating that with letters. . . . or, you could do a draw for a holiday in Majorca or something like that. (Line manager, private sector, CS3)*

Although this manager's comments suggest that he would like to reward employees' commitment, he fails to acknowledge that individuals vary in the extent to which they can tolerate being unwell without their performance being affected, and that people faced with the same symptoms might react differently.

At public sector organisations, a key concern was the maintenance of a good work profile to ensure long-term promotion prospects were not harmed.

> *In my experience, I think most people will struggle on, but there are a few people who won't make the effort. Most people will because they know if they're not there, somebody else has got to pick their work up and it just puts extra pressure on other people . . . I think HR monitor that as well. It's competency related pay. . . . part of that competency is the fact that your sickness level is below average (for the organisation) or below a certain level. So, if during the year your sickness level creeps above that, then you'll lose that entitlement. (Supervisor, public sector)*

Workplace culture At CS3, older employees and managers taught younger ones that they should discuss problems, get them sorted out and turn up for work and that it was not the 'done thing' to go off sick. This was the 'work ethic' passed down from worker to worker and impacted on the decision to be absent

Personally mediated presenteeism (personal motivation)

Personally mediated presenteeism reflecting individuals' internal drivers (such as their moral perspective on letting their colleagues, clients and the organisation down; or how they perceived absence might impact on their own career prospects) was widespread. There was less evidence of personal commitment to the workplace at organisations where employees felt coerced into being at work, such as at CS1 where the impact of the policies and procedures played a much greater role.

Commitment to colleagues and clients Employees in the public sector case studies experienced greater conflicting emotions over whether to attend work when they felt ill than occurred in the private sector case studies. Many did not want to let down their colleagues by being absent. They felt strongly committed to their organisation and loyal to the team who they perceived they had left to cover their job or duties.

Commitment to work was also strong when the general public were involved, although employees often felt that attending work with what they saw as a contagious illness was at odds with their desire not to pass on germs. Employees ended up feeling guilty both for taking time off work and for attending when sick:

> *some might argue, 'Oh, it's only a cold' but if you're going around somewhere where people are trying to get better is it a good thing? . . . It's a job to decide at times. Sometimes if you feel a bit yucky and you think, 'I'm coughing and sneezing' or something like that, do you or don't you, come in? Well I don't like being off any more than what I have to be but you just feel a little bit of responsibility towards other people . . . you can pass it on to somebody on the Ward and they could pass it on to a patient. (Employee, public sector; CS2)*

Numerous interviewees from all case studies expressed concern about employees attending work with short-term, contagious illnesses like colds, flu, stomach bugs, diarrhoea and sickness. It was frequently felt to be an irresponsible and undesirable practice that might result in more people becoming absent. Although the majority of employees and some managers categorically stated that if a person was ill they should not be at work, individuals' definitions over what constitutes a level of illness that prevents work varied.

Personal progress Some employees suggested that taking time off might be viewed as an indicator of poor performance and might impact on their promotion prospects.

> *'I don't want to blot my copy book'. (Employee, private sector, CS3)*

The perception that taking time off sick as a sign of under-performance was not always explicitly stated, but was often subtly evident in informal conversations, particularly in private sector organisations. 'High pressure' environments, with little spare capacity to accommodate absence, where employees held very specific or specialised roles and needed to be present to carry out essential tasks for the organisation to function at full capacity, were more likely to have a workplace culture that supported presenteeism.

Variants of presenteeism

Our findings suggest that the 'model' of presenteeism (Figure 1) needs to be seen as dynamic set of interactions, fluctuating according to circumstances. Although an individual might at one time have a low threshold for presenteeism, displaying a laissez faire attitude to absence, at another time the threshold may be raised because of additional work pressures, or internal pressures. For example, at case study sites CS3 and CS4 employees were required to work large amounts of overtime to conduct maintenance and for which they earned extra money, attendance was expected and every employee had a designated role (so both individual and organisational motivators to work even though an employee might be unwell); at these times there was very little absence. Following such periods, absence often increased (reduced workplace pressure and less to lose personally if a day or two of sickness absence taken in order to recover from the period of hard work). It might be argued that presenteeism increased during the time of high pressure, when organisational expectations are much higher, whereas during less pressured times, presenteeism reduces and absenteeism may increase.

HR staff and managers also experienced conflicting pressures regarding presenteeism. Here, one HR officer weighs up the financial costs of absence against the human costs including the possible consequences of attending work unwell or unfit.

> the cost of sickness absence ... [includes] the hard costings in terms of monetary value but also the impact on other people. So if Jack's off sick then John who sits next to him will have to cover some of his work. ... That puts additional strain on John so as well as the financial costs, there's the human costs as well ... (However) if somebody is signed off sick and is told not to work, medical advice, we do have people on site here, who will go against that advice and still come into work and insist that they're fit enough to do the job ... that's never an acceptable course of action. ... if somebody makes an error of judgement which is caused in part by the fact that they're operating at less than 100 per cent of their normal efficiency and they make a serious error then the impact could be enormous, so we discourage that. (HR officer, private sector, CS4)

Institutionally mediated presenteeism was characteristic of work environments with strongly enforced organisational policies, as described in previous research (Aronsson *et al.*, 2000; Grinyer and Singleton, 2000; Hansson *et al.*, 2006). In such organisations, presenteeism is fuelled by the threat of withdrawal of sick pay, trigger policies which hint at disciplinary action, and return-to-work interviews that are seen as punitive rather than supportive. In addition, incentives, such as bonuses and risks to career prospects, provide a further source of potential stress.

Policies and procedures which make employees feel insecure about their financial stability, employment or promotion prospects may create stress, tension, low morale and, at worst, employee antipathy towards the organisation itself. This is likely to affect well-being in the workplace, not only bringing employees into work when unwell but also potentially reducing their overall productivity and adversely affecting the wider organisational climate.

Individuals returning to work on light or modified duties, or phased returns, following long-term absence, often did so because they had been encouraged by their employers to return or because their entitlement to sick pay was running out. Despite being back in the workplace and re-engaging with work, these individuals may not yet be fully 'productive'. Some interviewees were sceptical about the purpose of bringing such individuals back to work before they had fully recovered, believing it was to keep sickness absence figures low rather than supporting the rehabilitation of the employee.

If you're ill there's nothing you can do, you're ill. You can't come to work. But there's a lot of these come in on light duties. What I feel is, come in to keep the sickness level down. I've seen lads in here hobbling in and I said 'what are you doing in?' He just came in and did nothing. (Employee, private sector, CS4)

Although the colleague described in the above extract was said to have come to work and 'did nothing', it may be that his presence at work served a rehabilitative function, whereas sitting at home and 'doing nothing' could be socially isolating and delay the return to work. Such perceptions may also reflect the area in which the colleague worked; for example, it might be more feasible for employees with desk jobs to return to work sooner than those with manual or physical jobs. Examples where this was the case were seen in both CS1 and CS2, where, for example, a manager who had returned to work early following an accident felt he had returned too soon, but because most of his job was desk-based, he felt that he had not suffered any negative effects.

There was at times a lack of understanding on the part of employees and managers about the purpose and benefit of phased return and modified working. Those who had benefited from such arrangements perceived that they had been provided with good support and valued the flexibility and understanding on the part of the organisation and managers. Despite the employee working at less than full capacity, the organisation was felt to be supporting their recovery and enabling them to return to their social network in the workplace quicker. This might be seen as promoting a positive form of presenteeism.

In contrast to the supported return to work approach discussed above, there were reports of employees feeling pressured to attend work despite not feeling they were ready or fully recovered. Such employees often felt unable to perform to their full capacity, and there appeared to be heightened feelings of stress, resentment and lack of organisational commitment. Some reported experiencing repeated problems with their health or had made themselves feel worse as they tried to struggle on.

Where work environments fostered personally mediated presenteeism there was a strong commitment to colleagues and clients and professional image. Personally mediated presenteeism was most common amongst public sector staff, although not exclusively.

The responsibilities associated with job role also influenced the decision to attend work, while others suggested taking absence was due to their commitment not to pass on illnesses to their colleagues or clients with whom they might work.

In contrast, there was much evidence at CS1 and CS2 that employees routinely attended work suffering from short-term ailments such as coughs, colds and stomach bugs. Many interviewees felt that they risked passing on illnesses to their colleagues and felt that their own performance was adversely affected. Indeed we found that presenteeism was a significant cause of poor performance and increased absence and that presenteeism itself was often seen as irresponsible by employees and line managers alike:

> We don't expect them to come in if they're unwell, if they can spread any coughs, sneezes or any illness, diarrhoea, vomiting, we don't want them in the workplace till they're fit and healthy to work. (Assistant manager, CS2)

It was clear that a balance needed to be struck between the needs of the service and the needs of its workforce. An insensitive approach from managers, for example, was more likely to increase presenteeism and reduce employee motivation and well-being at work. With a workplace culture that consistently placed pressure on its employees to be in work, we might assume that employees would, despite being physically present, simply become mentally disengaged.

DISCUSSION

By studying nine diverse organisations, we were able to examine all of the concepts described in previous research and summarised in our model of presenteeism. Our findings supported the idea that there are two distinct types of presenteeism, *institutionally mediated presenteesim*, which was more prevalent in the private sector organisations and related to organisational pressures (Grinyer and Singleton, 2000; Chatterji and Tilley, 2002; Taylor *et al.*, 2003; Hansson *et al.*, 2006) and *personally mediated presenteeism* which was more common in the public sector organisations (Shamansky, 2002; Aronsson and Gustafsson, 2005; Dew *et al.*, 2005; Dixon, 2005).

We also found that the model derived from the literature was too simplistic. We listened to a vast array of perspectives on presenteeism and it became evident that there are many mediating factors which will promote or discourage presenteeism in a number of different circumstances. These factors work on an individual level in a dynamic manner so that while one person in an organisation might be discouraged from practising presenteeism, another may not think twice about it.

Mediating factors, such as fear of passing on illness to colleagues and clients were common across all organisations, as was the perception that attending work when unfit was not acceptable as it may increase organisational illness and hinder recovery. In addition, we found that early rehabilitation of employees might have some positive aspects, the underlying reasoning (simply to reduce figures or to support employees at their own pace?) affected how positive the organisation was about such policies.

Other common factors were how supported an employee felt (by their manager and organisation as a whole), what the particular circumstances were in the organisation and what was required of a person at work (for example, would they be missed; would absence impact on others; would they lose money?)

Our study refines earlier research, elucidating the fluctuating nature of presenteeism, depending on individual and organisational context. Early rehabilitation policies, for example, support Black's (2008) assertion that work is good for us and for some, the policies did appear to benefit the organisation and employee alike, when implemented with mutual consent, support and understanding. Such policies may also increase employee commitment and feelings of well-being and could reduce the propensity for employees to become disengaged from the workplace. However, where the motivation is simply to reduce absence statistics they may increase the problem of presenteeism giving managers problems with running an effective and productive service.

The impact of presenteeism on productivity is, however, hard to measure. Although previous research has suggested that the loss of productivity is greater with presenteeism than absenteeism (Grinyer and Singleton, 2000; Dixon, 2005; Main *et al.*, 2005; Caverley *et al.*, 2007), this study demonstrates the complexity of the relationship between these two things. For example, in the case of rehabilitation, where policies are well thought-out and are designed to support the individual, the organisation accepts that the employee is going to be less productive for a while but this may contribute to investing in their long-term commitment. Both employee and organisation are entering a reciprocal arrangement, one by returning to work early, the other by providing support and helping re-socialise the employee; both reap the benefits in the long term (the organisation may be more efficient by doing this as it reduces staff turnover costs, retraining costs, promotes workforce stability, employee loyalty and group cohesiveness). Employees returning to work voluntarily and being supported back in to work have less opportunity to drop out of the work market or to lose their self-confidence, jobs or skills and social network that their workplace provides, while the organisation holds on to the established experience and expertise of that individual. Such linkages are hard to understand if absence and presence are treated simply as opposites.

In contrast, we also found a lack of overt employee support in several organisations. If an employee feels unwell but fears taking sickness absence, then this might increase the likelihood that they attend work but feel disengaged. This fits with Samuel and Wilson's (2007) finding that employers who encouraged staff to take sick leave and were sympathetic to their illness promoted higher staff morale and loyalty. Certainly in organisations with more proactive employee support and less pressure placed on absent employees, employee well-being and commitment to their work place appeared higher.

We would suggest that organisations tailor their solutions for different people, teams and settings within an organisation and use multiple ways of assessing productivity and efficiency, moving away from the tendency to use absence data, introducing measures which tap into employee attitudes and views of their own productivity and even ask how often they attend work sick.

This study has provided further evidence that there is complex decision-making that underlies sickness absence and presenteeism and has sought to dispel some of the negative connotations that the term presenteeism has gained in order to capture the subtle differences between voluntary and institutional presenteeism, those who are 'under-performing' in the workplace and the fact that some aspects of 'presenteeism' may be beneficial, a concept that has not been explored previously. It has offered an alternative future for presenteeism, one which recognises that, like absenteeism, some can be positive and some can be negative but that it is not the act itself that should be managed and controlled, but the organisation's response to those who are participating in it.

The organisations that agreed to participate in this study cannot be considered to be representative of those across the UK economy; for example, no small enterprises were included. They were, indeed, self-selected on the basis that they were keen to improve well-being at work and were at different stages of creating improved health and well-being packages in their workplace. The fact that presenteeism loomed large here suggests that it is more of a feature across the economy generally; there is some evidence that it may also be a feature of the recession that began in 2007. Future research would need to cover a range of other organisations to further assess the extent and determinants of presenteeism. The present article has identified some antecedents and has shown how presenteeism is deeply embedded in organisational practice.

REFERENCES

Aronsson, G. and Gustafsson, K. (2005). 'Sickness presenteeism: prevalence, attendance-pressure factors and an outline of a model for research'. *Journal of Occupational and Environmental Medicine, 47*: 9, 958–966.

Aronsson, G., Gustafsson, K. and Dallner, M. (2000). 'Sick but yet at work. An empirical study of sickness presenteeism'. *Journal of Epidemiology and Community Health, 54*: 502–509.

Black, C. (2008). *Working for a Healthier Tomorrow*, http://www.workingforhealth.gov.uk/documents/working-for-a-healthier-tomorrow-tagged.pdf, accessed 18 November 2009.

Caverley, N., Barton Cunningham, J. and MacGregor, J.N. (2007). 'Sickness presenteeism, sickness absenteeism, and health following restructuring in a public service organization'. *Journal of Management Studies, 44*: 2, 304–319.

Chatterji, M. and Tilley, C.J. (2002). 'Sickness, absenteeism and sick pay'. *Oxford Economic Papers, 54*: 669–687.

CIPD Survey (2005). *Absence Management*, http://www.cipd.co.uk, accessed 18 November 2009.

Dew, K., Keefe, V. and Small, K. (2005). ' "Choosing" to work when sick: workplace presenteeism'. *Social Science and Medicine,* 60: 2273–2282.

Dixon, K. (2005). 'Weighing the costs of presenteeism: recognise the signs and repair the damage of employee burnout'. *Chief Executive-New York,* 209: 22–23.

Grinyer, A. and Singleton, V. (2000). 'Sickness absence as risk-taking behaviour: a study of organisational and cultural factors in the public sector'. *Health, Risk and Society,* 2: 1, 7–21.

Hansson, M., Bostrom, C. and Harms-Ringdahl, K. (2006). 'Sickness absence and sickness attendance – what people with neck or back pain think'. *Social Science and Medicine,* 62: 2183–2195.

James, P., Cunningham, I. and Dibben, P. (2002). 'Absence management and the issues of job retention and return to work'. *Human Resource Management Journal,* 12: 2, 82–94.

Jenneh, T. (2006). 'Mondial UK reduces absence and increases productivity: a collaborative approach to managing health and well-being'. *Human Resource Management International Digest,* 14: 5, 31–33.

Kivimaki, M., Leino-Arjas, P., Luukkonen, R., Riihimaki, H., Vahtera, J. and Kirjonen, J. (2002). 'Work stress and risk of cardiovascular mortality: prospective cohort study of industrial employees'. *British Medical Journal,* 326: 7369, 857.

Main, C., Glozier, N. and Wright, I. (2005). 'Validity of the HSE stress tool: an investigation within four organisations by the Corporate Health and Performance Group'. *Occupational Medicine,* 55: 3, 208–214.

Patton, M. (1990). *Qualitative Evaluation and Research Methods,* 2nd edn, Newbury Park, CA: Sage Publications.

Pilette, P. (2005). 'Presenteeism in nursing: a clear and present danger to productivity'. *Journal of Nursing Administration,* 35: 6, 300–303.

Pollitt, D. (2006). 'Pressure management keeps down the stress at Toshiba UK: company strives to be among the UK's best employers'. *Human Resource Management International Digest,* 14: 5, 29–30.

Pollitt, D. (2007). 'Cadbury's runs smoothly under pressure: wellness programme keeps IT project on track'. *Human Resource Management International Digest,* 15: 1, 14–16.

Ramsey, R. (2006). ' "Presenteeism" a new problem in the workplace'. *Supervision,* 67: 8, 14–17.

Samuel, R.J. and Wilson, L.M. (2007). 'Is presenteeism hurting your workforce?'. *Employee Benefit Plan Review,* 61: 11, 5–7.

Schultz, A. and Edington, D.W. (2007). 'Employee health and presenteeism: a systematic review'. *Journal of Occupational Rehabilitation,* 17: 3, 547–579.

Shamansky, S.L. (2002). 'Editorial: presenteeism . . . or when being there is not being there'. *Public Health Nursing-Cambridge,* 19: 2, 79–80.

Steers, R. and Rhodes, S. (1978). 'Major influences on employee attendance: a process model'. *Journal of Applied Psychology,* 63: 391–407.

Taylor, P., Baldry, C., Bain, B. and Ellis, V. (2003). ' "A unique working environment": health, sickness and absence management in UK call centres'. *Work, Employment and Society,* 17: 3, 435–458.

Unison (1999). *Tackling Sick. Absence Policies,* http://www.unison.org.uk, accessed 18 November 2009.

Van Amelsvoort, L.G.P.M., Spigt, M.G., Swaen, G.M.H. and Kant, I. (2006). 'Leisure time physical activity and sickness absenteeism; a prospective study'. *Occupational Medicine,* 56: 3, 210–212.

Waddell, G. and Burton, K. (2006). *Is Work Good for Your Health and Wellbeing?,* London: TSO.

JOURNAL ARTICLE QUESTIONS

Journal Article 1

1. Think of at least four types of people who should be interested in this article, and why?

2. Why do you think 'previous studies' have been more simplistic in their approaches to the issue of absenteeism and presenteeism.

3. Suggest two strengths and two weaknesses of the paper.

PART 2

INDIVIDUAL DIFFERENCES AND THEIR RELEVANCE TO WORK

2 Perception, personality and values

3 Learning, reinforcement and self-management

4 Motivation and empowerment

Journal article: Parker, S. K., Bindl, U. K. and Strauss, K. (2010), Making things happen: a model of proactive motivation. *Journal of Management*, **36**(4), 827–856.

In this section of the book we explore a range of topics comprising the psychological perspective on organizational behaviour, in which the essential focus is on the individual person. An important tradition within OB has identified links between individual attributes and behaviour at work. Some writers stress individual uniqueness based on our own life experiences but others have sought to group people by personality type or preferred styles of learning. This latter perspective has led to a preponderance of psychometric testing enabling organizations to identify and choose the 'right person', from their point of view. We will examine the validity of such psychometric predictions and also consider the important ethical considerations involved.

In the following chapters, we will highlight the importance of individual attributes within the performance equation. We will also delve into the specific topic areas of *perception* – the process by which we select, interpret and respond to information from the world around us – *personality, learning* and *motivation*. While we will show how individual attributes can impact on the way we work, this relationship is two-sided. In later sections of the book we examine how features of organizations in turn affect individuals' experience of work. In Chapter 5, for example, we indicate how the ways in which work is designed and organized will impact on the individual worker and their attitudes. So the relationship between individual attributes and work arrangements is a reciprocal one.

CHAPTER 2

Perception, personality and values

LEARNING OBJECTIVES

After studying this chapter you should be able to:

- explain the individual performance equation
- comprehend the perceptual process and its importance in determining workplace attitudes and behaviour
- discuss personality characteristics that distinguish individuals
- define and understand the nature of values and attitudes and their importance within organizational behaviour.

POLITICS IN THE TV SPOTLIGHT

On 15 April 2010 the first live televised debate between three major UK political leaders took place during the General Election campaign. This was a widely anticipated forum, certainly in media circles, with keen interest in the outcome and effect on the campaign. In the event, the initial effects were indeed dramatic in terms of immediate reaction. Two opinion polls conducted by YouGov for *The Sun* newspaper and ComRes for ITV news called Nick Clegg, the Liberal Democrat party leader, the clear 'winner' of the debate. Clegg's performance was analysed in  subsequent days, with suggestions that viewers' positive perceptions of him were in part due to his effective projection both to the immediate and television audience, for example by looking directly at the cameras and use of questioners' names when responding to them.[1] Nick Clegg's performance at the debate also had a clear impact on the parties' standing in opinion polls at that time. One survey of 400 people while they watched the debate[2] recorded a 14% rise in those intending to vote Liberal Democrat, coupled with a 3% drop in support for both the Labour and Conservative parties.

These significant shifts in public opinion point to the role of *perception* in influencing people's attitudes and behaviour – a topic we go on to present at length in this chapter. In an important sense, Clegg's success was due to increased exposure and recognition when he was given 'equal billing' with the two larger parties, and the inclusion of the Liberal Democrats in the TV debates had only been subject to agreement by other party leaders. So many people may have watched Clegg talk at length for the first time when they viewed the debate. The effect of perception on public opinion was also evident in previous US Presidential elections. It was held to have been a significant factor in the close 1960 race when John F. Kennedy was judged the winner of a debate by those who saw it on television – but not by those who listened on radio, where a majority judged the seemingly less photogenic Richard Nixon to have won.[3] In OB terms we can apply the lessons of these political debates to numerous situations involving the management of people; from recruitment and selection to performance appraisal and even dismissal. We often only have brief opportunities to gain impressions of potential and actual employees, so an in-depth knowledge of how the perceptual process works is invaluable.

Personality also played an important part in the 2010 UK General Election as politics came to be increasingly presidential in nature. All the party leaders were subject to personality assessment in the media which included hostile reactions, for example, to the-then Prime Minister Gordon Brown's recorded comments after meeting a member of the public in Rochdale. It became possible to view the election as akin to an extended job interview for a chief executive role with issues of personality and trust very much to the fore. Personality is an important concept in OB terms and we go on to consider it in this chapter – with a full consideration of *leadership* in Chapter 9.

At the time of the first television debate on 15 April, Nick Clegg had noted that there was a long way to go before the British public gave their final verdict on 6 May. The election result showed that the boost to Liberal Democrat ratings after the 15 April debate had quickly diminished, although the nature of the result enabled the formation of a coalition government including the Liberal Democrats, in which Nick Clegg became Deputy Prime Minister. The 2010 General Election result may have been influenced in part by voter perceptions of the party leaders but it also reinforced the key importance of *values*; that is people's consistent beliefs on issues which are important to them. We will show how people's values can be an important factor in influencing work-related attitudes and behaviour at work later in this chapter. Given that political debates should centre on deep-rooted ideas on the nature of society, the fact that these televised events had less impact in determining the election result than was predicted immediately after the debates was reassuring to many observers. In OB, people's values influence their attitudes and behaviour in important ways, so, as we will see, a focus on values is pivotal to an understanding of our subject area.

Questions

1. How important is an individual's personality as a factor in successful performance in a job interview or business presentation? Give reasons for your conclusions.
2. A number of reality television programmes, such as *Big Brother*, involve the 'eviction' of contestants from the programme by viewers. However, viewers' perceptions, as evidenced by their votes, often differ sharply from the perceptions contestants have of each other. How could we explain such discrepancies?

INTRODUCTION

Personality *is the overall profile or combination of traits that characterize the unique nature of a person.*

Values *are global beliefs that guide actions and judgements across a variety of situations.*

In Chapter 1 we saw how managers' work involves sustaining high performance levels among workers. We also examined some key issues – for example globalization and changing employer–employee relations – which reinforced the need to ensure that individuals are both willing and able to work effectively. Accordingly, it is important that managers have a good understanding of individual attributes and what makes people different. In this chapter we will examine in detail three broad categories important in our study of organizational behaviour: individual perception, **personality** characteristics and values and attitudes. As students or as managers of people, it is extremely important to understand your own values and how they differ from those held by others. This is especially the case in pluralist societies increasingly common in Europe. In a pluralist society we particularly need to understand differences in perceptions between people from different cultural backgrounds.

Consequently, in this chapter we also examine **values** and **attitudes** as they relate to the workplace. These three concepts: *perception*, *personality* and *values and attitudes* are critical to your understanding of individuality in the workplace.

A review of the concepts listed above also brings into focus some issues surrounding the nature of OB as a subject, as introduced in Chapter 1. Consider, for example, from the topic of perception, the picture of a woman contained in Figure 2.1. Do you see an old woman, a young woman or both in Figure 2.1? Differences in response to this picture, first published in 1915,[4] can be explained by *psychological factors*, for example the ways our sensory systems operate, leading some of us to see one image while others perceive another – even when we are looking at the same object as in this case. However, another important notion within perception, as we will see, is stereotyping; namely the tendency to attribute perceived group characteristics to individual members of that group. In order to understand a **stereotype**, we need to refer to the subject of *sociology*.

*An **attitude** is a predisposition to respond in a positive or negative way to someone or something in your environment.*

Figure 2.1: Old/young woman.

*A **stereotype** is a view of an individual person or group which is derived from assumed wider characteristics, e.g. Italians are emotional.*

For example, Linehan,[5] in explaining the underrepresentation of women in international management roles, noted that women often found it difficult to secure international assignments due in part to concerns regarding their acceptability in a second culture. So stereotyped views within society (interestingly in this case originating in the 'home' location) contribute to the perpetuation of the **glass ceiling** phenomenon in international management.

In Chapter 1 we also suggested that OB research would need to employ a range of methods in order to capture the reality of people's working lives. Positivist style methods, for example, could be used to explore aspects of perception such as understanding of how our perceptual thresholds operate (consider, for example, how we screen out the sound of a ticking clock after a period of time). Such a topic is amenable to experimental study, maybe varying the audibility of clocks while exploring the impact of demographic variables such as age. Much work in the field of **ergonomics** might usefully be based on this type of positivist style research. In contrast, the interpretivist tradition could be used to

*The **glass ceiling** refers to an invisible barrier that stops women from attaining senior positions within organizations. It can involve unstated or unofficial views of women and their roles at work.*

Ergonomics *involves the application of scientific principles to the interaction between humans and their work environment including task and work areas, including physical layout, work systems and scheduling.*

highlight the deeper perceptions of workers – see, for example, the work by Kiely and Henbest[6] who conducted two extended case studies providing rich data on how female workers actually perceived sexual harassment, based on conversations with the workers in question – although these authors also used questionnaires to build up a broader view of this topic.

INDIVIDUAL PERFORMANCE FACTORS

In Chapter 1 we presented the organizational behaviour model that helps us explain and predict human behaviour in the workplace. As discussed, the performance equation (see Figure 1.1) views performance as the result of the personal attributes of individuals, the work effort they make and the organizational support they receive. The multiplication signs reinforce the key point that all three factors must be present for high performance to be achieved. Every manager can usefully understand how these three factors can affect performance results.

We will go on to use this equation as the theoretical guide for the material presented in this chapter. Notice that:

- individual attributes relate to a capacity to perform;
- work effort relates to a willingness to perform;
- organizational support relates to the opportunity to perform.

Individual attributes

Several broad categories of attributes create individual differences that are important in the study of organizational behaviour. These include demographic or biographic characteristics (for example, gender, age or ethnic background); competency characteristics such as aptitude/ability, or what a person can do (see our discussion of learning in Chapter 3); personality characteristics (the features that affect an individual's characteristic behaviour); and the values, attitudes and perceptions that influence how we interpret the world. The relative importance of these topics depends on the nature of the job and its task requirements. When seeking to achieve organizational goals – or the goals of those who control organizations – individual attributes should ideally match task requirements to facilitate job performance (Figure 2.2).

Work effort

Motivation to work *refers to the forces within an individual that account for the level, direction and persistence of effort expended at work.*

To achieve high levels of performance, even people with the right individual attributes must have the willingness to perform; that is, they must display adequate work effort. For many reasons, different individuals display different levels of willingness to perform. **Motivation to work** describes the forces within an individual that account for the level, direction and persistence of effort expended on work. A highly motivated person will tend to work hard. Level of effort refers to the amount of energy that is put forth by

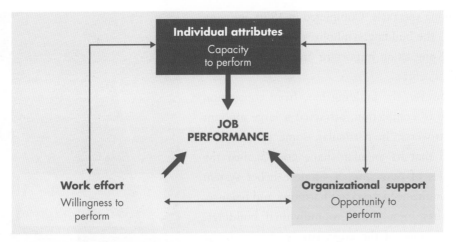

Figure 2.2: Dimensions of individual performance factors.
Source: Suggested by Melvin Blumberg and Charles D. Pringle (1982), The Missing Opportunity in Organizational Research: Source implications for a theory of work performance. *Academy of Management Review*, 7, 565.

the individual (for example, a high or low level of effort to complete a task). Direction refers to an individual's choice when presented with a number of alternatives (for example, quality versus quantity) and persistence refers to the length of time a person is willing to persevere with a given action (trying to achieve a goal or alternatively abandoning it when it is found difficult to attain the goal). The topic of motivation and managers' role in this process is complex and will be analysed in depth in Chapter 4.

Organizational support

The third component of the individual performance equation is organizational support.[7] Even people whose individual characteristics satisfy job requirements and who are highly motivated to exert effort may not be good performers in reality because they do not receive adequate support in the workplace. Organizational behaviour researchers refer to such inadequacies as **situational constraints** and these may include poor time planning, inadequate budgets, problems with work technology ('the system is down again' is an all too common lament), unclear instructions, unfair levels of expected performance and inflexibility of procedures.

> **Situational constraints** *are organizational factors that do not allow workers to perform adequately.*

Let us now turn to the first set of variables in our model – individual difference and attributes – and examine three topics in particular: *perception, personality* and *values and attitudes.*

PERCEPTION AND ATTRIBUTION

What do you see when you look at The Bank of China tower building in Hong Kong? This striking building occupies a prominent place on the foreshore of Hong Kong Island. When viewed across the harbour from Kowloon, especially when illuminated at night, it provides a stunning spectacle. Completed in 1990, in many respects the building symbolizes the emergence of Hong Kong as an important and thriving global financial centre.

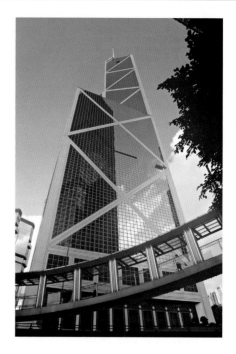

However, the building has, from conception through to completion, attracted a large amount of controversy. In particular, some people have claimed that its angular shape goes against the principles of *feng shui*, a Chinese belief system based on the need to secure harmony and balance, which has been linked to individual buildings. Thus portions of the cross bars endemic to the tower's structure have been altered to create diamond shapes rather than the earlier X shapes, which were considered inauspicious. When it was noted that the basic orientation of its sharp angles was towards Government House, the former headquarters of the last British Governor, Chris Patten, willow trees were reportedly planted in front of this older building in order to ward off any bad luck emanating from its new neighbour.

We perceive the world in different ways. One of the authors is familiar with the skyscrapers along the Hong Kong shore and regards the Bank of China tower as a beautiful building. But he does not have a lifelong knowledge of *feng shui*, which could cause him to perceive the building in a quite different way. No one perception is 'right' in any objective sense and, as can be seen from this example, the ways in which we view the world can be influenced by our cultural background, an important point to recognize in our increasingly interconnected business world.

Perception *is the process through which people receive, organize and interpret information from their environment.*

The concept of **perception** relates to the process by which people select, organize, interpret, retrieve and respond to information from the world around them (Figure 2.3). This information is gathered from the five senses of sight, hearing, touch, taste and smell.

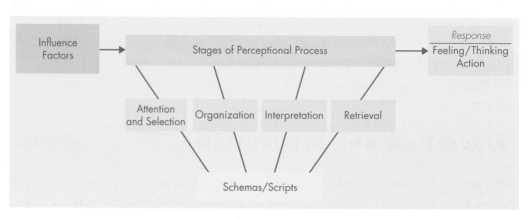

Figure 2.3: The perceptual process.

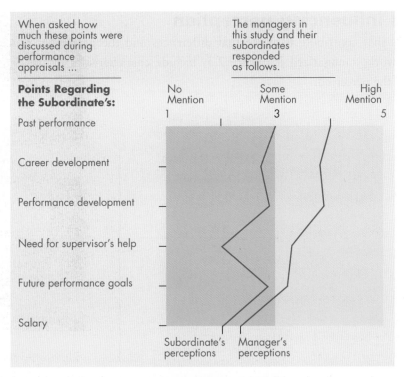

Figure 2.4: Contrasting perceptions between managers and their subordinates: the case of the performance appraisal interview.

Mullins suggests that; 'perception is the root of all organizational behaviour; any situation can be analysed in terms of its perceptual connotation.'[8] We support this conclusion in this book, as perception and reality are not necessarily the same thing. It is people's *perception* of reality that provides the fuel which drives their attitude formation and possibly their actual behaviour.

Through perception, people process information inputs into responses involving feelings and action. Perception is a way of forming impressions about oneself, other people and daily life experiences. It also serves as a screen or filter through which information passes before it has an effect on people. The quality or accuracy of a person's perceptions, therefore, has a major impact on his or her responses to a given situation. It is therefore entirely appropriate that perception is the first substantive OB topic analysed in this book.

Within the OB arena, perceptual responses are also likely to vary within an organizational setting, for example between managers and subordinates. Consider Figure 2.4, which depicts contrasting perceptions of a performance appraisal between managers and subordinates.

Rather substantial differences exist in the two sets of perceptions. In this case, managers who perceive that they already give adequate attention to past performance, career development and supervisory help are unlikely to give greater emphasis to these points in future performance appraisal interviews. In contrast, their subordinates are likely to experience continued frustration because they perceive that these subjects are not being given sufficient attention.

Factors influencing perception

The factors that contribute to perceptual differences and the perceptual process among people at work, summarized in Figure 2.5, include characteristics of the perceiver, the setting and the perceived.

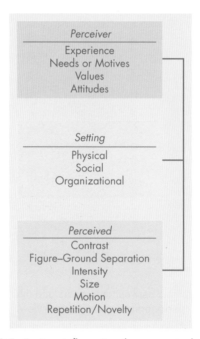

Figure 2.5: Factors influencing the perceptual process.

The perceiver

*A **perceptual set** comprises those factors that predetermine an individual's ability to perceive particular stimuli and respond in characteristic ways.*

A person's past experiences, needs or motives, personality, values and attitudes may all influence the perceptual process. Psychologists call these factors an individual's **perceptual set**. For example, a person with a strong achievement need will tend to perceive a situation in terms of that need. If you see doing well in a university course as a way to help meet your achievement need, for example, you will tend to emphasize that aspect when prioritizing your study responsibilities, social life, recreational activities or intimate relationships. You are more likely to attend classes regularly than another student whose priorities reflect the importance of other needs. A person with a negative predisposition towards someone with red hair might react antagonistically if interviewing someone of this description for an employment post. Such a stance might be dysfunctional (the redhead might be the best qualified candidate); it is certainly unethical. However, that interviewer's perceptual set may influence his or her attitudes – and consequently behaviour – at a subliminal level. These and other perceiver factors influence the various aspects of the perceptual process.

The setting

The physical, social and organizational context of the perceptual setting can also influence the perceptual process. Hearing the word 'fire' might lead you to behave quite differently in a classroom than if you were a spectator at a military tattoo. The British television programme *Blackadder Goes Forth*, set against the backdrop of the First World War, made great comic play out of naming one of its characters Captain Darling. His superior officer, using the social convention of the time, called him by his surname each time they spoke. The juxtaposition of the word 'darling', popularly a term of endearment, with the formal military *milieu* of the programme was used to considerable comic effect. The anomalous context, as perceived by the viewer, thus brought out a specific reaction.

The perceived

Characteristics of the perceived person, object or event – such as contrast, intensity, size, motion and repetition or novelty – are also important in the perceptual process. For example, one mainframe computer among six PCs will be perceived differently from one of six mainframe computers. Five students talking in the back row of a lecture theatre will be more easily perceived by the lec-

turer than 300 students quietly taking notes in the same room due to *contrast*. Intensity can vary in terms of brightness, colour, sound and movement. A bright red sports car stands out from a group of grey saloons; whispering or shouting stands out from ordinary conversation. This concept is known as figure–ground separation, and it depends on which image is perceived as the background and which as the figure. For an illustration, look at Figure 2.6. What do you see? Faces or a vase?

In the matter of size, very small or very large people tend to be perceived differently and more readily from average-sized people. Similarly, in terms of motion, moving objects are perceived differently from stationary objects. If you look out of a window on to a street, any moving vehicle will more readily capture your attention than those that are stuck in traffic or parked. Advertisers meanwhile hope that an advertisement's repetition or

Figure 2.6: Figure–ground illustration.

frequency will positively influence people's perception of a product. Finally, the novelty of a situation affects its perception. Tiger Woods's emergence as a world-class golf star may have led to him being perceived differently due to his mixed race ethnicity, as top players in the sport had previously been overwhelmingly white.

Stages of the perceptual process

So far we have discussed key factors influencing the perceptual process. Now we will dissect *stages* involved in processing the information that ultimately determines a person's perception and reaction, as shown previously in Figure 2.3.

The information-processing stages are divided into information attention and selection, organization of information, information interpretation and information retrieval.

Attention and selection

Controlled processing *refers, within the topic of perception, to conscious decisions made to pay attention to certain stimuli while ignoring others.*

Screening *is the umbrella term for the ways we selectively perceive objects and people.*

Our senses are constantly bombarded with so much information that if we don't screen it we quickly become incapacitated with information overload. Selective screening lets in only a tiny proportion of all the information available. Some of the selectivity comes from **controlled processing** – consciously deciding what information to pay attention to and what to ignore. In this case, the perceivers are aware that they are processing information. Think about the last time you were at a noisy restaurant and screened out all the sounds but those of the person with whom you were talking. If this occurred then that person is probably special to you. 'Cherry's cocktail party effect' describes a situation when you selectively perceive a communication because it is important to you – for example across a crowded room you hear your name; you are immediately alert because it is *your name –* and we are all, inevitably, the centre of our own universes!

In contrast to controlled processing, **screening** can also take place without the perceiver's conscious awareness. For example, you may drive a car without consciously thinking about the process of driving; you may be thinking about a problem you are having with your coursework instead. In driving the car, you are affected by information from the world around you, such as traffic lights and other cars, but you don't pay conscious attention to that information. Such selectivity of attention and automatic information processing works well most of the time when you drive, but if a nonroutine event occurs, such as a pedestrian running into the road, it is hoped that you can quickly shift back into controlled processing mode.

Organization

Schemas *are cognitive frameworks developed through experience.*

Even though selective screening takes place in the attention stage, it is still necessary to find ways to organize the information efficiently. **Schemas** help us do this. Schemas are cognitive frameworks that represent organized knowledge about a given concept or stimulus developed through experience.[9] A self schema contains information about a person's own appearance, behaviour and personality. For instance, a person with a decisiveness schema tends to perceive himself or herself in terms of that aspect, especially in circumstances calling for leadership.

Person schemas refer to the way individuals sort others into categories, such as types or groups, in terms of similar perceived features. The term 'prototype', or 'stereotype' is often used to represent these categories; it is an abstract set of features commonly associated with members of that category. Once the **prototype** is formed, it is stored in long-term memory; it is retrieved when it is needed for a comparison of how well a person matches the prototype's features. For instance, you may have a 'good worker' prototype in mind, which includes hard work, intelligence, punctuality, articulateness and decisiveness; that prototype is used as a measure against which to compare a given worker. Stereotypes may be regarded as prototypes based on such demographic characteristics as gender, age, disability, nationality or ethnic origin. **Stereotyping** has a generally negative connotation. But it is difficult to avoid in reality. It is one more manifestation of perceptual organization – we seek to close off meaning by taking short cuts in person perception. We are all truly unique, with an infinite number of individual differences. But in business settings, particularly in large organizations, it may not be realistic to truly know a co-worker (if such a thing is ever possible) and stereotyping offers us a way to define reality. A person may be female, Italian, in her twenties, a marketing executive and blonde – so we try to construct a complete mental picture of her by locating her within these groups and the assumptions we make about these groups. This simplifies the inherently complex activity of understanding a fellow human being and provides us with comforting predictions of her future behaviour – which may well turn out to be entirely false.

A prototype is a perception of a person based on group characteristics, from which the individual person may diverge.

Stereotyping describes the process by which we attribute characteristics to an individual based on our understanding of wider groups, e.g. she is Italian therefore she is an emotional person.

A script schema is defined as a knowledge framework that describes the appropriate sequence of events in a given situation.[10] For example, an experienced manager would use a script schema to think about the appropriate steps involved in running a meeting. Finally, person-in-situation schemas combine schemas built around persons (self and person schemas) and events (script schemas).[11] Thus, a manager might organize his or her perceived information in a meeting around a decisiveness schema for both himself or herself and a key participant in the meeting. Here, a script schema would provide the steps and their sequence in the meeting; the manager would push through the steps decisively and call on the selected participants periodically throughout the meeting to respond decisively. Note that, although this approach might facilitate organization of important information, the perceptions of those attending might not be completely accurate because the decisiveness element of the person-in-situation schema did not allow the attendees enough time for open discussion.

As you can see in Figure 2.3, schemas are not only important in the organization stage; they also affect other stages in the perception process. Furthermore, schemas rely heavily on automatic processing to free people up to use controlled processing as necessary. Finally, as we will show, the perceptual factors described earlier as well as the distortions to be discussed shortly, influence schemas in various ways.

Interpretation

Once your attention has been drawn to certain stimuli and you have grouped or organized this information, the next step is to uncover the reasons behind the actions. That is, even if your attention is called to the same information and you organize it in the same way your friend does, you may interpret it differently or make different attributions about the reasons behind what you have perceived. For example, as a manager, you might attribute compliments from a friendly subordinate to his being an eager worker, whereas your friend might interpret the behaviour as insincere flattery. Cultural differences become important here. Hall's concept of low-context and high-context cultures,[12] incorporates differences in communication style including nonverbal communication. A manager on an interview panel from a low-context society such as Denmark could interpret lack of eye contact from an interviewee as evasiveness. However, if that interviewee were from a high-context country – China provides an example in Hall's model – they might regard eye contact as a form of rudeness and avoid it on the grounds of wishing to be polite. We cannot be aware of all such culturally derived nuances of behaviour. For example, one of the authors was asked not to write comments on an essay by a Hindu student in red because the colour symbolized death in her culture; it was not surprising that he was previously unaware of this specific significance of red ink. However, a good manager must be alert to the *possibility* of misinterpreting cues from people from other cultures – they cannot be parochial – or 'culture-blind' in the globalized 21st century business world. This is also, of course, true for other workers in non-managerial roles who operate either outside their own indigenous culture or in diverse multicultural work settings.

OB IN ACTION

The emergence of China as a major economic player has led to a plethora of guides for conducting business in that country and with Chinese nationals elsewhere. Such guides typically note the importance of nonverbal cues, which play an important role in communication within Chinese culture. Indirect communication is preferred over explicit spoken or written messages. The memoirs of ex-US President Richard Nixon record his initial difficulty in decoding messages from the Chinese Communist Party Chairman Mao Tse Tung during Nixon's visit to China in 1972. A double translation was needed; firstly from Mandarin to English, and secondly from the allegorical style of speech

used by Mao into the direct information-based mode of language favoured by Nixon, before the latter statesman could comprehend what his counterpart had said. As noted before, in Hall's model China is a high-context culture whereas the US is low-context in this regard, so these perceptual misunderstandings might be expected.

Retrieval

So far, we have discussed the stages of the perceptual process as if they all occurred at the same time. However, to do so ignores the important component of memory. Each of the previous stages forms part of that memory and contributes to the stimuli or information stored there. The information stored in our memory must be retrieved if it is to be used. This leads us to the retrieval stage of the perceptual process summarized in Figure 2.3.

All of us at times find it hard to retrieve information stored in our memory. More commonly, our memory decays so that only some of the information is retrieved. Schemas play an important role in this area. They make it difficult for people to remember things not included in them. For example, based on your prototype about the traits comprising a 'high-performing employee' (hard work, punctuality, intelligence, articulateness and decisiveness) you may overestimate these traits and underestimate others when you are evaluating the performance of a subordinate whom you generally consider good. Thus, you may overestimate the person's decisiveness because it is a key part of your high-performance prototype.

Indeed people are as likely to recall nonexistent traits as they are to recall those that are really there. Furthermore, once formed, prototypes may be difficult to change and tend to last a long time.[13] Most importantly, this distortion can cause major problems in terms of performance appraisals and promotions, not to mention numerous other interactions both of a work and nonwork variety. At the same time, as we have seen, such prototypes allow you to 'chunk' information and reduce overload. Thus, prototypes are a double-edged sword.

Response to the perceptual process

Throughout this chapter we have shown how the perceptual process influences numerous OB responses. Figure 2.3 classifies such responses into thoughts, feelings and actions. For example, in Korea the exchange of business cards holds deep symbolic meaning and there are a series of stages bound up in the process; cards should be held in both hands and read thoroughly, just two steps in what is a very important social interaction. Anyone new to Korea might hope that any mistake would be forgiven and understood by their hosts. Nonetheless as you cover the other OB topics in the book, you also should be alert to the importance of perceptual responses covering thoughts, feelings and actions.

Common perceptual distortions

Figure 2.7 provides a summary of selected common kinds of distortions, some of which have already been referred to in this chapter. In all cases such distortions can render the perceptual process inaccurate and affect the lives of others in a profound way. These are stereotypes and prototypes, **halo effects**, **selective perception**, **projection**, **contrast effects** and **self-fulfilling prophecy**.

The **halo effect** within interpersonal perception occurs when our perception of another person is framed on the basis of a single striking favourable characteristic (the rusty halo phenomenon occurs when the characteristic is perceived negatively).

Selective perception refers to the ways in which we categorize and organize stimuli, leading us to perceive the world in a unique way.

Projection involves projecting our own emotions or motives on to another person. It is an example of a perceptual error.

Contrast effects occur within the process of perception when an object or person is perceived due to it standing out from its surroundings or group.

A **self-fulfilling prophecy** occurs when a prophecy comes true simply because it has been made. For example, if we label people in a particular way, they will behave in the expected manner.

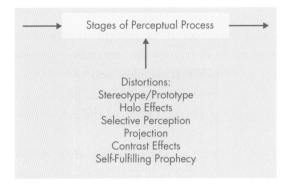

Figure 2.7: Distortions occurring in perceptual process stages.

Stereotypes or prototypes

Earlier, when discussing person schemas, we described stereotypes, or prototypes, as useful ways of combining information in order to deal with information overload. At the same time, we pointed out how stereotypes can cause inaccuracies in retrieving information, along with some further problems. In particular, stereotypes obscure individual differences; that is, they can prevent managers, or indeed anyone else, from getting to know people as individuals and from accurately assessing their needs, preferences and abilities. Research results show the errors that can occur when stereotypes are relied on for decision making. Nevertheless, stereotypes continue to inform both attitudes and practice at senior management level.

Halo effects

A halo effect occurs when one attribute of a person or situation is used to develop an overall impression of the individual or situation. Like stereotypes, these distortions are more likely to occur in the organization stage of perception. Halo effects are common in our everyday lives. When meeting a new person, for example, a pleasant smile can lead to a positive first impression of an overall 'warm' and 'honest' person. Alternatively, someone dropping a chocolate ice cream on to their shirt just before being called into a selection interview may run the risk of negative perception on the part of interviewers; the single striking stain on clothing being an example of the 'rusty halo' variant of this effect. The result of a halo effect is the same as that associated with a stereotype, however individual differences are obscured.

Halo effects are particularly important in the performance appraisal process because they can influence a manager's evaluations of subordinates' work performance. For example, people with good attendance records tend to be viewed as intelligent and responsible; those with poor attendance records are considered poor performers. Such conclusions may or may not be valid. Equally you may question the wisdom of eating a chocolate ice cream just before an interview! Ultimately it is the manager's job to try to form true impressions rather than allowing halo effects to result in biased and erroneous evaluations.

OB IN ACTION

Steven J. Karau, Associate Professor of Management at Southern Illinois University, has studied gender stereotyping in the US and Sweden. His study, conducted jointly with a Swedish academic Eric Hansen, involved asking college students in these two countries to correlate a number of traits as they perceived them to apply to men in general, women in general or middle managers. His hypothesis, based on previous research, was that so-called manager traits overlapped more with male traits than female traits. This is termed the 'think manager – think male effect'.

However, Karau's study found that the think manager – think male effect only held true for male raters – perhaps an expected finding – and that interestingly this effect was much less apparent in Sweden than in the US.

Steven Karau believes that his work can improve work opportunities for women, stating that: 'my hope would be for organizations to rely more directly on people's qualifications and to become aware of potential contaminating factors in their judgements in order to make better hiring and promotion decisions such that every person has a chance to go as far as their talents will take them.'[14]

Here, we reiterate our previous message: both managers and employees need to be sensitive to stereotypes; they must also attempt to overcome them and recognize that an increasingly diverse workforce can be a truly competitive advantage. It is also illuminating to record the cultural differences thrown up by Karau's study. In Chapter 1 we saw that Hofstede's classifications of culture included the masculine/feminine dimension, with Sweden identified as a feminine society, so we may find some corroboration of Hofstede's work in this study.

Selective perception

Selective perception is the tendency to single out those aspects of a situation, person or object that are consistent with one's needs, values or attitudes. Its strongest impact occurs in the attention stage of the perceptual process. This perceptual distortion was identified in a classic research study involving executives in a manufacturing company.[15] When asked to identify the key problem in a comprehensive business policy case, each executive selected problems consistent with his or her functional area work assignments. For example, most marketing executives viewed the key problem area as sales, whereas production people tended to see the problem as one of production and organization. These differing viewpoints would affect how the executives approached the problem; they might also create difficulties once these people tried to work together to improve things.

In a more recent study, 121 middle- and upper-level managers attending an executive development seminar programme expressed broader views in conjunction with an emphasis on their own function. For example, a chief financial officer indicated an awareness of the importance of manufacturing and an assistant marketing manager recognized the importance of accounting and finance along with each of their own functions.[16] This more recent research demonstrated very little perceptual selectivity. The researchers were not, however, able to state definitively what accounted for the differing results.

These results suggest that selective perception is more important at some times than at others. Managers should be aware of this characteristic and test whether or not situations, events or individuals are being selectively perceived. The easiest way to do this is to gather additional opinions from other people. When these opinions contradict a manager's own, an effort should be made to check the original impression.

Projection

Projection is the assignment of one's own personal attributes to other individuals; it is especially likely to occur in the interpretation stage of perception. A classic projection error is illustrated by managers who assume that the needs of their subordinates coincide with their own needs. Suppose, for example, that you enjoy responsibility and achievement in your work. Suppose, too, that you are the newly appointed manager of a group whose jobs seem dull and routine. You may move quickly to expand these jobs to help the workers achieve increased satisfaction from more challenging tasks because you want them to experience things that you, personally, value in work. But this may not be a good decision. If you project your needs onto the subordinates, individual differences are lost. Instead of designing the subordinates' jobs to best fit their needs, you have designed their jobs to best fit *your* needs. The problem is that the subordinates may be quite satisfied and productive doing jobs that seem dull and routine to you. Their own psychological contracts may lead them to be happy with the relative exchange between inputs and outcomes. Projection can be controlled through a high degree of self-awareness and empathy – the ability to view a situation as others see it. This, of course, ties in with the concept of emotional intelligence introduced in Chapter 1.

Contrast effects

Earlier, when discussing 'the perceived', we mentioned how a bright red sports car would stand out from a group of grey saloons because it contrasts with them. Here, we show the perceptual distortion that can occur when, for example, a person gives a talk following a strong speaker or is interviewed for a job following a series of mediocre applicants. We can expect a contrast effect to occur when an individual's characteristics are contrasted with those of others recently encountered who rank higher or lower on the same characteristics. Clearly, both managers and other employees need to be aware of the possible perceptual distortion the contrast effect may create in many work settings. It is emphatically not impossible to overcome this problem but awareness is necessary in the first instance.

Self-fulfilling prophecies

A final perceptual distortion that we consider is the self-fulfilling prophecy – the tendency to create or find in another situation or individual that which you expected to find in the first place. A self-fulfilling prophecy is sometimes referred to as the 'Pygmalion effect', named after a mythical Greek sculptor who created a statue of his ideal mate and then made her come to life.[17] His prophecy came true! Through self-fulfilling prophecies you also may create in the work situation that which you expect to find.

Self-fulfilling prophecies can have both positive and negative results for you should you be involved in managing others. Suppose you assume that your subordinates prefer to satisfy most of their needs outside the work setting and want only minimal involvement with their jobs. Consequently, you are likely to provide simple, highly structured jobs designed to require little involvement. Can you predict what response the subordinates would have to this situation? Their most likely response would be to show the lack of commitment you assumed they would have in the first place. Thus, your initial expectations are confirmed as a self-fulfilling prophecy. Self-fulfilling prophecies can have a positive side however. Students introduced to their teachers as star pupils do better on achievement tests than do their counterparts who lack such a positive introduction.

OB IN ACTION

A particularly interesting example of the self-fulfilling prophecy is shown in the research carried out by Eden and Shani in a military setting in Israel. One set of senior officers was told that, according to test data, some members of their assigned crews had exceptional abilities but others were only average. In reality, the crew members were assigned randomly, so that the two test groups were equal in ability. Later, the commanding officers reported that the so-called exceptional crew members performed better than the 'average' members. As the study revealed, however, the commanders had paid more attention to and praised the crew members for whom they had the higher expectations.[18]

The self-fulfilling effects in the cases documented above argue strongly for managers to adopt positive and optimistic approaches to people at work. This is also shown by Manzoni and Barsoux[19] who identified the mirror image 'set up to fail' syndrome. Here managers were found to micromanage and control those employees perceived as weak (often on the basis of a single incident), which led to a downward spiral with such employees losing confidence, resulting in turn in depressed levels of performance.

Managing perceptions

To be successful, managers must understand that everyone is different in terms of the ways they perceive the external world. In order to maximize their own performance, those who manage others should also be aware of the implications of the topic for themselves through an awareness of perceptual processes, the stages involved and the impact the perceptual process can have on their own and others' responses. They must also be aware of what roles the perceiver, the setting and the perceived have in the perceptual process. Particularly important with regard to the perceived is the concept of impression management – for managers and others.

Impression management

Impression management is a person's systematic attempt to behave in ways that will create and maintain desired impressions in the eyes of others. First impressions are especially important and influence how people respond to one another. Research demonstrates how quickly individuals on a selection panel make up their minds about individuals.[20] More generally, impression management is influenced by such activities as associating with the 'right people', doing favours to gain approval, flattering others to impress them, taking credit for a favourable event, apologizing for a negative event while seeking a pardon, agreeing with the opinions of others and downplaying the severity of a negative event.[21] In the 1960s an American social psychologist Erving Goffman[22] illuminated fascinating instances of how workers in the public eye – for example waiters – would consciously manipulate their own behaviour in view of what was expected by customers, partly in order to maximize gratuities. One can also argue that managers learn how to use these activities to enhance their own images and are sensitive to their use by their subordinates and others in their organizations. In this context, job titles are particularly important.

Distortion management

During the attention and selection stage, managers should be alert to balancing automatic and controlled information processing. Most of their responsibilities, such as performance assessment and clear communication, will involve controlled processing, which will take time away from other job responsibilities. Along with more controlled processing, managers need to be concerned about increasing the frequency of observations and about obtaining representative information rather than simply responding to the most recent information about a subordinate or a production order, for instance. In addition, managers should not fail to seek out disconfirming information that will help provide a balance to their typical perceptions.

The various kinds of schemas and prototypes and stereotypes are particularly important at the information organizing stage. Managers should strive to broaden their schemas or should even replace them with more accurate or complete ones.

At the interpretation stage, managers need to be especially attuned to the impact of attribution on information; we discuss this concept further in the next section. At the retrieval stage, managers should be sensitive to the fallibility of memory. They should recognize the tendency to rely too much on schemas, especially prototypes or stereotypes that may bias information storage and retrieval.

Throughout the entire perception process, managers and, once again we stress, all workers, should be sensitive to the information distortions caused by halo effects, selective perception, projection, contrast effects and self-fulfilling prophecies, in addition to the distortions caused by stereotypes and prototypes.

Attribution theory

Earlier in the chapter we mentioned attribution theory in the context of perceptual interpretation. Attribution theory aids in this interpretation by focusing on how people attempt to (1) understand the causes of a certain event, (2) assess responsibility for the outcomes of the event and (3) evaluate the personal qualities of the people involved in the event.[23] In applying attribution theory, we are especially concerned with whether one's behaviour has been internally or externally caused. Internal causes are believed to be under an individual's control – you believe Marie's performance is poor because she is lazy. External causes are seen as coming from outside a person – you believe Sarfraz's performance is poor because his machine has not been upgraded with the latest software.

The importance of attributions

According to attribution theory, three factors influence this internal or external determination: *distinctiveness*, *consensus* and *consistency*. Distinctiveness considers how consistent a person's behaviour is across different situations. If Marie's performance is low, regardless of the technological capabilities of her computer, we tend to give the poor performance an internal attribution; if the poor performance is unusual, we tend to assign an external cause to explain it.

Consensus takes into account how likely all those facing a similar situation are to respond in the same way. If all the people using machinery like Sarfraz's perform poorly, we tend to give his performance an external attribution. If other employees do not perform poorly, we attribute his performance to internal causation.

Consistency concerns whether an individual responds the same way across time. If Marie has a batch of low-performance figures, we tend to give the poor performance an internal attribution. In contrast, if Marie's low performance is an isolated incident, we attribute it to an external cause.

Attribution errors

In addition to these three influences, two errors have an impact on internal versus external determination – the fundamental **attribution error** and the self-serving bias.[24] Figure 2.8 provides data from a group of healthcare managers. When supervisors were asked to identify, or attribute, causes of poor performance among their subordinates, the supervisors more often chose the individual's internal deficiencies – lack of ability and effort – rather than external deficiencies in the situation, such as lack of support. This demonstrates the fundamental attribution error – the tendency to underestimate the influence of situational factors and to overestimate the influence of personal factors in evaluating someone else's behaviour. When asked to identify causes of their own poor performance, however, the supervisors overwhelmingly cited lack of support – an external, or situational, deficiency. This indicates the self-serving bias – the tendency to deny personal responsibility for performance problems but to accept personal responsibility for performance success.

Attribution errors *occur within the process of perception and relate to the reasons we attribute to events and behaviour. A common attribution error is to overemphasize the contribution of our own efforts and abilities when explaining our successes and, contrastingly, to attribute negative occurrences to outside influences such as bad luck.*

Cause of Poor Performance by Their Subordinates	Most Frequent Attribution	Cause of Poor Performance by Themselves
7	Lack of *ability*	1
12	Lack of *effort*	1
5	Lack of *support*	23

Figure 2.8: Healthcare managers' attributions of causes for poor performance.

To summarize, we tend to overemphasize other people's internal personal factors in their behaviour and to underemphasize external factors in other people's behaviour. In contrast, we tend to attribute our own success to our own internal factors and to attribute our failure to external factors.

The managerial implications of attribution theory can be traced back to the fact that perceptions influence responses. For example, a manager who feels that subordinates are not performing well and perceives the reason to be an internal lack of effort is likely to respond with attempts to 'motivate' the subordinates to work harder; the possibility of

OB IN ACTION

Following the European Champions League soccer final on 17 May 2006, in which FC Barcelona defeated the London club side Arsenal 2–1, both Arsenal's then star striker Thierry Henry (he swapped clubs in 2007) and team manager Arsene Wenger attributed their side's defeat to decisions made by the match officials in the game. Henry was quoted as saying 'I don't know if the referee was wearing a Barcelona shirt because they kicked me all over the place. If the referee did not want us to win he should have said so from the off. Some of the calls were strange. I believe the referee did not do his job. I would have liked to see a proper referee.'[25] Manager Wenger said 'My biggest regret is that the first [Barcelona] goal was offside. It's difficult to lose the game on a wrong decision. It was offside and it is proven on TV.'[26] Without going into the intricacies of the referee and his assistant's decision making, we have here – in the context of emotional reactions immediately following a dramatic sporting event – examples of attribution theory in action. And yet there were other factors influencing the result, including some missed chances to score by Arsenal players. Arsene Wenger acknowledged that his team had two or three good chances to increase their 1–0 lead in the course of the same interview cited here. Frank Rijkard, who was Barcelona coach at the time, contrastingly emphasized the role of his team's goalkeeper Victor Valdes in the side's triumph, drawing attention to key saves made by that player. Here we see how attribution of success is related to internal factors, in this case a team member's skill.

changing external, situational factors that may remove job constraints and provide better organizational support may be largely ignored. This oversight could sacrifice major performance gains. Interestingly, because of the self-serving bias, when they evaluated their own behaviour, the supervisors in the earlier study indicated that their performance would benefit from having better support. Thus, the supervisors' own abilities or willingness to work hard were not felt to be at issue.

Attributions across cultures

Research on the self-serving bias and fundamental attribution error has been carried out in cultures across the world with varying results.[27] In Korea, for example, the self-serving bias was found to be negative; that is, Korean managers attribute workgroup failure to themselves to a far greater extent – 'I was not a capable leader' – rather than to external causes. In India, the fundamental attribution error overemphasizes external rather than internal causes for failure. Certain cultures, such as that of the US, tend to overemphasize internal causes and underemphasize external ones. Such overemphasis may result in negative attributions toward employees. These negative attributions, in turn, can lead to disciplinary action, negative performance evaluations, transfers to other departments and overreliance on training, rather than focusing on such external causes as lack of workplace support.[28] Employees, too, take their cues from managerial misattributions and, through negative self-fulfilling prophecies, may reinforce managers' original misattributions. Employees and managers alike can be taught attributional realignment to help deal with such misattributions (see Effective Manager 2.1).[29]

EFFECTIVE MANAGER 2.1

Keys in managing perceptions and attributions

- Be self-aware.
- Seek a wide range of differing information.
- Try to see a situation as others would.
- Be aware of different types of schemas.
- Be aware of perceptual distortions.
- Be aware of self and other impression management.
- Be aware of attribution theory implications.

The critical importance of perception

You may have wondered how the concept of perception was relevant to OB. We trust that you are now convinced that it is highly relevant. Individuals perceive the world in different ways. We are unique in the ways we select, organize, interpret and retrieve information from the environment. Our perceptions of the world predate our attitudes and conceivably our actual behaviour. The psychological contract, introduced as an important concept in Chapter 1, is essentially a perceptual mindset. We tend to perceive other people with reference to our own perceptual worlds, so an awareness of the nature of perception can help us to better understand other people. Such an ability is crucial to securing strong organizational performance.

OB IN ACTION

In November 2006, the Supreme Court in Delhi was asked to rule on whether Indian Airlines could reasonably dismiss air cabin crew for being too fat. The Court was asked to consider the cases of 11 stewardesses who had been 'grounded' for allegedly carrying too much weight. One such victim, found to be 1.9 kg above her height/weight threshold, and faced with the prospect of losing her job, went on a crash diet but subsequently described her experience as personally demeaning and alien to the dignity of Indian culture. However, an Indian Airlines spokesperson located the company's policy within the imperative of commercial survival. One competitor, Kingfisher Airlines, actively markets female cabin crew in scarlet shoes and short red skirts as part of its brand image. Indian Airlines also point to weight as an indicator of fitness, a company source noting that: 'Staff need to be fit enough to control crazy guys who are trying to take over the flight.'[30]

PERSONALITY DIFFERENCES AMONG INDIVIDUALS

Personality is the overall profile or combination of traits that characterize the unique nature of a person.

The second basic attribute of individuals we will consider in this chapter is *personality*. We use the term **personality** to represent the overall profile or combination of characteristics that capture the unique nature of a person as that person reacts to and interacts with others. Personality combines a set of physical and mental characteristics that reflect how a person looks, thinks, acts and feels. Understanding personality contributes to an understanding of organizational behaviour by helping us to see what shapes individuals, what they can do (competency) and what they will do (motivation). One might expect there to be a predictable interplay between an individual's personality and their tendency to behave in certain ways. A common expectation, for example, is that introverts (people who are more interested in their private thoughts and feelings than in their external environment) tend to be less sociable than extroverts. Personality is a vital individual attribute for managers to understand.

Personality determinants

An important question in looking at personality is what determines it. Is personality inherited or genetically determined? Or are personality attributes determined by experience? You may have heard someone say something like 'she acts like her mother'. Or someone may argue that: 'Paulo is the way he is because of how he was raised' or indeed: 'Yasmin is a born leader'. These arguments illustrate the nature/nurture controversy – that is, is personality determined by heredity (or genetic endowment) or one's environment? Figure 2.9 shows that these two forces actually operate in combination. Heredity consists of those factors that are determined at conception, and includes physical characteristics and gender in addition to personality factors. Environment consists of cultural, social and situational factors.

Figure 2.9: Heredity and environmental links with personality.

Heredity

Psychologists acknowledge that the mind is made up of three domains: the cognitive domain (such as skills and learned behaviour), the affective domain (emotions) and the conative domain (instinctive approaches). Conative actions are those derived from striving instincts. Previous studies of components of the mind often ignored the notion of conation or instinct. Instinct is described as inherited patterns of unreasoned and unchangeable responses to particular actions and behaviours. At the beginning of modern psychology, both emotion and conation were considered central to its study. However, interest in these topics declined as measuring overt behaviour and cognition received more attention. The notion of instinct as the primary source of motivation was abandoned for several reasons, the common one being that this may place human beings on the same level as other animals.[31] Striving instincts are subconscious and immeasurable. They may nonetheless form an important component of the ways in which a person acts, or more pertinently, *the ways in which they would like to act.*

Psychodynamic theory

The pioneering work of Freud[32] put forward the view that personality is composed of thoughts and drives emanating from the **unconscious.** Freud's view was that our minds were firstly governed by the pleasure principle, or *id*, to use his own terminology. We are driven by this principle, which could manifest itself in sexual desire, need for nourishment or aggression (Freud was one of the psychologists who believed that human beings have a dark or 'shadow' side to their nature). The second aspect of our mental states was termed the *ego*; this essentially comprises the rational, problem-solving ways in which we consciously cope with our environments, governing the reality of our lives. The third element of our mental functioning is the *superego*, defined as our learned sense of how we should behave – or how we think other people think we should behave. This reflexive notion of behaviour involves our awareness of society's norms, which we learn through childhood. So our individual personality evolves dynamically over time – hence the term psychodynamic.

The term **unconscious,** *within Freud's theory of personality, refers to basic desires below the conscious level, which drive our behaviour and potentially conflict with values learned through socialization.*

Freud's theory of personality is also psychodynamic in that he identifies a series of *stages* through which all people progress in their childhood. He proposed that our experiences in our early years are important determinants of our adult behaviour. The stages, including the oral, anal, phallic and genital, refer to those areas of the body that form pleasure centres for the child. Freud believed that the stages correlate with specific ages in childhood and that overindulgence or deprivation at any stage will result in difficulties when that individual reaches adulthood. For example, an anally retentive personality is associated with meanness and an excessive desire for control. If one accepts this reading of personality development, it provides a novel (albeit for some a far-fetched) model for explaining behaviour in organizations.

There is considerable debate concerning the relative impact of heredity and environment – particularly childhood experiences on personality. The most general conclusion is that heredity sets the limits on just how much personality characteristics can be developed, whereas the environment determines development within these limits. The limits appear to vary from one characteristic to the next.

OB IN ACTION

In 2005, two British psychologists, Belinda Board and Katrina Fritzon[33] interviewed and administered psychological tests to 39 senior UK business executives. They compared these executives' psychological profiles with psychiatric patients at the high-security Broadmoor prison, which is the abode of some of the country's most infamous criminals, including at least one of Britain's most notorious serial killers. Somewhat disturbingly, Board and Fritzon found that three out of 11 identified personality disorders (PDs) were more apparent in the executive sample than among the Broadmoor patients. These were:

- Histrionic PD manifestations which included charm, insincerity, manipulativeness and egocentricity.
- Obsessive-compulsive disorder (OCD). Here symptoms numbered perfectionism, dictatorial behaviour, excessive devotion (in these cases to work) and rigidity.
- Narcissistic PD involving lack of empathy for others, grandiosity and independence.

This interesting research may explain what has become known as 'toxic manager syndrome' – disturbingly, many people can personally confirm the existence of such figures. One can also speculate on what internal forces have driven such individuals on to their current career success. Maybe Freud's vision of the destructive side of human behaviour is not so fanciful after all!

The nomothetic (traits) approach to personality

Organizational behaviour literature typically stresses the way of understanding personality that centres on traits and characteristics. This so-called *nomothetic* approach is popular within the business studies canon, possibly because it enables students of business and practising managers to identify and classify personality according to recognizable characteristics. It is an approach that lends itself easily to adoption within work organizations in terms of policy and practice. In the US and UK, a desire to measure individual differences as part of selection and remuneration policies means that nomothetic assumptions concerning personality will be familiar to you if you have lived and worked in those countries. Research indicates that **psychometric testing** (a logical follow-on from the nomothetic view) is used more or less frequently in particular societies.[34] In Chapter 1 we noted that Hofstede distinguished between individually and group-oriented societies. There is less of a desire to focus on the identification of individual differences in societies stressing group cohesion – such as Portugal and Greece – so managers there may be less concerned with putting the nomothetic approach into operation at the workplace.

The essence of the **nomothetic** view of personality is that it can best be understood by identifying the ways in which our personality varies from others. It proposes that it is possible to identify a set of dimensions along which we can all be classified and compared. These dimensions are called *traits*. Furthermore the traits cluster in a consistent fashion to create types. For example, traits of practicality and risk taking are typically found together within a single personality and form part of the extrovert type.[35] The nomothetic approach considers that personality is relatively unchanging; traits remain constant even in changing circumstances and can be captured through questionnaires and psychometric testing more generally.

In this section we will consider some of the personality traits that have been linked with behaviour in organizations. Firstly, we will outline the 'big five personality dimensions', and we will follow this with a discussion of other key characteristics that have attracted considerable research interest.

Psychometric testing *involves an attempt to extract an individual's key characteristics via controlled measures such as personality inventories.*

Nomothetic *approaches to understanding personality locate individuals within types on the basis of their traits. There is also a belief that personality is stable and unchanging, possibly as a result of inherited characteristics.*

Five key dimensions of personality

In a fascinating study of how we describe people's personalities, researchers identified 17 953 English-language terms that had been used over the years.[36] They sorted the terms into groups with similar meanings and finally distilled them into five key dimensions of personality. Research has generally confirmed the relevance of each dimension to behaviour in organizations:

- *Extroversion–introversion:* the degree to which individuals are oriented to the social world of people, relationships and events as opposed to the inner world (respectively). Extroverts tend to be outgoing, talkative and sociable, whereas introverts are generally quieter and happier spending time alone or with a few close friends.
- *Conscientiousness:* the extent to which individuals are organized, dependable and focused on detail, rather than disorganized, less reliable and lacking in perseverance.

- *Agreeableness:* the extent to which individuals are compliant, friendly, reliable and helpful, versus disagreeable, argumentative and uncooperative. One measure of this dimension is the Employee Reliability Scale.[37] Low-reliability individuals tend to be hostile towards rules, have feelings of detachment from others and are thrill-seeking, impulsive and socially insensitive. Those with high scores have favourable attitudes to teamwork, helping others, punctuality and are more adaptable.
- *Emotional stability:* the degree to which individuals are secure, resilient and calm, versus anxious, reactive and subject to mood swings.
- *Openness to experience:* the extent to which individuals are curious, open, adaptable and interested in a wide range of things, versus resistant to change and new experiences, less open to new ideas and preferring routine.

It might be assumed that employers and human resource managers in particular might commonly wish to recruit workers who are agreeable, stable and open to experience. While this would probably apply in most scenarios, we should allow for the reverse being true. The nomothetic trait approach could be used in many ways by organizations: the essence of this approach is that it is possible to identify stable traits in a predictive way. The traits that are sought would vary according to the situation.

Locus of control

One influential facet of personality is found in Rotter's concept of locus of control, which measures the internal–external orientation of a person – that is, the extent to which a person feels able to affect his or her life.[38] This notion does not sit easily within the nomothetic approach and shows how our personalities are influenced by feelings and thoughts deriving from our early influences and experiences. It is nonetheless a useful illustration of the potential importance of identifiable features in explaining personality and the actions people pursue. **Locus of control** refers to the general conceptions people have about whether events are controlled by themselves primarily, which indicates an *internal orientation*, or by outside forces or their social and physical environment, which indicates an *external orientation*. Internals, or people with an internal locus of control, believe they control their own fate or destiny. In contrast, externals, or people with an external locus of control, believe much of what happens to them is beyond their control and is determined by environmental forces.

For example, 'internals' would agree with statements like 'people's misfortunes result from the mistakes they make' and 'by taking an active part in political and social affairs, people can control world events'. On the other hand, 'externals' would agree with statements such as 'many of the unhappy things in people's lives are partly due to bad luck' and 'as far as world affairs are concerned, most of us are the victims of forces we can neither understand nor control'.

In the work context, at the general level, internals seek more information, experience stronger job satisfaction, perform better on learning and problem-solving tasks, have greater self-control and are more independent than externals.

Locus of control is the internal–external orientation – that is, the extent to which people feel able to affect their lives.

Authoritarianism/dogmatism

Both 'authoritarianism' and 'dogmatism' deal with the rigidity of a person's beliefs. A person high in authoritarianism tends to adhere rigidly to conventional values and to obey recognized authority. This person is concerned with toughness and power. People high in dogmatism see the world as a threatening place. They often regard legitimate authority as absolute, and accept or reject others according to how much they agree with accepted authority. Superiors possessing these dogmatic traits tend to be rigid and closed.[39]

We may expect highly author-  itarian individuals to present a special problem because they are so susceptible to obeying authority that they may behave unethically in their eagerness to comply.[40] Authoritarianism has been directly linked with 'crimes of obedience' and unethical behaviour.[41] For example, authoritarianism is a required trait in military organizations throughout the world. One recent example of a crime of obedience was the abuse of Iraqi prisoners by US soldiers at Abu Ghraib, and there have been many historical examples including genocide in Cambodia and the 1968 My Lai massacre in Vietnam.[42]

However, authoritarianism is not confined to the military; for example, under instruction, Arthur Andersen employees shredded documents to cover up the impending corporate scandal that allegedly led to the demise of one of the US's largest accountancy organizations and sparked the ENRON scandal.[43]

Machiavellianism

Another interesting personality dimension is **Machiavellianism**, which owes its origins to Niccolo Machiavelli. The very name of this 16th-century author evokes visions of a master of guile, deceit and opportunism in interpersonal relations. Machiavelli earned his place in history by writing *The Prince*, a nobleman's guide to the acquisition and use of power.[44] From its pages emerges the personality profile of a Machiavellian – that is, someone who views and manipulates others purely for personal gain.

Machiavellians *are people who view and manipulate others purely for personal gain.*

Manipulation is a basic drive for some people in social settings. And although some people view manipulation of others as being deceitful and even sinful, others see manipulation as an important attribute for career success in an organization. Thus, it is easy to see why Machiavelli's ideas have been both so avidly read and so heavily criticized over the years.[45]

Personality and stress

We find a useful application of the nomothetic model of personality within the topic of stress. In OB terms, stress refers to a negative and possibly damaging emotional state experienced if people feel they cannot cope with demands placed on them at work.[46] This is a specific adaptation of a more general term which characterizes stress in terms of demand and strain (as, for example, placed on a bridge by traffic).

One model for understanding the effects of stress takes as its centre point personality type and difference. Two personality types are identified: Type A and Type B.[47] The importance within the subject of stress is that individuals exhibiting Type A personality characteristics are more prone to experience stress acutely – in contrast to Type Bs.

Some typical Type A and B behaviour patterns are set out below:[48]

TYPE A:
- competitive
- ambitious
- never late for appointments
- try to do many things at once
- hide feelings

TYPE B:
- uncompetitive
- unambitious
- casual about appointments
- take one thing at a time
- express feelings

As can be seen, we have here a typically bi-polar model of personality, which evokes elements of the 'big five' classification referred to earlier, in that we can all be located within particular personality types and then compared to others in this regard. As was the case with the big five model, it should be noted that some people may not fall into the extremes of either the A or B types; rather exhibiting a more balanced profile. The Type A and B classification nonetheless provides a good example of the nomothetic school of personality as it can play out in practical terms. It purports to show how people's response to stress can vary according to personality type.

The causes of stress are numerous and include the nature of work (what demands are made of workers in their job role(s) and how much control they have over their work), organizational culture (see Chapter 7), interpersonal relationships at a group level (Chapter 8) and changes at the macro-social level; for example the impact of economic downturn (see Chapter 1). In this case we see a link with personality offering opportunities to assess how stress-prone workers are. It should be noted that stress is not necessarily perceived as a bad thing – we all need a level of stimulation to perform. However, individual differences – in both perception and personality – can mean that some people are more likely to experience negative consequences such as burnout than others. An individual classed as introverted might also find a job with many social contacts stressful, so in general terms it is valuable to link people to jobs by considering their propensity to feel stress acutely.

The idiographic approach to personality

The nomothetic approach to understanding personality predominates in business and management literature but we should also recognize the potential contribution of an alternative conception of the subject known as the *idiographic* view. It is also useful to locate this tradition within a process-relational view of individuals.[49] Here people are conceived as having developing identities and enacting their worlds – in other words our personalities emerge and develop in the light of our experiences. Cooley, an American psychologist writing in the early 20th century, termed this idea the 'looking glass self'. We find this idea plausible in explaining our everyday lives. For example, if you tell jokes and people habitually laugh at your jokes, this will reinforce your self-image as a sociable extrovert. If, on the other hand, your attempts to amuse are met with baffled silence or, even worse, disdain and abuse, then your self-image is likely to change along with your behaviour. The famous psychologist Carl Rogers[50] found that adjusted individuals were able to cope with changes in their self-concept. A flexible notion of one's self, recognizing that it can change over time and in new circumstances, will result in positive feelings and a psychologically healthy person.

 COUNTERPOINT

The windows to the soul – or a selection criterion?

Research published in 2007 by two Swedish academics concludes that patterns in individuals' irises can be an indicator of their personality. Mats Larsson, who led this project at Orebo University in Sweden,[51] claims that the genes involved in the development of this part of the eye also determine part of the brain's frontal lobe, which in turn is said to influence our personality. The eyes of 428 people were analysed and the personalities of these individuals 'tested'. Intricate patterns in the iris were found to be linked to personality features – for example, densely packed crypts (the wavy lines radiating from the pupil) were associated with open and empathetic personality traits.

Mats Larsson and his team have not suggested possible applications of these findings. However, it is conceivable that they could be used in the course of employee selection in future as the study is potentially strong on predictive validity – the extent to which findings predict future behaviour.

This study highlights the rise of genetic explanations of personality. In common with other scientific findings in the field of genetics, it brings forward important ethical issues.

Would you be happy to have your eyes scanned as part of a selection process and what would your reaction be if you were turned down for a job because of your eye markings? You might accept the judgement as scientifically valid or you could, alternatively, regard such a practice as an outrageous and unwarranted intrusion. More generally, what is your reaction to the possible use of genetic criteria such as this within business?

*The **idiographic** approach to understanding personality focuses on individual uniqueness. It regards personality as potentially shifting according to an individual's self-image and experiences.*

The **idiographic** approach to personality is less amenable to easy application within the workplace. Its central tenets are summarized below:

- individuals are unique complex entities and should not be located within typologies;
- personality should be understood as a complete entity (one should not focus on particular traits);
- people's personalities, closely related to their self-image, can change – sometimes radically – due to experience.

The idiographic approach implies that one needs a deep understanding of any one individual in order to capture their personality. This, of course, becomes difficult in an employee selection process that will probably be constrained by time and budget. But there are some methods that fall within this tradition. Thematic apperception tests (TATs), involve presenting someone with a photograph or other image, usually depicting a group of people, and asking him or her to imagine what is happening in terms of the dynamics between the people shown. It is claimed that TATs clearly evoke what is actually present in someone's mind although we are heavily dependent on people's honesty here. If their reaction is that they want to murder the people in the picture, how likely are they to reveal this thought if appointment to a desired job depends on it? Assessment centres use a collection of methods possibly including personality tests, group and team leadership activities, physical endurance tasks and work simulation. Such a combined range of measures administered over several days may go some way to creating a wider, more varied picture of someone's personality as it is manifested in different situations. Overall, idiographic approaches to personality are more closely associated with the *interpretivist* tradition in OB, set out in Chapter 1, and research methods aligning with that philosophical approach.

Earlier in this chapter we referred to the concept of *impression management*. It was suggested that individuals may seek to affect other people's impression of them in order to present a particular image of themselves – see our discussion of Goffman's work in this context. In this sense our *persona* – or projected image of ourselves – is what others see, and we can present that part of ourselves which we feel is appropriate to the situations we find ourselves in. The idiographic approach to personality can be understood via the metaphor of a Russian doll. There are a number of layers of personality, from the surface image we present through to the deep and real 'us'; our deepest dreams and fears which are known only to ourselves.

The idiographic approach to understanding personality is more challenging for managers to take on board not because it is difficult to conceptualize; many of you may relate to it well on an intuitive level. It is challenging to put into effect in work organizations though, as it implies an in-depth knowledge of individuals, including their development and 'inner lives' which can be difficult to achieve in reality. However, the idiographic view of personality also serves a warning against the use of quick and easy solutions based on psychometric testing which attempt to place individuals in suitable jobs and predict their performance.

Emotional competence

Another topic relevant to the study of individual difference at work is that of emotion. Until fairly recently emotions were given very little attention by researchers in organizational behaviour. Generally speaking, emotions were seen as impediments to sound decision making and an ordered approach to workplace relations. This kind of thinking is quickly being replaced by a view that sees emotions as a normal part of our workplace experiences. In fact, recent research has revealed the centrality of emotions to all areas of human functioning.[52] For example, to make decisions we are guided by our values, which are in turn based on our emotions. Reasoning and emotion are intertwined.

Emotional intelligence, introduced in Chapter 1, is one aspect of our emotional functioning that complements cognitive forms of intelligence. It is a form of *social intelligence* that allows us to monitor and shape our emotional responses and those of others. For many people, it is even more important than cognitive intelligence for success in life. Daniel Goleman popularized the concept of emotional intelligence in 1995 with the publication of his book on the topic, although others had been researching the area for some time.[53]

We now turn to the specific dimensions that make up emotional intelligence. A sound place to start is with the research instruments that are under development to assess it. There are several of these and each has a slightly different way of constructing and defining the dimensions or components of emotional intelligence. The oldest and most well researched was developed by Reuven Bar-On as a self-report instrument of emotional wellbeing.[54] It includes various measures of self-awareness and regard, interpersonal competence, adaptability, stress management and general mood state. An instrument that focuses more closely on awareness and management of emotions is the Multifactor Emotional Intelligence Scale (MEIS).[55] Please also refer to this scale on our website: **www.wileyeurope.com/college/french.** The four dimensions on the MEIS are as follows:

- identifying emotions – awareness of, and the ability to identify, the emotions you and others are feeling;
- using emotions – the capacity to weigh up the emotional aspects of values and attitudes when confronting problems and making decisions;
- understanding emotions – the ability to understand complex emotions and to recognize how emotions pass through stages over time;
- managing emotions – the ability to exercise self-control and self-regulation, and to empathize with and influence others.

Emotion management *is exercising emotional self-control and self-regulation influenced by the context in which individuals find themselves.*

Emotion management is an important organizational concern. Emotion can be viewed as a valuable resource to be harnessed in order to gain employee commitment (willingness) and a competitive advantage. Some researchers have the pessimistic view that emotion can be commodified via a 'commercialization of intimate life'.[56] Others celebrate the recognition of emotion as a vital part of organizational life, and harness these energies in a positive way to improve customer service and counteract employees' emotional exhaustion.[57]

Emotion is a lived interactional experience with an organizational dark side. For example, emotional burnout in front-line service work, the everyday stresses and strains of organizational life and the difficulty of working with bullies or harassers are realities that any employee can face. However, emotion cannot (and arguably should not) be controlled by the organization. Employees are social beings who enter the organization with life histories and experiences. They may take up organizationally prescribed roles, experience frustrations and often have to present themselves very differently to customers or clients. There is no clear divide between public and private worlds of emotion.[58]

Perhaps one of the most emotionally exhausting professions is nursing. Often nurses cannot show publicly their private emotions. For example, when a nurse cares for a particular patient during the process of dying, and especially when he or she has cared for this person for a long period of time, the nurse will experience a strong emotional response to the patient's death. At the same time, the nurse is likely to care for several other patients in the ward. In consideration of his or her other patients, the nurse cannot share these private emotions. Thus, to be effective, nurses need to be highly competent social actors and emotion managers.

Emotion constantly crosses boundaries between self and society, private and public, formal and informal. Employees continually juggle their mixed emotions in order to both enjoy and endure the rigours of organizational life. Managing employee emotions in the workplace includes recognizing the potential transformative power of human action. Managers also need to recognize the emotive forces that inhibit organizationally desirable behaviours. For this, managers themselves need to be emotionally competent. As is often

RESEARCH IN OB

Look at the article by Kahn *et al.* on our website **www.wileyeurope.com/college/french** examining the topic of burnout amongst teachers in the US. Note the multifaceted nature of burnout including emotional exhaustion, cynicism and concerns with efficacy. It is also interesting to record Kahn *et al.*'s finding that emotional support from supervisors and co-workers was a particularly important factor in dealing with symptoms of burnout. As positive emotional support increased, emotional exhaustion, cynicism and worries concerning efficacy decreased. The healing effect of emotional support worked for all personality types (see the next section for a full discussion of this concept). This research study lends support to the validity of the performance equation discussed earlier, with in this case, specific corroboration of the importance of organizational support.

the case in OB, this concept has attracted criticism from within the academic community, one commentator viewing it as 'old wine in new bottles'[59] and questioning whether *qualities* of emotional intelligence – for example self-awareness – are actually different from *competencies* that they are held to affect – such as accurate self-assessment. However, some evidence points to emotional intelligence as a powerful influence on job performance. One study[60] identified ten emotional competencies as the prime distinguishing capabilities of successful teams operating in a chemical company in Germany.

INDIVIDUAL DIFFERENCES AND WORKPLACE DIVERSITY

Increasing diversity is creating unparalleled workplace challenges. Significant variations are occurring in skill levels, education, physical abilities, cultural backgrounds, lifestyles, personal values, individual needs, ethnicity and social values. This increasing diversity is changing the mix of skills required to manage the workforce effectively.

EFFECTIVE MANAGER 2.2

In a situation where you are asked to work with workplace diversity, for example implementing a diversity management programme:

- Examine current structures and processes – do they harbour any systemic biases to disadvantage some groups? Whose priorities do they reflect? Who is excluded (for example, from decisions made in corridors or on the golf course)?
- Take a long-term view – attitudes may need to change and this will not happen overnight.
- Obtain support for change from the top (commitment, resources, money, time), as nothing will change without it.
- Obtain the involvement of all those who will be affected by change.

The benefits of a workplace that is open to diversity are:

- With shortages of skilled labour in some occupational areas, recruitment of staff is easier for organizations that welcome diversity.
- Diverse workplaces have contacts with customers and business partners from a wider range of cultures and groups.
- Diverse perspectives bring creativity and innovation.
- Problems are solved using a wider range of ideas and perspectives.

Organizations that can incorporate the opportunities created by diversity into their business strategies and management practices can gain a significant competitive advantage.

Essentially, managers need to ensure that everyone in the organization is sensitive to individual differences and to seek innovative ways to match increasingly diverse workers with job requirements. This may mean developing innovative recruiting strategies to attract new sources of labour and creating flexible employment conditions to better use the increasingly diverse range of workers.

The organization also needs to use various aspects of education and training in working with diverse employees, using a broad range of programmes, from basic skills to workshops designed to encourage managers and employees to value those with different demographic backgrounds. Note that training should be ongoing. Some organizations involve managers in conducting the training, to help provide a feeling of responsibility for making workplace diversity successful.

Look at Figure 2.10, which depicts the performance equation, building on Figure 1.1 on p. 11.

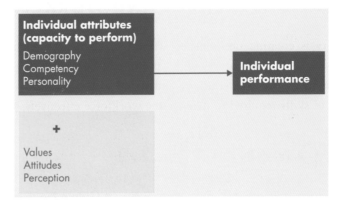

Figure 2.10: The individual performance equation.

Notice that we include two more important individual attribute variables:

- values
- attitudes

We will now discuss these variables in more detail.

VALUES

Values can be defined as broad preferences concerning appropriate courses of action or outcomes. As such, they reflect a person's sense of right and wrong, or what 'ought' to be.[61] 'Equal rights for all' and 'people should be treated with respect and dignity' are examples of values held by people. Values tend to influence attitudes and behaviour. If, for example, you value equal rights for all and you work for an organization that manifestly treats its managers much better than it does its other workers, you may form the attitude that your organization is an unfair place to work, and you may seek employment elsewhere.

Sources and types of values

People's values develop as a product of the learning and experiences they encounter in the cultural setting in which they live. Because learning and experiences differ from one person to another, value differences result. Such differences are likely to be deep seated and difficult (although not impossible) to change; many have their roots in early childhood and the way in which a person was raised.[62]

Psychologist Gordon Allport and his associates developed a classification of human values in the early 1930s.[63] However, although that classification had a major impact on the literature, it was not specifically designed for people in a work setting. More recently Meglino and associates have developed a values schema aimed at people in the workplace.[64] There are four values in this classification:

- achievement – getting things done and working hard to accomplish difficult things in life;
- helping and concern for others – being concerned with other people and helping others;
- honesty – telling the truth and doing what you feel is right;
- fairness – being impartial and doing what is fair for all concerned.

The Meglino framework was developed from information obtained in the workplace, where these four values were shown to be especially important. Thus, the framework has been viewed as particularly relevant for studying organizational behaviour.

Another typology of values is provided by Shalom Schwartz (1992).[65] Schwartz's ten basic human values are set out below with brief accompanying comments on how these are followed through in typical behaviour:

- *Achievement* (striving for personal success);
- *Benevolence* (wishing to foster harmony within a group);
- *Conformity* (avoiding behaviour likely to harm others);
- *Hedonism* (seeking pleasure and gratification);
- *Power* (looking to gain social status, prestige and control over others);
- *Security* (seeking safety, stability and social order);
- *Self-direction* (gaining independence in thought and action);
- *Stimulation* (seeking excitement and novelty);
- *Tradition* (accepting and respecting customs, e.g. cultural and religious);
- *Universalism* (promoting the welfare of all people and nature).

Schwartz proposed that values would typically be enduring. We rank values in order of importance. They can also be regarded as 'portable' in that we carry them through our daily lives in which they can be activated by a particular situation. For example, a couple may be driving to an anniversary meal – underpinned by values of benevolence and hedonism. If, however, one party was highly oriented towards universalism, s/he might be compelled to abandon the journey and instead head for an animal shelter if they saw an injured pigeon en route.

In OB terms, Schwartz's classification has potential explanatory value – think, for example, of the likely values held by a full-time skydiver! The whole idea of values is revisited in Chapter 4 when we look at the topic of motivation.

Importance of values

Values are important to managers and to the field of organizational behaviour because they have the potential to influence workplace attitudes, behaviour and outputs. In addition, values can be influential through value congruence, which occurs when individuals express positive feelings on encountering others who exhibit values similar to their own. When values differ, or are incongruent, conflicts may result over such things as goals and the means to achieve them. The Meglino value schema was used to examine value congruence between leaders and followers. The researchers found greater follower satisfaction with the leader when there was such congruence in terms of achievement, helping, honesty and fairness values.

Now turn to Table 2.1. The values reported here are based on responses from a sample of US managers and human resource professionals.[66] The responding organizational specialists were asked to identify the work-related values they believed to be most important to individuals in the workforce, both now and in the near future. The nine most popular values are listed in the table. Even though individual workers place their own importance on these values, and many countries have diverse workforces, this overall characterization is a good place for managers to start when dealing with employees in the new workplace.

However, we should be aware of applied research on value trends over time. Values change as the world is changing. For example, the 9/11 tragedies will have changed value ranking. When employees talk about security, this is no longer assumed to be financial security but also personal security at work. Employment on the 79th floor of an office building may be more an issue of concern than it would have been before 11 September 2001.

ATTITUDES

Like values, attitudes are an important component of organizational behaviour. Attitudes are influenced by values but they focus on specific people or objects, whereas values have a more general focus. 'Employees should be allowed to participate' is a value. Your positive or negative feeling about your job as a result of the participation it allows, is an attitude. An attitude is a predisposition to respond in a positive or negative way to someone or something in our environment. When you say that you 'like' or 'dislike' someone or something you are expressing an attitude. One important work-related attitude is job satisfaction (see Chapter 5). This attitude expresses a person's positive or negative feelings about various aspects of their job and/or work environment.

Regardless of the specific attitude considered, it is important to remember that an attitude, like a value, is a concept or construct; that is, one never sees, touches or actually isolates an attitude. Rather, attitudes are *inferred* from the things people say (informally or formally) or do (their behaviour).

1 Recognition for competence and accomplishments	People want to be seen and recognized, both as individuals and teams, for their value, skills and accomplishments. They want to know that their contribution is appreciated.
2 Respect and dignity	This value focuses on how people are treated — through the jobs they hold, in response to their ideas, or by virtue of their background. The strong support for this value indicates that most people want to be respected for who they are; they want to be valued.
3 Personal choice and freedom	People want more opportunity to be free from constraints and decisions made for and about them by authorities. They want to be more autonomous and able to rely more on their own judgement. They wish to have more personal choice in what affects their lives.
4 Involvement at work	Large portions of the workforce want to be kept informed, included and involved in important decisions at work, particularly where these decisions affect their work and quality of life at work.
5 Pride in one's work	People want to do a good job and feel a sense of accomplishment. Fulfilment and pride come through quality workmanship.
6 Lifestyle quality	People pursue many different lifestyles and each person wants theirs to be of high quality. Work policies and practices have a great impact on lifestyle pursuits. The desire for time with family and time for leisure were strongly emphasised.
7 Financial security	People want to know that they can succeed. They want some security from economic cycles, rampant inflation or devastating financial situations. This appears to be a new variation on the desire for money—not continual pursuit of money, but enough to feel secure in today's world, enjoy a comfortable lifestyle and ride out bad times.
8 Self-development	The focus here is on the desire to improve continually, to do more with one's life, to reach one's potential, to learn and to grow. There is a strong desire by individuals to take initiative and to use opportunities to further themselves.
9 Health and wellness	This value reflects the ageing workforce and increased information on wellness. People want to organise life and work in ways that are healthy and contribute to long-term wellness.

Table 2.1: The top nine work-related values.

Source: Jamieson, D. and O'Mara, J. (1991), *Managing Workforce 2000*, Jossey-Bass: San Francisco, pp. 28–29. Reproduced by permission of John Wiley & Sons, Inc.

Components of attitudes

Study Figure 2.11 carefully. This shows attitudes as accompanied by antecedents and results. The beliefs and values antecedents in the figure form the cognitive component of an attitude: the beliefs, opinions, knowledge or information a person possesses. Beliefs represent ideas about someone or something and the conclusions people draw about them; they convey a sense of 'what is' to an individual. 'My job lacks responsibility' is a belief shown in Figure 2.11. Note that the beliefs may or may not be accurate. 'Responsibility is important' is a corresponding aspect of the cognitive component that reflects an underlying value. In Chapter 1 we introduced the concept of the psychological contract, we can now see that, as a belief, it is essentially subjective – it is the individual's perception of the belief's reality that is most important.

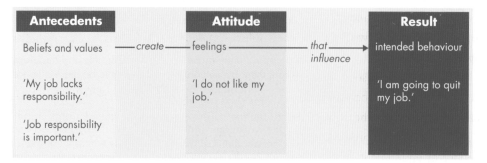

Figure 2.11: A work-related example of the three components of attitude.

The affective component of an attitude is a specific feeling regarding the personal impact of the antecedents. This is the actual attitude, such as 'I do not like my job'. The behavioural component is an intention to behave in a certain way based on specific feelings or attitudes. This intended behaviour is a predisposition to act in a specific way, such as 'I am going to quit my job'. In summary, the components of attitudes systematically relate to one another as follows:[67]

Beliefs and values → attitudes → behaviour.

Attitudes and behaviour

Look again at Figure 2.11. It is essential to recognize that the link between attitudes and behaviour is tentative. An attitude results in intended behaviour. This intention may or may not be carried out in a given circumstance. For example, a person with a favourable attitude towards unions would, one might assume, be likely to articulate positive opinions about unions. However, other practical factors in a given situation may override their intentions. For example, hearing a good friend say negative things about unions may lead to the suppression of the tendency to say something positive in the same conversation. The person has not changed his favourable attitude in this case, but nor has he carried out the associated intention to behave.

Even though attitudes do not always predict behaviour, the link between attitudes and potential or intended behaviour is important for managers to understand. Think about your work experiences or conversations with other people about their work. It is not uncommon to hear concerns expressed about someone's 'bad attitude'. These concerns typically reflect displeasure with the behavioural consequences with which the poor attitude is associated. As we will show in subsequent chapters, unfavourable attitudes in the form of low job satisfaction can result in costly labour turnover. Unfavourable attitudes may also result in absenteeism, tardiness and even impaired physical or mental health. One of the manager's responsibilities, therefore, is to recognize attitudes and to understand both their antecedents and their potential implications.

Attitudes and cognitive consistency

One additional avenue of research on attitudes involves cognitive consistency; that is, the consistency between a person's expressed attitudes and actual behaviour. Let us go back to the example depicted in Figure 2.11. A person in this illustration has an unfavourable attitude towards a job. She knows and recognizes this fact. Now assume that her intentions to leave are not fulfilled and that she continues to work at the same job each day. The result is an inconsistency between the attitude (job dissatisfaction) and the behaviour (continuing to work at the job).

Festinger, a noted social psychologist, uses the term **cognitive dissonance** to describe a state of inconsistency between an individual's attitudes and his or her behaviour.[68] Let us assume that you have the attitude that recycling rubbish is good for the economy but you do not recycle. Festinger predicts that such an inconsistency results in discomfort and a desire to reduce or eliminate it. There are three ways of achieving this reduction or elimination:

Cognitive dissonance *is a state of perceived inconsistency between a person's expressed attitudes and actual behaviour.*

* Changing the underlying attitude. You decide that recycling really is not a major priority for you as you now believe it has no impact on climate change.
* Changing future behaviour. You start recycling.
* Developing new ways of explaining or rationalizing the inconsistency. For example, recycling is good for the environment but you do not recycle because recycling bags and new rubbish collection procedures require more resources than are actually saved through recycling.

A NEW SET OF VALUES AND ATTITUDES: GLOBAL MANAGERIAL COMPETENCIES

The increasingly globalized nature of business, set out in Chapter 1, which often involves us dealing routinely with people from other cultures, means that managers and other workers must understand and respond to customers, governments and competitors from different parts of the world. To be successful, global managers in particular must develop key global and cultural competencies: cultural self-awareness, cultural consciousness, ability to lead multicultural teams, ability to negotiate across cultures and a global mindset.[69]

* Cultural self-awareness. The starting point for cultural sensitivity is an understanding of the influence of one's own culture. A clear appreciation of one's own cultural values, assumptions and beliefs is a prerequisite for developing an appreciation of other cultures.[70]
* Cultural consciousness. A critical requirement for global managers is the ability to adapt to cultural requirements and manage cultural diversity.[71]
* The ability to lead multicultural teams. This requires working collaboratively with people with different cultural perspectives and developing cultural sensitivity.[72]
* The ability to negotiate across cultures. Global managers are required to negotiate with people from different countries and cultures. Negotiating styles and approaches vary substantially with each culture.[73]

Culture shock *describes a series of stages experienced by people when they encounter a new cultural setting. It is normally depicted as a U-curve with initial elation followed by negative feelings, succeeded in turn by recovery and adjustment.*

• A global mindset. An essential global management competency has been described as 'global thinking', a 'global mindset' or a 'global perspective'. Managers need to appreciate the strategic implication of global business and develop a long-term orientation. A global mindset allows a manager to scan the global environment from a very broad perspective.[74]

A re-evaluation of our own culturally derived values and attitudes may result in some psychological disorientation. Writers on cross-cultural management have drawn attention to the concept of **culture shock** in this context.[75] We see that many managers are able to cope with culture shock and emerge as even more effective performers. Note that the re-evaluation of their values and a recognition of cultural difference within the process of culture shock is necessary, if sometimes traumatic, if they are to succeed in their job roles. Here we have a potent illustration of the relationship between values, attitudes and job performance.

CONCLUSION

Thus far we have discussed individual differences in terms of perception, personality, values and attitudes. All of these areas within OB are important in that they underlie so many of our routine experiences at work. For example, the way we perceive stimuli, whether these take the form of objects or other people, informs our attitudes and behaviour – perception is the springboard to what we do in our lives. An understanding of individual differences can also have a positive effect in terms of work and organizational performance. In this context turn back to the individual performance equation on p. 108. Employees' capacity to perform depends on individual attributes (such as perception and personality) that are influenced by values and attitudes. So an understanding of individual differences is critical to the study of OB and also helps us to understand some underpinnings of both individual and organizational performance.

SUMMARY

LEARNING OBJECTIVE 1
The individual performance equation

The individual performance equation views performance as the result of the personal attributes of individuals, the work efforts they put forth and the organizational support they receive. *Individual* performance factors are highlighted in the equation: performance = individual attributes × work effort × organizational support. Individual factors regarded as crucial within OB are our perceptual world, personality characteristics and held values and attitudes. Work effort is reflected in the motivation to work. Organizational support consists of a wide range of organizational support mechanisms, such as work technology, resources and an enabling organizational structure that provide the opportunity for an individual to perform if they have the capacity and willingness.

LEARNING OBJECTIVE 2
The perceptual process

Individuals do not perceive the world, including other people in it, in an identical fashion. This means that we select, organize, interpret and retrieve information from the environment in unique ways. Our perceptions are influenced by a number of factors, including social and physical aspects of the situation as well as personal factors such as needs, experience, values, attitudes and personality. An awareness of the perceptual process can help us more easily understand how other people may perceive a situation and enable us to minimize common perceptual distortions. Stereotypes are not always inaccurate but they frequently are, so should be avoided. You probably wish to be understood as an individual rather than as a member of a wider category; other people will wish this too so an awareness of stereotyping can help us deal with others in a better way.

LEARNING OBJECTIVE 3
Personality characteristics of individuals

Personality captures the overall profile or combination of characteristics that represent the unique nature of a person as that person reacts to and interacts with others. We expect there to be a predictable interplay between an individual's personality and a tendency to behave in certain ways. The nomothetic view of personality focuses on identifying and measuring traits important in organizational behaviour, including locus of control, authoritarianism/dogmatism, Machiavellianism and the oft-cited 'big five' personality dimensions. The contrasting idiographic approach to this topic emphasizes our individual uniqueness including an individual's self-concept. It allows for personality change in response to our experiences, so plays down the importance of fixed traits. This is conceivably a deeper view of personality in academic terms but is more challenging to put into operation in the organizational setting.

Idiographic concepts such as impression management, persona and role link into a recent preoccupation with the role of emotion at work, emotion management and emotional intelligence.

LEARNING OBJECTIVE 4
Values and attitudes

Values are global concepts that guide actions and judgements across a variety of situations. Values are especially important in organizational behaviour because they can influence performance outcomes directly. They can also have an indirect influence on behaviour by means of attitudes and perceptions. While treated as characteristics of individuals in this chapter, values can also reflect differences among various societal and organizational cultures – see also Chapter 7. Attitudes are influenced by values but focus on specific people or objects; in contrast, values have a more global focus. Attitudes are predispositions to respond in a positive or negative way to someone or something in one's environment. They operate through intended behaviour to influence actual behaviour or other variables.

Values and attitudes which foster a global mindset, cultural awareness and the ability to lead multicultural teams are especially useful given long-term trends affecting work organizations.

CHAPTER 2 STUDY GUIDE

Now that you have read this chapter, you should be able to apply and further develop your knowledge by undertaking the following activities set out over the next few pages: test your knowledge questions, an individual activity and an end-of-chapter case study.

Please also go to this book's website: **www.wileyeurope.com/college/french** to find further material which will enhance your understanding and enable you to assess your knowledge.

TEST YOURSELF

1. Outline and explain the individual performance equation used in this chapter.
2. Identify the factors influencing an individual's capacity to perform. Why is each of these important?
3. Which factors influence the perceptual process and how do they do so?
4. List and briefly explain the dimensions of personality put forward as the so-called 'big five' traits.
5. Identify Schwartz's ten basic human values. How can a knowledge of these values help explain people's behaviour at work?
6. Personality testing is widely used as a recruitment and selection strategy. What are the advantages and disadvantages of such a strategy and why? Please use examples in your answer.
7. What do you understand by the idiographic approach to understanding personality? How useful could this approach be when applied to work situations?
8. Colleges and universities are 'workplaces' for generating, acquiring and sharing new knowledge. There is great diversity within the student population, but this may not be used in the classroom teaching strategies that you experience. Develop a 'diversity management programme' suitable for use by teachers and lecturers in the classroom, which would reflect the diversity of the student group and capitalize on its potential within this group to enhance learning. Explain the ideas behind your diversity management programme.
9. Explain the relevance of emotional intelligence and emotional management to the workplace. Illustrate your answer with examples.
10. 'Workplace values and attitudes typically undergo significant change from one generation of workers to the next.' Do you agree? Explain and give examples.

INDIVIDUAL ACTIVITY[76]

Personal values

For the following 16 items, rate how important each one is to you. Write a number between 0 and 100 on the line to the left of each item.

Not important			Important				Very important	
0	10	20	30	40	50	60	70	80	90	100

_____ 1. An enjoyable, satisfying job

_____ 2. A high-paying job

_____ 3. A strong intimate relationship

_____ 4. Meeting new people; social events

_____ 5. Involvement in community activities

_____ 6. Religion and spirituality

_____ 7. Exercising, playing sports

_____ 8. Intellectual development

_____ 9. A career with challenging opportunities

_____ 10. Nice cars, clothes, home etc.

_____ 11. Spending time with family

_____ 12. Having several close friends

_____ 13. Volunteer work for not-for-profit organizations, like a medical charity

_____ 14. Meditation, quiet time to think and contemplate

_____ 15. A healthy balanced diet

_____ 16. Educational reading, and/or self-improvement programmes.

Below, transfer the numbers beside each of the 16 items to the appropriate column, then add the two numbers in each column.

Professional	Financial	Family	Social
1. _____	2. _____	3. _____	4. _____
9. _____	10. _____	11. _____	12. _____
Totals _____	_____	_____	_____

Community	Spiritual	Physical	Intellectual
5. _____	6. _____	7. _____	8. _____
13. _____	14. _____	15. _____	16. _____
Totals _____	_____	_____	_____

The higher the total in any area, the higher the value you place on that particular area. The closer the numbers are in all eight areas, the more well rounded you are; that is, your values encompass a number of areas.

Think about the time and effort you put into your top three values. Is it sufficient to allow you to achieve the level of success you want in each area? If not, what can you do to change the situation? Is there any area in which you feel you should have a higher value total? If yes, which area? What can you do to realize this wish?

Case Study

MEDIZIN AG

Medizin AG is the fully owned German subsidiary of a large pharmaceutical company whose headquarters are in Canada. It manufactures a wide range of both prescription and 'over-the-counter' medicines. The company also invests heavily in research and development (R&D) in the hope of becoming a world player in pharmaceuticals.

The board of directors at Medizin AG at the German plant located in Gelsen-kirchen are comprised of older males and this is also true of executive management posts within this subsidiary. The rest of the workforce consists of around 60 staff members, including highly qualified scientists and technicians involved with R&D, technically skilled pharmaceutical workers and a general factory workforce with seven different nationalities represented. In addition, administration is carried out by four female clerical officers.

Recently business has not been going well. Medizin AG has been finding it difficult to compete with overseas companies which manufacture medicines more cheaply, including strong competition from companies located in the Czech Republic, Portugal and Indonesia. At the moment, 95% of the skilled pharmaceutical workers in the plant are full-time permanent employees. To cut costs, senior managers have decided that the skilled pharmaceutical workers must work on a more flexible basis. The plan is to re-employ 50% of those workers as casual employees, which will result in a decrease in direct costs. The general factory workforce will be reduced by 30%. In addition, Medizin AG plans to set up an Internet business so that it can sell some products directly to the public, both in Germany and more widely, in the hope that it can cut more staff, including two of the clerical officers. These proposals will have to be discussed with the Works Council (including employee representatives) at the company within German codetermination law.

Questions

1. How are the employees at Medizin AG likely to perceive the proposed changes? Identify some ways in which perceptions could differ *within* the workforce.
2. What behaviours are you expecting from the skilled workers in response to the strategies proposed by the managers?
3. You are at the beginning of your studies in organizational behaviour. What additional knowledge about human behaviour (beyond that covered in this chapter) would help you to better understand the problems at Medizin AG and to propose suitable solutions?

Based on Drugs Inc, in Wood, J., Zeffane, R., Fromholtz, M. and Fitzgerald, J. (2006), *Organizational Behaviour: Core Concepts and Applications*, John Wiley & Sons: Milton, Queensland.

SUGGESTED READING

Arnold, J., Randell, R. *et al.* (2010), *Work Psychology, Understanding Human Behaviour in the Workplace*, 5th edn, FT Prentice Hall: Harlow. This book provides a useful outline of the nature of work psychology and the ways this discipline can be applied in a workplace setting.

Goffman, E. (1959), *The Presentation of Self in Everyday Life*, Penguin: Harmondsworth. This original source book contains numerous evocative examples of how workers present themselves to others by adopting roles and using fixed props as an actor would in a dramatic production.

END NOTES

1. Winnett, A. & Porter, R. (2010), TV election debate: Nick Clegg's star rises in great showdown, *Daily Telegraph*, 16 April.

2. Hope, C. (2010), General Election 2010: Liberal Democrats surge after Nick Clegg's TV debate performance, *Daily Telegraph*, 16 April.

3. www.museum.tv/eotusection.kennedy-nixon (accessed 4 July 2010).

4. Hill, W. E. (1915), *Puck*, 6 November.

5. Linehan, M. (2005), Women in international management, in *International Human Resource Management: A Critical Text* (eds H. Scullion and M. Linehan). Palgrave Macmillan: Basingstoke.

6. Kiely, J. & Henbest, A. (2000), Sexual harassment at work: experiences from an oil refinery. *Women in Management Review*, **15** (2), 65–77.

7. Wagner, J. A. III & Hollenbeck, J. R. (1998), *Organizational Behaviour*, 3rd edn, Prentice Hall: Upper Saddle River, NJ, p. 59.

8. Mullins, L. J. (2010), *Management and Organizational Behaviour*, 9th edn, FT Prentice Hall: Harlow, p. 209.

9. Cronshaw, S. F. & Lord, R. G. (1987), Effects of categorization, attribution and encoding processes in leadership perceptions. *Journal of Applied Psychology*, **72**, 97–106.

10. Ibid.

11. Hunt, J. G. (1991), *Leadership: A New Synthesis*, Sage: Newbury Park, CA.

12. Hall, E. T. (1990), *Understanding Cultural Differences*, Intercultural Press: Yarmouth, ME.

13. Hunt, J. G, Baliga, B. R. & Peterson, M. P. (1988), Strategic Apex leader scripts and an organizational life cycle approach to leadership and excellence. *Journal of Management Development*, 7, 61–83.

14. See www.news.siu.edu/news/August06/080 306sm6063, (accessed 26 May 2007).

15. Dearborn, D. W. & Simon, H. A. (1958), Selective perception: a note on the departmental identification of executives. *Sociometry*, **21**, 140–144.

16. Walsh, J. P. (1988), Selectivity and selective perception: an investigation of managers' belief structures and information processing. *Academy of Management Journal*, **24**, 453–470.

17. Sterling Livingston, J. (1969), Pygmalion in management. *Harvard Business Review*, July/August, 81–89.

18. Eden, D. & Shani, A. B. (1982), Pygmalion goes to boot camp. *Journal of Applied Psychology*, **67**, 194–199.

19. Manzoni, J.-F. & Barsoux, J.-L. (2002), *The Set Up to Fail Syndrome: How Good Managers Cause Great People to Fail*, Harvard Business School Press: Boston, MA.

20. Anderson, N. & Shackleton, V. (1993), *Successful Selection Interviewing*, Blackwell: Oxford.

21. Gardner, W. L. & Martinko, M. J. (1988), Impression management in organizations. *Journal of Management*, June, 332.

22. Goffman, E. (1959), *The Presentation of Self in Everyday Life*, Penguin: Harmondsworth.

23. Kelley, H. H. (1972), Attribution in Social Interaction, in *Attribution: Perceiving the Causes of Behaviour* (eds E. E. Jones, D. E. Kanouse, H. H. Kelley *et al.*), General Learning Press: Morristown, NJ.

24. Harvey, J. H. & Weary, G. (1984), Current issues in attribution theory and research. *Annual Review of Psychology*, 35, 427–459.

25. http://soccernet.espn.go.com/news/story, (accessed 26 May 2007).

26. Ibid.

27. Steers, R. M., Bischoff, S. J. & Higgins, L. H. (1992), Cross cultural management research. *Journal of Management Inquiry*, December, 325–326.

28. Crant, J. M. & Bateman, T. S. (1993), Assignment of credit and blame for performance outcomes. *Academy of Management Journal*, February, 7–27.

29. Fosterling, F. (1985), Attributional retraining: a review. *Psychological Bulletin*, November, 496–512.

30. Gentleman, A. (2006), India grounds hostesses who are 'too fat to fly', *Observer*, 5 November.

31. Kolbe, K. & Kolbe, D. (1999), Management by instinct leads the way to change, www.kolbe.com/info_center/articles.cfm, (accessed 9 November 2007).

32. Freud, S. (1935), *A General Introduction to Psychoanalysis*, Carlton House: New York.

33. Board, B. J. & Fritzon, K. (2005), Disordered personalities at work. *Psychology, Crime and Law*, 11 (1), 17–32.

34. Perkins, S. J. & Shortland, S. M. (2006), *Strategic International Human Resource Management*, 2nd edn, Kogan Page: London.

35. Eysenck, H. J. (1970), *The Structure of Human Personality*, 3rd edn, Methuen: London.

36. Allport, G. & Odbert, H. (1936), Trait names: a psycholexical study. *Psychological Monographs*, 47, 211–214.

37. Hogan, J. & Hogan, R. (1988), How to measure employee reliability. *Journal of Applied Psychology*, 74, 273–279.

38. Rotter, J. B. (1966), Generalized expectancies for internal versus external control of reinforcement. *Psychological Monographs*, 80, 1–28.

39. Hellriegel, D., Slocum, J. W. Jr & Woodman, R. W. (2004), *Organizational Behaviour*, 11th edn, West Publishing Co.: St Paul, Minnesota.

40. Wagner, J. A. III & Hollenbeck, J. R. (1995), *Management of Organizational Behaviour*, Prentice Hall: Englewood Cliffs, NJ, Ch. 4.

41. Hamilton, V. L. & Kelman, H. C. (1990), *Crimes of Obedience: Towards a Social Psychology of Authority and Responsibility*, Yale University Press: London.

42. Kelman, H. C. (2005), The policy context of torture: a social-psychological analysis. *International Review of the Red Cross*, 87 (857).

43. Waldmeir, P. (2005), Anderson conviction overturned, *Financial Times* (London), 1 June, p. 15.

44. Machiavelli, N. (1961), *The Prince*, trans. George Bull, Penguin: Harmondsworth.

45. Cyriac, K. & Dharmaraj, R. (1994), Machiavellianism in Indian management. *Journal of Business Ethics*, 13 (4), 281–286.

46. Arnold, J. & Randell, R. *et al.* (2010), *Work Psychology: understanding human behaviour in the workplace*, 5th edn, Harlow: FT Prentice Hall.

47. Lee, C., Ashford, S. J. & Jamieson, L. F. (1993), The effects of Type A behaviour dimensions and optimism on coping strategy, health and performance. *Journal of Organizational Behavior*, 14, 143–157.

48. Cooper, C. L., Sloan, S. & Williams, S. (1988), *Occupational Stress Indicator: The Manual*, Windsor: NFER/Nelson.

49. Watson, T. J. (2006), *Organising and Managing Work*, 2nd edn, FT Prentice Hall: Harlow.

50. Rogers, C. R. (1947), Some observations on the organization of personality. *American Psychologist*, **2**, 358–368.

51. Larsson, M., Pederson, N. L. & Stattin, H. (in press), Associations between iris characteristics and personality in adulthood. *Biological Psychology*.

52. Herkenhoff, L. (2004), Culturally tuned emotional intelligence: an effective change management tool? *Strategic Change*, **13** (2), 73.

53. Goleman, D. (2000), *Working with Emotional Intelligence*, Bantam: New York.

54. Bar-On, R. (2001), Emotional intelligence and self-actualization, in *Emotional Intelligence in Everyday Life: A Scientific Inquiry* (eds J. Ciarrochi, J. Forgas & J. D. Mayer), Psychology Press: New York.

55. Mayer, J. D. & Salovey, P. (1997), What is emotional intelligence? In *Emotional Development and Emotional Intelligence* (eds P. Salovey & D. J. Sluyter), Basic Books: New York.

56. Hochschild, A. (2003), *The Commercialization of Intimate Life*, University of California Press: Berkeley, Los Angeles.

57. Kinnie, N., Hutchinson, S. & Purcell, J. (2000), Fun and surveillance: the paradox of high commitment management in call centres. *International Journal of Human Resource Management*, **11** (5), 967–985.

58. Bolton, S. (2005), *Emotion Management in the Workplace*, Palgrave Macmillan: Basingstoke.

59. Stock, R. (2003), Watch those emotions – they're the new IQ, *Sunday Star Times* (Wellington, New Zealand), 21 December.

60. Jacob, P. E., Flink, J. J. & Schuchman, H. L. (1962), Values and their function in decision making. *American Behavioral Scientist*, **5** (9), 6–38.

61. Rokeach, M. & Ball Rokeach, S. J. (1989), Stability and change in American value priorities, 1968–1981. *American Psychologist*, May, 775–784.

62. Allport, G., Vernon, P. E. & Lindzey, G. (1931), *Study of Values*, Houghton Mifflin: Boston, MA.

63. Ibid.

64. Meglino, B. M., Ravlin, E. C. & Adkins, C. L. (1992), The measurement of work value congruence: a field study comparison. *Journal of Management*, **1** (1), 33–43.

65. Schwartz, S. H. (1992), Universals in the Content and Structure of Values, Theory and Empirical Tests in 20 Countries, in *Advances in Experimental Social Psychology* (ed. M. Zanna), Vol. 25, pp. 1–65, New York: Academic Press.

66. Jamieson, D. & O'Mara, J. (1991), *Managing Workforce 2000*, Jossey-Bass: San Francisco, pp. 28–29.

67. Fishbein, M. & Ajzen, I. (1975), *Belief, Attitude, Intention, and Behaviour: an Introduction to Theory and Research*, Addison-Wesley: Reading, MA.

68. Festinger, L. (1957), *A Theory of Cognitive Dissonance*, Stanford University Press: Palo Alto, CA.

69. Cant, A. G. (2004), Internationalizing the business curriculum: developing intercultural competence. *Journal of American Academy of Business*, **5** (1/2), 177–182.

70. Adler, N. J. (2002), *International Dimensions of Organizational Behaviour*, 4th edn, South-Western College Publishing, Thomson Learning: Cincinnati, OH.

71. McCall, M. W. & Hollenbeck, G. P. (2002), *Developing Global Executives: the Lessons of International Experience*, Harvard Business School: Boston, MA.

72. Broeways, M.-J. and Price, R. (2008), *Understanding Cross-Cultural Management*, FT Prentice Hall: Harlow.

73. Hyman, R. (2003), Varieties of capitalism, national industrial relations systems and transnational challenges, in *International Human Resource Management* (eds A.-W. Harzing & J. van Ruysseveldt), Sage: London.

74. Bartlett, C. A. & Ghoshal, S. (1998), *Managing Across Borders: The Transnational Solution*, 2nd edn, Random House: London.

75. French, R. (2010), *Cross-Cultural Management in Work Organizations*, 2nd edn, CIPD: London.

76. Lussier, R. N. (1993), Human Relations in Organizations: a skill building approach, 2nd edn, Richard D. Irwin: Homewood, IL. © The McGraw-Hill Companies, Inc. Reproduced by permission.

CHAPTER 3

Learning, reinforcement and self-management

LEARNING OBJECTIVES

After studying this chapter you should be able to:

- identify the various general approaches to learning
- explain organizational behavioural modification and how reinforcement strategies are involved in it
- discuss social learning theory and behavioural self-management
- examine modern forms of learning
- discuss the concept of the learning organization.

A PUNISHMENT OR A REWARD?

Bob Segers works for a major US car manufacturer based in Chicago. The company has operated a quality management approach for the last decade, in which each 'cell' (or department) is responsible for its own output standards and quality checking. His performance has recently changed, resulting in a poorer standard of quality of his work. As well as letting himself down, he is also letting the production team down.

His team leader (cell leader) calls him over for a chat, and simply says: 'Bob, take the day off tomorrow.' (Bob takes the following day off and receives his full pay for the day.) There is no extra cover arranged to fill the gap that Bob's absence will create.

This example illustrates the difficulties involved in attempting to change employees' behaviour. In this instance, how could Bob perceive the order from his team leader to stay home and to what extent is having the next day off seen as a punishment? There could also be cultural dimensions to this topic area. How would the instruction given by this team leader be perceived by a fellow worker in Spain, France, the UK, China or another country – more of a punishment than a reward?

INTRODUCTION

This chapter will focus on learning that takes place primarily within the workplace or in workplace-related activities. The concept of reinforcement and learning theories will then be considered, leading to an exploration of the concept of self-management.

THE NATURE OF LEARNING

The growth of literature surrounding workplace learning, knowledge management and core competence in the workplace is testament to the need to link learning with competitive advantage. According to Hamel,[1] 'A company's value derives not from things, but from knowledge, knowhow, intellectual assets, competencies – all embodied in people.' Similarly, if an organization's expertise (skill set, knowledge, capabilities, core competence and so forth) is standing still, then the company will not improve and, by definition, will not remain competitive.

Some organizational philosophies may still be based upon a predominantly instructional training approach whereby remedial action needs to take place to put something right. However, if it isn't broken and no fixing is needed, then no development activity will take place. Training interventions therefore only take place when the need is significant or the consequences deemed important (like essential health and safety training).

Contrary to this philosophy is the **lifelong learning** approach within organizations, adopting a much more developmental approach to training *and* development. If employees are seen as an important asset within the organization, then they need to be developed and nurtured, so that this asset can be maximized.

Malone[2] defines training as 'a planned and systematic way of improving a person's knowledge, skills and attitudes so that he or she can perform the current job more competently'. Malone's definition of development is 'the process of preparing a person to take on more onerous responsibilities or equip him or her for future promotion within the organization'. The same author's definition of learning is 'the process which brings about persistent change in behaviour. Learning gives a person increased competence to deal successfully with his or her environment as by acquiring knowledge, skills and attitudes'.

Learning can be defined more simply as a relatively permanent change in behaviour that occurs as a result of experience. The critical question for the management of organizations is how this impacts upon performance.

Learning relies upon the acquisition of the requisite skills or competencies to perform a task, job or role. Whereas performance includes learning and the motivation to engage in behaviour appropriate to apply to learning.

Lifelong learning *adopts the philosophy that we learn throughout our lives, and that learning does not cease when we reach a certain age.*

LEARNING AND PERFORMANCE

Why are there continued references to learning in textbooks and journal articles when, ultimately, learning has to manifest itself somewhere in organizations? It could be argued that learning is almost an unconscious process or an unobservable process that occurs through a person's introspection and reflective thought processes, and may not manifest itself immediately in observable actions.

One model that is useful in understanding people at work is the 'duck pond' analogy (see Figure 3.1), which differentiates between differing levels of observable and unobservable aspects of learning. At the top level, the surface water is clear and behaviours are observable. For example, a cashier who makes errors processing a purchase, resulting in the supervisor having to annul the sale and then re-input the sale.

The problem with this cashier may be that they panic with certain types of purchase (e.g. multiple payment methods), so their attitude is that they are going to make an error, and subsequently they do so. In order to affect behaviour, there may be a need to impact upon the values, attitudes and beliefs (some of which are entrenched in the deep and murky water) that the individual holds in order to impact upon performance (completing the task successfully). Learning is a complex area, and when addressing individuals we may consider their abilities, attitudes, competencies, their behaviours, their learning styles, their personality and many more aspects before considering how best they may learn within an organizational setting.

There is also the need to consider how people learn within both group/team and organizational settings. This chapter concentrates primarily on individual learning but the importance of team learning and **organizational learning** cannot be underestimated.

Organizational learning *is the process of acquiring or developing new knowledge that modifies or changes behaviour and improves organizational performance.*

Figure 3.1: The duck pond analogy.

The concepts of the 'learning organization' and 'teaching organization' are addressed later in this chapter.

LEARNING APPROACHES

It would be foolhardy to think that all learning in organizations is planned, systematic, structured and predictable. There are four general approaches to learning that have differing philosophical and historic principles:

- classical and operant conditioning
- cognitive learning
- social learning
- modern approaches to learning.

Each approach offers useful insights into understanding organizational behaviour.

Classical conditioning and operant conditioning

Behaviourists, such as Pavlov and Skinner, emphasize 'behaviour' as their central focus, not thoughts or feelings. Their emphasis is upon observation of behaviour.

Classical conditioning is a form of learning through association that involves the manipulation of stimuli to influence behaviour. Ivan Pavlov, a Russian psychologist, taught dogs to salivate at the sound of a bell by ringing the bell when feeding the dogs. The sight of the food naturally caused the dogs to salivate. Eventually, the dogs 'learned' to associate the bell ringing with the presentation of meat and to salivate at the ringing of the bell

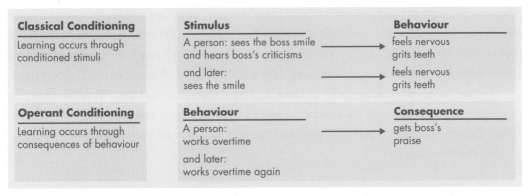

Figure 3.2: Differences between classical and operant conditioning approaches for a boss and subordinate.

alone. Such 'learning' through association is so common in organizations that it is often ignored until it causes considerable confusion. Look at Figure 3.2.

The key is to understand a stimulus and a conditioned stimulus. A **stimulus** is some-thing that incites action and draws forth a response (the meat for the dogs). The trick is to associate one neutral potential stimulus (the bell ringing) with another initial stimulus that already affects behaviour (the meat). The once-neutral stimulus is called a *conditioned stimulus* when it affects behaviour in the same way as the initial stimulus. In Figure 3.2, the boss's smiling becomes a conditioned stimulus because of its linkage to his criticisms.

Operant conditioning, popularized by Burhuss Frederic (B.F.) Skinner, is an extension of the classical case to much more practical affairs.[3] It includes more than just a stimulus and a response behaviour. **Operant conditioning** is the process of controlling behaviour by manipulating its consequences. Classical and operant conditioning differ in two important ways. First, control in operant conditioning is via manipulation of consequences. Secondly, operant conditioning calls for examining antecedents, behaviour and consequences. The *antecedent* is the condition leading up to or 'cueing' behaviour. For example, in Figure 3.2, an agreement between the boss and the employee to work overtime as needed is an ante-cedent. If the employee works overtime, this would be the *behaviour*, while the *consequence* would be the boss's praise.

A boss who wants a behaviour, such as working overtime, to be repeated must manip-ulate the consequences. The basis for manipulating consequences is E. L. Thorndike's law of effect.[4] The **law of effect** is simple but powerful: behaviour that results in a pleasant outcome is likely to be repeated, while behaviour that results in an unpleasant outcome is not likely to be repeated. The implications of this law are rather straightforward. If, as a supervisor, you want more of a behaviour, you must make the consequences for the indi-vidual positive.

Note that the emphasis is on consequences that can be manipulated rather than on consequences inherent in the behaviour itself. Organizational behaviour research often emphasizes specific types of rewards that are considered by the **reinforcement** perspective to influence individual behaviour. *Extrinsic rewards* are positively valued work outcomes

*A **stimulus** is something that incites action.*

__Operant conditioning__ is the process of controlling behaviour by manipulating its consequences.

*The **law of effect** refers to Thorndike's observation that behaviour that results in a pleasant outcome is likely to be repeated; behaviour that results in an unpleasant outcome is not likely to be repeated.*

__Reinforcement__ is the administration of a consequence as a result of behaviour.

that are given to the individual by some other person. They are important external reinforcers or environmental consequences that can substantially influence a person's work behaviours through the law of effect. Figure 3.3 presents a sample of extrinsic rewards that managers can allocate to their subordinates.[5] Some of these rewards are contrived, or planned, rewards that have direct costs and budgetary implications. Examples are pay increases and cash bonuses. A second category includes natural rewards that have no cost other than the manager's personal time and effort. Examples are verbal praise and recognition in the workplace.

Contrived Rewards: Some Direct Cost		Natural Rewards: No Direct Cost	
refreshments	promotion	smiles	recognition
piped-in music	trips	greetings	feedback
nice offices	company car	compliments	asking advice
cash bonuses	paid insurance	special jobs	
merit pay increases	stock options		
profit sharing	gifts		
office parties	sport tickets		

Figure 3.3: A sample of extrinsic rewards allocated by managers.

Reinforcement strategies

Organizational behaviour modification *is the systematic reinforcement of desirable work behaviour and the nonreinforcement or punishment of unwanted work behaviour.*

Extinction *is the withdrawal of the reinforcing consequences for a given behaviour.*

Positive reinforcement *is the administration of positive consequences that tend to increase the likelihood of repeating the behaviour in similar settings.*

We now bring the notions of classical conditioning, operant conditioning, reinforcement and extrinsic rewards together to show how the direction, level and persistence of individual behaviour can be changed. This combination is called OB Mod after its longer title of **organizational behaviour modification**. OB Mod is the systematic reinforcement of desirable work behaviour and the nonreinforcement or punishment of unwanted work behaviour. OB Mod includes four basic reinforcement strategies: positive reinforcement, negative reinforcement (or avoidance), punishment and **extinction**.

B. F. Skinner and his followers advocated **positive reinforcement** – the administration of positive consequences that tend to increase the likelihood of repeating the desirable behaviour in similar settings. For example, a Texas Instruments manager nods to a subordinate to express approval after she makes a useful comment during a sales meeting. Obviously, the boss wants more useful comments. Later, the subordinate makes another useful comment, just as the boss hoped she would.

To begin using a strategy of positive reinforcement, we need to be aware that positive reinforcers and rewards are not necessarily the same. Recognition, for example, is both a reward and a potential positive reinforcer. Recognition becomes a positive reinforcer only if a person's performance later improves. Sometimes, rewards turn out not to be positive reinforcers. For example, a supervisor might praise a subordinate in front of other group members for finding errors in a report. If the group members then give the worker the silent treatment, however, the worker may stop looking for errors in the future. In this case, the supervisor's 'reward' does not serve as a positive reinforcer.

To have maximum reinforcement value, a reward must be delivered only if the desired behaviour is exhibited. That is, the reward must be contingent on the desired behaviour. This principle is known as the **law of contingent reinforcement**. In the Texas Instruments example, the supervisor's praise was contingent on the subordinate's making constructive comments. Finally, the reward must be given as soon as possible after the desired behaviour. This is known as the **law of immediate reinforcement**.[6] If the TI boss waited for the annual performance review to praise the subordinate for providing constructive comments, the law of immediate reinforcement would be violated.

Now that we have presented the general concepts, it is time to address two important issues of implementation. First, what do you do if the behaviour approximates what you want but is not exactly on target? Second, is it necessary to provide reinforcement each and every time? These are issues of shaping and scheduling, respectively.

If the desired behaviour is specific in nature and is difficult to achieve, a pattern of positive reinforcement, called **shaping**, can be used. Shaping is the creation of a new behaviour by the positive reinforcement of successive approximations leading to the desired behaviour. For example, new machine operators in the Ford Motor casting operation in Ohio must learn a complex series of tasks in pouring molten metal into the casting in order to avoid gaps, overfills or cracks.[7] The moulds are filled in a three-step process with each step progressively more difficult than its predecessor. Astute master craftspersons initially show neophytes how to pour the first step and give praise based on what they do correctly. As the apprentices gain experience they are given praise only when all of the elements of the first step are completed successfully. Once the apprentices have mastered the first step, they progress to the second. Reinforcement is given only when the entire first step and an aspect of the second step are completed successfully. Over time, apprentices learn all three steps and are given contingent positive rewards immediately for a complete casting that has no cracks or gaps. In this way, behaviour is shaped gradually rather than changed all at once.

Positive reinforcement can be given according to either continuous or intermittent schedules. **Continuous reinforcement** administers a reward each time a desired behaviour occurs. **Intermittent reinforcement** rewards behaviour only periodically. These alternatives are important because the two schedules may have very different impacts on behaviour. In general, continuous reinforcement elicits a desired behaviour more quickly than does intermittent reinforcement. Thus, continuous reinforcement would be important in the initial training of the apprentice casters. At the same time, continuous reinforcement is more costly in the consumption of rewards and is more easily extinguished when reinforcement is no longer present. In contrast, behaviour acquired under intermittent reinforcement lasts longer upon the discontinuance of reinforcement than does behaviour acquired under continuous reinforcement. In other words, it is more resistant to extinction. Thus, as the apprentices master an aspect of the pouring, the schedule is switched from continuous to intermittent reinforcement.

As shown in Figure 3.4, intermittent reinforcement can be given according to fixed or variable schedules. *Variable schedules* typically result in more consistent patterns of desired behaviour than do fixed reinforcement schedules.

The **law of contingent reinforcement** is the view that for a reward to have maximum reinforcing value, it must be delivered only if the desired behaviour is exhibited.

The **law of immediate reinforcement** states that the more immediate the delivery of a reward after the occurrence of a desirable behaviour, the greater the reinforcing effect on behaviour.

Shaping is the creation of a new behaviour by the positive reinforcement of successive approximations to the desired behaviour.

Continuous reinforcement is a reinforcement schedule that administers a reward each time a desired behaviour occurs.

Intermittent reinforcement is a reinforcement schedule that rewards behaviour only periodically.

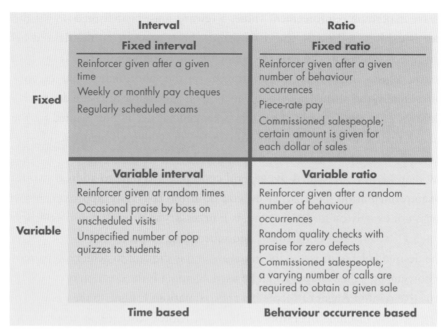

Figure 3.4: Four types of intermittent reinforcement schedules.

Fixed-interval schedules provide rewards at the first appearance of a behaviour after a given time has elapsed. *Fixed-ratio schedules* result in a reward each time a certain number of the behaviours have occurred. A *variable-interval schedule* rewards behaviour at random times, whereas a *variable-ratio schedule* rewards behaviour after a random number of occurrences. For example, as the apprentices perfect their technique for a stage of pouring castings, the astute masters switch to a variable-ratio reinforcement.

A second reinforcement strategy used in OB Mod is **negative reinforcement** or avoidance – the withdrawal of negative consequences, which tends to increase the likelihood of repeating the desirable behaviour in similar settings. For example, a manager at McDonald's regularly nags a worker about his poor performance and then stops nagging when the worker does not fall behind one day. We need to focus on two aspects here: the negative consequences followed by the withdrawal of these consequences when desirable behaviour occurs. The term 'negative reinforcement' comes from this withdrawal of the negative consequences. This strategy is also sometimes called *avoidance* because its intent is for the person to avoid the negative consequence by performing the desired behaviour. For instance, we stop at a red light to avoid a traffic ticket, or a worker who prefers the day shift is allowed to return to that shift if she performs well on the night shift.

A third OB Mod strategy is **punishment**. Unlike positive reinforcement and negative reinforcement, punishment is intended not to encourage positive behaviour but to discourage negative behaviour. Formally defined, punishment is the administration of negative consequences or the withdrawal of positive consequences that tend to reduce the likelihood of repeating the behaviour in similar settings. The first type of punishment is illustrated

Negative reinforcement *is the withdrawal of negative consequences, which tends to increase the likelihood of the behaviour being repeated in similar settings; it is also known as avoidance.*

Punishment *is the administration of negative consequences or the withdrawal of positive consequences, which tends to reduce the likelihood of repeating the behaviour in similar settings.*

by a fast-food manager who assigns a tardy worker to an unpleasant job, such as cleaning the toilets. An example of withdrawing positive consequences is a fast-food manager who docks the employee's pay when she is tardy.

Some scholarly work illustrates the importance of punishment by showing that punishment administered for poor performance leads to enhanced performance without a significant effect on satisfaction. However, punishment seen by workers as arbitrary and capricious leads to very low satisfaction as well as low performance.[8] Thus, punishment can be handled poorly, or it can be handled well. Of course, the manager's challenge is to know when to use this strategy and how to use it correctly.

Finally, punishment may be offset by positive reinforcement received from another source. It is possible for a worker to be reinforced by peers at the same time that the worker is receiving punishment from the manager. Sometimes the positive value of such peer support is so great that the individual chooses to put up with the punishment. Thus, the undesirable behaviour continues. As many times as an experienced worker may be verbally reprimanded by a supervisor for playing jokes on new employees, for example, the 'grins' offered by other workers may well justify continuation of the jokes in the future.

Does all of this mean that punishment should never be administered? Of course not. The important things to remember are to administer punishment selectively and then to do it right.

The final OB Mod reinforcement strategy is *extinction* – the withdrawal of the reinforcing consequences for a given behaviour. For example, Jack is often late for work and his co-workers cover for him (positive reinforcement). The manager instructs Jack's co-workers to stop covering for him, withdrawing the reinforcing consequences. The manager has deliberately used extinction to get rid of an undesirable behaviour. This strategy decreases the frequency of or weakens the behaviour. The behaviour is not 'unlearned'; it simply is not exhibited. As the behaviour is no longer reinforced, it will reappear if reinforced again. Whereas positive reinforcement seeks to establish and maintain desirable work behaviour, extinction is intended to weaken and eliminate undesirable behaviour.

Figure 3.5 summarizes and illustrates the use of each OB Mod strategy. They are all designed to direct work behaviour toward practices desired by management. Both positive and negative reinforcement are used to strengthen the desirable behaviour of improving work quality when it occurs. Punishment is used to weaken undesirable behaviour leading to high error rates and involves either administering negative consequences or withdrawing positive consequences. Similarly, extinction is used deliberately to weaken undesirable behaviour leading to high error rates when it occurs. Note also, however, that extinction is used inadvertently to weaken the desirable behaviour of low error rates. Finally, these strategies may be used in combination as well as independently.

Reinforcement and employee rights

Whilst the effective use of reinforcement strategies can help manage human behaviour at work, these approaches are also susceptible to a range of criticisms.

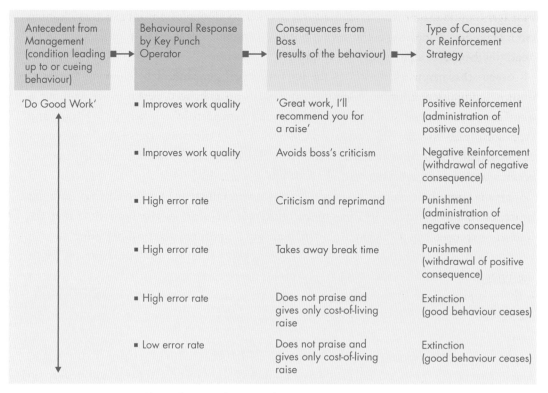

Figure 3.5: Applying reinforcement strategies.

RESEARCH IN OB

Look at the article by Makin and Sutherland which can be accessed on our companion website. Note how these researchers have applied a behavioural approach to a real-life organizational problem, in this case reducing accidents at work. They showed how employees were encouraged to report the full range of accidents and accident-related activities by using positive rewards – reporting was in itself regarded as a positive behaviour and was rewarded accordingly. As a result of this intervention, the company in question experienced a significant drop in work-related accidents, resulting in a far safer working environment.

Managerial use of these approaches is not without criticism, however. For example, some reports on the 'success' of specific programmes involve isolated cases that have been analysed without the benefit of scientific research designs. It is hard to conclude definitively whether the observed results were caused by reinforcement dynamics. In fact, one critic argues that the improved performance may well have occurred only because of the goal setting involved – because specific performance goals were clarified and workers were individually held accountable for their accomplishment.

Another major criticism rests with the potential value dilemmas associated with using reinforcement to influence human behaviour at work. For example, some critics may argue that the systematic use of reinforcement strategies leads to a demeaning and dehumanizing view of people that stunts individual growth and development. A related criticism is that managers abuse the power of their position and knowledge by exerting external control over individual behaviour. Advocates of the reinforcement approach attack the problem head on: they agree that behaviour modification involves the control of behaviour, but they also argue that behaviour control is part of every manager's job. The real poser is how to ensure that manipulation is done in a positive and constructive fashion.

Burnout *is a negative felt emotion relating to one's work. It is characterized by emotional exhaustion, cynicism and doubts regarding self-efficacy.*

The roots of reinforcement theory are embedded in the Scientific Management Approach, whereby employees are expected to carry out tasks in ways dictated to them. If the expectation is that managers control situations at work, based on the adoption of reward and punishment interventions, then these actions will continue, allowing little opportunity for the employee to develop themselves and reflect upon their own working practices and performance. It is therefore unlikely that creativity and innovation will result, and the employee will await their next metaphorical electric shock or food pellet!

 **IN ACTION**

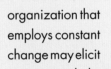

To what extent does control over the environment impact upon the ability to learn?

According to Ramirez,[9] the ability of humans to learn is impaired if they feel as though they cannot control their environment. Seligman's controversial experiments on dogs in the 1960s and 1970s led by accident to the concept of 'learned helplessness'. Seligman[10] set up experimental laboratories, whereby dogs were restrained in a harness and administered several shocks, which were paired with a conditioned stimulus (as in traditional classical conditioning experiments). The dogs were then placed in a shuttle box. They could avoid shocks by jumping over a barrier. These experiments then turned to operant conditioning. About a third of all dogs in the experiments (out of the 150 total sample) failed to jump the barrier and hence avoid the shock. Seligman argued that this prior exposure to inescapable shock had interfered with the dogs' ability to learn, even though escape and therefore avoidance of shock was possible.

Learned helplessness can take part in everyday working life, where employees feel that they have little control over their working environment. An organization that employs constant change may elicit certain psychological states in its employees.

Consider, for example, the case of **burnout**. Within the medical profession in the UK, high rates of burnout have been encountered with nurses.[11] Whilst there is a line of argument to link burnout with clinical depression and specific types of personality traits, employees in certain high stress occupational areas are more susceptible to burnout. Burnout may result in an employee simply not being able to face their work or place of work any more, they have simply 'had enough'. Like Seligman's dogs, employees simply give up.

Questions

1. To what extent does Seligman's work negate the work of behaviourists such as Pavlov and Skinner?
2. Can you identify examples of 'learned helplessness' in the workplace which you have either observed or experienced yourself?

Cognitive learning

Cognitive learning *is a form of learning achieved by thinking about the perceived relationship between events and individual goals and expectations.*

Cognitive learning is learning that is achieved by thinking about the perceived relationship between events and individual goals and expectations. The process motivation theories reviewed in Chapter 4 help to illustrate how this learning perspective is applied to the work setting. These theories are concerned with explaining how and why people decide to do things by examining the ways in which people come to view various work activities as perceived opportunities to pursue desired rewards, to eliminate felt inequities and the like. These cognitive explanations of learning differ markedly from the behaviourist explanations of operant conditioning.

Social learning

Social learning *is learning that is achieved through the reciprocal interaction between people and their environments.*

Social learning is learning that is achieved through the reciprocal interactions among people, behaviour and environment. Social learning theory is expressed in the work of Albert Bandura[12] and uses such reciprocal interactions to integrate operant and cognitive learning approaches; that is, environmental determinism and self-determinism are combined. Behaviour is seen not simply as a function of external antecedents and consequences, or as being caused by only internal needs, satisfaction or expectations (see Chapter 4), but as a combination of the two. Social learning theory stresses our capacity to learn from re-enforcement and punishments experienced by other people and ourselves. Figure 3.6 illustrates and elaborates on this reciprocal interaction notion.

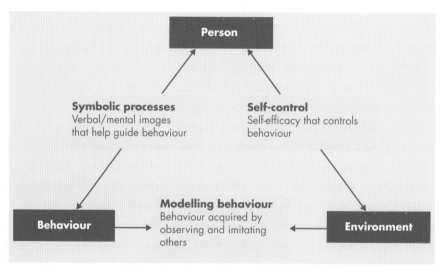

Figure 3.6: Social learning model.

Source: Adapted form Kreitner, R. and Luthans, F. (1984) *Organizational Dynamics*, Autumn, p. 55.

In Figure 3.6, the individual uses modelling or vicarious learning to acquire behaviour by observing and imitating others. The person then attempts to acquire these behaviours by modelling them through practice. The 'models' could be the person's parents, friends or even well-known celebrities. In the work situation, the model may be a manager or co-worker who demonstrates desired behaviours. Mentors or senior workers who befriend more inexperienced protégés can also be very important models.

Although mentors or role models may come from diverse sources, the shortage of appropriate mentors or role models is often a concern in the contemporary workplace. Indeed, some have argued that a shortage of mentors for women in management is a major constraint on their progression up the career ladder. It is also a leading reason why many women are leaving the corporate world and moving into self-employment.[13]

The field of Coaching and Executive Coaching has developed considerably over the last few decades. In the UK, the Chartered Institute of Personnel and Development (CIPD) reported in its 2010 Learning and Development Survey[14] that over 80% of its sample was using coaching as a development tool. In its simplest form, coaching can be considered to be a means to develop an employee's skill and knowledge in order to enhance their performance.

The CIPD differentiate coaching from mentoring by arguing that mentoring involves a longer term relationship, and there may be more explicit reciprocal benefits.

Self-efficacy and social learning

The symbolic processes depicted in Figure 3.6 are also important in social learning. Words and symbols used by managers and others in the workplace can help communicate values, beliefs and goals and therefore serve as guides to a person's behaviour. A 'thumbs up' or other symbol from the boss, for example, lets you know your behaviour is appropriate.

At the same time, an individual's self-control is important in influencing his or her behaviour. Self-efficacy is an important part of such self-control. People with high self-efficacy believe that:

- they have the necessary ability for a given job;
- they are capable of the effort required;
- they are motivated to perform the required behaviour;
- no outside events will hinder them from obtaining their desired performance level.[15]

In other words, high self-efficacy people believe they can manage their environmental cues and consequences and their cognitive processes to control their own behaviour. People with low self-efficacy believe that, no matter how hard they try, they cannot manage their environment well enough to be successful. If you feel self-efficacious as a student, for example, a low grade on one test will encourage you to study harder, talk to the lecturer or do other things to enable you to perform well the next time. In contrast, a person low in self-efficacy might drop the course or give up studying.

Even people who are high in self-efficacy do not control their environment entirely. As a manager, you can have an impact on the environment and other factors shown in Figure 3.5 (even though the impact is less than in the operant approach). This is especially the case in influencing another person's self-efficacy. A manager's expectations and peer support can go far in increasing a worker's self-efficacy and feelings of control.

EFFECTIVE MANAGER 3.1

Points for managers to consider in applying social learning theory[16]

- Identify appropriate job behaviours.
- Help employees select an appropriate behavioural model for behavioural modelling.
- Work with employees to meet the requirements of the new behaviours.
- Structure the learning situation to enhance learning of the necessary behaviours.

- Provide appropriate rewards (consequences) for workers who perform the appropriate behaviours.
- Engage in appropriate managerial actions to maintain the newly learned behaviours.

Social learning theory and behavioural self-management

Social learning theory is applied in the workplace to encourage employees to help manage or lead themselves. Table 3.1 shows some possible self-management strategies. Notice how these strategies build on social learning theory to emphasize both behavioural and cognitive focuses. Their use is designed to enhance self-efficacy and the worker's feeling of self-control. For example, 3M (the company that manufactures Post-It notes) encourages employees to apply behavioural self-management actions (such as those listed in Table 3.1) wherever possible. People are encouraged to 'work outside the box' to facilitate new product innovations.[17] Many high-profile sporting organizations throughout the world use sports psychologists to teach players the strategies listed in Table 3.1.[18]

Self-management is a social learning theory that can be applied by behaviour-focused strategies and cognitive-focused strategies. However, self-management for an organizational member includes managing inconsistencies between individual and organizational expectations and goals.

It is evident that self-management includes self-reflection or introspection, where individuals contemplate their thoughts, feelings and actions. In the organizational context, self-reflection can lead to the discovery of incongruence between organizational goals and personal expectations. These **intrapersonal conflicts** often involve actual or perceived pressures from incompatible goals or expectations of the following types. *Approach conflict* occurs when a person must choose between two positive and equally attractive alternatives. An example is having to choose between a valued promotion in the organization or a desirable new job with another organization. *Avoidance conflict* occurs when a person must choose between two negative and equally unattractive alternatives.

An example is being asked either to accept a job transfer to another town in an undesirable location or to have your employment with an organization terminated. *Approach-avoidance conflict* occurs when a person must decide to do something that has both positive and negative consequences. An example is being offered a higher paying job but one whose responsibilities will entail unwanted demands on your time.

Intrapersonal conflict *is conflict that occurs within the individual as a result of actual or perceived pressures from incompatible goals or expectations.*

Behaviour	Strategy
	Behaviour-focused strategies
Self-setting goals	Setting goals for your own work efforts
Managing cues	Arranging and altering cues in the work environment to facilitate your desired personal behaviours
Rehearsing	Physically or mentally practising work activities before you actually perform them
Self-observing	Observing and gathering information about specific behaviours that you have targeted for change
Self-rewarding	Providing yourself with personally valued rewards for completing desirable behaviours
Self-punishing	Administering punishments to yourself for behaving in undesirable ways (This strategy is generally not very effective.)
	Cognitive-focused strategies
Building natural rewards into tasks	Redesigning where and how you do your work to increase the level of natural rewards in your job. Natural rewards that are part of, rather than separate from, the work (that is, the work, like a hobby, becomes the reward) result from activities that cause you to feel: – a sense of competence – a sense of self-control
Focusing thinking on natural rewards	Purposely focusing your thinking on the naturally rewarding features of your work
Establishing constructive thought patterns	Establishing constructive and effective habits or patterns in your thinking (for example, a tendency to search for opportunities rather than obstacles embedded in challenges) by managing your: – beliefs and assumptions – mental imagery – internal self-talk

Table 3.1: Self-management strategies.

This chapter has emphasized workers as individuals. However, many of the self-management strategies can also be extended to self-managed teams, which are discussed later in the book. Managers are seeking strategies designed to increase the use of human potential in the workplace. Many Western organizations have experienced the downsizing of the past decade, and now they are giving increased attention to new approaches designed to increase worker productivity. Organizations are being designed to have flatter structures, provide increased worker empowerment and offer greater opportunities for self-management – all strategies designed to increase the use of the workplace's human resource. Manz and Sims (1989) argue that all employees have the potential to lead themselves, and if so, can then impact upon the need for additional levels of organizational structure.[19]

Experiential learning theory

'The best way to learn things is by doing them' is the tenet of experiential learning theory. Through reflection, people can draw conclusions and possibly then act differently (learn). Kolb[20] argues that learning is an iterative process and involves a learning cycle, whereby individuals experience, interpret, generalize and test things.

Individuals may have a preference for any of the four aspects included in this model. Some individuals spend little or no time reflecting on their experiences and may repeat the same mistakes time and time again, whilst others may spend too much time reflecting and not actually complete very much in practical terms. A balance of the four aspects may provide a more suitable approach to learning.

Kolb has extended his research to link the learning cycle with personality types. For further reading, please see Kolb, D. (1984), *Experiential Learning*, Prentice Hall: Englewood Cliffs, NJ; Honey, P. and Mumford, A. (2006), *Learning Styles Questionnaire*, Peter Honey Publications.

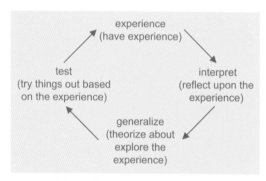

Figure 3.7: Kolb's experiential learning cycle.
Source: Kolb, D. (1984) *Experiential Learning*, Prentice-Hall: Englewood Cliffs, NJ.

OB IN ACTION

Experiential learning in practice

You have been tasked to provide training on workplace bullying to a group of ten engineers, from a diversity of engineering disciplines. Three of your group are from the 'ready, fire, aim' school of thinking and like to experiment a great deal, go through various testing and see if the results work. They often like to go on gut reaction. Four of your engineers like to theorize a great deal and prefer to use conceptual models, mind maps and introduce mathematical-type formulae where possible. The other three engineers like to spend a great deal of time reflecting on a problem, par-

ticularly reflecting from their own experience. By considering Figure 3.7, think about how you would manage these three distinct sets of learning styles presented in terms of the type of training that you may provide and how you might provide that training. In an ideal scenario, we may expect these engineers to go through each of the four stages presented in order to arrive at a reasonable solution.

OB IN ACTION

Career development at Fujitsu

In 2006, an employee survey carried out by global IT services company Fujitsu Services revealed that many members of staff felt it was not doing enough to support their career development. There were opportunities for development, but staff felt that Fujitsu was not delivering in this area.

London and Wilmslow based learning and development consultancy Academee came up with the idea for a Career Mapping Tool, an interactive online application that presents career planning information in an easy-to-understand and accessible way. Users can move through potential career paths from one job role to another, and as they do so, a list of required competencies for that job is generated.

A diagnostic section was added to help employees identify their career preferences and motivations, as well as a skills gap analysis tool, the results of which fed into a personal development plan. Other features include a development options menu, to show what kind of learning and development choices are available. These range from professional qualifications to what Fujistu describe as 'light touch suggestions', like reading the *Financial Times* to increase financial awareness in a situation where a formal finance training programme isn't appropriate.

Fujitsu also provides a 'new opportunities' website that enables users to subscribe and receive e-mail notification of any appropriate roles that come up.

Question

1. How are Fujistu using career development as a means of facilitating individual learning?

Source: Taking the pathways to learning, training and coaching today, 1 June 2008, http://www.xperthr.co.uk/

Modern forms of learning

There can be little doubt that the rate of technological advance in this millennium is phenomenal and continues to increase in speed and complexity. The growth of **e-learning** and blended learning continues to fascinate academics and professional bodies like the Chartered Institute of Personnel and Development (UK).

In the CIPD's 2005 *Learning and Development Survey*, they found that over half of respondents (companies) (54%) reported that they use e-learning, and a further 39% said they had plans to introduce it in the coming year.[22] According to the CIPD, the following are the major listed uses of e-learning:

- IT training (70%);
- technical training (45%);

e-learning *is Learning that is delivered, enabled or mediated using electronic technology for the explicit purpose of training in organizations.*[21]

- health and safety (34%);
- induction (33%).[23]

E-learning is utilized less for:

- management training (23%);
- interpersonal skills training (13%);
- diversity (9%);
- foreign languages (7%);
- team building (3%).

Whilst e-learning is not a panacea for all learning methods, it is how it is used which may provide some useful benefits.

OB IN ACTION

Mobiles as learning devices – M-learning

'M-learning' may be the way forward according to James Foster, director of development at Mezzo Films. Foster works with both public and private sector companies and provides mobile training programmes for clients. He believes that social factors are a driving force, especially with young people, who are happy to use mobile technology in order to learn new things.

'The way companies are trying to get staff engaged with training and learning is changing. People are looking for different ways of spreading knowledge and want more responsibility for their own learning,' Foster argues.

Mezzo has developed several systems that use personal media players, PC-based videos and satellite TV channels to train staff. Accessibilty is the key issue here.

The main reported benefits are convenience and cost, which, for clients such as the UK National Health Service, is very important during cost-cutting times. Similarly, the time spent off wards is kept to

a minimum. Wigham (2008) cites a consortium of northern UK universities which have provided some of their students with T-Mobile web-enabled telephones to support their learning and complete assessments while on work placements.[25]

However, caution has to be exercised as mobile learning is still evolving and may still be at a relatively early stage of its development. The rate of technological advancement may determine future progress.

Questions

1. What are the potential barriers to M-learning as a learning process?
2. Are M-learning tools only suited to a particular age band?

Source: the material on M-learning is taken from Wigham, R. (2008) Mobile Learning: Learning as you go, *Training and Coaching Today*, 1 March, RBI Publishing.

Vaughan Waller, director of Waller Hart Learning Architects, argues that e-learning is still used more inappropriately than appropriately, and that 'it works best when it's kept short and is designed so the learner is made to think, analyse and dig deeper, not just read-and-do multiple choice questions.'[24]

Having access to information and data is important but it needs to attract the recipient's attention and interest. Other forms of e-learning such as **blended learning** may prove attractive to employers and employees alike.

The question arises as to the reasons behind these findings and, more importantly, how e-learning is fully evaluated as a learning process.

Blended learning is an approach that blends, mixes or combines online learning with classroom instruction, coaching or mentoring [26]

THE LEARNING ORGANIZATION

The human race has experienced more rapid changes since the early 1980s than in the rest of humanity's existence. During the next 20 years or so, this pace of change is likely to accelerate. The challenge for organizations in this rapidly changing environment is to be flexible and adaptable enough to cope because not only growth but, perhaps more importantly, organizational survival depends on these responses. This section introduces the concepts of the learning organization and the teaching organization.

The 'learning organization' was popularized by Peter Senge in his book *The Fifth Discipline*.[27] He argued that a learning organization is a medium to enhance the development and use of knowledge at an individual level and, consequently, at an organizational level. Such knowledge will lead to organizational change. Learning organizational models are attempting to harness this potential for change in order to achieve competitive advantage.

Organizational learning refers to the process of becoming a learning organization and can be conceptualized as acquiring or developing new knowledge that modifies or changes behaviour and improves organizational performance.

Underlying the concept of a learning organization is a belief that organizations can be transformed by improving communication processes and techniques so as to enrich relationships among members.

Organizational learning is the process of acquiring or developing new knowledge that modifies or changes behaviour and improves organizational performance.

Creating a learning organization

Managers can create a learning organization by:[28]

- Building a powerful shared vision of future growth that will provide the focus for learning and a benchmark for future achievements.
- Developing strategies and action plans that will inspire the commitment of all personnel to achieve the future goals of the organization.
- Making extensive use of a continuous process of consultation to achieve consensus and unity of thought.
- Encouraging continual renewal of all organizational structures and processes.
- Employing systems thinking to ensure the organization focuses on both internal and external factors driving the change.

- Creating self-directed teams of employees that are supported to make decisions at appropriate levels.

The degree to which an organization can successfully create a learning environment can be measured by examining:

- the relationship between the employee and the organization;
- the value placed on the employee and their organizational contribution;
- employee ownership and acceptance of responsibility; and
- employee empowerment.

OB IN ACTION

Airline soars with new e-learning environment

For Cathay Pacific Airways, the move to e-learning is part of a larger cultural shift away from passenger participation toward employee initiative. Integral to this is the development of 'Learner's World'.

Cathay Pacific executives invested a large amount of money in its e-business as part of its plan to be Asia's leading e-business airline. The key principle around Learner's World is for employees to be enabled to control their own performance development.

According to Graham Higgins, manager of Cathay Pacific's learning and development team, the concept of flexible benefits was critical. 'We need to give them (employees) choice, control and the ability to tailor the learning process to their own needs.' Higgins chose NetDimension's Enterprise Knowledge Platform (EKP) as the airline's learning management system. This system enrols students, tracks their progress, delivers tests and reports costs, and can do so in any language. The flexibility of the software was commended by Higgins.

One example quoted is how staff keep themselves familiarized with airport layouts, so that if they have to be pulled out in an emergency, incident or disruption, they will know their way around. Higgins stated that they created a virtual tour using 3-D imagery, so that an employee can refresh their memory by walking virtually through the restricted and non-restricted areas of the airport.

The trick for Cathay Pacific was to get employees to buy into the process voluntarily. The process therefore had to be of interest to employees, for example by the creation of an online travel desk where staff could enter their comments on hotels that they had stayed in. This process proved very popular because of the frequency of staff travel and the need for feedback.

EKP was just the first part of the process for Cathay Pacific and, according to Higgins, they are now looking to personalize issues and seek collaboration from training managers on course content and methodology, so that employees take charge of their learning, drive their careers forward and improve customer service.

In the near future, NetDimensions, with direct input from Cathay Pacific, will unveil a new Web-based exam environment that features high-level security, publishing and assessment capabilities.

Questions

1. To what extent is Cathay Pacific doing anything different in terms of employee learning?

2. What impact will 'testing' have upon employees' willingness to participate and commit to 'Learner's World'?

The amount of learning that takes place is important to individuals, teams and organizations but the depth of learning is also important. Adaptation from learning may be an important factor in gaining competitive advantage. The concepts of **single-loop learning** and **double-loop learning** are important factors to consider.

Single-loop learning is more of a passive approach to learning and may be linked more readily to an operational focus, whereas double-loop learning involves deeper questioning (a more critical approach) as to why certain actions or activities take place in the way that they do. Double-loop learning may also occur more readily in a strategic context. Another differentiator may be that single-loop learning operates more effectively in a static, safe environment, where organization change is marginal, as opposed to a rapidly changing, complex environment for double-loop learning. Organizations wishing to maximize their employees' knowledge and competences need to consider how learning takes place and what mechanisms they have to support it.

Organizations may have in place various infrastructures, like strategic human resource development strategies and plans, **knowledge management** systems, group development plans, personal development plans (for individuals) and competence-based learning approaches and mechanisms. The question arises as to how these are translated into output and performance, continuous improvement and motivational drivers. Creating a 'learning culture' will depend on the whole organizational infrastructure and should not just simply be a company wish or mantra in the mission statement.

Certain preconditions are essential if a successful learning environment is to be created through these new communication processes:[29]

- *Trust.* All organizational members must believe they can rely on an individual's word (spoken or written). Trust permeates all organizational relationships and strongly influences all aspects of coordination and control. Managerial actions – such as encouraging supportive rather than defensive behaviour, aligning goals among and between organizational members, managing information flows and avoiding stereotyping – assist in building a trusting environment.
- *Commitment.* The company must develop an emotional and intellectual commitment to its actions and achievements.
- *Perceived organizational support.* Organizational support reinforces a bond between the organization and its employees and creates a sense of involvement with organizational objectives. An emphasis on relationship building and organizational support also reinforces the growth of trust and commitment.

Single-loop learning is learning by rote, with an emphasis on memorization rather than comprehension.

Double-loop learning is learning that involves innovation and creativity, by going beyond the basic line of questioning and thinking outside of the box.

Knowledge management focuses on processes designed to improve an organization's ability to capture, share and diffuse knowledge in a manner that will improve business performance.

LEARNING SUMMARY

What do the terms 'learning' and 'learning organization' mean? In common usage, people generally equate them with acquiring facts. However, acquired information needs to be interpreted and translated into usable knowledge. For organizations, knowledge acquisition is tied up with systems for codifying and disseminating information. But the real meaning of learning is much broader than this. It encompasses the subtle changes that take place when people, individually or collectively, reinterpret or *reframe* their experiences and modify their behaviour accordingly.

EFFECTIVE MANAGER 3.2

Managers in action

Garvin argues that managers need to follow the four steps set out below in pursuit of building a learning organization:[30]

1. Foster an environment that is conducive to learning. There needs to be time for reflection and analysis so that strategic plans can be considered, customer needs considered and work systems assessed. Management need to free up opportunities for employee learning. Training in brainstorming, problem solving, evaluating experiments and other core learning skills can make employees doubly productive.

2. Open up boundaries and stimulate the exchange of ideas. Conferences, meetings, project teams, crossing boundaries and/or linking with customers and suppliers ensure a fresh flow of ideas and ultimately the consideration of competing perspectives.

3. The creation of learning forums is the next step. Programmes or events need to be designed with explicit learning goals in mind, such as strategic reviews, systems audits and international benchmarking reports. Employees are required to wrestle with new knowledge and consider its implications.

4. Move learning higher on the organizational agenda, shifting away from continuous improvement toward a commitment to learning, resulting in the 3Ms – meaning, management and measurement of learning.

Learning organizations can only enable competitive advantage via learning if 'knowledge' exists and can be identified as important to the organization. In addition, this knowledge then needs to be *transferable* and a learning organization needs to transfer it better than comparable organizations.[31]

Knowledge acquisition and transfer are problematic, as gaining knowledge tends to be self-referential (based on what is known within the organization). Knowledge sharing is vitally important to a learning organization, as having a 'shared vision' underpins the collective nature of the organizational learning process. The problem is that when an organization's members are all moving the same way, they may very well move in the wrong direction and 'actively damage the future direction of the company'.[32] This means that despite all intentions of being 'open' to external feedback and responsive to specific and general organizational environments, organizational decision making is likely to be reactive. This reactivity is in direct contrast to an organizational learning process that is meant to be proactive. Therefore, knowledge development to enable competitive advantage, on the scale anticipated by learning organizations, is somewhat idealistic. The process may legitimate ineffective and circular processes and may hinder the desire to become a learning organization – it is unlikely that transformation will occur.

Difficulties may also occur with learning and well-intentioned attempts to create a 'learning organization' because existing mental models limit our ability to be adaptive.[33] Mental models can provide a link between individuals and collectives as they provide a context for interpretation of knowledge. Recent research in the UK, regarding the role of strongly held mental models in a team environment suggested that individual and organizational mental models may ultimately prevent desired creativity for innovation.[34] Strongly shared mental models are potentially 'closed' to new stimuli; little new knowledge can emerge and radically different and creative ideas are likely to be rejected. Hence, behaviour modification is unlikely to be achieved.

Learning is a subjective process encompassing the absorption of new knowledge through emotional, intuitive and reflective filters and mental models. Real learning is a lifelong process and requires the skills of self-management, self-knowledge and self-evaluation.

THE TEACHING ORGANIZATION

The 1990s saw the rise to prominence of the learning organization. Learning is a necessary competence but it is insufficient to assure market leadership. The companies that have outperformed competitors and increased shareholder returns have been those able to move beyond being learning organizations to become **teaching organizations**.

The two types of organization have many similarities. Fundamental to both is the common objective that every person within the organization continually acquires new knowledge and appropriate skills. However, the distinguishing aspect of a teaching organization is its ability to be more agile and to build more continuity into its successes. This is a direct consequence of a teaching organization's added focus on passing on learning experiences and knowledge; that is, a teaching organization aims to convey learning experiences to others, thereby allowing the organization to achieve and maintain success. Leaders in teaching organizations feel responsible for sharing their knowledge with other staff as a means of helping the organization to develop a knowledge base rapidly and accurately, infused with hands-on experience.

A teaching organization aims to pass on learning experiences to others, thereby allowing the organization to achieve and maintain success.

The constant focus on developing people to become leaders allows a teaching organization to become more agile and responsive to changes because its members are always armed with the necessary knowledge and knowhow to deal with new situations. An added benefit is the continuity of smooth leadership successions, preventing the potential disruption that a leadership change can entail.

CONCLUSION

Developing core work skills and ensuring lifelong learning for all is a massive undertaking for any country, even the richest ones, and can only be achieved over a very long time-frame, if ever. It is a target that is continually moving out of reach.[35]

The requirement for countries and organizations will be how to maximize development and, by definition, learning of their inhabitants/employees. A sophisticated understanding of how people learn will assist in this process. The motivation to learn and develop may be expected to come from within individual employees rather than being imposed upon them from above. The ideal scenario for an employer is that its employees are self-starters, do not require much supervision, are receptive to learning and change and manage to be innovative and creative at the same time. The organization's role is to help nurture the employees' talent so as to produce the desired outputs.

SUMMARY

LEARNING OBJECTIVE 1
Four general approaches to learning

Learning is a relatively permanent change in behaviour resulting from experience. It is an important part of reward management. The four general approaches to learning are classical conditioning, operant conditioning, cognitive learning and social learning. Modern managers need to understand the principles of cognitive learning, which relate to the motivational theories discussed in Chapter 4, to operant conditioning, which is achieved when the consequences of behaviour lead to changes in the probability of its occurrence, and to social learning.

LEARNING OBJECTIVE 2
Organizational behaviour modification and reinforcement strategies

Reinforcement is the means through which operant conditioning takes place. Its foundation is the law of effect, which states that behaviour will be repeated or extinguished, depending on whether the consequences are positive or negative. Reinforcement is related to extrinsic rewards (valued outcomes that are given to the individual by some other person) because these rewards serve as environmental consequences that can influence people's work behaviours through the law of effect.

Organizational behaviour modification uses four reinforcement strategies to change behaviour: positive reinforcement, negative reinforcement (avoidance), punishment and extinction. Positive reinforcement is used to encourage desirable behaviour; the administration of positive consequences tends to increase the likelihood of a person repeating a behaviour in similar settings. Positive reinforcement should be contingent (administered only if the desired behaviour is exhibited) and immediate (as close in time to the desired behaviour as possible).

Negative reinforcement, or avoidance, is used to encourage desirable behaviour; the withdrawal of negative consequences tends to increase the likelihood that a person will repeat a desirable behaviour in similar settings.

Punishment is the administration of negative consequences or the withdrawal of positive consequences, which tends to reduce the likelihood of a given behaviour being repeated in similar settings. Punishment is used to weaken or eliminate undesirable behaviour, but problems can occur. One must therefore be especially careful to follow appropriate reinforcement guidelines (including the laws of contingent and immediate reinforcement) when using it. Punishment is likely to be more effective if combined with positive reinforcement.

Extinction is the withdrawal of the reinforcing consequences for a given behaviour. It is often used to withhold reinforcement for a behaviour that has previously been reinforced. This is done to weaken or eliminate the undesirable behaviour. It is an especially powerful strategy when combined with positive reinforcement.

LEARNING OBJECTIVE 3
Social learning theory and behavioural self-management

Social learning theory advocates learning through the reciprocal interactions among people, behaviour and environment. Therefore, it combines operant and cognitive learning approaches. Behavioural self-management builds on social learning theory to emphasize both behavioural and cognitive foci with a special emphasis on enhancing a worker's self-efficacy and feeling of self-control. Self-management is useful in treating workers both as individuals and as part of self-managed teams.

LEARNING OBJECTIVE 4
Modern forms of learning

E-learning has changed the way that individuals and organizations can access and distribute knowledge and learning. Due to societal changes in the way that communication occurs, employees may begin to learn 'outside normal working time'. E-learning may not suit all types of learning activity or intervention but it can allow greater flexibility in terms of access. Blended learning involves a combination of online learning with classroom instruction, or possibly other supportive interventions like coaching or mentoring.

LEARNING OBJECTIVE 5
Learning organizations and teaching organizations

A learning organization is one in which members recognize the importance of communicating new knowledge for the benefit of the organization. Such an environment can be encouraged if trust, commitment and a perception of organizational support exist. A teaching organization is highly similar to a learning organization; the difference lies in the focus on continuity in the passing on of necessary knowledge and knowhow from leaders to other members of the organization. This ensures that a teaching organization is always agile and able to maintain its success.

CHAPTER 3 STUDY GUIDE

Now that you have read this chapter, you should be able to apply and further develop your knowledge by undertaking the following activities set out over the next few pages: test your knowledge questions, an individual activity and an end-of-chapter case study.

Please also go to this book's website: www.wileyeurope.com/college/french to find further material which will enhance your understanding and enable you to assess your knowledge.

TEST YOURSELF

1. Explain the 'law of effect'.
2. What are extrinsic rewards and how are these related to learning and reinforcement?
3. Distinguish between 'negative reinforcement' and 'punishment'. Summarize the main features of a learning organization.
4. Describe the classical conditioning process and provide examples of its impact on behaviours and emotions.
5. Mentoring, based on social learning theory, is often used to teach less experienced managers new skills. Discuss the operation and efficacy of mentoring programmes in the contemporary workplace.
6. Punishment strategies should be used sparingly by managers. Explain why.
7. What are some cultural issues to consider when using incentives for the purpose of achieving greater performance?
8. Critically analyse the difference between 'a learning organization' and 'organizational learning.'
9. As you have read in this chapter, punishment is a management tool that continues to be used in the workplace despite increasing concerns about its effectiveness. Using the library and other resources you have access to, research the following questions and either write a 1000-word report on your findings, or complete a 20-minute presentation of your findings to the class. Thinking of your own workplace (or one you are familiar with):
   a. How frequently is punishment used? Give examples.
   b. Explain the behavioural and emotional response to punishment.
   c. How does punishment prevent undesirable behaviour from reoccurring?
   d. Do you think that punishment has a place in modern workplaces? Why or why not?
10. Find an organization online that publicizes its employee rewards. How does the organization motivate its employees? Would you like to work for this organization? Why or why not? Compare your answer with those from others in your class and discuss why your answers may be the same or different.

What, when and how I learn[36]

Objective

To gain a greater understanding of what, when and how individuals learn.

Total time: 40 minutes.

Instructions

Think of *four* different things that you have learned that were, and still are, important to you. Now, for each one, think carefully about *what* you learned, *when* you learned, *how* you learned and, lastly, what it was that most *helped you learn it*. To help you with this, you might like a few ideas. What you learned and when are straightforward, but how and what helped most are a little more complicated!

In terms of the 'how' part of the question, think about this. Did you learn whatever it was by reading about it, being told about it, being shown how to do it, by trial and error, by practising it, by thinking about it, from film or video or any other medium, by research or by a combination of these or any other ways of learning? Were you taught by somebody else or did you learn it on your own? Were you in a group? Was the process formal or informal and did you have to undergo some kind of testing or accreditation? Did you learn in a way not given here? If so, what was it?

For the part of the question that asks what helped you learn, decide which factors you believe most helped you to learn. Was it your interest? Did you have a particularly inspiring teacher or instructor? Was there some kind of reward or sanction to be applied if you did or did not succeed? Or perhaps it was a target that you set yourself? Is there anything else that you can define that caused you to *want* to learn, helped you to keep learning and supported your successful learning? It will be worthwhile considering which factors were internal (that is, from within yourself) and which were external (from the job, peer pressure, fashion or anything else).

Now fill out the following table. To think about how you learn, place a tick under the heading that describes you best.

To obtain a better understanding of how you learn, think about these questions:

- How do I learn best – alone, in a group, with an instructor, from books, by doing, by watching, by any other way or by a lot of different ways?
- What makes me want to learn?
- What gets me started on learning?
- What keeps me learning?
- What stops me learning?
- How do other people affect my learning?

Now reflect on how you learn. How can you improve the way you are learning?

	Always	Most times	Seldom	Never
I memorize things easily				
I work out the meaning of things				
I notice what is around me				
I ask questions and think about the answers				
I use sources of information (the media, libraries, etc.)				
I measure what I find out against things I know				
I see links between things				
I choose how best to do things				
I use information and experience to choose solutions				
I act when I have decided				
I think about consequences				
I select important bits of information				
I enjoy learning new things				
I share what I learn				

TRAINING AT CONVERGYS CONTACT CENTRES, INDIA[1]

Background

Convergys is the world's largest operator of call or contact centres. It was established in its current form in 1998 and grew out of the US Cincinnati Bell telecommunications company. Revenue in 2005 was $2.58 billion and there are four operating divisions: customer management (the contact centre business), employee care (outsourced personnel activities, including payroll, benefits, learning and recruitment), information management (IT outsourcing, with specialisms in billing platforms) and finance and accounting (the outsourcing business recently acquired from Deloitte).

Currently Convergys operates over 65 contact, service and data centres worldwide. The largest number of service centres (54) is in North America where the company was founded. There are seven centres in India (the subject of this case study) and six in the Philippines. Total capacity in India is some 6000 'seats', which, given shift-working arrangements, means that some 9000 people are employed by Convergys in the country.

Programmes (the term used to describe a discrete activity centred around a product, service or market) are delivered for overseas clients. Convergys operates 'third party' centres for clients as opposed to 'captive centres' where a contact centre is established in India solely to meet the needs of the overseas parent company. The challenge therefore is to ensure that staff have both the technical and business knowledge to assist the client's customers and the communication skills and empathy so that this is put across in a way that leaves a positive and favourable impression.

Recruitment and retention

In its centres of operation (three in Gurgaon on the outskirts of Delhi and one each in Mumbai, Bangalore, Pune Thane and Hyderabad) Convergys is a prominent employer. The largest centre at Gurgaon, for example, has over 2000 agents (the term used for the staff who deal with client calls). As has been well observed, India has a current surfeit of capable and ambitious young people leaving its education system. Though the recruitment market is becoming more competitive, Convergys remains an 'employer of aspiration' for those who wish to work for the leader in the global contact centre business.

The majority of staff are young, mainly in their early 20s and half are female. Given that the majority of calls come from North America, much of the work takes place from

---

[1] This material has been taken from the 'Helping People Learn – case studies' (2008) section of the website: **www.cipd.co.uk**, with the permission of the publisher, the Chartered Institute of Personnel and Development, London. The author is Martyn Sloman.

Source: **www.cipd.co.uk/helpingpeoplelearn/_casestudies/_intcnvrgys.htm.**

Case Study

evening until early morning and the company puts a lot of resources into providing meals, transport and security. For many staff it will be their first job since leaving full-time education. Much of the initial induction is therefore focused on the transition to work – what the company offers and what is expected from the employee. Retention rates can be a problem: some people leave after a transitory period to move on to a different career or into higher education. Others simply 'don't know why they joined'. However, given the need for staff to acquire the knowledge and skills demanded by clients, Convergys puts a considerable effort into training, as Gyan Nagpal, Organizational Development Director based in Gurgaon, puts it: 'If an organization engages with its staff, offering them a career with prospects and progression, they will stay and develop.'

Initial training

After the initial induction, which typically lasts two days, the new agent will be supervised through two training modules. Both last three or four weeks and it can therefore be up to seven weeks before the new joiner takes their first customer-facing call.

The first module is designed to increase 'cultural sensitivity' to the country where the calls will originate, and to understand the context in which the client operates. All staff have English as a spoken language, and dealing with variations in accent is an issue in two respects. First, the agent needs to be comfortable understanding the caller's accent: five different groups of accents have been identified from North American callers alone. The second issue is the agent's accent – an element of 'accent neutralization' can be needed. Although, as Gyan Nagpur puts it: 'A person can't change their accent in three weeks even if it was necessary. We emphasize the need for clarity and encourage our agents to speak more slowly.'

Those modules are delivered in the classroom in groups of approximately 20 people, with feedback offered from the trainer and peers. Recording devices and audio support the programme. The second module, which is, again, classroom based, also introduces technology-based training screens. The module is focused on the client's products and systems and the questions that are likely to arise. Much of the detail is determined by the client's requirements and, whereas some clients are keen to avoid any situation where a customer sees a difference in approach between the client's home staff and the agent in India, others are less concerned. The nature of the client's product often determines the depth of understanding that the agents need to have.

Before they can deal with the client's customers over the phone, all agents must acquire both the generic skills of client handling and the specific knowledge to answer the underlying request. Agents are brought up to speed in an efficient and timely way: driving minimum 'time to competence' measures is an important consideration.

Ongoing support: the role of the team leader

Convergys's contact centres operate a relatively flat management structure and the normal progression for the agents is to the role of team leader: typically a team leader will have 15 to 20 direct reports. Team leaders are invariably chosen from high-performing agents, so their technical understanding of contact centre work will be good. However, for many the management of staff will be a new challenge.

From start to finish, the training period for new team leaders can be as long as 90 days. The classroom component of this training is delivered in five day modules. Critical elements include the modules that focus on staff development – one of the five day modules is mainly centred on coaching – and modules on tools that the team leader will use to monitor and drive performance. Feedback to agents regarding their call-handling capability is critical to the team and to the business's success and the team leader must have the skills and confidence to perform this task.

As part of the preparation for the new role, during this 90-day period, team leaders are required to undertake 13 modules of online e-learning (from two to four hours each). The majority of the modules have been specifically developed by Convergys, as the organization increasingly deploys e-learning as a preferred means of training delivery within a blended approach. Convergys acquired Digitalthink, a US-based e-learning organization in 2004, and has used these skills to deploy a learning portal that is available for Convergys agents throughout the world.

Convergys recognizes that the quality and motivation of its agents is critical to the success of the organization. The delivery of focused training in a cost-effective, globally consistent fashion drives higher standards of service from Convergys's centres, whilst simultaneously reducing turnover and the associated bottom-line costs.

Questions

1. How would you describe the type of training that Convergys offer in terms of learning theory?
2. How would you evaluate the way in which Convergys carries out its training?

SUGGESTED READING

Harrison, R. (2009), *Learning and Development,* CIPD: London. This book provides a useful combination of theory and practice. It takes a contemporary approach and provides a range of useful perspectives on individual and organizational learning.

END NOTES

1. Hamel, G. (2009), MT master class. *Management Today,* 1 July, 22.

2. Malone, S. A. (2003), *Learning About Learning: An A to Z of Training and Developmental Tools and Techniques,* CIPD: London.

3. For some of B. F. Skinner's work, see Skinner, B. F. (1948), *Walden Two,* Macmillan: New York; Skinner, B. F. (1953), *Science and Human Behaviour,* Macmillan: New York; Skinner, B. F. (1969), *Contingencies of Reinforcement,* Appleton-Century-Crofts: New York.

4. Thorndike, E. L. (1911), *Animal Intelligence,* Macmillan: New York, p. 244.

5. Adapted from Luthans, F. & Kreitner, R. (1985), *Organizational Behaviour Modification and Beyond,* Scott, Feresman: Glenview, IL.

6. Both laws are stated in Miller, K. L. (1975), *Principles of Everyday Behaviour Analysis,* Brooks/Cole: Monterey, CA, p. 122.

7. Example based on Price, B. & Osborn, R. (1999), *Shaping the Training of Skilled Workers,* working paper, Department of Management, Wayne State University: Detroit, MI.

8. Korukonda, A. R. & Hunt, J. G. (1989), Pat on the back versus kick in the pants: an application of cognitive inference to the study of leader reward and punishment behaviour. *Group and Organizational Studies,* **14** (3), 299–324.

9. Ramirez, E., Maldonado, A. & Martos, R. (1992), Attribution modulate immunization against learned helplessness in humans. *Journal of Personality and Social Psychology,* **62**, 139–146.

10. Seligman, M. E. P. & Maier, S. F. (1976), Learned helplessness: theory and evidence. *Journal of Experimental Psychology: General,* **105** (3), 46.

11. Cordes, C. L. & Dougherty, T. W. (1993), A review and integration of research on job burnout. *Academy of Management Review,* **18** (4), 621–654.

12. Bandura, A. (1977), *Social Learning Theory,* Prentice Hall: Englewood-Cliffs, NJ.

13. Mattis, M. (2004), Women entrepreneurs: out from under the glass ceiling. *Women in Management Review,* **19** (3), 154.

14. CIPD (2010), *CIPD Learning and Development Survey 2010,* accessed through http://www.cipd.co.uk/subjects/lrnanddev/general/_Learning_and_development_summary.htm (accessed 22 september 2010).

15. Peterson, T. & Amn, R. (2005), Self efficacy: the foundation of human performance. *Performance Improvement Quarterly,* **18** (2), 5–18.

16. See Zalesny, J. D. & Ford, J. K. (1990), Extending the social information processing perspective: new links to attitudes, behaviours and perceptions. *Organizational Behaviour and Human Decision Processes,* **47**, 205–246; Gist, M. E., Schwoerer, C. & Rosen, B. (1989), Effects of alternative training methods on self-efficacy and performance in computer software training. *Journal of Applied Psychology,* **74**, 884–891; Sutton, D. D. & Woodman, R. W. (1989), Pygmalion goes to work: the effects of supervisor expectations in a retail setting. *Journal of Applied Psychology,* **74**, 943–950; Gist, M. E. (1989), The influence of training method on self-efficacy and idea generation among managers. *Personnel Psychology,* **42**, 787–805.

17. Manz, C. C. & Sims, H. Jr (1990), *Superleadership,* Berkley Books: New York.

18. McLean, T. (2000), How to find the right frame of mind. *Financial Times,* 22 April, p. 22; Johnson, A. & Gilbert, J. (2004), The psychological uniform: using mental skills in youth sport. *Strategies,* **18** (2), 5–9; Improving the

performance of expert workers. *Journal for Quality and Participation,* 27 (1), 9–11.

19. Manz, C. C. & Sims, H. P. (1990) op.cit.

20. Kolb, D. (1984), *Experiential Learning,* Prentice Hall: Englewood Cliffs, NJ.

21. CIPD website: www.cipd.co.uk/subjects/lrnanddev/elearning/elearnprog.htm?IsSrchRes=1, (accessed 29 November 2007).

22. op.cit.

23. CIPD website: www.cipd.co.uk/subjects/ training/general/trdev2005 (accessed 30 November 2007).

24. Weekes, S. (2007), E-Ureka! Online learning comes of age, *Personnel Today,* 24 July, RBI Publishing.

25. Wigham, R. (2008), Mobile learning: learning as you go. *Training and Coaching Today,* 1 March, RBI Publishing.

26. Allison, R. (2002), *The ASTD E-Learning Handbook,* McGraw-Hill: New York.

27. Senge, P. (1992), *The Fifth Discipline,* Random House: Sydney.

28. Barker, R. T. & Caramata, M. R. (1998), The role of communication in creating and maintaining a learning organization: preconditions, indicators and disciplines. *Journal of Business Communication,* 35 (4), 443–467.

29. Blackman, D. & Henderson, S. (2005), Why learning organizations do not transform. *The Learning Organization Journal,* 12 (1), 42–56; Lee-Kelley, L. & Blackman, D. (2005), More than shared goals: the impact of mental models on team innovation and learning. *Journal of Innovation and Learning,* 2 (1), 11–25; Blackman, D. (2001), Is knowledge acquisition and transfer realisable? *Electronic Journal of Radical Organization Theory,* 7 (1), www.mngt.waikato.ac.nz/research/ejrot.

30. Garvin, D. A. (1993), Building a learning organization. *Harvard Business Review,* July–August, pp. 78–91.

31. Blackman, D. & Henderson, S. (2005) op.cit.

32. Blackman, D and Henderson, S. (2005) op.cit.

33. Lee-Kelley, L. & Blackman, D.(2005), op. cit.

34. Lee-Kelley, L. and Blackman, D. (2005) op.cit.

35. 'Learning and Training for work in the knowledge society' 2003:13 International Labour Office. Geneva.

36. Extracted from National Institute of Adult Continuing Education, 'Your life, your work, your future', www.niace.org.uk/research/edp/ leonmatall2.doc, (accessed 30 November 2007).

CHAPTER 4

Motivation and empowerment

LEARNING OBJECTIVES

After studying this chapter you should be able to:

- discuss the complexities of motivating and empowering today's workforce
- explain the difference between the two main types of motivation theories – content and process
- outline the major theoretical contributions from the content theories of motivation of Maslow, Alderfer, McClelland and Herzberg
- explain the process theories of motivation, including equity theory and expectancy theory
- explain how managers can use an integrated model of content and process motivation theories to enhance productivity and human resource maintenance
- explain how the four drives and self-concept models may add to our understanding of individual motivation
- explain how pay can be used as an extrinsic reward to motivate employees
- discuss empowerment and explain how the empowerment process works.

HOW DO I MOTIVATE MY OSTRICH WORKERS?

'I'm the Human Resource manager of a medium-sized company, I've been here for five years and, up until about 12 months ago, the organization was characterized by its many highly driven individuals. The company was growing fast and there was always a great appetite for people to develop their skill sets and help move the company forward.

'As the downturn has started to have an impact, however, a lot of workers have begun to stagnate as the company's growth has slowed. Whereas previously everyone was pushing for promotion and eager to move up the ladder, opportunities have now dried up. The tendency among our people now is to stick their heads in the sand, get on with their jobs quietly and simply try to avoid redundancy by not rocking the boat. How do I re-energize my people and bring back the sort of ambition and hunger for development that helped the company succeed in recent years?'[1]

Questions
1. What explanations would you give for the behaviour of the employees in this case?
2. What advice would you give the HR manager as to how they might re-motivate their staff?

INTRODUCTION

One of the keys to effective management lies in harnessing the motivation of employees in order to achieve the organization's goals and objectives, but how do managers achieve this? Is there a simple formula such as the ten-step approach suggested in Effective Manager 4.1, or is there one key ingredient that motivates all individuals? Many managers still believe that the key to motivation is money; people work for money therefore higher pay equals higher productivity. But is this true even in an economic downturn or does job security become the primary motivator as the opening case suggests? Research over 50 years into the subject of employee motivation provides evidence that, although money can motivate individuals, motivation depends on a wide variety of variables, which could include age, gender, socio-economic circumstances, job design and culture. Motivation is a complex issue involving a combination of both intrinsic and extrinsic factors yet the pressure on organizations to harness this motivation into employee productivity has never been greater because of the turbulent business environment, intensity of competition created by globalization, demographic changes and technological development. This chapter discusses several motivation theories and the concept of employee engagement and empowerment in terms of how they may contribute towards increasing productivity and the quality of working life as well as considering how motivation and pay are linked. The theories in this chapter are an important foundation for the ideas to be developed throughout the rest of this book.

EFFECTIVE MANAGER 4.1

Ten ways to motivate your staff:

- Keep them involved.
- Push autonomy, but be available.
- Tell them when they're doing well.
- Keep the buzz quotient high…
- …but see the upside of mellow.
- Take them out for lunch.
- Introduce flexible working.
- Promote only talented people.
- Hold a good bash once in a while.
- Do your own job well.[2]

WHAT IS MOTIVATION?

Motivation to work *refers to the forces within an individual that account for the level, direction and persistence of effort expended at work.*

Before looking at the separate theories, two key points should be made. First, **motivation to work** refers to forces within an individual that account for the level, direction and persistence of effort expended at work. Within this definition of work motivation:

- *level* refers to the amount of effort a person puts forth (for example, a lot or a little);
- *direction* refers to what the person chooses when presented with a number of possible alternatives (for example, to exert effort on achieving product quality or product quantity);
- *persistence* refers to how long a person sticks with a given action (for example, to try for product quantity or quality and to give up when it is difficult to attain).

Second, motivation to work (or willingness to perform) is one of three components of the individual performance equation (the other two are the capacity to perform and organizational support), which were presented in Chapters 1 and 2. High performance in the workplace depends on the combination of these three individual performance equation factors (as will be emphasized later in the chapter when motivation theories are integrated).

MOTIVATING ACROSS CULTURES

Whilst motivation is a key concern in organizations everywhere, the theories are largely developed from a North American perspective. So in examining them we must remember that they are subject to cultural limitations and contingencies.[3] Indeed, the determinants of motivation and the best ways to deal with it are likely to vary considerably across the world. For example, an individual pay rise might prove 'motivational' as a reward in one culture but not in another. Thus, in researching, studying and using motivation theories we should be sensitive to cross-cultural issues. We must avoid being parochial or ethnocentric by assuming that people in all cultures are motivated by the same things in the same ways.[4]

MOTIVATING AND EMPOWERING THE WORKFORCE

Regardless of culture each employee is different, each organization's workforce may have different characteristics, and at different times or in different locations there may be different circumstances that affect motivation and empowerment strategies in different ways. In order to meet the challenge of motivating employees, managers must be concerned with the context in which this is being done. Managers also need to understand the challenges of the work effort–motivation cycle.

Organizations that fail to recognize contextual factors and their implications for workplace motivation risk losing their best people to more exciting, satisfying or rewarding opportunities elsewhere. Managers also need to understand the challenges of the work effort–motivation cycle, creating a positive organizational climate in which employees are motivated to achieve high levels of work performance.

This challenge is examined in more detail in Figure 4.1. The figure shows how an individual's willingness to perform is directly related to the needs, expectations and values of the individual and their link to the incentives or aspirations presented by the organization's reward system. Rewards fulfil individual goals such as financial remuneration and career advancement.

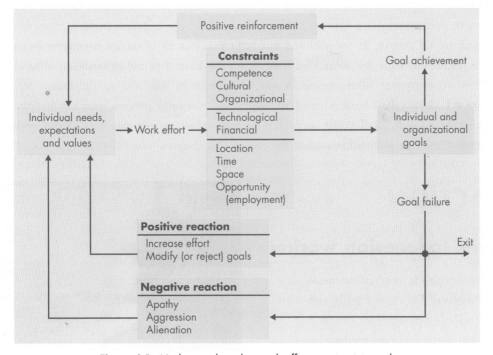

Figure 4.1: Understanding the work effort–motivation cycle.

The degree of effort expended to achieve these outcomes will depend on:

- the individual's willingness to perform, and his or her commitment to these outcomes in terms of the value attached to a particular outcome;
- the individual's competency or capacity to perform the tasks;
- the individual's personal assessment of the probability of attaining a specific outcome;
- the opportunity to perform (which is central to empowerment, discussed later in the chapter).

A number of organizational constraints or barriers, if not minimized, may restrict levels of individual performance.

Figure 4.1 shows that if the outcome or goal is attained, then the individual experiences a reduction in pressure or tension and goal attainment positively reinforces the expended effort to achieve the outcome. As a result of this positive experience, the individual may repeat the cycle. On the other hand, if the outcome is frustrated after a reasonable passage of time (for example, when no career progression has occurred), then the individual experiences goal frustration and arrives at a decision point. The individual is presented with three alternatives:

- exit from the organization;
- renew attempts at goal achievement, or modify or abandon the goals;
- adopt a negative response to the frustration experience and perform at below-optimum level.

The challenge for managers is to create organizations in which the opportunities to perform through competency building and empowerment are maximized and the impediments to performance are kept to a minimum to avoid the negative consequences of goal frustration. Of course, as we outlined in Chapter 1, not all of us are managers or aspire to be. However, with the subject of motivation we have a prime example of why OB is relevant to everyone. Who among us has no interest in why we do the things we do? Figure 4.1 shows the complexity of the work motivational process and emphasizes the importance of individual needs, expectations and values as key elements of this process. Some of these issues are addressed in the rest of this chapter.

OB IN ACTION

Motivating the Indonesian worker

In Indonesia motivation depends strongly on more personal factors than those of the West. Family, religion, health and other so-called personal factors often determine an Indonesian manager's performance on a daily basis. Western preoccupation with money as the prime mover in work performance does not apply well to Indonesia. Most Indonesian employees are motivated by two factors: *Gengsi* (appearance), here being the appearance of increasing status rather than money; and *Asal Bapak Senang* (keep the boss happy), in this case working diligently to please their superior.

In Indonesia, money is important because it is closely tied to position and status. When one has a senior, powerful position, one gains the accoutrements of power. These include company cars and mobile phones, golf club memberships, nice houses and holidays and, of course, money. These indicators of wealth stem and flow from the position, not from the performance. Indonesian employees are motivated by the appearance of increasing status. Western ideas of connecting performance to salary are not well understood. Promotion, and therefore increasing wealth and status, should be based on loyalty and seniority, not work performance in the minds of most managers.

Indonesian managers are also motivated by their loyalty to a superior. By maintaining and developing personal relationships between superior and subordinate, you develop the basis for the motivation of the employee to contribute more to the success of the company as embodied by his or her superior.

Western businesspeople have a very strong future-time sense. Indonesian employees normally have a very strong past- and present-time sense. If an Indonesian employee has enough money to cover present expenses and desires, offering more money solely based on future performance will not usually affect motivation. It is often the case that an employee who receives a performance bonus will not continue at a high level of performance until further funds are needed, thus confusing the expatriate manager expecting a Pavlovian stimulus–response reflex.

So an expatriate manager should motivate Indonesian subordinates by showing an understanding of Indonesian business culture, by giving paternalistic protection, by instructing their subordinates on the proper and desired method of behaviour in the company clearly and regularly and by giving support and encouragement (including emergency financial aid) without having to be asked. These outward signs of a mature and productive superior–subordinate relationship are all that sophisticated and experienced expatriate managers in Indonesia normally need to motivate their staff.[5]

CONTENT AND PROCESS MOTIVATION THEORIES

The two main approaches to the study of motivation, developed since the 1950s and still widely promoted today, are known as the content and process theories.

Content theories are primarily concerned with what it is within individuals or their environment that energizes and sustains behaviour. In other words, what specific needs or motives within an individual or their environment energize individual behaviour? We use the terms 'needs' and 'motives' interchangeably to mean the physiological or psychological deficiencies that one feels a compulsion to reduce or eliminate. If you feel very hungry (a physiological need), you will feel a compulsion to satisfy that need by eating. If you have a need for recognition (a psychological need), you may try to satisfy that need by working

Content theories *of motivation offer ways to profile or analyse individuals to identify the needs that are assumed to motivate their behaviour.*

hard to please your boss. Content theories are useful because they help managers to understand what people will and will not value as work rewards or need satisfiers.

The **process theories** strive to provide an understanding of the thought or cognitive processes that take place within the minds of individuals to influence their behaviour. Thus, a content theory may suggest that security is an important need. A process theory may go further by suggesting how and why a need for security could be linked to specific rewards and to the specific actions that the worker may need to perform to achieve these rewards. Process theories add a cognitive dimension by focusing on individuals' beliefs about how certain behaviours will lead to rewards such as money or promotion; that is, the assumed connection between work activities and the satisfaction of needs.[6]

Process theories of motivation seek to understand the thought processes that take place in the minds of people and how these act to motivate their behaviour.

Higher-order needs are esteem and self-actualization needs in Maslow's hierarchy.

Lower-order needs are physiological, safety and social needs in Maslow's hierarchy.

Content theories

Maslow, Alderfer, McClelland and Herzberg proposed four of the better-known content theories. Each of these content theories has made a major contribution to our understanding of work motivation. Some have provided a basis for more complex theorizing in later years.

Maslow's hierarchy of needs theory

Abraham Maslow's 'hierarchy of needs' theory (Figure 4.2) identifies five distinct levels of individual needs from self-actualization and esteem at the top (**higher-order needs**) to social, safety and physiological requirements at the bottom (**lower-order needs**). Maslow

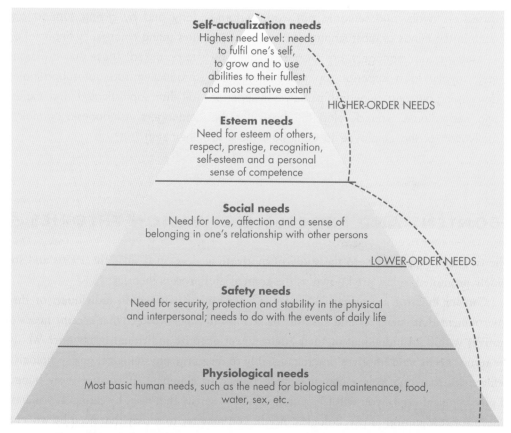

Self-actualization needs
Highest need level: needs to fulfil one's self, to grow and to use abilities to their fullest and most creative extent

HIGHER-ORDER NEEDS

Esteem needs
Need for esteem of others, respect, prestige, recognition, self-esteem and a personal sense of competence

Social needs
Need for love, affection and a sense of belonging in one's relationship with other persons

LOWER-ORDER NEEDS

Safety needs
Need for security, protection and stability in the physical and interpersonal; needs to do with the events of daily life

Physiological needs
Most basic human needs, such as the need for biological maintenance, food, water, sex, etc.

Figure 4.2: Higher-order and lower-order needs in Maslow's hierarchy of needs.

assumes that some needs are more important (potent) than others and must be satisfied before other needs can serve as motivators. Thus, the physiological needs must be satisfied before the safety needs are activated, the safety needs must be satisfied before the social needs are activated, and so on.

The physiological needs are considered the most basic; they consist of needs for such things as food and water. Individuals try to satisfy these needs before turning to needs at the safety level, which involve security, protection, stability and so on. When these needs are active, people will look at their jobs in terms of how well they satisfy these needs.

The social needs of a sense of belonging and a need for affiliation are activated once the physiological and safety needs are satisfied. The higher-order needs depicted in Figure 4.2 consist of the esteem and self-actualization needs – that is, being all that one can be. Here, challenging work and recognition for good performance assume centre stage. Implications of these needs at work are set out in Effective Manager 4.2 on p. 174.

Maslow: the research

Whilst Maslow's theory has proved popular with managers, there is limited research evidence to support his theory; in fact Maslow himself even questioned its applicability to organizational behaviour.[7] Some research suggests that there is a tendency for higher-order needs to increase in importance over lower-order needs as individuals move up the managerial hierarchy.[8] However, other studies suggest that individuals still place the greatest emphasis on lower-order needs (particularly money) even though they are fully achieving higher-order needs.[9] Other studies report that needs vary according to a person's career stage,[10] the size of the organization[11] and even geographic location.[12] Generally, there is no consistent evidence that the satisfaction of a need at one level will decrease its importance and increase the importance of the next higher need.[13]

To what extent does Maslow's theory apply only to Western culture? In many developing nations, the satisfaction of lower-order needs, such as basic subsistence and survival needs, consumes the entire lifetimes of many millions of individuals, with little opportunity to progress to higher-level need satisfaction. But in societies where regular employment is available, basic cultural values appear to play an important role in motivating workplace behaviour. In those countries high in Hofstede's uncertainty avoidance, such as Japan and Greece, security tends to motivate most employees more strongly than does self-actualization. Workers in collectivist-oriented countries, such as Pakistan, tend to emphasize social needs.[14] In general, a person's frame of reference will determine the order of importance of their needs, and societal culture influences that frame of reference.[15] With the increasing diversity of the workforce throughout Europe, we must also be careful to consider ethnic or other cultural groups within countries. For example, in the UK the traditional mix of ethnic groups – Asian, Chinese, black and white – is now being complemented by the influx of workers from eastern European ethnic groups, all of whom could present different cultural contexts for motivation. The circumstances of different sections of the population may also make a difference to motivation, as the following example shows.

▶ COUNTERPOINT

Satisfying generational needs – reality or myth?

Content motivation theories present us with a range of ways of understanding the needs of employees in the workplace but are these sufficient? It seems that the ways we talk about employee motivation are growing and in particular making distinctions between different groups of employees such as the differences between the generations. It has been argued that young employees (aged 16–24) need a lot more mentoring, constant feedback and team-work, while older workers (aged 50+) might need more help embracing new technology.[16] Whilst there has been an increasing interest in genera-tional needs, there are those such as Jim Bright, an Australian academic, who don't like measuring personnel needs by generational differences. Bright argues differences in life stages can be used to help measure the characteristics of different cohorts of people. Young people today are no different to those living 100 years ago, in that they want to have new experiences, interesting and challenging work and to be well rewarded for it. Thus, this theory follows that there will always be a 'younger generation' with certain needs in any society. Bright says the needs of workers will change at other life stages, such as when they start families or have greater domestic and financial respons-ibilities. Rather than needs being determined by generation, the stage of their lifecycle may dictate their needs. More importantly organizations need to see people as individuals and respond to indi-vidual needs as best they can – often by being as flexible as they can.[17]

One reason why there has been increased focus on the generational debate is that with increasing globalization and skills shortages (despite the global economic downturn) there is more competi-tion for talented employees. This competition has meant employers have had to be more sensitive to the needs of employees or potential employees in order to attract, retain and motivate talent.[18]

Questions

1. The 'life stage' explanation of needs suggests that people's needs change over time. How might this statement differ if you adopted an approach based on different needs for different generations?

2. In what ways can employers respond effectively and flexibly to all the individual needs their workers may have?

ERG theory *categorizes needs into existence, relatedness and growth needs.*

Existence needs *arise from a desire for physiological and material wellbeing.*

Alderfer's ERG theory

Clayton Alderfer's **ERG theory** (Figure 4.3) is also based on needs but is more flexible than Maslow's theory in three basic respects.[19] First, the theory collapses Maslow's five need cat-egories into three: **existence needs** relate to a person's desire for physiological and material wellbeing; **relatedness needs** represent the desire for satisfying interpersonal relationships; and **growth needs** are about the desire for continued personal growth and development. Second, where Maslow's theory argues that individuals progress up a needs hierarchy as a result of the satisfaction of lower-order needs (a satisfaction–progression process), ERG theory includes a 'frustration–regression' principle, whereby an already satisfied lower-level need can become activated when a higher-level need cannot be satisfied. Thus, if a person is continually frustrated in their attempts to satisfy growth needs, relatedness needs will again surface as key motivators. Third, according to Maslow, a person focuses on one need at a time. In contrast, ERG theory contends that more than one need may be activated at the same time.

Relatedness needs are about the desire for satisfying interpersonal relationships.

Growth needs relate to the desire for continued personal growth and development.

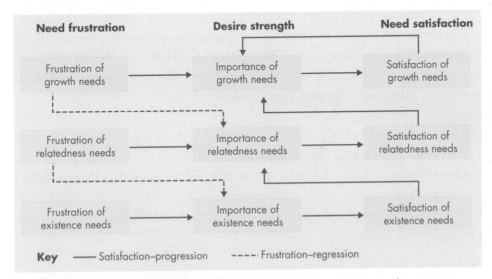

Figure 4.3: Clayton Alderfer's ERG theory: satisfaction–progression, frustration–regression components of the ERG theory.

Source: Wallace, M. J. Jr and Szilagyi, A. D. Jr (1982), *Managing Behaviour in Organizations*, Scott Foresman & Company: Glenview, IL.

ERG: the research

Research appears to provide better supporting evidence for ERG theory than Maslow's theory. However, the research is relatively limited and includes disclaimers,[20] so additional research is needed to support its validity. One article provides evidence for the ERG need categories and reports additional findings – for example, growth needs were greater for respondents with more highly educated parents, and women had lower strength of existence needs and higher strength of relatedness needs than men.[21] The combined satisfaction–progression and frustration–regression principles provide the manager with a more flexible approach to understanding human needs than does Maslow's strict hierarchy. Importantly, Alderfer's theory emphasizes that performance constraints outside the control of the individual (see Figure 4.1), or innate disposition (such as lack of competence or low intrinsic work motivation) may cause a decline in effort or negative behaviour. Managers thus need to examine the workplace environment continually to remove or reduce any organizational constraint that will restrict opportunities for personal growth and development.

McClelland's acquired needs theory

In the late 1940s, psychologist David I. McClelland and his colleagues began experimenting with the Thematic Apperception Test (TAT) as a way of measuring human needs.[22] The TAT, as mentioned in Chapter 2, is a projective technique that asks people to view pictures and write stories about what they see. It is normally associated with personality testing. McClelland, however, used it to collect data on motivation. In one case, McClelland showed three executives a photograph of a man sitting down and looking at family photos arranged on his work desk. One executive wrote of an engineer who was daydreaming about a family outing scheduled for the next day. Another described a designer who had picked up an idea for a new gadget from remarks made by his family. The third described an engineer who was intently working on a bridge-stress problem that he seemed sure to solve because of his confident look.[23] McClelland identified three themes in these TAT stories, with each corresponding to an underlying need that he believes is important for understanding individual behaviour. These needs are:

* **need for achievement** (nAch) – the desire to do something better or more efficiently, to solve problems or to master complex tasks;
* **need for affiliation** (nAff) – the desire to establish and maintain friendly and warm relations with others;
* **need for power** (nPower) – the desire to control others, to influence their behaviour or to be responsible for others.

McClelland's basic theory is that these three needs are acquired over time, as a result of life experiences. Individuals are motivated by these needs, which can be associated with different work roles and preferences. The theory encourages managers to learn how to identify the presence of nAch, nAff and nPower in themselves and in others and to create work environments that are responsive to the respective need profiles of different employees.

McClelland: the research

The research lends considerable insight into nAch, in particular McClelland's theory challenges and rejects the research of other psychologists such as Erikson[24] who suggest that the need to achieve is a behaviour that is only acquired and developed during early childhood: if it is not obtained then it cannot easily be learned or achieved during adult life. McClelland maintains that the need to achieve is a behaviour that an individual can acquire through appropriate training in adulthood. For example, McClelland trained businesspeople in Kakinda, India, to think, talk and act like high achievers by having them write stories about achievement and participate in a business game that encouraged achievement. The businesspeople also met with successful entrepreneurs and learned how to set challenging goals for their own businesses. Over a two-year period following these activities, the people from the Kakinda study engaged in activities that created twice as many new jobs as those who did not receive training.[25]

Other research also suggests that societal culture can make a difference in the emphasis on nAch. Anglo-American countries such as the UK, the US, Canada and Australia (countries weak in uncertainty avoidance and high in masculinity) tend to follow the high nAch pattern. In contrast, strong uncertainty, high femininity countries, such as Portugal and Chile, tend to follow a low nAch pattern. There are two especially relevant managerial applications of McClelland's theory. First, the theory is particularly useful when each need is linked with a set of work preferences (Table 4.1). Second, if these needs can truly be acquired, it may be possible to acquaint people with the need profiles required to succeed in various types of jobs. For example, McClelland found that the combination of a moderate to high need for power and a lower need for affiliation enables people to be effective managers at higher levels in organizations. Lower nAff allows the manager to make difficult decisions without the undue worry of being disliked.[26] High nPower creates the willingness to have influence or impact on others, though misuse of that power may result in sabotage by those mistreated or prevented from rising to the top of the organization.[27] Other more recent studies have found that the satisfaction of these needs, particularly self-esteem, had a significant influence on the job performance of senior managers.[28]

Individual needs	Work preference	Example
High need for achievement	Individual responsibility; challenging but achievable goals; feedback on performance	Field salesperson with a challenging quota and the opportunity to earn individual bonus; entrepreneur
High need for affiliation	Interpersonal relationships; opportunities to communicate	Customer service representative; member of a work unit that is subject to a group wage bonus plan
High need for power	Influence over other persons; attention; recognition	Formal position of supervisory responsibility; appointment as head of special task force or committee

Table 4.1: Work preferences of persons high in need for achievement, affiliation and power.

Herzberg's two-factor theory

Frederick Herzberg took a different approach to examining motivation. Using a 'critical incident' interviewing technique, Herzberg simply asked workers to comment on two statements:[29]

- 'Tell me about a time when you felt exceptionally good about your job.'
- 'Tell me about a time when you felt exceptionally bad about your job.'

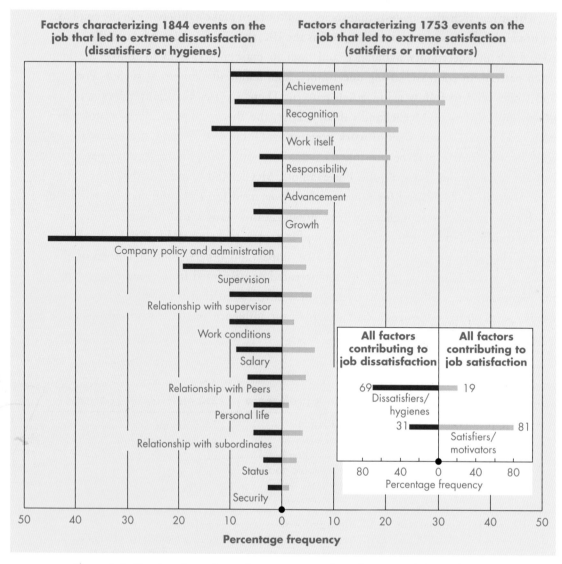

Figure 4.4: Herzberg's two-factor theory: sources of satisfaction and dissatisfaction as reported in 12 investigations.

Source: Reprinted by permission of *Harvard Business Review*. Adapted from Herzberg, Z. (1987), One more time: how do you motivate employees? *Harvard Business Review*, September/October © 2002 Harvard Business School Publishing Corporation. All Rights Reserved.

The motivator–hygiene theory distinguishes between sources of work dissatisfaction (hygiene factors) and satisfaction (motivators); it is also known as the two-factor theory.

After analysing nearly 4000 responses to these statements (Figure 4.4), Herzberg and his associates developed the two-factor theory, also known as the **motivator–hygiene theory**. They noticed that the factors identified as sources of work dissatisfaction (subsequently called 'dissatisfiers' or 'hygiene factors') were different from those identified as sources of satisfaction (subsequently called 'satisfiers' or 'motivator factors').

According to Herzberg's two-factor theory, an individual employee could be simultaneously both satisfied and dissatisfied because each of these two factors has a different set of drivers and is recorded on a separate scale. According to Herzberg's measurement the two scales are:

1. Satisfaction   No satisfaction
2. Dissatisfaction   No dissatisfaction

Effective managers have to achieve two distinct outcomes as discussed below: to maximize the job satisfaction of the people who work for them and, similarly, to minimize their job dissatisfaction.

Satisfiers or motivator factors

To improve satisfaction, a manager must use **motivators**, as shown on the right side of Figure 4.4. These factors are related to **job content**; that is, what people do in their work. Adding these satisfiers or motivators to people's jobs is Herzberg's link to performance. These are also known as intrinsic rewards and cover such things as sense of achievement, recognition and responsibility. According to Herzberg, when these opportunities are absent, workers will not be satisfied and will not perform well. Building such factors into a job is an important topic and it is discussed at length in the next chapter.

Dissatisfiers or hygiene factors

Hygiene factors are associated with the **job context**; that is, they are factors related to a person's work setting. Improving working conditions (for example, special offices and air conditioning) involves improving a hygiene or job-context factor. It will prevent people from being dissatisfied with their work but will not make them satisfied. Table 4.2 shows other examples of hygiene factors in work settings.

Motivators (motivator factors) are satisfiers that are associated with what people do in their work.

Job content refers to what people do in their work.

Hygiene factors (hygienes) are dissatisfiers that are associated with aspects of a person's work setting.

Job context refers to a person's work setting.

Hygiene factors	Examples
Organizational policies, procedures	Attendance rules
Holiday schedules	
Grievance procedures, Performance appraisal methods	
Working conditions	Noise levels, Safety
Personal comfort, Size of work area	
Interpersonal relationships	Co-worker relations, Customer relations Relationship with boss
Quality of supervision	Technical competence of boss
Base salary	Hourly wage rate or salary

Table 4.2: Sample hygiene factors found in work settings.

As Table 4.2 shows, salary or money is included as a hygiene factor. This is perhaps surprising and is discussed further in the next section.

Money: motivator or hygiene factor?

Herzberg found that a low salary makes people dissatisfied but that paying people more does not satisfy or motivate them. It is important to bear in mind that this conclusion derives from data finding that salary had considerable cross-loading across both motivators and hygiene factors (see the bars that cross the central vertical line at zero percentage frequency in Figure 4.4). Because most of the variance could be explained within the hygiene or job context group of factors, Herzberg concluded that money was not a motivator. The theme of money as an extrinsic reward is discussed more fully later in the chapter.

Herzberg: the research and practical implications

There has been much debate on the merits of the two-factor theory.[30] While Herzberg's continuing research and that of his followers support the theory, some researchers have used different methods and are unable to confirm the theory. It is therefore criticized as being method-bound – that is, supportable only by applying Herzberg's original method. This is a serious criticism because the scientific approach requires that theories be verifiable when different research methods are used. Perhaps the most powerful critique was offered by Vroom, who postulated that the critical incident method used by Herzberg may have resulted in respondents generally associating good times in their jobs with things under their personal control, or for which they could give themselves credit. Bad times, on the other hand, were more often associated with factors in the environment, or under the control of management.[31]

Herzberg's theory has also met with other criticisms:

- the original sample of scientists and engineers probably is not representative of the working population;
- the theory does not account for individual differences (for example, the impact of pay according to gender, age and other important variables);
- the theory does not clearly define the relationship between satisfaction and motivation.[32]

Such criticisms may contribute to the mixed findings from research conducted outside the US. In New Zealand, for example, supervision and interpersonal relationships were found to contribute significantly to satisfaction and not merely to reducing dissatisfaction. Certain hygiene factors were cited more frequently as satisfiers in Panama, Latin America and a number of countries other than the US. In contrast, evidence from countries such as Finland tends to confirm US results.[33] In view of globalizing workforces, these distinctions may have significant importance for managers endeavouring to motivate their employees.

However, the theory does have value. For example, it may help to identify why a focus on job environment factors (such as special office fixtures, piped-in music, comfortable lounges for breaks, high base salaries and other monetary-based rewards schemes) often do not motivate. This has led to many companies rethinking these types of schemes as the above example demonstrates. It also draws strong attention to the value of job design and motivation, as discussed in the next chapter.

OB IN ACTION

The 'green' corporation – is it just a public relations exercise?

There are numerous examples of employers 'going green'. For example, Nike has invested millions to find a way to produce its 'air' trainers without the use of greenhouse gases;[34] Richard Branson has pledged £2 million from the profits of the transportation businesses in his Virgin group to help combat global warming by investing in sustainable energy sources; and global giant Unilever makes public its contributions to carbon dioxide and hazardous wastes as well as funding projects in many countries to fight the ills of water shortages, poverty and climate change.[35] So is this just a public relations exercise? On the face of it this might be the case, as recent survey evidence in the UK suggests that 60% of employers that have adopted a green approach to managing their company car fleet were motivated to do so by the desire to enhance their organization's image.

However the same UK survey suggests that there is increasing demand from employees for their employer to be environmentally responsible and that a third of employees, particularly younger employees (aged 18–24), would change jobs in order to obtain a greener benefits package. The three most attractive green benefits among respondents are: incentives to move to sustainable energy use; discounts on green or recycled products; and public transport discounts.

It seems that employers may be taking note, as green benefits are an increasingly important component of the reward package for many employers, with demand growing as environmental awareness becomes more widespread.[36] For example, staff at IT giant Cisco who choose greener company cars or preventive healthcare schemes are rewarded with extra cash;[37] Nottingham City Council offers a range of benefits and incentives to encourage staff to use public transport including tax-free bus travel and bicycle purchase or hire; and Getronics UK and Thomsons Online Benefits offer employees the opportunity to offset their carbon dioxide emissions through donations to environmental charities.[38] But the benefits aren't just financial, telecoms firm BT claims it has identified a direct link between involving employees in climate change and improving staff engagement and retention.[39] It seems that environmental issues are firmly on the agenda and could be one way for employers to motivate and engage staff.

Process theories

The various content theories still emphasize the 'what' aspect of motivation; that is, they try to look for ways of improving motivation by dealing with deprived needs. They do not emphasize the thought processes concerning 'why' and 'how' people choose one action over another in the workplace. For this, we must turn to *process motivation theories*. Two well-known process theories are equity theory and expectancy theory.

Equity theory

Equity theory
*is based on the
phenomenon of
social comparison
and posits that
because people
gauge the
fairness of their
work outcomes
compared with
others, any felt
inequity will result
in an unpleasant
feeling which the
individual will be
driven to remove
through a variety
of possible actions.*

Equity theory is based on the phenomenon of social comparison and is best known through the writing of J. Stacy Adams.[40] Adams argues that when people gauge the fairness of their work outcomes compared with those of others, felt inequity is a motivating state of mind. That is, when people perceive inequity in their work, they experience a state of cognitive dissonance and they will be aroused to remove the discomfort and to restore a sense of felt equity to the situation. Inequities exist whenever people feel that the rewards or inducements they receive for their work inputs or contributions are unequal to the rewards other people appear to have received for their inputs. For the individual, the equity comparison or thought process that determines such feeling is:

Individual rewards/individual inputs $\xleftrightarrow{\text{comparison}}$ Others' rewards/others' inputs

Resolving felt inequities

**Felt negative
inequity** *exists
when individuals
feel they have
received relatively
less than others
have in proportion
to work inputs.*

A **felt negative inequity** exists when individuals feel that they have received relatively less than others have in proportion to work inputs. **Felt positive inequity** exists when individuals feel that they have received relatively more than others have.

Both felt negative and felt positive inequity are motivating states. When either exists, the individual will likely engage in one or more of the following behaviours to restore a sense of equity:

**Felt positive
inequity** *exists
when individuals
feel they have
received relatively
more than others
have.*

- change work inputs (for example, reduce performance efforts);
- change the outcomes (rewards) received (for example, ask for an increase in salary);
- act to change the inputs or outputs of the comparison person (for example, get a co-worker to accept more work);
- change the comparison points (for example, compare self with a different co-worker);
- psychologically distort the comparisons (for example, rationalize that the inequity is only temporary and will be resolved in the future);
- leave the situation (for example, change departments or quit).

Equity theory predicts that people who feel either under-rewarded or over-rewarded for their work will act to restore a sense of equity.

Adams's equity theory: the research

The research of Adams and others, accomplished largely in laboratory settings, lends tentative support to this prediction.[41] The research indicates that people who feel overpaid (feel positive inequity) have been found to increase the quantity or quality of their work, while those who are underpaid (feel negative inequity) decrease the quantity or quality of their work. The research is most conclusive about felt negative inequity. It appears that people are less comfortable when they are under-rewarded than when they are over-rewarded, which is hardly surprising.

RESEARCH IN OB

Fair dues

Are people more upset about perceived inequities when money is involved? Sanford DeVoe from the University of Toronto and Sheena Lyengar from Columbia University have recently found that employees' perceptions of how fairly they are being rewarded depend on whether they are getting bonuses in the form of goods or money.

Participants in their research were asked to read a scenario about a manager handing out equal rewards to ten employees with vastly different performance records. In some scenarios the participants were told that the manager divided up 20 boxes of chocolates or 20 extra days of holiday equally among employees, in others they were told cash bonuses or credit card reward points were equally divided. Participants were then asked to rate the fairness of the manager's behaviour on a nine-point scale, where one was extremely unfair and nine was extremely fair.

The researchers found that these egalitarian tactics won higher average fairness values for chocolates and holidays than for monetary rewards. The researchers suggest that something about monetary rewards made people feel more strongly that they should reflect individual effort.[42]

Managing the equity dynamic

Figure 4.5 shows that the equity comparison intervenes between a manager's allocation of rewards and their impact on the work behaviour of staff. Feelings of inequity are determined solely by the individual's interpretation of the situation.

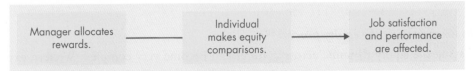

Figure 4.5: The equity comparison as an intervening variable in the rewards, satisfaction and performance relationship.

Thus, it is incorrect to assume all employees in a work group will view their annual pay rise as fair. It is not how a manager feels about the allocation of rewards that counts; it is how the recipients perceive the rewards that will determine the motivational outcomes of the equity dynamic. Fairness in this context also focuses on both **distributive justice** – the perceived fairness of the amount of the reward employees received – and **procedural justice** – the perceived fairness of the process used to determine the distribution of awards among employees. Research mainly carried out in the US found that workers place greater emphasis on the perceived fairness of the system rather than the actual pay rise itself.[43] Another study of senior managers supports this view and goes further in suggesting that

Distributive justice *refers to the perceived fairness of how rewards are allocated.*

Procedural justice *refers to the perceived fairness of the process used to determine the distribution of rewards.*

they place little value on comparisons with other employees and are only concerned about whether the system has fairly rewarded them for their performance.[44] The challenge for management is, then, in creating a process that is seen to be fair because perceived equity can foster job satisfaction and performance. In contrast, rewards that are received with feelings of negative inequity can damage these key work results. The burden lies with the manager to take control of the situation and make sure that any negative consequences of the equity comparisons are avoided, or at least minimized, when rewards are allocated.

EFFECTIVE MANAGER 4.2

Higher-Order Needs

Self-Actualization
Highest need level; need to fulfill oneself; to grow and use abilities to fullest and most creative extent.

Esteem
Need for esteem of others; respect, prestige, recognition, need for self-esteem, personal sense of competence, mastery.

Lower-Order Needs

Social
Need for love, affection, sense of belongingness in one's relationships with other persons.

Safety
Need for security, protection, and stability in the physical and inter-personal events of day-to-day life.

Physiological
Most basic of all human needs; need for biological maintenance; need for food, water and sustenance.

* Recognize that an employee is likely to make an equity comparison with colleagues when especially visible rewards, such as pay, promotions and so on, are being allocated.
* Anticipate felt negative inequities.
* Communicate to each individual your evaluation of the reward, an appraisal of the performance on which it is based, and the comparison points you consider to be appropriate.

Steps for managing the equity process

Managing the equity dynamic across cultures can become very complex. Western expatriates working in multinational corporations typically adopt an individual frame of reference when making equity comparisons. For local employees in Eastern cultures, the value placed on rewards and the weighting attributed to a specific outcome may vary considerably from Western norms. The group, not the individual, is the major point of reference for such equity comparisons and if a multinational corporation tries to motivate by offering individualized rewards, employees may not respond as expected.[45]

Expectancy theory

Victor Vroom's expectancy theory[46] seeks to predict or explain the task-related effort expended by a person. The theory's central question is: 'What determines the willingness of an individual to exert personal effort to work at tasks that contribute to the performance of the team and the organization?' Figure 4.6 illustrates the managerial foundations of expectancy theory.

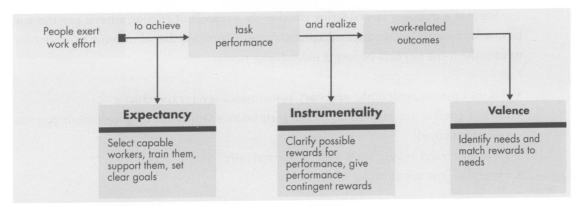

Figure 4.6: Key terms and managerial implications of Vroom's expectancy theory.

Individuals are viewed as making conscious decisions to allocate their behaviour towards work efforts and to serve self-interests. The three key terms in the theory are as follows.

- **Expectancy:** the probability that the individual assigns to work effort being followed by a given level of achieved task performance. Expectancy would equal '0' if the person felt it was impossible to achieve the given performance level; it would equal '1' if a person was 100% certain that the performance could be achieved.
- **Instrumentality:** the probability that the individual assigns to a given level of achieved task performance leading to various work outcomes that are rewarding for them. Instrumentality also varies from '1' (meaning the reward outcome is 100% certain to follow performance) to '0' (indicating that there is no chance that performance will lead to the reward outcome).
- **Valence:** the value that the individual attaches to various work reward outcomes. Valences form a scale from –1 (very undesirable outcome) to +1 (very desirable outcome).

Expectancy theory argues that work motivation is determined by individual beliefs about effort–performance relationships and the desirability of various work outcomes from different performance levels. Simply, the theory is based on the logic that people will do what they can do when they want to.[47] If you want a promotion and see that high performance can lead to that promotion, and that if you work hard you can achieve high performance, you will be motivated to work hard.

Multiplier effects and multiple outcomes

Vroom posits that motivation (M), expectancy (E), instrumentality (I) and valence (V) are related to one another by the equation: $M = E \times I \times V$.

This relationship means that the motivational appeal of a given work path is sharply reduced whenever any one or more of these factors approaches the value of zero. Conversely, for a given reward to have a high and positive motivational impact as a work outcome, the expectancy, instrumentality and valence associated with the reward must all be high and positive.

Expectancy is the probability that the individual assigns to work effort being followed by a given level of achieved task performance.

Instrumentality is the probability that the individual assigns to a level of achieved task performance leading to various work outcomes.

Valence represents the values that the individual attaches to various work outcomes.

Expectancy theory argues that work motivation is determined by individual beliefs about effort–performance relationships and the desirability of various work outcomes from different performance levels.

Suppose a manager is wondering whether the prospect of earning a merit pay rise will be motivational to a subordinate. Expectancy theory predicts that motivation to work hard to earn the merit pay will be low if individuals:

- feel they cannot achieve the necessary performance level (expectancy);
- are not confident a high level of task performance will result in a high merit pay rise (instrumentality);
- place little value (valence) on a merit pay increase;
- experience any combination of these.

Expectancy theory is able to accommodate multiple work outcomes in predicting motivation. As shown in Figure 4.7, the outcome of a merit pay increase may not be the only one affecting the individual's decision to work hard. Relationships with colleagues may also be important, and they may be undermined if the individual stands out from the group as a high performer. Although merit pay is both highly valued and considered accessible to the individual, its motivational power can be cancelled out by the negative effects of high performance on the individual's social relationships with colleagues. One of the advantages of expectancy theory is its ability to help managers account for such multiple outcomes when trying to determine the motivational value of various work rewards to individual employees.

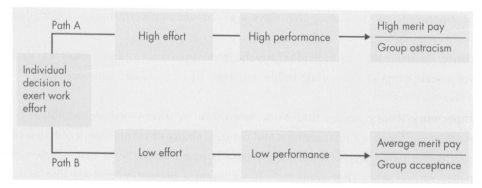

Figure 4.7: An example of individual thought processes as viewed by expectancy theory.

Vroom: managerial implications

The managerial implications of Vroom's expectancy theory are summarized in Table 4.3. Expectancy logic argues that a manager must try to understand individual thought processes, then actively intervene in the work situation to influence them. This includes trying to maximize work expectancies, instrumentalities and valences that support the organization's production purposes. In other words, a manager should strive to create a work setting in which the individual will also value work contributions serving the organization's needs as paths towards desired personal outcomes or rewards.

Expectancy term	The individual's question	Managerial implications
Expectancy	'Can I achieve the desired level of task performance?'	Select workers with ability; train workers to use ability; support individual ability with organizational resources; identify performance goals.
Instrumentality	'What work outcomes will be received as a result of the performance?'	Clarify psychological contracts; communicate performance–reward possibilities; confirm performance–reward possibilities by making actual rewards contingent on performance.
Valence	'How highly do I value the work outcomes?'	Identify individual needs or outcomes; adjust available rewards to match these.

Table 4.3: Managerial implications of expectancy theory.

In terms of outcome valence, the manager can identify individual needs or outcomes important to each individual, then try to adjust available rewards to match these. In this sense the theory can be universally applied. Each individual may be different, though different cultural patterns of values will affect valence of rewards across cultures. It may also be possible to change the individual's perceptions of the valence of various outcomes, as shown in Effective Manager 4.3.

EFFECTIVE MANAGER 4.3

Tips for influencing the perceived valence of work outcomes:
- find out the currently valued outcomes for each employee;
- determine the outcomes that are currently available to them;
- discuss how well the two sets match, and examine similarities between each individual's list and your list;
- show how some available outcomes may be more desirable or less undesirable than the worker thinks (for example, promotion may be available but the employee currently does not desire it because he or she feels uncomfortable with it).

Vroom: the research
There is a great deal of research on expectancy theory and good review articles are available.[48] Although the theory has received substantial support, the terminology used by psychologists is often difficult to understand and apply. Rather than suggesting that the

underlying theory is inadequate, researchers indicate that problems of method and measurement may cause their inability to generate more confirming data. Thus, while awaiting the results of more sophisticated research, experts seem to agree that expectancy theory is a useful insight into work motivation.

One of the more popular modifications of Vroom's original version of the theory distinguishes between **extrinsic** and **intrinsic rewards** as two separate types of possible work outcomes.[49] Extrinsic rewards are positively valued work outcomes that the individual receives from some other person in the work setting. An example is pay. Workers typically do not pay themselves directly; some representative of the organization administers the reward. In contrast, intrinsic rewards are positively valued work outcomes that the individual receives directly as a result of task performance; they do not require the participation of another person. A feeling of achievement after accomplishing a particularly challenging task is one example. The distinction between extrinsic and intrinsic rewards is important because each type demands separate attention from a manager seeking to use rewards to increase motivation.

> **Extrinsic rewards** are positively valued work outcomes that the individual receives from some other person in the work setting.
>
> **Intrinsic rewards** are positively valued work outcomes that the individual receives directly as a result of task performance.

Integrating content and process motivation theories

Each of the theories presented in this chapter is potentially useful for the manager. Although the equity and expectancy theories have special strengths, current thinking argues for a combined approach that points out where and when various motivation theories work best.[50] Thus, before leaving this discussion, we should pull the content and process theories together into one integrated model of individual performance and satisfaction.

First, the various content theories have a common theme, as shown in Figure 4.8. Content theorists disagree somewhat as to the exact nature of human needs but they do agree that:

Individual needs $\xrightarrow{\text{activate}}$ tensions $\xrightarrow[\text{influence}]{\text{that}}$ attitudes and behaviour.

Maslow	Alderfer	McClelland	Herzberg
Needs hierarchy	**ERG theory**	**Acquired needs theory**	**Two-factor theory**
Self-actualization	Growth	Need for achievement	Motivators and satisfiers
		Need for power	
Esteem			
Social	Relatedness	Need for affiliation	Hygienes and dissatisfiers
Safety and security			
Physiological	Existence		

Figure 4.8: Comparison of content motivation theories.

The manager's job is to create a work environment that responds positively to individual needs. Poor performance, undesirable behaviour and/or decreased satisfaction can be partly explained in terms of 'blocked' needs, or needs that are not satisfied on the job. The motivational value of rewards (intrinsic and extrinsic) can also be analysed in terms of 'activated' needs to which a given reward either does or does not respond. Ultimately, managers must understand that individuals have different needs and place different importance on different needs. Managers must also know what to offer individuals to respond to their needs and to create work settings that give people the opportunity to satisfy their needs through their contributions to task, work unit and organizational performance.

Porter and Lawler's model

Figure 4.9 is a model that goes further to integrate content and process theories. The model, as proposed by Lyman W. Porter and Edward E. Lawler, is an extension of Vroom's original expectancy theory.[51] The figure is based on the individual performance equation (see Chapter 1). Individual attributes and work effort and the manager's ability to create a work setting that positively responds to individual needs and goals all affect performance. Whether a work setting can satisfy needs depends on the availability of rewards (extrinsic and intrinsic). The content theories enter the model as the manager's guide to understanding individual attributes and identifying the needs that give motivational value to the various work rewards allocated to employees. Managers are also interested in promoting high levels of individual satisfaction as a part of their concern for human resource maintenance. Motivation, performance and satisfaction can all occur when rewards are allocated on the basis of past performance (that is, when rewards are performance contingent) but motivation can also occur when job satisfaction results from rewards that are felt to be equitably allocated. When felt negative inequity results, satisfaction will be low and motivation will be reduced. Thus, the integrated model includes a key role for equity theory and recognizes job performance and satisfaction as separate but potentially interdependent work results.[52]

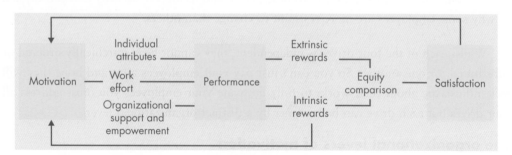

Figure 4.9: Predicting individual work performance and satisfaction: an integrated model.

OTHER PERSPECTIVES ON MOTIVATION

In recent years more work has developed to explain other dimensions that contribute to our understanding of motivation. These extend beyond what is traditionally explained by content and process theories. A complex interplay of factors can affect motivation. Two of these are the four basic drives of motivation and the idea of self-concept.

The four basic drives of motivation are the drive to acquire, the drive to bond, the drive to comprehend and the drive to defend.

The four basic drives of employee motivation

Advances and research in the neurosciences, biology and evolutionary psychology have allowed us to learn more about the human brain and how it may influence our behaviour. This has led to researchers from the Harvard Business School putting forward a new model of human motivation. Nitin Nohria, Boris Groysberg and Linda Eling Lee postulate that people are guided by four basic emotional needs, or drives, that are a product of our common evolutionary heritage.[53] These drives underlie everything that we do.

1. *The drive to acquire.* We are all driven to acquire scarce goods that bolster our sense of wellbeing. The drive applies to physical goods like money, experiences such as travel and events that improve our social status such as promotion. It is also relative in that we always compare what we have with others and we always want more.
2. *The drive to bond.* When met this is associated with strong positive emotions like love and caring and when not met, with negative ones like loneliness. At work the drive to bond accounts for the enormous boost in motivation when employees feel proud of the organization and for their loss of morale when the institution lets them down.
3. *The drive to comprehend.* We want to make sense of the world around us, to produce theories and accounts that make events comprehensible and suggest reasonable actions and responses. At work this accounts for the desire to make a meaningful contribution and explains why employees are motivated by jobs that challenge them and allow them to learn and grow.
4. *The drive to defend.* We naturally defend ourselves, our family and friends our property and accomplishments. This drive manifests itself not just as aggressive or defensive behaviour but also in a quest to promote justice and feelings of security and can explain why some employees are more resistant to change than others.

Whilst each of the four drives is independent, they cannot be hierarchically ordered or substituted for one another. So you can't just pay your employees a lot and hope they will feel enthusiastic about their work; to fully motivate your employees you must address all four drives but each drive can be best met by a distinct organizational lever.

The organizational levers of motivation

1. *The reward system.* The drive to acquire is most easily satisfied by an organization's reward system – how effectively it discriminates between good and poor performers, ties rewards to performance and gives the best people opportunities for advancement.

2. *Culture*. The most effective way to fulfil the drive to bond – to engender a strong sense of camaraderie is to create a culture that promotes teamwork, collaboration, openness and friendship.

3. *Job design*. The drive to comprehend is best addressed by designing jobs that are meaningful, interesting and challenging.

4. *Performance management and resource allocation processes*. Fair, trustworthy and transparent processes for performance management and resources allocation help to meet people's drive to defend.

The role of the direct manager

In their research to support their theory, Nohria, Groysberg and Lee found that employees attributed as much importance to their boss's meeting their four drives as to the organization's policies; that is to say, they recognized that their manager had control over how company policies and processes were implemented and they expected their manager to do their best to address all four drives within the constraints that the organization imposed. However, employees were realistic about what managers could not do.

The model posits that employee motivation is influenced by a complex system of managerial and organizational factors, but the research suggests that an organization's ability to fulfil all four basic emotional needs will lead to increased motivation, which they argue can boost company performance. Two notes of caution need to be made here, firstly it is, as yet, only a theory developed from survey evidence from employees of successful companies, and secondly as yet the theory has not been tested (that is to say, there is no empirical evidence), but it does add an interesting new dimension to the debate on motivation.

Self-concept

Self-concept is the concept that individuals have of themselves as physical, social and spiritual or moral beings. The self-concept approach comes from personality theory. It focuses on using the concept of the self as an underlying force that motivates behaviour, which gives it direction and energy and sustains it. Self-concept is derived from many influences including family, social identity and reference groups, education and experience. Generally speaking, these aspects of personality are a guide to our behaviour and help us to decide what to do in specific situations. So, for example, young people may choose to study medicine or dentistry at university, or to enter the family business, because that is what was always expected of them and has therefore become an important part of their identity. Rewards such as money and status may be secondary considerations. Many acts are done out of a sense of responsibility, integrity or even humour, which relate to the self-concept aspect of personality.[54] This sort of approach would help to explain the nurse who waits with the relatives of a critically injured patient for hours after his/her shift is completed; or the person who works the shift of a friend who is studying for exams. It may also explain why more employees seek to work for ethical employers.

Self-concept is the concept that individuals have of themselves as physical, social and spiritual or moral beings.

OB IN ACTION

What motivates NHS workers?

Career development and the opportunity to improve working practices provide the greatest job satisfaction for National Health Service (NHS) staff, according to a report into what motivates its employees. The survey, which canvassed more than 9000 staff from 48 NHS trusts and a range of GP practices, also found that providing support for workers to do a good job and adequate resources to deliver quality care are key to increasing motivation. The NHS plans to use the report evidence to develop policies and practices that help staff feel valued, empowered and able to make an even greater difference to patient care than they do already.[55]

In contrast to a focus on needs or cognitive thought processes to explain motivation, the self-concept approach relies on other ways of understanding motivation to explain the full range of motivated behaviour. People may also draw on the values they hold and the way that these values are a guide to behaviours that seem right or appropriate for them. For example, people internalize values that are espoused by the professional group (or the organization) to which they belong. Behaviours consistent with such values might include saving lives and property at considerable personal risk, exposing unethical financial practices despite censure from management, facing personal hardship or leaving a well-paid job because the company's values differ from their own.

Having identified many content and process theories and an integrated model of these two approaches, as well as the ideas of self-concept and personal values in motivation, it is a good time to reflect on how managers may be able to realistically implement all these in the workplace. The following 'Counterpoint' raises some points about the complexity and difficulties of motivating employees.

▶ COUNTERPOINT

Knowing and engaging our workers

When managers or scholars discuss workplace motivation, they tend to talk about it as if work, and a single workplace, is the only place where people exert effort towards fulfilling needs, achieving rewards and/or living life according to their self-concept. The idea that you can get to know your employees and work out what motivational needs they have, then find ways to help them satisfy those needs, can over-emphasize the importance of work in motivating people and simplify the complex circumstances and working arrangements that exist in today's workforce.

It is to be expected that employers would want some return on their motivational strategies. To do so employers need to invest time, money and other resources into employees who are 'engaged' with the company. The idea of 'employee engagement' helps to link up motivation with the workplace attitudes of organizational commitment, job satisfaction and advocacy (those who speak highly of their own organization as an employer and of its products, services and brand). Studies in the US and Canada reveal that companies with disengaged employees have significant productivity losses, while those with engaged employees have higher revenue, customer loyalty and profits.[56]

The idea that in the new-style workplace employees are all engaged may be problematic because many remain for only a short time, have links with more than one organization and/or have mixed feelings about their employment. These include an increasing number of casual or part-time employees, who in turn include the 'well-heeled itinerants' who are working multiple jobs (such as some university academics who hold three or more concurrent jobs).[57] Loosely engaged professionals often move from one contracted job to another,

many working as free agents. Older workers may be torn between the pressures to continue working, at least part-time, and their desire to retire. At the other end of the age spectrum, a survey of generation Y employees (aged 16–24) found that they were very likely to change jobs if their expectations were not met in an organization.[58] People who work remotely or operate in a virtual workplace may lack engagement with the organization. For example, 4000 software consultants at Wipro, an Indian IT company, operate from and between customer sites outside of India.[59]

Also, it is important to remember that people do not spend all their lives at work and other things in their lives may drive behaviour as much as their work. Whether they play sport, work in their gardens, act in a voluntary capacity in a community organization or pursue further study, they are involved in motivation outside the workplace.

Questions

1. How might an employee's needs be satisfied outside the workplace and, if this occurs, how would it affect the needs that employees seek to satisfy in the workplace?

2. Why might casual employees, those with multiple jobs, older employees, generation Y and virtual and professional workers be less engaged than other employees and what could an employer do to seek to motivate these different cohorts?

MANAGING PAY AS AN EXTRINSIC REWARD

In the next chapter we discuss more fully the nature of intrinsic motivation and job satisfaction; in this chapter we will now look more closely at pay as an extrinsic reward. As we have already said, extrinsic rewards are positively valued work outcomes that the individual receives from some other person. Pay is an especially complex extrinsic reward. It can help organizations attract and retain highly capable workers and it can help satisfy and motivate these workers to work hard to achieve high performance, but if workers are dissatisfied with the salary, pay can also lead to strikes, grievances, absenteeism, turnover and sometimes even poor physical and mental health. The various aspects of pay make it an especially important extrinsic reward.[60]

Multiple meanings of pay

To use pay effectively as a reward a manager must understand why it is important to people. Various OB theories recognize multiple meanings of pay and the potential of these meanings to vary from one person or situation to another. When it comes to the relationship between pay and job satisfaction, for example, each of the following theories (which were discussed in general earlier in the chapter) offers a slightly different perspective.

According to Maslow's hierarchy of needs theory, pay is a unique reward that can satisfy many different needs. It is used directly to satisfy lower-order needs, such as the physiological need for food, and it is of symbolic value in satisfying higher-order needs, such as ego fulfilment.

According to McClelland's acquired needs theory, pay is an important source of performance feedback for high-need achievers. It can be attractive to people with a high need for affiliation when offered as a group bonus and it is valued by the high need-for-power person as a means of 'buying' prestige or control over others.

According to Herzberg's two-factor theory, pay in the form of a base wage or salary can prevent dissatisfaction but cannot lead to motivation (although merit pay rises given as special rewards for jobs done well can cause increased satisfaction and motivation). However, Herzberg's research does show that pay crossloads across both his hygiene and motivating factors. This finding recognizes that many of the respondents in Herzberg's research perceived money as a motivating factor.

Expectancy and equity theories, as well as the various reinforcement strategies, give additional insight into the multiple meanings of pay and their potential relationships to job performance. These ideas (summarized in Table 4.4) show how pay can serve as a motivator of work effort when properly managed. This phrase is the real key; for pay to prove successful as a reward that is truly motivational to the recipient, it must be given:

• contingent on the occurrence of specific and desirable work behaviours, and
• equitably.

Merit pay and a variety of emerging creative pay practices are applications that need to be dealt with in more detail.

Merit pay

Merit pay is a compensation system that bases an individual's salary or wage increase on a measure of the person's performance accomplishments during a specified time period.

Edward Lawler's research has contributed greatly to our understanding of pay as an extrinsic reward. His research generally concludes that for pay to serve as a source of work motivation, high levels of job performance must be viewed as the path through which high pay can be achieved.[61] **Merit pay** is defined as a compensation system that bases an individual's salary or wage increase on a measure of the person's performance accomplishments during a specified time period. That is, merit pay is an attempt to make pay contingent on performance.

Theory	The meaning of pay
Equity theory	Pay is an object of social comparison. People are likely to compare their pay and pay increases with those received by others. When felt inequity occurs as a result of such comparisons, work effort may be reduced in the case of negative inequity, or increased in the case of positive inequity.
Expectancy theory	Pay is only one of many work rewards that individuals may value at work. When valence, instrumentality and expectancy are high, pay can be a source of motivation. However, the opportunity to work hard to obtain high pay will be viewed in the context of other effort–outcome expectancies and the equity dynamic.
Reinforcement theory	Pay is one of the extrinsic rewards that a manager may use to influence the work behaviour of employees. Through the techniques of operant conditioning, pay can be used as a positive reinforcer when the laws of contingent and immediate reinforcement are followed.

Table 4.4: The multiple meanings of pay as viewed from a performance perspective.

For some time now, research has supported the logic and theoretical benefits of merit pay but it also indicates that the implementation of merit pay plans is not as universal or as easy as we may expect.[62]

To work well, a merit pay plan must:

- be based on realistic and accurate measures of individual work performance;
- create a belief among employees that the way to achieve high pay is to perform at high levels;
- discriminate clearly between high and low performers in the amount of pay reward received;
- avoid confusing 'merit' aspects of a pay increase with 'cost-of-living' adjustments.

These guidelines are consistent with the basic laws of reinforcement and the guidelines for positive reinforcement discussed in Chapter 3.

However, total quality management guru W. Edwards Deming has long been a critic of pay-for-performance schemes. Deming argues that, because performance is difficult to measure, all employees should receive a traditional salary or wage, and that all future pay rises should be administered uniformly across the company to encourage cooperation and team-work. There are potential problems in linking pay to performance. However, many human resource experts and headhunters emphasize the importance of rewarding high performers for a private company's ability to attract top talent in a competitive global marketplace.

Paying for performance

The concept of linking pay with performance is controversial. Most employers would agree that quality employees deserve higher pay than underperforming employees. However, exactly what constitutes a 'quality employee' is problematic. Performance measurements are largely based on the perceptions of immediate supervisors; they are subjective and not based on specific criteria, and therefore can cause a sense of unfairness for many employees. In addition, the low inflation economies that exist in western Europe create more problems because the difference between an average and high-performing employee may only translate into a 2–3% difference in the pay increase. So is pay a motivator? In summary it depends on a number of factors, some of which are outlined in the following 'Counterpoint'.

COUNTERPOINT

But it's all about money deep down isn't it?

The link between money and motivation remains complex and inconclusive. This lack of clear evidence is compounded by the problem that, when asked, employees often understate the importance of pay; that is to say, it is much more important in people's actual choices and behaviours than it is in their self-reports of what motivates them.[63] It is also evident that the link between money and motivation depends on a number of other variables such as time, career stage, level in the organization, age and culture. One longitudinal study found that employees' motivational preferences vary over time, with today's workers placing greater emphasis on more extrinsic factors with 'good wages' still being the top motivator for the majority of employees.[64] Another, in the hospitality industry, found that where jobs offer no variety and little intrinsic job satisfaction, employees are overwhelmingly motivated by money alone.[65] In Britain, 83% of human resources directors believed that younger employees were more motivated by flexible hours and career development programmes than by more traditional benefits such as money.[66] This was supported in a survey by the DTI that found that over 46% of respondents would chose flexible working over money as a benefit[67] and although money was reported to be the main motivator for young people in the Far and Middle East, work ethic and mastery were ranked higher in North and South America.[68] Robbins suggests that money can be considered to act as a 'scorecard' that enables employees to assess the value their employer places on them in comparison to others and as a medium of exchange allowing employees to purchase whatever 'needs satisfying' things they desire.[69] Other research develops this comparative concept further, arguing that it's not absolute salary but comparative salary that motivates employees. Put simply, it doesn't matter so much what you are paid, more how much you are paid in comparison to others.[70] This concept is the basis of equity theory, which we have already discussed in this chapter.

Questions

1. How much does money motivate you in your choice of job?
2. Would you change jobs for an increase in salary alone?
3. Would you change jobs in order to work more flexibly even if it meant a cut in salary?

Creative pay practices

So how can employers effectively use financially based rewards to motivate their staff? Merit pay plans are but one attempt to enhance the positive value of pay as a work reward and to use it as a positive reinforcer, but some argue that merit pay plans are not consistent with the demands of today's organizations because they fail to recognize the high degree of task interdependence among employees, as illustrated particularly in total quality management programmes. Still others contend that the nature of any incentive scheme should be tied to the overall organizational strategy and the nature of the desired behaviour; for example, the pay system of an organization that needs highly skilled individuals who are in short supply should emphasize employee retention rather than performance.[71]

Many organizations facing increased competition, in an attempt to become more competitive by getting more from their workers, use varying creative incentive schemes either singly or in combination. Such nontraditional practices are becoming more common in organizations with increasingly diverse workforces and a growing emphasis on total quality management or similar setups.[72] These creative schemes can include skill-based pay, profit-sharing plans, lump-sum pay increases, bonus share schemes and flexible benefit plans. Table 4.5 depicts a variety of remuneration methods available to employers.

Pay practice	Description
Skill-based pay	A pay system that rewards people for acquiring and developing job-relevant skills that relate to organizational needs.
Gain-sharing plans	A pay system that links pay and performance by giving workers the opportunity to share in productivity gains through increased earnings.
Lump-sum pay increases	A pay system in which people elect to receive their annual wage or salary increase in one or more lump-sum payments.
Bonus share schemes	A share plan to reward high-performing executives.
Flexible benefit plans	Pay systems that allow workers to select benefits according to their individual needs.

Table 4.5: Creative pay practices.

There is a growing trend away from rewarding performance solely by financial outcomes. Many companies are now incorporating nonfinancial outcomes, such as a flexible benefit plan, into this performance-based pay equation. Additional criteria such as improved customer service, employee satisfaction with managerial style and increased market share are being added to the equation to obtain a clearer and more comprehensive profile of the measurement of effective managerial performance.[73] The following 'OB in Action' looks at how the effectiveness of incentives varies with different cultural and economic contexts.

OB IN ACTION

Paying for performance?

The concept of linking pay with performance is controversial. It can lead to inequities which are hard to reconcile. Financial workers' bonuses, in particular, have come under the spotlight as a result of the global banking crisis of 2008. Many have asked how bonuses running into the millions can be justified when governments have had to make bailouts that have cost taxpayers hundreds of billions around the world. In London there has been a 350% rise in bonuses since 2000, at a time when the value of the FTSE 100 has dropped by 25%; four of the biggest US investment banks were reportedly planning to pay their staff in 2010 nearly $100 billion (£61.5 billion) in salary and bonuses; while RBS, 84% owned by the British taxpayer, still paid its staff bonuses despite making substantial losses.

RBS's boss, Stephen Hester, said that he had to pay bonuses, which will cost the bank an estimated £1.5 billion, to stop bankers leaving for higher rewards at rival institutions. But is this true? Boris Groysberg, Associate Professor of Organizational Behaviour at Harvard Business School, thinks not. He argues that Wall Street and the City are wedded to the idea that success depends on the talent and flair of individual bankers, but his widespread analysis into investment banking suggests that it isn't. 'Exceptional performance is far less portable than is widely believed,' he says. 'We found that mobile stars [bankers who leave one company for another] experienced an immediate degradation in performance that persisted for at least five years. Thus their exceptional performance at their prior employer appears to have been more firm-specific than is generally appreciated.'

Which leads us to the other argument often made in favour of dishing out bonuses: the idea that lump sums are a great way to enhance performance. Another survey by Harvard academics Nancy Katz and Michael Beer asked more than 200 senior executives in more than 30 countries about their bonus intentions – only to discover that the vast majority of those executives thought that bonuses had little or no effect on how their employees or businesses performed.[74]

EMPOWERMENT

Much of the motivational theory discussed in this chapter has addressed the question of what management can do to ensure employees positively contribute to the achievement of organizational goals. This chapter has emphasized the influence of extrinsic rewards such as pay in motivating staff to perform; however, in the workplace in the 21st century, workers may not just be searching for money but also for recognition, involvement and a heightened sense of self-worth. The employer is often looking for a 'can do' mentality among employees that lessens the need for managerial control.

Empowerment can meet these requirements. Empowerment is the process by which managers delegate power to employees to motivate greater responsibility in balancing the achievement of both personal and organizational goals. The key question for managers is how to facilitate employees' individual and joint contributions to the organization and their own development. Empowerment focuses on liberating, not controlling, human energy, and on balancing the achievement of personal and organizational goals. Managers commonly attempt these processes by delegating more power to employees and encouraging them to take on leadership roles in the organization.

> **Empowerment** *is the process by which managers delegate power to employees who therefore have an enhanced view of their work and role within the organization.*

IN ACTION

Barnardo's New Zealand, part of the children's charity founded in the UK in the 19th century, has 1000 staff and nearly 800 contract workers. These employees play an important role in helping to achieve the organization's charitable objectives such as looking after children in difficult circumstances. The organization understands the importance of both employee engagement and staff having passion for the work they do. While staff are trained in best practice, Barnardo's cannot impose corporate values and beliefs on workers. Murray Edridge, the CEO, operates by giving employees accountability and a mandate to do the best they can, while providing sufficient support to help them do so. He says the idea of leading by making others powerful underpins much of what Barnardo's is doing. The organization has a very simple and brief strategy plan and risk framework and the 'overriding' objectives are aimed at *enabling* and *entrusting* employees to operate effectively.[75]

The concept of empowerment is founded on the belief that everyone has an internal need for self-determination and a need to cope with environmental demands directly. This suggests that appropriate empowerment strategies can raise the perception of low **self-efficacy**. Self-efficacy refers to a person's belief that they can perform adequately in a situation. It refers to a state of mind or mentality,[76] which is why its relationship with empowerment strategies is important. Empowerment strategies are designed to improve self-efficacy by providing employees with greater autonomy and by increasing knowledge and control over factors directly related to job performance.

> **Self-efficacy** *refers to a person's belief that they can perform adequately in a situation.*

Some work on empowerment has identified the following stages (see Figure 4.10) in the empowerment process:[77]

- *Stage 1:* Identify the conditions contributing to low self-efficacy. This could include organizational factors (such as poor communication systems and an impersonal bureaucratic climate); supervisory style factors (such as authoritarianism, an emphasis on failure or lack of communication of reasons for action or inaction); reward factors (such as rewards that are not performance based, or the low incentive value of rewards) and

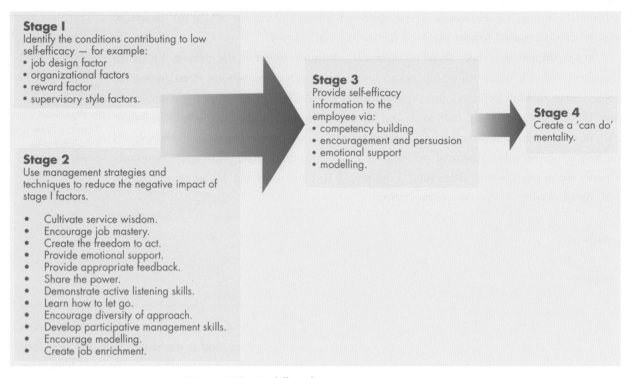

Figure 4.10: Modelling the empowerment process.

job design factors (such as unclear roles, unrealistic goals, low levels of participation and low job enrichment).

• *Stage 2:* Employ empowerment strategies and techniques that help to vest substantial responsibility in the hands of the individual who is closest to the problem requiring a solution.

  • *Cultivate a 'service wisdom'.* Trained and multiskilled employees should be able to handle nonroutine situations, to understand the bigger picture and how their role affects other employees and the achievement of organizational goals.

  • *Encourage job mastery.* Provide coaching, training and appropriate experiences to ensure successful job performance.

  • *Create a freedom to act.* Treat employees as if they own their jobs, devolving power so employees can adequately resolve problems. Managers should set appropriate boundaries to the freedom to facilitate successful employee job performance without creating inappropriate licence.

  • *Provide emotional support.* Employees must feel that if they act within the designated boundaries then managers will support their actions even if they make mistakes. Such support helps reduce stress and anxiety through clearer role definition, task support and concern for employee wellbeing.

  • *Provide appropriate feedback.* Employees need regular and detailed feedback so they know how they are performing against managerial expectations.

- *Share the power.* Share as much power as possible, allowing for employee experience, education and task difficulty.
- *Demonstrate active listening skills.* Learn to listen to feedback from experienced employees because the person performing the task often has the best ideas on process improvement.
- *Learn how to let go.* Treat employees as partners and equals rather than as subordinates and know when to let go when their work is successfully helping the business move in the right direction.
- *Encourage diversity of approach.* Employees should have the discretion to use various job styles and methods provided they meet agreed organizational standards for the work.
- *Develop participative management skills.* Encourage employees to participate in major decisions that affect their daily working lives directly.
- *Encourage modelling.* Employees should be able to observe and model their work on examples of 'best practice' performance in particular skills and competency-based areas relevant to their own work assignments.
- *Create job enrichment.* Enrich jobs by making employees more accountable and responsible for key aspects of their work performance.

- *Stage 3:* Provide self-efficacy information directly to the employee. This stage focuses on modifying employee behaviour and increasing the self-efficacy belief. Four approaches have been identified:

  - *Competency building.* Structure training and organizational learning so that employees acquire new skills through successive, moderate increments in task complexity and responsibility.
  - *Encouragement and persuasion.* Use verbal feedback and other persuasive techniques to encourage and reinforce successful job performance.
  - *Emotional support.* Provide emotional support for employees and minimize emotional arousal states such as anxiety, stress and the fear associated with making mistakes. Mistakes should be seen as part of the learning process.
  - *Modelling.* Allow employees to observe workers who perform successfully on the job.

  Both stages 2 and 3 are designed to remove and eradicate the conditions identified in stage 1, and to develop the positive feelings of self-efficacy within the individual employee.

- *Stage 4.* Create a 'can do' mentality and an empowering experience for the employee. If stages 2 and 3 are successful, then they will increase the employee's effort–performance understanding. As we saw earlier in the chapter, expectancy theories of motivation are essential for high and sustained levels of performance. Here, performance is linked directly to the positive mentality of the individual.

RESEARCH IN OB

In view of the potential importance of this topic for individual worker satisfaction, wellbeing and organizational performance, it will be no surprise to readers to learn that there is a rich body of research within OB attempting to demonstrate the relative validity of models of motivation discussed in this chapter. You may wish to look at our website **www.wileyeurope.** **com/college/french** and in particular at the article by Kuuvas examining the links between commitment, different forms of pay administration and motivation among knowledge workers in Norway. Typical of research in this field, Kuuvas's study points to the complexity of the topic, noting several links between reward and employee attitude.

CONCLUSION

Theories and models of motivation often contain quite different underlying assumptions on how similar and different humans are in terms of work motivation. They also appear at times to pose different questions – content theories focusing on *what* motivates whereas process theories look at *how* we come to be motivated or not by examining links between our expectations (including equitable treatment) and behaviour. An integrated model comprising elements of both traditions may help in terms of predicting behaviour and enhancing performance. The relationship between pay and motivation is complex and recent work has stressed empowerment as an important concept within this subject area.

SUMMARY

LEARNING OBJECTIVE 1
Motivating and empowering today's workforce

In the contemporary world a key challenge is to motivate and empower workers towards productive performance. With ageing populations, labour shortages and mobile workforces, organizations will need to understand how to motivate and empower employees in order to attract and retain them and to enhance performance.

LEARNING OBJECTIVE 2
Difference between content and process motivation theories

There are two main types of motivational theories – content and process. Content theories examine the needs that individuals have. Their efforts to satisfy those needs are what drive their behaviour. Process theories examine the thought processes that people have in relation to motivating their behaviour.

LEARNING OBJECTIVE 3
Content theories of motivation

The content theories of Maslow, Alderfer, McClelland and Herzberg emphasize needs or motives. They are often criticized for being culturally biased and caution should be exercised when applying these theories in non-Western cultures.

Maslow's hierarchy of needs theory arranges human needs into a five-step hierarchy: physiological, safety, social (the three lower-order needs), esteem and self-actualization (the two higher-order needs). Satisfaction of any need activates the need at the next higher level and people are presumed to move step by step up the hierarchy. Alderfer's ERG theory has modified this theory by collapsing the five needs into three: existence, relatedness and growth. Alderfer also allows for more than one need to be activated at a time and for a frustration–regression response. McClelland's acquired needs theory focuses on the needs for achievement (nAch), affiliation (nAff) and power (nPower). The theory argues that these needs can be developed through experience and training. People high in nAch prefer jobs with individual responsibility, performance feedback and moderately challenging goals. Successful executives typically have a high nPower that is greater than their nAff. Herzberg's two-factor theory treats job satisfaction and job dissatisfaction as two separate issues. Satisfiers, or motivator factors, such as achievement, responsibility and recognition, are associated with job content. An improvement in job content is expected to increase satisfaction and motivation to perform well. In contrast, dissatisfiers, or hygiene factors, such as working conditions, relations with co-workers and salary, are associated with the job context. Improving job context does not lead to more satisfaction but is expected to reduce dissatisfaction.

LEARNING OBJECTIVE 4
Process theories of motivation

Process theories emphasize the thought processes concerning how and why people choose one action over another in the workplace. Process theories focus on understanding the cognitive processes that act to influence behaviour. Although process theories can be very useful in explaining work motivation in cross-cultural settings, the values that drive such theories may vary substantially across cultures and the outcomes may differ considerably.

Equity theory points out that people compare their rewards (and inputs) with those of others. The individual is then motivated to engage in behaviour to correct any perceived inequity. At the extreme, feelings of inequity may lead to reduced performance or job turnover. Expectancy theory argues that work motivation is determined by an individual's beliefs concerning effort–performance relationships (expectancy), work–outcome relationships (instrumentality) and the desirability of various work outcomes (valence). Managers, therefore, must build positive expectancies, demonstrate performance–reward instrumentalities and use rewards with high positive valences in their motivational strategies.

LEARNING OBJECTIVE 5
Integrating content and process motivation theories

The content theories can be compared, with some overlap identified. An integrated model of motivation builds from the individual performance equation developed in Chapter 1 and combines the content and process theories to show how well-managed rewards can lead to high levels of both individual performance and satisfaction.

LEARNING OBJECTIVE 6
Other perspectives on motivation – four drives and self-concept

The four drives theory of motivation recognizes that employees do their best work when their basic emotional drives to acquire, bond, comprehend and defend are met. In harnessing these four drives with organizational levers, employee motivation and performance can be improved. Theories that focus on self-concept seek to describe motivation that cannot be readily explained by content and process theories. Self-concept is an aspect of personality that describes the concept individuals have of themselves as physical, social and spiritual or moral beings. This self-conception guides their behaviour.

LEARNING OBJECTIVE 7
Managing pay as an extrinsic reward

Managing pay as an extrinsic reward is particularly important as pay has multiple meanings – some positive and some negative. As a major and highly visible extrinsic reward, pay plays a role in reinforcement and in the motivation theories. Its reward implications are especially important in terms of merit pay.

LEARNING OBJECTIVE 8
Empowerment and the empowerment process

Empowerment is the process by which managers delegate power to employees to motivate greater responsibility in balancing the achievement of personal and organizational goals. For employees who experience low self-efficacy, managers can implement strategies to improve the employees' feelings of self-worth and their capacity to improve their performance.

CHAPTER 4 STUDY GUIDE

Now that you have read this chapter, you should be able to apply and further develop your knowledge by undertaking the following activities set out over the next few pages: test your knowledge questions, an individual activity and an end-of-chapter case study.

Please also go to this book's website: **www.wileyeurope.com/college/french** to find further material which will enhance your understanding and enable you to assess your knowledge.

TEST YOURSELF

1. Define 'work motivation' and identify the role of motivation in the individual performance equation.
2. Compare the 'needs' in Alderfer's and McClelland's theories of motivation.
3. Explain the key differences between the expectancy and the equity theories of motivation.
4. Describe each of the four stages in the empowerment process.
5. What challenges might there be in motivating (a) young unskilled workers and (b) highly talented and experienced middle-aged workers?
6. Assuming that an organization successfully retains its older employees, what can it do to motivate them?

7. 'It is impossible to know what employees want but if you give them good salaries or wages they can use the money to find ways to fulfil their own needs. Employers do not need to worry about anything else.' Discuss this statement.

8. Explain the application of the integrated model of motivation to each of the following occupational groups at an early career stage: police officers and marketing research professionals.

9. Discuss ways in which (a) a major retail store could empower its retail assistants in their jobs and (b) a bank could empower its cashiers in their work.

10. Imagine that you are the manager of a small furniture design and manufacturing company. Several of the staff members have complained that the rewards and benefits provided by the company are inequitable. What practical steps can you take to evaluate current policies and practices, or to ensure that perceptions of inequity are rectified?

11. What are some of the ethical issues to consider when linking pay and performance?

12. 'The need theories of motivation are culturally based.' Discuss this statement, examining in detail one of the need theories of motivation. In answering this question, you are encouraged to read an original work of the theorist associated with the theory you choose, such as David McClelland's *The Achieving Society*, or the works of Douglas McGregor and Abraham Maslow given in the end notes for this chapter.

13. Many companies in the service sector – large hotels and resorts, for example – are implementing empowerment strategies to improve the quality of service provided to residents and guests. Search the Internet for an example of such a company, with particular emphasis on strategies used to empower front-line staff.

INDIVIDUAL ACTIVITY

Are you motivated to work hard at your studies?

Fill out the following tables based on your work as a university or college student. This exercise should help to explain the level of effort you put into your studies at university or college, while also clarifying the way the expectancy theory of motivation is intended to work.

Connection 1: Expectancy (people's perception that a chosen course of action will result in desired outcomes).

How often do you feel that the following statements are true in your own case? Place a tick under the appropriate heading.

	Never	Sometimes	Often	Always
Spending twice as many hours on an assignment results in a higher grade.				
Studying consistently throughout the term leads to better results.				
Participating in class activities enhances my understanding of the subject or improves my grades.				
Being organized helps me handle the demands of being a student.				

Connection 2: Instrumentality (probability that your performance will result in various rewards and outcomes).

How likely are you to receive the following rewards if you work hard (put in the hours, study consistently, participate, try to be organized)? Place a tick under the appropriate heading.

	Never	Not very likely	Fairly likely	Very likely
A better academic record/transcript.				
More/better employment options.				
Peer acceptance.				
Sense of accomplishment.				
Building my knowledge/skills.				
Feeling good about myself.				
Avoidance of pressure and stress.				
A 'pat on the back' from my parents/family.				
Reward – holiday, dinner out etc.				
Other (specify).				

Connection 3: Valence (value of the reward outcome to you).

How important are each of the following rewards to you? Place a tick under the appropriate heading.

	Not important	Moderately important	Fairly important	Very important
A better academic record/transcript.				
More/better employment options.				
Peer acceptance.				
Sense of accomplishment.				
Building my knowledge/skills.				
Feeling good about myself.				
Avoidance of pressure and stress.				
A 'pat on the back' from my parents/family.				
Reward – holiday, dinner out etc.				
Other (specify).				

After you have completed the above sections, review your responses in the light of what expectancy theory tells us about motivation:

- What do your responses in the 'expectancy' section tell you about your level of confidence in your abilities, or the things that have discouraged/encouraged you in the past?
- Refer to your responses in the 'instrumentality' section. What do they tell you about the rewards you experience from your studies? Are they predominantly extrinsic, intrinsic or a mix of both?
- Compare the rewards you experience (or expect to experience) from your studies with the rewards you value from the 'valence' section. How well do they match one another? Are there any rewards that you value highly but do not expect to receive?
- Assess the 'multiplier effect' to explain the level of effort you put into your studies. Compare your results with those of others in the class. If your motivation to study is low, what can you do to improve it?
- Are the class selections motivators or hygiene factors? As a class, discuss whether you agree with Herzberg's two-factor theory.

Case Study

LONDON ELECTRICITY GROUP GIVES A HELPING HAND TO EMPLOYEE MOTIVATION

London Electricity (LE) Group's staff-volunteering programme, Helping Hands, made an impact right from its introduction – not only by contributing to communities, but also by building employee motivation, skills and a common identity across the business. The group is committed to sustainability and corporate responsibility (CR), understanding that this can both benefit the communities in which the company operates and drive fundamental business performance. Corporate community investment is part of this wider CR approach and includes encouraging employee volunteering with a focus on education and employability.

Active in the community

London Electricity Group has always been active in the community. The catalyst for board-level support and strategic direction, however, was a Business in the Community Seeing is Believing visit in Southwark, London, when the chief executive and other top managers were brought face-to-face with pressing social issues, and recognized the potential role of education and employability for neighbourhood renewal.

This led to the launch of 'Helping Hands', its first formal group-wide employee-volunteering scheme, which included the offer to all employees of two days' paid work time for volunteering. By the end of the first year, LE Group had achieved over 24% staff involvement across the group, rising to an impressive 50% within the Sunderland customer-service centre, at Doxford, all in line with the aim that Helping Hands becomes an important part of the corporate culture.

Business benefits of volunteering

The group executive understands the business benefits of volunteering and the company is committed to being a respected employer because the acquisition and retention of a talented and satisfied workforce is fundamental to business success. LE Group believes that Helping Hands directly contributes towards this. Feedback so far indicates that the programme is having a positive effect on motivation within the company and is also helping to build key skills. The scheme is seen as a dynamic and evolving initiative.

LE Group has four key stated corporate values, one of which is to excel in corporate responsibility and to work for sustainable development. Helping Hands is contributing to this. The objectives for the programme are to:

- complement existing training and management development;
- support and enhance the company's existing community investment;

Source: Viewpoint (2003), *Human Resource Management International Digest*, **11** (4), 35–37. Reproduced by permission of Emerald Insight.

- improve its contribution to specific social and economic issues, especially education, homelessness and regeneration; and
- enhance the company's reputation among its stakeholders.

The programme has been driven both through clear executive leadership and the natural take-up by employees.

Dedicated team

Helping Hands, along with the wider corporate community investment, is managed by a small dedicated team and delivered throughout the group by a network of coordinators within business units. The volunteering policy and information on getting involved are set out in publications and on an intranet, which includes a database of volunteering opportunities. Helping Hands works through partnerships to meet its aims and objectives. Schools are close to offices and are all in education action zones, releasing matched public-sector funding from regeneration budgets, through primary school and secondary school volunteering programmes.

Skill development is a fundamental objective. Senior managers, managers and graduates are all asked to contribute towards a community project through in-house training programmes. These range from team challenges to mentoring and enterprise programmes with schools. Community involvement is included in employee performance appraisals and career-development plans.

A central community-affairs budget of almost £500000 is supplemented by charitable gifts and community investment within business units. The actual level of total community investment across the group in 2001 reached 1.6% of pretax profits, and was included in the company's first corporate responsibility report in 2002. The report involved a new measurement regime including the London benchmarking group model and the business impact review group.

Positive impact on society

Helping Hands is designed to encourage and raise the capacity of employees to make a positive impact on society, specifically through education and employability. In its first eight months, 4665 hours of paid work time were completed. Of this, almost 60% was directed towards volunteering in more than 30 primary and secondary schools, all in education action zones. This leveraged more than £42500 from various public regeneration budgets. More than 140 children benefited from literacy and numeracy programmes, and 65 children were mentored. The value of this work in schools has been recognized in an Ofsted school inspection report. Employees have also taken on team challenges, such as developing school play areas and decorating classrooms. The company's Sunderland customer service centre has pioneered a graduate programme that matches university graduates within LE Group with high-potential year 11 pupils, to raise their aspirations and motivation. The company also arranges activity days at primary and secondary schools, which promote the workplace relevance of basic numeracy and literacy skills. Community activities also tackle adult employability and lifelong learning. Interview skill days are held for tenants from the Aylesbury estate in Southwark – principally for mothers keen to get back to work – with some participants taken on for short-term work placements. The company also looks for opportunities to link the education and employability activity, Helping Hands volunteering and sponsorship.

Increased loyalty to the company

LE Group recognizes the value of an active community programme to drive business perform- ance by building a vibrant workforce and customer base. Some 90% of volunteers confirm that doing so makes them feel more positive about working for the company, on the basis of the skills gained, the sense of responsibility and increased motivation. Senior managers have had the opportunity to apply problem-solving and strategy skills in entirely new contexts.

Helping Hands was put together in conjunction with the company's employer group – a team of senior executives who look at how to acquire, retain and develop a talented work- force. The programme also helps to build the company's group identity across business units, which is a major priority as the company grows across geographical locations and cultures. The scheme also encourages communication and team building within departments. Finally, Helping Hands and the broader community programme is a major factor driving positive media coverage for the company. The LE Group chief executive, Vincent de Rivaz, com- mented: 'Along with the rest of the executive, I am committed to finding ways in which all parts of the group can play a positive role in the community. It is no longer enough just to give cash – to give our skills and time is one of the most important ways we are able to have an impact and to make our contribution to the sustainable improvement of our community.'[78]

Questions

1. How do you think the Helping Hands programme contributes to employee motivation?
2. In what ways may these types of volunteering schemes satisfy higher-order needs as described by Maslow?
3. In what ways has the scheme been of benefit to the employer and the employees who have taken part and how might you sell these to other employers?
4. Is there a relationship between such volunteering schemes and work performance and, if so, what is it?

SUGGESTED READING

All OB books devote considerable time and space to motivation as a topic and many provide remarkably similar coverage. One recent textbook takes an innovative approach by locating motivation within the domain of leaders and leadership, with use of interesting examples and images. This is: Clegg, S., Kornberger, M. and Pitsis, T. (2005), *Managing and Organizations*, Sage: London.

Griffin, R. W and O'Leary-Kelly, A. M. (2004), *The Dark Side of Organisational Behaviour*, Jossey-Bass (Wiley) provides a framework for understanding current thinking on the negative consequences of organizational behaviour.

END NOTES

1. Chartered Institute of Personnel and Development (2009), How do I motivate my ostrich workers? *People Management Magazine,* 21 May, p. 38, CIPD: London.

2. *Management Today,* Brainfood: Ten Ways To Motivate your staff, 16 January 2006, p. 14.

3. Hofstede, G. (1993), Cultural constraints in management theories. *Academy of Management Executive,* **7** (February), 81–94.

4. Hofstede, G. (1984), *Cultural consequences: international differences in work-related values,* abridged edition. Sage: Beverley Hills.

5. Whitefield, G. B. 'Ask EOS' http://www. expat.or.id/business/employeemotivation.html (accessed 1 March 2010).

6. Campbell, J. P., Dunnette, M. D., Lawler, E. E. III & Weick, K. E. Jr (1970), *Managerial Behaviour Performance and Effectiveness,* McGraw-Hill: New York, Chapter 15.

7. Maslow, A. H. (1943), A theory of human motivation. *Psychological Review,* **50** (4), 370–396.

8. Porter, L. W. (1963), Job attitudes in management: II. Perceived importance of needs as a function of job level. *Journal of Applied Psychology,* **47** (April), 141–148.

9. Manolopoulos, D. (2006), What motivates R&D professionals? Evidence from decentralized laboratories in Greece. *International Journal of HRM,* **11,** 4 April, 616–647.

10. Hall, D. T. & Nougaim, K. E. (1968), An examination of Maslow's need hierarchy in an organizational setting. *Organizational Behaviour and Human Performance,* **3,** 12–35.

11. Porter, L. W. (1963), Job attitudes in management: IV. Perceived deficiencies in need fulfillment as a function of size of company. *Journal of Applied Psychology,* **47** (December), 386–397.

12. Ivancevich, J. M. (1969), Perceived need satisfactions of domestic versus overseas managers. *Journal of Applied Psychology,* **54** (August), 274–278.

13. Wahba, M. A. & Bridwell, L. G. (1974), Maslow reconsidered: a review of research on the need hierarchy theory. *Academy of Management Proceedings,* 514–520; Lawler, E. E. III & Shuttle, J. L. (1973), A causal correlation test of the need hierarchy concept. *Organizational Behaviour and Human Performance,* **7,** 265–287.

14. See Adler, N. J. (1991), *International Dimensions of Organizational Behaviour,* 2nd edn. PWS-Kent: Boston, MA, p. 153; Hodgetts, R. M. & Luthans, F. (1991), *International Management.* McGraw-Hill: New York.

15. Adler, op. cit., Ch. 11.

16. 'Ageing population will demand more private/public cooperation'. *Management* New Zealand: August 2007, pp 6–7.

17. Stock, P. (2007), 'Generation y is not a mutation'. *Human Resources,* 27 November, p. 3.

18. Donaldson, C. (2007), 'Much ado about nothing: generational change'. *Human Resources,* 27 November, p. 3.

19. See Alderfer, C. P. (1969), An empirical test of a new theory of human needs. *Organizational Behaviour and Human Performance,* **4,** 142–175; Alderfer, C. P. (1972), *Existence, Relatedness, and Growth.* The Free Press: New York; Schneider, B. & Alderfer, C. P. (1973), Three studies of need satisfaction in organizations. *Administrative Science Quarterly,* **18,** 489–505.

20. Tracy, L. (1984), A dynamic living systems model of work motivation. *Systems Research,* **1,** 191–203; Rauschenberger, J., Schmidt, N. & Hunter, J. E. (1980), A test of the need hierarchy concept by a Markov model of change in need strength. *Administrative Science Quarterly,* **25,** 654–670.

21. Alderfer, C. P. & Guzzo, R. A. (1979), Life experiences and adults' enduring strength of desires in organizations. *Administrative Science Quarterly,* **24,** 347–361.

22. Sources pertinent to this discussion are McClelland, D. C. (1961), *The Achieving Society*. Van Nostrand: New York; McClelland, D. C. (1962), Business, drive and national achievement. *Harvard Business Review*, **40** (July/August), 99–112; McClelland, D. C. (1966), That urge to achieve. *Think*, (November/December), 19–32; Litwin, G. H. & Stringer, R. A. (1966), *Motivation and Organizational Climate*. Division of Research, Harvard Business School: Boston, MA, pp. 18–25.

23. Harris, G. (1971), To know why men do what they do: a conversation with David C. McClelland. *Psychology Today*, **4** (January), 35–39.

24. Erikson, E. H. (1963), *Childhood and Society*, 2nd edn. Vintage: New York.

25. Miron, P. & McClelland, D. C. (1979), The impact of achievement motivation training in small businesses. *California Management Review*, Summer, 13–28.

26. McClelland, D. C. & Burnham, D. H. (1976), Power is the great motivator. *Harvard Business Review*, **54** (March/April), 100–110; McClelland, D. C. & Boyatzis, R. E. (1982), Leadership motive pattern and long-term success in management. *Journal of Applied Psychology*, **67**, 737–743.

27. Kelly, C. M. (1987), The interrelationship of ethics and power in today's organizations. *Organizational Dynamics*, **5** (Summer); Farrell, C. (1986), Gutfreund gives Salmon's young lions more power. *Business Week*, **32** (20 October); Solomon, J. (1987), Heirs apparent to chief executives often trip over prospect of power. *Wall Street Journal*, **29** (24 March).

28. Arnolds, C. A. & Boshoff, C. (2003), Compensation, esteem, valence and job performance: an empirical assessment of Alderfer's ERG theory. *International Journal of Human Resource Management*, **13** (4 June), 687–719.

29. The complete two-factor theory is well explained by Herzberg and his associates in Herzberg, F., Mausner, B. & Synderman, B. B. (1967), *The Motivation to Work*, 2nd edn. John Wiley & Sons: New York. See also Herzberg, F. (1968), One more time: how do you motivate employees? *Harvard Business Review*, **46** (January/February), 53–62.

30. See House, R. J. & Wigdor, L. A. (1967), Herzberg's dual-factor theory of job satisfaction and motivation: a review of the evidence and a criticism. *Personnel Psychology*, **20** (Winter), 369–389; Kerr, S., Harlan, A. & Stogdill, R. (1974), Preference for motivator and hygiene factors in a hypothetical interview situation. *Personnel Psychology*, **27** (Winter), 109–124.

31. Vroom, V. H. (1963), *Work and Motivation*. John Wiley & Sons, Ltd: Chichester.

32. See King, N. (1970), A clarification and evaluation of the two-factor theory of job satisfaction. *Psychological Bulletin*, July, 18–31; Dunnette, M., Campbell, J. & Hakel, M. (1967), Factors contributing to job satisfaction and job dissatisfaction in six occupational groups. *Organizational Behaviour and Human Performance*, May, 143–174; House & Wigdor, op. cit.

33. Adler, op. cit., Ch. 6; Adler, N. J. & Graham, J. T. (1989), Cross cultural interaction: the international comparison fallacy. *Journal of International Business Studies*, Fall, 515–537; Herzberg, F. (1987), Workers' needs: the same around the world. *Industry Week*, 27 September, 29–32.

34. Holmes, S. (2006), Nike goes for the green. *Business Week*, 25 September, 106.

35. Beatty, S. (2006), Big Green Investment. *Wall Street Journal*, 22 September, 2.

36. Carty, M. (2008), Green benefits in focus: Cutting edge practice at 3 organizations. *IRS Employment Review*, Iss. 901 24/7/2008.

37. *Personnel Today* (2009) Incentives plans to boost Cisco green agenda, 24 February, RBI.

38. Carty, M. (2008), op. cit.

39. *Personnel Today* (2008), BT links green scheme to staff retention, 25 March, RBI.

40. See, for example, Adams, J. S. (1963), Toward an understanding of inequality. *Journal of Abnormal and Social Psychology*, **67**, 422–436; Adams, J. S. (1965), Inequity in social exchange, in *Advances in Experimental Social Psychology*, vol. 2 (ed. L. Berkowitz). Academic Press: New York, pp. 267–300.

41. See Toronto Sun Publishing Corporation, *Wall Street Journal*, 9 March 1990, pp. B1–B2.

42. *Economist* (2010), Fair Dues – employees sniff out unfairness when money is involved. *Economist*, 13 February, 77.

43. Folger, R. & Konovsky, M. A. (1989), Effects of procedural and distributive justice on reactions to pay raise decisions. *Academy of Management Journal*, 32, 135–148.

44. Adler op. cit.

45. Dowling, P., Schuler, R. & Welch, D. (1994), *International Dimensions of Human Resource Management*. Wadsworth: Melbourne.

46. Vroom, V. H. (1964), *Work and Motivation*. John Wiley & Sons, Inc.: New York.

47. For an excellent review see Mowday, R. T. (1987), Equity theory predictions of behaviour in organizations, in *Motivation and Work Behaviour*, 4th edn (eds R. M. Steers & L. W. Porter). McGraw-Hill: New York, pp. 89–110.

48. Salancik, G. R. & Pfeffer, J. (1978), A social information processing approach to job attitudes and task design. *Administrative Science Quarterly*, 23 (June), 224–253.

49. See Mitchell, T. R. (1974), Expectancy models of job satisfaction, occupational preference and effort: a theoretical, methodological, and empirical appraisal. *Psychological Bulletin*, 81, 1053–1077; Wahba, M. A. & House, R. J. (1974), Expectancy theory in work and motivation: some logical and methodological issues. *Human Relations*, 27 (January), 121–147; Connolly, T. (1976), Some conceptual and methodological issues in expectancy models of work performance motivation. *Academy of Management Review*, 1 (October), 37–47; Mitchell, T. (1980), Expectancy-value Models in Organizational Psychology, in *Expectancy, Incentive and Action* (ed. N. Feather), Erlbaum: New York.

50. Mitchell, T. R. (1982), Motivation – new directions for theory, research and practice. *Academy of Management Review*, 7 (January), 80–81.

51. Porter, L. W. & Lawler, E. E. III (1968), *Managerial Attitudes and Performance*, Richard D. Irwin: Homewood, IL.

52. This integrated model is not only based on the Porter and Lawler model but is consistent with the kind of comprehensive approach suggested by Evans in a recent review. See Evans, M. G. (1986), Organizational behaviour: the central role of motivation, in Yearly Review of Management (eds J. G. Hunt & J. D. Blair). *Journal of Management*, 12, 203–222.

53. Nohria, N., Groysberg, B. & Lee, L. (2008), Employee Motivation. *Harvard Business Review*, 86 (7/8), 78–84.

54. For further explanation of alternatives to process and content theories of motivation, see Leonard, N., Beauvais, L. & Scholl, R. (1999), Work motivation: the incorporation of self-concept-based processes. *Human Relations*, 52 (8), 969–998; McKenna, R. (2000), Identity, not motivation: the key to employee-organisation relations, in *Management and Organizational Behaviour* (eds R. Wiesner & B. Millett). John Wiley & Sons: Brisbane, pp. 35–45.

55. Chubb, L. (2008), Improvements are key motivation for NHS staff. *People Management Magazine*, 23 June, CIPD: London.

56. Samson, K. (2004/5), Research off the map. *HR Monthly*, December/January, 34–35.

57. Macken, D. (2004), My job-juggling career. *The Weekend Australian Financial Review*, 6–7 March, 25.

58. YOYOY (2006), *IRS Employment Review*, issue 845, 4.

59. Lui, J. (2004), Asia Pacific 25: not by price alone. *Managing Information Strategies*, (special annual issue), 73–86.

60. Spinelli, M. A. & Gray, G. R. (2003), How important is compensation for job satisfaction of retail trainers? Some evidence. *Employee Benefit Plan Reviews*, 58 (5), 29.

61. Lawler, E. E. III (1981), *Pay and Organizational Development*, Addison-Wesley: Reading, MA.

62. Lawler, E. E. III (1971), *Pay and Organizational Effectiveness*, McGraw-Hill: New York; Lawler (1981), op. cit.; Lawler, E. E. III (1987), The design of effective systems, in *Handbook of Organizational Behaviour* (ed. J. W. Lorsch), Prentice Hall: Englewood Cliffs, NJ.

63. Rynes, S., Gerhart, B. & Minette, K. (2004), The importance of pay in employee motivation: discrepancies between what people say and what they do. *Human Resource Management*, 43 (4), 381–394.

64. Wiley, C. (1997), What motivates employees according to 40 years of motivation surveys.

International Journal of Manpower, **18** (3), 263–280.

65. Weaver, T. (1988), Theory M: Motivating with money. *Cornell HRA Quarterly*, **29** (3), 40–45.

66. YOYOY (2006), op. cit.

67. See DTI (2003), *Balancing Work and Family Life: Enhancing Choice and Support for Parents*. HMSO: London; DTI (2002), *More People Want Flexible Hours than Cash, Company Car or Gym*. HMSO: London.

68. Furnham, A., Kirkaldy, B. D. & Lynn, R. (1994), National attitudes to competitiveness, money and work amongst young people: first, second and third world differences. *Human Relations*, **47** (1), 119–132.

69. Robbins, S. P. (1996), *Organizational Behaviour*, Prentice Hall: Englewood Cliffs, NJ.

70. Furnham, A. & Booth, T. (2006), *Just for the Money: What really motivates us at work*, Cyan Books: London.

71. Pearce, J. L. (1987), Why merit pay doesn't work: implications from organizational theory, in *New Perspectives on Compensation* (eds D. B. Balkin & L. R. Gomez-Mejia), Prentice Hall: Englewood Cliffs, NJ, pp. 214–224; Lawler, E. E. III (1989), Pay for performance: making it work. *Compensation and Benefits Review*, **21** (1), 55–60.

72. See Boyle, D. C. (1992), Employee motivation that works. *HR Magazine*, **37** (10), 83–89.

73. Weinberg, N. (2002), Hidden treasure, *Forbes*, 28 October, 58.

74. Sanghera, S. (2010), Do bankers' bonuses really work? *The Times*, 21 January.

75. Edridge, M. (2007), Lessons for Corporates. *Management*, August, 19.

76. Gist, M. E. (1987), Self-efficacy: implications in organizational behaviour and human resource management. *Academy of Management Review*, **12**, 472–485; Bandura, A. (1987), Self-efficacy mechanism in human agency. *American Psychologist*, **37**, 122–147.

77. Conger, J. A. & Kanungo, R. N. (1988), The empowerment process: integrating theory and practice. *Academy of Management Review*, **13** (3), 471–482.

78. Lussier, R. N. (1993), *Human Relations in Organizations: a skill building approach*, 2nd edn. Richard D. Irwin: Homewood, IL. © The McGraw-Hill Companies, Inc. Reproduced by permission.

Journal Article

MAKING THINGS HAPPEN: A MODEL OF PROACTIVE MOTIVATION

Sharon K. Parker, *University of Western Australia*

Uta K. Bindl and Karoline Strauss, *University of Sheffield*

Being proactive is about making things happen, anticipating and preventing problems, and seizing opportunities. It involves self-initiated efforts to bring about change in the work environment and/or oneself to achieve a different future. The authors develop existing perspectives on this topic by identifying proactivity as a goal-driven process involving both the setting of a proactive goal (proactive goal generation) and striving to achieve that proactive goal (proactive goal striving). The authors identify a range of proactive goals that individuals can pursue in organizations. These vary on two dimensions: the future they aim to bring about (achieving a better personal fit within one's work environment, improving the organization's internal functioning, or enhancing the organization's strategic fit with its environment) and whether the self or situation is being changed. The authors then identify "can do," "reason to," and "energized to" motivational states that prompt proactive goal generation and sustain goal striving. Can do motivation arises from perceptions of self-efficacy, control, and (low) cost. Reason to motivation relates to why someone is proactive, including reasons flowing from intrinsic, integrated, and identified motivation. Energized to motivation refers to activated positive affective states that prompt proactive goal processes. The authors suggest more distal antecedents, including individual differences (e.g., personality, values, knowledge and ability) as well as contextual variations in leadership, work design, and interpersonal climate, that influence the proactive motivational states and thereby boost or inhibit proactive goal processes. Finally, the authors summarize priorities for future research.

Keywords: proactive; proactivity; motivation; self-regulation; initiative; work behavior

Because our team is a new team, the Process Map that we've got for our task is quite out of date really. It was done quite a while ago and the systems and the business have changed since then.…I suggested that the people that work the tasks write their own Process Map as they're doing it and then we all get together in a room and say "this is my process, this is yours" and just re-do the whole thing.

Call center agent, energy company

Corresponding author: Sharon K. Parker, UWA Business School, The University of Western Australia, M261, 35 Stirling Highway, Crawley WA, 6009, Australia

E-mail: Sharon.Parker@uwa.edu.au

Taken from: Journal of Management, 36: 827. Originally published online 14 May 2010. doi: 10.1177/01492063 10363732, reprinted by permission of Sage Publication.

Being proactive is about taking control to make things happen rather than watching things happen. It involves aspiring and striving to bring about change in the environment and/or oneself to achieve a different future (Bindl & Parker, in press-b; Grant & Ashford, 2008). Proactivity has three key attributes: It is self-starting, change oriented, and future focused. The call center agent described above has taken it on herself (self-starting) to aim to improve work processes (change the situation) to enhance effectiveness in the longer term (achieve a different future).

The call centre example shows being proactive is meaningful at the lowest levels of organizations. Proactivity is also relevant at the highest levels: Deluga (1998) showed that U.S. presidents vary in their proactivity and that proactive presidents are rated by historians as more effective in leading the country than are passive presidents. This study concurs with wider evidence that proactivity can enhance work place performance (for a meta-analysis, see Fuller & Marler, 2009) as well as generate positive outcomes beyond work performance, such as obtaining employment (Kanfer, Wanberg, & Kantrowitz, 2001) and career satisfaction (Seibert, Kraimer, & Crant, 2001).

But where does proactivity come from? Why are some people proactive in improving their work context whereas others are more focused on actively sculpting their own careers? Can a manager enhance employees' job proactivity? Understanding how proactivity is motivated is our focus in this article. To set the scene, we review ways of conceptualizing proactivity.

BACKGROUND TO PROACTIVITY AS A CONCEPT

Traditional theories of motivation and performance, such as equity theory and goal setting theory, have tended to consider employees as passive, reactive respondents to their context. For example, early goal setting theory largely assumed that goals are given to individuals and need to be accepted by them, and expectancy theory focused on the rewards and outcomes allocated by the organization. However, there has been a growing recognition of the role that employees play in actively shaping and influencing their environment. For example, employees can set goals for themselves and create their own rewards (Crant, 2000; Frese & Fay, 2001; Grant & Ashford, 2008).

One of the most important active work concepts to be introduced into the literature is "personal initiative." Kring, Soose, and Zempel (1996: 38) defined personal initiative as a constellation of behaviors with the following attributes: consistent with the organization's mission, a long-term focus, goal directed and action oriented, persistent in the face of barriers and setbacks, and self-starting and proactive. A stream of research has focused on this concept, showing, for example, that personal initiative is affected by the work context (for a review, see Frese & Fay, 2001). In addition to proactive forms of work performance such as personal initiative (also see Griffin, Neal, & Parker's, 2007, concept of proactive performance), proactive concepts have been identified in the literature on organizational citizenship, such as taking charge (Morrison & Phelps, 1999) and change-oriented citizenship (Choi, 2007). Similarly, the work design literature has increasingly aimed to account for employees' agency in shaping their tasks, jobs, and roles (Parker, Wall, & Jackson, 1997; Wrzesniewski & Dutton, 2001). Other topic areas in which employees' active role has been acknowledged include the literatures on organizational change (e.g., Dutton & Ashford, 1993, on issue selling; Scott & Bruce, 1994, on innovation), organizational socialization (Ashford & Cummings, 1985), and career development (e.g., Rousseau, Ho, & Greenberg, 2006).

This phenomenon-oriented approach to proactivity has certainly enriched the understanding of these constructs. However, it has been increasingly recognized that there are potential commonalities in these disparate concepts. An initial approach to integration was to identify "proactive personality" as a determinant of proactive behavior across many different domains. Bateman and Crant (1993: 105) defined a proactive person as someone with a "relatively stable behavioral tendency" to initiate change in the environment. This personality-based approach assumes proactive individuals are proactive across multiple contexts and over time, regardless of the contingencies of a situation. Much research has shown that proactive personality is associated with positive outcomes across many domains, such as job performance (Thompson, 2005), career success (Seibert *et al.*, 2001), and charismatic leadership (Crant & Bateman, 2000).

A further development has been to recognize that there are likely common motivational processes across different types of proactive behavior, beyond proactive personality as a driver (Crant, 2000; Frese & Fay, 2001; Grant & Ashford, 2008; Parker & Collins, 2010). Parker, Williams, and Turner (2006: 636) suggested that "despite different labels and theoretical underpinnings, concepts that relate to individual-level proactive behavior typically focus on self-initiated and future-oriented action that aims to change and improve the situation or oneself." Building on this definition, as well as on Frese and colleagues' description of personal initiative as an action sequence (Frese & Fay, 2001), Grant and Ashford (2008) suggested that proactivity is not a unique set of behaviors, such as particular feedback seeking behaviors, but rather is most usefully considered as a process involving anticipating, planning, and striving to have an impact. As such, proactivity is not purely extrarole, as some have suggested, but all tasks can be carried out in a more or less proactive way: "The key criterion for identifying proactive behavior is not whether it is in-role or extra-role, but rather whether the employee anticipates, plans for, and attempts to create a future outcome that has an impact on the self or environment" (Grant & Ashford, 2008: 9). Griffin *et al.* (2007) similarly argued that team-oriented behaviors such as helping and organization-oriented behaviors such as loyalty can be carried out more or less proactively.

Thus, in moving on from considering a proliferation of proactive concepts across many domains, a consensus has begun to emerge that proactivity is a future-focused, change-oriented way of behaving, or a process. In this article, we further develop this perspective by identifying proactivity as a goal-driven process involving both setting a proactive goal (proactive goal generation) and striving to achieve that proactive goal (proactive goal striving). We identify a range of proactive goals that individuals can pursue. We then identify "can do," "reason to," and "energized to" motivational states as prompting proactive goal generation and goal striving within particular domains. We use this model to discuss more distal antecedents of proactive behavior. The overall model is summarized in Figure 1. Finally, we identify future research directions, based on the model and extending beyond it.

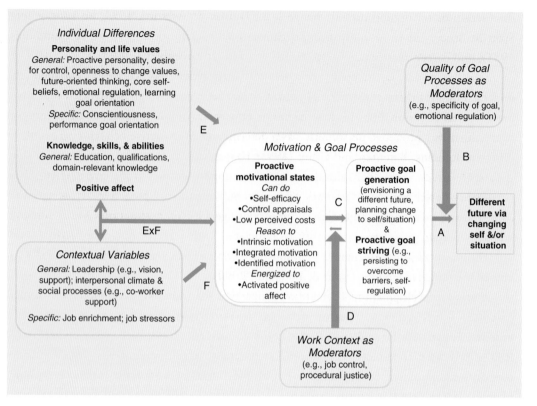

Figure 1: Model of Proactive Motivation Process and Antecedents.

PROACTIVITY AS A GOAL-DRIVEN PROCESS

Our primary perspective is that proactive action is motivated, conscious, and goal directed. Thus, to understand what prompts, stifles, and shapes proactivity, one can look to motivation theories, particularly to self-regulation theory (Bandura, 1991), which in turn draws on other theories such as goal-setting theory (Locke & Latham, 1990) and expectancy theory (Vroom, 1964). We recognize evidence that individuals' goals are hierarchically organized into two broad systems (Kanfer & Ackerman, 1989): Individuals anticipate desired future states or outcomes and develop strategies to reach those goals (goal generation) and then mobilize and monitor their day-to-day behaviors to attain their goals (goal striving).

Goal generation processes are those by which an individual allocates his or her time or energy across behaviors or tasks, including selecting goals and planning activities to achieve them (Locke & Latham, 1990). Goal generation processes occur prior to task engagement, creating a "road map for action" (Chen & Kanfer, 2006).

Proactive goal generation involves envisioning and planning, under one's own volition, the goal to bring about a new and different future by changing the self and/or the environment. Thus, proactive goal generation is self-initiated: The individual acts on his or her own volition rather than as the result of a specification or direction given by someone else. The degree of self-initiation varies from initiating one's own end (e.g., coming up with a new work goal) to accepting a specified end but initiating the means (e.g., introducing a new product as requested but in a way that uses one's initiative; Grant & Ashford, 2008).

This self-initiation both signals and expresses psychological ownership of the change target (Wagner, Parker, & Christianson, 2003).

Proactive goal generation involves at least two processes: envisioning and planning (Bindl & Parker, 2009; also see Frese & Fay, 2001; Grant & Ashford, 2008, who identified related processes). Envisioning involves perceiving a current or future problem or opportunity, and imagining a different future that can be achieved by actively addressing this problem or opportunity. Envisioning involves anticipating future outcomes and mentally representing and imagining a person, situation, or event at some forward point in time (Grant & Ashford, 2008). Although there are many future states that an individual might envisage, an empirical study by Parker and Collins (in press) identified three higher order categories of individual-level proactive behavior at work. Each varies in the future the individual is aiming to create.

The first category is proactive person–environment (PE) fit behavior, which encompasses proactive goals to achieve a better fit between one's own attributes and those of the internal work environment. For example, to achieve demand–abilities fit (when individuals have the knowledge, skills, and other resources demanded by the environment), individuals can actively gather information about their performance or engage in proactive feedback seeking (Ashford & Black, 1996). Likewise, individuals can proactively achieve supplies–values fit (when the environment supplies the attributes desired by an individual) by actively negotiating changes in their job so that it better fits their skills, abilities, and preferences, or job-role negotiation (Ashford & Black, 1996).

Proactive work behavior, the second category, involves proactive goals to improve the internal organizational environment (Parker & Collins, in press). Taking charge to improve work methods (Morrison & Phelps, 1999) and proactive problem solving (Parker, Williams, et al., 2006) are example behaviors in this category. Griffin et al. (2007) identified three types of proactive work behavior: improving one's individual tasks (e.g., introducing more efficient work methods), improving one's tasks as a team member (e.g., making suggestions to improve team working), and improving one's tasks as a member of the organization (e.g., participating in projects to improve organization-wide practices).

The third higher order category is proactive strategic behavior, and this involves taking control and bringing about change to improve the organization's strategy and its fit with the external environment. Issue selling, in which managers proactively aim to influence the formation of strategy in organizations (Dutton & Ashford, 1993), and strategic scanning (Parker & Collins, in press), in which employees proactively survey the fit between the organization and its environment, are example behaviors.

Having envisioned a different future, the process of planning involves the individual deciding on which actions to take to achieve this future (Bindl & Parker, 2009). In broad terms, we suggest the envisioned future can be achieved by changing the self, such as the individual developing his or her new skills, building new networks, and acquiring more information, or by changing the situation, such as revising work methods, influencing his or her peers, or persuading a leader to change strategic direction. In many situations, the plans for achieving the envisioned future state will involve changing both the self and

	Envisioned Future Outcome[a]		
Locus of change	Greater compatibility between one's own attributes and the organizational environment (proactive person–environment fit behavior)	Improved functioning of the internal organizational environ-ment (proactive work behavior)	Improved strategic fit between the organization and its environment (proactive strategic behavior)
Changing oneself	Seek out feedback from supervisor to enhance performance; establish meeting with supervisor to identify career opportunities; seek out new projects to develop skills	Seek out feedback from supervisor to enhance performance; identify and acquire new technological skills in anticipation of a new IT system; build relationships with managers from other departments	Identify and select a coach to improve strategic thinking; build networks to learn about competitors; enhance knowledge about industry developments by seeking out new partners
Changing others or the situation	Negotiate an i-deal prior to job entry that fits individual needs; renegotiate work load demands with supervisor; craft job duties to enhance meaning	Introduce new work methods; change the communication system for the team; establish a committee to review the organization's absence policies	Persuade leaders to change strategy; restructure the organization to position for potential threat against competitors; change strategic focus to exploit emerging markets

Table 1: Illustrative Proactive Goals That Arise Out of Proactive Goal Generation.

the situation. In Table 1, we show illustrative proactive goals that arise from considering both what it is the individual aims to achieve (the envisioned future) and how the individual plans to bring about that future outcome (the locus of change).

Proactive Goal Striving

Drawing on Kanfer and Ackerman (1989), we define proactive goal striving as the behavioral and psychological mechanisms by which individuals purposively seek to accomplish proactive goals. Generating a proactive goal without striving is not proactive per se, as it does not produce an impact on oneself or the environment.

Bindl and Parker (2009) identified enacting and reflecting as two key elements of proactive goal striving. Enacting is the overt action individuals engage in to achieve their proactive goal. In the case of an employee wishing to improve a process, enacting might involve persuading colleagues about the advantages of the strived-for change and finding new ways of moving forward in the face of obstacles. Not all enacted action will appear proactive, especially in isolation. For example, in taking charge to improve the way a team works, an individual might consciously withhold his or her view to allow other team members to speak. Likewise, an individual might adapt to a problematic situation in the short term while building alliances to change the situation in the longer term. In this vein, Berg,

Wrzesniewski, and Dutton (2010) argued that proactive job crafting both requires and triggers adaptive behavior, such as adjusting one's expectations.

Effective self-regulation is important when enacting proactive goals, such as keeping focused on the task rather than being distracted by off-task demands. Bringing about change is often challenging and likely involves a need to persist (Frese & Fay, 2001)—often more so than task-compliant or reactive action does (Sheldon & Elliot, 1999). As we discuss shortly, proactive action often stems out of personally held beliefs about what is important, or a strong ownership, which likely creates the resilience for persisting. At the same time, the greater engagement of the self also suggests potentially stronger emotions, and therefore emotional regulation is likely to be very important when pursuing self-set goals (Kanfer & Kantrowitz, 2002).

Reflecting is a further phase of proactive goal striving (Bindl & Parker, 2009; Frese & Fay, 2001). Reflecting consists of an individual's efforts to understand the success, failure, or consequences of his or her proactive behavior. These efforts ultimately serve as information that leads an individual to sustain or modify the proactive goals set by an individual or to modify his or her efforts to achieve those goals (Gollwitzer, 1990). Individuals tend to remain with an action if they believe they are satisfactorily progressing toward their goal (Carver & Scheier, 1998). Given that achieving proactive goals is often highly ambiguous, intensive reflecting processes are likely to facilitate judgments as to whether a proactive goal should be maintained or modified (Gollwitzer, 1990).

In sum, individuals generate and strive for a range of proactive goals that vary both in the future they are trying to achieve through change and the locus of change (self or situation) for achieving that future. As we depict in Figure 1, these proactive goal processes will lead to a different future and change to the extent that individuals engage in both proactive goal generation and goal striving (Path A). In addition, attributes of the goals generated and the quality of the striving process will influence the extent to which a different future and change is achieved (Path B). For example, theory and evidence suggest that proactive goals will be more likely to result in effective striving, and hence achievement of the goal, if they are specific and challenging (Locke & Latham, 1990), are learning focused rather than solely performance oriented (Dweck, 1986), and include subgoals and planning (Chen & Gogus, 2008). Likewise, the more that striving to achieve a proactive goal involves effective self-regulation, such as dealing with emotions associated with setbacks and engagement in appropriate reflection, the more likely that proactive goals will continue to be pursued rather than abandoned.

Importantly, we have thus far not considered where the impetus for setting and striving for a proactive goal in a particular domain comes from. It is to this we now turn.

PROACTIVE MOTIVATION STATES

Why does one individual decide to take the risk of implementing a new work method whereas another individual instead focuses on actively shaping his or her career path within the organization? The fact that an individual might pursue proactive goals to achieve one future-oriented outcome but not another shows it is insufficient to focus on personality as the sole motivator of proactive action. One needs to understand the individual's motivational state in the corresponding context and in relation to the envisioned future. It is therefore important to consider proactive motivation states that are more proximal to goals and action. It is these states that drive goal generation and striving (Figure 1, Path C), and it is largely through these states that more distal variables—personality and other individual differences (Path E), the work context (Path F), and the interaction of individual differences and context (Path ExF)—have their influence.

In the proactivity literature, most attention has been given to what we refer to as "can do" and "reason to" motivational states (e.g., Parker, Williams, *et al.*, 2006). The can do state maps onto theories focused on expectancy, such as self-efficacy theory and control theory, in which the main question is, "Can I do this?"; the reason to state maps onto theories based on why people engage (in behavior), or valence (e.g., Do I want to do this? Why should I act?), such as theories concerned with self-determination, flow, interest, and goal orientation. Some theories recognize both. For example, expectancy-value theories (e.g., Eccles *et al.*, 1983) propose ways in which both expectations of success (can do) and subjective task value (reason to) influence goals. We next review evidence that proactive goal regulation is influenced by can do and reason to motivational states. We then discuss the role of affect and propose an "energized to" pathway.

Can Do Motivation

Can do motivation includes self-efficacy perceptions (Can I do it?), control appraisals and attributions (e.g., How feasible is it?), and the perceived costs of action (e.g., How risky is it?).

Drawing on self-regulation theory, scholars have proposed that setting a proactive goal is likely to involve a deliberate decision process in which the individual assesses the likely outcomes of his or her behaviors (Morrison & Phelps, 1999; Parker, Williams, *et al.*, 2006). A belief that one can be successful in a particular domain, or high self-efficacy, is likely to be especially important in proactive goal generation because being proactive entails quite a high potential psychological risk to the individual. Using one's personal initiative and taking charge to improve work methods, for example, involve changing the situation, which can often be met by resistance and skepticism from others. Likewise, active feedback seeking involves risks to individuals' ego and perceived image (Ashford, Blatt, & VandeWalle, 2003). Individuals therefore need to feel confident they can both initiate proactive goals and deal with their consequences before they act. Self-efficacy has also been shown to enhance persistence and increase individuals' willingness to overcome obstacles (Bandura, 1997), both of which have been suggested as important for successful proactive action (Frese& Fay, 2001).

In support of this reasoning, meta-analytic studies show that job-search self-efficacy is positively linked with proactive job search (Kanfer *et al.*, 2001). Similarly, judgments of the perceived capability to go over and beyond the prescribed job tasks ("role-breadth self-efficacy"; Parker, 1998) predict proactive behaviors such as the suggestion of improvements (Axtell, Holman, Unsworth, Wall, & Waterson, 2000) and proactive problem solving and idea implementation (Parker, Williams, *et al.*, 2006).

General perceptions of self-efficacy have also been shown to be positively related to taking charge (Morrison & Phelps, 1999) as well as to personal initiative (Frese, Garst, & Fay, 2007), although in a study that included both general job-related self-efficacy and role-breadth self-efficacy, Ohly and Fritz (2007) found that only the latter predicted proactive work behavior. This study supports the importance of specific capability perceptions for the relevant target of impact. Furthermore, in one of the only studies to separate goal generation from goal striving, Bindl and Parker (2009) found that role-breadth self-efficacy uniquely predicted each of proactive envisioning, planning, enacting, and reflecting, which concurs with the wider motivation literature that shows self-efficacy enhances both goal generation and striving (Bandura, 1997).

In addition to confidence in specific and relevant capabilities being important, it is important to believe that the behavior at stake will lead to the desired outcome (Vroom, 1964). In regard to proactive work behavior, Frese and Fay (2001) identified as important for personal initiative individuals' expectations that they feel they control the situation and have an impact on the outcomes. Individuals with high control appraisals were proposed to maintain a strong sense of responsibility, to not give up easily, to search for opportunities to act, to have high hopes for success, and to actively search for information. In a longitudinal study, Frese, Garst, and Fay (2000, cited in Frese & Fay, 2001) found that control appraisals led to greater personal initiative. Interestingly, Parker, Williams, *et al.* (2006) did not find that control appraisals contributed to predicting proactive work behavior over and above self-efficacy perceptions and flexible role orientation, suggesting further research is needed to assess the incremental validity of control appraisals. It is also unknown as to whether control appraisals are equally important in both proactive goal generation and goal striving. For example, high control appraisal might be most important for maintaining high levels of effort after setbacks. With low perceived control, difficulties might be interpreted as signaling that the goal is not attainable and thus lead to goal disengagement. Control appraisals are also likely to assume more importance for pursuing proactive goals that involve changing the situation (bottom row of Table 1) than for proactive action that mostly focuses on changing aspects of oneself (top row of Table 1).

The perceived cost of behavior is also relevant to can do motivation (Eccles & Wigfield, 2002). Perceived costs refer to the negative aspects of engaging in the task, such as fear of failure (or success) and the opportunities lost by focusing on this action rather than another. Aspinwall (2005) suggested that individuals will not engage in proactive coping if they perceive the effort involved as too costly in terms of time, money, energy, or other resources relative to the gain they may provide. Kanfer and Ackerman (1989) argued that goal striving, such as staying on track, requires attentional resources that are finite. Thus, individuals might judge the costs of proactive action as excessive, thereby failing to set proactive goals, or they might set off to achieve a proactive goal but realize that the costs involved are too high and revise their goals accordingly.

One would expect that the perceived costs of proactive action will depend on the scope of the envisioned future outcome (e.g., the number of people involved) and whether the primary focus of change is the self or the situation. Considering Table 1, for proactive goals in the top left-hand corner that involve changing the self to achieve better fit within one's environment, the perceived costs will likely revolve around self-oriented concerns, such as the threat to one's ego of making mistakes. For example, individuals' motives to protect or enhance their ego and avoid threats to their image influence the extent and nature of proactive feedback seeking (Ashford, Blatt, & VandeWalle, 2003). In contrast, potential costs associated with setting out to restructure the organization to enhance strategic fit (bottom right-hand side of Table 1) likely involve not only image- and ego-oriented concerns but also other-oriented, or prosocial, concerns about the possible wasted time and effort of many individuals or even threatened job security if the wrong action is taken.

Reason To Motivation

Although can do theories are important, these theories do not deal with why individuals select or persist with particular proactive goals. People might feel able to improve work methods, for example, but have no compelling reason to do so. Individuals therefore need to want to be proactive or see value associated with being proactive to achieve a different future. When goals are imposed or prescribed via some external regulation, there is already a reason to carry out the goal—it is expected or necessary. For self-initiated goals, however, the reason to element cannot be taken for granted. As Griffin *et al.* (2007) suggested, proactive work behavior is often most important in "weak" situations (Mischel & Shoda, 1995) in which individuals have high levels of discretion, goals are not tightly specified, the means for achieving them are uncertain, and attainment is not clearly linked to rewards. Under such circumstances there needs to be a strong internal force driving the potentially risky behavior of proactivity. Moreover, temporal construal theory suggests that the desirability of future goals (the "why" of an action) is a stronger determinant than feasibility (the "how" of an action) when goals are in the longer term rather than the near term (Liberman & Trope, 1998). The why aspects of an action are more abstract, high level, and related to meaning than are how aspects and hence are more resistant to change as well as more robust (Wegener, Vallacher, Kiersted, & Dizadjii, 1986). Thus, reason to motivation might be more important in proactive goal processes than can do states, particularly for very long-term oriented proactive goals.

Reason to motivation is well recognized in existing theory, such as the concept of utility judgments in expectancy theory (Vroom, 1964). Utility judgments, or how well a task relates to current and future goals such as career goals, drive individuals' goal commitment and their determination to reach the goal (Eccles *et al.*, 1983). We recognize the role of utility judgments in driving proactive processes in our model, but we also go beyond this theory and identify additional reason to pathways. We draw on self-determination theory (Deci & Ryan, 2000) because, by definition, proactive behavior is autonomous (self-initiated) rather than externally regulated by contingencies outside the person. As self-determination theory proposes, different types of autonomous motivation can drive proactive goal processes, as we elaborate next.

First, individuals will be more likely to set and strive for proactive goals when they find their tasks enjoyable, intrinsically interesting, or a source of flow. Self-determination theory proposes that humans are motivated to maintain an optimum level of stimulation and thus have basic needs for competence, autonomy, and relatedness. Being proactive can increase challenge, thereby fulfilling individuals' basic needs for competence and autonomy. An example of proactivity generated by intrinsic motivation is individuals who voluntarily, often in their own time, engage in the development of new open-source software because they find it intellectually stimulating (Lakhani & Wolf, 2003). In a related vein, proactivity can be motivated by the experience of flow, which is when an individual narrows his or her focus to an activity in which he or she feels immersed, forgetting time, tiredness, and everything but the activity (Csikszentmihalyi, 1988). Because challenge needs to be relatively high before flow is possible (Massimini & Carli, 1988), individuals need increasingly greater challenge to experience flow. The desire for flow can therefore prompt proactive action, such as crafting a job to take on more difficult tasks, or striking an i-deal with a supervisor to get involved in new, challenging projects (Rousseau *et al.*, 2006).

Individuals also pursue proactive goals even if they are not especially enjoyable or intrinsically motivating. Self-determination theory proposes a process of internalization or integration in which the individual "takes in" a value, contingency, or regulation (internalization) or transforms that regulation into his or her own so that it subsequently emanates from the self (integration). The most autonomous form of extrinsic motivation is integrated regulation in which "people have a full sense that the behavior is an integral part of who they are, that it emanates from their sense of self and is thus self-determined" (Gagné & Deci, 2005: 335). Thus, a second reason to set and strive for proactive goals is to fulfill important life goals or express values that are central to the self. For example, individuals with a "calling" are those for whom work is seen as inseparable from life, who work not for money or career advancement alone but for fulfillment and because the work is seen as socially valuable (Wrzesniewski, McCauley, Rozin, & Schwartz, 1997). Those with a calling are proposed to engage in active job crafting (Wrzesniewski & Dutton, 2001) because of their high investment in the work. According to the self-concordance model (Sheldon & Elliot, 1999), goals consistent with individuals' core values and interests are associated with enhanced goal striving. Thus, the more the envisioned future is central to one's identity or values, the more one will be motivated to bring about that future. For example, if one's identity is tightly bound up in one's team or organization, one will feel ownership for improving that team or organization (Gagné & Deci, 2005) and therefore will be likely to set proactive work goals or proactive strategic goals. In contrast, if one has an extremely strong career identity, one is likely to pursue proactive career management or person-environment fit goals.

Proactive goals not only are linked to current identities but also can be motivated by future-oriented identities. Strauss, Griffin, and Parker (2009) identified the concept of "future work self," an imagined, hoped-for future identity that captures an individual's hopes and aspirations in relation to his or her career. Like other possible future and past identities, future work selves serve as a standard against which the present self can be compared (Carver & Scheier, 1998) and constitute "motivational resources that individuals can use in the control and direction of their own actions" (Oyserman & Markus, 1990: 122).

Strauss *et al.* showed that future work selves pertaining to individuals' careers were associated with more proactive career oriented behaviours such as career planning.

A further autonomous form of motivation is "identified regulation" in which an individual consciously values the behavioral goal or regulation such that the action is accepted or owned as personally important. Identified regulation is similar to the utility judgment in expectancy theory as well as to the instrumental motive in the feedback seeking literature (Ashford *et al.*, 2003). Thus, a third reason that individuals will pursue proactive goals is because they recognize that change toward the envisioned future outcome is important, for themselves and/or for others. For example, the more that an individual perceives that feedback will be diagnostically useful to achieving his or her goals, the more he or she engages in feedback seeking (Ashford *et al.*, 2003). As a further example, a nurse might identify a way to help speed up the discharge of a patient, not because this is an enjoyable task (intrinsic motivation) nor because this is fundamental to his or her identity as a carer (integrated motivation) but because he or she accepts the importance of patient flow for the effective functioning of the hospital (identified motivation).

Significantly, in addition to the nurse understanding the importance of the goal, he or she must accept personal responsibility for the goal. It is not enough to believe that proactive action is important, however, to then consider that the action is "someone else's job." Relevant to this perspective is the concept of flexible role orientation (Parker *et al.*, 1997) in which individuals report ownership and feel responsibility for problems and goals beyond their immediate tasks. Parker and Ohly (2008) suggested that flexible role orientation can be seen as indicative of the process of internalization in which individuals "take on" external values and regulatory structures. Individuals with flexible role orientations define their role broadly and thus experience a sense of accountability for broader goals beyond completing their core tasks. Evidence suggests individuals with a flexible role orientation are indeed more likely to engage in proactive work behavior (Parker, Williams, *et al.*, 2006). Related concepts, such as felt responsibility for change (Fuller, Marler, & Hester, 2006; Morrison & Phelps, 1999), also reflect employees' internalization of values relevant to change and, as such, predict proactive work behavior (Fuller *et al.*, 2006).

Autonomous motivation, including intrinsic, integrated, and identified forms, thus provides reasons to pursue change to achieve a different future. As to which motivational form is most powerful, Koestner and Losier (2002) showed that intrinsic motivation resulted in better performance when tasks were interesting but that autonomous extrinsic motivation (identified or integrated) yielded better performance when the tasks were not so interesting yet were important and required discipline or determination, as is likely to be the case for much proactive goal striving. As we discuss later, it might be that more than one "reason to," or multiple motivation forms, provides a flexible motivation base sufficient to stimulate proactive goals and to see them through.

Energized To Motivation

In addition to the "cold" motivational states of can do and reason to, "hot" affect-related motivational states can affect proactive behavior. Core affect refers to momentary, elementary feelings that combine both valence and activation (Russell, 2003). Later, when we discuss distal antecedents, we consider how affect can influence proactivity indirectly, via can do and reason to states. Here, we focus on the more direct mechanisms by which positive affect can affect the setting of and striving for proactive goals.

Seo, Barrett, and Bartunek (2004; Seo, Bartunek, & Feldman Barrett, 2009) theorized, and found empirical support for the theory, that positive core affect activates an approach action tendency, and others have shown that positive affect broadens individuals' momentary action–thought repertoires (Fredrickson, 1998; Isen, 1999). Positive affect promotes the setting of more challenging goals (Hies & Judge, 2005) and helps individuals engage with a more problematic future (Oettingen, Mayer, Thorpe, Janetzke, & Lorenz, 2005). For all these reasons, positive affect should enhance the likelihood that individuals set proactive goals. Core affect also potentially promotes more effective proactive goal striving. The cognitive broadening and flexibility that come with positive affect (for a review, see Isen, 1999) bode well for more creative ways of dealing with problems that can arise during proactive goal striving. For example, positive affect raises the chance that people will pursue win–win outcomes to problem solving because they are better able to see possibilities, think innovatively, and flexibly reason about trade-offs (Carnevale & Isen, 1986). Likewise, positive affect can influence goal revision during proactive goal regulation by increasing openness to feedback (Gervey, Igou, & Trope, 2005). In support of these theoretical arguments for the role of affect in proactive goal generation, Bindl and Parker (2009) found that individuals' average positive affect was especially important in predicting employees' envisioning of proactive work goals. In support of an affect pathway more generally, Fritz and Sonnentag (2009) showed that positive affect promotes taking charge behaviors that day as well as on the following day. Similarly, Ashforth, Sluss, and Saks (2007) reported a positive association between positive affectivity and proactive PE fit behaviors such as information seeking, feedback seeking, job-change negotiation, and networking.

It has further been suggested (Bindl & Parker, in press-a) that activated positive affect, such as feeling enthusiastic, is more important for stimulating proactive action than is inactivated positive affect, such as feeling contented. A high degree of activation increases the amount of effort put into a behavior by increasing the experience of energy (Brehm, 1999). In contrast, evidence suggests that feelings of contentment tend to be associated with inactivity and reflection (Frijda, 1986). For this reason, we identify "energized to" as the key direct affect pathway influencing goal generation and striving across a range of proactive goals. Preliminary evidence supports this thesis in relation to proactive work behavior (Parker, 2007). We later discuss how inactivated positive affect and activated negative affect might also have a role to play.

SUMMARY AND MODERATING INFLUENCES

Can do, reason to, and energized states motivate the setting of proactive goals and/or striving to achieve these goals (Figure 1, Path C). Both can do and reason to states need to align with the particular target. For example, although self-efficacy is important in both cases, the self-efficacy that drives efforts to change work methods (role-breadth self-efficacy) is different from the self-efficacy that drives efforts to seek a job (job-search self-efficacy). Likewise, although identified motivation is apparent in both cases, one nurse might proactively aim to improve the way his or her team works because working in a positive atmosphere is very important, whereas another nurse might negotiate new project opportunities because getting ahead in his or her career is very important. We have also suggested that the reasons for pro-activity extend beyond the purely instrumental. An individual might introduce a new work method because he or she enjoys his or her work so immensely (intrinsic motivation) and/or his or her job is so central to him or her that improving its effectiveness is part of "who he or she is" (integrated motivation). Finally, we suggested that activated positive affect influences proactivity by broadening cognition and by promoting approach tendencies. We expect this energized to pathway to be more general, such that activated positive affect stimulates the pursuit of proactive goals regardless of the envisioned future state or locus of change (also see the concept of "free activation" in Frijda, 1986).

Thus far we have assumed that if an individual is motivated to be proactive, then he or she will set and pursue proactive goals. However, aspects of the work context can intervene to prevent individuals high in can do, reason to, and energized to motivations from being proactive (Figure 1, Path D). One of the most important inhibitors of proactive work behavior is a lack of job control. Situations low in job control leave little scope for individual antecedents to influence behavior (Mischel & Shoda, 1995). For example, Binnewies, Sonnentag, and Mojza (2009) found a stronger relationship between feeling recovered in the morning and engaging in proactive behavior during the day for employees with a high level of job control than for those with low control. Low job control appears to stifle employees' proactivity, regardless of their level of recovery.

A further situational factor, procedural justice, has been shown to influence whether and how motivational states lead to proactive behaviors. McAllister, Kamdar, Morrison, & Turban (2007) showed individuals are more likely to take charge when they are not only high in role breadth self-efficacy but also perceive their organization as high in procedural justice. It appears that having fair procedures ensures that individuals feel safe to be proactive, whereas a lack of procedural justice might render proactive action as overly risky.

In addition to these contextual factors influencing whether motivation translates into goal-oriented action (Figure 1, Path D), the work context can enhance or reduce proactive action through affecting motivation (Figure 1, Path F), as we elaborate next.

DISTAL ANTECEDENTS OF PROACTIVE GOAL PROCESSES

Consistent with prior research (Frese & Fay, 2001; Parker, Williams, et al., 2006), we discuss how distal antecedents can affect proactive action via motivational states (Figure 1, Paths E, F, ExF). Distal antecedents include individuals' personality, values, knowledge, skill, and abilities as well as job design, leadership, and social processes. Where research exists, we describe how distal antecedents vary according to the envisioned future and the locus of change of the proactive goal. We thus distinguish between general antecedents (see Figure 1) that have been shown to influence most types of proactive behavior and specific antecedents that have primarily been associated with one or a few types of proactive behavior.

Individual Differences in Personality and Values

The most frequently investigated trait in relation to proactivity is *proactive personality*, or the tendency of an individual to be relatively unconstrained by situational forces in effecting environmental change. Given its emphasis on taking control and bringing about change, proactive personality should predict multiple proactive goals. This appears to be so. Proactive personality predicts network building (Thompson, 2005), proactive socialization (Ashford & Cummings, 1985), career initiative (Seibert *et al.*, 2001), and proactive work behaviors such as taking charge, problem prevention, and voice (Parker & Collins, in press). A meta-analysis by Fuller and Marler (2009) shows the consistency of these effects across many studies. Mediation analyses also show that proactive personality has its effects via both can do states (job-search self-efficacy in Brown, Cober, Kane, Levy, & Shalhoop, 2006; role-breadth self-efficacy in Parker, Williams, *et al.*, 2006) and reason to states (motivation to learn in Major, Turner, & Fletcher, 2006; flexible role orientation in Parker, Williams, *et al.*, 2006).

The question of whether proactive personality is the most important trait for all proactive goals, however, needs further attention. Studies have typically examined proactive personality as the sole trait, without controlling for other correlated traits. In an exception to this trend, Parker and Collins (in press) found that although there were significant zero-order correlations between proactive personality and proactive PE fit behaviors such as career initiative, job-role negotiation, and proactive feedback seeking, when considered alongside other traits proactive personality was less important for these behaviors. Instead, *conscientiousness* was a stronger predictor of proactive person–environment fit behaviors. These authors explained this finding in terms of proactive personality having a strong situational-change focus, whereas the person–environment fit behaviors tend to involve changing the self rather than the situation. At the same time, they recognized that conscientious individuals, because of the strong "industrious element" of conscientiousness that is about being hardworking and dependable (Roberts, Chernyshenko, Stark, & Goldberg, 2005), will want to achieve a good fit within the organization. Other studies have similarly found conscientiousness to predict proactive PE-fit behaviors, such as career planning (Carless & Bernath, 2007) and information seeking (Tidwell & Sias, 2005).

Beyond proactive personality and conscientiousness, which seem particularly important for situationally oriented and self-oriented proactive goals, respectively, a further relevant individual difference variable is the *desire for control*. Ashford and Black (1996) found individuals high in desire for control reported more networking, job-change negotiation, information seeking, and other proactive socialization tactics. The authors reasoned that in a highly uncertain situation such as job entry, individuals with a high desire for control will be active in attempting to attain greater certainty. Although this research was conducted in the context of proactive socialization, we would expect desire for control to influence other proactive goals. Control perceptions are essential for feeling self-efficacy (can do) as well as for autonomous motivation (reason to).

There is some evidence that *openness to change life values* provide a reason for an individual to set and to strive for proactive goals. Life values are emotion-linked beliefs that represent desirable, trans-situational goals or modes of conduct that promote these goals (Schwartz, 2010). Openness to change life values emphasizes independence of thought, which is relevant to the self-starting nature of proactivity, as well as readiness for change, which is relevant to the change-oriented nature of proactivity. For individuals with strong openness to change values, being proactive is a way of expressing these values. Moreover, according to Schwartz (2010), openness to change values is also anxiety free rather than anxiety based, which increases the resources available for proactive goal striving. Such an argument is consistent with Parker and Collins' (2009) preliminary finding that individuals with strong openness to change values report higher levels of proactive work behavior. In a related study, psychologically conservative individuals, who favor an authoritarian way of upbringing and who are politically conservative, report lower personal initiative, perhaps because they see less reason to engage in change (Fay & Frese, 2001).

Learning goal orientation is a further relevant individual difference variable that appears to influence multiple proactive goals. Individuals who are high in learning goal orientation—that is, who have a preference to understand or master new aspects (Dweck, 1986)—have been found to be more likely to engage in proactive feedback seeking (Tuckey, Brewer, & Williamson, 2002), likely because they find feedback less risky (can do) and more valuable (reason to) than individuals without a strong emphasis on learning. Parker and Collins (in press) also showed individuals with a learning goal orientation report higher engagement in proactive work behaviors such as taking charge and individual innovation, which they attributed to the role of learning goal orientation in promoting the persistence and recovery from setbacks that are needed to bring about work change.

At the same time, Parker and Collins (in press) showed that those with a strong *performance orientation,* who prefer to gain favorable, and to avoid negative, judgments of their competence, were less likely to engage in proactive work behavior or proactive strategic behavior. For performance-oriented individuals, being proactive likely means going out of the comfort zone and engaging in behaviors with uncertain outcomes, reducing can do motivation. The perceived costs of being proactive in changing the situation for individuals with a high performance orientation might well be too high; negative feedback will be threatening to their ego and image, and they will be highly concerned about failure (Tuckey *et al.*, 2002). Performance orientation, however, appears less inhibiting of PE fit proactive goals: Parker and Collins reported no significant association of performance goal orientation with feedback inquiry or career initiative. Indeed, individuals with a strong performance goal orientation reported higher engagement in feedback monitoring, which is a more covert, observational tactic of feedback seeking. Individuals with a strong performance goal orientation appear to want to manage their PE fit in indirect ways that are the least "threatening" to their ego or, in VandeWalle and Cummings's (1997) terms, least costly for self-presentation. It thus appears that although learning goal orientation is associated with a range of proactive goals, the effects of performance goal orientation on proactivity can be negative or positive, depending on the type of proactive goal.

A further category of traits and values that predict proactivity is those concerned with *future-oriented thinking* (Parker & Collins, in press). Where the behaviors needed for success are uncertain, or where outcomes might have negative elements such as resistance from others, individuals require a much stronger focus on the future (Aspinwall, 2005). Consistent with this reasoning, Parker and Collins (in press) showed that employees who are high in consideration of future consequences, the extent to which one considers distant versus immediate consequences (Strathman, Gleicher, Boninger, & Edwards, 1994), reported greater proactivity. This finding particularly applied in the case of proactive strategic behavior, which requires a long time frame and, perhaps, has the most uncertain outcomes of proactivity in the workplace. Likewise, Aspinwall, Sechrist, and Jones (2005) found that optimism, a form of future-oriented thinking, predicted people's engagement in anticipatory coping and preparation for Y2K. Interestingly, not all future-oriented thinking is relevant for proactive behavior. In an application of fantasy realization theory (Oettingen et al., 2005), Rank and Bayas (2008) found that dwelling about the future (i.e., ruminating about obstacles to future success) impaired innovative action.

In addition, personality aspects related to one's *core beliefs about the self* (e.g., resilience, core self-evaluations) and those related to *emotional regulation* (e.g., reappraisal, rather than suppression strategies) likely help drive the goal-striving process. Positive beliefs about the self can enhance perceptions that one can deal with barriers or obstacles (enhancing can do motivation) and emotional regulation might allow the more effective management of occasional negative affect (enhancing reason to motivation). Consistent with this reasoning, Johnson, Kristof-Brown, Van Vianen, De Pater, and Klein (2003) showed that people with positive core self-evaluations proactively build social networks, and Kanfer et al. (2001) showed self-esteem was important for proactive job search. The role of core beliefs about the self for other proactive goals has not yet been examined.

Individual Differences in Knowledge, Skills, and Abilities

Job qualifications predict greater personal initiative (Fay & Frese, 2001), and *education* predicts more proactive job-search behavior (Kanfer et al., 2001) as well as more speaking out with suggestions (LePine & Van Dyne, 1998). Multiple pathways likely explain these links, such as that individuals high in cognitive ability have a stronger perception of their capabilities (can do motivation) and therefore set more proactive goals as well as likely think flexibly and thereby effectively manage the change process during proactive striving. Drawing on broader literature, one would also expect that experience, such as past success or failure in achieving proactive goals as well as the attributions given to these outcomes, will influence can do perceptions (e.g., via self-efficacy and perceived cost) and reason to perceptions (e.g., via anticipated positive affect).

Domain-relevant knowledge is also an important antecedent (Fay & Frese, 2001). Dutton, Ashford, O'Neill, and Lawrence (2001) identified as critical for issue selling relational knowledge (e.g., understanding "who will be affected by the issue"), normative knowledge (e.g., understanding "what kinds of meetings are considered legitimate decision forums"); and strategic knowledge (e.g., understanding "what the organization's goals are"). Likewise, Howell and Boies (2004) found that contextual knowledge facilitated innovation champions' framing of ideas to promote them.

Positive Affect

Affect influences can do and reason to states (Seo *et al.*, 2004) and thereby boosts individuals' proactivity through these pathways. Positive affect influences can do pathways because it leads individuals to focus on positive outcomes of behaviors (e.g., such as via mood congruence recall effect), thereby generating higher expectancy judgments for these outcomes (Wegener & Petty, 1996) as well as higher self-efficacy (Tsai, Chen, & Liu, 2007). Moreover, positive affect promotes intrinsic motivation (reason to), which we argued above is an important driver of proactive goals. Thus, when people experience positive affect, they tend to see tasks as richer and more varied (Kraiger, Billings, & Isen, 1989) and report more intrinsic motivation (Isen & Reeve, 2005). There is also evidence that positive affect fosters the internalization of regulations (identified and integrated motivation). Isen and Reeve (2005) found that positive affect led individuals to engage in more responsible behaviors, such as completing uninteresting tasks that needed to be done. In addition, positive affect influences utility judgments during decision making (Schwarz, 1990) and leads individuals to more strongly value the positive outcomes of behaviors (Damasio, 1994).

Positive affect thus appears to enhance individuals' beliefs that they can set and strive for proactive goals as well as their reasons to do so. As we described earlier, there is good evidence that positive affect predicts proactive work behavior and some types of proactive PE fit behavior, although the precise mechanisms have not yet been investigated.

Contextual Variables

When it comes to the role of the context in motivating proactive goal pursuit, existing research is rather imbalanced. Relatively few studies consider how the context shapes active feedback seeking, career initiative, and other such behaviors aimed at achieving a better fit between the individual and the organization (see Ashford *et al.*, 2003). The research on these behaviors that exists mostly focuses on the social context, including climate and leadership. Climate and leadership are also important for fostering proactivity to improve organizational functioning and strategy, but for the latter types of proactive goals, work design is also key, as we elaborate next.

Work design appears especially important in promoting proactive work behavior. *Enriched jobs* with autonomy and complexity play a key role in influencing perceptions of control over the work environment, as well as self-efficacy to go beyond the core, and thus influence can do proactive motivation. Several longitudinal studies have shown that job enrichment predicts role-breadth self-efficacy (Axtell & Parker, 2003; Parker, 1998; Parker *et al.*, 1997) and that this type of self-efficacy mediates the link between job enrichment and proactivity (Parker, Williams, *et al.*, 2006). Job enrichment is also likely to influence reason to motivation. For example, enriched jobs create conditions under which individuals experience enjoyment and flow and are thus intrinsically motivated to be proactive in their work. Enriched jobs also enhance individuals' sense of the impact and meaningfulness of their work (Grant, 2007) and promote flexible role orientations (Parker *et al.*, 1997), both processes of internalization that then lead to integrated and identified regulation of proactivity to improve work processes. In line with these arguments, job autonomy, complexity, and control have been consistently shown to predict proactive work behaviors, including personal initiative (e.g., Frese *et al.*, 2007; Rank, Carsten, Unger, & Spector, 2007) idea implementation (Parker, Williams, et al, 2006), and suggesting improvements (Axtell *et al.*, 2000). Enriched jobs also promote energized to states. For example, Salanova and Schaufeli (2008) found that job resources (job control, feedback, and variety) predicted personal initiative via feelings of vigor and dedication. One reason, therefore, that job enrichment might be so key for proactive work behavior is that it influences can do, reason to, and energized to pathways.

Interestingly, Fuller *et al.* (2006) found that job autonomy did not uniquely predict felt responsibility for bringing about constructive change in work methods, which in turn predicted proactive work behaviors, whereas one's hierarchical position in the organization was important. These authors suggest that those in higher positions have greater initiated task interdependence, as well as change expectations, associated with their role. This explanation makes intuitive sense, although it is unclear why autonomy was less important in this study.

Job stressors such as time pressure and situational constraints also influence proactive work behavior, although not necessarily in the way one might expect. Conceptual research (Frese & Fay, 2001) and empirical studies (e.g., Fritz & Sonnentag, 2009; Ohly *et al.*, 2006) suggest that stressors can prompt greater initiative to improve work methods. Drawing on control theory (Carver & Scheier, 1998), researchers have argued that stressors indicate a mismatch between a desired and an actual situation. Employees then engage in proactive behavior to decrease this discrepancy. Support for this idea also comes from the feedback seeking literature. Employees are more likely to actively seek feedback when they experience role ambiguity and contingency uncertainty (Ashford & Cummings, 1985), likely because feedback helps to reduce the associated uncertainty.

Leadership plays a role in shaping motivation for a range of proactive goals. Rank, Nelson, Allen, and Xu (in press) found transformational leadership to be positively related to followers' innovative work behaviors, and Belschak and Den Hartog (in press) reported similar positive relationships between transformational leadership and organizationally oriented proactive behavior. Consistent with evidence from the wider literature that links leadership and self-efficacy (van Knippenberg, van Knippenberg, De Cremer, & Hogg, 2004), Strauss, Griffin, and Rafferty (2009) showed that team leaders' transformational leadership predicted followers' role-breadth self-efficacy, which in turn predicted team member proactivity. Evidence also implicates a reason to pathway. Strauss, Griffin, and Rafferty (2009) found that senior leaders' transformational leadership predicted employees' organizational commitment and in turn their organizationally oriented proactivity. Vision has been identified as a key element of transformational leadership for proactivity. Vision provides a discrepancy between the ideal situation and the current situation, thereby providing a motivational force for proactive action. Griffin, Parker, and Mason (in press) found that, for followers high in role-breadth self-efficacy, vision predicted greater employee proactive work behavior over time.

Other types and forms of leadership have also been shown to be important. For example, studies have shown that high-quality leader–member exchange predicts individual innovation (Janssen & Van Yperen, 2004) and voice (Burris, Detert, & Chiaburu, 2008). Likewise, Dutton, Ashford, O'Neill, Hayes, and Wierba (1997) identified top management's willingness to listen as important for issue selling, and researchers have shown that a supervisor can influence individuals' feedback seeking through reducing fears of potential image costs (see Ashford *et al.*, 2003). However, other studies have reported no unique relationship between supportive leadership and proactive motivation or behavior (Frese, Teng, & Wijnen, 1999; Parker, Williams, *et al.*, 2006). One explanation offered for these findings is that supportive leadership influences followers' proactive behavior indirectly (e.g., by increasing job enrichment), and once these variables are accounted for, supportive leadership might have no further role (Parker, Williams, *et al.*, 2006). Alternatively, if the leaders are passive in their personality, they might be "supportive," but not in ways that stimulate proactivity.

Interpersonal climate and social processes, such as peers' support of their proactive actions, can influence can do and reason to pathways. Low psychological safety or poor intra-group relations can make it seem overly risky to engage in proactive behavior—the perceived costs are too high. On the other hand, positive relationships not only generate positive affect but also can lead to internalization of team goals and, hence, to greater identified motivation. Evidence suggests that positive relationships within the work group predict voice (LePine & Van Dyne, 1998), and individuals engage in more issue selling if they have a good relationship with the person to whom they are selling the issue (Ashford, Rothbard, Piderit, & Dutton, 1998). Feeling supported by coworkers (Griffin *et al.*, 2007; Kanfer *et al.*, 2001) or supported by the organization (Ashford et al, 1998) positively relates to various proactive behaviors at work. In a study of wire makers, Parker, Williams, *et al.* (2006) showed that trust in coworkers was associated with a more flexible role orientation, which in turn predicted self-reported proactivity. Broader social processes, such as group norms, group goals, and normatively framed feedback, have had relatively little attention in the proactivity literature thus far. An exception is Ashford and Northcraft (1992), who showed that norms regarding how often people typically seek feedback subsequently influence the frequency of feedback seeking.

Interaction Between Individual and Contextual Antecedents of Proactivity

As depicted in Figure 1 (Path ExF), distal individual differences and situational factors interact to affect proactive work motivation and goal processes. These ways of interaction can be explained by trait activation theory (Tett & Burnett, 2003), which suggests that personality traits affect work behavior as responses to relevant, situational cues. Individuals are thus more likely to behave in a way consistent with their predisposition if the situation stimulates aspects of this predisposition. For example, task-related and organizational aspects of the job can provide cues that activate personality to influence job performance. In this vein, Fuller *et al.* (2006) reported that access to resources predicted voice via felt responsibility for change only for individuals with proactive personalities; there was no such relationship for those who were low in proactive personality. Likewise, Parker and Sprigg (1999) reported that only individuals with a proactive personality responded positively (with low strain) to active jobs (high demands and high control), with the implication that enriching work might benefit only those predisposed to respond to this type of change. Similarly, in favorable situations, individuals high in proactive personality are more likely to seek feedback (Kim & Wang, 2008) and are more likely to perceive their job as satisfying (Erdogan & Bauer, 2005) than are less proactive individuals.

Work-related cues may further compensate for a lack of corresponding dispositional characteristics, or vice versa (see behavior plasticity theory; Brockner, 1988). For instance, Rank and colleagues (in press) found transformational leadership was associated more strongly with individual innovation for those with lower levels of self-presentation propensity or organization-based self-esteem. In this case, leadership appeared to play a compensatory role for particular dispositions. Similarly, LePine and Van Dyne (1998) showed that individuals with low self-esteem are more strongly influenced by favorable situational characteristics, such as high levels of group autonomy, for voice behavior. Strong disposition may also compensate for a weak situation, as characterized by poor leadership. For instance, Grant and Sumanth (in press) found in a sample of fundraisers that high dispositional trust propensity and prosocial motivation were associated with higher levels of initiative at work, even if supervisors were not seen as trustworthy.

CONCLUSIONS AND WAYS FORWARD

In 2000, Crant (2000: 435) argued that proactivity "has not ... emerged as an integrated research stream. ... There is no single definition, theory, or measure driving this body of work." Crant's review helped to address this situation. We hope the current article progresses the quest for integration even further. We discuss contributions of our model, as well as ways forward, next.

Contributions of Our Model and Related Research Directions

Individuals do not just wait to be told what to do, nor do they act only when a problem occurs. Rather, they can take charge, anticipate opportunities and problems, and actively shape themselves and/or the situation to bring about a different future. We identified a range of proactive goals (Table 1) that vary in the future being envisioned and the extent to which the locus of change is the self or the situation. We also suggested proactivity requires a goal generation process, in which individuals envision and plan a different future, as well as a goal-striving process in which individuals execute behaviors and reflect on progress. The more effectively individuals engage in goal generation (e.g., the more that the proactive goal is specific and challenging) and goal striving (e.g., the more that individuals regulate their emotions), the more likely that a different future, and change, will be achieved. Of course, achieving a different future outcome is not automatically positive, or perceived to be so, for either the individual or the organization. As we discuss later, a range of factors can influence whether proactivity in fact leads to positive outcomes.

Our goal-oriented approach highlights the need to focus on processes other than enacting, which has thus far been the focus of proactivity research. Little attention has been given to the self-regulation process during proactivity, despite the fact that bringing about change is often a struggle, incurring resistance and setbacks. We do not know what leads individuals to discard proactive goals, what gives individuals the strength to persist during a difficult proactive goal, and whether escalation of commitment to a proactive goal occurs as a result of striving. For example, antecedent-focused emotion regulation, with its focus on reappraising a negative situation in the onset of negative emotion, should sustain proactive action, whereas response-focused emotion regulation, with its focus on suppressing negative emotions, decreases well-being and will likely lead individuals to abandon their proactive goals because of feelings of depletion (Hobfoll, 1989).

Our model identifies can do and reason to motivational states as leading individuals to set and strive for specific proactive goals. If an individual believes he or she can implement an improved work method and has a strong reason to do so, he or she is likely to pursue proactive goals to improve organizational functioning. Other individuals might similarly believe they can engage in proactive work behavior without undue cost yet see it as more important to enhance their career and therefore direct their energy toward proactive feedback seeking. Evidence is especially compelling for the can do pathway; several studies have shown that specific forms of self-efficacy motivate specific proactive action.

There is rather less attention in existing research on the reasons why individuals are proactive. We particularly recommend a focus on how external goals are internalized, on the role of identity, and on how multiple motivations might play out. Evidence from education suggests the combination of intrinsic regulation with identified or integrated regulation might be the most powerful: Intrinsic motivation promotes a focus on the task and results in feelings such as excitement, whereas identification facilitates a focus on the long-term significance of the action and promotes persistence (Deci & Ryan, 2000). We also know little about the combination of autonomous and controlled regulation in regard to proactivity, such as the case of a software developer who enjoys innovating (intrinsic regulation) and receives a bonus for each innovation (extrinsic regulation).

The motivational implications for proactivity of introjected regulation—a further type of controlled regulation (Deci & Ryan, 2000) that we did not discuss above—is worth attention. Introjected regulation involves individuals sanctioning their own behavior such that behavior is regulated by approval-based pressures based on guilt, anxiety, and self-esteem maintenance (Rigby, Deci, Patrick, & Ryan, 1992). Although this form of motivation comes from within, the behavior is not perceived as freely chosen and is considered to be externally regulated. The prediction from self-determination theory is clear: Introjected regulation will not motivate proactivity and could even suppress it. This speculation is consistent with the finding that a strong performance goal orientation (in which individuals have a strong emphasis on approval) is negatively linked to proactive work behaviors (Parker & Collins, in press). However, introjected regulation might in some situations promote proactivity, particularly when self-enhancement motives are concerned with enhancing the positivity of one's self-evaluation (Leary, 2007) rather than only avoiding negative self-evaluations. For example, self-improvement motives motivate individuals to gain useful information on their performance and prompt proactive feedback seeking (Ashford *et al.*, 2003). Thus, how self-enhancement motives operate for proactivity might depend on whether individuals are trying to avoid negative self-evaluations or rather to gain positive evaluations.

A further contribution of our model is its focus on activated positive affect as a predictor of proactivity. Being a relatively less explored pathway, several areas now need attention. One avenue is the possible role of activated negative affect. Feelings of frustration and anger might stimulate proactive action, in part as a way of relieving these feelings. This idea is consistent with evidence we presented above that job stressors can prompt proactive action because of the desire to reduce discrepancy with a goal. However, because negative affect has been shown to narrow cognitive processing, proactive behavior stimulated by feelings of anger might be restricted in its focus. For example, a teacher experiencing frustration over excess marking might change marking methods to make them more efficient but might be less likely to come up with more radical curriculum changes. In addition, the effect of negative affect on proactivity could depend on individuals' coping: Individuals who experience activated negative affect with a problem-focused coping style might engage in proactivity that is directed at improving a situation, whereas individuals who lack active coping mechanisms might be unable to envision and plan for proactive solutions when experiencing negative emotions. We also suggest considering the role of inactivated positive affect, such as feelings of contentment. Few studies have examined this dimension (the most commonly used measure of positive affect, the Positive Affect Negative Affect Schedule, includes only activated positive affect). Frijda (1986) suggested that low arousal positive affect predicts reflection, suggesting its possible role in promoting learning while striving to achieve a proactive goal. We also recommend considering how others' affect might influence an individual's proactivity through processes such as signaling and emotional contagion. For example, negative affect displayed by others—particularly anger—can create fear and exhaustion in the target of the anger as well as in uninvolved bystanders (Rupp & Spencer, 2006), thereby potentially stifling the proactivity of the target and bystanders. Finally, we suggest that anticipated affective outcomes of striving for a goal based on previous experiences (Baumeister, Vohs, DeWall, & Zhang, 2007) can function to either motivate or demotivate proactive behavior.

Having set out can do, reason to, and energized to pathways, we then proposed that more distal antecedents (individual differences, context) affect the pursuit of proactive goals via these motivational pathways. Our model will help both to develop a better understanding of why antecedents have the effects they do and to identify distal antecedents that have thus far not been considered. For example, individual differences such as need for cognition and curiosity are likely to assume a more important role than has been hitherto considered because curious, exploring-oriented individuals will see fewer costs of being proactive (can do motivation) and will be more likely to intrinsically enjoy exploring possible new futures (reason to motivation). Likewise, accountability has also been suggested to be important for proactive work behavior (Grant & Ashford, 2008), providing a clear "reason to" be proactive, although thus far this has not been investigated.

Social processes as antecedents to proactivity need further investigation, especially for proactive goals that involve changing the situation and therefore implicate interdependent others. How colleagues and leaders support or undermine proactive behavior, how individuals are resilient (or not) to such interpersonal forces, and how proactive employees use social networks to achieve change are all pertinent questions. In addition, although there has been some linking of social processes to PE fit behaviors, little attention has been given to other contextual antecedents of these proactive goals. For example, scholars have speculated about how diversity in a team influences feedback seeking, but this speculation remains untested (see Ashford *et al.*, 2003). We also advocate attention to reward systems. Based on findings from their meta-analysis, Deci, Koestner, and Ryan (1999) suggested that if rewards and feedback provide informational aspects, they convey self-determined competence and thereby enhance intrinsic motivation, whereas if rewards and feedback are controlling, this prompts an external perceived locus of causality and lowers intrinsic motivation. How such findings apply to proactivity is unknown.

Directions Beyond the Proposed Model

We recommend continuing to build bridges across proactivity research in the different domains, as we have done here, as well as going further to draw stronger links between proactivity and related fields such as entrepreneurship, innovation, and stress management. We also encourage researchers to continue to compare proactive behaviors to more passive forms of work behavior (e.g., Griffin *et al.*, 2007). As an example, citizenship behaviors can be executed more or less proactively, but thus far most conceptualizations of citizenship have been rather passive (e.g., helping on request) rather than proactive (e.g., anticipating the needs of others). Studies that assess proactive citizenship acts and compare them to passive citizenship acts would be fruitful (see Choi, 2007).

It is important to note that we did not focus here on outcomes. We summarized at the outset of our article solid evidence that proactivity predicts a range of positive outcomes. Nevertheless, proactivity is not always judged as positive for performance by supervisors, such as when the proactive individual lacks situational judgment (Chan, 2006) or when the individual is high in negative affect or weak on prosocial motives (Grant, Parker, & Collins, 2009). There is scope to more deeply consider what factors moderate the effectiveness of proactivity, for both the organization and the individual (for a more detailed consideration of outcomes, see Bindl & Parker, in press-b). A further important avenue concerns proactivity at the team and organization levels. A few team-level studies show that team proactive behavior relates to team effectiveness (e.g., Kirkman & Rosen, 1999), and at the organization level proactivity has been found to predict preventive approaches to the environment (Aragon-Correa, 1998). However, research into team-level or organizational-level proactivity is overall rather scant, despite the fact that the antecedents might differ at these levels. For example, Williams, Parker, and Turner (2009) identified the diversity in proactive personality within teams as important. Teams with greater diversity of team members' trait proactivity reported less favorable team climates, suggesting the diversity caused unhelpful conflict within the team, thereby inhibiting proactivity.

The methods of inquiry also need attention. Although there are some longitudinal field studies (e.g., Frese *et al.*, 2007; Parker, 1998) and diary studies that track intraindividual change over time (e.g., Fritz & Sonnentag, 2009; Sonnentag, 2003), more longitudinal studies are needed to better understand temporal processes and to capture dynamic effects. Laboratory studies will also be useful for investigating the micro processes of goal generation and striving. We also recommend intervention studies, which help to provide guidance to practitioners as to how to intervene to boost proactivity. For example, Raabe, Frese, and Beehr (2007) showed that a career self-management training intervention enhanced individuals' active career self-management, and Parker, Johnson, and Collins (2006) showed that the introduction of an advanced nursing role during overtime shifts boosted junior doctors' proactive care and taking charge behavior.

A further challenge is how to assess proactivity. Fuller and Marler (2009) showed stronger associations between proactive personality and outcomes when same-source measures were used, suggesting possible inflation because of common-method variance. Nevertheless, self-ratings also might have advantages in this topic area. First, because of its emphasis on change, proactive behavior can be uncomfortable or threatening and can be assessed negatively by peers and supervisors (Frese *et al.*, 1997). Second, if one is interested in the whole goal process, self-ratings are important for assessing nonobservable elements such as envisioning and reflecting (see Bindl & Parker, 2009). Other approaches to try to overcome some of the challenges of assessing proactive behavior include the use of interview judgments based on detailed interviews (Frese *et al.*, 1997), using context-specific scenario-based approaches (Parker, Williams, *et al.*, 2006), and using a situational judgment test (Bledow & Frese, 2009). Judging proactivity based on a one-off observation (e.g., a meeting) could also be inappropriate; observations across the entire goal process might well be needed.

In sum, great strides have been taken in the past decade to clarify the meaning of proactivity in the work place, and to demonstrate the value of this way of behaving for enhancing job performance, career success, socialization and other important outcomes. We focused here on developing a model to help understand more about what motivates the generation and pursuit of proactive goals. We hope our can do, reason to, and energized to model of proactive goal regulation provides a useful integrating framework for identifying how to cultivate individual proactivity, through modifying the work context and/or by recruiting individuals with attributes that are likely to make things happen.

REFERENCES

Aragon-Correa, J. A. 1998. Strategic proactivity and firm approach to the natural environment. *Academy of Management Journal*, 41: 556–567.

Ashford, S. J., & Black, J. S. 1996. Proactivity during organizational entry: The role of desire for control. *Journal of Applied Psychology,* 81: 199–214.

Ashford, S. J., Blatt, R., & VandeWalle, D. 2003. Reflections on the looking glass: A review of research on feedback-seeking behavior in organization. *Journal of Management,* 29: 773–799.

Ashford, S. J., & Cummings, L. L. 1985. Proactive feedback seeking: The instrumental use of the environment. *Journal of Occupational Psychology,* 58: 67–79.

Ashford, S. J., & Northcraft, G. B. 1992. Conveying more (or less) than we realize: The role of impression management in feedback seeking. *Organizational Behavior and Human Performance,* 53: 310–334.

Ashford, S. J., Rothbard, N. P., Piderit, S. K., & Dutton, J. E. 1998. Out on a limb: The role of context and impression management in selling gender-equity issues. *Administrative Science Quarterly,* 43: 23–57.

Ashforth, B. E., Sluss, D. M., & Saks, A. M. 2007. Socialization tactics, proactive behavior, and newcomer learning: Integrating socialization models. *Journal of Vocational Behavior,* 70: 447–462.

Aspinwall, L. G. 2005. The psychology of future-oriented thinking: From achievement to proactive coping, adaptation, and aging. *Motivation and Emotion,* 29: 203-235.

Aspinwall, L. G., Sechrist, G. B., & Jones, P. R. 2005. Expect the best and prepare for the worst: Anticipatory coping and preparations for Y2K. *Motivation and Emotion,* 29: 357–388.

Axtell, C. M., Holman, D. J., Unsworth, K. L., Wall, T. D., & Waterson, P. E. 2000. Shop-floor innovation: Facilitating the suggestion and implementation of ideas. *Journal of Occupational and Organizational Psychology,* 73: 265–285.

Axtell, C. M., & Parker, S. K. 2003. Promoting role breadth self-efficacy through involvement, work redesign and training. *Human Relations,* 56: 113–131.

Bandura, A. 1991. Social cognitive theory of self-regulation. *Organizational Behavior and Human Decision Processes,* 50: 248–287.

Bandura, A. 1997. *Self-efficacy: The exercise of control.* New York: Freeman.

Bateman, T. S., & Crant, J. M. 1993. The proactive component of organizational-behavior: A measure and correlates. *Journal of Organizational Behavior,* 14: 103-118.

Baumeister, R. E, Vohs, K. D., DeWall, C. N., & Zhang, L. 2007. How emotion shapes behavior: Feedback, anticipation, and reflection, rather than direct causation. *Personality and Social Psychology Review,* 11: 167–203.

Belschak, E D., & Den Hartog, D. N. in press. Different foci of proactive behavior: The role of transformational leadership. *Journal of Occupational and Organizational Psychology.*

Berg, J. M., Wrzesniewski, A., & Dutton, J. E. 2010. Perceiving and responding to challenges in job crafting at different ranks: When proactivity requires adaptivity. *Journal of Organizational Behavior,* 31: 158–186.

Bindl, U. K., & Parker, S. K. 2009. *Investigating self-regulatory elements of proactivity at work.* Working paper, Institute of Work Psychology, University of Sheffield, Sheffield, UK.

Bindl, U. K., & Parker, S. K.in press-a. Feeling good outperforming well? Psychological engagement and positive behaviors at work. In S. Albrecht (Ed.), *The handbook of employee engagement: Models, measures and practice*. Cheltenham, UK: Edward Elgar.

Bindl, U. K, & Parker, S. K. in press-b. Proactive work behavior: Forward-thinking and change-oriented action in organizations. In S. Zedeck (Ed.), *APA handbook of industrial and organizational psychology*. Washington, DC: American Psychological Association.

Binnewies, C, Sonnentag, S., & Mojza, E. J. 2009. Daily performance at work: Feeling recovered in the morning as a predictor of day-level job performance. *Journal of Organizational Behavior,* 30: 67–93.

Bledow, R., & Frese, M. 2009. A situational judgment test of personal initiative and its relationship to performance. *Personnel Psychology,* 62: 229–258.

Brehm, J. W. 1999. The intensity of emotion. *Personality and Social Psychology Review,* 3: 2–22.

Brockner, J. 1988. *Self-esteem at work: Research, theory, and practice*. Lexington, MA: Lexington Books.

Brown, D. J., Cober, R. T, Kane, K, Levy, P. E., & Shalhoop, J. 2006. Proactive personality and the successful job search: A field investigation with college graduates. *Journal of Applied Psychology,* 91: 717–726.

Burris, E. R., Detert, J. R., & Chiaburu, D. S. 2008. Quitting before leaving: The mediating effects of psychological attachment and detachment on voice. *Journal of Applied Psychology,* 93: 912–922.

Carless, S. A., & Bernath, L. 2007. Antecedents of intent to change careers among psychologists. *Journal of Career Development,* 33: 183-200.

Carnevale, P. J. D., & Isen, A. M. 1986. The influence of positive affect and visual access on the discovery of integrative solutions in bilateral negotiation. *Organizational Behavior and Human Decision Processes,* 37: 1–13.

Carver, C. S., & Scheier, M. F. 1998. *On the self-regulation of behavior*. Cambridge, UK: Cambridge University Press.

Chan, D. 2006. Interactive effects of situational judgment effectiveness and proactive personality on work perceptions and work outcomes. *Journal of Applied Psychology,* 91: 475–481.

Chen, G., & Gogus, C. I. 2008. Motivation in and of work teams: A multilevel perspective. In R. Kanfer, G. Chen, & R. D. Pritchard (Eds.), *Work motivation: Past, present, and future. The organizational frontiers series*: 285-318. New York: Routledge.

Chen, G., & Kanfer, R. 2006. Toward a system theory of motivated behavior in work teams. In B. M. Staw (Ed.), *Research in organizational behavior* (Vol. 27): 223–267. Greenwich, CT: JAI.

Choi, J. N. 2007. Change-oriented organizational citizenship behavior: Effects of work environment characteristics and intervening psychological processes. *Journal of Organizational Behavior,* 28: 467–484.

Crant, J. M. 2000. Proactive behavior in organizations. *Journal of Management,* 26: 435–462.

Crant, J. M., & Bateman, T. S. 2000. Charismatic leadership viewed from above: The impact of proactive personality. *Journal of Organizational Behavior*, 21: 63–75.

Csikszentmihalyi, M. 1988. The flow experience and its significance for human psychology. In M. Csikszentmihalyi & I. S. Csikszentmihalyi (Eds.), *Optimal experience: Psychological studies of flow in consciousness*: 15–35. Cambridge, UK: Cambridge University Press.

Damasio, A. R. 1994. *Descartes' error: Emotion, reason, and the human brain*. New York: Avon Books.

Deci, E. L., Koestner, R., & Ryan, R. M. 1999. A meta-analytic review of experiments examining the effects of extrinsic rewards on intrinsic motivation. *Psychological Bulletin*, 125: 627–668.

Deci, E. L., & Ryan, R. M. 2000. The "what" and "why" of goal pursuits: Human needs and the self-determination of behavior. *Psychological Inquiry*, 11: 227–268.

Deluga, R. J. 1998. American presidential proactivity, charismatic leadership, and rated performance. *Leadership Quarterly*, 9: 265–291.

Dutton, J. E., & Ashford, S. J. 1993. Selling issues to top management. *Academy of Management Review*, 18: 397–428.

Dutton, J. E., Ashford, S. J., O'Neill, R. M., Hayes, E., & Wierba, E. E. 1997. Reading the wind: How middle managers assess the context for selling issues to top managers. *Strategic Management Journal*, 18: 407–423.

Dutton, J. E., Ashford, S. J., O'Neill, R. M., & Lawrence, K. A. 2001. Moves that matter: Issue selling and organizational change. *Academy of Management Journal*, 44: 716–736.

Dweck, C. S. 1986. Motivational processes affecting learning. *American Psychologist*, 41: 1040–1048.

Eccles, J. S., Adler, T. E, Futterman, R., Goff, S. B., Kaczala, C. M., Meece, J. L., *et al.* 1983. Expectancies, values, and academic behaviors. In J. T. Spence (Ed.), *Achievement and achievement motivation*: 5–146. San Francisco: Freeman.

Eccles, J. S., & Wigfield, A. 2002. Motivational beliefs, values, and goals. *Annual Review of Psychology*, 53: 109–132.

Erdogan, B., & Bauer, T. N. 2005. Enhancing career benefits of employee proactive personality: The role of fit with jobs and organizations. *Personnel Psychology*, 58: 859–891.

Fay, D., & Frese, M. 2001. The concept of personal initiative: An overview of validity studies. *Human Performance*, 14: 97–124.

Fredrickson, B. L. 1998. What good are positive emotions? *Review of General Psychology*, 2: 300–319.

Frese, M., & Fay, D. 2001. Personal initiative (PI): An active performance concept for work in the 21st century. In B. M. Staw & R. M. Sutton (Eds.), *Research in organizational behavior* (Vol. 23): 133–187. Amsterdam: Elsevier.

Frese, M., Kring, W., Soose, A., & Zempel, J. 1996. Personal initiative at work: Differences between East and West Germany. *Academy of Management Journal*, 39(1): 37–63.

Frese, M., Garst, H., & Fay, D. 2007. Making things happen: Reciprocal relationships between work characteristics and personal initiative in a four-wave longitudinal structural equation model. *Journal of Applied Psychology*, 92: 1084–1102.

Frese, M., Teng, E., & Wijnen, C. J. D. 1999. Helping to improve suggestion systems: Predictors of making suggestions in companies. *Journal of Organizational Behavior*, 20: 1139–1155.

Frijda, N. H. 1986. *The emotions*. Cambridge, UK: Cambridge University Press.

Fritz, C, & Sonnentag, S. 2009. Antecedents of day-level proactive behavior: A look at job stressors and positive affect during the workday. *Journal of Management*, 35: 94–111.

Fuller, B., Jr., & Marler, L. E. 2009. Change driven by nature: A meta-analytic review of the proactive personality literature. *Journal of Vocational Behavior*, 75: 329–345.

Fuller, B., Jr., Marler, L. E., & Hester, K. 2006. Promoting felt responsibility for constructive change and proactive behavior: Exploring aspects of an elaborated model of work design. *Journal of Organizational Behavior*, 27: 1089–1120.

Gagné, M., & Deci, E. L. 2005. Self-determination theory and work motivation. *Journal of Organizational Behavior*, 26: 331–362.

Gervey, B., Igou, E. R., & Trope, Y. 2005. Positive mood and future-oriented self-evaluation. *Motivation and Emotion*, 29: 269–296.

Gollwitzer, P. M. (1990). Action phases and mind-sets. In E. T. Higgins & R M. Sorrentino (Eds.), *Handbook of motivation and cognition* (Vol. 2): 53–92. New York: Guilford.

Grant, A. M. 2007. Relational job design and the motivation to make a prosocial difference. *Academy of Management Review*, 32: 393–417.

Grant, A. M., & Ashford, S. J. 2008. The dynamics of proactivity at work: Lessons from feedback-seeking and organizational citizenship behavior research. In B. M. Staw & R. M. Sutton (Eds.), *Research in organizational behavior* (Vol. 28): 3–34. Amsterdam: Elsevier.

Grant, A. M., Parker, S. K., & Collins, C. G. 2009. Getting credit for proactive behavior: Supervisor reactions depend on what you value and how you feel. *Personnel Psychology*, 62: 31–55.

Grant, A. M., & Sumanth, J. J. in press. Mission possible? The performance of prosocially motivated employees depends on manager trustworthiness. *Journal of Applied Psychology*.

Griffin, M. A., Neal, A., & Parker, S. K. 2007. A new model of work role performance: Positive behavior in uncertain and interdependent contexts. *Academy of Management Journal*, 50: 327–347.

Griffin, M. A., Parker, S. K., & Mason, C. M. in press. Leader vision and the development of adaptive and proactive performance: A longitudinal study. *Journal of Applied Psychology*.

Hobfoll, S. E. 1989. Conservation of resources: A new attempt at conceptualizing stress. *American Psychologist*, 44: 513–524.

Howell, J. M., & Boies, K. 2004. Champions of technological innovation: The influence of contextual knowledge, role orientation, idea generation, and idea promotion on champion emergence. *Leadership Quarterly*, 15: 123–143.

Ilies, R., & Judge, T. A. 2005. Goal regulation across time: The effects of feedback and affect. *Journal of Applied Psychology*, 90: 453–467.

Isen, A. M. 1999. On the relationship between affect and creative problem solving. In S. Russ (Ed.), *Affect, creative experience, and psychological adjustment*: 3–17. Philadelphia: Taylor & Francis.

Isen, A. M., & Reeve, J. 2005. The influence of positive affect on intrinsic and extrinsic motivation: Facilitating enjoyment of play, responsible work behavior, and self-control. *Motivation and Emotion*, 2: 295–323.

Janssen, O., & Van Yperen, N. W. 2004. Employees' goal orientations, the quality of leader–member exchange, and the outcomes of job performance and job satisfaction. *Academy of Management Journal*, 47: 368–384.

Johnson, E. C., Kristof-Brown, A. L., Van Vianen, A. E. M., De Pater, I. E., & Klein, M. R. 2003. Expatriate social ties: personality antecedents and consequences for adjustment. *International Journal of Selection and Assessment*, 11: 277–289.

Kanfer, R., & Ackerman, P. L. 1989. Motivation and cognitive abilities: An integrative/ aptitude-treatment interaction approach to skill acquisition. *Journal of Applied Psychology*, 74: 657–690.

Kanfer, R., & Kantrowitz, T. M. 2002. Emotion regulation: Command and control of emotion in work life. In R G. Lord, R. J. Klimoski, & R. Kanfer (Eds.), *Emotions in the workplace*: 433–471. San Francisco: Jossey-Bass.

Kanfer, R., Wanberg, C. R., & Kantrowitz, T. M. 2001. Job search and employment: A personality-motivational analysis and meta-analytic review. *Journal of Applied Psychology*, 86: 837–855.

Kim, T. Y., & Wang, J. 2008. Proactive personality and newcomer feedback seeking: The moderating roles of supervisor feedback and organizational justice. In M. A. Rahim (Ed.), *Current topics in management* (Vol. 13): 91–108. London: Transaction Publishing.

Kirkman, B. L., & Rosen, B. 1999. Beyond self-management: Antecedents and consequences of team empowerment. *Academy of Management Journal*, 42: 58–74.

Koestner, R., & Losier, G. F. 2002. Distinguishing three ways of being highly motivated: A closer look at introjection, identification, and intrinsic motivation. In E. L. Deci & R. M. Ryan (Eds.), *Handbook of self-determination research*: 101-121. Rochester, NY: University of Rochester Press.

Kraiger, K., Billings, R. S., & Isen, A. M. 1989. The influence of positive affective states on task perceptions and satisfaction. *Organizational Behavior and Human Decision Processes*, 44: 12–25.

Lakhani, K. R., & Wolf, R. G. 2003. *Why hackers do what they do: Understanding motivation and effort in free/open source software projects*. MIT Sloan working paper no. 4425–03, Massachusetts Institute of Technology, Cambridge.

Leary, M. R. 2007. Motivational and emotional aspects of the self. *Annual Review of Psychology*, 58: 317–344.

LePine, J. A., & Van Dyne, L. 1998. Predicting voice behavior in work groups. *Journal of Applied Psychology*, 83: 853–868.

Liberman, N., & Trope, Y. 1998. The role of feasibility and desirability considerations in near and distant future decisions: A test of temporal construal theory. *Journal of Personality and Social Psychology, 75:* 5–18.

Locke, E. A., & Latham, G. P. 1990. *A theory of goal setting and task performance.* Englewood Cliffs, NJ: Prentice Hall.

Major, D. A., Turner, J. E., & Fletcher, T. D. 2006. Linking proactive personality and the Big Five to motivation to learn and development activity. *Journal of Applied Psychology, 91:* 927–935.

Massimini, F., & Carli, M. 1988. The systematic assessment of flow in daily life. In M. Csikszentmihalyi & I. S. Csikszentmihalyi (Eds.), *Optimal experience: Psychological studies of flow in consciousness:* 266-287. Cambridge, UK: Cambridge University Press.

McAllister, D. J., Kamdar, D., Morrison, E. W., & Turban, D. B. 2007. Disentangling role perceptions: How perceived role breadth, discretion, instrumentality, and efficacy relate to helping and taking charge. *Journal of Applied Psychology, 92:* 1200–1211.

Mischel, W., & Shoda, Y. 1995. A cognitive–affective system theory of personality: Reconceptualizing situations, dispositions, dynamics, and invariance in personality structure. *Psychological Review, 102:* 246–268.

Morrison, E. W., & Phelps, C. C. 1999. Taking charge at work: Extrarole efforts to initiate workplace change. *Academy of Management Journal, 42:* 403–419.

Oettingen, G., Mayer, D., Thorpe, J. S., Janetzke, H., & Lorenz, S. 2005. Turning fantasies about positive and negative futures into self-improvement goals. *Motivation and Emotion, 29:* 237–267.

Ohly, S., & Fritz, C. 2007. Challenging the status quo: What motivates proactive behavior? *Journal of Occupational and Organizational Psychology, 80:* 623–629.

Ohly, S., Sonnentag, S., & Pluntke, F. 2006. Routinization, work characteristics and their relationships with creative and proactive behaviors. *Journal of Organizational Behavior, 27:* 257–279.

Oyserman, D., & Markus, H. R. 1990. Possible selves and delinquency. *Journal of Personality and Social Psychology, 59:* 112–125.

Parker, S. K. 1998. Enhancing role breadth self-efficacy: The roles of job enrichment and other organizational interventions. *Journal of Applied Psychology, 83:* 835–852.

Parker, S. K. 2007. *How positive affect can facilitate proactive behavior in the workplace.* Paper presented at the annual meeting of the Academy of Management, Philadelphia.

Parker, S. K., & Collins, C. G. 2009. *Life values, goal orientations, and proactive behavior in the work place.* Paper presented at the conference of the Academy of Management, Chicago.

Parker, S. K., & Collins, C. G. 2010. Taking stock: Integrating and differentiating multiple proactive behaviors. *Journal of Management.* Advance online publication, doi: 10.1177 /0149206308321554

Parker, S. K., Johnson, A., & Collins, C. G. 2006. *Enhancing proactive patient care: An intervention study.* Paper presented at the annual meeting of the Academy of Management, Atlanta.

Parker, S. K., & Ohly, S. 2008. Designing motivating work. In R Kanfer, G. Chen, & R D. Pritchard (Eds.), *Work motivation: Past, present, and future*: 233–384. New York: Routledge.

Parker, S. K., & Sprigg, C. A. 1999. Minimizing strain and maximizing learning: The role of job demands, job control, and proactive personality. *Journal of Applied Psychology*, 84: 925–939.

Parker, S. K., Wall, T. D., & Jackson, P. R. 1997. "That's not my job": Developing flexible employee work orientations. *Academy of Management Journal*, 40: 899–929.

Parker, S. K., Williams, H. M., & Turner, N. 2006. Modeling the antecedents of proactive behavior at work. *Journal of Applied Psychology*, 91: 636–652.

Raabe, B., Frese, M., & Beehr, T. A. 2007. Action regulation theory and career self-management. *Journal of Vocational Behavior*, 70: 297–311.

Rank, J., & Bayas, N. 2008. *Applying fantasy realization theory to organizational behavior: Future-related thinking, leadership and innovation.* Paper presented at the annual meeting of the Academy of Management, Anaheim, CA.

Rank, J., Carsten, J. M., Unger, J. M., & Spector, P. E. 2007. Proactive customer service performance: Relationships with individual, task, and leadership variables. *Human Performance*, 20: 363–390.

Rank, J., Nelson, N. E., Allen, T. D., & Xu, X. in press. Leadership predictors of innovation and task performance: Subordinates' self-esteem and self-presentation as moderators. *Journal of Occupational and Organizational Psychology*.

Rigby, C. S., Deci, E. L., Patrick, B. C, & Ryan, R M. 1992. Beyond the intrinsic–extrinsic dichotomy: Self-determination in motivation and learning. *Motivation and Emotion*, 16: 165–185.

Roberts, B. W., Chernyshenko, O., Stark, S., & Goldberg, L. 2005. The structure of conscientiousness: An empirical investigation based on seven major personality questionnaires. *Personnel Psychology*, 58: 103–139.

Rousseau, D. M., Ho, V. T, & Greenberg, J. 2006. I-deals: Idiosyncratic terms in employment relationships. *Academy of Management Review*, 31: 977–994.

Rupp, D. E., & Spencer, S. 2006. When customers lash out: The effects of customer interactional injustice on emotional labor and the mediating role of discrete emotions. *Journal of Applied Psychology*, 91: 971–978.

Russell, J. A. 2003. Core affect and the psychological construction of emotion. *Psychological Review*, 110: 145-172.

Salanova, M., & Schaufeli, W. B. 2008. A cross-national study of work engagement as a mediator between job resources and proactive behaviour. *International Journal of Human Resource Management*, 19: 116–131.

Schwartz, S. H. 2010. Basic Values: How they motivate and inhibit prosocial behavior. In Mario Mikulincer & P. R. Shaver (Eds.), *Prosocial motives, emotions, and behavior: The better angels of our nature*: 221–241. Washington, DC: American Psychological Association.

Schwarz, N. 1990. Feelings as information: Informational and motivational functions of affective states. In E. T. Higgins & R. M. Sorrentino (Ed.), *Handbook of motivation and cognition: Foundations of social behavior* (Vol. 2): 527–561. New York: Guilford.

Scott, S. G., & Bruce, R. A. 1994. Determinants of innovative behavior: A path model of individual innovation in the workplace. *Academy of Management Journal*, 37: 580–607.

Seibert, S. E., Kraimer, M. L., & Crant, J. M. 2001. What do proactive people do? A longitudinal model linking proactive personality and career success. *Personnel Psychology*, 54: 845–874.

Seo, M.-G., Barrett, L. F., & Bartunek, J. M. 2004. The role of affective experience in work motivation. *Academy of Management Review*, 29: 423–439.

Seo, M.-G., Bartunek, J. M., & Feldman Barrett, L. 2009. The role of affective experience in work motivation: Test of a conceptual model. *Journal of Organizational Behavior*. Advance online publication. doi:10.1002/job.655

Sheldon, K. M., & Elliot, A. J. 1999. Goal striving, need satisfaction, and longitudinal well-being: The self-concordance model. *Journal of Personality and Social Psychology*, 76: 482–497.

Sonnentag, S. 2003. Recovery, work engagement, and proactive behavior: A new look at the interface between nonwork and work. *Journal of Applied Psychology*, 88: 518–528.

Strathman, A., Gleicher, F., Boninger, D. S., & Edwards, C. S. 1994. The consideration of future consequences: Weighing immediate and distant outcomes of behavior. *Journal of Personality and Social Psychology*, 66: 742–752.

Strauss, K., Griffin, M. A., & Parker, S. K. 2009. *Future work selves: How hoped for and feared selves motivate behavior in organizations*. Working paper, Institute of Work Psychology, University of Sheffield, Sheffield, UK.

Strauss, K., Griffin, M. A., & Rafferty, A. E. 2009. Proactivity directed toward the team and organization: The role of leadership, commitment, and confidence. *British Journal of Management*, 20: 279–291.

Tett, R. P., & Burnett, D. D. 2003. A personality trait-based interactionist model of job performance. *Journal of Applied Psychology*, 88: 500–517.

Thompson, J. A. 2005. Proactive personality and job performance: A social capital perspective. *Journal of Applied Psychology*, 90: 1011–1017.

Tidwell, M., & Sias, P. 2005. Personality and information seeking: Understanding how traits influence information seeking behaviors. *Journal of Business Communication*, 42: 51–77.

Tsai, W. C, Chen, C. C, & Liu, H. L. 2007. Test of a model linking employee positive moods and task performance. *Journal of Applied Psychology*, 92: 1570–1583.

Tuckey, M., Brewer, N., & Williamson, P. 2002. The influence of motives and goal orientation on feedback seeking. *Journal of Occupational and Organizational Psychology*, 75: 195–216.

van Knippenberg, D., van Knippenberg, B., De Cremer, D., & Hogg, M. A. 2004. Leadership, self, and identity: A review and research agenda. *Leadership Quarterly*, 15: 825–856.

VandeWalle, D., & Cummings, L. L. 1997. A test of the influence of goal orientation on the feedback-seeking process. *Journal of Applied Psychology*, 82: 390–400.

Vroom, V. H. 1964. *Work and motivation.* New York: John Wiley.

Wagner, S. H., Parker, C. P., & Christianson, N. D. 2003. Employees that think and act like owners: Effects of ownership beliefs and behaviors on organizational effectiveness. *Personnel Psychology,* 56: 847–858.

Wegener, D. T, & Petty, R. E. 1996. Effects of mood on persuasion processes: Enhancing, reducing, and biasing scrutiny of attitude-relevant information. In L. L. Martin & A. Tesser (Eds.), *Striving and feeling: Interactions among goals, affect, and self regulation:* 329–362. Mahwah, NJ: Lawrence Erlbaum.

Wegner, D. M., Vallacher, R. R, Kiersted, G., & Dizadjii, D. 1986. Action identification in the emergence of social behavior. *Social Cognition,* 4: 18–38.

Williams, H., Parker, S. K., & Turner, N. 2009. *What makes a proactive team?* Working paper.

Wrzesniewski, A., & Dutton, J. E. 2001. Crafting a job: Revisioning employees as active crafters of their work. *Academy of Management Review,* 26: 179–201.

Wrzesniewski, A., McCauley, C, Rozin, P., & Schwartz, B. 1997. Jobs, careers, and callings: People's relations to their work. *Journal of Research in Personality*, 31: 21–33.

JOURNAL ARTICLE QUESTIONS

Journal Article 3 — Some unintended consequences of job design

1. What are the main unintended consequences of job design discussed in this paper.
2. How do these manifest themselves in tasks that involve team working?
3. What recommendations does the author make for future research in this area?

PART 3

MANAGING THE ORGANIZATION

Journal article: Johns, G. (2010), Some unintended consequences of job design, *Journal of Organizational Behavior*, **31**, 361–369.

In this section of the book we shift our focus to a more macro-level. We seek to examine a range of topics which show how individual employees are affected by external factors within their working environment. In Chapter 5 for example, we summarise evidence linking the nature of work and peoples' jobs with their attitudes and subsequent performance. In this chapter we go on to identify and discuss social trends and patterns that inform current debates on work in many societies – for example flexible working and work–life balance.

At this stage we also switch the stage of OB to the organizational level. We examine important features of organizations such as their *structure* and *culture*. In a sense our study of organizations at this macro-level can lead us to conclude that organizations are entities in their own right; in other words they are more than the sum of their parts. Nonetheless, whereas all organizations may be understood by reference to structure and culture, each organization is unique in these regards and its characteristic shape, values and beliefs will have been developed by individual actors through an emerging process of negotiation. In this way, the macro-level analysis contained in this part of the book links back to earlier sections dealing with individual attributes and group and/or team dynamics.

Students may find topics such as organizational structure and culture to be less immediately engaging than the psychology-based subject areas dealt with in Part 2. Nonetheless they are highly relevant to our experience of work ... someone employed within a classical bureaucratic structure for example, will find that the structural pattern there will impact on their everyday experience of work in powerful ways. Such topics are also crucial in assessing how organizations work effectively within the task performance element of management set out in Chapter 1.

CHAPTER 5

Changing worlds and the design of work

LEARNING OBJECTIVES

After studying this chapter you should be able to:

- explain the concept of intrinsic motivation
- compare and contrast the alternative job design strategies and link them to intrinsic work rewards
- discuss the job characteristics model employing job diagnosis techniques as an approach to job enrichment
- explain how goal-setting theory is linked to job design
- examine flexibility and its relevance to job design

THROWING OUT THE RULES OF WORK? CHALLENGING THE PRESENTEEISM CULTURE AT BEST BUY

Imagine a job like this: no problem taking time off to play golf during normal working hours; able to start and finish work at times convenient for you; physical attendance at meetings is optional; able to work from home and no one looking over your shoulder asking where you are. It's not fiction but fact at Best Buy, the American electronics retailer that has recently opened stores in the UK.

What started as a covert management experiment in 2003 – so secretive that even the Chief Executive was unaware of it – is now part of the everyday culture at Best Buy's headquarters in Minneapolis, USA. The goal was to develop a workplace culture defined by results rather than attendance. The firm's ROWE (Results-Only Work Environment) has changed the rules for many employees, giving people the freedom 'to work whenever they want, wherever they want, as long as they get their work done'. It's output-focused and results orientated, not a rules-driven culture. So how does it work?

Well, great, if you ask those participating (60% of workers have taken up the ROWE option). Kelly McDevitt, an online promotions manager, leaves early to pick her son up from school; Chad Achen, online orders manager, often leaves early to catch an afternoon movie; Mark Wells, an e-learning specialist, sleeps late whenever he wants; whilst Steve Hance, employee relations manager, can participate in conference calls whilst he's out fishing 'No one at Best Buy really knows where I am,' he explains 'Nor do they really care. It used to be I had to schedule my life around my work, now I schedule my work around my life.'

It's also great if you look at the numbers, average voluntary turnover has fallen drastically whilst productivity in the departments adopting ROWE has increased by an average of 35%. In addition, the company has made savings on office space as employees no longer have to attend a set place of work. Senior Vice President J. T. Thompson comments 'For years ... I was always looking to see if people were here when I should have been looking at what they were getting done.' For her part Cari Ressler, one of two HR professionals behind the idea, says: 'The old way of managing and looking at work isn't going to work any more. We want to revolutionize the way work gets done. Work should be something you do, not a place you go.' 'Eighty per cent of lost productivity can be attributed to "presenteeism",' she argues, 'employees who believe simply turning up is half the job done. With ROWE people at all levels stop doing any activity that is a waste of their time, the customers' time and the company's money.'

But before we get carried away, this approach is not without criticism, 'the lack of fixed schedules at Best Buy cannot exist in a competitive global market' says one critic, whilst another asks how do you measure the effect of one employee needing a quick answer from another but wasting time chasing them down because they don't know where they are?

Could it work in the UK and Europe? Flexible working, according to David Woodward, is still seen by many as idealistic and unworkable. He cites a 2009 report by the Equality and Human Rights Commission that found that 40% of British men believed that a request for flexible working would negatively affect their chances of promotion. It appears then that a significant change in attitudes to work is still needed if the ROWE concept is to have wider appeal.[1]

Questions

1. How do these more flexible working arrangements help employees deal with their work–life balance?
2. What are the advantages and disadvantages of ROWE for the employee?
3. What challenges does ROWE place on managers in managing their subordinates? How might you overcome these?
4. If you were employed by Best Buy would you participate in ROWE? Explain your reasoning behind your answer.

INTRODUCTION

Our society and the nature of workplaces are continuously changing, generating forces that impact upon how workers experience their work and their workplaces. Coupled with this are significant changes in the demographic makeup of our society (such as an ageing population) and changing attitudes to work that are having an impact within the workplace. Whilst the Best Buy example may be a somewhat radical approach, it does illustrate the need for organizations to challenge traditional thinking about employee motivation and the design of jobs and to gain deeper appreciation of how the job itself can affect an individual's motivation and job satisfaction. Organizations have moved well beyond simply trying to improve worker performance by offering limited extrinsic rewards such as higher wages or promotion. There is more focus now on responding to the intrinsic rewards that employees get from doing their jobs and on the goals that can help to guide and motivate them in their work. Designing the work to maximize employee outcomes is fundamental to this process.

In Chapter 4 we discussed motivation in relation to intrinsic and extrinsic rewards. We also emphasized various aspects of reinforcement and different kinds of pay plans as extrinsic rewards. In this chapter we give special emphasis to intrinsic rewards and how to use job design, goal setting and flexible work arrangements to improve intrinsic job satisfaction. The theoretical aspects of job design are explained and job design theories or approaches (such as job characteristics, socio-technical, socio-information and multi-skilling) are examined to demonstrate how the design of jobs can have an impact on workers. The alignment and achievement of organizational goals through a process of goal setting is also considered, as these affect employees' jobs and their motivation, satisfaction and performance within them. Finally, a discussion of flexible work arrangements explores how the very arrangements in which workers are employed are being reconsidered and modified. These new arrangements take into account the demands that employees make; they enhance the quality of their working lives and also enhance their capacity to work productively for their organizations.

INTRINSIC MOTIVATION

Intrinsic work rewards were defined in Chapter 4 as those rewards that an individual receives directly as a result of task performance. One example is the feeling of achievement that comes from completing a challenging project. Such feelings are individually determined and integral to the work. The individual is not dependent on an outsider, such as a manager, to provide these rewards or feelings.

This concept is in direct contrast to extrinsic rewards, such as pay and conditions, which are externally controlled. The unique nature of intrinsic rewards can be seen when a social worker says: 'My working conditions are bad and my colleagues are boring but I get a sense of satisfaction out of helping my clients.'[2]

Intrinsic work rewards,[3] are a very important part of motivating and satisfying employees in the workplace. Herzberg's two-factor theory of motivation in Chapter 4 particularly draws attention to the importance of intrinsic job content factors in improving satisfaction in the job (while extrinsic job context factors can lead to dissatisfaction). His ideas will be discussed further in this chapter when job enrichment is considered. Intrinsic work rewards play a key part in effective job design. The example above illustrates that people can be motivated simply because they enjoy the experience of accomplishing tasks. This is described as **intrinsic motivation**, which is a desire to work hard solely for the pleasant experience of task accomplishment.

When we discussed extrinsic rewards in Chapter 4, we saw the manager as responsible for allocating extrinsic rewards such as pay, promotion and verbal praise to employees and for controlling general working conditions. To serve in this capacity, a manager must be good at evaluating performance, knowing what rewards employees value and giving these rewards to employees contingent upon work performance.

Managing intrinsic work rewards presents an additional challenge for the manager. Still acting as an agent of the organization, the manager must design jobs for individual employees so that intrinsic rewards become available to them as a direct result of feedback gained from working on assigned tasks. That is not to say that every manager should design every job to provide every employee with the maximum opportunity to experience intrinsic work rewards. This chapter will help you to understand:

* when people may desire intrinsic work rewards;
* how to design jobs for people who desire greater intrinsic work rewards;
* how to motivate those people who do not desire intrinsic work rewards.

> **Intrinsic motivation** *is a desire to work hard solely for the pleasant experience of task accomplishment.*

TRADITIONAL APPROACHES TO JOB DESIGN

A job is one or more tasks that an individual performs in direct support of an organization's production purpose. Well-designed jobs can facilitate both the quality of task performance and job satisfaction, partly through intrinsic motivation. Additional aspects of human resource performance, such as absenteeism, commitment and turnover, may also be influenced.

Job design *is the planning and specification of job tasks and the work setting in which they are to be accomplished.*

Job design involves the planning and specification of job tasks and the work setting designated for their accomplishment. This definition includes both the specification of task attributes and the creation of a work setting for these attributes. It includes all the structural and social elements of the job and their impact on employee behaviour and performance. The objective of job design is to help make jobs meaningful, interesting and challenging. For the organization it is essential that jobs are properly designed in order to reduce stress, improve performance and enhance motivation and job satisfaction so that they can compete effectively in the global market.[4] The manager's responsibility is to design jobs that will motivate the individual employee. Figuratively speaking, this is properly done when:

Individual needs + task attributes + work setting → performance and satisfaction.

Between 1900 and 1950 there were many developments in management theories that ranged from scientific studies of job efficiency to studies that were more concerned with the human response to the job. Four major approaches to job design were identified. Each approach was prescriptive in nature and assumed that all workers would respond to the strategies in the same manner. None of these approaches made allowance for variation in the motivational potential of the individual worker. The approaches were:

- job simplification
- job enlargement
- job rotation
- job enrichment

Job simplification

Job simplification *involves standardizing work procedures and employing people in clearly defined and specialized tasks.*

Job simplification involves standardizing work procedures and employing people in clearly defined and specialized tasks. The machine-paced car assembly line is a classic example of this job design strategy.

This approach, deriving from the scientific managers such as Frederick Taylor, involves simplified jobs that are highly specialized and usually require an individual to perform a narrow set of tasks repetitively. The potential advantages include increased operating efficiency (which was the original intent of the job simplification approach), low-skill and low-cost labour, minimal training requirements and controlled production quantity.

Some possible disadvantages of this 'de-skilling' include loss of efficiency due to low-quality work, high rates of absenteeism and turnover and the need to pay high wages to get people to do unattractive jobs. For most people, simplified job designs tend to be low in intrinsic motivation. The jobs lack challenge and lead to boredom. In Chapter 1 we saw how Braverman went further in his analysis of de-skilling, seeing it as a deliberate strategy by owners and managers of organizations to strengthen their own power position relative to that of workers. In Chapter 10 we examine the strategic contingencies model of power, which suggests that power accrues to those who are in control of key attributes or tasks central to the organization's functioning and survival. De-skilled workers within this framework have sharply reduced potential power.

In today's high-technology age, a natural extension of job simplification is complete automation – allowing a machine to do the work previously accomplished through human effort. This approach increasingly involves the use of robots and sophisticated computer applications based on expert systems and artificial intelligence. The Walgreens pharmacy chain in the US increased the rate of packing shipments from its distribution centre to its stores by more than 800% with its use of robots.[5] More recently, computer applications such as menus on call centre help lines and the directed prompts and menus of bank cash machines have replaced tasks previously done by human effort.

Job enlargement

Job enlargement emerged in the 1950s when many managers sought a job design strategy to reduce the boredom associated with the job simplification approach. The aim is to increase the breadth of a job by adding to the variety of tasks performed by a worker. Task variety is assumed to offset some of the disadvantages of job simplification, thereby increasing job performance and satisfaction for the individual. Job enlargement increases task variety by combining into one job two or more tasks previously assigned to separate workers. The only change in the original job design is that a worker now does a greater variety of tasks.

Job enlargement involves increasing task variety by combining into one job tasks of similar skill levels that were previously assigned to separate workers.

Often job enlargement has not lived up to its promise. For example, if a graphic designer who has been designing business brochures and posters is also given the task of preparing book-cover layouts, the job has been enlarged even if the same basic technique of using computer design software is used. The designer's supervisor would still secure the business, conduct meetings with the client and oversee the tasks, so there is no more responsibility. Job enlargement may add variety and alleviate boredom with mundane tasks but there may be limits to how much it might stimulate and satisfy the designer.

Job rotation

Like job enlargement, job rotation increases task variety but generally it does so by periodically shifting workers among jobs involving different tasks at similar skill levels. Job rotation can be arranged around almost any time period, such as hourly, daily or weekly schedules. For example, a nurse may be rotated on a monthly basis, looking after geriatric patients one month, surgical patients the next and rehabilitation patients each third month.

Job rotation involves increasing task variety by periodically shifting workers among jobs involving different tasks at similar levels of skill.

However, as with job enlargement, the results have sometimes been disappointing. If a rotation cycle takes employees through a series of the same old jobs, the employees simply experience many boring jobs instead of just one. The nurse may still be doing the same repetitive tasks of checking pulses and taking blood pressure and temperatures in each ward. In different wards there may be different tasks such as checking and changing wound dressings or feeding patients in geriatrics, but overall the tasks may still seem routine.

Job rotation may decrease efficiency because people spend more time changing but it can add to workforce flexibility. Staff can be moved from one job to another and this is currently often the primary purpose of job rotation. Employers have a more adaptable workforce to accomplish work tasks when employees are on holiday or sick leave; or when they move from the organization.

Perhaps the greatest weakness in the application of job rotation in the 1950s was that workers tended to be rotated horizontally (expanding the scope of the job) – that is, across tasks that demanded similar skill profiles. In other words, just as with enlargement, there was a **horizontal loading** of tasks, which means that the breadth of the job is increased by the addition of a variety of tasks. Research (for example in Denmark) continues to show that, although job-rotation schemes are widely used, they do little to enhance employee motivation and job satisfaction because of this horizontal loading.[6] Since the mid-1970s, job rotation has become an important part of work experience and corporate acculturation. New employees are often rotated around the company and across different divisions to gain a better understanding of the corporate structure and corporate work and communication networks. Many graduate training programmes in the UK include what is known as 'Cook's Tour' of planned job rotation as part of their training programme, allowing graduates to experience all aspects of the business including a period spent working on the shop floor before being given their first substantive appointment. Job rotation can often involve **vertical loading**, which enables increasing job depth by adding responsibilities, like planning and controlling, which were previously held by supervisors. Such experience often contributes to employee development and helps overcome many limitations of the earlier approaches to job rotation. China, for example, has used rotation schemes to send employees from central urban locations into rural areas to keep in touch with the needs of rural communities.[7] Global companies in China such as Kone, Standard Chartered and Schering all offer job rotation as a feature of employment on their careers pages.[8] Vertical loading is a key aspect of job enrichment.

Horizontal loading *involves increasing the breadth of a job by adding to the variety of tasks that the worker performs.*

Vertical loading *involves increasing job depth by adding responsibilities, like planning and controlling, previously held by supervisors.*

Job enrichment

Frederick Herzberg, whose two-factor theory is discussed in Chapter 4, suggests that it is illogical to expect high levels of motivation from employees whose jobs are designed according to the rules of simplification, enlargement or rotation (with horizontal loading). Herzberg asks, '[Why] should a worker become motivated when one or more "meaningless" tasks are added to previously existing ones or when work assignments are rotated among equally "meaningless" tasks?'[9] Rather than pursuing one of these job design strategies, Herzberg recommends that managers practise job enrichment.

Job enrichment is the practice of building motivating factors into job content. This job-design strategy differs from the previous ones in that it seeks to expand job content by adding planning and evaluating duties (normally performed by the manager) to the employee's job. The changes that increase the 'depth' of a job involve vertical loading of the tasks, as opposed to the horizontal loading involved in job enlargement and much job rotation.

Job enrichment *is the practice of building motivating factors into job content.*

The seven principles guiding Herzberg's approach to job enrichment are listed in Table 5.1. Each principle is an action guideline designed to increase the presence of one or more motivating factors. Remember, in the job enlargement and rotation strategies, managers tend to retain all responsibility for work planning and evaluating; in contrast, the job enrichment strategy involves vertical loading, which allows employees to share in these planning and evaluating responsibilities, as well as doing the actual work.

Principle	Motivators involved
1. Remove some controls while retaining accountability	Responsibility and achievement
2. Increase the accountability of individuals for their own work	Responsibility and recognition
3. Give a person a complete natural unit of work (module, division, area and so on)	Responsibility, achievement and recognition
4. Grant additional authority to employees in their activities; provide job freedom	Responsibility, achievement and recognition
5. Make periodic reports directly available to the worker rather than to the supervisor	Recognition
6. Introduce new and more difficult tasks that the individual has not previously handled	Growth and learning
7. Assign to individuals specific or specialized tasks; enable them to become experts	Responsibility, achievement, recognition and advancement

Table 5.1: Herzberg's principles of job enrichment.

On the face of it, job enrichment seems appealing. However, it has some problems:

- Little, if any, diagnosis of the jobs is undertaken before they are redesigned.
- Cost–benefit data concerning job enrichment are not often reported and it may not always be worth it. Much of the time it is expensive to implement, especially if work flows need to be redesigned and facilities or equipment changed.
- Situational factors specifically supporting job enrichment have often not been systematically assessed.
- Many reports of the success of job enrichment have been evangelical in nature; that is, the authors overstate benefits and understate problems. There are few reported failures in the literature, possibly as a result of such bragging.
- Evaluations of job enrichment programmes too often have not been conducted rigorously using the appropriate scientific method.

- Many trials of job enrichment have been undertaken with hand-picked employees, rather than a random sample of employees representing differing skill profiles and job environments.
- Job enrichment theory fails to recognize and emphasize that individuals may respond differently to job enrichment and that not all individuals will like it.
- Job enrichment falls into that category of workplace innovations that is much talked about but not widely practised. Despite the plethora of literature defining job enrichment, only a small number of case studies have actually been reported.[10]

The various strategies of job design are summarized on a continuum in Figure 5.1. This figure shows how the strategies differ in their degree of task specialization and as sources of intrinsic work rewards. The availability of intrinsic rewards is lowest for task attributes associated with simplified jobs, and highest for enriched jobs. Task specialization is higher for simplified jobs and lower for enriched jobs.

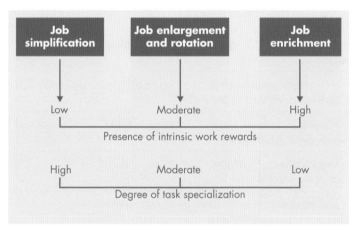

Figure 5.1: A continuum of job design strategies.

The four basic approaches to job design (simplification, enlargement, rotation and enrichment), as shown in Figure 5.1, have provided vital insights into the complexity of effective job design. Collectively, they are an important platform for later theorists. However, the common factor underlying these approaches is that they are 'static'; that is, they assume that all individuals will respond in the same, positive manner to these approaches. They fail to recognize the 'dynamic' nature of individual behaviour – that workers can and will respond in a variety of ways to the implementation of any innovative job design approach. To be effective, a manager needs to be able to understand, identify and predict how an individual employee will respond to any job redesign approach.

THE JOB CHARACTERISTICS MODEL

Pioneering work by Turner and Lawrence and Hulin and Blood in the 1960s began to look at the role of individual differences in job design.[11] They were trying to understand how an individual would respond to job redesign. That work led to the diagnostic approach – a technique developed by Richard Hackman and Greg Oldham and which is the basis of their job characteristics model (sometimes abbreviated to JCM). This model addresses job design in a contingency fashion.[12] The diagnostic job design approach, which generated considerable research in the 1980s, recognizes that there will be differences in the way any group of individuals responds to a change in the design of their jobs.

The current version of this approach to job enrichment, as depicted in Hackman and Oldham's **job characteristics model**, is shown in Figure 5.2. Five core job characteristics are identified as task attributes of special importance in the diagnosis of job design. A job that is high in these core characteristics is said to be enriched. The core job characteristics are:

*The **job characteristics model** identifies five core characteristics (skill variety, task identity, task significance, autonomy and job feedback) as having special importance to job designs.*

- *Skill variety* – the degree to which the job requires an employee to undertake a variety of different activities and use different skills and talents.
- *Task identity* – the degree to which the job requires completion of a 'whole' and identifiable piece of work (that is, it involves doing a job from beginning to end with a visible outcome).
- *Task significance* – the degree to which the job is important and involves a meaningful contribution to the organization or society in general.
- *Autonomy* – the degree to which the job gives the employee substantial freedom, independence and discretion in scheduling the work and determining the procedures used in carrying it out.
- *Job feedback* – the degree to which carrying out the work activities results in the employee obtaining direct and clear information on how well the job has been done.

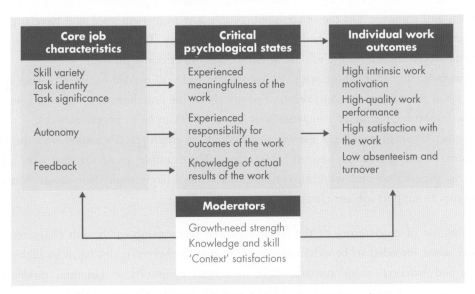

Figure 5.2: Job design implications of job characteristics theory.

Source: Adapted from Hackman, J. R. and Oldham, G. R. (1975), Development of the Job Diagnostic Survey. *Journal of Applied Psychology,* **60**, 159–170. Reproduced by permission of Richard Hackman.

Hackman and Oldham state further that three critical psychological states must be realized for people to develop intrinsic work motivation. These are:

- experienced meaningfulness in the work;
- experienced responsibility for the outcomes of the work;
- knowledge of actual results of the work activities.

These psychological states represent intrinsic rewards that are believed to occur and to influence later performance and satisfaction when the core job characteristics are present in the job design.

Individual differences: moderators of the job characteristics model

The job characteristics model recognizes that the five core job characteristics do not affect all people in the same way. Unlike many earlier theories of job design, the job characteristics model recognizes individual differences in response to changes in job design. A number of factors will influence the manner in which any individual employee responds to changes in the design of his or her job. These factors are called 'job design moderators'. Figure 5.2 shows three important individual difference moderators:

- *Growth-need strength.* This is the degree to which a person desires the opportunity for self-direction, learning and personal accomplishment at work. It is similar to Maslow's esteem and self-actualization and Alderfer's growth needs. The theory predicts that people strong in growth-need will respond positively to enriched jobs, experiencing high internal motivation, high growth satisfaction, high-quality performance and low absenteeism and turnover. On the other hand, people low in growth-need will have negative reactions and will find enriched jobs a source of anxiety. They are likely to be at risk of being 'overstretched' in the job and possibly balking at doing the job.[13]
- *Knowledge and skill.* Those with the knowledge and skill needed for performance in an enriched job are predicted to respond positively to the enrichment. Once again, we see how important a sense of competency or self-efficacy can be to people at work.
- *Context satisfaction.* This is the extent to which an employee is satisfied with the kind of contextual factors emphasized by Herzberg. For example, those satisfied with salary levels, supervision and working conditions are more likely than their dissatisfied colleagues to support job enrichment.

This list of moderators of the work outcome relationship of the job characteristics model is not intended to be exhaustive because many other variables (such as high-order needs and workers' value systems) have also been examined as potential moderators of reactions to these job dimensions.[14] In general, people whose capabilities match the requirements of an enriched job are likely to experience positive feelings and to perform well; people who are inadequate or who feel inadequate in this regard are likely to have difficulties.

The following 'OB in Action' looks at the increasing importance of having jobs that will attract and retain talented global workers.

For the organization that invests in talented employees it is important to be sure that the job offered is sufficiently enriched, satisfying and motivating to retain the employees into the future, although this cannot, of course, be guaranteed as talented workers may continue to seek new opportunities. For example, president of ANZ China, Andrew McGregor, says that the bank's really good people are headhunted at least weekly. At ANZ China (in locations such as Shanghai), many Chinese workers have gained 'Western' experience in the bank. In order to retain these workers, he tries to promote exchanges with Australian bank workers to enhance their global experience. In the context of mobile global workers there will also be a need to consider cultural differences for workers from different backgrounds in any job placement or design. McGregor, for example, has found that, although his Chinese workers adapt to less hierarchical organizational structures, it is difficult to foster feedback and open discussion with them because of their respect for people in higher positions.[15] One might expect this given Hofstede's findings on cultural differences set out in Chapter 1.

The shortage of knowledge workers continues despite the recent global economic downturn and is also being exacerbated by demographic changes, in particular the likely brain drain as the 'baby boomers' near retirement,[16] and the underutilization of part-time workers, particularly women, in the workforce through the 'hidden brain drain.' The UK's Equality and Human Rights Commission argued that the incidence of flexible working practices needs to be extended in order to take full advantage of these often highly qualified and experienced workers.[17] These themes are explored later in the chapter.

OB IN ACTION

Attracting and retaining talented global workers

'Talent is elusive – it's everywhere yet nowhere as talent shortages continue to persist in many countries and industry sectors,' that's according to Manpower Inc. They surveyed over 35 000 employers across 36 countries to determine the impact of talent shortages on today's labour markets and the results of their fifth annual Talent Shortage Survey 2010 revealed that 31% of employers worldwide are having difficulty filling positions due to the lack of suitable talent available.[18]

Other survey evidence supports Manpower's findings. In South Africa a severe shortage of

mining engineers is predicted to hamper future growth of the industry;[19] The so-called 'brain drain' has caused major shortages of information technology and e-business professionals, particularly in western Europe; in the UK, highly skilled foreign workers have been used to plug the gaps in health-care, IT and managerial work; and at the other end of the scale, the influx of unskilled migrant workers from eastern Europe has boosted the UK economy by filling vacancies in agriculture, hotel and catering industries that UK workers don't want to do.[20] Skills shortages have also contributed to the trend of shifting business activities overseas, in particular many banks and other major organizations have outsourced call centre operations to India, and to a lesser extent to the Philippines and China.[21]

Although the current global economic situation has increased the number of overall job seekers worldwide, there is still a notable talent shortage in many countries and industry sectors. So the immediate problem is not the *number* of potential candidates. Rather, it is a *talent mismatch*: there are not enough sufficiently skilled people in the right places at the right times. Simultaneously, employers are seeking ever-more-specific skill sets and com-binations of skills – not just technical capabilities alone, but perhaps in combination with critical thinking skills or other qualities that will help drive the company forward. As a result, the 'right' person for a particular job is becoming much harder to find. And the problem shows no signs of easing.[22]

There can be considerable incentives for mobile workers to move to where the best jobs can be found – there is often competition between countries for the best workers. In India the expan-sion of the financial services market has meant that there has been increasing competition for English-speaking graduates, resulting in severe skills shortages and annual turnover rates in call centres as high as 150%.[23] Attracting 'talent' and retaining good employees is widely discussed in contemporary business literature because of its importance to organizational success but job design is also important in this context. Knowledge-based economies can contribute towards changing job design so that organizations can offer jobs that will attract the most talented workers. These workers are often highly qualified and can afford to seek out jobs that offer them meaning, responsi-bility and opportunities for personal advancement and improvement. Survey evidence in the UK sug-gests that if job rotation schemes are not present, these workers will simply move on.[24]

A job diagnostic survey is a questionnaire used to examine each of the dimensions of the job characteristics model.

A motivating potential score is a summary of a job's overall potential for motivating those in the workplace.

Testing and the motivating potential score

Hackman and Oldham developed the **job diagnostic survey** questionnaire to test each of the dimensions in their job characteristics model, as shown in Figure 5.2. They also devel-oped a **motivating potential score** (MPS) to summarize a job's overall potential for motiv-ating those in the workplace. You can calculate this score using the following formula:

$$\text{MPS} = (\text{variety} + \text{identity} + \text{significance}) / 3 \times \text{autonomy} \times \text{feedback}$$

The scores for each of the dimensions come from the job diagnostic survey and show the great importance of autonomy and feedback in providing the results shown in Figure 5.2. The MPS is especially useful for identifying low-scoring jobs that may benefit most from redesign.

The research

Considerable research has been done on the job characteristics approach. The approach has been examined in a variety of work settings, including banks, dental practices, telephone companies and such organizations as IBM and Texas Instruments. Job-design studies using this approach have also been reported in the Netherlands[25] and the UK.[26] More recently, evidence from India suggests a positive correlation between the job characteristics model and work-to-family enrichment.[27]

A comprehensive review of the approach shows that:[28]

- On average, job characteristics affect performance but not nearly as much as they affect satisfaction.
- It is important to consider growth-need strength. Job characteristics influence performance more strongly for high growth-need employees than for low growth-need employees. The relationship to growth-need is about as strong as that to job satisfaction.
- Employee perceptions of job characteristics are different from objective measures and from those of independent observers. Positive results are typically strongest when an overall performance measure is used, rather than a separate measure of quality or quantity.

Effective Manager 5.1 summarizes some guidelines for implementing a job enrichment programme and for reviewing the process.

EFFECTIVE MANAGER 5.1

Guidelines for implementing a programme of job enrichment

Consider a job to be a candidate for job enrichment only when evidence exists that job satisfaction and/or performance is either deteriorating or open for improvement. Use a diagnostic approach and proceed with actual job enrichment only when:

- employees view their jobs as deficient in one or more of the core job characteristics;
- extrinsic rewards and job context are not causing dissatisfaction;
- cost and other potential constraints do not prohibit job design changes necessary for enrichment;
- employees view core job characteristics positively;
- employees have needs and capabilities consistent with new job designs.

Whenever possible, conduct a careful evaluation of the results of job enrichment to discontinue the job design strategy (if necessary) or to make constructive changes to increase its value. Expect that enrichment will also affect the job of the supervising manager because duties will be delegated. Do not feel threatened or become anxious or frustrated. If needed, get help for required personal work adjustments.

Experts generally agree that the job diagnostic approach which forms the basis of Hackman and Oldham's job characteristics model is useful. A series of implementation concepts for the enrichment of core job characteristics is outlined in Figure 5.3 and some impacts of enriching core job characteristics are listed in Table 5.2. However, these experts urge caution in applying the technique, emphasizing that it is not a universal panacea for job performance and satisfaction problems. It can fail when job requirements are increased beyond the level of individual capabilities and/or interest. It can also raise issues of changes in remuneration – if employees are taking on more responsibility, should they be paid more? In summary, jobs high in core characteristics (especially as perceived by employees) tend to increase both satisfaction and performance, particularly among high growth-need employees. The following 'Counterpoint' looks at how job enrichment may overtax employees and increase the imbalance between the working and personal lives of employees (work–life balance is also discussed further later in the chapter).

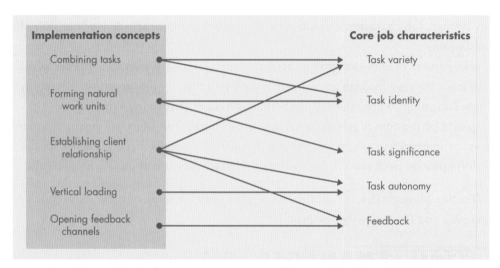

Figure 5.3: Implementation concepts and the core job characteristics.

Source: Derived from Hackman, J. R., Oldham, G. and Purdy, K. (1975), A new strategy for job enrichment. *California Management Review*, **17** (4), 62.

	Enriched	*Unenriched*
Skill variety	Decided own strategy for performing task and changed strategy at will.	Were provided with explicit instructions for task to perform and strategy to use (e.g. 'first, open letters').
Task identity	Formed into groups of ten; performed all necessary operations on a certain proportion of customer requests.	As an individual, performed just one of these operations on all requests.
Task significance	Were briefed about importance of their jobs and how they fitted into the organization as a whole.	Received no formal instruction.
Autonomy	Chose length and timing of breaks. Performed own inspections at intervals they determined.	Except for breaks, stayed at workplace throughout the day. Had work periodically checked by inspectors.
Feedback	Saw productivity posted on scoreboards at end of each day.	Received no specific information about performance level.

Table 5.2: Sample core job characteristics for enriched and unenriched jobs.

COUNTERPOINT

Enrichment and work–life balance in the 'real world'

The notion of job design and job enrichment transforming the working lives of people is commendable. However, in reality there are much more complicated factors involved and the job experience for many people, although perhaps more stimulating, challenging and satisfying, may also be much more stressful and difficult.

The suggestions for job enrichment in Table 5.2 look very reasonable. The opportunity for developing more skills, for completing more parts of the task, for having autonomy and feedback and viewing your job as significant in the organization are commendable. Many people are experiencing enriched jobs in many organizations. More skills are acquired and required to do the job. Jobs are less routine and more autonomous and people take responsibility for much of their own work. They are often given a sense of identity with the task and feel their work is significant. But how does this fit into the real world of longer working hours and pressures for balance between work and home?

While endeavouring to improve jobs on the one hand, it would appear that organizations can also be major contributors to making individual workers' lives very difficult. In many countries people are being required to work longer hours. In the EU long working hours are still a key feature of working life for many workers; despite the introduction of the European Working Time Directive, over 10% of all employees still work more than 48 hours a week.[29] Workers in eastern and southern Europe (particularly in the hospitality and construction industry) work the longest; for example 64% of workers in Romania work in excess of 45 hours per week and senior managers in all member states typically work more than 48 hours.[30] In Australia the difference between perception of working life and

the reality was clearly illustrated by a survey of young graduates. The survey found that 58% of employers expected graduates to work up to 50 hours a week with very few (8%) paying overtime. In contrast, only 45% of graduates had any expectation that they would be required to work these hours.[31] Companies might talk actively about enriched jobs and work–life balance but we need to take some stock of how these changes really affect people. Given more responsibility in enriched jobs, many people will work harder to do what is required for the job, even when it involves working longer hours. A number of studies in the UK and across Europe all show that although working longer hours improves pay prospects, it does not improve career prospects and has a significant affect on work satisfaction, feelings of wellness and work–life balance.[32] However, increasing hours were also linked to increasing employee consultation, involvement in decision making, career opportunities and awareness of organizational direction. It seems that when there is some 'say' in their work and a desire for career success, workers may be more prepared to work long hours and sacrifice some balance between their work and home lives.[33]

Questions

1. How and why would an enriched job cause an employee to work longer hours?

2. What responsibility do managers have to ensure their employees do not work excessive hours and experience excessive stress?

3. Is there any value in organizations providing flexible work arrangements if, at the same time, they are encouraging employees (intentionally or unintentionally) to work longer hours?

SOCIO-TECHNICAL JOB DESIGN

Socio-technical job design *is the design of jobs to optimize the relationship between the technology system and the social system.*

Technology can sometimes constrain the ability to enrich jobs. **Socio-technical job design** recognizes this problem and seeks to optimize the relationship between the technology system and the social system. This is achieved by designing work roles to integrate with the technology system. Best known is the semiautonomous work group approach, by which self-managed or autonomous work teams perform a job previously done on the assembly line (these teams are discussed in Chapter 8).

It is difficult and costly to modify technology in an existing factory, and to change work practices and job design across the entire organization, so the socio-technical approach often works more effectively in a 'Greenfield' site (that is, a new site with no established work practices).

Since the mid-1990s some managers have begun to question the costs of maintaining and developing this socio-technical approach in some factories because of the rising costs associated with rapid knowledge obsolescence and multiskilling the workforce. However, this is not always a problem, or organizations can take action to minimize this effect. For example, while Boeing has different cockpits on its different aircraft, Airbus's strategy is to have the same cockpit on all the models in its fleet. This means that pilots require much less re-skilling when they move between different aircraft models. More research on the costs and benefits of the approach in contemporary environments and of strategies to minimize problems is needed to address such criticisms.

SOCIAL INFORMATION AND JOB DESIGN

The social information-processing approach *argues that individual needs, task perceptions and reactions are a result of socially constructed realities.*

Gerald Salancik and Jeffrey Pfeffer have reviewed the literature on the job diagnostic approach to job design.[34] They question whether jobs have stable and objective characteristics that individuals perceive and to which they respond predictably and consistently. As an alternative, their **social information-processing approach** argues that individual needs, task perceptions and reactions are a result of socially constructed realities. Thus, social information in the workplace influences employees' perceptions of the job and their responses to it (see Chapter 2 for a fuller discussion of the topic of perception). It is much like a student's perception of a class. Several of the student's friends may tell her that the lecturer is bad, the content is boring and the class requires too much work. The student may then think that the critical characteristics of the class are the lecturer, the content and the workload and that they are all bad. All of this may take place before the student has even set foot in that class and may substantially influence the student's class perception and response, regardless of the characteristics in the job characteristics approach.

Research on the social information-processing approach provides mixed results. Essentially, the results show that social information processing does influence task perceptions and attitudes, but the kinds of job characteristics described earlier remain very important.

MULTISKILLING

Multiskilling programmes help employees become members of a flexible workforce and acquire an array of skills needed to perform multiple tasks in a company's production or customer-service function. The cross-training and multiskilling of employees allow them to assume broader responsibilities so they are better equipped to solve problems. When a team member is absent there is always someone who can take over the role. When suggestions for process improvements are required, members of the team have the requisite skills and expertise to make highly valued contributions. The training programme in the following 'OB in Action' illustrates this.

OB IN ACTION

A training initiative to broaden the skills of staff at the Marriott's Marble Arch Hotel in London UK has helped employees become more flexible. The training scheme, which was offered to all 150 staff, enabling them to develop the skills needed in different departments, thus improving their ability and enabling them to become more flexible through the introduction of multiskilling. This was mutually beneficial as it allowed staff to move across departments but also increased opportunities and readiness for promotion or movement sideways within the organization. The scheme that helped the hotel win a British Hospitality Association 'Excellence through People Award' has now been incorporated into the induction process. All new staff now receive a two-week cross-training programme, which gives them the skills and flexibility to be able to work in a range of departments. The scheme is also available to staff looking to develop skills.[35]

Multiskilling is an innovative work practice that has helped improve organizational performance by 30–40% in some cases. Strong links between a multiskilled workforce and improved productivity have been identified. More recently, the skills matrix has been used to measure employees' skill levels and compare them to the desired levels, which are often an upward-moving target. Multiskilling has also helped some organizations such as Barrett Developments, the UK's largest house builder, survive the recession, minimizing job and skills losses and increasing flexibility. Apprentice roofers, for example, are now expected to be able to fit solar panels as part of their job.[36]

Overall, employees in a flexible workforce benefit from having a challenging and varied work experience, more control over their work environment, higher skill levels, higher pay opportunities and greater marketability in the job market.

GOAL-SETTING THEORY

Goal setting
*is the process
of developing,
negotiating and
formalizing an
employee's targets
and objectives.*

A reasonable question for any employee to ask an employer is: 'What is it you want me to do?' Without clear and appropriate goals, employees may suffer a direction problem and be unable to channel their work energies towards the right goal. Many sportsmen and women use goal setting to focus their training and motivation, as the next 'Research in OB' box illustrates.

Similar problems are found in many workplaces. Proper setting and clarification of task goals can eliminate, or at least reduce, these and other problems. **Goal setting** involves building challenging and specific goals into jobs and providing appropriate performance feedback.

RESEARCH IN OB

Many people associate goal setting with New Year's resolutions, and are quick to dismiss it as ineffective, since most well-intentioned, if vague, resolutions have failed before the end of January. Most such resolutions are perfect examples of how **not** to set goals. However, goal setting has been widely used in sports psychology to help top athletes to improve their performance. In sports, as well as in life, it is very important to set goals for yourself.

Michael Johnson did just this in the course of a spectacular career. He rewrote the record books when he became the only man ever to win both 200m and 400m Olympic gold medals at the 1996 Olympics. At times he was, quite literally, 'in a class of his own'. However, according to Johnson in his book *Slaying the Dragon*, his achievements were based not purely on talent but on hard physical conditioning, mental strength, a clear vision of where he wanted to go and a plan of how to get there. His book is an insight into how he mobilized his talent through effective goal setting. Not everyone has

the talent to be a Michael Johnson, but anyone can achieve significant improvements in performance by means of effective goal setting.

But many people struggle to achieve their goals unless someone else provides the impetus to pursue the goal. For example, some individuals will tell you that they can only lose weight if they join a club such as Weight Watchers, or choose to stay up all night to complete an assignment the night before it's due in because they can't seem to motivate themselves any earlier.

So how might sports psychology help? Academics at Sheffield Hallam University argue that techniques used by high-flying athletes can help improve employee engagement and performance. Ambitious long-term goals such as winning an Olympic medal are broken down into shorter-term targets that are easier to reach, winning a specific race for example, that celebrate their achievements rather than focus on financial rewards.[37] These are coupled with 'positive self-talk', this means telling yourself you can do something even if it seems out of reach and 'visualization' techniques to help in achievement of goals. Paula Radcliffe used visualization techniques on the way to winning the New York Marathon, in the pursuit of her goal she visualized herself celebrating her win holding her baby daughter.

Looking at issues such as mental toughness, performance under pressure and creating a winning mindset are priorities for sports scientists in helping athletes achieve their goals and it helps to build our resilience at work. For instance, if Roger Federer has to play a match point on Wimbledon's centre court, how does he manage to focus? Are there aspects of this single-mindedness that someone can use if they have to give a complex presentation, for example?

Research on goal setting in the worlds of business and in sport and exercise has consistently shown that it can lead to enhanced performance. In fact, evaluation of the data from a whole series of experiments showed that goal setting led to performance enhancement in 78% of sport and exercise research studies, with moderate to strong effects.[38]

Goal setting is the 'process of developing, negotiating and formalizing the targets or objectives that an employee is responsible for accomplishing'.[39] Expanding job design to include goal setting results in specific task goals for each individual. These task goals are important because they have a link with task performance. Over a number of years, Edwin Locke developed a set of arguments and predictions concerning this link. This set of predictions serves as the basis for goal-setting theory. Locke's research and that of others provides considerable support for the following predictions:[40]

1. Difficult goals are more likely to lead to higher performance than are less difficult ones because they encourage effort that leads to greater outcomes. However, if the goals are seen as too difficult or as impossible, the relationship with performance no longer holds. An individual is likely to cease trying if the goal is unattainable.

2. Specific goals are more likely to lead to higher performance than are no goals or vague or general ones. Setting a specific goal of selling ten refrigerators a month should lead to better performance than a simple 'do your best' goal.

3. Task feedback, or knowledge of results, is likely to motivate people towards higher performance by encouraging the setting of higher performance goals. Feedback lets people

know where they stand and if they are on or off course in their efforts; for example, think about how eager you are to find out how well you have done in an examination.

4. Goals are most likely to lead to higher performance when people have the abilities and the feelings of self-efficacy required to accomplish them. Individuals must believe that they are able to accomplish the goals and feel confident in their abilities.

5. Goals are most likely to motivate people towards higher performance when they are accepted and there is commitment to them. One way of achieving such acceptance or commitment is by participating in the goal-setting process. You then feel a sense of 'ownership' of the goals. However, Locke and Latham report that goals assigned by someone else can be equally effective. The assigners are likely to be influential authority figures. Also, the assignment implies that the employee can actually reach the goal. Third, assigned goals are often a challenge. Finally, assigned goals help define the standards people use to attain personal satisfaction with their performance.[41] According to Locke and Latham, assigned goals only lead to poor performance when they are curtly or inadequately explained.[42]

Goal setting: follow-up research

Research using and extending the five predictions discussed is now quite extensive. Indeed, there is more research for goal setting than for any other theory related to work motivation.[43] Nearly 400 studies have been conducted in several countries, including Australia, the UK, Germany, Japan and the US.[44] Locke and Latham and their associates have been at the forefront of this work and have recently integrated their predictions into a more comprehensive framework that links goals to performance. We show a simplified version of the Locke and Latham framework in Figure 5.4.

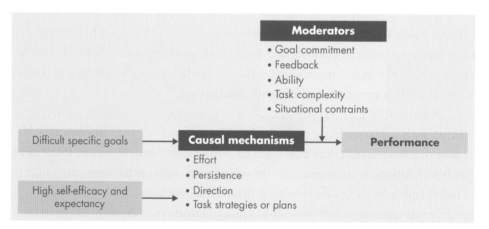

Figure 5.4: Simplified Locke and Latham goal-setting framework.

Source: Adapted from Locke, E. A. and Latham, G. P. (1990), Work motivation and satisfaction: light at the end of the tunnel. *Psychological Science*, 1 (4), 244. Reproduced by permission of Blackwell Publishing.

Starting at the left we see the difficult, specific goals mentioned earlier in predictions 1 and 2. These are joined by high self-efficacy (mentioned in prediction 4 and emphasized in Chapters 2 and 4) and high expectancy (discussed as a part of expectancy motivation theory in Chapter 4). The argument is that these factors operate through the linking mechanisms of effort, persistence, direction and task strategies or plans to affect performance. At the same time, the moderators of goal commitment (prediction 5), feedback (prediction 3), ability (prediction 4), task complexity and situational constraints also operate to strengthen or weaken the relationship between goals and performance.

Locke's predictions concerning goal setting are still relevant. However, they have now been embedded in the simplified framework in Figure 5.4. That framework includes some ideas discussed in the motivation chapter and relates to concepts from expectancy theory, as shown in our discussion in the previous paragraph of the role of expectancy and self-efficacy. Further, although our simplified framework does not show it, Locke and Latham argue that the instrumentality concept from expectancy theory (that is, that performance leads to rewards) operates through the link between challenging goals and valued rewards.[45] Again, the basic tenets of expectancy theory prove useful in explaining work behaviour. This relationship has sometimes led to the treatment of goal-setting theory as a process motivation theory, in addition to the equity and expectancy theories discussed in Chapter 4. Furthermore, the task-complexity notion discussed earlier suggests a link with job enrichment. As more enrichment is built into a job, the job becomes more complex and probably calls for new task strategies or plans. Finally, Locke's fourth prediction links goal-setting theory with ability as an individual attribute and with self-efficacy, which is so important in social learning theory.[46]

Goal setting and MBO

When we speak of goal setting and its potential to influence individual performance at work, the concept of management by objectives (MBO) immediately comes to mind. This approach has been widely used in many large organizations in both the public and private sectors.[47] In Europe and the US many senior executives have performance-based contracts that identify clear goal-achievement milestones for each year.

Management by objectives involves managers working with their employees to establish performance goals and plans that are consistent with higher level work unit and organizational objectives.[48] When this process is followed throughout an organization, MBO helps to clarify the hierarchy of objectives as a series of well-defined means–end chains.

Figure 5.5 shows a comprehensive view of MBO. The concept is consistent with the notion of goal setting and its associated principles (as already discussed). Notice how joint supervisor–employee discussions are designed to extend participation from the point of initial goal establishment to the point of evaluating results in terms of goal attainment. Key issues for mutual goal setting are summarized in Effective Manager 5.2.

In addition to the goal-setting steps previously discussed, a successful MBO system calls for careful implementation. This means that the previous steps are translated into the kinds of strategies or plans, mentioned earlier, that will lead to goal accomplishment.

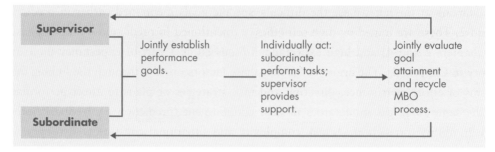

Figure 5.5: The management by objectives (MBO) process.

Employees must have freedom to carry out the required tasks; managers may have to carry out considerable coaching and counselling. As with other applied organizational behaviour programmes, managers should be aware of MBO's potential costs as well as its benefits.

EFFECTIVE MANAGER 5.2

Key issues for mutual goal setting in an MBO programme

- What must be done? Start with higher level goals, job descriptions stating tasks to be performed, outcomes expected, necessary supplies and equipment and so on.
- How will performance be measured? Time, money or physical units are often used to measure performance. If the job is more subjective, emphasize behaviours or actions believed to lead to success.
- What is the performance standard? Start with previous performance or the average performance of others doing this job. Where these

measures do not exist, use mutual supervisor–subordinate judgement and discussion.
- What are the deadlines for the goals? Discuss deadlines in terms of daily, weekly or longer terms.
- What is the relative importance of the goals? Not all goals are equally important. The manager and employee should decide the goal ranking together.
- How difficult are the goals? Watch especially for high task complexity and multiple goals. Come up with a clearly agreed decision.

Despite substantial research based on case studies of MBO success, such research has not always been rigorously controlled and it reports mixed results.[49] In general, and as an application of goal-setting theory, MBO has much to offer. But it is not easy to start and keep going. MBO may also need to be implemented organization-wide if it is to work well.[50]

KEY PERFORMANCE INDICATORS

The concept of individual goal setting has been further developed over the past few years to introduce the concept of **key performance indicators** (KPIs) – standards against which individual and organizational performance can be measured.

Such measurement is a step in the benchmarking process taken by companies wanting to achieve superior performance in a formal and structured way. High performance has been linked to improved business performance, which has been strongly associated with improvements in recognizing and using an organization's key performance indicators. In the UK, the government's national standard for HR activity 'Investors in People' (IIP) is underpinned by the concept of KPIs. Investors in People is a continuous improvement activity designed to help organizations of any size or type to achieve their business object-ives through its people investment. IIP involves companies achieving ten KPIs in order to gain the award, although the award is not prescriptive as it encourages organizations to achieve the standard in their own way. Over 30 000 have done so since the scheme began in 1993.[51]

Key performance indicators *are standards against which individual and organizational performance can be measured.*

The use of such indicators in employee remuneration packages has been popular.[52] Using performance appraisals, an employee's pay is structured according to their achieve-ment of individual key performance indicators that cascade down from organizational ones. The individual's contribution to the organization can thus be measured because the indicators provide a benchmark against which an employee can be judged. The use of per-formance appraisals holds employees accountable for their achievements.

A key performance indicator must therefore be Specific, Measurable, Achievable, Real-istic and Time-framed (SMART) in the same way that goal-setting targets in general need to be SMART.[53] It depends on the nature of the employee's job, the industry in which the employee works, the strategic direction and goals of the company and the bottom line of the organization.

The common use of key performance indicators to measure quantifiable targets also extends to qualitative issues, such as staff initiative and communication skills. For example, the Australian National Maritime Museum's KPIs include quantitative targets, such as number of visitor interactions, as well as qualitative ones, such as reputation (assessed by focus groups).[54]

RETHINKING WORK PATTERNS – FLEXIBLE WORKING

Attempting to enhance worker satisfaction through job redesign involves mostly intrinsic factors related to doing the job. Employee satisfaction (as well as avoidance of dissatis-faction) can also be achieved by changing job conditions, such as the timing or number of working hours and work location. For example, the employee may experience a more acceptable working environment (extrinsic change) if working hours are flexible enough to allow the achievement of other (personal) goals. This, in turn, may affect the employee's levels of work motivation and performance (intrinsic changes) because they are more satis-fied with their job environment. The key drivers and practices of flexible work arrange-ments are now presented.

Major drivers of changing work arrangements

For many the design of jobs in the modern workplace is not about the nature of the job itself, but more about work arrangements or how and when the job is done. Flexibility in the workplace is about developing modern working practices to fit the needs of the 21st century. Flexible working opportunities can be good for everyone – both employers and employees have the flexibility to organize their working arrangements in a way that suits them. The opening case study at Best Buy is one example of how employers are restructuring work arrangements in order to attract, retain and motivate staff in an increasingly competitive market. Governments have also recognized the need for change in working practices; for example in the EU, the European Employment Strategy has, since the mid-1990s, been driving through changes that focus on the introduction of more flexible working practices. 'Policies on career breaks, parental leave and part-time work as well as flexible working arrangements which serve the interest of both employers and employees are of particular importance.'[55] This strategy is a key feature of the Lisbon Treaty which came into force on 1 December 2009 as the European Union recognizes the need for modern workplaces to optimize their working methods to both efficiently and effectively meet today's challenges in today's world.[56] In the UK, government initiatives have been in place for over ten years now to promote the benefits of more flexible working practices. Survey evidence found that 91% of respondents felt that: 'people work their best when they can balance their work and other aspects of their lives.'[57]

The world of work has seen enormous economic and social changes. Flexible working is good for businesses, families, older workers, carers and a growing population who want a better balance between work and home life. There is a wealth of evidence to support this, and the recession has created a climate where there is an even stronger appetite for the business case for flexible working. Organizations that use flexible strategies in the workforce have the potential to reap many benefits including:

- higher retention of staff and thus higher retention of organizational knowledge;
- less absenteeism;
- more capacity to meet peak demand and more capacity to service client demands outside normal hours;
- more contented, productive, committed and motivated employees;
- more diverse and qualified workforces.[58]

Work–life balance *refers to a concern which people have with balancing work hours with other responsibilities including caring for children or adults. It has become a key issue for employers with the advent of 24/7 societies and customers' expectations of where and when services should be provided for them.*

Flexible work practices can assist individual workers in dealing with their work in the context of the following drivers.

Changing family lifestyles and work–life balance

The prevalence of households where both partners are working (dual-income families) and the rising number of one-parent families, along with increasing hours worked, exacerbate the problems of balancing work and nonwork pressures. At the heart of the European strategy is the growing concern about demographic changes, the detrimental effects of long working hours and the view that **work–life balance** isn't just for mothers but for all employees. Substantial benefits can be gained for both employees and employers in considering the work–life balance for workers in very many different ways, as the following examples show.

Even simple measures can reduce the pressures on staff as they struggle to fulfil personal and work goals in the limited time available to them. For example, car parts manufacturer

Autoliv has set up a prayer room in its workplace to assist its many Muslim workers to participate in necessary religious activities.[59]

OB IN ACTION

B&Q, the home improvement retailer which employees nearly 40 000 people at over 300 stores across the UK, is committed to helping its employees to pursue their careers as well as feeling fulfilled in their personal lives. The company has long been known for welcoming older workers into its workforce, but its flexible approach to working practices in general means that the company has attracted and retained a diverse workforce. More than 60% of employees work flexible or part-time hours. The company has no length of service criteria for requesting flexibility and the majority of its policies are open to everyone regardless of their caring responsibilities. Term-time only contracts, for example, are available not only to parents, but also grandparents in recognition of the caring role that many of them have. Other working patterns that the company offers its workforce include: part-time working; job sharing; staggered start and finish times; split shifts and home and remote working for some employees. Why do it? B&Q argues that having flexible working practices contributes to employee engagement and commitment, which translate into improved customer satisfaction and profitability.[60]

Occupational stress and work patterns

With the emphasis on cost cutting and downsizing that has prevailed over the past few decades, where employees in many organizations are expected to 'do far more with less' it is hardly surprising that one of the major adverse influences on job satisfaction and work performance is the increasing incidence of **stress** at work.[61] In Europe the introduction of the Working Time Directive in 1998 was intended to reduce the maximum number of hours employees should work; however, many workers throughout Europe continue to work long hours. In the UK, survey evidence suggests that over 50% of employees worked some hours in addition to their fixed standard hours (an additional nine hours average for full-time workers),[62] with many professional workers still working more than 48 hours per week, often with unpaid overtime,[63] and nearly 20% of men and 6% of women were working excessively long hours on a regular basis.[64] Two-thirds of employees report putting in unpaid overtime in a climate of frozen pay and threat of redundancies where their employers do not appreciate their extra effort and are treated like dispensable commodities.[65] Thus the real working conditions of so many employees, with increased pressure to work harder and longer, are associated with rising levels of work stress and burnout, and it is not surprising that stress as an issue is becoming more prevalent.[66] Three

Stress is a state of tension experienced by individuals facing extraordinary demands, constraints or opportunities.

European studies support this view, concluding that the main causes of workplace stress are related to deficiencies in the design and management of work.[67] Some organizations are responding by offering extended breaks from the workplace, such as sabbatical leave, to help employees cope more effectively.[68] Others, as discussed later in this chapter, are beginning to see the benefits of offering their employees more flexible working arrangements. Stress at work is discussed further in Chapter 2.

Changing levels and modes of employment

Throughout the 1980s and into the 1990s, rising levels of unemployment dominated and impacted on work security and workload. After a period of stability in the late 1990s and early 2000s, where unemployment figures stabilized or decreased, unemployment has started to rise again and continues to do so as the world economy slowly recovers from recession triggered by the global banking crisis. For example, unemployment levels across the Eurozone (those using the Euro) had risen sharply to 10.1% in April 2010 compared to 7.3% in April 2009 and across the whole of the 27 EU member states unemployment rose to 23 million.[69] There are now four million fewer jobs than at the start of the banking crisis and there are significant variations between countries; for example, the UK's unemployment rate rose to 7.9% in April 2010 compared to nearly 20% in Spain and Estonia.[70]

Against this background the unemployment rates for women continue to be less than those for men, this may be because more full-time jobs have been lost than part time, but it is also a reflection of the significant increase in part-time working in the EU since 2002; in the UK alone, some 7.3 million people now work part time. This shift away from permanent full-time work is also reflected in the rise of fixed-term contract and agency employees working within Europe. Despite the recession there is still an increasing emphasis being placed on work–life balance and demographic changes, in particular the ageing workforce in Europe.[71] Labour shortages continue in some areas as well as the free movement of migrant workers within the EU. For example in Italy there is a severe shortage of nurses, which has resulted in immigration laws being relaxed for care workers, and in Sweden there is growing concern that 60% of all nurses are over 44 years of age.[72]

Ageing population and changing retirement patterns

The population in western Europe is ageing (16% over the age of 65)[73] and yet the labour market participation rates are declining sharply for men and women from their mid-50s onwards.[74] In the UK it is predicted that by 2033, 23% of the population will be aged 65 and over and only 16% aged 16 or younger. In addition, there is a sharp tapering of people in the workforce of those between 30–40 years old due to low birth rates in the 1970s.[75] Employees aged 50 or over now form 27% of the UK workforce.[76] These statistics, along with the introduction of the legislation on ageism in October 2006 and the raising of the State retirement age, have led many UK employers into rethinking their retirement strategies. There is also increasing pressure on social services, meaning that is vital for employees to continue working beyond retirement age and that as many older employees as possible are retained in the workforce. Flexible working options need to be explored to help retain the productive skills of many older workers whilst simultaneously offering them a new balance between work and lifestyle, as survey evidence indicates that respondents are more than willing to work beyond retirement providing they can work more flexibly.[77] Offering them part-time work, phased retirement or contracted work will also help to retain older workers.[78] UK retailers such as Asda, Tesco and B&Q have long been champions of the older worker, but UK employers as diverse as the Nationwide Building Society, Derby City Council and the Ministry of Defence have all introduced practical measures to support the recruitment and retention of older workers.[79] This trend is also reflected in Europe: Polyfelt in Austria, Dell Inc. in Slovenia, Zemat in Poland and Volvo in Sweden are just a few of the companies that have strategies under way.[80] The following examples illustrate some of these.

OB IN ACTION

The Danish supermarket chain Netto is one of the largest supermarket chains operating in Denmark and the rest of Scandinavia, as well as having a presence in Germany and the UK. Like many other retailers, it has initiated policies in order to attract and retain older employees. Older customers like to deal with older employees, so the company has recruited a more age diverse workforce. They believe that hiring employees who represent each age category optimizes customer satisfaction and profitability. Netto has also created three so-called 'senior supermarkets' where at least half of the employees in the supermarket are over 50 years old. This contrasts with the normal staffing in Netto's supermarkets where most of the employees are very young. After a period of implementation, the senior supermarkets have proven to fully measure up to the standards and profitability of the best supermarkets in the Netto chain. Personnel expenses are relatively higher in the senior supermarkets due to a greater degree of part-time and special arrangements, but costs of sick leave are much lower in the senior supermarkets. Furthermore, the senior supermarkets perform excellently in Netto's customer satisfaction surveys. There are no plans to open more senior supermarkets. Rather,

Netto intends to use the experience to create a higher age diversity in all its supermarkets in order to gain the advantages and benefits deriving from retaining older employees.[81]

Fars and Frosta Sparbank is the largest independent savings bank in Sweden. As part of its age diversity policy (over 20% of its workforce are over 55), a mentoring scheme was set up whereby experienced workers aged 55+ act as mentors to younger employees. Whilst the older workers pass on their wealth of knowledge and experience, the younger employees are able to reciprocate by contributing valuable knowledge relating to economics and computers. This sharing of knowledge has helped provide both personal development and knowledge transfer within the organization as well as improving the work environment, customer growth and the bank's public image.[82]

Telework
principles relate to work conducted remotely from the central organization using information technology

Changing technology and the capacity to work remotely

Information technology enables many changes to the way in which work is organized and located. Work can often be location independent and in reality there may be no need for the employee and the employer to meet regularly. **Teleworking** and working remotely from the office have been extensively discussed over many years[83] and, despite a slow takeup, have been increasing in popularity in the past few years. It is seen by many as a way to reduce overhead costs, as the Renault example in the following 'OB in Action' box illustrates.

OB IN ACTION

Renault, the French car manufacturer, first introduced teleworking and hot-desking at its Paris sites in 2007 in order to reduce costs. Under the original agreement employees were able to work between two and four days a week at home, but were required to spend one day a week in their offices where they would no longer have a designated work space but would hot-desk, sharing a desk with several other colleagues.

Today, Renault has more than 400 teleworkers and the programme is such a huge success that it has been extended to other sites. It is also more flexible; employees, for example, can now work any number of days away from the office and not necessarily from their main residence.

For the employee the benefits are the achievement of a better balance between work and private lives, reduced commuting, fatigue and stress as well as enabling them to organize their assignments in a more flexible way. For Renault it has not only helped reduce costs but has helped improve employee commitment and satisfaction. It has also contributed to Renault's efforts to promote sustainable development, particularly by helping to cut pollutant emissions from transport.[84]

Types of flexible work arrangements

As already mentioned, the introduction of more flexible working patterns figures highly in the European Employment Strategy,[85] and in the UK, The Employment Act of 2002 gave parents and carers the right to request more flexible working from their employer. Some of the important work options to emerge from the trends already outlined include a compressed work week, annualized hours, zero hours, flexitime, job sharing and teleworking or remote working. Employers are increasingly recognizing the business case for introducing more flexible working patterns[86] but, more importantly here, nearly all these options are designed to influence employee satisfaction and to serve as both extrinsic and intrinsic motivating devices by helping employees to balance the demands of their working and nonworking lives. In our fast-changing society these arrangements are becoming more important as a way of dealing with our increasingly diverse workforce.

The compressed work week

A **compressed work week** is any scheduling of work that allows a full-time job to be completed in fewer than the standard five days (the assumed five-day norm may, however, in itself be an outdated concept). The most common form of compressed work week is the '4–40'; that is, 40 hours of work accomplished in four 10-hour days, but can include other forms, such as nine days in a fortnight. In the UK this pattern of work is more common in the public sector, for example Medway Council allows employees to work nine days over a fortnight (74 hours), but is becoming more widespread, with one-fifth of employers reporting they operate compressed hours for some staff. This may often be as part of a wider flexible working package; the bank Lloyds TSB in the UK allows staff to compress their working week into fewer than five days,[87] and the chemical firm Bayer also has a compressed working week as one of its flexible working options.[88] Added time off is the key benefit for the employee, with the individual often benefiting from increased leisure time, more three-day weekends, free week days to pursue personal business and lower commuting costs. The organization can benefit, too, through reduced energy consumption during three-day shutdowns, lower employee absenteeism, improved recruiting of new employees and the extra time available for building and equipment maintenance, although results are inconsistent.[89]

> A **compressed work week** is any scheduling of work that allows a full-time job to be completed in fewer than the standard five days.

OB IN ACTION

Chris Ainslie is a father of three and managing director of BT Global Partners, a business with sales of more than £500 million a year. From Monday to Thursday, he works ten-hour days. Then he switches off his laptop and mobile and devotes Friday and the weekend to family and outside interests. Ainslie made his four-day week a condition of accepting a senior job with the telecommunications company when he was headhunted in 2005. He does it in 40 hours by 'ruthless prioritization', self-discipline and delegation. 'I make decisions far more quickly. I've never been more efficient than I am now.' In his three years in the job, his directorate's revenues have doubled internationally and grown 14% in the UK, while profit margins have risen from 18% to 23%. The key business benefits are the creation of a group of seven experienced deputies, who take it in turn to run the business when Ainslie is away and increased employee satisfaction levels in his division.[92]

The potential disadvantages of the compressed work week include increased fatigue from the extended work day and family adjustment problems for the individual and, for the organization, increased work scheduling problems and possible customer complaints due to breaks in work coverage. One study found that reaction to the compressed work week was most favourable among employees who had participated in the decision to compress the work week, who had had their jobs enriched as a result of the new schedule and who had strong higher-order needs. The enrichment occurred because fewer employees were on duty at any one time and job duties were changed and enriched to accommodate this reduction.[90] A further interesting finding is employees' seeming reluctance to subsequently seek employment under the typical standard-hours model of five days/40 hours, once they have experienced the lifestyle changes associated with a compressed work week.[91]

Annualized hours

Annualization *is a scheme whereby employees' working time and pay are scheduled and calculated over a period of a year.*

Annualization or 'annualized hours' schemes allow employees' working time (and pay) to be calculated and scheduled over a period of a year. Pay is equalized each month but working hours vary. Annualization is a means of achieving working time flexibility, which has proved increasingly popular in a number of European countries in recent years, and which has been promoted by EU policy and recommendations.[93] In Denmark, 67% of employees in the private sector have access to this work pattern,[94] meanwhile in Finland, 14% of workers in the private sector have annualized contracts.[95] In the UK, around 5% are engaged on annual hours contracts.[96] For example, ground staff at Aberdeen City Council work 1924 hours a year, which allows them to work longer hours in the growing seasons,[97] whilst the bank Alliance and Leicester introduced annualized contracts for its branch staff that accommodated staff preferences, including school term time only working, with an agreed fixed number of working hours to be scheduled throughout the year.[98]

Zero-hours contracts

A zero-hours contract can be defined as an arrangement where the worker is not guaranteed any work at all but in some way is required to be available as and when the employer needs that person. Wide-ranging flexibility is the main motive for employing workers on zero-hours contracts. In the UK many employers (around 22%) use zero-hours contracts in order to deal with work fluctuations, particularly seasonal variations. In mainland Europe, though, there is little evidence for this pattern of work. Although there are now a growing number of employers using zero-hours contracts as a way to retain staff in the challenging business environment created by the recession.[99]

The advantages of this type of working for the employer are reduced costs and greater flexibility. For many workers this is a very flexible arrangement with a good degree of choice over when and whether or not they work. However, in reality, employers have been criticized for treating employees on zero-hours contracts less favourably than other staff in terms of pay and conditions of service.[100] For many adopting a critical perspective within OB, zero-hours contracts constitute a clear case of significant exploitation of workers.

Job sharing

Another alternative work pattern is **job sharing**, whereby one full-time job is assigned to two or more people, who then divide the work according to agreements made between or among themselves and with the employer.[101] Under this scheme a job can be 'shared', which may require a high degree of coordination and communication between job-sharing partners, or it may be 'split', which requires little cooperative interaction and coordination. Some jobs require a careful job-sharing approach, whereas in other cases a job split approach can work effectively. Work options such as job sharing and permanent part-time help facilitate a better balance between work and family life. Job sharing often entails split weeks, with each person working half a week, or split days, with each person working half a day, although it may also be a weekly or monthly arrangement.

Job sharing has a lot to offer for the creation of a family-friendly workplace. Yet in the UK only 2% of employees are employed on a job-sharing basis.[102] Organizations benefit from job sharing when they are able to attract talented people who would otherwise be unable to work. For example in the teaching profession, two members of staff are able to teach one class. Whilst many organizations in the UK report that any employee can ask to job share, in practice it is more common in the public sector and tends to be concentrated in secretarial/clerical and administrative positions.[103]

Some job sharers report less **burnout** and claim to feel recharged each time they report for work. Finding the right partnership is very important, however, because the 'sharers' must work well with each other.[104] A more recent and somewhat controversial development of this scheme is 'family job sharing', which has been introduced by McDonald's. Here husbands, wives, children and grandparents can job share and swap shifts without notifying management in advance. Introduced to help to tackle the problem of absenteeism, this type of workplace flexibility could increase job satisfaction and help workers to achieve a better work–life balance.[105]

Flexible working hours or flexitime

There is much debate as to what actually constitutes flexible working, with some commentators including the whole range of non-standard working patterns within their definitions. True **flexible working** allows employees to 'exercise a choice in relation to personal circumstances and work demands but compatible with the achievement of business objectives'[106] but in reality this translates into a more limited daily flexitime 'that gives employees some choice in the timing of work and nonwork activities.'[107] Flexitime is perhaps the most widely adopted work option in Western economies, although data about it are not always clear. In Europe there are sharp differences in practice; in northern European countries workers can choose to adapt working time to their needs to a large extent (around half of employees say they can do so with or without certain limits), which is in sharp contrast to southern and eastern European countries, where more than 75% of employees have no possibility whatsoever of adapting their work schedules, as they are set by the company.[108] Other evidence suggests that flexible working, particularly part-time working and flexitime, is widespread in Europe and set to increase further.[109]

Job sharing *is the assignment of one full-time job to two or more people, who divide the work according to agreements made between themselves and the employer.*

Burnout *is a negative felt emotion relating to one's work. It is characterized by emotional exhaustion, cynicism and doubts regarding self-efficacy.*

Flexible working hours *(flexitime) is any work schedule that gives employees daily choice in the timing of work and nonwork activities.*

In the UK, survey evidence is often contradictory; on the one hand, one survey stated that less than one in two workers have any control over their working hours,[110] with the TUC finding that this lack of flexibility was as high as 77%,[111] while on the other hand, 51% of employees apparently now have access to flexitime schemes.[112] Changes in legislation giving parents the right to request flexible working in some form (not just flexitime) mean that 91% of UK employees in theory have access to flexible working.[113] What is perhaps of more concern is the number of workers who have lower job satisfaction because they cannot work more flexibly. Nearly 6.5 million UK workers could be using their skills more fully if more flexible working was available in the UK.[114] Approximately half of all part-time workers, both men and women, have previously held jobs requiring higher levels of skills or qualifications or more managerial or supervisory responsibility, and a third say they could easily work at a higher level.[115] The impact of people working below their potential has implications for the economy because of lost productivity and is particularly important given the current downturn. It is estimated that this waste of talent costs the economy up to £23 billion.[116]

Interestingly, the global recession has also provided more opportunities for flexible working as a means to minimize redundancy. In their recent research, King's College London found that 28% of organizations had increased flexible working arrangements and 21% had increased part-time working.[117] The CBI found that the most popular response to the recession was to increase the use of flexible working. Their report found that more than two-thirds of employers had increased flexible working or intended to in the near future.[118] In this respect the recession may have acted as a catalyst for a sustained shift in the growth of flexible and part-time work. However, one can question whether this trend produces any real benefits for the employees affected.

The potential advantages of flexible working are listed in Table 5.3.

Organizational benefits	Individual benefits
Lower absenteeism	More time for leisure and personal business, e.g. dentist, bank and better timing of commuting
Reduced tardiness	Less commuting time
Reduced turnover	Higher job satisfaction
Higher work commitment	Greater sense of responsibility
Higher performance	Easier personal scheduling

Table 5.3: Organizational and individual benefits of flexible working hours.

Proponents of flexible working argue that the discretion it allows workers in scheduling their own hours of work encourages them to develop positive attitudes and increased commitment to the organization. Research tends to support this position.[119] For example, a CIPD survey found that employees who are satisfied with their work–life balance and those on flexible contracts are more engaged with their work than those who are dissatisfied or not working flexibly,[120] but 52% of men and 48% of women say they want to work more flexibly;[121] more than 1 in 10 employees would like to work fewer hours;[122] and 45% of survey respondents had changed their jobs in order to work more flexibly.[123] It seems then that flexible working is highly desired by many workers because it helps in achieving a better work–life balance and, as the following 'OB in Action' suggests, can lead to greater levels of satisfaction with life in general.

OB IN ACTION

How happy are you?

In today's busy world, time is a scarce and highly valued commodity, having sufficient time to fulfil both professional and personal goals – raising children, caring for older relatives, maintaining social and family contacts – is a crucial element in determining a good quality of life. However, findings from the European Quality of Life Survey indicate that work–life balance remains an elusive goal for many working Europeans, but people are happier when they are in employment. However much we complain about having to go to work, it seems that Europeans with a job enjoy greater life satisfaction that those without. People are also happiest when they are part of a couple with children and can rely on family support. They are even happier

if the work–family conflict they experience is not too acute. Finding the right balance through more flexible working practices could, it seems, make us all happier, as women who are employed and who experience little pressure in reconciling their domestic and professional responsibilities are the happiest group of all.[124]

Remote working and the virtual office

As the example at Renault illustrated, it is now clear that the traditional office is no longer the sole focal point of employee activity.[125] Advances in communication and information technology, as well as changing attitudes towards trusting employees, are leading to more work being undertaken in 'virtual offices' remote from the central workplace. Workers can work from home, work while travelling on a train, in a hotel overseas or many other locations. Despite lack of physical proximity to each other, workers in different locations are able to interact extensively with each other. There are numerous options and forms of teleworking. The most common is working from home but other options enable workers to work from well-equipped hotels, resorts, offices, telecentres and vehicles. All these options involve telework principles whereby a worker is enabled, in various ways but especially through information technology, to work remotely from the central organization.

Further definition is required of those who qualify as remote workers in any statistical count of such workers and data collection must become more accurate. Although teleworking has expanded substantially over the past decade, much of this can be accounted for by the inclusion of sales staff and 'white van men' whose jobs have always taken them on the road but who can now keep in touch with their base using a laptop and mobile phone. Teleworking also tends to be concentrated amongst professional and managerial staff that can be 'trusted' to work from home.[126]

Trying to gain an accurate picture is difficult as surveys differ on who they count as teleworkers. In Europe just over 11% of employees usually or sometimes work from home. While the proportion of employees who usually work from home is higher for women, the share of those sometimes working from home is higher for men. The share of home-based teleworking is considerably higher in the original 15 member states (EU15). The highest percentages can be found in the Netherlands, Denmark, France and Sweden. In the Netherlands, 9% of employed people work more than one full day each week in home-based teleworking. Just over half (51%) of teleworkers in the EU15 feel that, without the option to telework from home, they could not do their job as well as they can with tele-work and 27% would have to reduce their working hours per week.[127]

Teleworkers work in virtual workplaces or offices. In virtual workplaces, productivity can rise substantially as a result of fewer interruptions and a quieter, more focused environment. The virtual office can offer more flexible work schedules, allowing employees to do work when and where they are most productive, whether early in the morning or late in the evening. It also fosters better customer service because virtual workers are constantly in the field in direct contact with their clients.

It is vital to match the right people to remote work. They must have disciplined work habits (or a facility to acquire them) and the knowledge and technical skills to be able to work effectively without supervision. They must also be motivated to continually improve their work skills on their own and to know when to call on outside support. Use of e-mail, Internet and software for work and work meetings is involved. Employees will benefit by saving in commuting time and expense and reducing personal expenditure on lunches, work clothes, laundry and so on. However, they may feel isolated from other employees and the workplace. They may be overlooked for training opportunities and promotions because they do not have a presence in the workplace. Managers and colleagues often do not believe that employees can work effectively at home without being supervised. However, survey evidence in the UK and India has shown that teleworkers are more productive and the quality of work increases.[128] Employees may be expected to work harder to prove the effectiveness of the arrangement and/or because working at home blurs the hours of attending to home and work duties. There can also be an expectation that being at home means workers can work at any time.[129] It can be unclear who should bear the cost of infrastructure for telework in the home (computers, printers, wireless or Internet broadband, air-conditioning, heating, lighting, etc.). It does appear that workers are often not knowledgeable enough to provide adequate data security and that technology failure can be a strong cause for terminating telework arrangements (with inability to download large files being an example of the problems that arise).[130]

When an employee becomes a teleworker, advantages accrue to the community through the reduction of travel, traffic and pollution, as well as by returning patterns of consumption to local neighbourhoods instead of city centres.[131]

For the organization, advantages include increased employee productivity and satisfaction; lower costs such as energy, providing office space and parking and access to a larger pool of highly skilled workers, many of whom may not be willing to cope with the demands of the traditional office environment (those in carer roles or with a physical disability, for example). The potential business costs and problems may include insurance, security, office safety, remote support and supervision. Insurance issues involving the home office can be complex because responsibilities are not always clear. Others are data confidentiality and security, because employees often have confidential client information in their home office and must be responsible for security and backing up data to the main office's network.[132]

 ## RESEARCH IN

Access our website **www.wileyeurope.com/college/french** for an interesting research article by Golden, examining how teleworking impacts on relationships with managers, co-workers and family and how these, in turn, affect job satisfaction. One can anticipate other studies going on to examine similar topics given the importance of this contextual development.

CONCLUSION

The 21st century work environment is subject to rapid and significant change. Job design, technological developments and radically altered work patterns such as virtual, remote and teleworking have resulted in new and, for many, exciting ways of organizing our working and nonworking lives.[133] There is considerable pressure on those people who run organizations to facilitate ways of working that both motivate employees and are cost effective. Workers' performance can be seen as strongly related to the context in which they carry out their tasks and roles.

SUMMARY

LEARNING OBJECTIVE 1
Intrinsic motivation
Intrinsic motivation is the desire to work hard solely for the pleasant experience of task accomplishment. It builds upon intrinsic work rewards, or those rewards that an individual receives directly as a result of task performance. They are self-motivating and do not require external reinforcement. Together these can be important components of job design.

LEARNING OBJECTIVE 2
Job design strategies and intrinsic work rewards

In theory, job design involves the planning and specification of job tasks and the work setting in which they are to be accomplished. The manager's responsibility is to fit individual needs with task attributes and the work setting so both performance and human resource maintenance are facilitated. Job design strategies include four broad alternatives. Job simplification standardizes work procedures and employs people in clearly defined and specialized tasks. Job enlargement increases task variety by combining two or more tasks previously assigned to separate workers. Job rotation increases task variety by periodically rotating employees among jobs involving different tasks. Job enrichment builds motivating factors into job content by adding planning and evaluating duties. The intrinsic work rewards made available by these strategies range on a continuum from low (job simplification) to high (job enrichment).

LEARNING OBJECTIVE 3
The job characteristics model and the diagnostic approach to job enrichment

The job characteristics model and the diagnostic approach to job enrichment recognize that not everyone wants an enriched job. Rather, they consider those with high and low growth needs and related concerns. They then look at the effect of five core job characteristics (ranging from skill variety to feedback from the job itself) on intervening critical psychological states that influence motivation, performance and satisfaction. The socio-technical approach to job design is also known as the semi-autonomous work group. The impact and role of technology is viewed as a factor in designing jobs, and steps are taken to optimize the relationship between technology and the social system to which employees belong. The social information-processing model argues that individual needs, task perceptions and reactions are a result of social constructions of reality. Multiskilling promotes the learning of a wide array of skills needed to perform multiple tasks within a company. Employees who are multiskilled are better equipped to shoulder greater responsibilities and to take over when another employee is absent.

LEARNING OBJECTIVE 4
Goal-setting theory and job design

Goal setting is the process of developing, negotiating and formalizing the targets or objectives that an employee is responsible for accomplishing. It includes predictions that link it to job design and that serve as the basis for goal-setting theory. These predictions emphasize challenging and specific goals, knowledge of results, ability, a feeling of self-efficacy to accomplish the goals and goal commitment or acceptance. A managerial technique that applies goal-setting theory is management by objectives (MBO). A manager and subordinate agree on individual goals that are consistent with higher level ones. A process is then implemented to monitor and assist the subordinate in task accomplishment, and the subordinate's performance is evaluated in terms of accomplished results. If implemented well, many positive aspects of goal-setting theory can be realized from MBO but effective MBO systems are difficult to establish and maintain. Key performance indicators provide a benchmark against which employees' goals can be measured.

LEARNING OBJECTIVE 5
Flexible work arrangements

There are a number of flexible work arrangements. The compressed work week allows full-time work to be completed in less than five days. Flexible working hours allow employees a daily choice in timing work and nonwork activities. Job sharing occurs when two or more people divide one full-time job according to an agreement among themselves and the employer. Flexitime, annual hours, job sharing and teleworking are all designed to enable workers to balance the competing demands on their time of work, leisure and education. These flexible work arrangements are becoming more important as a way of obtaining the services of an increasingly diverse workforce requiring a family-friendly workplace in our rapidly changing society. Information and communication technologies have had a significant impact on organizational design. The capabilities of this technology and lessening costs mean that the technology can often be taken with the worker or to the worker. This enables workers to work while travelling to and/or from their homes. Such teleworking allows work to be conducted remotely from the central organization using information technology. These methods have several potential benefits, especially for those with childcare or other care duties, or for those with physical disabilities. For all employees it can involve reductions in employee expenditure on travel to work, lunches and work clothes, as well as saving on time. The potential costs are increased isolation of employees and poorer communication and knowledge sharing, as well as costs like insurance and establishment of home offices. Data confidentiality and security and local government zoning laws can also present potential problems.

CHAPTER 5 STUDY GUIDE

Now that you have read this chapter, you should be able to apply and further develop your knowledge by undertaking the following activities set out over the next few pages: test your knowledge questions, an individual activity and an end-of-chapter case study.

Please also go to this book's website: **www.wileyeurope.com/college/french** to find further material which will enhance your understanding and enable you to assess your knowledge.

TEST YOURSELF

1. What is the difference between intrinsic rewards and extrinsic rewards?
2. Explain the difference between job enlargement and job enrichment.
3. List and define the core job characteristics.
4. Explain the differences between job sharing and voluntary reduced work time.
5. Consider a situation in which you performed a duty for someone – for example, doing an assignment, doing a job for your supervisor or even doing a favour for a friend. List the rewards you obtained from completing the duty. Distinguish between the intrinsic and extrinsic rewards.

6. Assume you are a university lecturer in this subject. You are designing an assignment for students. Consider the assignment design as being a job design. Use the job characteristics model to design an assignment that will maximize the intrinsic motivation for students doing the assignment. Explain the advantages of your assignment design.

7. Think about and explain how much your current 'job' (studying at college or university) involves social information processing. Provide two examples.

8. In view of the listed predictions on goal setting provided in this chapter, how would you set goals for yourself in completing a subject in your course? How do you think your tutor could be involved in this process of goal setting for you?

9. Consider the principles of teleworking. How much of your study requires you to be located at your college or university and how much of it do you undertake remotely? Explain the role that information technology plays in enhancing this process. Discuss, based on your experience as a student, whether you think you would work effectively as a teleworker or telecommuter in the workforce.

10. Think about a job with which you have some familiarity (for example, a bank clerk, shop assistant or teacher). Explain what advantages or disadvantages you would see for (a) that person, (b) the employer and (c) you as the customer if that person was working flexible hours.

11. Many organizations have strongly developed conditions to support workplace flexibility for employees. Find two organizations in your community and investigate what flexible work arrangements they provide for their employees; evaluate their apparent effectiveness.

12. Hewitt Associates, a global HR outsourcing company, announces each year the 'best employers' list for countries such as China, Hong Kong, India, the Philippines, Malaysia, Singapore, Thailand, Australia and New Zealand – and for Asia in general. In 2004, for Australia and New Zealand, Sales Force topped the list, with Bain International, Cisco Systems, Flight Centre and Seek ranking as highly commended. Analyse the characteristics of these 'best' employers (from your country of interest) in terms of their jobs and job-related practices. (Note that there are other relevant or similar awards, such as *Fortune* magazine's awards for work–life balance.)

INDIVIDUAL ACTIVITY[134]

Job design preference

Instructions

People differ in what they like and dislike about their jobs. Listed below are 12 pairs of jobs. For each pair, indicate which job you would prefer. Assume that everything else about the jobs is the same – pay attention only to the characteristics actually listed for each pair of jobs. If you would prefer the job in column A, indicate how much you would prefer it by putting a check mark in a blank to the left of the neutral point. If you would prefer the job in column B, check one of the blanks to the right of neutral. Check the neutral blank only if you find the two jobs equally attractive or unattractive. Try to use the neutral blank sparingly.

Column A

Column B

1. A job that offers little or no challenge.

Strongly   Neutral   Strongly

A job that requires you to be completely isolated from co-workers.

2. A job that pays well.

Strongly   Neutral   Strongly

A job that allows considerable opportunity to be creative and innovative.

3. A job that often requires you to make important decisions.

Strongly   Neutral   Strongly

A job in which there are many pleasant people to work with.

4. A job with little security in a somewhat unstable organization.

Strongly   Neutral   Strongly

A job in which you have little or no opportunity to participate in decisions that affect your work.

5. A job in which greater responsibility is given to those who do the best work.

Strongly   Neutral   Strongly

A job in which greater responsibility is given to loyal employees who have the most seniority.

6. A job with a supervisor who sometimes is highly critical.

Strongly   Neutral   Strongly

A job that does not require you to use much of your talent.

7. A very routine job.

Strongly   Neutral   Strongly

A job in which your co-workers are not very friendly.

8. A job with a supervisor who respects you and treats you fairly

Strongly   Neutral   Strongly

A job that provides constant opportunities for you to learn new and interesting things.

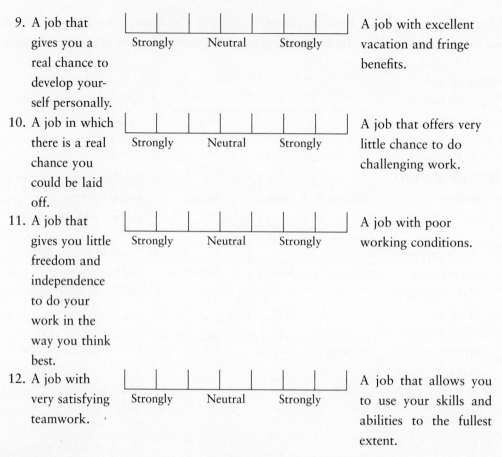

9. A job that gives you a real chance to develop yourself personally. | Strongly — Neutral — Strongly | A job with excellent vacation and fringe benefits.

10. A job in which there is a real chance you could be laid off. | Strongly — Neutral — Strongly | A job that offers very little chance to do challenging work.

11. A job that gives you little freedom and independence to do your work in the way you think best. | Strongly — Neutral — Strongly | A job with poor working conditions.

12. A job with very satisfying teamwork. | Strongly — Neutral — Strongly | A job that allows you to use your skills and abilities to the fullest extent.

Interpretation

People differ in their need for psychological growth at work. This instrument measures the degree to which you seek growth-need satisfaction. Score your responses as follows:

Add up all of your scores and divide by 12 to find the average. If you score above 4.0, your desire for growth-need satisfaction through work tends to be high and you are likely to prefer an enriched job. If you score below 4.0, your desire for growth-need satisfaction through work tends to be low and you are unlikely to be satisfied or motivated by an enriched job.

For items 1, 2, 7, 8, 11 and 12 give yourself the following points for each item:

1	2	3	4	5	6	7
Strongly prefer A			Neutral			Strongly prefer B

For items 3, 4, 5, 6, 9 and 10, give yourself the following points for each item:

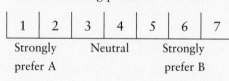

7	6	5	4	3	2	1
Strongly prefer A			Neutral			Strongly prefer B

Source: Reprinted by permission from Hickman, J. R. and Oldham, G. R. (1974), *The Job Diagnostic Survey: An Instrument for the Diagnosis of Jobs and the Evaluation of Job Redesign Projects*, technical report 4, Yale University, Department of Administrative Sciences: New Haven, CT.

TELEWORKING AT BRITISH TELECOM

British Telecom (BT) is one of the largest employers of 'flexible workers' in the UK. Nearly 2000 teleworkers at BT were surveyed as part of an EU-wide project on sustainable working. Perhaps the most striking finding from this survey was that a large majority of the respondents said they worked longer hours than they did in their office-bound existence. Yet they also said that their quality of life had improved. In some cases this could equate

to more than 15 extra hours per week and many said that they worked from home when they would be too ill to go into the office.

The profile of the respondents to the survey followed that typically found in the UK of middle-aged men in managerial or sales jobs. They worked largely from home or split their time between home, BT offices and clients' premises. Only 8% still had a main office and only 1% a dedicated office desk.

British Telecom has particularly encouraged middle management and above to work remotely because they tend to be motivated, are able to organize their work and are not paid overtime. For the managers themselves, 77% said that they chose to do so because they had more flexibility about when and where they worked. It also appears that they get more work done because the home is quieter than the office. 'I'd forgotten what it was like to read documents without my fingers in my ears', said one respondent who had previously worked in an open-plan office.

Improved quality of life is one of the key benefits, with teleworkers no longer being out of the house for over 12 hours per day they can also combine work with doing the shopping or ironing or taking children to school. This leaves them with more 'quality time' in the evening and at weekends and less stress in their relationship. Some say that their female partners have been able to return to work as a result. 'I can hang out the washing and prepare the evening meal when I finish work', says one worker. The downside to this can be lack of social interaction and knowledge exchange with fellow workers as well as the feeling of isolation and the fear that not being seen in the office will hinder future advancement.[135]

Questions

1. Why do you think that teleworkers report greater satisfaction with work despite working longer hours?
2. Would you accept a home-based job on graduation? What are your reasons for your choice?
3. Consider an office-based job with which you are familiar. How would this need to be redesigned in order to allow the job occupant to work remotely?
4. What issues exist for the organization in managing the remote worker and how can they be addressed effectively?

SUGGESTED READING

It is useful to recognize that topics contained in this chapter can be viewed from the perspective of human resource management (HRM) as well as from an OB vantage point. Look at relevant sections of the following book for an HRM treatment of the issue of flexibility at work:

Pilbeam, S. & Corbridge, M. (2006), *People Resourcing Contemporary HRM in Practice*, 3rd edn, FT Prentice Hall: Harlow.

Harris, L. (2003), Home-based Teleworking and the Employment Relationship: Managerial Challenges and Dilemmas. *Personnel Review*, **32** (4), 422–437. This journal article points to a range of practical implications when introducing teleworking and highlights the need for effective managerial interventions.

END NOTES

1. Sources and quotes from Conlin, M. (2006), Smashing the Clock. *Business Week*, 11 December, 60–68; The Pros and Cons of Flex-time. *Business Week*, January 2007, 7; Woodward, D. (2010), Beat The Clock, www.Director.co.uk (accessed 14 June 2010); Bloomberg Business Week (2008), Smashing the Clock, 11 December, www.businessweek.com (accessed 14 June 2010); Kiger, P. J. (2009), Throwing out the rules of work, www.workforce.com/section/09/feature24/54/28/ (accessed 14 June 2010).
2. Aldag, R. J. & Brief, A. P. (1977), The intrinsic–extrinsic dichotomy: toward conceptual clarity. *Academy of Management Review*, **2**, 497–498.
3. See Tosi, H. L., Rizzo, J. R. & Carroll, S. J. (1990), *Managing Organizational Behaviour*, 2nd edn, Harper & Row: New York, Ch. 8.
4. Garg, P. & Renu, R. (2006), New model of job design: motivating employees' performance. *Journal of Management Development*, **25** (6), 572–587.
5. Based on an example presented in Lawler, E. E. III (1973), *Motivation in Work Organizations*, Brooks/Cole: Monterey, CA, pp. 154–155.
6. Eriksson, T. & Ortega, J. (2006), The adoption of job rotation: testing theories. *Industrial and Labour Relations Review*, **59** (4), 653–666.
7. *Hong Kong Standard*, August 1990, p. 6.
8. Kone China, *Careers – working at Kone*, www.kone.com (accessed 9 January 2006); Standard Chartered (2006), *Careers – building your career*, www.standardchartered.com.cn/

career/byc_tra.html (accessed 9 January 2006); Schering China, *Career – FAQs*, www.schering.com.cn (accessed 9 January 2006).
9. Herzberg, F. (1968), One more time: how do you motivate employees? *Harvard Business Review*, **46** (January/February), 53–62.
10. See Hackman, J. R. (1975), On the coming demise of job enrichment, in *Man and Work in Society*, (eds E. L. Cass & F. G. Zimmer), Van Nostrand: New York.
11. See Hulin, C. L. and Blood, M. R. (1968), Job enlargement, individual differences, and worker responses. *Psychological Bulletin*, **69**, 41–55; Blood, M. R. & Hulin, C. L. (1967), Alienation, environmental characteristics and worker responses. *Journal of Applied Psychology*, **51**, 284–290; Turner, A. N. & Lawrence, P. R. (1965), *Industrial Jobs and the Worker: An Investigation of Responses to Task Attributes*, Harvard Graduate School of Business Administration: Boston, MA.
12. For a complete description and review of the research, see Hackman, J. R. & Oldham, G. R. (1980), *Work Redesign*, Addison-Wesley: Reading, MA.
13. See Hackman, J. R., Oldham, G., Janson, R. & Purdy, K. (1975), A new strategy for job enrichment. *California Management Review*, **17** (4), 60.
14. See discussion on research into job design moderators in Luthans, E. (1985), *Organizational Behaviour*, McGraw-Hill: New York.

15. Rance, C. (2005), The long march. *HR Monthly*, April, 22–29.

16. Brain drain likely as baby boomers near retirement. *Personnel Today*, 4 October 2006.

17. Equal Opportunities Commission (2005), *Britain's Hidden Brain Drain*, EOC: London. (Note the EOC has been replaced by the Equality and Human Rights Commission.)

18. Manpower Inc. (2010) 5th Annual Talent Shortage Survey: NY Manpower Inc. http://www.manpower.com/research/research.cfm (accessed 29 June 2010).

19. AllAfrica.com (2010) New Mining Survey Warns of Serious Skills Shortages. http://allafrica.com/stories/201003020677.html (accessed 29 June 2010).

20. BBC News (2007) Migrant Workers help the UK Economy. BBC London: http://news.bbc.co.uk/1/hi/business/6766003.stm (accessed 29 June 2010); *Foreign Labour in the United Kingdom: Patterns and Trends* (2001), Labour Market Trends.

21. Maiden, M. (2005), Banks want to do the mess for less. *Sydney Morning Herald*, Business and Money section, 5–6 February, p. 46.

22. Manpower Inc op. cit.

23. Wusterman, L. A. (2005), A Passage to India; off-shoring in financial services. *IRS Employment Review*, Issue 831.

24. Berry, M. (2005), Employees sure to walk out if opportunity doesn't knock. *Personnel Today*, 19 April.

25. Van der Vegt, G., Emms, B. & Van de Vliert, E. (1998), Motivating effect of task and outcome interdependence in work teams. *Group and Organisation Management*, 23 (2), 124–143.

26. Lee-Ross, D. (1998), A practical theory of motivation applied to hotels. *International Journal of Contemporary Hospitality Management*, 10 (3).

27. Baral, B. & Bhargava, S. (2009), Work–family enrichment as a mediator between organizational interventions for work–life balance and job outcomes. *Journal of Managerial Psychology*, 25 (3), 274–300.

28. See Hackman, J. R. and Oldham, G. (1975), Development of the job diagnostic survey. *Journal of Applied Psychology*, 60, 159–170.

29. European Industrial Relations Observatory Online (2010) *Commission consults social partners on working time directive review.* http://www.eurofound.europa.eu/eiro/2010/04/articles/eu1004019i.htm (accessed 29 June 2010).

30. European Foundation for the Improvement of Living and Working Conditions (2005), *Fourth European Working Conditions Survey*, http://www.eurofound.europa.eu (accessed 29 June 2010).

31. Graduates not in the real world. *HR Monthly*, December 2004–January 2005, p. 7.

32. European Foundation for the Improvement of Living and Working Conditions (2005), op. cit.

33. Langford, P. & Parkes, L. (2005), Debunking the myths around work–life balance. *Human Resources*, 3 May, p. 14.

34. See Salancik, G. & Pfeffer, J. (1977), An examination of need-satisfaction models of job attitudes. *Administrative Science Quarterly*, 22, 427–456; Salancik, G. & Pfeffer, J. (1978), A social information processing approach to job attitude and task design. *Administrative Science Quarterly*, 23, 224–253.

35. Adapted from Marriot Hotel wins Excellence Through People Award. *Personnel Today*, 13 November 2001.

36. Craig, T. (2010) Case Study – Coping with recession at Barrett Developments. *Personnel Today*, 19 January 2010.

37. O'Reilly, S. (2008) Motivation: Winning ways to success. *Personnel Today*, 5 February 2008.

38. Singer, R, Hausenblas, H. & Janelle, C. (Eds) (2001), *Handbook of Sport Psychology*, John Wiley & Sons, Inc.: New York.

39. Locke, E. A., Shaw, K. N., Saari, L. M. & Latham, G. P. (1981), Goal setting and task performance: 1969–1980. *Psychological Bulletin*, 90 (July/November), 125–152; see also Latham, G. P. & Locke, E. A. (1979), Goal setting – a motivational technique that works. *Organizational Dynamics*, 8 (Autumn), 68–80; Latham, G. P. & Steele, T. P. (1983), The motivational effects of participation versus goal-setting on performance. *Academy of Management Journal*, 26, 406–417; Erez, M. & Kanfer, F. H. (1983), The role of goal

acceptance in goal setting and task performance. *Academy of Management Review*, 8, 454–463.

40. Ibid.

41. See Locke, E. A. & Latham, G. P. (1990), Work motivation and satisfaction: light at the end of the tunnel. *Psychological Science*, 1 (4) (July), 240–246.

42. Ibid.

43. Ibid.

44. For a complete review of goal-setting theory and research, see Locke, E. A. & Latham, G. P. (1990), *A Theory of Goal Setting and Task Performance*, Prentice Hall: Englewood Cliffs, NJ.

45. See Locke, E. A. & Latham, G. P. (1990), Work motivation and satisfaction. *Psychological Science*, July, 241.

46. Ibid., pp. 240–246.

47. Schuster, F. & Kendall, K. (1974), Where we stand – a survey of Fortune 500. *Human Resources Management*, Spring, 8–11.

48. For a good review of MBO, see Raia, A. P. (1974), *Managing by Objective*, Scott Foresman: Glenview, IL; The criticisms are summarized well in Kerr, S. (1976), Overcoming the dysfunctions of MBO. *Management by Objectives*, 5 (1).

49. Pinder, C. C. (1984), *Work Motivation Theory, Issues, and Applications*, Scott Foresman: Dallas, TX, p. 169.

50. Based on Cypress Semiconductor Corporation. *Harvard Business Review*, July/August 1990, 88–89.

51. Investors in People UK (2006), see www.investorsinpeople.co.uk (accessed 29 June 2010).

52. Roberts, P. (1998), Sharing the secrets of success. *Australian Financial Review*, 3 July, p. 42.

53. Moodie, A.-M. (1998), Career surfing now the new wave. *Australian Financial Review*, 22 May, p. 58.

54. Australian Maritime Museum, *Strategic plan 2003–2006*, www.anmm.gov.au/stratplan.htm (accessed 29 June 2010).

55. EU Directive 1995, cited in Hardy, S. and Adnett, N. (2002), The parental leave directive; towards a family friendly social Europe?

European Journal of Industrial Relations, 8 (2), 157–172.

56. Eurofound website http://www.europa.eu/ lisbontreaty (accessed 5 July 2010).

57. Work–life Balance – Changing Patterns in a Changing World (2000), DfEE: London.

58. The Work and Age Trust, *Flexible employment*, http://www.eeotrust.org.nz/worklife/flex_employment.shtml (accessed 29 June 2010), p. 6.

59. Foster, C. (2005), Tackling the long-hours culture. *Equal Opportunities Review*, 1 April.

60. Human Resource Management International Digest (2008) *Employee engagement "does it" for B&Q*, 16 (2), 12–15.

61. Arnold, J., Cooper, C. L. & Robertson, I. T. (2004), *Work Psychology: Understanding Human Behaviour in the Workplace*, 5th edn, FT Prentice Hall: Harlow.

62. DfEE (2000), *Work–life Balance: Results from the Baseline Survey*, HMSO: London.

63. CIPD Survey (2000), *Married to the Job*, CIPD: London.

64. Trade Union Congress (2008) *Return of the Long Hours Culture*, June 2008, TUC London.

65. *Economist* (2010) Overstretched, *Economist*, 395, Issue 8663.

66. Stress is becoming the biggest problem in European companies. *Financial Times*, 8 May 2000.

67. European Foundation for the Improvement of Living and Working Conditions (2001), *Third European Survey on Working Conditions*, EU0101292F; Cox, T., Griffiths, A. & Rial-Gonzalez, E. (2000), *Research on Work-related Stress*; Armstrong, J. (2001), *Workplace Stress in Ireland*, ICTU.

68. Wood, J. & Duffie, J. (1982), Sabbatical: a strategy for creating jobs. *New Ways to Work Newsletter*, 2 (1), 5–6; Wood, J. & Duffie, J. (1982), Sabbatical: a strategy for creating jobs (part II). *New Ways to Work Newsletter*, 2 (2–3), 5–6.

69. See http://epp.eurostat.ec.europa.eu and www.euroufound.europa.eu/ (accessed 29 June 2010).

70. Office for National Statistics (2010) http://www.statistics.gov.uk (accessed 5 July 2010).

71. European Foundation for the Improvement of Living and Working Conditions (2009), *Annual Review of Working Conditions in Europe 2008–9*.

72. See www.eurofound.europa.eu/ (accessed 29 June 2010).

73. Eurostat (2006), *Statistics in Focus: Population and Social Conditions 2006*.

74. European Industrial Relations Review (2006), *Report seeks to encourage flexible working*, Issue 384/1/1.

75. ONS (2010), www.statistics.gov.uk (accessed 24 March 2010).

76. Kersley, B., Alpin, C., Forth, J. *et al.* (2006), *Inside the Workplace Findings from the 2004 Workplace Employment Relations Survey*, Routledge: London.

77. 'Flexible working a top priority for UK workers', press release, 3 October 2005, www.manpower.co.uk (accessed 29 June 2010); Chartered Institute of Personnel and Development (2005), *Tackling Age Discrimination in the Workplace*, October, CIPD: London.

78. IRS Employment Review (2005), *Extending Working Life*, Issue 838.

79. *IRS Management Review* (2001), Employing Older Workers: The Practice, Issue 21.

80. European Foundation for the Improvement of Working Conditions (2007), www.eurofound.europa.eu/ (accessed 29 June 2010).

81. Eurofound (2010) http://www.eurofound.europa.eu/ewco/reports/TN0407TR01/TN0407TR01_2.htm (accessed 5 July 2010).

82. Eurofound (2010) Case study on a comprehensive approach: Fars and Frosta Sparbank Sweden, http://eurofound.europa.eu/areas/populationandsociety/cases/se001.htm (accessed 28 June 2010).

83. Nilles, J. (1976), *The Telecommunications-transportation Tradeoff: Options for Tomorrow*, John Wiley & Sons, Inc.: New York.

84. IRS (2007), France: Teleworking, hot desking and outsourcing at Renault, *European Employment Review*, Issue: 398 01/03/2007; AutoMK (2010), *Renault broadens its teleworking program* (retrieved 5 July 2010 from http://www.automk.com/thread-125436-1-1.html

85. Hardy, S. & Adnett, N. (2002), The parental leave directive; towards a family friendly social Europe? *European Journal of Industrial Relations*, **8** (2), 157–172.

86. DfEE (2000), *Work–life Balance – Changing Patterns in a Changing World*, HMSO: London.

87. *IRS Employment Review* (2002), The way we work now, Issue 755.

88. Bayer's staff free to choose own working hours. *Personnel Today*, 28 May 2006.

89. Latack, J. C. & Foster, L. W. (1985), Implementation of compressed work schedules: participation and job redesign as critical factors for employee acceptance. *Personnel Psychology*, **38**, 75–92.

90. Cohen, A. R. & Gadon, H. (1978), Alternative Work Schedules: Integrating Individual and Organizational Needs, Addison-Wesley: Reading, MA, pp. 38–46; see also Pearce, J. L. & Newstrom, J. W. (1980), Toward a conceptual clarification of employee responses to flexible working hours: a work adjustment approach. *Journal of Management*, **6**, 117–134.

91. Wood, J. (1977), *Altered Work Week Study*, unpublished PhD thesis, Department of Educational Administration, University of Alberta, Canada.

92. Equality and Human Rights Commission (2009) Working Better: Meeting the changing needs of families, workers and employers in the 21st century, March.

93. European Foundation for the Improvement of Living and Working Conditions (2007), *Annualized hours in Europe*.

94. Danish Employers' Federation, Danish *Arbeydsgiverforening*.

95. Confederation of Finnish Industry, *Teollusus y a tyon*.

96. Incomes Data Services Report (2004), *Annual Hours*, February.

97. IRS Employment Review (2002) *The way we work now*, Issue 755.

98. IRS Management Review (1998), *Variable-hours Schemes*, Issue 9.

99. Wolff, C. (2010), *IRS flexible working survey 2010: benefits, issues and making it work.* IRS employment review, 22 March 2010.

100. Ibid.

101. Wood, J. & Wattus, G. (1987), The attitudes of professionals towards job sharing. *Australian Journal of Management*, **12** (2), 103–121.

102. IRS Employment Trends (1998), *Two heads are better than one: a survey of job sharing*, Issue 661.

103. Ibid.

104. Job shares can mean two brains for the price of one. *Management Today*, August 1998, p. 10.

105. Adler, R. (2006), Beware the risks of job sharing. *Personnel Today*, 28 February.

106. Pilbeam, S. & Corbridge, M. (2006), *People Resourcing: HRM in Practice*, 3rd edn, FT Prentice Hall: Harlow.

107. France aims to make job sharing work. *The Australian*, 23 August 1996.

108. Parent-Thirion, A., Fernández Macías, E., Hurley, J. & Vermeylen, G. (2005), *Fourth European Working Conditions Survey*. European Foundation for the Improvement of Living and Working Conditions: Dublin.

109. Brewster, C., Mayne, L. & Tregaskis, O. (1997), Flexible working in Europe. *Journal of World Business*, **32** (2), 133–151.

110. Doyle, J & Reeves, R. (2003), *Time Out, The Case for Time Sovereignty*, The Work Foundation: London.

111. Trade Union Congress (2006), *Challenging Times: Flexibility and Flexible Working in the UK*.

112. EHRC Equality and Human Rights Commission (2010), *Flexible working: working for families working for business*, EHRC: London.

113. Ibid.

114. Equal Opportunities Commission (2007), *Working outside the box*; Equal Opportunities Commission (2005), Flexible working for all should be the norm, *Equal Opportunities Review*, IRS Issue 146, 1 October.

115. Equal Opportunities Commission investigation taken from Working Families (2005) Hours to Suit: The Hidden Brain Drain; The Women and Work Commission (2006) *Shaping a Fairer Future*.

116. EHRC op. cit.

117. EHRC op. cit.

118. Confederation of British Industry (CBI) (2009) *Employment Trends Survey: Easing Up*.

119. Pearce, J. L., Newstrom, J. W., Dunham, R. B & Barber, A. E. (1989), *Alternative Work Schedules*, Allyn & Bacon: Boston.

120. Rruss, T., Soane, E. & Edwards, C. (2006), *Working Life: employee attitudes and engagement*, Chartered Institute of Personnel and Development research report, London.

121. Equal Opportunites Commission (2007) *Working outside the box*.

122. Trade Union Congress (2006), *Challenging Times: Flexibility and Flexible Working in the UK*.

123. CIPD (2002), *Work, Parenting and Careers*, CIPD: London.

124. European Foundation for the Improvement of Living and Working Conditions (2010), *How are you? Quality of Life in Europe*.

125. Gray, M., Hodson, N. & Gordon, G. (1993), *Teleworking Explained*, John Wiley & Sons, Inc.: New York.

126. Crail, M. (2006), Teleworking: where reality and urban myth collide. *IRS Employment Review*, Issue 80, 1 December.

127. European Foundation for the Improvement of Living and Working Conditions (2003), *Third European Working Conditions Survey*.

128. Crail, M. (2006), Teleworking: where reality and urban myth collide. *IRS Employment Review*, Issue 80, 1 December.

129. Australian Telework Advisory Committee (ATAC) (2005), *Telework in Australia* (II), March, pp. 17–18.

130. Ibid., pp. 19–20.

131. Telework New Zealand, alternatives and choices, www.telework.co.nz/Alternatives.htm (accessed 29 June 2010).

132. Kepcyk, R. H. (1999), Evaluating the virtual office, *Ohio CPA Journal*, **58** (2), 16–17.

133. European Foundation for the Improvement of Living and Working Conditions (2003), *Third European Working Conditions Survey*.

134. Hackman, J. R. & Oldham, E. R. (1974), *The job diagnostic survey: an instrument for the diagnosis of jobs and the evaluation of job redesign projects*; technical report 4, New Haven, CT, Yale University Dept. of Administrative Sciences; Hackman, J. R. & Oldham, E. R. (1975), Development of the Job, Diagnostic Survey. *Journal of Applied Psychology*, **60**, 159–170. Reprinted by permission.

135. Adapted from Maitland, A. (2002), Inside track: a long day at home, *Financial Times*, 21 October and EU's Sustel project website, www.sustel.org (accessed 29 June 2010).

CHAPTER 6

Organizational structure and design

LEARNING OBJECTIVES

After studying this chapter you should be able to:

- define and compare organizational design and structure and discuss the relationship between them
- explain the basic factors that impact upon designing organizational structures and what organizational designs may emerge
- describe the different types of organizational goals and different methods of controlling and coordinating the activities of organizational members
- define vertical specialization and explain what is meant by chain of command, unity of command and span of control
- describe and compare different patterns of horizontal specialization used by organizations
- describe some of the emerging forms of organization design and their implications for the individuals within them.

AN AVOIDABLE TRAGEDY?

The world's worst chemical disaster occurred in Bhopal in the early hours of 3 December 1984, resulting in the death of 2500 people[1] and permanent injury to 100000 people.[2] The cause of this disaster at the Union Carbide Plant in India is still in debate, with Union Carbide arguing that it was industrial sabotage by a disgruntled employee.

Eckerman argues that the causes were twofold – economic pressures (affecting safety procedures) and plant design (linked to the policies and systems in place).

Initially, operators at the plant had to be either science graduates or hold a diploma in engineering, but later, eight weeks of training was deemed to be sufficient to commence work. Workers and operators were given more responsibility than their training and competence equipped them to cope with. In 1982 most of the original operators had resigned and workers from other plants were asked to undergo training, which by that stage comprised 14 days in total. These new recruits were asked to take charge of a regular plant operator's position independently. Workers' knowledge was affected by acts of secrecy, with manuals kept in safe custody and the plant operating manual only available in English.

During the training period, technicians were treated as casual labourers and, even after training, only paid an hourly rate. Technicians who accepted a job at the Bhopal plant received formal documentation informing them that they would undergo six months of training, but in practice, after five weeks of instruction, they were asked to stop the training and take on a fully fledged plant operator's role.

Operators who demonstrated unquestioning loyalty were invariably selected before others for promotion. Demands by workers for extra safety measures led to warnings that appointments could be terminated. There were lapses of safety measures, with some contract workers carrying out dangerous work without safety equipment and others routinely exposed to toxic chemicals.

There were reductions in personnel from 1983 to 1984 in order to lower costs. Early retirement was encouraged. Three hundred temporary workers were laid off and another 150 permanent workers were put into a pool to be assigned jobs as needed. The operating shifts were cut from twelve to six and the maintenance shifts from six to two. The positions of second shift supervisor and third shift maintenance supervisor had been eliminated just a few days before the disaster. On the night of 3 December 1984 there were no trained engineers on site. The responsible production supervisor who was on duty had been transferred from a Carbide battery plant only a month before.

On the night of the disaster, the supervisor from the day shift had left instructions on flushing the pipes leading from the tanks to the vent gas scrubber. However, he forgot to mention that the slip bends should have been placed at the end of the pipes. Then the worker cut off the water and the supervisor told him to clean the filters. When the worker turned on the water, it came out of only three of the four drain-cocks.

The worker was told that the night shift worker would turn off the water. The ensuing result is one of terrible tragedy and loss of life.

Questions

1. To what extent was this tragedy attributable to poor job design and training?
2. Could this tragedy have been avoided by appropriate organizational design linked to job responsibilities?
3. How could the organization have put in place safety measures and procedures to avoid individual sabotage?

_____

Source: Adapted primarily from Eckerman, I. (2006), The Bhopal disaster 1984 – working conditions and the role of trade unions. *Asian-Pacific Newsletter on Occupational Health and Safety*, **13**, 48–49.

INTRODUCTION

Every organization needs to decide how to divide its work or activities, how to coordinate all work-related activities and how to control these activities to ensure that goals are achieved. The organization must consider its external environment and the internal systems and processes used to transform inputs to outputs. These differences help to explain, for example, why a football club is different from a manufacturing company. A manager of any organization must ensure consistency between the structure of the organization, the scale of its operations, the tasks at hand, the needs of all stakeholders and the strategic direction of the organization. This consistency between structure and operations distinguishes successful organizations from less successful ones.

In this chapter we will first explain the difference between organizational structure and organizational design and then consider the various factors that may impinge upon the design; that is, the scale of the organization, the technology it uses, its environment and its strategy. Collectively they will all influence how the structural elements are combined into a suitable design for the **organization**. Certain emerging forms of organizational design are presented at the end of the chapter but we must remember that every organization will be unique.

The basic structural attributes of organizations include the different types of goals that organizations develop and implement. They also involve the techniques used to effect control and coordination within organizations. Other structural considerations relate to how the organization allocates authority and manages the chain of command and how labour is divided into organizational units. These elements are, in essence, the building blocks of structure. They reflect various choices that can be made when organizing how work is to be done and goals are to be achieved. Understanding all these elements is necessary to predict how they affect employee behaviour.

An **organization** *is a collectivity with a relatively identifiable boundary, a normative order, ranks of authority, communications systems and membership coordinating systems; this collectivity exists on a relatively continuous basis in an environment and engages in activities that are usually related to a set of goals; the activities have outcomes for organizational members, the organization itself and society.*[3]

ORGANIZATIONAL STRUCTURE AND DESIGN

Organizational structure and **organizational design** are very closely related. The process of choosing and implementing a structural configuration is referred to as organizational design.[4] Organizational executives should adjust the structural configuration of their organizations to best meet the challenges faced at any given point in time.

Formal structure shows the intended configuration of positions, job duties and lines of authority among different parts of the enterprise. This structure emerges from the process of designing the organization. It reflects the goals of the organization and also reflects the contingency factors that impact on the organization design, such as the organization's size, environment, technology and strategy. The formal structure also involves the decisions that are made about who has authority, how the organization and its members will be divided up to achieve tasks and how activities will be controlled and coordinated. We emphasize the word 'formal' simply because the intentions of organizational designers are not always fully realized. While no formal structure can provide the detail needed to show all the activities within an organization, it is still important because it provides the foundations for managerial action; that is, it outlines the jobs to be done, the people (in terms of position) who will perform specific activities and the ways in which the total task of the organization will be accomplished.

Organization charts are diagrams that depict the formal structures of organizations. A typical chart shows the various positions, the position holders and the lines of authority that link them to one another. The top half of Figure 6.1 is a partial organization chart for a small regional university.

The chart allows university employees to locate their positions in the structure and to identify the lines of authority linking them with others in the organization. In this figure, the head of financial services reports to the registrar and secretary, who reports to the vice-chancellor (the chief executive officer of the university). Such charts predominate in representing organizational structures. However, there has been some criticism that they only show lines of authority and the division of the organization into different units. An alternative means of mapping organizational activities has been developed by Mintzberg and Van der Heyden. Their organigraphs show how an organization works, what it does and how people, products and information interact. This can bring more insight, or at least a different perspective, to explaining the behaviour of people in organizations. The bottom half of Figure 6.1 shows a simple organigraph for teaching in a university.

In summary, organizational design involves the choices made about how to structure the organization and the implementation of those choices. The formal structure explains in more detailed ways how the structural elements are configured. The terms 'organizational structure' and 'organizational design' are sometimes used interchangeably. Since organizational design is a structural configuration, the reasons for this are quite apparent. In the following sections, we will examine basic ways of understanding the design choices and structural features of organizations.

Organizational design is the process of choosing and implementing a structural configuration for an organization.

The **formal structure** is the intended configuration of positions, job duties and lines of authority among the component parts of the organization.

Organization charts are diagrams that depict the formal structures of organizations.

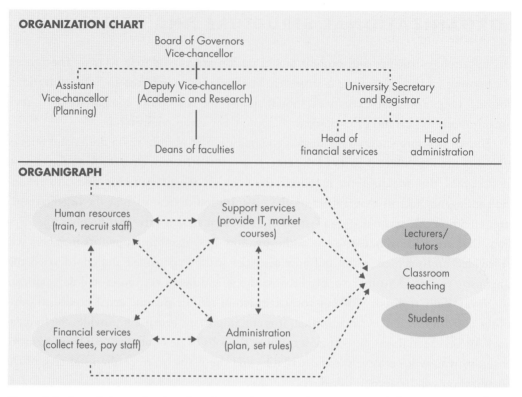

Figure 6.1: A partial organization chart for a university and an organigraph for university teaching. *Source:* Organigraph developed from Mintzberg, H. and Van der Heyden, L. (1999) Organigraphs: drawing how companies really work, *Harvard Business Review*, September/October, 87–94. Copyright © 1999 the Harvard Business School Publishing Corporation, all rights reserved. Reprinted by permission of *Harvard Business Review*.

Factors influencing organizational design

Some particular factors will have an impact on the choices made when designing the organization: scale, technology, environment and strategy. This analysis will identify the way in which these factors impact and their implications on design. Some of the possible design outcomes that may emerge are described at the end of the chapter.

The more individuals in an organization, the more possible interconnections among them and the less the likelihood of direct interpersonal contact between everyone. Thus, as organizations grow, their structure is likely to become more complex. More advanced electronic communication methods and policies, rules and procedures are used as substitutes for direct supervision, both to save money and to ensure consistency. Larger organizations can be more efficient, with potential economies of scale in production and services through repetition, but then there is more need to break tasks down into parts, to allocate authority and to make sure everything and everyone is acting in a coordinated way to achieve the organization's goals. Larger organizations often have more products, production processes, geographic locations and so on. This additional complexity calls for more sophisticated organizational designs.

Technology

Organizations are said to arrange their internal structures to meet the dictates of their dominant 'technologies' or work flows; this is known as the **technological imperative**.[5]

Technology is the combination of resources, knowledge and techniques that creates a product or service output for an organization. The match between structure and technology is important for the successful design of organizations. Thompson[6] and Woodward[7] present different classifications that illustrate the possible diversity in technology and these are shown in Table 6.1. For example, Woodward's successful small-batch and continuous-process plants have flexible structures with small work groups at the bottom; more rigidly structured plants are less successful. In contrast, successful mass production operations are rigidly structured and have large work groups at the bottom.

There are other possible technologies that can be described. For example, with more flexible manufacturing systems there is a trend towards more 'mass customization', where

*The **technological imperative** is the idea that if an organization does not adjust its internal structure to the requirements of technology, it will not be successful.*

***Technology** is the combination of resources, knowledge and techniques that creates a product or service output for an organization.*

Thompson	
Intensive technology	Involves a team of highly interdependent specialists using a variety, but no certain, techniques to produce the desired outcomes for nonroutine problems or situations. Because the problem is unique there are no standard operating procedures and there must be mutual adjustments to deal with it. Examples include the team in a hospital emergency room and a research development laboratory.
Mediating technology	Links parties that want to become interdependent, such as wholesalers who link producers and retailers. Also, banks link creditors and depositors, and store money and information to facilitate such exchanges. Interdependent depositors and creditors rely on each other through pooled activity of the bank. If one creditor defaults on a loan, no one depositor is injured.
Long-linked technology	The way to produce the desired outcomes is known so the task is broken into sequential, interdependent steps. An example is the high-volume car assembly line.
Woodward	
Small-batch	A variety of custom products, such as tailored suits, are made to fit customer specifications. The machinery and equipment used are generally not elaborate, but considerable craftsmanship is often needed. For example, producing a unique marketing campaign or television movie.
Continuous-process	Producing a few products with considerable automation in an ongoing process. Examples include automated chemical plants and oil refineries.
Mass production	Similar to Thompson's long-linked technology; produces one or a few products using an assembly-line type of system. The work of one group depends on that of another, the equipment is typically sophisticated and the workers are given detailed instructions. Cars and refrigerators are produced in this way.

Table 6.1: Thompson's and Woodward's classifications of technology.

custom adjustments are possible even in a mass production process. Such a process would allow an infinite variety of goods and services unique to customer requirements.

Environment

An effective organizational design reflects powerful external forces as well as the desires of employees and managers. There are two main sets of parameters we can use to explain the environment. First, as open systems, organizations need to receive various inputs from their environment and sell various outputs to their environment. Environments can be labelled as either:

- *General* – that is, the set of cultural, economic, legal–political and educational conditions found in the areas in which the organization operates. These can include different global economies and markets.
- *Specific* – which involves the mix of owners, suppliers, distributors, government agencies and competitors with which it interacts.

Another basic concern in analysing the environment of the organization is its complexity. Environmental complexity is the estimated magnitude of the problems and opportunities in the organization's environment, as evidenced by the combination of the following three main factors that emerge uniquely, in the context of each organization, from the general and specific environments:[8]

- *Environmental richness.* The environment is richer when the economy is growing and improving, customers are spending more and investors investing more; when individuals are improving their education and others the organization relies upon are also prospering. Organizational survival is easier, there is more dynamism and there are more opportunities for change. The opposite is decline, which occurs in economic recession. Typically, workers may be laid off and the number of working units and managers may be reduced.
- *Environmental interdependence.* The link between external interdependence and organizational design is often subtle and indirect. The organization may coopt powerful outsiders onto its board of directors and/or adjust its design strategy to absorb or buffer the demands of a more powerful external element. For example, it may include a public relations unit to deal with public pressures or to lobby government for policy change. Because of increasing internationalization, many organizations face a number of 'general environments' and maintain highly complex and diffuse interdependencies with them.
- *Uncertainty and volatility.* In times of change, investments quickly become outmoded and internal operations no longer work as expected. The obvious organizational design response to uncertainty and volatility is to opt for a more flexible structure. However, these pressures may run counter to those that arise from large size and technology and the organization may continue to struggle while adjusting its design a little at a time.

OB IN ACTION

Pause for thought!

To what extent do environmental influences, including internal ones, affect the organization? Mobach[9] argued that 'Organizations do not only use their building to sit dry and comfortable, but in many cases they actively seek to structure the work, improve the performance, and express their corporate identity through architectural design. It appears that organization and architecture have a lot in common.' Mobach goes on to argue that a building construction (or reconstruction) can support organizational design or change and improve current organizational processes and outcome.

To what extent does ergonomics have an impact when considering a holistic approach to organizational design? Why have some institutions, such as banks, adopted more open-plan architectural layouts for their business, and to what extent does this layout affect organizational culture?

OB IN ACTION

Going global

Businesses are increasingly engaging with global markets. This affects both the markets to which they sell their goods and services and also the labour market they rely on to produce them. The implications for businesses can be significant in terms of opening up new markets or seeking favourable alliances or outsourcing arrangements. But moving into new countries means moving into new environments too, which can add to the diversity of political, cultural and economic scenarios that the business managers and employees must understand and succeed in.

According to an international survey conducted by PricewaterhouseCoopers (PwC), offshore expansion is an increasing trend among banks and financial services companies, with more than 80% of financial services companies offering some form of offshore operation. Such offshore operations involve setting up a business in a foreign country, setting up a joint venture or outsourcing their business to another company in the foreign country. India and China are the two most popular countries for such outsourcing, especially in IT functions. Others include Ireland, Romania and the Philippines. Outcomes are not always favourable, however, with more than 15% of the respondents dissatisfied with the cost savings they achieved.[10]

Strategy

Organizational strategy is the process of positioning the organization in its competitive environment and implementing actions to compete successfully. The study of linking strategy, organizational design and performance has a long tradition in organizational analysis. While it cannot be covered extensively here, the important point is that the organization's strategy will be driving its goals and vision, and an organizational design must be established to achieve the vision. For example, an organization may be endeavouring to become a market leader by having the cheapest or best value-for-money product. Alternatively, it may be trying to differentiate its product from others. In other words, the degree to which the organization's strategy is aiming to produce standardized products, and the narrow or broad scope of the organization's business, may impact on the design choices that are made.

Another issue of strategy involves the organization building on and refining its unique experience and competencies; that is, competency-based strategies. Business practices that have built up over time and proved a key to the success of a business or the competence of employees may well be factors upon which the business should focus and make design decisions. For example, the design may need to be flexible and allow employees the scope to make decisions, such as where the organization is trying to capitalize on employee creativity in innovating new products. In other cases, it may be more important to have relatively rigid, formalized structures with more rules and controls.

ORGANIZATIONAL GOALS, CONTROL AND COORDINATION

The first of the structural building blocks are organizational goals. In an organization, people are organized into a structure in order to work together to achieve organizational goals. This involves breaking people and tasks up into units, allocating authority and making other decisions about how things are done. Two other components of structure are control and coordination, which provide ways of ensuring that these subdivided activities can be brought together to achieve the organizational goals.

Organizational goals

Organizations may be viewed as entities with goals. The goals they pursue are multifaceted and often conflict with, or overlap, one another. These goals are common to individuals within an organization though their reasons for involvement in the organization are partly about serving their own individual interests. There are two types of organizational goals. The first centres on how the organization intends to serve particular groups in society, or with social responsibility, serve society as a whole. The second focuses on organizational survival.

Organizations are inevitably involved in some 'type of business', whether or not it is profit-oriented. They operate to provide products, services, infrastructure or wealth, for example. **Output goals** define the organization's type of business and are the basis of the mission statements that organizations often use to indicate their purposes. These can form the basis for long-term planning and strategies and may help prevent huge organizations from diverting too many resources to peripheral areas.

Some organizations may provide benefits to the society as a whole but most target their efforts towards a particular group or groups. The main recipients of the organization's efforts are the primary beneficiaries.

Primary beneficiaries are particular groups expected to benefit from the efforts of specific organizations.

Political organizations serve the common good, while culturally based organizations such as churches may emphasize contributions to their members. Social service organizations such as hospitals are expected to emphasize quality care to patients. In Japan, long-time workers are typically placed at the centre of the organization with an expectation that through them and their secure employment there will be economic growth for the country. Many larger organizations have found it useful to review, clarify and state carefully their type of business.

In the process of serving society there is an expectation of corporate social responsibility; that is, the organization or corporation has an obligation to behave in ethical and moral ways. Organizations contributing to societal goals are given broader discretion and may obtain some control over resources, individuals, markets and products at lower costs. Organizations are typically expected to take action to improve society in a socially responsible way, or at least to avoid damaging it. Social responsibility is exhibited towards small and large social beneficiaries for a range of reasons, both altruistic and related to the organization's reputation. It is important for organizations to maintain society's trust and confidence if they wish to avoid negative impacts on their operations.

Organizations also face the immediate problem of just making it through the coming years. **Systems goals** are concerned with the internal conditions that are expected to increase the organization's survival potential. The list of systems goals is almost endless because each manager and researcher links today's conditions to tomorrow's existence in a different way. However, for many organizations the list includes growth, productivity, stability, harmony, flexibility, prestige and, of course, human resource maintenance. For some businesses, analysts consider market share and current profitability to be important systems goals. Other studies suggest that innovation and quality also may be considered important.

Systems goals *are goals concerned with conditions within the organization that are expected to increase its survival potential.*

In a practical sense, systems goals represent short-term organizational characteristics that higher-level managers wish to promote. Systems goals must often be balanced against one another; for instance, a productivity and efficiency drive may cut the flexibility of an organization. Different parts of the organization may be asked to pursue different types of systems goal. Higher-level managers, for example, may expect to see their production operations strive for efficiency, while pressing for innovation from their research and development laboratory and promoting stability in their financial affairs. Systems goals provide a 'road map' to assist in linking together various units of an organization to ensure its survival. Well-defined systems goals are practical and easy to understand, focusing the manager's attention on what needs to be done.

Control

Control *is the set of mechanisms used to keep actions and outputs within predetermined limits.*

Control is one of the basic management functions and is involved with ensuring the organization achieves what it is intended to achieve. Control is the set of mechanisms used to keep actions and/or outputs (based on predetermined organizational goals) within predetermined limits. Control deals with setting standards, measuring results against standards and instituting corrective action.

The control process that is used in activities such as accounting and production is depicted in Figure 6.2.

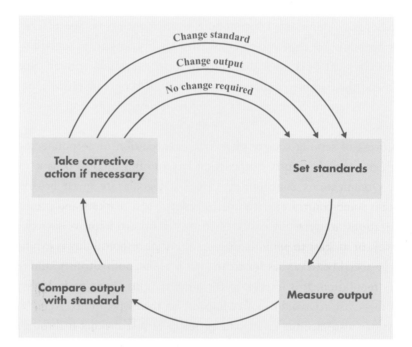

Figure 6.2: The business control process.

Note the iterative nature of the process; in other words, controlling activities within an organization is an ongoing process. Note also that once the actual output is compared with the objective or standard that has been set, the manager may need to decide whether to adjust the standard (if it proves unrealistic or unachievable) or produce a different level of output in step with the standard. For a given project, actual expenditure (output) may be exceeding the budget (standard), so the manager will need to take measures to reduce ongoing costs for the project in some way.

While controls are needed in all organizations, just a few controls may go a long way. Astute managers need to be aware of the danger of too much control in the organization, as noted in Effective Manager 6.1.

Output controls *are controls that focus on desired targets and allow managers to use their own methods for reaching defined targets.*

Output controls

Developing targets or standards, measuring results against these targets and taking corrective action are all steps involved in developing output controls. **Output controls** focus on desired targets and allow managers to use their own methods for reaching defined targets.

EFFECTIVE MANAGER 6.1

Signs of too much control

Astute managers look for the signs that too much control or inappropriate controls have been placed on their units. They look for:

- too much emphasis on one measured goal to the exclusion of all others;
- too much emphasis on the quick fix and an unwillingness to look for underlying causes of problems or new opportunities;

- a tradition of across-the-board cuts rather than reductions linked to demands, constraints and opportunities;
- too many vague and unrealistic expectations that breed defeat;
- raising of quotas without reward for employees, particularly after employee suggestions for change are implemented.

Most modern organizations use output controls as a part of an overall method of managing by exception; that is, when identification of a problem triggers corrective actions. Such controls are popular because they promote flexibility and creativity, as well as facilitating dialogue about corrective action.

There is an important link between controls and goals but it is not necessarily simple or one way. The links are complex and encompassing. Goals define what is to be achieved and they influence the controls set in place to ensure that the goals are met. Controls may also have an impact on goals. For example, output goals may be revised if targets cannot realistically be met. Controls over the manner in which tasks are done may also have an impact on an organization's systems goals, especially if there is little choice over the controls. For example, an organization may be obliged to comply with certain requirements of government legislation such as those relating to workplace safety, or with the requirements of an allied organization such as a supplier, major customer or alliance partner.

Process controls

Few organizations run on output controls alone. Once a solution to a problem is found and successfully implemented, managers do not want the problem to recur, so they institute **process controls**. Process controls attempt to specify the manner in which tasks will be accomplished. There are many types of process control, but three groups have received considerable attention.

Process controls *are controls that attempt to specify the manner in which tasks will be accomplished.*

Policies, rules and procedures

Most organizations have a variety of policies, rules and procedures in place at any time. Usually, we think of a policy as a guideline for action that outlines important objectives and broadly indicates how an activity is to be performed. A policy allows for individual discretion and minor adjustments without direct clearance by a higher-level manager. Many organizations have a stated policy towards cultural diversity, for example, which not only outlines their goals for increasing the diversity of the workforce but also specifies the procedures to be used in recruiting staff. Bear in mind that a policy is a statement of intent only and relies on employees following the rules and procedures.

Rules and procedures are more specific, rigid and impersonal than policies. They typically describe in detail how a task or series of tasks is to be performed. They are designed to apply to all individuals under specified conditions. Most car dealers, for example, have detailed instruction manuals for repairing a new car under warranty. They must follow strict procedures to obtain reimbursement from the manufacturer for warranty work that they have undertaken.

Other examples of rules and procedures include requirements for employees to:

* have someone countersign approval for payments;
* wear certain apparel for certain jobs;
* follow particular steps for cleaning equipment (such as coffee machines) or conducting regular maintenance checks (such as of electrical equipment).

Rules, procedures and policies are employed as substitutes for direct managerial supervision, leaving managers to focus on exceptional incidents or unique problems. Under the guidance of written rules and procedures, the organization can specifically direct the activities of many individuals. It can ensure virtually identical treatment across even distant work locations. McDonald's hamburgers and fries, for example, taste much the same whether they are purchased in Greece, London, Hong Kong, Moscow or Sydney, simply because the ingredients and the cooking methods follow standardized written rules and procedures.

Formalization and standardization

Formalization refers to the written documentation of rules, procedures and policies to guide behaviour and decision making. It is often used to simplify jobs: for example, written instructions allow individuals with less training to perform comparatively sophisticated tasks. Formalization is the written documentation of work rules, policies and procedures.

Written procedures may also be available to ensure a proper sequence of tasks is executed, even if this sequence is only performed occasionally.

Standardization *is the degree to which the range of actions in a job or series of jobs is limited.*

Most organizations have developed additional methods for dealing with recurring problems or situations. **Standardization** is the degree to which the range of allowable actions in a job or series of jobs is limited. It involves the creation of guidelines so similar work activities are repeatedly performed in a similar fashion and employees know what they can and cannot do. In some cases there may be no need for formalization and standardization; rules and regulations may unnecessarily hinder workers' progress in their jobs.

In other cases they may be vital for ensuring equity, fair treatment of clients or safety. Typically, a worker's job requirements and limits are clearly defined in a job description and these often form part of a broad pattern of jobs. However, if you wanted highly creative workers to be innovative in the development of a new product, for example, putting them into straitjacketed jobs might not gain the desired behaviours from them.

OB IN ACTION

Working to rule[11]

Consider the following comparisons of the definitions of the term 'work to rule' for the four countries below, and then review the questions provided.

Greece: *aperyía zílou*
Form of industrial action in which employees, having previously agreed between themselves to do so, collectively exhibit exaggerated care in the execution of work. In practice, the effect is to reduce output or to hinder the functioning of services. Working to rule, which has not been encountered in Greece, is a lawful form of strike although the element of a cessation of work is absent. As it constitutes strike action, it would mean the loss of pay throughout its duration.

Netherlands: *stiptheidsactie*
A form of industrial action in which employees collectively slow down the pace of work through exaggeratedly meticulous observance of rules and regulations. It is therefore mostly used in situations where voluminous and detailed sets of working rules are to be found, which mainly tends to be in the public sector. A work to rule is also seen as a less aggressive form of action than, for example, a strike or sit-in and its use reflects a less serious degree of dissension between employer and employees.

Sweden: *paragrafarbete* A Situation in which employees follow all rules and regulations to the letter while working. This usually means that the work is performed with more meticulous care and hence more slowly than usual, possibly but not necessarily in conjunction with a go-slow, which results in delays. Working to rule is done openly and is usually a way of exerting pressure on the employer, in which case it often constitutes a form of industrial action. As such, it is lawful if organized by a union but this is never so in practice. Working to rule is extremely rare in Sweden.

UK: *work to rule*
A form of collective industrial action in which workers collectively slow down the pace working through scrupulous and detailed observation of orders, works rules or health and safety regulations. This form of action is most frequently used in the public service sector, where large and detailed sets of working rules are often found. Despite the fact that such action involves conforming to rules it may be held by the courts to constitute a breach of contract by the employees concerned.

Questions

1. Organizations and governments produce policies on the basis that people are rational, responsible and rule/law abiding. How would we operate different working practices in the four different countries?

2. What are the implications for management in dealing with employees who work to rule?

Quality management

Another way to institute process controls is to establish a quality management process. Quality management emerged from the total quality management (TQM) movement founded by W. Edwards Deming. The heart of Deming's approach is to institute a process approach to continual improvement based on statistical analyses of the organization's operations. All levels of management are to be involved in the quality programme; managers are to improve supervision, train employees, retrain employees in new skills and create a structure that will push the quality programme. The emphasis is on training, learning and consistency of purpose, which appear to be important lessons and all organizations need to be reminded of this constantly.

Coordination

In order to enhance the operation of the organization, there must be ways to get all the separate activities, people and units working together. Coordination is the set of mechanisms that an organization uses to link the actions of its units into a consistent pattern. The greater the specialization in the organization, the greater the need for effective coordination. Much of the coordination within a unit is handled by its manager. Smaller organizations may rely on their management hierarchy to provide the necessary consistency but as the organization grows, managers become overloaded. The organization then needs to develop more efficient and effective ways of linking work units to one another. Coordination methods can be personal or impersonal.

Personal methods of coordination

Personal methods of coordination produce synergy by promoting dialogue, discussion, innovation, creativity and learning, allowing the organization to address the particular needs of distinct units and individuals simultaneously. Perhaps the most popular of the wide variety of personal methods is direct contact between and among organizational members. Typically, this involves the development of an effective informal network of contacts within the organization; for example, direct personal communication and e-mail.

Committees, although generally costly and sluggish, are effective for mutual adjustment across unit heads, for communicating complex qualitative information and for helping managers whose units must work together to adjust schedules, work loads and work assignments to increase productivity. Taskforces are typically formed with limited agendas and involve individuals from different parts of the organization identifying and solving problems that cut across different departments. Another personal method of coordination involves developing a shared set of values that allows organizational members to predict accurately the responses of others to specific events. There is no magic involved in selecting the appropriate mix of personal coordination methods and tailoring them to the individual skills, abilities and experience of employees. Managers need to know the individuals involved and their preferences.

Effective Manager 6.2 provides some guidelines for understanding how different personal methods can be tailored to match different individuals.

EFFECTIVE MANAGER 6.2

Selecting personal coordination styles

The astute manager must recognize the following important differences in matching up workers:

- individuals and representatives of departments often have their own views of how best to move towards organizational goals;
- some individuals emphasize immediate problems and move towards quick solutions while others stress underlying problems and longer-term solutions;

- given that each department develops its own unique vocabulary and standard way of communicating, the coordination method chosen should recognize such potential differences and include many opportunities for direct exchange;
- there are often pronounced departmental and individual preferences for formality.

Source: Adapted from Lawrence, P. R. and Lavsch, J. W. (1967), *Organization and environment, Managing differentiation and Integration*, Richard D. Irwin: Homewood, IL.

Impersonal methods of coordination

Impersonal coordination methods are often refinements and extensions of process controls, with an emphasis on formalization and standardization. Most larger organizations have written policies and procedures, such as schedules, budgets and plans, which are designed to mesh the operations of several units into a whole. Some other examples of impersonal methods of coordination are:

- Cross-departmental work units that coordinate the efforts of diverse functional units.
- Management information systems (MIS) that coordinate and control the operations of diverse subordinate units. These are computerized substitutes for schedules, budgets and the like. In some firms, MIS still operate as a combined process control and impersonal coordination mechanism. In the hands of astute managers, MIS become an electronic network, linking individuals throughout the organization. Using decentralized communication systems, supplemented with the telephone, fax machine and e-mail, a manager can greatly improve coordination.

Two broad types of organizational design that reflect the degree of control and coordination in an organization (as well as the allocation of authority, which is considered in the next section) are mechanistic and organic. A mechanistic design is an organizational structure that tends to emphasize authority and control, as well as specialization in jobs. Organizations of this type stress rules, policies and procedures, specify techniques for decision making and emphasize well-documented control systems backed by a strong middle management and supported by a centralized staff. In an organic design there is more flexibility in how things are done, with fewer rules and procedures; there is even flexibility in how elements of the structure can change quickly in response to changing circumstances. More responsibility is placed in the hands of workers, who are seen as competent and/or expert at what they do.

VERTICAL SPECIALIZATION

Vertical specialization
is a hierarchical division of labour that distributes formal authority and establishes how critical decisions will be made.

In most larger organizations, there is a clear separation of authority and duties by hierarchical rank. This separation represents **vertical specialization**, which is a hierarchical division of work that distributes formal authority and establishes where and how critical decisions will be made. This division creates a hierarchy of authority, and a chain of command, that arranges work positions in order of increasing authority. We will also discuss another form of division of labour in the next section on horizontal specialization.

The distribution of formal authority is evident in the responsibilities typically allocated to managers. Top managers or senior executives plan the overall strategy of the organization and plot its long-term future. Middle managers guide the daily operations of the organization, help formulate policy and translate top management decisions into more specific guidelines for action. Lower-level managers supervise the actions of employees to ensure implementation of the strategies authorized by top management and compliance with the related policies established by middle management. When allocating authority or specializing vertically, one feature of organizational structure can be explained. That is, those organizations that have many levels in their hierarchies can be described as tall. Others that have very few levels can be described as flat.

We also consider organizations in terms of how centralized or decentralized they are. The degree of centralization of decision-making authority is high if discretion to spend money, recruit people and make similar decisions is retained further up the hierarchy of authority. The more such decisions are delegated, or moved down the hierarchy of authority, the greater is the degree of decentralization.

Applying these characteristics to mechanistic and organic designs, we can make the following general (but not the only possible) observations about design. Visually, mechanistic organizations tend to have a tall hierarchy and may resemble a tall, thin pyramid with centralized decision-making senior staff at the top. Taller or more vertically specialized structures have more managers per worker. This may mean closer and tighter control over workers, with formal communication through several layers of hierarchy that can be slow and distorted. People might get frustrated waiting for approval in tall structures and feel unable to take responsibility for their own work.

Mechanistic design emphasizes vertical specialization, hierarchical levels, tight control and coordination through rules, policies and other impersonal methods.

Organic design is an organizational structure that emphasizes horizontal specialization, an extensive use of personal coordination and loose rules, policies and procedures.

Organic organizations are more likely to have a flatter structure because more responsibility is delegated down to workers. Flatter organizations with fewer layers of hierarchy and authority and fewer managers generally permit submanagers and employees more discretion; they decentralize decision making and loosen control.

OB IN ACTION

Empowered or enslaved?

During the 1980s the concept of 'empowerment' was popular in various companies, including the automobile industry in the UK. The organization chart was deliberately turned upside down to demonstrate graphically the change in company philosophy, culture and approach. An example of a car-servicing garage is shown in Figure 6.3.

The case in question involves a garage in South Wales (UK) dealing with customer service and repairs. Traditionally in this company, when customer service assistants encountered problems, they consulted their manager for a decision. Any problem that incurred a cost in excess of £500 required the general manager's approval. A month after the empowerment policy was brought in, Stephen Williams, one of the customer service assistants on the front desk, was confronted by an angry customer, asking for a replacement rear windscreen wiper to be put on their car. Stephen looked at the organizational chart that both he and customers could see (clearly and proudly displayed at the customer service desk) and duly replaced the wiper free of charge. A few minutes later, he was called into his manager's office and told that he should have sought permission before taking the decision that he did. Stephen challenged this approach stating that he was empowered to take this decision. His manager clarified that he was empowered to take the decision provided that it did not incur any charge to the organization.

Questions

1. What do you think Stephen's perception of the reversed organizational chart is likely to be?
2. What is the customer services manager's role under the new 'structure'?

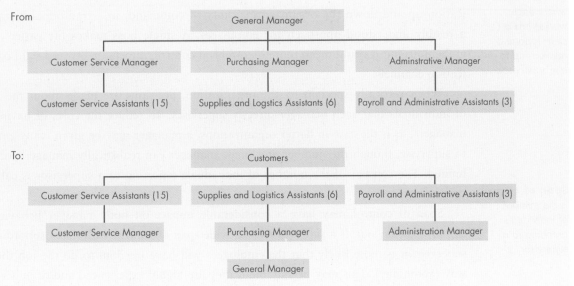

Figure 6.3: Inverted organization chart for a car-servicing garage.

Generally speaking, greater decentralization provides higher subordinate satisfaction and a quicker response to problems and may give workers a sense of ownership and greater levels of motivation in their work. Decentralization also assists in the on-the-job training of employees for higher-level positions.

Australia's leading accommodation website is an example of an organization that has made decisions about authority allocations.

Wotif.com began in 1999 when its founder and CEO Graeme Wood was asked to help a hotelier fill vacant rooms. He pioneered the selling of last-minute accommodation via the Internet. Now Wotif.com has 6000 hotels (or similar accommodation venues) on its books in 36 global locations and the website attracts nearly two million user sessions a month (translating into more than 100 000 monthly bookings). There are 100 employees internationally in Brisbane, Canada, New Zealand, Singapore and the UK. Wood has maintained a flat structure in the organization, with a focus on participation. He believes in keeping lines of communication completely open – a casual and accessible organization structure where anyone can talk to anyone else whenever they like.

Two other organizational characteristics that emerge from vertical specialization (though other factors might also contribute) are unity of command and span of control.

Unity of command and span of control

As already indicated, with vertical specialization, executives, managers and supervisors are hierarchically connected through the 'chain of command'. Individuals are expected to follow their supervisors' decisions in the areas of responsibility outlined in the organization chart. Traditional management theory suggests that each individual should have one supervisor and each unit should have one leader. Under these circumstances there is a unity of command. **Unity of command** is considered necessary to avoid confusion, to assign accountability to specific individuals and to provide clear channels of communication up and down the organization. Unity of command, in a traditional hierarchy, is a readily understood approach for employees. A single boss makes life easier and less ambiguous but it could mean more hierarchical control, impersonality and rigid communication channels.

Unity of command *is the situation in an organization where each worker has a clear reporting relationship to only one supervisor.*

When vertically specializing the organization, decisions are made about the number of individuals that each manager directly supervises. To reduce the costs of having many managers, as is the case in flatter organizations, a manager may be given many employees to supervise, though the number any single manager can realistically manage is obviously limited. The concept of the number of individuals reporting to a supervisor is called the **span of control**.

Span of control *is the number of individuals reporting to a supervisor.*

Span of control may have a considerable impact on both manager behaviour and employee behaviour. If a supervisor has a wide span of control with many subordinates to supervise, it is more likely that the employees will have freedom to do the job their own way (autonomy). This may be suitable if they are highly experienced and/or in a very creative role. Control may be looser and people may have a higher satisfaction level (but not necessarily a higher performance level).

Narrower spans of control are expected when tasks are complex, when employees are inexperienced or poorly trained and/or when tasks call for team effort.

Unfortunately, narrow spans of control yield many levels in the organizational hierarchy. The excessive number of levels is not only expensive (typically requiring more managers), but also makes the organization unresponsive to necessary change. A research study based on data collected from 74 manufacturing organizations found that differentiating mechanisms such as high job specialization and narrow spans of control led to poor integration of design manufacturing processes.[12]

HORIZONTAL SPECIALIZATION

Control, coordination and vertical specialization are only part of the picture. Managers must divide the total task into separate duties and group similar people and resources. Different groups or people do different parts of the larger operation. Look again at Figure 6.1 and note the two work groups reporting to the university secretary and registrar. **Horizontal specialization** is the division of labour that establishes work units or groups within an organization; it is often referred to as the process of departmentalization. In the following section we will examine three forms of horizontal specialization – by function, division and matrix – and also look at some 'mixed' or 'hybrid' forms that can emerge.

Horizontal specialization *is the division of labour through the formation of work units or groups within an organization.*

Line personnel are work groups that conduct the major business of the organization. Staff personnel are groups that assist the line units by performing specialized services for the organization.

Prior to doing this it is valuable to consider the difference between the terms 'line' and 'staff'. In an organization line personnel conduct the major business that directly affects the organization. In universities, academic staff, or in factories the workers who make the goods, are line workers. In contrast, staff personnel assist the line units by providing specialized expertise and services, such as accounting, human resources and public relations. The dotted lines on the organization chart depicted in the top of Figure 6.1 denote staff relationships, whereas the solid lines denote line relationships (teaching in the faculties is the major business of the university).

Line personnel are likely to feel more directly involved with the operations of the organization, especially if they can clearly see their part in achieving the organization's goals (task significance and task identity from the job characteristics model are particularly relevant). However, a common behavioural consequence is that there tend to be different perspectives between the line and staff groups. Staff personnel are often accused of interfering with line work with their unnecessary forms and procedures (although often they are trying to accomplish important things such as financial audits, legal compliance, payrolls and so on). Line personnel say they just want to get on with the job and lower-level managers, in particular, resent the demands or requirements of staff personnel. Inter-group and interpersonal conflict can be common (see Chapter 8).

Departmentalization by function

Grouping individuals by skill, knowledge and action yields a pattern of functional departmentalization and represents the most commonly used arrangement.

Figure 6.4 shows the organization chart for a supermarket chain, where each department has a technical speciality considered necessary for efficient operation. The organization is divided into four main functional groups – financial services, customer and marketing services, distribution and logistics and company support services – and within each of these groups employees in different sections or departments undertake separate and specialized tasks. In business organizations generally, marketing, finance, production and personnel are important functions. In many small organizations, this functional pattern dominates; for instance, Apple Computer used this pattern early in its development. Functional units or departments are often criticized as encouraging functional 'silos' that stand alone for too much of the time and discourage cooperative and coordinated behaviour. People working in functional departments tend to develop narrow interests, limited perspectives, competitive behaviour, unique language and cultures and a propensity to pass problems on to other sections.

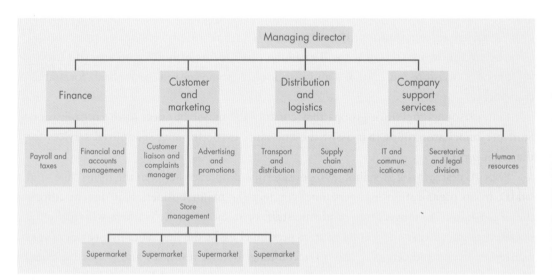

Figure 6.4: A functional pattern of departmentalization for a supermarket chain.

Table 6.2 summarizes the advantages (and disadvantages) of a functional pattern. With all these advantages, it is not surprising that the functional form is extremely popular, being used in most organizations, despite some disadvantages. Organizations that rely on functional specialization may expect the following tendencies to emerge over time:

- an emphasis on quality from a technical standpoint;
- rigidity with respect to change, particularly if change within one functional area is needed to help other functional areas;
- difficulty in coordinating the actions of different functional areas, particularly if the organization must continually adjust to changing external conditions.

Advantages	Disadvantages
1. It can yield clear task assignments that are consistent with an individual's training.	1. It may reinforce the narrow training of individuals and lead to boring and routine jobs, e.g. accounts processing. Communication across technical areas is difficult, and conflict between units may increase. Lines of communication across the organization can become complex.
2. Individuals within a department can easily build on one another's knowledge, training and experience. Facing similar problems and having similar training facilitates communication and technical problem solving.	2. Complex communication channels can lead to 'top management overload'. Top management may spend too much time and effort dealing with cross-functional problems.
3. It provides an excellent training ground for new managers, who must translate their academic training into organizational actions.	3. Individuals may look up the organizational hierarchy for direction and reinforcement rather than focusing on products, services or clients. Guidance is typically sought from functional peers or superiors.
4. It is easy to explain. Most employees can understand the role of each unit, even though many may not know what individuals in a particular function do.	

Table 6.2: Major advantages and disadvantages of functional specialization.

Departmentalization by division, geography and customer

Alternatively, a divisional departmentalization may group individuals and resources by products, services and/or clients/customers. Figure 6.5 shows a divisional pattern of organization grouped around products (automotive parts such as transmissions and engines), regions (European, Asia-Pacific and South American) and customers (government accounts, corporate accounts and university/college accounts) for three divisions of a large international organization. This pattern is often used to meet diverse external threats and opportunities.

Many larger, geographically dispersed organizations that sell to national and international markets use departmentalization by geography. The savings in time, effort and travel can be substantial, and each territory can adjust to regional differences.

Divisional departmentalization is the grouping of individuals and resources by product, service and/or client. Departmentalization by geography is the grouping of individuals and resources by geographical territory. Departmentalization by customer is the grouping of individuals and resources by client.

Organizations that rely on a few major customers may organize their people and resources by client. The idea is to focus attention on the needs of the individual customer.

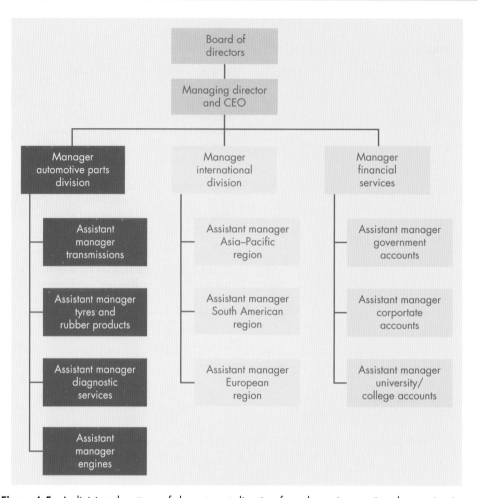

Figure 6.5: A divisional pattern of departmentalization for a large international organization.

To the extent that customer needs are unique, departmentalization by customer can also reduce confusion and increase synergy. Organizations expanding internationally may also divisionalize to meet the demands of complex host-country ownership requirements.

The major advantages and disadvantages of divisional specialization are summarized in Table 6.3. In organizations in which satisfying the demands of outsiders is particularly important, the divisional structure may provide the desired capabilities. This pattern can help improve customer responsiveness for organizations that operate in many territories, produce quite different products and services, serve a few major customers or operate internationally. Organizations that rely on divisional specialization can generally expect the following tendencies to occur over time:

- an emphasis on flexibility and adaptability to the needs of important external units;
- a lag in the technical quality of products and services compared with that of functionally structured competitors;
- difficulty in achieving coordination across divisions, particularly where divisions must work closely or sell to each other.

Advantages	Disadvantages
1. It provides adaptability and flexibility in meeting the demands of important external groups.	1. It does not provide a pool of highly trained individuals with similar expertise to solve problems and train new employees.
2. It allows for spotting external changes as they are emerging.	2. It can lead to a duplication of effort as each division attempts to solve similar problems.
3. It provides for the integration of specialized personnel deep within the hierarchy.	3. Divisional goals may be given priority over the health and welfare of the overall organization; divisional organizations may have difficulty responding to corporation-wide threats.
4. It focuses on the success or failure of particular products, services, clients or territories.	4. Conflict problems may arise when divisions attempt to develop joint projects, exchange resources, share individuals or 'transfer price' one another for goods and services.
5. To the extent that this pattern yields separate 'business units', top management can pit one division against another; for instance, Procter & Gamble has traditionally promoted friendly competition among product groups.	

Table 6.3: Major advantages and disadvantages of divisional specialization.

Branch offices

Having geographically remote offices or branches can be an important part of doing business in different locations (nationally or internationally). However, there can be problems in keeping in contact with head office. As Sean Spence (business mentor and consultant) says: 'Mutual contempt is highly corrosive.' He recommends regular visits to the branch offices to maintain face-to-face contact. Such visits can be very effective.

Departmentalization by matrix

From the aerospace industry, a third, unique, form of departmentalization was developed; it is now called a **matrix structure**.[13]

In the aerospace industry projects are technically complex and they involve hundreds of subcontractors located throughout the world. Precise integration and control is needed across many sophisticated functional specialities and corporations. This is often more than a functional or divisional structure can provide. Thus, departmentalization by matrix uses both the functional and divisional forms simultaneously.

Figure 6.6 shows the basic matrix arrangement for an aerospace programme. Note the *functional* departments (production, marketing and engineering) and the *project* efforts representing the two elements of the matrix structure.

Workers and supervisors in the middle of the matrix have two bosses – one functional and one a project boss. For example, if you are one of the people in the marketing function and in the Vulcan project, you would report to the marketing manager but you would also

> *A matrix structure is a combination of functional and divisional patterns in which an individual is assigned to more than one type of unit.*

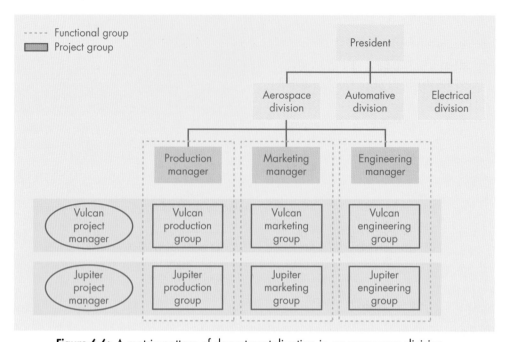

Figure 6.6: A matrix pattern of departmentalization in an aerospace division.
Source: Hodgetts, R. and Luthans, F., (1997) *International management*, McGraw-Hill, New York.

report to your Vulcan project manager. Thus, the matrix breaks the 'unity of command' principle that is central to bureaucratic hierarchy. Each person in a project team has two bosses. The project manager will be responsible for the person's contribution to the project. The department manager will be responsible for the person's:

• general career development
• pay
• promotion prospects within the organization
• contributions to the work of the department if/when there are gaps in their project team duties.[14]

It is also possible that some people in such an industry work outside this matrix structure. As you can see from the figure, there may be some people who work in the functional departments (production, marketing and engineering) but who are not necessarily also in a project team.

The major advantages and disadvantages of the matrix form of departmentalization are summarized in Table 6.4. The key disadvantage is the loss of unity of command. Individuals can be unsure as to what their jobs are, to whom they should report for specific activities and how various managers are to administer the effort. It can also be an expensive method because it relies on individual managers to coordinate efforts deep within the organization.

In Figure 6.6, note that the number of managers almost doubles compared with the number in either a functional or a divisional structure. Despite these limitations, the matrix structure provides a balance between functional and divisional concerns. Many problems can be resolved at the working level, where the balance between technical, cost, customer and organizational concerns can be rectified.

Advantages	Disadvantages
1. It combines strengths of both functional and divisional departmentalization.	1. It is expensive.
2. It helps to provide a blending of technical and market emphasis in organizations operating in exceedingly complex environments.	2. Unity of command is lost (because individuals have more than one supervisor).
3. It provides a series of managers able to converse with both technical and marketing personnel.	3. Authority and responsibilities of managers may overlap, causing conflicts and gaps in effort across units and inconsistencies in priorities.
	4. It is difficult to explain to employees.

Table 6.4: Major advantages and disadvantages of a matrix structure.

Many organizations also use elements of the matrix structure. Special project teams, coordinating committees and taskforces, for example, can be the beginnings of a matrix. A large advertising firm could use project teams for major client contracts. Yet, these temporary structures can be used within a predominantly functional or divisional form without upsetting unity of command or recruiting additional managers.

Mixed forms of departmentalization

As the matrix concept suggests, it is possible to departmentalize by two different methods at the same time but the matrix form is not the only possibility. Organizations often use a mixture of departmentalization forms; it may be desirable to divide the effort (group people and resources) by two methods at the same time to balance the advantages and disadvantages of each. Consider the example in Figure 6.7.

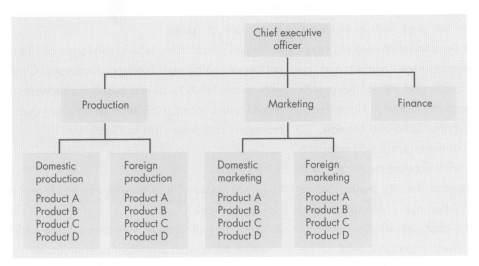

Figure 6.7: Partial organization chart showing a mixed form of departmentalization.
Source: Hodgetts, R. and Luthans, F., (1997), *International Management*, New York, McGraw-Hill Companies Inc. Reproduced by permission.

Notice that this organization has overall functional units (that is, production, marketing and finance) but that work is divided on a divisional basis (that is, domestic and foreign) within each functional area. Thus, departmentalization can take different permutations. Another example might be a geographically departmentalized organization that has functional departments within each major geographical area.

EMERGING FORMS OF ORGANIZATIONAL DESIGN

Every organization will develop a unique design in response to its scale, technology, environment and strategic aims and in terms of the choices it makes about goals, control, coordination and vertical and horizontal specialization. Other factors may also have an impact on design, such as the history of the organization, sudden changes, mergers and acquisitions and geographical locations.

OB IN ACTION

Pierre Lafarge was born in Switzerland and speaks French, German, Spanish, Italian and English fluently. As a recent business studies graduate, he went for an interview in Belgium in order to secure employment with one of the largest global human resources (HR) consulting firms, with their headquarters based in Strasbourg.

He realized after securing the job as an HR advisor that he was interviewed by a recruitment agency working for the global HR firm. There was a formal induction for the post, with a two-week intensive work-related induction delivered in Dubai. Pierre received an employment contract and an e-mail account. He was charged with assisting with the running of client accounts, based in Hong Kong, Los Angeles, Brussels, Paris, Sofia and London.

He was notified that the organization adopts a matrix structure, with each account managed by a regional manager (based in the city mentioned) as well as a client account manager (there are several hundred client accounts and over 40 client account managers). Client account managers tend to be very mobile and typically operate from at least four countries.

Communication within the company tends to occur via e-mail, but where needed, video conferencing is arranged. There are a series of 'virtual office' sites, where messages can be left and work coordinated between employees. Contact with clients tends to be via telephone networks but face-to-face contact is allowed when client account managers authorize visits to clients.

Questions

1. To whom does Pierre go when he has a problem with his work?
2. What sort of problems is Pierre likely to face within the current organizational structure?

In this section we will consider some recognizable types of organizational design in the contemporary world. They are not necessarily new or unimagined but they do illustrate some generally occurring design trends for organizations. Common forms are the simple design, the bureaucracy, the divisionalized organization and the conglomerate. However, there are distinctions in the design of organizations even within these categories; for example, variations in the degree of organic or mechanistic design in bureaucracies. Figure 6.8 illustrates these popular basic designs. Other forms of organization design also emerge, such as alliances, virtual organizations, core-ring designs and adhocracies. These, and their impact on the people working within such organizations, will be briefly examined.

The simple design

The **simple design** is a configuration involving the specialization of individuals and units. That is, vertical specialization and control typically emphasize levels of supervision without elaborate formal mechanisms (such as rule books and policy manuals) and the majority of the control based with the manager. One or two ways of organizing departments are used, and coordination mechanisms are often personal.

*A **simple design** is a configuration involving one or two ways of specializing individuals and units.*

The organization visually resembles a 'pyramid' with few staff individuals or units (see the simple design at the top of Figure 6.8).

The simple design is appropriate for many small organizations, such as family businesses, retail stores and small manufacturing companies,[15] as these have few people, little necessity for coordination, specialized tasks and hierarchical control. The strengths of the simple design are simplicity, flexibility and responsiveness to the desires of a central manager (in many cases, the owner). A simple design relies on the manager's personal leadership, so this configuration is only as effective as the senior manager.

The bureaucracy

The simple design is a basic building block of all organizations. However, as the organization grows, additional layers of management and more specialized departments are added. Line and staff functions are separated and the organization may begin to expand its territorial scope. In this way, larger organizations become much more structurally complex than small ones.[16]

A bureaucracy is an ideal form of organization whose characteristics include a division of labour, hierarchical control, promotion by merit with career opportunities for employees and administration by rule.

The nature of the organization changes as layers of management increase, as the division of labour and coordination mechanisms become more elaborate and as formal controls are established. In addition to the single senior manager there are other 'levels' of management exercising varying degrees of authority.

The famous German sociologist Max Weber suggested that large organizations would thrive if they relied on legal authority, logic and order.[17] Weber argued that relying on a division of labour, hierarchical control, promotion by merit with career opportunities for employees and administration by rule was a superior option to the simple design. While Weber knew the bureaucracy he was designing was an ideal type and that it could

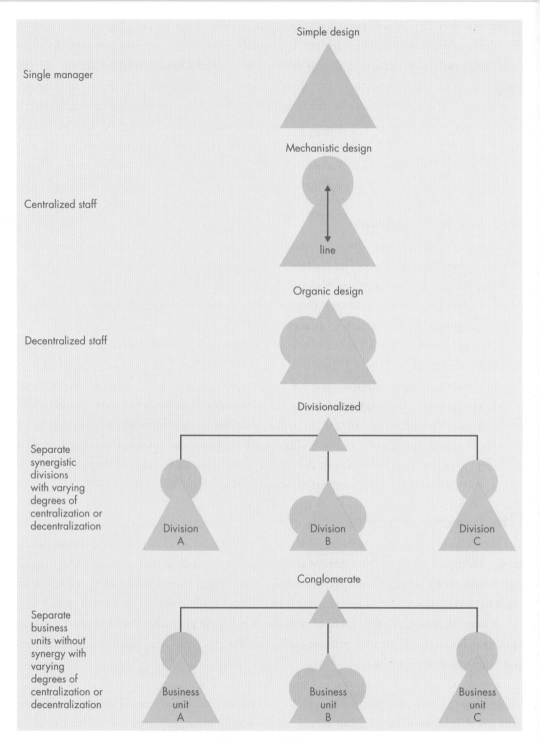

Figure 6.8: Visual depiction of different design options.

not always be perfect, he believed that efficiency, fairness and more freedom for individual expression within the organization would be important outcomes. Bureaucracies are often criticized for being too rule-bound and procedural and some organizations seek to reduce the impact of this, as the following example illustrates. Effective Manager 6.3 also indicates some of the dysfunctional tendencies of bureaucracies.

EFFECTIVE MANAGER 6.3

The natural dysfunctional tendencies of a bureaucracy

All large organizations must systematically work to minimize the dysfunctional characteristics of the modern bureaucracy. Among these dysfunctions are tendencies to:

- overspecialize and neglect to mitigate the resulting conflicts of interest resulting from specialization;
- overuse the formal hierarchy and emphasize adherence to official channels rather than problem solving;

- assume senior managers are superior performers on all tasks and rulers of a political system, rather than individuals who should help others reach goals;
- overemphasize insignificant conformity that limits individual growth;
- treat rules as ends in and of themselves rather than as poor mechanisms for control and coordination.

All large organizations are bureaucratic to some extent, although there are variations in the ways they are designed. The following discussion shows some possible variations on bureaucratic design.

Machine bureaucracies (characterized by mechanistic design features, as in Figure 6.8) are popular in industries with large-scale operations, such as banks, insurance companies and government offices. However, when the organization is viewed as too rigid and centralized, employees may feel constrained and the organization may be hindered in its capacity to adjust to external changes or new technologies. The inherent problems of such mechanistic command-and-control type structures are often overlooked by companies that try to resolve problems by frequent restructuring instead of fundamental changes in design.

On the other hand, a professional bureaucracy often relies on organic features in its design.[18] Universities, hospitals, consulting firms, libraries and social services agencies typically adopt this design. A professional bureaucracy looks like a broad, flat pyramid with a bulge in the centre for the professional staff (refer again to Figure 6.8, organic design). Power rests with knowledge and the experience of professionals but control is enhanced by the standardization of professional skills and the adoption of professional routines, standards and procedures. Given that this design emphasizes lateral relations and coordination, centralized direction by senior management is less intense. Although not as efficient as the mechanistic design, this design is better for problem solving, serving individual customer needs and detecting external changes and adjusting to new technologies (but sacrifices responsiveness to central management direction).[19]

The balance of technological and environmental demands can have an impact on the 'mix' of mechanistic and organic features in a bureaucracy. A bureaucracy can have an organic core with a mechanistic shell. While the technology of the organization may call for an organic design to promote flexibility, creativity and innovation, there may be environmental demands that lead to the development of a series of top-level and mechanistic staff units (for example, in response to powerful external groups). This strange design of mechanistic staff units at the top with organic line units towards the middle and bottom of the organization can protect the organization externally, while allowing responsible internal operations (see Figure 6.9).

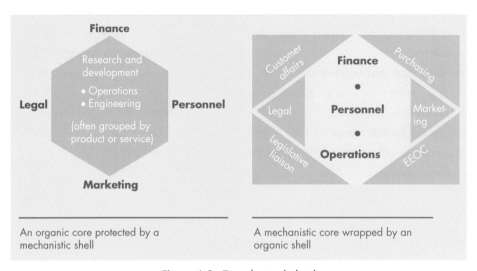

An organic core protected by a mechanistic shell

A mechanistic core wrapped by an organic shell

Figure 6.9: Two design hybrids.

A bureaucracy can also have a mechanistic core with an organic shell. Very large organizations with technologies that call for mechanistic designs and economies of scale are vulnerable to environmental uncertainty and volatility. A partial solution to the problem is to wrap these inflexible cores within organic staff units. The staff units often attempt to change the external conditions by moderating the volatility in the specific environment and to absorb or buffer as many changes as possible. This latter option is found most often in organizations that must balance efficient production with flexible marketing and design operations. The assembly line is mechanistically structured, yet products may be designed by more organically structured teams.

RESEARCH IN OB

Many research studies have sought to indicate the relative appropriateness of different organizational forms to diverse settings and environments. Look at our website: www.wileyeurope.com/college/french for one such example. In their study, Ramanujam and Rousseau examine the extent to which organizational arrangements in hospitals affect their success.[20] The researchers approach the topic recognizing that hospitals can, in many cases, fall far short in applying state-of-the-art clinical knowledge and management practices. Here we have an example of academic research that focuses on a critically important practical area.

Divisionalized organizations

Many very large organizations find that neither the mechanistic nor the organic designs are suitable for all their operations. Adopting a machine bureaucracy would overload senior management and yield too many levels of management,[21] but adopting an organic design would mean losing control and becoming too inefficient. Even in the same industry, some business activities may call for an organic structure, whereas others call for a mechanistic one. The solution is the **divisionalized design**, by which the organization establishes a separate structure for each business or division.

The classic divisional organization was created for General Motors by Alfred Sloan, who divided the company's operations into divisions for designing and producing Chevys, Oldsmobiles, Pontiacs, Buicks and Cadillacs.[22]

Each division was treated as a separate business; each business competed against the others. In the divisionalized organization, all the businesses are coordinated by a comparatively small centralized team that provides support such as financial services and legal expertise. Senior line management provides direction and control over the presumably 'autonomous' divisions. In very large organizations, this approach can free top management to establish strategy and concentrate on large, long-term problems. Divisional heads run their own businesses and compete for resources, yet each enjoys the support (financial, personnel, legal and so on) of the larger parent.

This structure is expensive because many similar staff and support units must be developed for each division but it allows the organization greater flexibility to respond to different markets and customers. However, tension between divisional management and senior management is often apparent. It is difficult for corporate executives and corporate staff to allow the divisions to operate as independent businesses. Over time, senior staff may grow in number and force 'assistance' on the divisions. Further, because divisions compete for common resources, coordination across divisions is also often difficult.

> **Divisionalized design** *is an organizational structure that establishes a separate structure for each business or division.*

The conglomerate

Organizations that own several unrelated businesses are known as **conglomerates**. The line between the divisionalized form and the conglomerate can often be confusing. For our purposes, the key question is whether there is synergy among the various businesses owned by the corporation. Synergies are potential links, as between computers and information systems, or between financing and vehicle rentals, that create an entity with an output greater than its individual parts. If there is synergy, we would call the organization divisionalized; if there is little synergy, the organization is a conglomerate.

Pure conglomerates have not done particularly well in the US, mainly because substantive knowledge of the various businesses is often needed for them to be successfully managed.[23]

Most scholars would argue against conglomerates and for a more synergetic approach but Wesfarmers has proved to be an exception. Highly diverse conglomerates are not popular because it is believed that they do not have the capacity to sustain advantage in a number of nonsynergetic areas. Wesfarmers is a corporate company with multiple business

> **Conglomerates** *are organizations that own several unrelated businesses.*

units in diverse and unrelated areas (for example, hardware, insurance and fertilizers), meaning there are fewer opportunities to capitalize on common areas of competency and expertise. Wesfarmers successfully 'parents' those different businesses but maintains a centralized control through an integrated system focused on shareholders. Important planning processes, project evaluation, performance measurement and remuneration are all used in this way. In effect, Wesfarmers incubates the businesses until a buyer comes along to buy the business and make use of synergetic opportunities with their own, existing, businesses.[24]

The core-ring organization

The pressure to enhance productivity in the last decades of the 20th century encouraged many organizations to 'downsize' or reduce their number of employees. While this trend appears to have slowed, possible large-scale reductions in employee numbers still make headlines, as the following example shows.

In mid-2005, Kimberly-Clark announced plans to cut 6000 jobs (around 10% of its workforce) and sell 20 plants (17% of its manufacturing facilities). Most of the plant closings were to be in North America and Europe. The move was part of a strategy to strengthen its diaper (nappy) and healthcare businesses and to expand its presence in emerging markets (such as India and China). The restructuring was designed to achieve economies of scale in existing manufacturing plants.[25]

The widespread practice of downsizing has led to the increased popularity of an organizational design known as the core-ring organization. The major driver behind this new core-ring organization is the greater need for flexibility in production. An organization adopting a core-ring design (Figure 6.10) takes on a two-tiered structure, in which the inner core workforce represents the high value-adding members of the organization.

These employees often have higher job security, higher salaries and better career paths. The second tier of this structure is also known as the flexible ring and it is made up of a contingent workforce. Contingent workers in this outer ring may supply specialized services to the organization on an ongoing basis and, as a result, have a relatively stable employment relationship with the core organization (at least for the duration of their contracts). Traditionally, such services would be contained within the core of a large bureaucratic organization but in the core-ring organization services such as cleaning, information technology and specialist consultants can be more cost-effectively contracted or outsourced.

The largest component of the outer ring consists of lower skilled, casual employees. Such employees typically experience lower job security, relatively lower pay and a lack of available career paths.[26]

Workers in this peripheral category may actually receive a higher hourly rate of pay than that of some core workers in the organization but on-costs such as holiday loadings, training costs, sick leave and other fringe benefits do not apply to them because they are employed on a just-in-time basis. From the casual employee's point of view, their employment can be very 'precarious' with little certainty about having a steady income, where the next day's work is coming from and whether the family can enjoy a holiday together (as they may be called in for work).

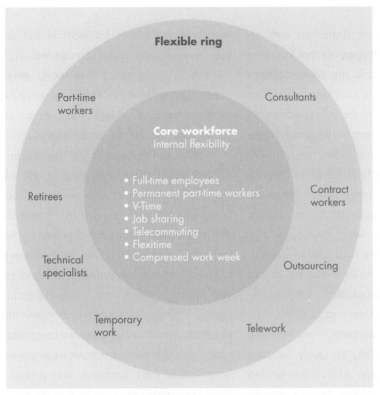

Figure 6.10: Core and peripheral workforce employment options.

Such workers are temporary; fluctuations in the size of this outer ring depend on prevailing levels of demand for the organization's products. These fluctuations may be due to changes in economic prosperity, market competition or other factors. For the organization, the core-ring design offers a flexible and cost-effective structure to adapt quickly to such variations in demand for a particular product. When product demand rises, the ring or contingent workforce can be rapidly expanded at short notice, given the high levels of unemployment in most OECD countries over the past decade. Given that organizations no longer expect demand patterns to be constant throughout the year, if demand falls, the contingent workforce can be cut back at short notice depending on the nature and the level of the work required.

▶ COUNTERPOINT

Structure for the people – a workers' market?

Organizational designs have often placed more emphasis on getting outcomes for the organization than considering how the structure benefits the people within it. Designs such as the core-ring model, where workers are seen as human just-in-time

inventory to be called upon or dispensed with on demand, reinforce this view. It appears that the main reason for casualized labour is the organization's bottom line. Casual employees cost less in terms of overheads, rights and benefits (such as leave and superannuation). While there are varying arguments about whether people are dissatisfied or not with being casual, there should perhaps be some concern about whether they are sufficiently productive, committed and motivated. It appears that having casual workers is one of very few ways employers can reduce fixed costs to compete in a global market. But for the workers themselves there is lack of job security and for the organizations there is potentially high turnover, recruitment and training costs.[27]

Designs do take into account how people might behave but they are less seriously focused on designing the organization to suit the preferences of its workers. If structural designs benefit the employees and increase their satisfaction and commitment (such as through empowerment and decentralized decision making) it is a bonus, but the key reason for such changes is ultimately productivity and performance. The fact that the increased productivity or performance might be related to job satisfaction in some way helps to justify the designs, but ultimately getting the most out of the workers is the driving aim of organizational design decisions.

However, with ageing populations and increasing labour shortages expected in a number of areas, organizations are now finding that they must respond to the expectations and requirements of valuable workers and potential workers. In any case, the on-call casuals may not always be so readily available.

There is increasing speculation about the ways in which organizations might endeavour to fulfil worker expectations (at least in the areas where they have trouble gaining required workers). With increasing acceptance that many employees are not happy at work, or that they want better work–life balance and/or less stress, organizations must reconsider the needs and satisfaction of workers in relation to the organizational design, just as we do with job design. We need to ask the following types of questions of our workers: Does the functional unit provide you with sufficient development and stimulation? Does the structure impede the way you can effectively relate to customers? Do you fulfil your needs for achievement and power? Can you manage stress and work–life balance in this position? These questions and many others could, in effect, reflect a customer focus on employees. In recent years, businesses have been conditioned to a 'shortage of jobs' scenario, with a pool of workers keen to get those jobs. Now, there is a trend towards a demand-driven labour market (where good workers are in demand) and organizations must compete for the best of them, just as they would for customers.

Questions

1. How do casual workers experience their work in organizations? What implications are there for their commitment to the organization and their motivation/satisfaction with it?
2. What features of organizational design and structure, as discussed in this chapter, would act as a motivator to you as a worker?
3. Can organizations design themselves so that they may attract and retain the right sorts of people, who will be satisfied and committed to stay? Why or why not?

The adhocracy

The influence of technological considerations can be clearly seen in small organizations and in specific departments within large ones. In some instances, managers and employees simply do not know the appropriate way in which to service a client or to produce a particular product. This is the extreme of Thompson's intensive type of technology and may be found in some small-batch processes where a team of individuals must develop a unique product for a particular client. Mintzberg suggests that the **adhocracy** may be an appropriate structure at these technological extremes.[28]

An adhocracy is characterized by:

- few rules, policies and procedures;
- very decentralized, shared decision making among members;
- extreme horizontal specialization because each member of the unit may be a distinct specialist;
- few levels of management;
- virtually no formal controls.

The adhocracy is particularly useful when an aspect of the organization's technology presents two problems: first, the tasks facing the organization vary considerably and provide many exceptions, as in a hospital and, second, when problems are difficult to define and resolve.[29]

The adhocracy places a premium on professionalism and coordination in problem solving, especially in solving technical problems. As such, adhocracies are often used as a supplement to other designs to offset their dysfunctional effects.[30]

Organizations use temporary taskforces, special committees and even contracted consulting firms to provide the creative problem identification and problem solving that the adhocracy promotes. Lotus Development Corporation, for instance, creates autonomous departments to encourage talented employees to develop software programs. Allied Chemical and 3M also set up quasi-autonomous groups to work through new ideas.

*An **adhocracy** is an organizational structure that emphasizes shared, decentralized decision making, extremely horizontal specialization, few levels of management, the virtual absence of formal controls and few rules, policies and procedures.*

OTHER STRUCTURAL ARRANGEMENTS

Many other forms of organizational design are emerging or exist. They often involve alliances of two or more organizations or networks of several organizations or of businesses within larger organizations. Some of these are now discussed and may be useful in describing some organizational or part-organizational designs.

Strategic alliances are announced cooperative agreements or joint ventures between two independent organizations. Often these agreements involve corporations that are headquartered in different nations.[31]

In high-technology areas, such as robotics, semiconductors, advanced materials (ceramics and carbon fibres) and advanced information systems, a single company often

Strategic alliances are announced cooperative agreements or joint ventures between two independent organizations.

does not have all the knowledge necessary to bring new products to the market. Often the organizations with the knowledge are not even in the same country. In this case, the organizational design must go beyond the boundaries of the organization into strategic alliances. New Zealand company Comvita is one example of a company that collaborates in alliances. It has signed an agreement with a UK wound-dressing manufacturer to produce its innovative wound dressings (they combine alginate or seaweed fibres with medical-grade manuka honey).[32] Another purpose for alliances is to provide goods in the supply chain.

Alliances exist in other forms in other countries. In Europe, for example, they are called informal combines or cartels; competitors work cooperatively to share the market, decrease uncertainty and create more favourable outcomes for all. The legality of such arrangements may vary between countries, depending on trade practices, laws and other regulations.

In Japan, strategic alliances among well-established organizations in many industries are quite common and linked in a network of relationships called a *keiretsu*. For example, organizations may be linked to each other directly via cross-ownership and through historical ties to one bank, such as with the Mitsubishi group. Alternatively, a key manufacturer may be at the hub of a network of supplier organizations, with long-term supply contracts and cross-ownership ties, such as Toyota. Similar arrangements exist elsewhere. The network organization involves a central organization that specializes in a core activity, such as design and assembly. It works with a comparatively small number of participating suppliers on a long-term basis for both component development and manufacturing efficiency. Chrysler is a leader in the development of these relationships.

A network organization is a delayered organization aligned around the complementary competencies of players in a value chain.

More extreme variations of this network design are also emerging to meet apparently conflicting environmental, size and technological demands simultaneously. Organizations are spinning off staff functions to reduce their overall size and concentrate their internal design on technological dictates. Network organizations are delayered and flexible, with freer and less formal communication, control and coordination. Activities are geared towards alignment with the value chain in the industry, with an array of complementary competencies and resources brought together to achieve the objectives of the network.[33]

Kaplan and Norton[34] refer to the 'Velcro Organization', which can be 'pulled apart then reassembled in new ways to respond to changing opportunities'.

Organizations have to be flexible to demands of the market that they are operating in, have an external as opposed to internal focus and act speedily when required. Moss-Kanter[35] uses the metaphor of large organizations being clumsy and slow to manoeuvre in her book *When Giants Learn to Dance*. We can imagine giants stepping on toes and being awkward. Agility and speed are important qualities to organizations operating in a complex and turbulent market. Similar analogies could be made likening large organizations to large oil tankers requiring several kilometres to stop or turn round.

OB IN ACTION

TNT

For delivery firm TNT, outsourcing seemed like the logical next step when members of the HR department were being stretched into areas of benefits administration that distracted them from their day-to-day tasks.

David Taylor, reward manager, explains: 'The resources in our HR department were being stretched as it was, and it would have been difficult for us to conduct a four-month communication programme across all staff for a new scheme.'

He was also keen on provider Personal Group's specialist ability in negotiating deals for employees, and wanted to give staff access to a greater range of benefits than were being arranged internally.

'The sheer buying power was important for us. The reality is that the provider represents a far greater number of staff than just at TNT. They can achieve discounts that are more valuable than we could achieve in isolation,' admits Taylor.

Maintaining control and owning the benefits package was a top priority for the reward team. It was important that even though a provider produced the package, it was sold as a TNT product.

'You can't outsource and then lose touch. It would not make sense to put your [company] name on something that you didn't really manage or control,' he adds.

Question

1. What aspects of an organization should not be outsourced?

Source: Golding, N. (2009) Making cost savings by outsourcing benefits provision, *Reward and Benefits Today*, 1 July, accessed through XPertHR.

Virtual organizations

Executives do not just face prospects for growth, more complex operations technology, new IT capabilities or a more complex environment one at a time. For some firms, all of these internal and external contingencies are changing simultaneously and changing dramatically. Facing dramatic changes across the board, how do firms keep sufficient consistency in the pattern of their actions and yet co-evolve with their environment? That is, what is the design option when everything is changing and changing quickly?

There is no simple answer but we can start by saying that firms do not do it alone. Some executives have started to develop what are called **virtual organizations**.[36] A virtual organization is an ever-shifting constellation of firms, with a lead corporation, that pool skills, resources and experiences to thrive jointly. This ever-changing collection most likely has a relatively stable group of actors (usually independent firms) that normally include customers, competitors, research centres, suppliers and distributors. There is a lead organization that directs the constellation because this lead firm possesses a critical competence

Virtual organizations comprise individuals, groups and businesses that work together across time and space.

that all need. This critical competence may be a key technology or access to customers. Across time, members may come and go, as there are shifts in technology or alterations in environmental conditions. It is also important to stress that key customers are an integral part of a virtual organization. Not only do customers buy but they also participate in the development of new products and technologies. Thus, the virtual organization co-evolves by incorporating many types of firms.

The virtual organization works if it operates by some unique rules and is led in a most untypical way. First, the production system yielding the products and services customers desire needs to be a partner network among independent firms where they are bound together by mutual trust and collective survival. As customer desires change, the proportion of work done by any member firm might change and the membership itself might change. In a similar fashion, the introduction of a new technology could shift the proportion of work among members or call for the introduction of new members. Second, this partner network needs to develop and maintain:

- an advanced information technology (rather than just face-to-face interaction);
- trust and cross-owning of problems and solutions; and
- a common shared culture.

Developing these characteristics is a very tall order but the virtual organization can be highly resilient, extremely competent, innovative and efficient – characteristics that are usually tradeoffs. The virtual organization can effectively compete on a global scale in very complex settings using advanced technologies.

The role of the lead firm is also quite unusual and actually makes a network of firms a virtual organization. The lead firm must take responsibility for the whole constellation and coordinate the actions and evolution of autonomous member firms. Executives in the lead firm need to have the vision to see how the network of participants will both effectively compete with a consistent enough pattern of action to be recognizable and still rapidly adjust to technological and environmental changes. Executives should not only communicate this vision and inspire individuals in the independent member firms but also treat members as if they were volunteers. To accomplish this across independent firms, the lead corporation and its members also need to rethink how they are internally organized and managed.

Based on a synthesis of successful management experiments by General Electric and its partners, a group of consultants and scholars put together a list of the changes firms need to consider if they are to compete globally in rapidly changing technical settings.[37] They used the buzz words of GE and labelled their package the 'boundaryless organization'. In essence, the challenge to management is to eliminate barriers vertically, horizontally, externally and geographically that block desired action. Specifically, an overemphasis on vertical relations can block communication up and down the firm. An overemphasis on functions, product lines or organizational units blocks effective coordination. Maintaining rigid lines of demarcation between the firm and its partners can isolate it from others. And, of course, natural cultural, national and geographical borders can limit globally coordinated action. The notion of a boundaryless organization is not to eliminate all boundaries but to make them much more permeable. We think the development of permeable boundaries is a key characteristic of all members of a virtual organization.

The notion of a virtual and boundaryless organization is very different from the conditions found in and across most corporations. A movement toward cooperating to compete and removing barriers calls on firms to learn.

EFFECTIVE MANAGER 6.4

Managing a virtual project

The following need to be carried out:

- establish a set of mutually reinforcing motives for participation, including a share in success;
- stress self-governance and make sure that there is a manageable number of high quality contributors;
- outline a set of rules that members can adapt to their individual needs;

- encourage joint monitoring and sanctions of member behaviour;
- stress shared values, norms and behaviour;
- develop effective work structures and processes via project management software;
- emphasize the use of technology for communication and norms about how to use it.

CONCLUSION

The current decade presents many challenges for organizations, particularly ones which have to grapple with tough economic climates. Primarily, it is the role of management to allow for adaptability and transformation in order to survive and compete. Daft (2010) argues that the key challenges facing organizations are: globalization, intense competition, rigorous ethical scrutiny, the need for rapid response, the digital workplace and increasing diversity.[38]

If the CEO of BP was asked his view of outsourcing, he may have produced a different response following the disastrous oil spill in the Gulf of Mexico in 2010!

In spite of all the learned knowledge that is available about designing organizations, in the end it all comes down to people, and the impact that culture has on organizational structure. The tripodic relationship between strategy, structure and culture cannot be underestimated. Whilst this perspective may focus to some extent upon internal issues, the external interface, together with all its unknowns and complexities, makes designing organizations (and constantly redesigning organizations) a highly challenging task.

SUMMARY

LEARNING OBJECTIVE 1
Formal structure and organizational design

Organizational design is the process of choosing and implementing a formal structural configuration (that is, a formal structure) for an organization. The structure is typically represented on an organizational chart. Structure defines the configuration of jobs, positions and lines of authority of the various component parts of the organization.

LEARNING OBJECTIVE 2
Factors for organizational design

Four main factors can be said to affect organizational design – scale, technology, environment and strategy. Scale is important since the number of people and the degree of division of labour and authority will have an impact on the complexity of the organization and the need for compensatory control and coordination mechanisms. Major distinctions in technology are the Thompson (intensive, long-linked, mediating) and Woodward (small batch, mass production, continuous processing) classification systems. The technology of the organization will have some impact on the chosen structure. Environmental differences have a large impact on the type of organizational design that works best. Both the general environment (background conditions) and specific environment (key actors and organizations) are important, as is environmental complexity (richness, interdependence and uncertainty and volatility in the organization/environment). The organizational design must support the strategy if it is to prove successful. Strategy positions an organization in its competitive environment. Strategies such as differentiating the business or leading the market in price and value or based on competency can have an impact on the organizational design.

LEARNING OBJECTIVE 3
Goals, control and coordination

Organizational goals include both output and systems goals. Output goals relate to the type of business the organization is engaged in; they are concerned with satisfying primary beneficiaries and corporate social responsibility. Systems goals establish a basis for organizational survival and prosperity. Control is the set of mechanisms the organization uses to keep action and/or outputs within predetermined levels. Output controls focus on desired targets and allow managers to use their own methods for reaching the desired target. Process controls (such as policies, rules, procedures, formalization and standardization) attempt to specify the manner in which tasks will be accomplished. Coordination is the set of mechanisms that an organization uses to link the actions of separate units into a consistent pattern. Coordination methods can be impersonal (such as centralized staff units) or personal (such as network development and taskforces). Organizational designs, overall, can be said to be mechanistic (involving many levels of authority, high levels of control and impersonal coordination) or organic (breakup of work horizontally, personal coordination and loose control).

LEARNING OBJECTIVE 4
Vertical specialization

Vertical specialization is the hierarchical division of labour that specifies formal authority and a chain of command. The organization's hierarchy can be said to be tall or flat, relating to the number of levels of management or authority in the organization. Organizational authority can also be centralized (concentrated at the top or centre of the organization) or decentralized (where decision making is pushed down to lower levels of the organization). Unity of command defines the situation in which each worker has a clear reporting relationship to only one supervisor. It lessens confusion and provides clear channels of communication. Span of control indicates the number of individuals reporting to a supervisor. Wide spans of control mean the supervisor supervises many people, whereas a supervisor with a narrow span of control will have few employees.

LEARNING OBJECTIVE 5
Horizontal specialization

Horizontal specialization is the division of labour that results in various work units or groups in the organization. The distinction between line and staff units can be particularly relevant to horizontal departmentalization. Line personnel conduct the major business of the organization while staff personnel assist in performing specialized supportive services. Three main types of 'departmentalization' are functional, divisional and matrix departmentalization. Each structure has advantages and disadvantages. Organizations may successfully use any type, or a mixture, as long as the strengths of the structure match the needs of the organization's goals.

LEARNING OBJECTIVE 6
Implications of emerging forms of work organization

Each organization's design will be unique. Smaller organizations often adopt a simple structure; larger organizations often adopt a bureaucratic form. The bureaucracy is an ideal form based on legal authority, logic and order rather than on individual supervision or tradition. Whilst most larger corporations are bureaucracies, they differ in the degree and combination of mechanistic and organic features.

Divisionalized organizations establish a separate structure for each business or division in the organization so that there is emphasis on coping with the particular aspects of that part of the business but also overall synergy. Conglomerates are organizations that own several unrelated businesses that do not have inherently synergetic advantages. Within divisionalized or conglomerate organizations, each business can develop different design features. The core-ring organization involves an inner core, relatively permanent, workforce with higher job security, higher salaries and better career paths. There is also a flexible outer ring of workers employed on a part-time or casual basis as required. They tend to have lower job security, lower pay and a lack of career paths. This approach enables the organization to achieve economies by adapting its employment levels to suit the circumstances. The adhocracy is a structural form that emphasizes shared, decentralized decision making, extreme horizontal specialization, few levels of management and few formal controls. Other organization designs include strategic alliances, networked organizations, virtual organizations and franchises.

CHAPTER 6 STUDY GUIDE

Now that you have read this chapter, you should be able to apply and further develop your knowledge by undertaking the following activities set out over the next few pages: test your knowledge questions, an individual activity and an end-of-chapter case study.

Please also go to this book's website: **www.wileyeurope.com/college/french** to find further material which will enhance your understanding and enable you to assess your knowledge.

TEST YOURSELF

1. Compare control and coordination and explain two types of each.
2. Explain the difference between mechanistic and organic organizations.
3. Explain and compare the types of technology identified by Thompson and Woodward.
4. What is a core-ring organization and why does it have an impact on the workforce?
5. Demonstrate the purpose of an organizational chart in terms of depicting horizontal and vertical specialization in an organization.
6. From the perspective of an employee, how might it be to work in the following situations (compare the choices in each of (a), (b) and (c)?
   (a) A functionally departmentalized organization compared to a functionally departmentalized organization with project teams in a matrix structure.
   (b) An organization that is highly decentralized compared with one that is highly centralized.
   (c) An organization that uses a mass production technology compared to a small batch organization.
7. In a large organization employing mostly highly educated professionals, what do you think might be the best approaches to achieving control over those professionals? Explain your answers.
8. Many organizations are becoming flatter, reducing levels of hierarchy and widening the span of control. What advantages and disadvantages would there be in this approach for an organization that relied on its employees to make judgements on customers' requests (for example, for loans, insurance claims or special consideration of circumstances in social welfare cases)?
9. What form of hybrid design might be necessary for an organization that is very large and must reach economies of scale, but also needs to adapt to environmental uncertainty? Explain your answer.
10. How would you describe the technology and organizational forms used in the following (it is acceptable to describe a mix of technologies and forms)? Explain your reasons.
    (a) an organization making a Hollywood movie.

(b) a large company building prefabricated homes and later assembling them on customers' land.

(c) a firm of solicitors and barristers.

(d) a multinational mining and steel producer.

11. Find two local organizations. Try to choose two different-sized organizations that have different processes – for example, retail and service industries. It would be best to avoid organizations that are branches of a bigger organization, as this would complicate your research. Give a brief overview of these two organizations and what they do and then compare and contrast them in terms of the following criteria: goals, control methods, vertical specialization, horizontal specialization and coordination methods. Also assess and compare the scale, environment, technology and strategy of the organizations to consider how this may have affected the design of the organizations.

12. Search the website of a major retail chain, analysing the chain in terms of the following elements of organizational structure:
   • statements of goals (output/system goals);
   • explanations or diagrams of the formal structure of the organization (organizational charts, number of layers in the hierarchy, span of control, apparent centralization/ decentralization);
   • different groups/sections in the organization (type of specialization into divisions or departments, line and staff personnel, casual and permanent components of the staff).

Assuming there are different business units within the organization, analyse the range of businesses or business units in the 'organization' and draw conclusions based on whether you find them synergetic (or not synergetic) in the design of the entire organization.

INDIVIDUAL ACTIVITY

Vertical and horizontal specialization: organizing XYZ Paper Company

XYZ does not have an organizational chart. The following is a list of its management position titles. Develop an organizational chart by dividing the total task into separate duties, grouping similar people and resources together in a division of labour that establishes specific work units/departments. Draw your organizational chart using both the job title and the letter in each box.

A sales manager

B accountants

C engineering department

D vice-president of personnel

E president

F credit manager

G product A manager (facial tissue, paper towels, napkins, etc.)

H product B supervisor

I vice-president of finance

J advertising manager

K vice-president of manufacturing

L quality-control manager

M product A supervisor

N product A sales supervisor

O purchasing manager

P training manager

Q data-processing manager

R vice-president of marketing

S product B manager (writing paper, envelopes, etc.)

T sales supervisor product B

U assistant to the president

After completing the organizational chart, answer the following questions.

1. What is the span of control for the president and each vice-president? Is it broad or narrow?
2. Identify the line and staff units and consider whether XYZ uses standardization.
3. What type of departmentalization does your organizational chart have?
4. Use the following criteria to consider whether the organizational design tends towards being organic or mechanistic.

Mechanistic	Organic
Stable predictable environment	Innovative unpredictable environment
Strict formal lines of authority	Flexible informal lines of authority
Centralized authority	Decentralized authority
Extensive use of managerial techniques	Minimal use of managerial techniques
Many rules and procedures	Few rules and procedures
Specialist jobs	Generalist jobs
Formal and impersonal coordination and control	Informal and personal coordination and control
Large batch or mass production technology	Made-to-order or long-run process technology
Functional departmentalization	Divisional departmentalization

DEFENCE FORCE RECRUITING

It has been described as Australia's largest recruiting exercise contract and it is arguably the only recruitment contract of its kind in the world. In 1997, with an eye on costs, the Australian Defence Force (ADF) began a review of its recruitment functions in the army, navy and air force. Its recommendations included investigating and trialling an outsourced recruitment programme.

Fast forward to 2005 and ADF recruiting is now a collaboration between the ADF and a civilian recruitment and change management consultancy known as Defence Force Recruiting (DFR), a business unit of Manpower. It is the first time that ADF uniformed staff have worked in collaboration with civilian staff under a civilian organization's management structure.

This extraordinary partnership evolved from a transition and change management programme that took place over two years across the nation.

Talk to the people involved and they'll say it was one of the most complex organizational and culture change opportunities in the Australian business environment. And so far the results are promising. As well as reducing costs the new arrangement has fostered a positive shift in culture. The new business improvement services structure encompassing human resources, learning and development and quality has been instrumental in creating an innovative culture where continuous improvement and learning is encouraged and supported throughout the organization.

Given the spread of the defence forces and the importance of a consistent national approach, DFR was created as an organization with a 'local national' approach. The organization is managed from a central headquarters with each regional office empowered to direct their resources as they see fit. Each area manager is encouraged to manage their business as if it were their own, with support and guidance available from headquarters if needed. Central requirements of the recruitment function such as target allocation, budget allocation and support for systems, processes and people are managed by headquarters.

Continuous improvement is a contractual requirement, with ISO 9001/2000 selected as the quality system for DFR. The contract also requires a percentage decrease in the cost of services.

The collaborative nature of DFR means that each group plays to its strengths. Civilian staff perform the majority of the management, planning and administration functions while

Source: Latham, S. (2005), On Manoeuvres. *HR Monthly,* April, 30–34. Reproduced by permission of Scott Latham, Vantage Point Solutions, Australia.

the ADF staff, and a small number of civilian staff, perform the shared function of candidate attraction, counselling and interviewing.

Each candidate is tested against medical and psychological standards provided by the military. These tests are undertaken by staff from the psychology services function and medical staff from the group's major teaming partner, Health Services Australia.

The final decision on whether a candidate is invited to join the defence force is made by an ADF member from the same service applied for. Enlistment of candidates and the appointment of officer candidates is a function retained by the ADF and is carried out by the senior military recruiting officer at each location.

A key feature of the organization's structure is that the staff perform their functions in operational cells, not roles.

Culturally, this approach to workplace relations emphasizes integrative yet individualistic systems. The manager in DFR is supported by the organizational structure to concentrate on employee participation, HR flow – of candidate and worker, reward systems and work organization – as opposed to reporting, representation, strategy and other hierarchical structural requirements. The operational worker in DFR can be used in a range of roles and functions to support the manager's mission.

The organization provides coaching, mentoring and flexible working environments, and the cells structure creates the environment where staff become skilled 'all-rounders' who are easily retrained and redeployed. This gives the DFR workforce the operational ability to be flexible and responsive.

Questions

1. What are the goals of the DFR and how does the structure support the achievement of the goals?
2. What type of horizontal specialization approach is used in the organization and how effective is it likely to be?
3. The defence forces are typically considered to have rule-bound, centralized and hierarchical organizations whereas DFR is said to be flexible and responsive. Discuss the differences between the 'typical' defence force (such as army or navy) and DFR, and the probable impacts on the defence-force personnel who now operate in DFR.

SUGGESTED READING

Crowther, D. & Green, M. (2004), *Organizational Theory*, CIPD: London. These authors provide a summary of the development of organizational theory across time and in different contexts. As such, they illuminate the ways in which forms of organizational structures are themselves located in time and space.

END NOTES

1. Rice, A. (2006), Bhopal revisited – the tragedy of lessons ignored. *Asian-Pacific Newsletter on Occupational Health and Safety*, **13**, 46–47.

2. Eckerman, I. (2006), The Bhopal disaster 1984 – working conditions and the role of trade unions. *Asian-Pacific Newsletter on Occupational Health and Safety*, **13**, 48–49.

3. Hall, R. H. (1996), *Organizations – Structures, Processes and Outcomes*, 6th edn, Prentice Hall: Englewood Cliffs, NJ, p. 30.

4. Osborn, R. N., Hunt, J. G. & Jauch, L. R. (1984), *Organization Theory: Integrated Text and Cases*, Krieger: Melbourne, FL, pp. 123–215.

5. Woodward, J. (1965), *Industrial Organization: Theory and Practice*, Oxford University Press: Oxford.

6. Thompson, J. D. (1967), *Organization in Action*, McGraw-Hill: New York.

7. Woodward, J., op. cit.

8. See Osborn, R. N. & Baughn, C. C. (1988), New patterns in the formation of US/Japanese cooperative ventures. *Columbia Journal of World Business*, **22**, 57–65.

9. Mobach, M. P. (2007), A critical systems perspective on the design of organizational space. *Systems Research and Behavioural Science*, **24**, 69–90.

10. Shifting business offshore growing. *Sydney Morning Herald*, 15 September 2005.

11. See: www.eurofound.europa.eu/emire/ UNITED%20KINGDOM/WORKTORULEEN. html; www.eurofound.europa.eu/emire/SWEDEN/ ANCHOR-PARAGRAFARBETESE.html; www. eurofound.europa.eu/emire/NETHERLANDS/ WORKTORULE-NL.html; www.eurofound. europa.eu/emire/GREECE/WORKTORULEGR. html (accessed 10 July 2007); Adapted from Deming, W. E. (1982), Improvement of quality and productivity through action by management. *Productivity Review*, Winter, 12–22; Deming, W. E. (1982), *Quality, Productivity and Competitive Position*, MIT Center for Advanced Engineering: Cambridge, MA.

12. Liker, J., Collins, P. & Hull, F. (1999), Flexibility and standardization: test of a contingency model of product design-manufacturing integration. *Journal of Product Innovation Management*, **16** (3), 248–267.

13. For a discussion of matrix structures, see Davis, S., Lawrence, P., Kolodny, H. & Beer, M. (1977), *Matrix*, Addison-Wesley: Reading, MA.

14. Open University (1984), *The effective manager. Unit 9: organizations,* p. 19.

15. See Mintzberg, H. (1983), *Structure in Fives: Designing Effective Organizations*, Prentice Hall: Englewood Cliffs, NJ.

16. For a comprehensive review, see Scott, W. R. (1987), *Organizations: Rational, Natural, and Open Systems*, 2nd edn, Prentice Hall: Englewood Cliffs, NJ.

17. Weber, M. (1947), *The Theory of Social and Economic Organization*, translated by A. M. Henderson & H. T. Parsons, The Free Press: New York.

18. Mintzberg, H., op. cit.

19. See Osborn, R. N., Hunt, J. G. & Jauch, L. R., op. cit., for an extended discussion.

20. Ramanujam, R. & Rousseau, D. R. (2006), The Challenges are Organizational Not Clinical. *Journal of Organizational Behavior*, **27** (7), 1–17.

21. See Clark, P. & Starkey, K. (1988), *Organization Transitions and Innovation-design*, Pinter Publications: London.

22. Osborn, R. N., Hunt, J. G. & Jauch, L. R., op. cit.

23. Ibid.

24. Kerin, P. (2005), The gold Wesfarmers. *Business Review Weekly*, 1–7 September, p. 32.

25. Kimberly-Clark to cut jobs. *Sydney Morning Herald*, 25 July 2005, www.smh.com.au/articles/-2005/07/25 (accessed 25 July 2005).

26. Champy, J. (1995), *Reengineering Management*, HarperCollins: Glasgow; Hammer, M. & Stanton, S. (1995), *The Reengineering Revolution: A Handbook*, HarperCollins: New York; Morgan, R. & Smith, J. (1996), *Staffing the New Workplace*, CCH: Chicago, IL.

27. Parker, L. op. cit. pp. 20–25.

28. Mintzberg, H., op. cit.

29. Perrow, C. (1986), *Complex Organizations: A Critical Essay*, 3rd edn. Random House: New York.

30. Osborn, R. N., Hunt, J. G. & Jauch, L. R., op. cit.

31. See Ettlie, J. (1990), Technology drives a marriage. *Journal of Commerce*, 16 March, p. 6.

32. Comvita: healing with honey in the UK. *National Business Review*, 14 July 2005, www.nbr.co.nz (accessed 14 July 2005).

33. Luthans, F. (2002), *Organizational Behaviour*, 9th edn, McGraw-Hill: Boston, MA, pp. 117–119.

34. Kaplan, R. S. & Norton, D. P. (2006), How to implement a new strategy without disrupting your organization. *Harvard Business Review*, March, 100–109.

35. Moss-Kanter, R. (1992), *When Giants Learn to Dance*, Routledge: New York.

36. The discussion of the virtual organization is based on Hedberg, B., Hahlgren, G., Hansson, J. & Olve, N. (2001), *Virtual Organizations and Beyond*, John Wiley & Sons, Inc.: New York.

37. This treatment of the boundaryless organization is based on Ashkenas, R., Ulrich, D., Jick, T. & Kerr, S. (1995), *The Boundaryless Organization: Breaking through the Chains of Organizational Structure*, Jossey-Bass: San Francisco.

38. Daft, R. L., Murphy, J. & Willmott, H. (2010), *Organization Theory and Design*, Cengage Learning: London.

CHAPTER 7

Organizational culture

LEARNING OBJECTIVES

After studying this chapter you should be able to:

- define the concept of organizational culture and be aware of its importance within the study of organizational behaviour (OB)
- explain the levels of cultural analysis in organizations and the notions of dominant cultures, subcultures and cultural diversity
- identify common types of organizational culture as outlined in existing literature
- be aware of possible functions of organizational culture and links with performance
- discuss alternative and critical perspectives on organizational culture
- consider the interrelationships between organizational and national culture.

'GOOGLERS' SHARE A CULTURE OF CHOICE

The Google corporation could, on several criteria, be described as one of the most successful businesses in the world in the early years of the 21st century. Formed by two Stanford University students, Larry Page and Sergey Brin, in 1998, the company, which is best known as an Internet search facility, has also broadened its activities into other areas including e-mail, social networking services and mobile phone operating systems.

Google has certainly grown rapidly in the short years since its foundation. In 2009, it employed just under 20 000 workers. However, its success lies not just in its rapid expansion. For the word Google has itself now entered the everyday language of millions of people across the world. A survey conducted by BrandZ in 2008 found that Google was the most powerful brand worldwide, while a *Forbes* magazine article from 2007 identified Google as the most desirable place to work in the USA.

To what extent is Google's success associated with the development of a distinctive organizational culture – the topic we go on to address in this chapter? Google's own promotional material undoubtedly lays stress on the distinctiveness and importance of its culture. The *'corporate information'* section of its website[1] stresses a 'small-company feel' within this large organization. To take one example, Google's headquarters offers the opportunity for open discussions over lunch as everyone is encouraged to eat in the same office café. Google's depiction of its own culture also identifies some striking artefacts that could be found in a typical Google work space.

In this chapter we will claim that organizational culture comprises different *levels*; namely the outer layer of observable culture (or 'the ways things are done around here'), together with the deeper levels of shared values and common assumptions. Google's website invites visitors to take a virtual tour of its headquarters in Mountain View, California. The tour shows, amongst other things, a piano, rubber exercise balls, bicycles, a gymnasium with weights, a massage room, football and pool tables. Roller hockey is played in the car park and both the café and assorted snack-rooms serve a range of 'healthy options'. So, all-in-all, there is a distinctive, and in many respects unusual, set of observable artefacts making up the outer layer of Google's organizational culture.

We will also see, however, how the outer level of a company's culture can be an expression of its more deeply-held values. Google has developed a strongly distinctive set of values and these values and core assumptions are reflected in its surface ways of working. Indeed, it is possible to claim that a typical Google workspace is designed to foster and reinforce desired corporate values. Google's website highlights the company's commitment to innovation, which in turn can only happen if everyone is comfortable sharing ideas and opinions. Office and indeed café layout can be pivotal to the reality of such sharing. Google's reputation as a good employer, bolstered by its emphasis on fun and good health, can also contribute to employees' effectiveness.

The depiction of language, symbols, physical layout, values, beliefs and ways of behaving set out here capture the essence of this company's organizational culture; in the case of Google, a highly distinctive and unusual one. Do such things matter or are they simply surface or even shallow manifestations of style?

In this chapter we will examine the concept of organizational culture, look at alternative critical perspectives on the topic and, in particular, show how an organization's culture can link to action and performance. In this context, we might assume that Google's culture helps to deliver success and, if this were no longer the case, would be subject to change in the future.

Source: http://www.google.co.uk/corporate/culture.html (accessed 30 December 2009).

INTRODUCTION

Organizational culture is defined as 'the system of shared values and beliefs that develops within an organization and guides the behaviour of its members.' As we see from the example of Google, the concept deals with nonquantifiable or even invisible aspects of organizational life – the so-called 'soft stuff'. But that does not mean that its importance should be minimized or even dismissed, as we shall attempt to show in this chapter. It is, in fact, a topic of much contemporary interest within OB, although the concept of culture has only recently been applied to organizations and the field of business studies more generally; significant contributions by Peters and Waterman,[2] and Schein,[3] for example, dating from 1982 and 1985 respectively. In 2009 there was a series of contributions to the literature on organizational culture; attesting to the continued topicality of the area. One article pointed to a link between an organization's culture and the level of trust employees had in their managers.[4] Another noted a correlation between types of organizational culture and successful attempts to create a learning organization (a concept we covered in Chapter 3).[5] These new studies joined a long tradition of work highlighting the benefits of developing a distinctive organizational culture in a thoughtful and even strategic way. There were also, interestingly, contributions published in 2009 which indicated the potentially negative and harmful impact of organizational culture. One study carried out in China showed how greater spending on research and development, and innovation initiatives more generally, would only have the desired positive effect if organizations' cultures were in tune with this new focus.[6] An article in the *People Management* journal meanwhile attributed the economic crisis which began in 2007 to counterproductive and unethical behaviour in parts of the financial services sector, which in turn, arose out of excessive risk-taking and

Organizational culture *is a system of shared beliefs and values that guides behaviour.*

target-setting typical of certain corporate cultures. These cultures were shown with hindsight to be unhealthy, and in this case, linked to very serious consequences worldwide.[7]

In the early decade of the 21st century it had become accepted that the notion of culture, as characterized by shared values and beliefs, formed an important part of the study of business and that culture impacted on the performance of work organizations – both positively and negatively. Prior to the 1980s, however, culture was studied primarily by anthropologists and sociologists at the macro-social level, focusing on the belief systems, values and specific human behaviour that distinguished one society from another. In 1980 Hofstede's ground-breaking work[8] sought to compare how work organizations operated in societies across the world, in the process identifying significant and systematic differences that impacted on the reality of working life and organizational arrangements. It is now generally accepted that societal culture – usually defined as national culture – is an important source of influence on work organizations. However, organizations are one significant subsystem *within* any society and so it can be said that they too can exhibit elements and features that make up their own culture. Thus it is important to have a firm understanding of the elements of organizational culture, what they represent and how some may link to competitive advantage, partly through securing employee commitment and resultant high performance levels.

Some commentators have gone further and suggested that a focus on organizational culture has become *essential* to an understanding of organizations.[9] Many managers now believe, for example, that a strong and unified organizational culture is the key to competitive advantage within their own sphere of operation. There is evidence that some successful organizations sustain continued growth and development by 'implanting' a strong culture that is shared and acted on by all members of the organization.[10] However, other commentators express concerns about striving for a strong organizational culture, because of the difficulties associated with reconciling strongly integrated belief systems with the need for creative thinking, innovation and the ability to cope with change.[11] Within OB there is also a view (which we will explore later in the chapter) that organizational culture represents an insidious attack on workers' freedoms in its stress on collective values and frequently involves attempts to alter people's identities. In earlier chapters we have alerted readers to important changes in the context facing many organizations, suggesting that old methods of command and control are increasingly being replaced by methods of participation and involvement. Managers in this scenario are becoming facilitators, helpers, guides and coaches. These changes require adjustment of individual, group and overall organizational value systems and affect an organization's culture. In such a setting the so-called 'soft stuff' bound up in the culture concept takes centre stage and assumes an ever-greater importance for everyone concerned.

This chapter considers the concept of organizational culture, how it manifests itself within organizations and its functions. We look at the observable aspects and values of organizational cultures and common assumptions about organizational culture and discuss the importance of subcultures, countercultures and the increasing diversity of organizational cultures. We will discuss the link between organizational culture and ethical behaviour and, finally, consider links between organizational and national culture.

In Chapter 1 we set out our strongly held view that organizational behaviour should be seen as an integrated subject comprising interrelated topic areas. This is most certainly true when we consider organizational culture. Developing a new organizational culture has been seen as a way of addressing existing problems and planning for improved performance. There is, therefore, an immediate link with the concept of *organizational change* which we address in Chapter 12. It is probable that a change in organizational culture will, in practice, be planned in conjunction with consideration of *organizational structures* (dealt with in Chapter 6) which support – or at least do not hinder – the change. As we will see, organizational culture also has a strongly interlinked relationship with *leadership* (Chapter 9), as leaders will have a critically important role in reinforcing and changing cultures. In conclusion, the topic of organizational culture should not be treated and understood in isolation; rather as part of an integrated approach to organizational behaviour.

THE CONCEPT OF ORGANIZATIONAL CULTURE

Just as a person's individual personality is unique, so no two organizational cultures are identical. Most significantly, management scholars and consultants increasingly believe that cultural differences can have a major impact on the performance of organizations and the quality of work–life experienced by their members. However, before we analyse this claim in more detail it is necessary to separate out layers or *levels* of organizational culture. A recognition of the multilayered nature of culture can go a long way towards bringing the topic into focus, as it highlights the fact that while some manifestations of culture can be easily observed, others, specifically the deepest aspects of common assumptions, may be difficult to uncover, not least because they are 'taken for granted' by members of that culture.

LEVELS OF CULTURAL ANALYSIS

Figure 7.1 graphically depicts three important levels of cultural analysis in organizations: observable culture, shared values and common assumptions. As noted earlier these are envisaged as layers (other explanatory metaphors include onions, icebergs, the earth's crust and cakes). Importantly, the deeper we get, the more difficult it is to discover the phenomenon from the surface.

The first level relates to **observable culture**, or 'the way we do things around here'.[12] These are the methods that the group has developed and imparts to new members – either explicitly, for example through induction programmes or more subtly via symbols and identification of heroes and villains. The observable culture includes the unique stories, ceremonies and corporate rituals that make up the history of a successful work group or the organization as a whole. It also includes symbols such as physical design, dress codes, logos and badges. Organizational cultural researchers look for patterns of behaviour or espoused cultural forms when trying to locate and capture this level of culture.

Observable culture *is behavioural patterns that a group displays and teaches to new members.*

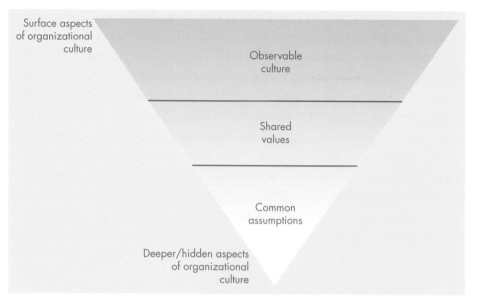

Figure 7.1: Three levels of analysis in studying organizational culture.

OB IN ACTION

In 2005 the Portuguese flag carrier airline TAP launched a new corporate image that the airline intended to reinforce its positioning as a modern global company while simultaneously highlighting its Portuguese character.[13] Its new look was intended, according to company sources, to translate the airline's prestige, balance and competitiveness, while adding attractiveness, lightness and joy to its corporate identity.

The new-look initiative included a new livery applied to its fleet but also the design and launch of new staff uniforms to be brought into service in 2007.[14]

Corporate uniforms can be one example of a clearly visible manifestation of a company's culture. In this sense organizations may wish their workers

to reflect organizational values; when followed to its logical extent, employees could be regarded as brand ambassadors.

In the case of TAP, staff are asked to wear uniforms that embody concepts as diverse as prestige, sophistication, lightness and joy.

The second level of analysis recognizes that **shared values** (for example, 'quality in this organization is our cornerstone to success' or 'we value innovative ideas' or 'we will provide the best possible care') can play a critical part in linking people and can provide a powerful motivational mechanism for members of that culture. Organizational values underpin the patterns for behaviour in observable cultural analysis, as in the case of the new TAP staff uniforms. Many consultants suggest that organizations should develop a 'dominant and coherent set of shared values'.[15] The term 'shared' in cultural analysis implies that the group is a whole. Every member may not agree with the shared values but they have all been exposed to them and have often been told they are important. Hence, many managers believe that cultivating a strong organizational culture will have a positive effect in gaining a competitive advantage. Shared values, such as wearing an airline uniform with pride, could have ties to values of the wider society. Unique and shared values can provide a strong identity, enhance collective commitment, provide a stable social system and reduce the need for controls. However, we also need to acknowledge the individual differences within a collective and the value of individuality to the overall organizational culture. Such stress on the positive aspects of shared values has always been common in school systems: from the 1980s onwards, however, writers such as Peters and Waterman extended the scope of the shared values argument to the adult world of work organizations.

> **Shared values** are the set of coherent values held by members of the organization that link them together.

At the deepest level of cultural analysis are **common assumptions**, or the taken-for-granted truths that collections of organizational members share as a result of their joint experience. In most organizational cultures there is a series of common assumptions known to everyone in the organization. However these may be implicit and unspoken. A study of farmers in the US,[16] showed how many farmers had work values instilled in them as young children; their parents, grandparents and great-grandparents all farmed. The working culture of farms was thus transmitted from one generation to another with seemingly little change occurring. Farmers continue to 'get up with the chickens' and work until dark. Long hours, self-reliance and the centrality of work in life are still pivotal to farmers' experiences and retirement at the age of 65 is rare. But it is debatable to what extent these deep-rooted common assumptions are frequently discussed or questioned; their very longevity may reinforce their embedded nature. Such common assumptions may plausibly bring us closer to understanding the culture of a farm than either observable artefacts or shared (documented) values.

> **Common assumptions** are the collection of truths that an organization's members share as a result of their joint experiences and that guide values and behaviour.

ORGANIZATIONAL CULTURE AND CLIMATE

We sometimes hear the terms organizational culture and organizational climate used to explain similar phenomena and with seemingly interchangeable meanings. Throughout this chapter we will refer to the term *organizational culture* as we see a subtle distinction between the two terms. We agree with a recent commentator[17] who concluded that while an organization's *culture*, in focusing on values and beliefs, provides a framework setting out appropriate and rewarded attitudes and behaviour, *climate* refers to the prevailing atmosphere in an organization, as perceived by its members. Climate therefore is the felt – or affective – dimension of culture. A positive climate is more likely where the values of an organization coincide with those of its members. If an organizational culture change programme does not take its members along – or if they do not 'buy-in' to such changes – then a negative climate can ensue.

DOMINANT CULTURE, SUBCULTURES AND COUNTERCULTURES

*A **dominant coalition** denotes the people who are in a strong position of power and influence within organizations at any one time. Dominant coalitions are shifting and can be replaced by others.*

In Chapter 1 we stressed that while organizations can have goals in the sense that they are legally defined entities, goals are in reality defined and put into effect by people. We also referred to the concept of a **dominant coalition**, namely those individuals and groups who hold power and influence in an organization at any one time. The culture of an organization will also be a reflection of these twin concepts. It is possible that an organization may have a single dominant culture articulated by a dominant individual or group and with a unitary set of shared assumptions, beliefs and actions. Those who view organizational culture as a unified phenomenon in which all cultural elements are consistent with one another are said to take an **integration perspective** on the topic. Within this perspective, organizational members, as directed by their leaders, jointly agree on 'the way things are done around here', resulting in cohesiveness, unity and harmony.

*The **integration perspective** views organizational culture as a system of shared meanings, unity and harmony.*

Most writers in this field, however, also draw attention to the existence of **subcultures** and **countercultures** and the significant role that they play. Their existence is important if we believe that organizations comprise disparate groups, which may possess their own values and beliefs that can, on occasion, bring them into conflict with other parties. This is termed the **pluralist** view of organizations – the term is also applied to analysis of the wider society.

***Subcultures** are unique patterns of values and philosophies within a group that are not inconsistent with the dominant culture of the larger organization or social system.*

Subcultures and countercultures

Subcultures represent groups of individuals with a unique pattern of values and philosophy that are not necessarily inconsistent with the organization's dominant values and philosophy. Strong subcultures are often found in high-performance taskforces, teams and special project groups in organizations. In addition, subculture formation has also been linked to educational background, professional identity and distinctive work paradigms.[18] The culture emerges to bind individuals working intensely together: organizational values and assumptions are shared but actions can be influenced differently by distinct occupational tasks. For example, in a hospital the shared assumption of 'doing things better' could underpin the common value of providing the best possible care for patients. However, the expressed 'care' is performed differently by different occupational groups, each with distinctive interpretations of what 'best care' means. For catering staff this may be providing a meal at the correct temperature; for surgeons it may mean removing the cause of illness and for the occupational therapist it may mean helping patients and their carers to achieve an improved quality of life. Because 'providing the best care' means different things to different individuals and groups, we must expect conflict to arise between occupational subcultures and this conflict is normal and by no means necessarily dysfunctional.

***Countercultures** are the patterns of values and philosophies that outwardly reject those of the larger organization or social system.*

*The **pluralist** view of organizations views them as being populated by individuals and groups that may have diverse aims and interests and that, as a result, can come into conflict with the dominant coalition and other groups.*

In contrast, countercultures have a pattern of values and a philosophy that reject the surrounding culture.[19] Within an organization, mergers and acquisitions may produce countercultures. Employers and managers of an acquired organization may hold values and assumptions that are quite inconsistent with those of the acquiring organization. This is often referred to as the 'clash of corporate cultures'.[20]

Mergers and acquisitions do not inevitably cause cultural clashes, although this may be a matter of opinion among different subcultures within the new organization. Understanding the importance of culture can also help a company to absorb or accommodate the cultures within the organizations that are acquired or merge, or to manage the complex interplays in alliances, company formations and employment relations.[21]

Whistleblowers *are employees, ex-employees or other people connected to an organization who report perceived misconduct on the part of that organization to a person or body who can take or initiate action.*

The ethical dimension

The tone of the preceding section may lead readers to regard countercultures as an intrinsically negative phenomenon. This would ignore the unethical conduct of dominant coalitions in many organizations. **Whistleblowers** could be regarded as lone members of countercultures, however few would view their role and activities in a pejorative way; on the contrary, many people might accord whistleblowers heroic status. As is often the case in OB, our own reality is filtered by perception, in this instance how we judge the values and actions of the dominant culture.

 IN ACTION

Would you have been a whistleblower at Parmalat?

The collapse of the Italian dairy company Parmalat in 2003 revealed an alleged culture of corruption amongst several key players in that organization. The founder, finance director, chief financial officer, auditor and legal consultant were among those who subsequently went on trial accused of financial corruption. Specific charges of market rigging, providing false accounting information and misleading the Italian stock market were brought against these individuals as representatives of the company. This became a corporate scandal. The scale of corruption uncovered in the company was both large and significant. An account supposedly held with the Bank of America by Parmalat's Cayman Island subsidiary Bonlat, understood to contain nearly four billion euros, did not, in fact, exist – information that led to the collapse of the company. The fallout from the Parmalat scandal was severe – it was a very important regional employer and the Italian government intervened to avoid further damage.

This scandal was uncovered through financial scrutiny but what if a whistleblower had emerged from within the company? He or she would have taken on the role of countercultural agent, as exposure was always likely to result in the end of the organization in its pre-2003 form. For many, any such whistleblower would have been justified in opposing the culture of the dominant coalition at Parmalat at that time.

Questions

1. Assess the desirability of whistleblowing in a case such as Parmalat with reference to the *deontological*, *consequential* and *character virtue* approaches to business ethics set out in Chapter 1.

2. If, as an employee, you had become aware of the alleged culture of corruption in this company, would you have acted as a whistleblower? Give reasons for your conclusions.

CORPORATE OR ORGANIC CULTURES?

The preceding discussion of dominant cultures, subcultures and countercultures opens up a wider debate within this subject area, namely whether an organization's culture can ever be designed or imposed by senior figures. One interesting distinction was put forward by Smircich,[22] who distinguished between culture as a *critical variable* as contrasted with culture as a *root metaphor.* Smircich's distinction has practical value for organizational designers as well as utility in expanding academic knowledge of the area. Her conclusion is that culture is often hierarchically defined (most frequently by managers) in an attempt to control aspects of organizational life and improve performance. In this way its status is elevated to that of critical variable; in other words it is regarded as a key factor in determining an organization's success. If we follow this interpretation of the concept then an organization's culture will be viewed as something that it 'has' and which can be changed through intervention – for example with a managed programme of culture change. This view underlies many attempts to alter a perceived existing culture – it can, for example, be frequently observed when public sector organizations are privatized. In such cases new or existing management teams are often concerned to build and instil a culture of customer service, which may, in reality or in their perception, have been lacking in the past. In contrast, Smircich's location of culture as root metaphor sees it as something 'that is' – in other words it has grown organically (hence the reference to roots) along with an organization's history, employees, technology and strategy. This second approach takes a social constructivist perspective on culture. If we believe that culture is a root metaphor then we have to acknowledge that there are multiple, rather than single, cultures within organizations and that cultures will be very difficult to change.

A corporate culture is an attempt by managers to deliberately create and mould organizational culture to achieve specified results.

Needle[23] draws a similar distinction between organizational culture representing the values, beliefs and principles of organizational members, which have grown within the context of a particular setting, and **corporate culture**, the latter term referring to cultures deliberately created by managers to achieve specified results. Those managers and academics who propound the value of corporate culture claim that strong unified cultures will play a key part in delivering success. We acknowledge the prevalence of the corporate culture view in management literature but lean towards the social constructivist view in this chapter. This regards culture (both at national and company level) as a concept that, in essence, grows organically – it derives, after all, from an agricultural metaphor – and is difficult to change in a top-down manner.

LEVELS OF CULTURE IN WORK SETTINGS

Look closely at Figure 7.1 again. We are viewing organizational culture from a social constructivist point of view, so we propose that important aspects of an organization's culture emerge from the collective experience of its members. These emergent aspects of the culture help make it unique and may well help provide a competitive advantage for the organization. Alternatively aspects of its emergent culture can inhibit its performance, particularly in a changing environment. Some of these features may be directly observed in day-to-day practices. Others may have to be discovered, for example by asking members to tell stories of important incidents in the history of the organization. We often learn about the unique aspects of organizational cultures through descriptions of very specific events.[24] By observing organizational symbols and rituals, listening to stories and asking organizational members to interpret what is going on, you can begin to understand that organization's culture or subcultures.

Stories, rites, rituals and symbols

Stories indicate the state of an organization's health. Stories offer evidence of unique qualities and characteristics that an organization is proud of. A story may be as simple as telling a new employee about the newly appointed worker who stood up to the CEO of the company and progressed quickly through the company because that CEO admired his or her courage (which may in turn be something that is considered to be an important quality of the company in question).[25] Perhaps one of the most important stories concerns the founding of the organization. The **founding story** often contains the lessons learned from the efforts of an embattled entrepreneur whose vision may still guide the firm. The story of the founding may be so embellished that it becomes a **saga**, a heroic account of accomplishments.[26] Sagas are important because they are used to tell new members the real mission of the organization, how the organization operates (at least in the eyes of managers) and how individuals can fit into the work environment. Rarely is the founding story totally accurate and it often glosses over some of the more negative outcomes along the way. If you have job experience, you may well have heard stories concerning the following questions: How will the boss react to a mistake? Can someone move from the bottom to the top of the company? What will get me dismissed? These are common story topics in many organizations.[27] Often the stories will provide valuable hidden information about who is 'more equal' than others, whether jobs are secure and how things are really controlled. The stories suggest how organizational members view the world and live together.

Among the most obvious aspects of organizational culture are **rites** and **rituals**. Rites are standardized and recurring activities that are used at special times to influence the behaviour and understanding of organizational members. Rituals are systems of rites. Rituals serve to establish boundaries and relationships between the stakeholders of an organization through the repetition of events, such as staff meetings or how long people take for lunch. In Japan, for example, it is common for workers and managers to start their work days together with group exercises and singing the 'company song'. Separately, the exercises and song are rites. Collectively, they form part of a ritual.

Rituals and rites may be unique to particular groups within the organization. Subcultures often arise from the type of technology deployed by the unit, the specific function being performed and the specific collection of specialists in the unit. The boundaries of the subculture may well be maintained by a unique language. Often the language of a

*The **founding story** is the tale of the lessons learned and efforts of the founder of the organization.*

*A **saga** is an embellished heroic account of the story of the founding of an organization.*

***Rites** are standardized and recurring activities used at special times to influence the behaviour and understanding of organizational members.*

***Rituals** are systems of rites.*

subculture, as well as its rituals and rites, emerges from the group as a form of jargon. In some cases, the special language starts to move outside the organization and enter the larger society. For example, the information technology (IT) industry is renowned for its use of technical language and, slowly, terms such as software, download, floppy, desktop, browser, hyperlink, icon, multimedia and online have become part of mainstream language. On the other hand, many of the IT industry's plentiful jargon terms have yet to find wide acceptance. One such term, used by personnel manning an IT help desk to point to a user problem, is 'PEBKAC' – 'Problem Exists Between Keyboard And Chair'.

Language is used to convey the meaning of an organizational culture, with particular words and phrases either being unique to an organization or having a particular meaning in that organization. It has been suggested that many conversations in organizations are making cultural statements when they convey what the company expects and wants to occur;[28] for example, language can convey meaning about daily routines and habits of employees. It can also be a valuable measure in highlighting possible subcultural differences within an organization. Consider again the role of language used in the Google example cited at the start of this chapter. An activity such as 'foozball' might be thought to convey a different cultural statement than use of alternative titles such as 'corporate bonding away day'.

A cultural symbol is any object, act or event that serves to transmit cultural meaning.

No discussion of corporate culture would be complete without mentioning the symbols found in organizations. A **cultural symbol** is any object, act or event that serves to transmit cultural meaning. Symbols can include the architecture of a building, the layout of offices and space assigned to employees, the décor of the offices and the general impression that is communicated to visitors by way of company name and size of the establishment. Although many such symbols are quite visible, their importance and meaning may not be. Other symbols include badges, prizes, organizational branding and stationery.

The physical layout of the office is an observable symbol of culture. For example, in an organization that values knowledge sharing, an open plan may express that value and encourage collegiality and camaraderie. However, a lack of privacy in the workplace can also affect people adversely and have a subliminal effect on what makes them secure and happy. So a culture may express its respect for employees in such an open-plan office if it makes an effort to provide at least acoustical and visual privacy. In a world in which many businesses are failing, physical space can express culture through the permanency and conservatism of its furnishings and décor. Consider again the attempt at Google to use architecture, layout and space to create a 'cool' workplace, which was a visible expression of the cultural values espoused by managers and, in this case, at least one worker who was a strong advocate of those values.

CULTURAL RULES AND ROLES

Organizational culture often specifies when various types of actions are appropriate and where individual members stand in the social system. These cultural rules and roles are part of the normative controls of the organization and emerge from its daily routines.[29] For instance, the timing, presentation and methods of communicating authoritative directives are often quite specific to each organization. In one organization meetings may be forums for dialogue and discussion, where managers set agendas and then let others offer new ideas, critically examine alternatives and fully participate. In another organization the 'rules' may be quite different. The manager goes into the meeting with fixed expectations. Any new ideas, critical examinations and the like are expected to be worked out in private before the meeting takes place. The meeting is a forum for letting others know what is being done and for passing out instructions on what to do in the future. Cultural rules and roles can become deeply ingrained in organizational behaviour, as they influence 'the way things are done around here', but sometimes, of course, they need to be changed.

OB IN ACTION

Open-plan offices are no silver bullet for teamwork

New research shows that it is not the layout and decoration of an office that determines how people cooperate. More important in this regard are the values that they embrace.

Heidi Lund Hansen, in research conducted by Consultancy within Engineering, Environmental Science and Economics (COWI) and Copenhagen Business School,[30] questions whether open-plan offices do promote cooperation and learning in workplaces. She found that open-plan office arrangements are managerial tools that will not result in improved communications without deeper analyses of organizational culture. Her research showed that, paradoxically, open-plan offices lead to task-related communication being relocated to designated meeting or conference rooms, thereby making them less inclusive to wider groups in the organization.

She also points out that the transparency of open-plan working may lead to a more powerfully controlled hierarchy, noting that: 'If the boss says, "hmm we have been having a lot of tea breaks, haven't we?", you get some indication that you are supposed to be sitting at your desk. And in the process, you foster a culture in which people sit in front of their monitors and quickly bring any dialogue to a conclusion.'

VALUES AND ORGANIZATIONAL CULTURE

Consider Figure 7.1 again. In order to describe the culture of an organization more fully, we have already stated that it is necessary to go deeper than the observable aspects. To many researchers and managers, shared values lie at the heart of organizational culture.

Shared values:

- help turn routine activities into valuable, important actions;
- tie the corporation to the important values of society;
- may provide a very distinctive source of competitive advantage.

John Weeks, a professor at the French-based INSEAD Business School, spent a year working at and studying the culture of a well-known British high street bank, known as 'Britarm' in the study, although its identity has since been revealed. He found a ritual of complaint in this bank, described as a culture of shocking negativity characterized by chronic criticism at all levels of the organization.[31] Weeks records that on no occasion did he hear the bank referred to positively by employees. Colleagues would moan to each other continually while managers openly expressed their cynicism regarding the company in front of staff. Britarm's performance in this period was good, however, and it might be thought that this was despite the complaining culture within its branches. Weeks, however, goes further and suggests that the negative culture may, in a roundabout way, link to success. He records his experience of being told that he now knew what it was really like to be a Britarm employee when enduring a stint in the uncomfortable surroundings of its securities centre. Weeks records that: 'if she was right then being a securities clerk at Britarm feels like basking in the warm glow of adversity with sympathizers all around. I felt more like a part of the team than I ever had before...The ritual of making derogatory remarks about some aspects of the bank and receiving empathy in return, is a glue that strengthens the bonds between the individual and the group.'

Once more we see the complexity of links between organizational culture, values and performance.[32] It is doubtful whether the paradoxical and convoluted logic of the Britarm example should be taken up as an example of good practice, though, and readers can themselves ponder whether they would wish to be part of such a moaning culture at work and what the long-term effects could be on their mental wellbeing.

Linking actions and values

Individuals collectively learn behaviours and concepts to help them deal with problems. In organizations what works for one person is often taught to new members as the correct way to think and feel. Important values are then attributed to these solutions to everyday problems. By linking values and actions, the organization taps into some of the strongest and deepest realms of the individual. The tasks that a person performs are not only given meaning but value; what one does is not only workable but correct, right and important.

Some successful organizations have been seen to share a number of common cultural characteristics. Figure 7.2 provides a list suggested by two well-known US management consultants, Terrence Deal and Allan Kennedy.[33] As you can see from the figure, organizations with 'strong cultures' possess broadly and deeply shared value systems. Increasingly, organizations are adopting values statements that express their commitment to such areas as customer service, product and service quality, creativity, innovation and social responsibility.

A widely shared philosophy. This philosophy is not an abstract notion of the future but a real understanding of what the organization stands for, often embodied in slogans.

A concern for individuals. This often places individual concerns above rules, policies, procedures and adherence to job duties.

A recognition of heroes. Heroes are individuals whose actions illustrate the shared philosophy and concerns of the company.

A belief in ritual and ceremony. Management understands that rituals and ceremonies are real and important to members and to building a common identity.

A well-understood sense of informal rules and expectations. Employees understand what is expected of them.

A belief that what employees do is important to others. Networking in order to share information and ideas is encouraged.

Figure 7.2: Elements of strong corporate cultures.

However, a strong culture can be a double-edged sword. Unique, shared values can:

- provide a strong corporate identity;
- enhance collective commitment;
- provide a stable social system;
- reduce the need for formal and bureaucratic controls.

Conversely, a strong culture and value system can reinforce a view of the organization and its environment. If dramatic changes are needed, it may be very difficult to change the organization.

COMMON ASSUMPTIONS AND ORGANIZATIONAL CULTURE

At the deepest level of organizational culture (refer once more to Figure 7.1), there are common understandings known to almost everyone in the corporation: 'we are different', 'we are better at...' and 'we have unrecognized talents'. These shared truths or common assumptions often lie dormant until actions violate them.

COMMON ASSUMPTIONS AND MANAGEMENT PHILOSOPHY

If culture is considered a variable that can be changed to affect an organization's competitive advantage (we have questioned this assumption to some extent), managers would need to recognize what can and what cannot be changed in the organization's culture. The first step is to recognize the group of managers as a subculture in itself. Senior managers often share common assumptions, such as 'we are good stewards', 'we are competent managers' or 'we are practical innovators'. In many organizations, broadly shared common assumptions of senior management go even further. The organization may have a well-developed **management philosophy**.

*A **management philosophy** links key goal-related issues with key collaboration issues to come up with general ways by which the organization will manage its affairs.*

A management philosophy links key goal-related issues with key collaboration issues and comes up with a series of general ways in which the organization will manage its affairs. A well-developed management philosophy is important because it establishes generally understood boundaries for all members of the organization; it provides a consistent way of approaching novel situations and it helps hold individuals together by assuring them of a known path towards success. In other words, a well-developed management philosophy is important because it links strategy with how the organization operates and thus helps an organization adapt to its environment. For example, Cisco Systems's strategy of growth, profitability and customer service is linked to empowering employees to generate the best ideas quickly; hiring the best people, with ideas and intellectual assets that drive success; and disseminating information to compete in an 'ideas world'.

Elements of the management philosophy may be formally documented in a corporate plan, a statement of business philosophy or a series of goals. Yet it is the unstated but well-understood fundamentals these written documents signify that form the heart of a well-developed management philosophy.

HOW CAN ORGANIZATIONAL CULTURE BE STUDIED?

Organizational culture researchers are interested in researching cultural manifestations while attempting to gather meaning about the patterns that link these manifestations. Studying manifestations includes researching the working environment of a culture; for example, the décor of the office, hierarchical structures and money earned by employees, as well as relationships between organizational members. Joanne Martin identifies four types of cultural manifestations, including cultural forms, formal practices, informal practices and content themes.[34]

Cultural forms are manifestations of organizational culture conveyed to employees. Tools used to convey observable culture include symbols, rituals, stories and language. For example, the 'employee-of-the-month' award or the story of how the company was founded help employees to identify with the organization's culture as these rituals and stories are all part of 'the way things are done here'. Symbols, such as branding (for example, the golden arches of McDonald's) have meaning. What does your company or university brand symbol on the top of any letterhead convey to you? This is a cultural form!

Formal practices are written down and are, on the surface, easily controllable by management. These practices can include structure, task and technology, policies and procedures and financial controls. The formal practices are all expressions of an organizational culture. Therefore, formal practices need to be observed when studying organizational culture.

Informal practices, by contrast, evolve through interaction, are not written down and take the form of social rules. Informal practices can include the time used for tea breaks throughout the day and the prevalence and acceptability of arriving at work a few minutes late or leaving work a few minutes early at the end of the day. Such informal practices serve to highlight possible contradictions within the formal practices that are written down but not always carried out.

Content themes are considered common threads of concern that underlie interpretations of several organizational cultural manifestations. Top companies may try to impress certain images on stakeholders and the general public; for example, by promoting respect for the environment in all business pursuits. Companies that include such values in the mission statement or on company websites are attempting to create positive associations with their brands. Often, the way that managers behave in organizations, such as showing a friendly yet competitive nature to the outside world, will communicate to observers the content themes (or the images the organization is attempting to create in an audience's mind) of a company being studied.[35]

The majority of cultural studies within organizations take place via information obtained from the views of those members in management positions. However, it is now widely recognized that organizational culture researchers must also extract information about how the organization works by providing members of the organization who do not hold such posts with a tool through which to express their opinions. This ensures the organizational culture research is conducted from multiple perspectives (see the section on alternative perspectives on organizational culture later in this chapter) and is more complete.

Quantitatively, cultural forms, formal practices and content themes can be measured by asking questions about the organization. This might take the form of an assessment of the general feelings and beliefs participants hold about the organization, their sense of affiliation with the organization and so on.[36] Content themes can be examined by questioning organizational/supervisory characteristics and by ranking the importance of organizational goals, reputation, engagement with the community and service quality. Formal practices are studied by analysing policies and procedures and how these are put into operation. Informal practices are rather more difficult to measure via questionnaire and are best revealed through interview and observation. Quantitative methods can include survey questionnaires.

Qualitatively, manifestations of organizational culture can be observed by participant observers, who may have discussions with organizational members via formal and informal interviews and focus groups, or alternatively may simply observe, with their status as researchers remaining unknown to the group. The researcher who is identified as such tends to examine patterns of behaviour, looks at consistencies and inconsistencies in behaviour and is particularly interested in patterns of behaviour that are more covert. The interviews can include questions about organizational reputation before and after employment. What has changed? This is important as inconsistencies in what is reported to members outside an organization and what members inside an organization actually experience may reveal important information about the covert behaviours. Furthermore, the way an employee portrays the organization to outsiders may differ depending on the position or the occupational group that the organizational member belongs to. This may reveal patterns of inconsistencies between occupational groups or subcultures. Interview questions can also examine 'accountability' in terms of who sets standards formally and what happens informally. This may highlight the importance of informal practices for the day-to-day functioning of an organization. Observations can reveal a great deal about the organization's reliance on formal and informal practices and organizational content themes. Interpretations help to make sense of interactions between organizational actors and occupational groups and ultimately the relations between organizational culture and overall organizational performance.

Many organizational culture researchers use a mix of quantitative and qualitative methods to obtain a complete picture of 'what is truly going on' in the organization.

In Chapter 1 we drew the distinction between the positivist and interpretative traditions in OB. As can be seen from the preceding paragraphs, although there has been some attempt to capture organizational culture via more scientific (or at least quantitative) research methods, the topic more readily lends itself to interpretive study, relying on more in-depth personal accounts and interpretations of culture and longer-term observation of life in a single case study organization.

OB IN ACTION

Traders deal in 'babes' and 'dragons'

In 1995, a British academic, Belinda Brooks-Gordon, made public the results of her research into the culture present in trading houses in the City of London.[37] Her findings revealed widespread sexist attitudes among male traders at that time. This was reflected in the language used to describe, categorize and indeed stigmatize female colleagues.

Women in this work environment were classified on the basis of perceived attractiveness coupled with imagined sexual availability, age and clothing worn. So-called 'babes' were young and attractive to members of the male workforce. 'Babes' were shown more courtesy than other female workers but had less credibility in career terms. A subgroup of 'babes' was termed 'goers'. These women were perceived to be sexually active, promiscuous and available. Females in the workplace regarded as less attractive were termed 'mums' and, according to the researcher, were mostly ignored by the men. However, women perceived as unattractive were labelled 'dragons' and the male workers felt they were entitled to be ruder to them in their everyday dealings. Any women understood to hold feminist views were termed 'lesbians', regardless of their known sexual orientation. The male traders were seemingly more respectful of women workers who they considered competed with them in terms of aggressive behaviour and also ability. This last group were referred to as 'one of the boys'.

It should be stressed that this, to many people doubtless unsavoury, picture of a particular work culture is time-framed – in other words it may no longer paint an accurate picture of life in trading houses in the 21st century. It is cited here in part to stress the methods used in the study. Brooks-Gordon worked 'under cover' in the course of her study and was thus able to unravel and put on public display aspects of organizational culture that were likely to remain invisible if other methods, such as questionnaires, were used.

TYPES OF ORGANIZATIONAL CULTURE

Although we have indicated that if cultures grow organically out of people's specific experiences and situations resulting in cultural *uniqueness*, some commentators have identified commonly found types of culture. Such typologies are useful in crystallizing our thoughts on the topic area and help to bring the subject to life. Nonetheless we should recognize that categorizing culture in this way, although enabling us to locate individual cultures along comparative (sometimes bipolar) frameworks, will not provide us with an in-depth knowledge of the development and workings of any individual culture.

Charles Handy's classification of types of organizational culture, dating from 1989,[38] distinguishes between the following four commonly found models:

- **Role culture.** In this type of culture, set rules, procedures and job descriptions dominate. People's power in such a setting is embedded in the *roles* they occupy. In particular, your position within a hierarchy is most likely to underlie your influence. The organization's culture is essentially a depersonalized one; it will continue to operate in a 'machine-like' way even if key staff move or are absent. To many readers this description will be redolent of the concept of bureaucracy set out in Chapter 6 and it is normal for role cultures to be structured in the form of a bureaucracy. It is often felt that public sector organizations, oriented by values of fairness and predictability, provide good examples of the role culture, although commercial organizations in which standardized processes are important – for example in the financial services sector – can also exhibit characteristics of the role culture model.

- **Power culture.** It is claimed that this type of culture can be found in small organizations that bear the mark of their founder or owner. This central figure continues to exercise power on a personalized basis, there are as few rules in place as possible and the central figure will attempt to recruit people who 'fit in' or in whom they see echoes of themselves. As organizations grow and become more complex, there is a tendency for this type of culture to evolve into more of a role culture model, although it is possible that it could endure in, for example, family firms even when they expand. More often, however, in a growing company, the central figure becomes more of a figurehead and exerts less day-to-day influence on the culture.

- **Person culture.** This model of culture is interesting in that it points to organizations that exist for their members' benefit. In this sense people use the infrastructure of an organization (space, IT networks and so forth) to help them achieve objectives within a 'pooled' network. This is a more unusual type of culture, but one recent contributor to the literature[39] suggested that it could be characteristic of barristers' chambers, architects' partnerships or could be how hospital consultants view their organizational setting. It might be thought, therefore, that this type of culture is centred (or revolves) around 'star performers' who are partly based in that organization.

- **Task culture.** In this type of culture, people are conceptualized and grouped together in terms of tasks or projects. A task orientation takes priority; people are brought together

Role culture *is a type of organizational structure in which set rules, task procedures and job descriptions are particularly important.*

Power culture *is a type of organizational culture in which a central figure exercises power on a personalized basis, there being relatively few formal rules in place.*

Person culture *is a type of organizational culture in which an organization exists for the benefits of members, particularly star performers. It has been located in barristers' chambers and other professional work settings.*

to work in teams for specific purposes rather than being located in functional or departmental areas as in role cultures. This culture could be found in the case of management consultancies or other client-based agencies.

Another typology of culture was developed by Deal and Kennedy.[40] These authors also identified four archetypal cultures set out below:

Process culture *is a type of organizational culture characterized by clear processes, which need to be followed correctly: it can be found in highly regulated sectors such as healthcare.*

Tough guy culture *is a type of organizational culture driven by a need to take quick decisions, leading to a preoccupation with risk taking and a competitive ethos.*

Work hard/ play hard culture *is a type of organizational culture that stresses the twin roles of performance and fun at work.*

Bet-your-company culture *refers to a type of organizational culture characterized by a long-term outlook in which significant levels of investment are made, the results of which may take many years to feed through.*

- **Process culture.** Organizations with this culture are concerned with ensuring that processes are clear and followed correctly. Highly regulated sectors such as healthcare, waste management and financial services might be driven by a need for precision and uniformity and therefore be associated with formal low-risk hierarchical cultures.
- **Tough guy culture.** This type of culture is underpinned by a need to take quick decisions leading to a preoccupation with risk taking and a competitive and resilient outlook. The 1987 Hollywood film *Wall Street* painted a picture of just such a workplace culture with the anti-hero lead character, played by Michael Douglas, memorably using the catchphrase 'lunch is for wimps' to evoke the mentality required to prosper in this type of setting – which was instilled in younger aspiring employees.
- **Work hard/play hard culture.** As the name indicates, organizations identified within this type stress the importance of 'fun' at work. They are also likely to be highly performance driven. Strong teamwork and a customer focus are also typically found in this cultural type.
- **Bet-your-company culture.** This type of culture is characterized by a long-term outlook. It was conceived by Deal and Kennedy as appropriate in high-risk but slow feedback situations. Very significant levels of investment may be seen, but it could be many years before the results are apparent. Space technology provides a good example, also highlighting the very high level of technical expertise often associated with the culture. Investment banking has also been included as an example – once again a long-term orientation will be important to success in this field. The cultural features of vision and durability will be exemplified in employees' attitudes in organizations linked to this type.

In Chapter 1 we indicated that many OB topics could be usefully understood with reference to a contingency perspective. The essence of contingency theory is that no one solution, model or perspective will always result in organizational effectiveness. Rather the specific features of the organization, or circumstances faced by it, should be taken into account. The typologies of organizational culture put forward by Handy and by Deal and Kennedy can be seen within the contingencies idea. No one type of culture will be effective in all situations, instead *it all depends*, for example, on an organization's size, stated aims, market and technology. It might, for example, be difficult in reality to avoid elements of role or process cultures (Handy and Deal and Kennedy's typologies show similarities) in the health sector, which is highly regulated, driven by a need to treat patients fairly and systematically and where processes, including patients' records, need to be carefully documented. However, dysfunctions of bureaucracy such as slowness, a departmental outlook and inflexibility may be more damaging in a small company exploring a new market and the founders of a company like this may wish to choose, instil and manage another culture – perhaps the work hard/play hard culture may be more suitable given the situation (contingencies) they face.

ALTERNATIVE PERSPECTIVES ON ORGANIZATIONAL CULTURE

Many studies of organizational culture adopt only one perspective of culture – the integrationist perspective, which we characterized earlier in this chapter as viewing culture in terms of shared meanings resulting in harmony and a supposed organization-wide consensus.[41] These studies tend either to focus on managers and professionals and/or to present managerial perspectives as representative of organizational culture as a whole. But if a study claims to represent the culture of an entire organization, then employees of diverse levels and functions should also be studied. This gives us an opportunity to include more than one perspective and to be inclusive of views of members throughout the organization, rather than presuming that an occupational group, a profession or a functional level represents all organizational voices. Although the integration perspective is the most commonly researched and published, there are additional perspectives. Two influential approaches are the differentiation and ambiguity perspectives.

Differentiation perspective

In contrast to the integration perspective, which is seen from a managerial functional point of view, the differentiation perspective views organizational culture as a system of shared beliefs in *different* groups (often differentiated by location, function, gender, ethnicity or other demographic variations). These group values are sometimes in tune with the dominant culture and sometimes not. Some researchers believe the differentiation perspective is similar to integration, but is manifested at lower organizational levels. This perspective is not only characterized by harmony but also by diversity and inconsistency.

Organizational anthropologists and social researchers believe that organizational cultures, even if they represent a system of shared meaning, are not uniform cultures but rather have sets

of subcultures, typically defined by departmental designations and geographical separation. Rather than finding harmony and unity, these researchers see diversity and inconsistency. Subcultures are not necessarily abnormal or deviant; they are natural outcomes of the different groups, departments and occupational cohorts within the organization. Such subcultures can enhance the dominant culture: they accept its core values but bring in other nonconflicting or countercultural values that directly challenge the values of the dominant culture. The tension between subcultures shapes the organizational culture itself. The formation of subcultures is sometimes called 'multiculturalism' in organizations.

Individuals develop differences in perception and opinion because of social bondings. Some of these relationships can span organizations. For example, plumbers in a large engineering factory can develop a shared relationship through their membership of a plumbing staff association.

In contrast to the integration perspective, the differentiation perspective sees organizations as characterized not just by harmony and unity but also by diversity and inconsistency. It accepts the possibility and value of internal conflict and suggests that this normally occurs due to the processes of differentiation and specialization common in modern organizations. As noted earlier, when organizations grow and mature they tend to become more complex, this complexity often taking the form of formal structural arrangements. But the subunits within organizations are very likely to develop their own cultures too.

Ambiguity/fragmentation perspective

The ambiguity or fragmentation perspective does not see clear-cut cultural groupings within organizations as the normal state; rather it views organizations and their members as typically experiencing a high level of ambiguity, as meanings differ both between individuals and within individuals over time. Meanings, values and behavioural norms are diverse because each individual independently assesses his or her environment. If consensus is observed then it is only momentary and such groupings soon dissolve. The ambiguity lies in the formation of associations between identities that are in a constant state of instability, lacking any form or pattern.[42] An ambiguity or **fragmentation perspective** suggests, therefore, that there are no clearly identified patterns of culture. Instead there is an ever-changing flow of consensus, divergent views and confusion. This view rejects the idea of 'shared meanings' in favour of the idea that people attribute meanings to phenomena in organizations. They interpret them in random, ambiguous ways, and sometimes the interpretations are shared or partially shared. This perspective further brings into question whether the attribution of meaning in organizations really falls neatly into categories, as suggested by much 'mainstream' organizational culture theory.

The fragmentation perspective sees attempts at cultural change along normative lines as having no effect, because the impact of any change will be absorbed. You cannot change the culture in any managed way, because change is continual.

The **fragmentation perspective** *views organizational culture as lacking any form of pattern as a result of differing meanings between individuals and within individuals over time.*

CULTURE AS CONTROL

Another alternative to the mainstream view of organizational culture stems from the work of Willmott.[43] This new twist on the concept saw culture as fundamentally an attempt by managers of organizations to control workers by shaping their identities. As such, organizational culture represents one more way of exercising managerial control following on from other control mechanisms such as leadership, motivation or organization structure. Willmott's argument is that this particular form of control is different, however, as it involves an attempt not just to control behaviour but also to alter the internal worlds of individuals – their *identities*. Grey,[44] writing in 2009, goes further in linking culture change management programmes with the totalitarian world depicted by George Orwell in his novel *Nineteen Eighty-Four*. For example, Orwell showed how a ruling political party attempted to distort meaning by creating a particular mode of language (Newspeak). This resulted in the invention of new terms, such as 'oldspeak', which meant thoughts not consistent with philosophies and policies espoused by the ruling party. At the same time Newspeak was characterized by euphemisms, which often contained meanings exactly opposite to what was denoted, so the Ministry of Truth was, in reality, responsible for issuing propaganda and lies. Grey sees parallels here with what he perceives as counterintuitive language contained in company mission statements and other manifestations of organizational culture change programmes. More seriously, he also questions whether organizational culture places the collective above the individual and whether it involves an insidious attack on freedoms. His thoughtful contribution concludes with self-reflection on how far we can take the *Nineteen Eighty-Four* analogy. If workers cannot, or do not wish to, conform to organizational culture, the worst that could happen to them (in most advanced societies) is that they would be dismissed – they wouldn't typically, as employees, be tortured or killed. Nonetheless, being sacked could be a very severe blow to many people depending on their circumstances and future prospects. In one further contribution, Watson[45] brings us back into focus by pointing out that work identities are only one part of our being. We suggest that you will, in reality, have multiple identities, for example as a Czech, female, married Catholic accountant; our work and everything that goes with it is important, but it is only one part of our lives. So if we are controlled through organizational culture then we are only partly controlled.

Hence, understanding multiple perspectives of culture involves us going beyond an understanding of shared values and beliefs in organizational members, as proposed by the integration perspective; it also includes having an in-depth insight into patterns of overt and covert behaviour that link patterns of integration, differentiation and ambiguity. Each of these perspectives can operate at any one time or at the same time.[46] Thus, by adding alternative perspectives, including radical approaches from critical management theory, organizational culture can be more comprehensively defined as 'the socially constructed patterns of behaviour that link expressions of organizational integration, group differentiation and individual ambiguities together. These patterns of behaviour reflect individual, group and organizational values and beliefs.'[47]

▶ COUNTERPOINT

Culture deteriorates in overcrowded prison[48]

An unannounced UK government inspection of Her Majesty's Prison at Leeds in Yorkshire in 2006 noted a deterioration in relationships between staff and prisoners since its last inspection. Specific problem areas highlighted by the visiting inspectors included:

- over a third of prisoners reported feeling unsafe; this figure rising to 43% for black and other minority ethnic prisoners;
- a high and mechanistic use of force;
- the segregation unit ran in a militaristic way, with insufficient support for prisoners at risk and an incident when an alleged assault on a prisoner had not been followed up;
- staff were heard referring to prisoners as 'bodies' or 'cons';
- black and ethnic minority prisoners continued to report 'undercover' racism and had no confidence in the race complaints system. Fewer than half of those surveyed believed staff treated them with respect;
- there were only spaces for 60% of prisoners and prisoners without work could spend 23 hours in their cells.

Anne Owers, Her Majesty's Chief Inspector of Prisons, said:

'This inspection shows how difficult it is to sustain progress in a crowded inner-city local prison, where cultures are hard to change and governors are preoccupied with crisis management. Under such pressure, officers tend to revert to their comfort zone, and governors are preoccupied with crisis management. Managers were aware of the task they faced, and conscious that some fundamental issues remained to be tackled However, achieving and sustaining lasting change will be difficult with current levels of overcrowding.'

Phil Wheatley, Director General of the Prison Service, said:

'The Chief Inspector makes it very clear that the main problems faced by HMP Leeds are exacerbated by the serious difficulties which overcrowding presents to busy local prisons. Leeds prison is working hard to address the feelings of insecurity experienced by prisoners and there is a very active safer prisons agenda currently in operation. The Governor is taking this agenda forward through projects such as the West Yorkshire Community Chaplains, which is working to deliver an inclusive approach to support prisoners and create a positive environment for black and ethnic minority prisoners.'

This 'Counterpoint' feature shows us that organizational culture is not only to be perceived in positive terms. Note also the impact of resource issues cited as having an impact both on the existing culture and attempts to change it. Consider the steps you would take if you were to embark on a further cultural change programme in this prison.

THE FUNCTIONS OF ORGANIZATIONAL CULTURE FOR MEMBERS

We have now introduced you to some alternative perspectives on this topic and wish to reinforce the importance of acknowledging multiple perspectives of organizational culture. However, returning to mainstream managerial views of the concept, it is undeniable that organizational cultures do have an element of functionality. In other words, organizational culture may be influenced by top management in order to achieve a competitive advantage. For example, ideally in your first managerial job, one of the old hands on the job will sit down with you and explain exactly what is to be done and how and why it is to be done. Experienced individuals know what to do and are aware of all the informal rules surrounding their roles in the organization.

Through their collective experience, members of an organization resolve two types of extremely important survival issues. The first is the question of external adaptation: what precisely needs to be accomplished and how can it be done? The second survival issue is the question of internal integration: how do members solve the daily problems associated with living and working together?

External adaptation

External adaptation involves reaching goals and dealing with parties external to the organization. These issues involve assessing the tasks to be accomplished, the methods used to achieve the goals and the ways of coping with success and failure.

External adaptation *is the process of reaching goals and dealing with outsiders.*

Through their shared experiences, members develop common views that help guide their day-to-day activities. Organizational members need to know the real mission of the organization, not just the pronouncements to key constituencies such as shareholders. Members will naturally develop an understanding of how they contribute to the mission via interaction. This view may emphasize the valued importance of human resources, or it may emphasize the role of employees as cogs in a machine or a cost to be reduced.

Closely related to the organization's mission and its view of staff contribution are the questions of responsibility, goals and methods. These need to be translated into specific contributions, identifying clearly what the organization is endeavouring to achieve in its external environment. Organizations often present numerous goals; for example, in relation to strategy or corporate social responsibility and establishing procedures and methods, including the selection of the 'right people' to achieve their aims. They will also define jobs and procedures that reflect their approaches to external adaptation.

In summary, external adaptation involves answering important instrumental or goal-related questions concerning coping with reality, such as:

- What is the real mission?
- How do we contribute?
- What are our goals?
- How do we reach our goals?

- What external forces are important?
- How do we measure results?
- What do we do if specific targets are not met?

Internal integration

Internal integration *is the creation of a collective identity and the means of matching methods of working and living together.*

The external adaptation questions help a collection of individuals cope with a changing environment; the organizational culture also provides answers to the problems of **internal integration**. Internal integration deals with the creation of a collective identity and with finding ways of matching methods of working and living together.

Through dialogue and interaction, members of an organization begin to characterize their world. They might see it as malleable or fixed, filled with opportunity or threatening. For instance, real progress towards innovation can begin when group members collectively believe that they can change important parts of the world around them and that what appears to be a threat is actually an opportunity for change.

Three important aspects of working together are:

- deciding who is a member and who is not;
- developing an informal understanding of acceptable and unacceptable behaviour;
- separating friends from enemies.

To work together effectively, individuals need to decide collectively how to allocate power, status and authority and to establish a shared understanding of who will get rewards and sanctions for specific types of actions.

Managers often fail to recognize these important aspects of internal integration. For example, a manager may fail to explain the basis for a promotion and to show why this reward, the status associated with it and the power given to the newly promoted individual are consistent with commonly shared beliefs. For example, at AstraZenica, a pharmaceutical company, the human resource (HR) managers surveyed employees' values in regard to affiliation with the company. They found that employees valued learning and development opportunities, competitive rewards, an energizing work environment and a successful business. So the HR department works in accord with building a capable, talented team with the potential for growth; building credibility by getting the fundamentals right; aligning the HR strategy with the business strategy; and understanding, communicating and measuring the return on investment (ROI) for HR initiatives. HR is committed to constantly reviewing and changing in response to business needs.[49] Although these don't seem to be unusual features, they are applied in the organization in a way that reveals real commitment to the values and principles that underpin them.

We have seen how organizational culture helps members by providing answers to important questions of external adaptation and internal integration. However, there is often an important difference in the answers to these questions between executives towards the top of the organization and members at the bottom. This may be because senior executives may owe their primary allegiance to their position in the organization. They may identify with the organization as a whole and may equate organizational and individual success; and they may want all others in the organization to believe much the same. They also expect to be very handsomely rewarded. On the other hand, less senior employees may see themselves as part of a larger, more varied and complex network of relationships. The job may be just an instrumental mechanism, such as a means of getting the financial rewards necessary to live. The distance between the values and beliefs of employees and those of their managers, expressed in the formation of distinct subcultures, may in itself be a cultural construct of an organization. Some organizations encourage their middle and senior managers to 'stay in touch with their floor workers' by taking on tasks usually done by employees.

This is in an effort to facilitate integration between managers and their employees. However, in practice, employees express a level of discomfort working closely with their managers on their own routine tasks. For example, research found that employees were reluctant to share a task or convey criticism directly to the manager when needed. In addition, managers felt isolated in performing their tasks and expressed discomfort about changing roles. The research concluded that in this organization efforts to facilitate boundary crossing were not very successful and may even reinforce occupational boundaries between managers and their employees.[50]

This finding signifies that, when attempting to initiate organizational culture, different perspectives need to be considered. Approaching organizational culture from a differentiation or fragmentation perspective will be more complex, but that may reflect the findings of organizational cultural research. Nevertheless, we cannot deny that most current management writing echoes (mostly consciously) the integration perspective, giving direction and prescriptions on how to manage an organization's culture.

MANAGERS' ROLE IN REINFORCING AND CHANGING CULTURE

Managers can help foster a culture that provides answers to important questions concerning external adaptation and internal integration. Recent work on the links between corporate culture and financial performance reaffirms the importance of an emphasis on helping employees to adjust to the environment. It also suggests that this emphasis alone is not sufficient. Nor is an emphasis solely on shareholders or customers associated with long-term economic performance. Instead, managers must work to emphasize all three issues simultaneously. Managers are also challenged to consider the challenges of approaching culture change in the same ways for both core and peripheral workforces. Peripheral workers often spend too little time in the company to be socialized into the culture and core workers may resent peripheral workers experiencing the same positive treatment that they receive. But so-called peripheral workers are also important to the organization and it is arguably unethical to treat them in a different way. This is likely to emerge as an increasingly important issue for all concerned: consider, for example, the increasing prevalence of 'teleworkers' – employees who spend a considerable amount of time working form home or remotely via telecommunications links. Sometimes managers adopt a two-tier approach to managing culture to deal with these differences.[51] Is this appropriate? It may be tempting for managers to attempt to revitalize an organization by dictating major changes rather than by building on shared values. Things may change a bit on the surface but a deeper look often shows whole departments resisting change and many key people who do 'buy in' for more or less understandable reasons to the new ways. Such responses may indicate that the responsible managers are insensitive to the effects of their proposed changes on shared values. They fail to ask if the changes are:

- contrary to important values held by participants within the organization;
- a challenge to historically important organization-wide assumptions;
- inconsistent with important common assumptions derived from the national culture(s) outside the organization.

All too often, executives are unable to realize that they, too, can be captured by the broadly held common assumptions within their organizations (see Effective Manager 7.1).[52] Top management may, for example, take a decision to introduce autonomous working teams to improve productivity and innovation, yet not face the reality that the organizational culture invests all authority in the executive management team. In such circumstances, the introduction of autonomous working teams can be disastrous, as decision-making responsibility will not be devolved to the team. Culture influences managerial behaviour as much as that of everyone else in the organization and astute managers who seek to manage culture will seek to understand it first.

EFFECTIVE MANAGER 7.1

Using organizational culture to help an organization compete

As more organizations are moving into volatile industries using advanced technology and confronting international competitors, managers may need to help their organizational culture adjust. Here are some pitfalls to avoid and some factors to emphasize when entering and competing in highly volatile, high-technology markets such as computing and biotechnology:

- When entering the market early, do not allow employees to become disenchanted when facing initial technical barriers and skill development challenges.
- When entering slowly, do not give competitors too big a lead – keep stressing to all employees the necessity of building technical and market skills.
- When adding new products to an existing market, take the opportunity to reassess approaches to decision making and management for both new products and old ones – challenge old routines.
- When adjusting to new markets with new products, avoid using 'conventional wisdom' and stress the development of new ways to compete.
- When entering the market, foster the Internet culture by embracing all forms of open communication in all possible media.

ORGANIZATIONAL AND NATIONAL CULTURE

There is very considerable scope for macro-social factors to affect organizational culture. In this respect national culture is itself a major influence on any organization operating within its boundaries. Societal-level culture can impact on workplaces in the following ways:

- Attitudes towards such things as individual responsibility, group harmony, ambiguity, displaying emotion openly and status will be embodied in the workplace by organizational actors, including those in positions of influence. These attitudes are culturally derived so that an organization will have its organizational culture influenced by wider society through its members' values.
- Institutional factors, for example the relative importance of trade unions in a particular society – itself deriving from a country's economic/political context, will set limits on how an organization operates in important ways, including aspects of its culture. For example, a litigious culture such as the US is likely to be manifested at organizational level in cultures that stress the protection of individual rights and formalized health and safety policies.

The links between national and organizational culture are made more complex when you consider the multicultural makeup of workforces within any one society. We are here looking at issues of imported cultures and cultural diversity.

Every large organization imports potentially important subcultural groupings when it recruits employees from the larger society. There is a range of strategies for dealing with this phenomenon. At one extreme, senior managers can merely accept these divisions and work within the confines of the larger culture – in other words informing staff that they will have to fit in to the overriding national culture and do things 'our way'. However, there are three primary difficulties with this approach. First, subordinated groups, such as members of a specific religion or ethnic group, may find it difficult to wholly assimilate in the new culture with a number of potentially deleterious consequences. Academics studying national culture[53] note that individuals' core values are formed at an early age (that is, within their 'home' culture) and will therefore be deeply rooted and potentially difficult to change. Second, the organization may lose valuable knowhow if it discourages diversity amongst its workforce. Third, organizations that accept and build on cultural diversity may find it easier to develop sound international operations. Conversely, for example, many Japanese organizations have had substantial difficulty adjusting to the equal treatment of women in their US and European operations.

A recent study found that people from different ethnic and gender groups filter and process information about organizational culture differently. This means that they may interpret the same cultural messages differently. Thus, attempts by management to manipulate cultural elements may need to take account of the fact that they will not always be universally and consistently understood. Management efforts to homogenize culture will almost inevitably result in subunit variations in interpretation and this is likely to contribute to the development of subcultures.[54]

In Europe multicultural populations are now a reality. In 2004 statistics showed that over 10% of the populations of Austria, Belgium, Germany, the Republic of Ireland, the Netherlands and Sweden were foreign born. The figure was highest in Switzerland, with 23.5% of its population originating from outside that country.[55] The clear indication is that cultural change within these societies has occurred within a short period of time. Therefore, it has become important for organizations to manage multiculturalism effectively. Robin Ely and David Thomas[56] discuss three paradigms for assessing an organization's level of openness to multiculturalism. First, the 'discrimination and fairness' paradigm looks at multiculturalism with respect to equal opportunity, fair treatment, recruitment and compliance with legislation by ensuring certain numbers of staff from ethnically diverse backgrounds are employed. This paradigm insists that individuals assimilate into the existing organizational culture and tends to lead to the development of potentially destructive subcultures (as ethnic differences are ignored or suppressed).

Second, the 'access and legitimacy' paradigm for an organization's level of openness to multiculturalism emphasizes gaining access to new and diverse markets by using cultural diversity within the organization. This may create a feeling of exploitation in staff as they are the 'token representative of their culture'. In addition, this differentiation of individuals from the group can lead to subculture development as differences are highlighted.

Third, the 'learning and effectiveness' paradigm for an organization's level of openness to multiculturalism incorporates elements of the other two paradigms. Additionally, this paradigm firmly connects diverse ethnicity to diverse approaches to work. According to Ely and Thomas, by creating openness, organizations will find that individuals from different national cultures do not feel devalued by assimilation into the existing organizational culture, nor will subcultures along ethnic lines be created.

Managing cultural diversity in organizations is a skill that contemporary managers must acquire. Many organizations run courses on multiculturalism to ensure knowledge and understanding of national and cultural differences. In addition, many organizations have courses for ethnically different groups and individuals, including language tuition related to the workplace. When we talk about cultural differences it is important not to overlook the importance of communication; many intercultural misunderstandings are the result of a lack of facility in a second language.

CONCLUSION

Organizational culture is an important topic within OB. It is concerned with the ways in which its members interpret the everyday realities of organizational life. Such interpretations can be an important influence upon behaviour. Some theorists and managers believe that a strong organizational culture can contribute to high performance and success. Whether or not this is consistently true, the study of organizational culture is key to an understanding of how organizations operate in the real world.

SUMMARY

LEARNING OBJECTIVE 1
What is organizational culture?

Organizational culture is defined as the system of shared values and beliefs that develops within an organization and guides its members' behaviour. It occupies an important role within OB, growing in importance since the 1980s in response to key trends within the business world. It is normally studied by using qualitative or ethnographic research methods in an attempt to capture the meanings that individuals and groups attach to culture.

LEARNING OBJECTIVE 2
Organizational culture and national culture

The concept of organizational culture is as important to the management of an organization as are strategy and structure. As the system of shared beliefs and values that guide and direct the behaviour of members links to macro-level national culture, this level of culture can have a strong influence on day-to-day organizational behaviour and performance. There are connections between organizational culture and national culture but each organizational culture is unique despite being embedded in a national culture.

LEARNING OBJECTIVE 3
Cultural levels, dominant cultures, subcultures and diversity

Culture can be analysed through its three components: observable culture – the behaviours that can be seen within an organization; shared values held by members of an organization; and, at the deepest level, common assumptions or truths developed and shared by members through their joint experiences in the organization. Dominant cultures are articulated by dominant individuals or groups. Organizations are also routinely characterized by subcultures among various work units and subsystems, as well as possible countercultures, which can be the source of potentially harmful conflicts.

LEARNING OBJECTIVE 4
Types of organizational culture

Although each organizational culture is necessarily unique, several writers have formulated typologies which establish commonly found forms of culture. In this chapter we have looked at the models put forward by Handy and Deal and Kennedy. Such models enable us to consider organizations we work in or know along a pre-existing continuum framework. This can be useful in crystallizing our thoughts on the topic, although it is rare that real-life organizations fit perfectly into any one category.

LEARNING OBJECTIVE 5
Does culture link to performance?

A well-developed culture can assist in responding to internal and external problems. Through common shared behaviours, values and assumptions, organizational members can clearly understand the organization's mission, strategies and goals in relation to the external environment. Culture also helps to achieve internal adaptation – the ability of members to work together effectively on organizational activities. A third function of culture is to help bring management and employees much closer together in their respective goals.

LEARNING OBJECTIVE 6
Critical perspectives on culture

It may be naïve and misleading to regard organizations as unified entities with one dominant culture to which everyone completely subscribes. The ambiguity and fragmentation perspectives alert us to more pluralist models of culture, which could be more realistic in many instances. If employees hold values that do not mirror those of dominant coalitions within organizations, this may not lead to conflict or confusion and differences in this regard may be a source of creativity and diversity which is otherwise positive, in terms of organizational performance.

CHAPTER 7 STUDY GUIDE

Now that you have read this chapter, you should be able to apply and further develop your knowledge by undertaking the following activites set out over the next few pages: test your knowledge questions, an individual activity and an end-of-chapter case study.

Please also go to this book's website: **www.wileyeurope.com/college/french** to find further material which will enhance your understanding and enable you to assess your knowledge.

TEST YOURSELF

1. What is organizational culture and what are the levels of analysing culture in organizations?
2. What functions do organizational cultures serve and how do subcultures and cultural diversity help in this?
3. What are some alternative perspectives of culture? Why is it important to view organizational culture from more than one perspective?
4. Describe some ethical issues that might be encountered when managing organizational culture.
5. You are a manager who wishes to encourage employees to make suggestions and contribute to new ideas. What aspects of culture could be manipulated to try to encourage this?
6. What observable elements of organizational culture can you identify from your own organization or an organization with which you are familiar?
7. Give examples of both formal and informal processes that occur in your organization or at your university. What can you say about the nonobservable culture in your organization?

8. In a small organization with 50 employees, senior management has espoused values of equality, respect and high performance for employees and customers. When the latest performance figures for the company are released, management's response is to call the staff to a general meeting and tell them they all have to 'lift their game' if they expect to retain their jobs. What comments can you make on the cultural features of the organization?

9. Your company has just merged with another that provides a similar service. What issues will emerge in relation to the merging of two organizational cultures and what can managers do to deal with them?

10. Examine the following values and visible elements of culture. What underlying assumptions do you think might exist 'beneath' these aspects of culture?

- Organization A values new ideas and selects its highest-performing employees for special monthly creative workshops. Organization B values new ideas and promises a prize of 4000 euros to any employee whose idea contributes clearly to increasing profits. Organization C values new ideas and encourages employees, as owners of shares in the company, to contribute ideas in their day-to-day work.

- Organizations D, E and F express the importance of high-performing employees. Organization D conducts annual performance reviews between supervisor and worker and if workers perform according to requirements, they are given an incremental increase in wages. Organization E conducts six-monthly reviews and more regular 'chats' between supervisor and worker. If the workers are not performing according to requirements they are asked to account for their low performance. In Organization F no reviews are conducted but workers and supervisors work closely together. If employees are demonstrating outstanding performance, their work is commended and publicized in the company newsletter. They also receive a bonus.

- In Organizations G and H an employee makes a significant mistake. In Organization G the manager speaks to the employee and tries to analyse the problem and find ways to overcome it. In Organization H the manager discusses the employee's mistake at a team meeting in front of all members of the group and expresses disappointment at his poor behaviour. The incident is also reported to senior management and recorded on the employee's file.

INDIVIDUAL ACTIVITY

Assessing your organization's culture

Choose an organization with which you are familiar. This 15-question survey has been developed to serve as a starting point for the analysis of organizational culture. Answer each true/false question according to what is true most of the time and answer based on how your organization actually acts – not how you would like it to be.

True/false questions

1. I know how my projects contribute to the success or failure of our organization.
2. Management here makes lots of announcements to employees.
3. I have colleagues from a wide variety of professional and personal backgrounds.
4. In this organization people who are not ready to be promoted after a certain length of time at their level are generally encouraged to leave.
5. Departments or teams compete with each other for our organization's resources.
6. When people are not getting along here it is a long time before we directly address the issue.
7. When it is time for me to learn a new skill, training is readily available at no cost to me.
8. When the boss tells us to 'jump!' we ask 'how high?'
9. It takes a long time for this organization to address customer concerns.
10. Many employees expect to work at this organization for their whole careers.
11. Senior management says the door is always open – and they mean it.
12. It is fun to work here.
13. We have three or fewer layers of management.
14. We have performance reviews less often than once a year.
15. Compensation and benefits are relatively low here.

Count your 'true' responses in each third of the quiz (questions 1–5, 6–10, 11–15). The section in which you have answered 'true' the most times corresponds to the culture type your organization most closely matches. If you have the same number of 'true' responses in more than one section, your culture matches this combination of types. Here is a list of primary advantages and potential pitfalls of each one.

For questions 1–5
If you had the most 'true' responses in this set of questions, your company has a deliberative/traditional culture.

Advantages:

- This culture tends to be intellectual and thoughtful.
- People in this type of organization often consider issues carefully prior to making a change.
- The organization probably has many formal systems, yet flexibly forms and reforms teams in accordance with immediate client needs.
- This cultural type regularly hires groups of new employees, generating a valuable flow of diverse talent with fresh perspectives.
- Senior management communicates frequently to employees.

Pitfalls:

Although plenty of communication usually flows from the top of this organizational type, management often does not indicate interest in feedback from all levels. Beyond making announcements from management, ask for regular feedback so you don't miss critical information and/or valuable innovations from your staff.

- Be careful that your organization does not discuss change for so long that you miss important opportunities to change for the better.
- Be aware of the cultural implications of fostering competition within a company. Internal competition may create resentment that drives costly turnover.

For questions 6–10

If you had the most 'true' responses in this set of questions, your company has an established/stable culture.

Advantages:

- This organization has most likely been around for a long time and/or is a family business. These organizations tend to have solid institutional memories, so they are not likely to waste resources by repeatedly 'reinventing the wheel'.
- This type of company has processes in place to address most situations.
- Organizations of this type tend to cultivate employees by encouraging development through mentoring programmes and/or formal training opportunities.
- This culture type is known for compensating its people relatively well.

Pitfalls:

- Typically this type of organization struggles to handle conflict well, often becoming either conflict avoidant or 'command and control'. If your organization tends to be conflict avoidant, it may be time to address those problems that are out of hand, or that have been out of hand in the past.
- 'Command-and-control' style leadership may yield feelings of disconnectedness among employees. Consider assessing employee morale immediately.
- Overall, this culture type tends to be wary of turnover so take a careful look at your organization and consider whether it is holding on to people who might best be let go.
- While established systems can be a positive sign of organizational health, make sure your processes are focused toward addressing customer needs in a timely manner. If your processes impede rapid resolution of customer problems, rework them right away.

For questions 11–15

If you had the most 'true' responses in this set of questions, your company has an urgent/seat-of-the-pants culture.

Advantages:

- This culture type features a positive work environment with tight bonds among employees.
- It is likely that an aspect of your organization's mission includes responding to crisis. People care deeply about the organization's mission and work hard to achieve the organization's goals.
- Employees who frequently hurry to beat the clock can create great results in a short time, provided that quality is a strong value in your organization.
- These organizations tend to have a flat structure that fosters communication and collaboration among employees and speeds the decision-making process.

Pitfalls:

- Minimum rewards (both tangible and intangible) and minimum feedback are common with this culture type. Rewards and recognition are important not only to generate loyalty but also to foster collaboration.
- The constant rush to get things done quickly can lead to burnout and increase the ever-present danger of losing talent.
- Although this type of culture generally features frequent upward communication and grassroots change, top-down communication tends to be inadequate. Beyond staying accessible, take time to share important messages and expectations with your entire staff to keep them motivated and moving in the right direction.
- Making decisions under intense time pressure may lead to a reduction in the quality of your products or services.

Is your type different from what you thought it would be? If so, you might have an unrealistic perception of your organization's character and values.

WE KNOW IT WHEN WE SEE IT

'You can take IKEA out of Smaland, but you can't take Smaland out of IKEA.' This statement is part of the opening section of IKEA's corporate website that focuses on the company's shared values, themselves an integral part of the company's culture. Smaland in Sweden, where Ingvar Kamprad founded the business that grew into the present-day IKEA, is characterized as a place that embodies the company's values. IKEA's website notes that: 'Simplicity, humility, thrift and responsibility are all evident in the lifestyle, attitudes and customs of the place where IKEA began. An example of the Smalanders' way of doing things is not to ask others what you should be doing, but to ask yourself and then get on with it!'[57]

An IKEA executive reinforces the importance of the company culture for employees, stating that successful employees are:

> '...people who accept our values and are willing to act on our ideas. They tend to be straightforward rather than flashy and not too status-conscious. They must be hardworking and comfortable dealing with everyone from the customer to the owner to the cashier. But perhaps the most important quality for an IKEAN is *odmujkhet*, a Swedish word that implies humility, modesty and respect for one's fellow man. It may be hard to translate but we know it when we see it.'[58]

Ingvar Kamprad is very clear that maintaining a strong IKEA culture is, in his judgement, one of the most crucial factors explaining IKEA's success. Values of togetherness and enthusiasm are supported by the company through open-plan office layouts and by laying out clear goals that co-workers can stand behind. Another espoused value, willpower, is defined as first agreeing on mutual objectives and then not letting anything stand in the way of actually achieving them. It is alternatively stated as involving a sense of knowing exactly what we want and exhibiting an irrepressible desire to achieve it.

IKEA's culture is viewed by the company itself as a strong culture 'living and based on a set of shared values'.[59] The organization claims that its togetherness and enthusiasm make it unique. Its recruitment section on the IKEA corporate website offers potential employees (termed co-workers) the prospect of fun at work and opportunities to contribute to the development of others. IKEA also wishes to build a diverse workforce, noting that 'we want to attract people from diverse nationalities, perspectives and approaches because we believe diversity makes IKEA a better place to work and to shop.'[60] The recruitment of suitable co-workers is clearly important to IKEA, as it views culture as emerging and being sustained by people enacting values.

Questions

1. To what extent is IKEA's culture, as depicted here, unique or can it be located within either Handy or Deal and Kennedy's typology of cultures?
2. If you were a manager in IKEA, what would you do to sustain the current culture?

Source: http://www.ikea-group.ikea.com/corporate/work/why.html

SUGGESTED READING

Gabriel, Y., Fineman, S. & Sims, D. (2009), *Organizing and Organizations*, 4th edn, Sage: London. In several chapters of this book, the authors provide some vivid examples of the day-to-day manifestations of organizational culture.

Peters, T. & Waterman, R. H. (1982), *In Search of Excellence*, Harper & Row: New York. This best-selling, albeit subsequently much-criticized, book sets out a clear view of the potential impact of organizational culture on performance.

END NOTES

1. google.co.uk/corporate/culture (accessed 30 December 2009).

2. Peters, T. & Waterman, R. H. (1982), *In Search of Excellence*, Harper & Row: New York.

3. Schein, E. H. (1985), *Organizational Culture and Leadership*, Jossey-Bass: San Francisco, CA.

4. Alston, F. & Tippett, D. (2009), Does a Technology-Driven Organization's Culture Influence the trust Employees Have in Their Managers? *Engineering Management Journal*, **21** (2), 3–10.

5. Fard, H. D., Rostamy, A. A. A. & Taghiloo, H. (2009), How types of Organisational Cultures Contribute in Shaping Learning Organisations. *Singapore Management Review*, **31** (1), 49–61.

6. Wang, S. Guidice, R., Tansky, J. W. & Wang, Z-M. (2009), The Moderating Role of Organizational Culture in Innovation: Evidence from China, *Academy of Management Proceedings (Conference Theme: Green Management Matters)*.

7. Foster-Back, P. (2009), The Light Brigade. *People Management*, 1 January, 28–30.

8. Hofstede, G. (2001), *Culture's Consequences*, 2nd edition, Sage: Thousand Oaks, CA.

9. Linstead, S. (2009), Managing Culture, in *Management and Organization a Critical Text* (eds S. Linstead, L. Fulop & S. Lilley), 2nd edn, Palgrave Macmillan: Basingstoke.

10. Den Hartog, D. & Verburg, R. M. (2004), High performance work systems, organizational culture and firm effectiveness. *Human Resource Management Journal*, **14** (1), 55–78.

11. Ibid.

12. Deal, T. & Kennedy, A. (1982), *Corporate Culture*, Addison-Wesley: Reading, MA.

13. See www.staralliance.com/en/meta/airlines/TP, (accessed 30 June 2007).

14. Ibid.

15. Peters, T. & Waterman, R. H. (1982), *In Search of Excellence*, Harper & Row: New York.

16. Lueders Bolwerk, C. A. (2002), The culture of farm work and its implications on health, social relationships and leisure in farm women and men in the United States. *Journal of Cultural Diversity*, **9** (4), 102–107.

17. Rollinson, D. (2008), *Organisational Behaviour and Analysis*, 4th edn, FT Prentice Hall: Harlow.

18. Fitzgerald, J. A. & Teal, A. (2004), Health reform and occupational sub-cultures: the changing roles of professional identities. *Contemporary Nurse*, **16** (1–2), 9–19.

19. Jones, R., Lasky, B., Russell-Gale, H. & Le Fevre, M. (2004), Leadership and the development of dominant and countercultures: a narcissistic perspective. *Leadership and Organization Development Journal*, **25** (1/2), 216.

20. Martin, J. & Siehl, C. (1983), Organization culture and counterculture. *Organizational Dynamics*, **12**, 52–64.

21. McColl, G. (2002), Toll's takeover touch. *Business Review Weekly*, 12–18 December, 40–41.

22. Smircich, L. (1983), Concepts of culture and organizational analysis. *Administrative Science Quarterly*, **28** (3), 339–358.

23. Needle, D. (2004), *Business in Context*, 4th edn, Thomson: London.

24. Schein, E. H. (1990), Organizational culture. *American Psychologist*, **45** (2), 109–119.

25. Martin, J. (1992), *Cultures in Organizations*, Oxford University Press: New York.

26. Geertz, C. (1973), *The Interpretation of Culture*, Basic Books: New York.

27. Byer, J. M. & Trice, H. M. (1987), How an organization's rites reveal its culture. *Organizational Dynamics*, Spring, 27–41.

28. McManus, K. (2003), The challenge of changing culture. *Industrial Engineer*, **35** (1), 18–19.

29. Den Hartog, D. N. & Verburg, R. M. (2004), High performance work systems, organizational culture and firm effectiveness. *Human Resource Management Journal*, **14** (1), 55–79.

30. See http://www.cowi.com/en/menu/news/newsarchive/bulidings/openplan (accessed 21 June 2007).

31. Weeks, J. (2003), *Unpopular Culture: the Culture of Complaint in a British Bank*, Chicago University Press: Chicago, IL.

32. Arnold, J. (2003), *Why Clever Companies Have the will to Whinge*, newsvote.bbc.co.uk-BBCNEWS/business, (accessed 1 July 2007).

33. Developed from Deal, T. & Kennedy, A. (1982), *Corporate Cultures: The Rites and Rituals of Corporate Life*, Addison-Wesley: Reading, MA.

34. Martin, J. (2002), *Organizational Culture: Mapping the Terrain*, Sage: Thousand Oaks, CA.

35. Ibid.

36. Degeling, P., Kennedy, J., Hill, M., *et al.* (1998), *Professional Sub-cultures and Hospital Reform*, Centre for Hospital Management and Information Systems Research, University of New South Wales: Sydney.

37. Traders deal in 'Babes and 'Dragons' (1995), *Independent*, 21 December.

38. Handy, C. (1989), *Understanding Organizations*, Penguin: Harmondsworth.

39. Brewis, J. (2007), Culture, in *Introducing Organizational Behaviour and Management* (eds K. Knights & H. Willmott), Thomson: London.

40. Deal, T. E & Kennedy, A. A. (1982), *Corporate Cultures: The Rites and Rituals of Corporate Life*, Addison-Wesley: Reading, MA.

41. Martin, J. (2002), *Organizational Culture: Mapping the Terrain*, Sage: Thousand Oaks, CA.

42. Ibid.

43. Willmott, H. (1993), Strength is ignorance, slavery is freedom: managing culture in modern organizations. *Journal of Management Studies*, **30** (5), 515–552.

44. Grey, C. (2009), *A Very Short, Fairly Interesting and Reasonably Cheap Book about Studying Organizations*, 2nd edn, Sage: London.

45. Watson, T. J. (2006), *Organising and Managing Work*, 2nd edn, FT Prentice Hall: Harlow.

46. Martin, J. (2002), *Organizational Culture: Mapping the Terrain*, Sage: Thousand Oaks, CA.

47. Fitzgerald, J. A. (2002), *Managing Health Reform: a Mixed Method Study into the Construction and Changing of Professional Identities*, unpublished PhD thesis.

48. *HMP Leeds – Culture Deteriorates in Overcrowded Prison*, http://press.homeoffice.gov.uk/press-releases (accessed 30 June 2007).

49. Donaldson, C. (2002), AstraZenica HR: a study in strategic people management. *Human Resources*, November, 12–14.

50. Fitzgerald, J. A. & Hinings, R. (2004), *Changing Professional Identities: Adjusting Professional Delineations in Health*. Paper presented at the International Federation of Scholarly Associations of Management (IFSAM) VIIth World Congress, Goteburg, Sweden.

51. Ogbonna, E. & Harris, L. C. (2002), Managing organizational culture: insights from the hospitality industry. *Human Resource Management Journal*, **12** (1), 33–53.

52. Cooper, A. C. & Smith, C. G. (1992), How established firms respond to threatening technologies. *Academy of Management Executive*, **6** (2), 56–69.

53. French, R. (2007), *Cross-Cultural Management in Work Organizations*, CIPD: London.

54. Helms, M. M. & Stern, R. (2001), Exploring the factors that influence employees' perceptions of their organization's culture. *Journal of Management in Medicine*, **15** (6), 415–425.

55. OECD (2007) *OECD Factbook*, OECD: Paris.

56. Ely, R. & Thomas, D. (2001), Cultural diversity at work: the effects of diversity perspectives on group processes and outcomes. *Administrative Science Quarterly*, **46** (2), 229–274.

57. See www.ikea-group.ikea.com/corporate/work/why.html, (accessed 5 July 2007).

58. Konzelmann, S. J., Wilkinson, F., Craypo, C. & Aridi, R. (2005), *The Export of National Varieties of Capitalism; The Cases of Wal-Mart and IKEA*. Working Paper No. 314, Centre for Business Research, University of Cambridge: Cambridge.

59. See www.ikea-group.ikea.com/corporate/work/why.html, (accessed 14 August 2007).

60. Ibid.

Commentary

SOME UNINTENDED CONSEQUENCES OF JOB DESIGN

GARY JOHNS*

By intent or default, all jobs have a design that constitutes a context for their incumbents, and that design is embedded in a larger work context. The purpose of this article is to examine the unintended and sometimes negative consequences of job designs and their related contexts. Several themes will emerge in what follows. First, the larger context in which jobs are embedded can either shape or countervail intended job design effects. Second, many job characteristics have a paradoxical double-edged quality. For example, the same autonomy that leads some academics to produce creative scientific breakthroughs enables others to produce crackpot ideas in the name of academic freedom. Third, the question *Job design for what purpose?* is important to answer. Thus, job designs that support high in-role performance might not support creativity or learning or citizenship or ethical behavior or employee health. Finally, the identity of job incumbents is an important but seldom examined factor in the consequences of job design.

The Fragility of Meaningfulness

In a comprehensive test of the Job Characteristics Model, Johns, Xie, and Fang (1992) found that experienced meaningfulness was a particularly robust mediator of the connection between all core job characteristics and work outcomes, a finding subsequently confirmed in a meta-analysis by Humphrey, Nahrgang, and Morgeson (2007). Given the potent affective and motivational properties of meaningfulness, it should play a key role in the design of jobs. However, research has shown that the contextual cues that stimulate meaningfulness can be rather subtle, and thus overlooked, that other aspects of job design or job context can damage inherent meaningfulness, and that people can extract meaningfulness from cues rather far removed from the intended design of the job.

On the surface, soliciting scholarship money for deserving students or detecting cancer would seem to be inherently meaningful tasks. However, as Grant and Parker (2009) imply, such jobs, as designed, often inadvertently isolate incumbents from beneficiaries in a way that attenuates empathy and motivation to help. Thus, in a field experiment, Grant and colleagues (Grant, Campbell, Chen, Cottone, Lapedis, & Lee, 2007) found that brief exposure to a scholarship recipient helped by their work significantly increased calling persistence (142%) and money accrued (171%) by fundraisers. Grant and Parker cite similar findings showing that radiologists exposed to photos of patients whose scans they were diagnosing reported more empathy and diagnosed more accurately (Turner, Hadas-Halperin, & Raveh, 2008).

* Correspondence to: Gary Johns, Department of Management, John Molson School of Business, Concordia University, 1455 de Maisonneuve Blvd. West, Montreal, Quebec, H3G 1M8, Canada. E-mail: gjohns@jmsb.concordia.ca
Taken from: *Journal of Organizational Behavior*, **31**, 361–369 (2010), Wiley-Blackwell.

What is important to underline in these examples is that apparently small changes in job design can have big effects (cf. Johns, 2006) by making salient the significance of the task at hand. For instance, as part of their jobs, Singapore Airlines cabin crew routinely report informal customer suggestions, complaints, and praise to their managers for transmission to the appropriate airline unit (e.g., the food and beverage department). The practice supplements formal customer surveys, allowing more fine-grained attention to customer needs (Wirtz, Heracleous, & Menkhoff, 2007). This rather minor job design feature enhances the meaningfulness of cabin crew work by emphasizing the relational aspects of the job (Grant & Parker, 2009) and providing knowledge of results as comments are acknowledged and innovations (e.g., the advent of in-flight e-mail) are implemented.

If organizations accidentally miss out supplying the cues that signal meaningfulness, they equally often intentionally engineer them out of jobs, but with unintended results. Thus, some readers might, for privacy concerns, agonize over calling attention to a needs-based scholarship recipient or circulating patient photos around the clinic or hospital, preempting the advantages of the interventions described earlier. Many years ago Hackman and Oldham (1980) recognized the tendency to subvert an otherwise good job design with a meaning-dampening design feature. In general, the core job design dimensions tend to be positively correlated. A signature exception is the high significance-low autonomy job profile. That is, the job is seen as being so important that the incumbent's autonomy is curtailed so that things do not get out of control, so that consequential mistakes are preempted. Firewalls that isolate employees from more direct forms of contact with clients are one such example. Under these conditions, incumbents will recognize and report their jobs as being significant. However, as noted earlier, meaningfulness as a psychological state is also cued by other core job characteristics, and the design of the entire job thus merits close attention. One is reminded in all of this of the "deadly combinations" of HR practices (such as team designs coupled with individual rewards) that Becker, Huselid, Pickus, and Spratt (1997) describe. Deadly combinations of job dimensions (e.g., high significance, low autonomy) deserve more attention. A place to start might be burnout-prone jobs such as teaching, nursing, and police work. Many aspects of these jobs actually signal a good motivational profile. Despite this, constraints in the form of bureaucratic red tape often thwart the desire to provide meaningful aid to beneficiaries (Grant & Parker, 2009).

The salutary effects of autonomy have often been observed. One of the unintended consequences that a reduction in autonomy often has is a diminution in learning or the motivation to execute learning, outcome variables that receive inadequate consideration in the domain of job design. In a definitive series of studies of advanced manufacturing technology, Wall and colleagues determined that increased operator autonomy (e.g., the freedom to bypass computer programming when necessary) contributed to superior performance and job satisfaction as well as less felt work pressure (e.g., Jackson & Wall, 1991; Wall, Corbett, Martin, Clegg, & Jackson, 1990; Wall, Jackson, & Davids, 1992). The studies strongly implicated enhanced learning as a key mediator of these effects. However, such control is routinely denied on the grounds that big mistakes could occur, thus damaging the meaningfulness of the work. Similarly, Parker, Wall, and Jackson (1997) show how curtailed autonomy can create a knowing-doing gap (Pfeffer & Sutton, 2000) by blocking the conversion of strategic knowledge into related work attitudes and behavior. Thus, under limited autonomy, employees exposed to training and persuasive communication understood the need for flexibility but failed to assume the broader role orientation that would lead them to enact such flexibility.

If some discrete job characteristics can inadvertently counter the positive effects of others, aspects of the larger work context can counter the effects of generally motivating job designs. On paper, Elsbach and Hargadon (2006) contend that professional jobs are generally designed so as to have the textbook qualities that stimulate creativity via intrinsic motivation. However, they further argue that grinding workload pressures often undermine the benefits of this traditional design for creativity. In particular, they describe how exaggerated skill variety can actually preempt task identity and how coping with grueling workload to maintain one's self-worth is a poor basis for extracting meaningfulness from a job. Hence, meaningfulness is undermined in a way that saps the intrinsic motivation deemed necessary for creativity.

The notion of identity (who am I?) is intimately tied to the meaningfulness of one's job. Research shows that some job design changes inadvertently threaten employees' identity and that employees are, on the other hand, capable of extracting meaningfulness from sources rather far removed from the formal design of their jobs. Eriksson-Zetterquist, Lindberg, and Styhre (2009) described the introduction of new Internet-based purchasing technology in a US-owned Swedish auto manufacturer. Although the system helped integrate the parent company's IT system and also facilitated certain aspects of their work, it ultimately threatened the professional identity of the Swedish firm's purchasing personnel. The alacrity with which the system was programmed to require signoffs and approvals threatened their professional autonomy, and the much-prized opportunity to interact personally with suppliers was curtailed by the system, damaging an important relational aspect of professional identity. In a telling example of how the larger context can inadvertently affect job design, many of the more fulfilling aspects of the purchasers' jobs were replaced by onerous audit and control tasks mandated by the passage in the US of the Sarbanes-Oxley Act. As such, an act meant to improve corporate governance in America ultimately helped damage job design in Sweden.

Researchers and managers will do well to understand that employees often extract meaning about their work from quarters well removed from the actual design of the job. Elsbach (2009) explains how toy car designers maintained their identities as cool, independent, iconoclastic, non-conformists despite the fact that they were cranking out designs for retail commodities produced in the millions according to rather rigid corporate specifications. Apparently, the actual job design was not the optimum for reinforcing a creative persona. Despite this, Elsbach found that designers worked hard to develop signature designs that defined their work and looked to admiration of these designs by peers and savvy expert collectors to affirm the meaningfulness of their work. In a similar vein, Ashforth and Kreiner (1999) explain how people who do "dirty work" to which some social stigma is attached derive ennobling meaning from the occupational and workgroup cultures in which their jobs are embedded. These examples illustrate the rather imprecise boundary between job designs and job contexts.

The Perils of Interdependence

Job designs based on teams are perhaps the most prominent manifestation of the shift that Grant and Parker (2009) note toward more relational job designs. In a trenchant critique of this trend aptly entitled *The Romance of Teams* Allen and Hecht (2004) assemble evidence that questions the universal performance benefits of teams. They then attempt to account for the persistent romance by citing literature that teams do provide certain social-emotional benefits (e.g., fulfillment of social needs, uncertainty reduction), and that they can lead to positive *attributions* (i.e., illusions) of team and individual member performance. Although these outcomes are of scholarly interest, they are not the goals that most firms have in mind when they adopt team designs. I will return later to the value of such an expansion of the criterion space when studying job design.

Teams, of course, can perform effectively when the underlying task requires true interdependence and the work is interesting (Hackman, 1987). However, one unintended consequence of teams concerns attendance dynamics. There is some evidence that team designs either elevate absenteeism or fail to lead to expected attendance improvements, a phenomenon that has been observed even when the teams were generally considered to be successful when judged by more narrow performance criteria (Harrison, Johns, & Martocchio, 2000). The reason for this is not clear, but some degree of collusion to take time off might be one factor (e.g., Xie & Johns, 2000). Also, any sample of teams will include some that don't gel, and the very worst scenario for attendance is observed in team designs where social integration breaks down or is never achieved (Johns, 2008). Such lack of social integration reduces social control and is particularly reflected in a lack of cohesion or a very diverse range of group opinion or sentiment. Thus, poor social integration in the face of a need for interdependence maximizes absence, as team members adopt a "do your own thing" mentality.

There have been occasional reports of "improvements" in attendance under team designs, but these effects suggest considerable contextual subtleties. Thus, Barker (1993) found that the conversion of circuit board work from assembly lines to self-managed teams led to considerable coercion by peers for good attendance. The team design fostered high identification with individual customers, a relational job design feature that is generally held to be motivating (enhancing client relationships, Hackman & Oldham, 1980) but in this case caused some coercion for attendance so as not to let customers down. On the other hand, Grinyer and Singleton (2000) reported that the conversion to teams in UK public sector work occasioned employees to engage in presenteeism, going to work when unwell, so as not to let team members down. Many employees felt that this practice exacerbated illness and elevated downstream absenteeism. In fact, a lack of backup is one of the best established job context correlates of presenteeism (Johns, in press), being a product of lean staffing, lack of cross-training, and other such manifestations of contemporary employment. Studying "lean teams" in a production environment, Parker (2003) found that any advantages of interdependence were likely offset by reduced autonomy and skill utilization, which in turn led to reduced organizational commitment. In her words, such teams are characterized more by multitasking than multiskilling.

Elsbach and Flynn (2008) discuss how job designs that stress collaboration with others have become the preferred means of managing creative professionals. Thus, it is thought that an interdependent mixture of ideas, perspectives, and disciplines is the key to enhanced creative output, and the ability to collaborate is a much touted quality in the performance appraisals of such professionals. There is indeed a corpus of research to support the idea that diverse collaboration fosters creativity. However, Elsbach and Flynn call attention to the paradox that work designs that stress collaboration are often at odds with the person- and role-based identities that are frequently held by creative professionals. In other words, strained fit is essentially engineered into many jobs designed around project work or cross-functional teams by virtue of the identities of the incumbents, which are often grounded in feelings of uniqueness, independence, purity of purpose, and self-affirmation. In a study of toy designers, Elsbach and Flynn (2008, p. 33) found that they "routinely withheld idea giving or idea taking behaviors in response to perceived or anticipated identity threats," although idea taking was perceived as more threatening. Consequently, the job design requirement to "deal with others" (Hackman & Oldham, 1980) was subverted. Aside from identity issues, Fried, Levi, and Laurence (2008) review evidence suggesting the need for a delicate balance between individual job design and team job design. For instance, highly motivating individual designs may deflect attention from interdependent work requirements.

The toy design study illustrates that interdependence might be initiated or received (Kiggundu, 1981; Morgeson & Humphrey, 2006). That is, employees might provide information to others (initiated interdependence) or receive information (received interdependence). In a network study of investment bankers, Gargiulo, Ertug, and Galunic (2009) showed that the distinction between these two forms of interdependence is not trivial. In particular, they found that dense social ties within a financial services firm enhanced individual performance among bankers who were habitual acquirers of information from colleagues and decreased performance when they were habitual providers of such information. Such sign changes, here indicating asymmetric interdependence, are common signals of the impact of context on organizational behavior (Johns, 2006). It will also be noted that information acquisition was evidently seen as boon by investment bankers and as bane by toy designers, evidently a function of occupational context and self-selection into that context. Flynn (2003) reported complex tradeoffs between social status versus productivity resulting from favor exchanges among engineers, highlighting that the outcomes of interdependence are most uncertain.

The Limits of Richness

Given the demonstrated benefits of rich, high-scope jobs (Fried & Ferris, 1987; Humphrey *et al.*, 2007), it might seem heretical to suggest that a job could be too rich. Yet certain trends in the domain of work, including intrusive information technology, the flattening of organizational structures, and the deification of clients by professional service firms, point to this possibility (see also Baron, 2010, on entrepreneurs). Most particularly worrisome are steroidal *ad hoc* job "designs" that hammer several jobs into one, prompted by an unfettered wave of mergers, acquisitions, downsizing, and restructuring. However, some evidence also points to occupational-level determinants of excessive job scope, in line with the findings of Dierdorff, Rubin, and Morgeson (2009) concerning how occupational context shapes managerial role requirements.

Intentionally sampling to maximize variation in job design, Xie and Johns (1995) found a u-shaped relationship between non-incumbent and incumbent-provided indicators of job scope and emotional exhaustion. Furthermore, the effect was most pronounced for those who perceived low-demands abilities fit. The fact that similar results were found for self-reported scope as well as two independent indicators of scope at the occupational level (*Dictionary of Occupational Titles* job complexity index; occupational prestige index) suggests that some occupations systematically shape the role requirements of job incumbents in ways that lead to negative outcomes (*cf.* Dierdorff *et al.*, 2009). It should be emphasized that such curvilinear relationships between job design and related job context features and various criteria are not uncommon when samples exhibit reasonable variance in these features. Thus, some time pressure is good for creativity, but not too much (Baer & Oldham, 2006), some job demands are good for psychological health, but not too many (Noblet & Rodwell, 2009), and some telecommuting is good for job satisfaction, but not too much (Golden & Viega, 2005). In their treatise on creativity among professionals, Elsbach and Hargadon (2006) actually go so far as to propose scheduling "mindless work" into the workday so as to counter the effects of too much richness.

As many indecisive PhD students searching for a dissertation topic have learned, even autonomy, generally safely prescribed as a positive job design feature, has its limits. This is because autonomy implies choices, and a surfeit of choices has been identified as a source of negative well-being (Schwartz, 2004). Thus, Chua and Iyengar (2006) review evidence that autonomy for choice is not always preferred by those of lower socioeconomic status and those from more interdependent cultures, and that excessive options for action can create stress and even dampen creativity. Although viable theories, such as activation theory (e.g., Gardner & Cummings, 1988) and Warr's (1987) vitamin model, predict curvilinear connections between certain job design features and certain work outcomes, tests for such effects are often neglected.

Other studies support linear versions of the too-much-of-a-good-thing thesis, particularly when personal and contextual moderators reflecting susceptibility are taken into account. Chen and Chiu (2009) observed that skill variety was negatively related to the exhibition of organizational citizenship behavior (OCB). Similarly, Raja and Johns (in press) found some evidence that high-scope job holders were less inclined to exhibit OCB if they were high in neuroticism or extraversion. Most worrisome are findings that high scope jobs are associated with cardiovascular disorder and increased health care use among Type A individuals and those high on hostility (Dwyer & Fox, 2000; Schaubroeck, Ganster, & Kemmerer, 2004). Fried, Melamed, and Ben-David (2002) found that high-scope jobs greatly exacerbated absenteeism among women working in noisy environments. Such context × context interactions are equally important to understand the boundary conditions for job design prescriptions, but except for demands × control, they have been less studied than person × context interactions.

The Research Agenda

What does this brief foray into some unintended consequences of job design suggest as a research agenda? In my opinion, it would be particularly valuable to extend the criterion space for such research to include the full range of variables that might be affected by job design. Early theory and research in this domain understandably concentrated on satisfaction, motivation, and performance, narrowly construed. Given the documented decline in the volume of job design research, there is clearly a missing generation of information on how job design might affect important criteria that have been studied more recently, including OCB, corruption, learning, proactivity, and creativity. To take just one example, I have read several anecdotal accounts of how downsizing, flat structures, and large spans have contributed to corruption in organizations by reducing oversight. At the same time, it has been opined that excessively narrow jobs preempt feelings of responsibility and lead to corruption. On reflection, these apparently contradictory assertions could both be true, but I am unaware of any actual research on this matter.

Job design is ultimately about the micro-context of work, and as I have noted elsewhere (Johns, 2006), examining multiple dependent variables is a potent way to better appreciate the subtle effects of context. In particular, attention needs to be devoted to those cases in which opposing effects on work outcomes are possible (e.g., the elevation of both creativity and stress). In addition, an expanded criterion space will force attention to the aforementioned paradoxes in job design. The extended parallel lives of the job characteristics model and the job demands-control model (the former focused on motivation and the latter on stress and health) illustrate the dysfunction of studying outcomes in isolation. Grandey and Diamond's (2010) excellent treatise on how differences in job design concerning interactions with the public can result in either meaningful work or debilitating emotional labor shows the value of thinking in terms of multiple dependent variables.

Some serious thought should be given to applying a configural approach to study job design. As a package, this approach accommodates non-linearity, synergy between variables, and equifinality better than regression-oriented approaches (Fiss, 2007). Thus, it simultaneously allows for "too much" of a job feature, identifies deadly and fortuitous combinations of job features, and allows for the almost certain probability that there is more than one way to design a job to stimulate creativity, OCB, or honesty. This issue of equifinality is especially important in light of the previous discussion of multiple outcomes of job design. Hence, there may be several designs that foster good in-role performance but considerably fewer that foster both in-role performance *and* creativity.

Finally, in the past, job design has too often been treated as a phenomenon rather isolated from its surroundings, resulting in some of the aforementioned unintended consequences. This is a natural but dysfunctional consequence of the very useful goal of distilling job design into a parsimonious number of generic characteristics that can be applied across jobs. Although it is possible to separate job designs from their contexts via detailed definitions and variance apportioning statistics, there would seem to be more traction gained by embracing the inherent connection of jobs to their larger contexts (Morgeson, Dierdorff, & Hmurovic, 2010). Earlier, it was noted how occupations dictate distinct role requirements that shape job design (Dierdorff *et al.*, 2009). Some good lessons about the unintended consequences of job design might be gleaned from examining a range of outcome variables for jobs in particular organizations that violate the contextual imperative implied by modal occupational norms for job design and role requirements. One expects that there will be some negative and some positive consequences to such deviations, the former signalling poor design judgment and the latter signalling a distinct form of competitive advantage.

I conclude with the simple observation that examining the unintended consequences of job design is one viable way to better understand jobs and the relationship of jobs to their larger context. In fact, the information content of the unexpected might exceed that of the expected.

Author biography

Gary Johns holds the Concordia University Research Chair in Management in the John Molson School of Business, Concordia University, Montreal, Canada. He has research interests in job design, presenteeism, absenteeism, personality, research methods, and the impact of context on organizational behavior.

REFERENCES

Allen, N. J., & Hecht, T. D. (2004). The 'romance of teams': Toward an understanding of its psychological underpinnings and implications. *Journal of Occupational and Organizational Psychology, 77,* 439–461.

Ashforth, B. E., & Kreiner, G. E. (1999). "How can you do it?" Dirty work and the challenge of constructing a positive identity. *Academy of Management Review, 24,* 413–34.

Baer, M., & Oldham, G. R. (2006). The curvilinear relation between experienced creative time pressure and creativity: Moderating effects of openness to experience and support of creativity. *Journal of Applied Psychology, 91,* 963–970.

Barker, J. R. (1993). Tightening the iron cage: Concertive control in self-managing teams. *Administrative Science Quarterly, 38,* 408–437.

Baron, R. A. (2010). Job design and entrepreneurship: Why closer connections = mutual gain. *Journal of Organizational Behavior, 31,* 370–378. DOI 10.1002/job.607

Becker, B. E., Huselid, M. A., Pickus, P. S., & Spratt, M. E (1997). HR as a source of shareholder value: Research and recommendations. *Human Resource Management, 36,* 39–7.

Chen, C.-C., & Chiu, S. E. (2009). The mediating role of job involvement in the relationship between job characteristics and organizational citizenship behavior. *Journal of Social Psychology, 149,* 474–494.

Chua, R. Y.-J., & Iyengar, S. S. (2006). Empowerment through choice? A critical analysis of the effects of choice in organizations. *Research in Organizational Behavior, 27,* 41–79.

Dierdorff, E. C, Rubin, R. S., & Morgeson, F. P. (2009). The milieu of managerial work: An integrative framework linking work context to role requirements. *Journal of Applied Psychology, 94,* 972–988.

Dwyer, D. J., & Fox, M. L. (2000). The moderating role of hostility in the relationship between enriched jobs and health. *Academy of Management Journal, 43,* 1086–1096.

Elsbach, K. D. (2009). Identity affirmation through 'signature style': A study of toy car designers. *Human Relations, 62,* 1041–1072.

Elsbach, K. D., & Flynn, F. D. (2008). Issues of identity in collaborations among professionals: A study of toy designers. Working paper 09-08. Graduate School of Management, University of California, Davis.

Elsbach, K. D., & Hargadon, A. B. (2006). Enhancing creativity through "mindless" work: A framework of workday design. *Organization Science, 17,* 470–483.

Eriksson-Zetterquist, U., Lindberg, K., & Styhre, A. (2009). When the good times are over: Professionals encountering new technology. *Human Relations, 62,* 1145–1170.

Fiss, P. C. (2007). A set-theoretic approach to organizational configurations. *Academy of Management Review, 32,* 1180–1198.

Flynn, F. J. (2003). How much should I give and how often? The effects of generosity and frequency of favor exchange on social status and productivity. *Academy of Management Journal, 46,* 539–553.

Fried, Y., & Ferris, G. R. (1987). The validity of the job characteristics model: A review and meta-analysis. *Personnel Psychology, 40,* 287–322.

Fried, Y., Levi, A. S., & Laurence, G (2008). Motivation and job design in the new world of work. In S. Cartwright, & C. L. Cooper (Eds.), *The Oxford handbook of personnel psychology* (pp. 586–611). Oxford: Oxford University Press.

Fried, Y., Melamed, S., & Ben-David, H. A. (2002). The joint effects of noise, job complexity, and gender on employee sickness absence: An exploratory study across 21 organizations—the CORDIS study. *Journal of Occupational and Organizational Psychology, 75,* 131–144.

Gardner, D. G., & Cummings, L. L. (1988). Activation theory and job design: Review and reconceptualization. *Research in Organizational Behavior, 10,* 81–122.

Gargiulo, M., Ertug, G., & Galunic, C. (2009). The two faces of control: Network closure and performance among knowledge workers. *Administrative Science Quarterly, 54,* 299–333.

Golden, T. D., & Viega, J. F. (2005). The impact of extent of telecommuting on job satisfaction: Resolving inconsistent findings. *Journal of Management, 31,* 301–318.

Grandey, A. A., & Diamond, J. A. (2010). Interactions with the public: Bridging job design and emotional labor perspectives. *Journal of Organizational Behavior, 31,* 338–350. doi: 10.1002/job.637

Grant, A. M., Campbell, E. M., Chen, G., Cottone, K., Lapedis, D., & Lee, K. (2007). Impact and the art of motivation maintenance: The effects of contact with beneficiaries on persistence behavior. *Organizational Behavior and Human Decision Processes, 103,* 53–67.

Grant, A. M., & Parker, S. K. (2009). Redesigning work design theories: The rise of relational and proactive perspectives. *Academy of Management Annals, 3,* 317–375.

Grinyer, A., & Singleton, V. (2000). Sickness absence as risk-taking behaviour: A study of organizational and cultural factors in the public sector. *Health, Risk & Society, 2,* 7–21.

Hackman, J. R. (1987). The design of work teams. In J. Lorsch (Ed.), *Handbook of organizational behavior* (pp. 315–342). Englewood Cliffs, NJ: Prentice-Hall.

Hackman, J. R., & Oldham, G. R. (1980). *Work redesign.* Reading, MA: Addison-Wesley.

Harrison, D. A., Johns, G, & Martocchio, J. J. (2000). Changes in technology, teamwork, and diversity: New directions for a new century of absenteeism research. *Research in personnel and human resources management, 18,* 43–91.

Humphrey, S. E., Nahrgang, J. D., & Morgeson, F. P. (2007). Integrating motivational, social, and contextual work design features: A meta-analytic summary and theoretical extension of the work design literature. *Journal of Applied Psychology, 92,* 1332–1356.

Jackson, P. R., & Wall, T. D. (1991). How does operator control enhance performance of advanced manufacturing technology? *Ergonomics, 34,* 1301–1311.

Johns, G. (2006). The essential impact of context on organizational behavior. *Academy of Management Review, 31,* 386–108.

Johns, G. (2008). Absenteeism and presenteeism: Not at work or not working well. In C. L. Cooper, & J. Barling (Eds.), *The Sage handbook of organizational behavior* (Vol. 1, pp. 160–177). London: Sage.

Johns, G. (in press). Presenteeism in the workplace: A review and research agenda. *Journal of Organizational Behavior.*

Johns, G., Xie, J. L., & Fang, Y. (1992). Mediating and moderating effects in job design. *Journal of Management, 18,* 657–676.

Kiggundu, M. N. (1981). Task interdependence and the theory of job design. *Academy of Management Review, 6,* 499–508.

Morgeson, F. P., Dierdorff, E. C., & Hmurovic, J. L. (2010). Work design *in situ:* Understanding the role of occupational and organizational context. *Journal of Organizational Behavior, 31,* 351–360. doi: 10.1002/job.642

Morgeson, F. P., & Humphrey, S. E. (2006). The Work Design Questionnaire (WDQ): Developing and validating a comprehensive measure for assessing job design and the nature of work. *Journal of Applied Psychology, 91,* 1321–1339.

Noblet, A. J., & Rodwell, J. J. (2009). Identifying the predictors of employee health and satisfaction in an NPM environment: Testing a comprehensive and non-linear demand-control-support model. *Public Management Review, 5,* 663–683.

Parker, S. K. (2003). Longitudinal effects of lean production on employee outcomes and the mediating role of work characteristics. *Journal of Applied Psychology, 88,* 620–634.

Parker, S. K., Wall, T. D., & Jackson, P. R. (1997). "That's not my job": Developing flexible employee work orientations. *Academy of Management Journal, 40,* 899–929.

Raja, U., & Johns, G. (in press). The joint effects of personality and job scope on in-role performance, citizenship behaviors, and creativity. *Human Relations*.

Pfeffer, J., & Sutton, R. I. (2000). *The knowing-doing gap: How smart companies turn knowledge into action*. Boston: Harvard Business School Press.

Schaubroeck, J., Ganster, D. C., & Kemmerer, B. E. (2004). Job complexity, "type A" behavior, and cardiovascular disorder: A prospective study. *Academy of Management Journal, 37,* 426–439.

Schwartz, B. (2004). *The paradox of choice: Why more is less*. New York: HarperCollins.

Turner, Y. N., Hadas-Halperin, I., & Raveh, D. (2008). *Patient photos spur radiologist empathy and eye for detail*. Paper presented at the annual meeting of the Radiological Society of North America.

Wall, T. D., Corbett, J. M., Martin, R., Clegg, C. W., & Jackson, P. R. (1990). Advanced manufacturing technology, work design, and performance: A change study. *Journal of Applied Psychology, 75,* 691–697.

Wall, T. D., Jackson, P. R., & Davids, K. (1992). Operator work design and robotics system performance: A serendipitous field study. *Journal of Applied Psychology, 77,* 353–362.

Warr, P. (1987). *Work, unemployment, and mental health*. Oxford: Oxford University Press.

Wirtz, J., Heracleous, L., & Menkhoff, T. (2007). Value creation through strategic knowledge management: The case of Singapore Airlines. *Journal of Asian Business, 23,* 249–263.

Xie, J. L., & Johns, G. (1995). Job scope and stress: Can job scope be too high? *Academy of Management Journal, 38,* 1288–1309.

Xie, J. L., & Johns, G. (2000). Interactive effects of absence culture salience and group cohesiveness: A multi-level and cross-level analysis of work absenteeism in the Chinese context. *Journal of Occupational and Organizational Psychology, 73,* 31–52.

JOURNAL ARTICLE QUESTIONS

Journal Article 2 — Making things happen a model of proactive motivation

1. Summarise what the authors mean by 'can do', 'reason to' and 'energized to' motivational states in relation to work motivation.
2. What influence does having a 'proactive personality' have on individual motivation?
3. What influence does the environment and context have on individual motivation?
4. What recommendations do the authors make for future research in this area?

PART 4

PEOPLE, PROCESSES AND PERFORMANCE

Journal article: Wei, L-Q., Liu, J., Chen, Y-Y and Wu, L-Z. (2010), Political Skill, Supervisor-Subordinate *Guanxi* and Career Prospects in Chinese Firms, *Journal of Management Studies*, **47**(3), 437–454.

In this final section of our book, we bring together some subject areas which might, at first sight, appear disparate. Groups, leadership, power and change have typically been approached as discrete areas in many treatments of OB. However, we contend that each is pivotal to an understanding of life within work organizations. In particular, these subject areas can be viewed as *processes* that underlie practices at work. In business and management terms, these processes – all of which involve relationships – will need to be shaped in order to achieve an organisation's aims; now and in the future. In this last sense we see that the processes identified in this part of our book are ongoing and require continual management.

Groups and teams form a key part of life in work organizations. Most activities taking place within organizations are dependent on coordination and cooperation that can only be achieved by people working together. In the twenty-first century, competitive pressures have led to a renewed concern on the part of managers to ensure that groups and teams perform to their full potential. At the same time, psychologists typically point to individuals' social needs; in other words many people seek to become members of groups and gain satisfaction and enjoyment from interacting with other humans. We place considerable stress therefore, on the topic of groups and teams, which we believe underlies its importance within OB. There is a strong body of evidence showing that individuals are affected by group membership, often behaving in atypical and surprising ways. Stanley Milgram's work on group conformity showing how many people were willing to administer what they believed to be fatal electric shocks if they thought other group members were also doing so, provides a striking example of this phenomenon. This in itself would justify an extended analysis of group and team working. In contemporary organizations it is moreover, critically important to understand how groups and teams contribute to organizational effectiveness. While their effect is potentially positive, we will also point out the possible negative or dysfunctional aspects of group working.

We also address several other processes intrinsic to work organizations, namely *leadership, power and politics* and *change*. We argue that an understanding of these concepts is crucial to making sense of the reality of organizations. These are dynamic (constantly changing) processes, which involve interplay between the members of organizations and are subject to impact from events and trends in wider society. We have argued for the adoption of a contingency perspective in these and other subject areas; in other words no one model or perspective can always result in organizational effectiveness; rather, different types of leadership influence strategy and approach to change and their success depends on the particular situation.

CHAPTER 8

Groups and teams

LEARNING OBJECTIVES

After studying this chapter you should be able to:

- define groups and teams and understand the differences between them
- understand and explain how effective group and team working can contribute to organizational performance
- define the dynamics and processes that occur within groups
- explain the key features of intergroup dynamics and why it is important that managers understand them
- explain the factors that affect team performance and cohesion
- discuss the range of teambuilding activities and approaches
- describe the main types of teams that exist in an organization.

HIGH FLYING TEAMWORK

Twenty years since women were first allowed to become pilots in the Royal Air force (RAF), Flight Lieutenant Kirsty Moore made the headlines in 2009 by becoming the first female aviator to join the world-renowned Red Arrows display team. The Red Arrows, who are the public face of the RAF, perform aerobatic displays in fast jets in over 50 countries. You have to be super fit, talented and experienced (over 1500 flying hours) to join the Red Arrows, but whilst Kirsty may have grabbed the headlines in being the first woman to be selected, what will keep her in the air will be teamwork.

The Red Arrows display team is all about mutual trust and precision while flying at high speeds. Take, for example, the 'Vixen Break' – the Reds approach the crowd in tight formation, wings just feet apart, manoeuvring at speeds of up to 400 mph (720 kph). With split-second timing, releasing their trademark coloured trails, the ten Hawk aircraft fan out to form a perfect pattern in the sky – the Vixen Break. Rising vertically, the pilots pull a gruelling 7g, clenching their stomach muscles to help withstand the force. From the ground it looks absolutely amazing. Flying in formation requires incredible teamwork and trust and the pilots practice these moves as a team for hundreds of hours in order to create the spectacle that wows audiences everywhere they go.

But it's not just the pilots who make the Red Arrows spectacular, there's a whole team behind every single display. Their skills and team spirit ensure that each performance is full of energy. All Red Arrow pilots are heavily dependent on the Ground Support team – 'the Blues' (so called because of their blue flying suits). The blues are the unseen heroes of the Red Arrows and care for the aircraft themselves as well as all the equipment that goes with them. Then there is the support team that is responsible for the extensive planning and organization behind the scenes and the 'Circus' team of Engineering support staff that maintain the aircraft when the Red Arrows are on tour. Without these dedicated support teams working together often in difficult circumstances and with tight timescales, pilots like Kirsty would never get in the air. So next time you see the Red Arrows don't just marvel at the spectacle but spare a thought for the teams that keep them in the air.[1]

Questions
1. How does team working influence the performance of the Red Arrows display team?
2. In what groups do you participate and how could they benefit from better team working?

INTRODUCTION

Gathering in groups has always been a characteristic of human behaviour. We work in groups in our families, neighbourhoods, communities and educational systems. Individuals seldom, if ever, behave without being influenced by the groups to which they belong. In organizations most activities that take place require some degree of coordination and cooperation that can only be achieved through individuals working together in groups and teams. The modern workplace places great value on change and adaptation, organizations are continually under pressure to find new ways of operating in the quest for higher productivity, total quality and service, customer satisfaction and better quality of working life. The challenge of remaining competitive in a global market has led to organizations restructuring with flatter structures, wider spans of control and general reductions in the layers of management and increasing empowerment of employees. All of these aspects lead to a greater need for organizations to tap the full potential of groups and teams more creatively as critical organizational resources.

Take the example of Apple Computers. When you send a text using your Apple iPhone or check your e-mails on your Apple laptop, it is worth remembering that a team created it. The original MacIntosh computer was the brainchild of Apple's co-founder Steve Jobs, but it was a team of high-achieving members who were excited and turned onto a highly challenging task that actually turned it into reality. Together they worked all hours and at an unrelenting pace. Housed in a separate building flying the Jolly Roger, the MacIntosh team combined youthful enthusiasm with great expertise and commitment to an exciting goal. The result: a benchmark computer produced in record time.[2] And that is what groups in organizations should be all about, working together to achieve common goals.

There is no doubt that an organization's success depends in a significant part on the performance of its internal networks of groups and teams. To meet competitive demands in challenging environments, the best organizations mobilize groups and teams in many capacities in the quest to reach their full potential as high-performance systems. Most organizational goals cannot be achieved by members working alone; thus most employees spend an increasing amount of work time working with others in groups. It is therefore essential that leaders in organizations understand the nature of groups and teams and how to harness the behaviours that will lead to better performance and effectiveness if they are to meet the challenging global business environment that exists today. This chapter will help you understand groups and teams and how they work, how they contribute to effective organizational performance and will provide you with the knowledge and skills to work in and manage groups and teams better.

GROUPS IN ORGANIZATIONS

There is no doubt that groups can be important sources of performance, creativity and enthusiasm for organizations but it takes the right membership, lots of commitment and great leadership to achieve these results consistently. Just putting people together does not guarantee success; the pathways to such success all begin with an understanding of groups in organizations.

WHAT IS A GROUP?

There is no single agreed definition of what constitutes a group. One of the most popular definitions by Schein defines a group in psychological terms 'as any number of people who interact with one another; are psychologically aware of one another; and perceive themselves to be a group.'[3] Handy puts this more simply 'as any collection of people who perceive themselves as a group.'[4] However, neither of these definitions encapsulate *why* people form groups at work, so perhaps a better definition here is that a **group** is a collection of two or more people who interact with one another regularly to achieve common goals. In a group within this definition, members:

*A **group** is a collection of two or more people who interact with each other regularly to achieve common goals.*

* are mutually dependent on one another to achieve common goals; and
* interact regularly with one another to pursue those goals over a sustained period of time.[5]

Groups are important resources that are good for both organizations and their members. They help organizations to accomplish important tasks. They also help to maintain a high-quality workforce by satisfying needs and expectations of their members. Consultant and management scholar Harold J. Leavitt is a well-known advocate for the power and usefulness of groups.[6] He describes 'hot groups' that thrive in conditions of crisis and competition and whose creativity and innovativeness generate extraordinary returns.[7] In general Leavitt points out the following benefits of group work:

* groups can guide and foster innovation and creativity;
* groups sometimes make better decisions than individuals do, and can help gain commitments needed to implement such decisions;
* groups can guide members and exert control over them;
* groups can help offset the negative effects of increasing organization size;
* groups can help organizations accomplish important tasks.

Whilst groups serve useful purposes in organizations, they can have various advantages and disadvantages which are summarized in Figure 8.1.

The success of organizations depends upon the success of its groups as well as the way networks of groups interlock and work with each other. Like individuals, groups must succeed for the organization to prosper in the long run, but what distinguishes an effective group from an ineffective one?

What is an effective group?

Effective groups are groups that achieve high levels of both task performance and human resource performance.

An **effective group** is one that achieves high levels of task performance, member satisfaction and team viability. With regard to task performance, an effective group achieves its performance goals – in the standard sense of quantity, quality and timeliness of work results. For a formal workgroup, such as a manufacturing team, this may mean meeting daily production targets. For a temporary group, such as a new policy working party, this may involve meeting a deadline for submitting a new organizational policy to the managing director. With regard to member satisfaction, an effective group is one whose

Advantages of groups	Disadvantages of groups
Groups bring together people for a specific purpose.	Some groups' specific purposes may conflict with the objectives of the organisation or with those of other groups.
Groups can achieve positive synergy.	Groups may result in negative synergy, especially when there are disruptive behaviours, ambiguous roles or interpersonal conflicts between group members.
Groups can become highly cohesive and high-performance entities.	Groups can become highly cohesive but work against organisational work goals.
Individuals can collaborate to achieve a joint goal.	Some people may be able to 'loaf' in groups while others do the work.
Groups of people with complementary skills, attitudes, experiences and viewpoints may enhance task accomplishment and decision making.	Groups of people with similar opinions and viewpoints may make uncreative or poor decisions while groups of people with extreme differences, or with strong subgroups, may experience dysfunctional levels of conflict in decision making.
People from collectivist societies are likely to work well in groups.	People from individualistic societies may not work well in groups.
Organising people into groups clarifies goals and activities and enables people to work together on large and complex tasks.	The more people are organised into specific task-related activities, the more they may become different from other groups working on different goals and activities, leading to problematic intergroup relations.
Groups can be an ideal collection of people to work on particular tasks.	Groups can be the wrong size or combination of people to accomplish what is necessary.
Informal groups can enable informal networks of individuals who support one another towards achieving organisational goals.	Informal groups can have members whose goals and behaviours conflict (intentionally or unintentionally) with organisational goals.

Figure 8.1: Potential advantages and disadvantages of groups.

Source: Wood, J.M., Zeffane, R.M., Fromholtz, M., Wiesner, R. & Creed, A., (2010), *Organisational Behaviour*, Second Australasian Edition, Milton Qld, John Wiley & Sons Australia Ltd.

EFFECTIVE MANAGER 8.1

Ten characterists of an effective group

1. A sense of urgency and direction; purpose and goals.
2. A lot of work at the start, setting a tone, setting a 'contract' and/or specifying a clear set of rules.
3. A broad sense of shared responsibility for the group outcomes and group process.
4. Effective approaches to recognizing problems and issues and making decisions.
5. A high level of commitment and trust among members.
6. A balance in satisfying individual and group needs.
7. A climate that is cohesive yet does not stifle individuality.
8. An ability to confront differences and deal with conflict.
9. An ability to deal with minority opinions effectively.
10. Communication patterns with a proven track record.

members believe that their participation and experiences are positive and meet important personal needs. They are satisfied with their tasks, accomplishments and interpersonal relationships. With regard to team viability, the members of an effective group are sufficiently satisfied to continue working well together on an ongoing basis and/or to look forward to working together again at some future point in time. Such a group has all-important long-term performance potential. For a permanent work group this means that the members work well together day after day; for a temporary work group, it means the members work well together for the duration of the assignment. A classic listing of the characteristics of an effective group is found in Effective Manager 8.1 below. You might want to review these in the context of groups that you participate in and consider whether your groups display some or all of these characteristics. How critical do you think these characteristics are for achieving effectiveness or desired outcomes for your group?

GROUP SYNERGY AND GROUP ACCOMPLISHMENTS

Synergy *is the creation of a whole that is greater than the sum of its parts.*

When groups are effective, they help organizations accomplish important tasks. In particular, they offer the potential for **synergy** – the creation of a whole that is greater than the sum of its parts. When synergy occurs, groups accomplish more than the total of their members' individual capabilities. Group synergy is increasingly required in order that organizations become and remain competitive and achieve long-term high performance in the dynamic 21st century business environment. There are several benefits that groups can bring to organizations. Groups can have performance advantages over individuals acting alone in three specific situations:[8]

- when there is no clear 'expert' in a particular task or problem;
- when problems are complex, requiring a division of labour and the sharing of information;
- when creativity and innovation are required because groups tend to make riskier decisions.

Groups are important settings where people learn from one another and share job skills and knowledge. The learning environment and the pool of experience within a group can be used to solve difficult and unique problems as well as develop and share competencies. Groups are also important sources of need satisfaction (discussed in Chapter 4) for their members. Opportunities for social interaction within a group can provide individuals with a sense of security, can provide emotional support for group members in times of special crisis or pressure and can help them experience self-esteem and personal involvement through group working.

At the same time that they have enormous performance potential, however, groups can also have problems. In essence, group problems can result in 'negative synergy'. A manager should endeavour to avoid these effects. The very word 'group', for example,

Social loafing *is the tendency of people not to work as hard in groups as they would individually.*

produces both positive and negative reactions. It is said that 'two heads are better than one', but also we are warned that 'too many cooks spoil the broth'. The issue here is how well group members work together to accomplish a task. This includes a concern about **social loafing**, also known as the 'Ringlemann effect' named after the German psychologist who first popularized the phenomenon. It is the tendency of people to work less hard in a group than they would individually.[9] In Ringlemann's specific example, people were asked to pull on a rope as hard as they could, first alone and then in a group.[10] He found that, on average, productivity dropped as more people joined the rope-pulling task. He suggested that people may not work as hard in groups because their individual contributions are less noticeable in the group context and they prefer to see others carry the workload.

Social loafing is also another name for freeloading, which occurs when a person is placed in a group and removed from individual accountability. Because of differences in the degree of individualism or collectivism in different national cultures (see Chapter 1), it is possible that social loafing might occur more in individualist societies than in collectivist societies, in which people focus on working together in groups. Obviously one of a manager's interests in studying organizational behaviour is to learn how to minimize social loafing and maximize the performance contributions of any group. Ways of dealing with social loafing or preventing its occurrence include the following:

- define roles and tasks to maximize individual interests;
- raise accountability by making individual performance expectations clear and identifiable;
- tie individual rewards to their performance contributions to the group.

FORMAL AND INFORMAL GROUPS

Before exploring the role of groups at work in further detail it is necessary to distinguish between particular *types* of group. A **formal group** is an official group that is designated by formal authority to serve a specific organizational purpose to which employees are formally assigned. A typical example is a work project headed by a manager and consisting of one or more subordinates. The organization creates such a group to perform a specific task, which typically involves the use of resources to create a product such as a report, decision, service or commodity. The head of a formal group is responsible for the group's performance, but all members contribute to the required work. Managers are typically seen as playing a key linchpin role that ties groups horizontally and vertically with the rest of the organization.[11] For example, a manager of a bank branch may be 'in charge' of the bank but will also be a member of another group in which he/she isn't the head.

Formal groups are 'official' groups that are designated by formal authority to serve a specific purpose.

Formal groups may be permanent or temporary. Permanent workgroups often appear on organization charts as departments (for example, the sales and marketing department), divisions (the consumer products division) or teams (the customer services team). Such groups can vary in size from very small departments or teams of just a few people to large divisions employing 100 or more people. As permanent workgroups, they are each officially created to perform a specific function on an ongoing basis. They continue to exist until a decision is made to change or reconfigure the organization for some reason. In contrast, temporary workgroups are task groups specifically created to solve a problem or perform a defined task. They often disband once the assigned purpose or task has been accomplished. Examples are the many temporary committees and taskforces that are important components of any organization.[12] Indeed, today's organizations tend to make more use of cross-functional teams or working parties for special problem-solving efforts. The HR manager, for example, might convene a task group to investigate the possibility of implementing flexible working for all employees. Usually, such temporary groups appoint a head who is held accountable for results. Another common form is the project team that is formed, often cross-functionally, to complete a specific task with a well-defined end point. Examples include installing a new computer system and introducing a new product modification.

Informal groups
are groups that emerge unofficially and are not formally designated as parts of the organization.

Informal groups emerge without being officially designated by the organization. They form spontaneously through personal relationships or special interests, not by any specific organizational endorsement. Friendship groups, for example, consist of people with natural affinities for one another. They tend to work together, take coffee and lunch breaks together and even socialize outside of the workplace. Interest groups consist of people who share common interests. These may be job-related interests, such as a desire to learn more about computers, or nonwork interests, such as leisure pursuits or sports. Informal groups often help people get their jobs done. Through their network of interpersonal relationships, they can do things more quickly and assist each other in ways that formal lines of authority fail to provide. They also help individuals satisfy needs such as social and security needs that are thwarted or otherwise left unmet in a formal group.

STAGES OF GROUP DEVELOPMENT

Whether one is part of a formal or informal group, the group itself, as shown in many research studies, will pass through a series of lifecycle stages.[13] Depending on the stage the group has reached, the leader and members can face very different challenges. The five stages of group development (see Figure 8.2) have been described as follows:[14]

- *Forming stage*. In the forming stage of group development, the primary concern is the initial entry of members into the group. Individuals may ask a number of questions as they begin to identify with other group members and with the group itself. Their concerns may include: 'What can the group offer me?' 'What will I be asked to contribute?' People are interested in getting to know each other and discovering what is considered acceptable behaviour, in determining the real task of the group and in defining group rules.
- *Storming stage*. The storming stage of group development is a period of high emotion and tension among the group members. During this stage, hostility and infighting may occur and the group typically experiences many changes. Alliances or cliques may form as individuals jockey for position and compete to impose their preferences on the group. Outside demands, including premature expectations for performance results, may create uncomfortable pressures. In the process, membership expectations tend to be clarified and attention shifts toward obstacles standing in the way of group goals. Individuals begin to understand one another's interpersonal styles and efforts are made to find ways to accomplish group goals while also satisfying individual needs.
- *Norming stage*. The norming stage of group development, sometimes called initial integration, is the point at which the group really begins to come together as a coordinated

unit. The turmoil of the storming stage gives way to a precarious balancing of forces. With the pleasures of a new sense of harmony, group members will strive to maintain positive balance. Holding the group together may become more important to some than successfully working on the group's tasks. Minority viewpoints, deviations from group directions and criticisms may be discouraged as group members experience a preliminary sense of closeness. Some members may mistakenly perceive this stage as one of ultimate maturity. In fact, a premature sense of accomplishment at this point needs to be carefully managed as a stepping stone to the next – higher level of group development.

- *Performing stage.* The performing stage of group development, sometimes called total integration, marks the emergence of a mature, organized and well-functioning group. The group is now able to deal with complex tasks and handle internal disagreements in creative ways. The structure is stable, and members are motivated by group goals and are generally satisfied. The primary challenges are continued efforts to improve relationships and performance. Group members should be able to adapt successfully as opportunities and demands change over time.

- *Adjourning stage.* A well-integrated group is able to disband, if required, when its work is accomplished. The adjourning stage of group development is especially important for the many temporary groups such as project teams that are increasingly common in the new workplace. Members of these groups must be able to convene quickly, do their jobs on a tight schedule and then adjourn – often to reconvene later if needed. Their willingness to disband when the job is done and to work well together in future responsibilities, group or otherwise, is an important long-run test of group success.

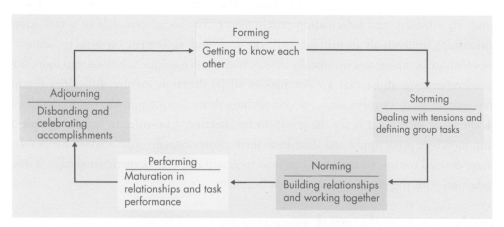

Figure 8.2: Five stages of group development.

FACTORS THAT AFFECT GROUP PERFORMANCE

One way to gain a better understanding of what it takes to become effective as a group and remain so is to view the group as an open system, as shown in Figure 8.3. This perspective depicts a group as an open system that interacts with its environment to transform group resource inputs into outputs. The environment here will consist of other individuals and groups with whom the group interacts within the organization. The group needs these resources in order to operate. The quality and strength of the input resources will affect the quality of the group output and long-term group effectiveness. A truly effective group will use resources in order to achieve its own goal but also help other groups attain theirs. Key group inputs include the nature of the task, goals, rewards, resources, technology, membership characteristics and group size.

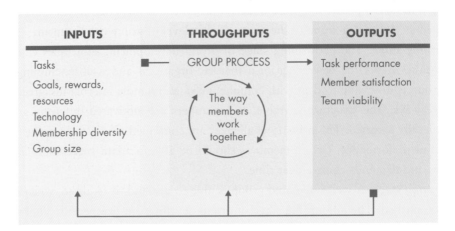

Figure 8.3: The work group as an open system transforming resource inputs into product outputs.

Nature of the group task

The tasks that groups are asked to perform can place different demands on them, with varying implications for group effectiveness. The technical demands of a group's task include its difficulty and information requirements. The social demands of a task involve relationships, individuals identifying with the task and agreement on how to achieve it. Tasks that are complex and technically demanding require unique solutions and more information processing; those that are complex in social demands involve difficulties reaching agreement on goals or methods for accomplishing them. Simply put, the more complex the task the more difficult it is for the group to be effective.[15] In order to master complexity, group members must apply and distribute their efforts broadly and actively cooperate to achieve desired results, in turn this can lead to group members experiencing high levels of satisfaction with the group and its accomplishments.

Goals, rewards and resources

Many of the insights discussed in Chapter 4 with regard to goals, needs and rewards can be applied to groups as well as individuals. Appropriate goals and well-designed reward systems can help establish and maintain the 'motivation' for the group members to work hard together in support of collective accomplishments. Conversely a group's performance, just like individual performance, can suffer when goals are unclear, insufficiently challenging or arbitrarily imposed. It can also suffer if goals and rewards are focused too much on individual-level instead of group-level accomplishments. Similarly it can suffer if adequate budgets, the right facilities, good work methods and best procedures as well as the right technology are not available.

OB IN ACTION

According to the CIPD[16] team reward 'is a just and equitable way to acknowledge the contribution made by people as team members or individuals' and with many believing that the key to successful organizational performance is teamwork, shouldn't we reward teams rather than individuals at work? Team working skills are a decisive factor when assessing and selecting new recruits.[17] Yet team pay remains a marginal reward practice even though it appears in theory to represent an ideal method of encouraging team working. So why isn't it more popular? Over 50% of organizations with team pay believe it contributes to improved performance, yet surveys suggest only 23% of employers operate a team-based bonus plan.[18] Where team pay has been introduced, employers argue that it has significantly boosted productivity whilst promoting teamwork. But it is also, as in the case of Fenner Dunlop, a UK manufacturer of conveyor belts, part of a wider reward package that gives team bonuses for productivity alongside individual rewards.[19] Others argue that whilst in theory it appears a good idea, in practice it is far too complicated and costly to implement. Most employers now manage individuals' pay progression by linking it to an assessment of an employee's performance and examining the skills and competencies that they apply to the job. Is the real problem that when it comes to pay there is no 'I' in teams, people want to be assessed and rewarded for their individual efforts and not on the performance of others? Perhaps then the way forward is to include team working as a key performance indicator when defining criteria for individual rewards?

Membership characteristics

The attributes of individual group members are also important inputs that may affect the way the group operates and its achievements. A group must have the right skills and competencies available for problem solving and to perform the task. Although talents alone cannot guarantee desired results, they establish an important baseline of performance potential. It is difficult to overcome the performance limits that result when the input competencies are insufficient to the task at hand. For example, if there is too much personal conflict it may distract the group's resources away from the task to be accomplished. In **homogeneous groups**, where members are very similar to one another, members may find it very easy to work together, however they may still suffer performance limitations if their collective skills, experiences and perspectives are not a good match for complex tasks. In **heterogeneous groups**, whose members vary in age, gender, race, experience, culture and the like, a wide pool of talent and viewpoints is available for problem solving. But this diversity may create difficulties as members try to define problems, share information and handle interpersonal conflicts. These difficulties may be quite pronounced in the short run or early stages of group development. Once members learn how to work together, however, research

Homogeneous groups are groups whose members have similar backgrounds, interests, values, attitudes and so on.

Heterogeneous groups are groups whose members have diverse backgrounds, interests, values, attitudes and so on.

confirms that diversity can be turned into enhanced performance potential.[20] The role of the manager is also important in channelling group diversity towards enhanced performance, as effective managers judge how and when to harness individual differences to foster or avoid conflict in their teams.[21] So are heterogeneous groups better than homogeneous groups? Well, that could depend on the task, as diversity has been found to improve performance in complex tasks but not in straightforward tasks[22] so the nature of the task to be completed may also need to be considered in forming effective work groups. Whatever the task, diversity will continue to present a challenge for groups and teams in the future.

Researchers also identify what is called the **diversity–consensus dilemma**. This is the tendency for increasing diversity among group members to make it harder for group members to work together, even though the diversity itself expands the skills and perspectives available for problem solving.[23] The challenge to group effectiveness in a culturally mixed multinational team, for example, is to take advantage of the diversity without suffering process disadvantages.[24] The following 'Counterpoint' provides another perspective on a phenomenon called 'homophily' that may also have an impact on group and, in particular, team working.

*The **diversity–consensus dilemma** refers to a tendency for diversity in group membership to make it harder for people to work together even though diversity itself expands a group's problem-solving capacity.*

Group size

The number of members in a group can also have an impact on group effectiveness. In larger groups more people are available to divide up the work and accomplish needed tasks. This can boost performance and member satisfaction. However, as a group continues to grow in size, communication and coordination problems often set in, such as increases in dissatisfaction, turnover, absenteeism and social loafing. Even logistical matters, such as finding time and locations for meetings, become more difficult for larger groups and can damage performance.[25] A good size for problem-solving groups is between five and seven members. A group with fewer than five may be too small to adequately share responsibilities. With more than seven, individuals may find it harder to participate and offer ideas. Larger groups are also more prone to possible domination by aggressive members and have tendencies to split into coalitions or subgroups.[26] Groups with an odd number of members may be more effective where speed of decision is paramount because they can use majority voting in order to resolve disagreements. But when careful deliberations are required and the emphasis is more on consensus, such as in jury duty or very complex problem solving, even-numbered groups may be more effective unless an irreconcilable deadlock occurs.[27]

▶ COUNTERPOINT

Too friendly to be effective?

As the old proverb goes, 'birds of a feather flock together.' Paul Davis has conducted research into the phenomenon of 'homophily' and its impacts in the workplace, including its effect in groups and teams. Homophily, a term coined in 1964 by Lazarfield

and Merton, describes the tendency of people to be with others who are similar to themselves in age, social background, ethnicity, gender, interests, geographic location and perhaps in other ways.[28]

We often draw attention to the need for diversity or heterogeneity in teams, so it can be seen that problems may arise when people cluster in smaller groups within a team. Doing this may undermine the benefits of diversity that might be gained in the team as it might inhibit the range of life experiences, ideas, opinions and attitudes that could be brought to the team process. There is another aspect to this phenomenon. Teambuilding encourages trust, camaraderie and working closely together, so it is possible that team members may become close and homophilic on the basis of their teams. That is, they may tend to cluster in their teams in other contexts, which could inhibit their capacity to gain from networking and/or working with others outside the team to achieve team tasks.

Davis's research showed that managers at a conference who did not know each other tended to sit next to people who were like themselves (based on outward features such as age, gender or cultural background). In another five-day workshop for a company, his research showed that people were six times more likely to arrive and sit with people from their own work area rather than with those from other work areas. They were slow to come back from breaks and on average 25 minutes a day was lost through this. Additionally,

work was often rushed, not taken seriously and of low quality. People spent some of their time 'off task' and sometimes the bare minimum on the task. When Davis intentionally mixed them up on the final day of the workshop, 14 out of 17 people were unhappy with the change and some were openly hostile. Yet they returned from breaks quicker (on average wasting only 12 minutes), spent more of the allotted time completing required tasks and produced better quality outcomes. A survey of the participants revealed that they achieved more away from their friends on the last day and were more focused. They networked more, took the workshop more seriously and put more effort into it. Only two of the 17 said they got nothing out of the change on the fifth day. The participants themselves acknowledged that they behaved differently when they worked with people with whom they had a lot in common.[29]

Questions

1. If homophily can affect team/group performance as described, should organizations pull back from the trend towards team-based management?

2. How can organizations build diverse but cohesive and effective teams?

3. What role is there for team leadership in managing the phenomenon of homophily?

Group and intergroup dynamics

The effectiveness of any group as an open system (depicted earlier in Figure 8.3) requires more than the correct inputs. It always depends also on how well members work together to use these inputs to produce the desired outputs. When we speak about people 'working together' in groups, we are dealing with issues of **group dynamics**; that is, the forces operating in groups that affect the way members relate to and work with one another.

Group dynamics *are the forces operating in groups that affect group performance and member satisfaction.*

Required behaviours *are those contributions the organization formally requests from group members as a basis for continued affiliation and support.*

George Homans described a classic model of group dynamics involving required and emergent behaviours. **Required behaviours** are those formally defined and expected by the organization.[30] For example, they may include such behaviours as punctuality, respect for customers and helping colleagues. **Emergent behaviours** are those that are derived from personal initiative in addition to what the organization asks of them. Emergent behaviours often include things that people do beyond formal job requirements and that help get the job done – for example, telephoning an absent member to keep him or her informed about what happened during a group meeting. Emergent behaviours are essential because it is unlikely that required behaviours will specify all the demands that arise in a work situation.

Emergent behaviours *are those things that group members do in addition to, or in place of, what is formally asked of them by the organization.*

Intergroup dynamics *are the dynamics that take place between groups, as opposed to within groups.*

The term **intergroup dynamics** refers to the dynamics that take place between two or more groups. Organizations would ideally operate as cooperative systems in which the various groups are willing and able to help one another as needed (this may not, of course, automatically occur in reality). An important managerial responsibility, therefore, is to make sure that groups work together to benefit the whole organization. Competition between groups can stimulate them to work harder, become more focused on key tasks, develop more internal loyalty and satisfaction or achieve a higher level of creativity in problem solving. Japanese companies, for example, often use competitive themes to motivate their workforces. At Sony, workers once rallied around the slogan: 'beat Matsushita whatsoever.'[31] Conversely, intergroup conflict may lead to group members focusing more on their animosities toward the other group than on the performance of important tasks.

GROUP COMMUNICATION AND DECISION MAKING

Groupthink *is the tendency of members in highly cohesive groups to lose their critical evaluative capabilities.*

Within groups communications and decision making are important functions. However, they are also important processes in the organization as a whole and for this reason they are dealt with within subsequent chapters in this book. It is important for us to acknowledge here that the dynamics of groups will affect the quality of decision making and communication and also that the functioning of groups (both in terms of task performance and group maintenance) will be affected by decision making and communication. One particular problem that can occur with group decision making is 'groupthink', when members of a highly cohesive group seek to conform and then come to think alike and/or become unwilling to be critical of one another's ideas and suggestions. This can result in poor and sometimes very costly decision errors, particularly at senior management level. Whilst many successful organizations have retained stable top teams for years, giving strategic continuity and working practices that serve the interests of stakeholders and shareholders, success can also breed over confidence and groupthink, making teams resistant to self-reflection and outside influence, which can ultimately lead to their downfall.[32] This and other group decision-making issues are discussed further in Chapter 10, but some of the many issues that might emerge are also highlighted in the following 'Counterpoint'. In terms of communication, the structure of groups and how group members work on tasks – that is, in an interactive, coactive or counteractive way – will relate closely to the types of communication networks that exist in the group: decentralized, centralized or restrictive, respectively.

▶ COUNTERPOINT

Meetings – the boredom factor

Before deciding who to invite to your next meeting, ask yourself whether you can avoid holding it in the first place. A radical proposal you may think, but only if you accept the current orthodoxy that meetings are an essential part of management.

In fact, while some meetings are essential, most are dispensable. There is credible evidence to suggest that communication and follow-up actually improve without meetings. To put it another way, meetings are often counterproductive.

Even worse is the tendency to acquiesce in whatever idea appears to have been adopted by others. This is the origin of so-called 'groupthink' – ideas that are not privately supported by any individual present, but take on a life of their own as the apparent will of the group. For instance, everyone in the room is sceptical about a new training proposal but no one has the courage to challenge it.

But are there alternatives to meetings, and would they work any better? Yes and yes, according to *Stop the Meeting I Want to Get Off*, by Scott Snair. Like several other experts on group dynamics, Snair argues that one-to-one conversations are more efficient.

How could it be faster to talk to ten people in succession than to talk to ten people at the same time?

Meeting with ten people at once is likely to be largely ineffective for the reasons discussed earlier, whereas shorter conversations with each of the ten people will achieve higher levels of communication, feedback and commitment. The one-to-ones are therefore more 'efficient' than the meeting because when someone speaks with you personally, you listen. You don't tend to drift mentally because you assume that the information is tailored to your needs. And, by default, you are also being made individually accountable.

In addition, one-to-ones are more effective because the listener has to make a contribution to the conversation. If asked a question, the listener has to engage with it mentally (by thinking) and physically (by articulating their thoughts).

Contrast this with the typical meeting. If asked a question, each member of the group of ten can remain silent without obvious breech of social etiquette; also, in a one-hour meeting involving ten people, only around ten minutes is directly relevant to each person present. The person calling the meeting may like to think that everyone should know everything being discussed, instead of giving each person only the information that is narrowly relevant to their personal role. After all, a general awareness of what others are doing would certainly be helpful wouldn't it?

But that is not how our brains function. We all specialize all of the time; we constantly filter out the 99% of information that we don't really need to know.[33]

Questions

1. What group dynamics phenomena help to explain why meetings are counterproductive?
2. If one-to-one conversations are more efficient than meetings (as claimed in the extract), is there any context in which group meetings would be necessary and/or effective?
3. If you had to call a meeting what actions would you take in order to ensure that your meeting was effective?

TEAM WORKING

*A **team** role is a pattern of behaviour characterizing the ways one team member interacts with others.*

In most literature and in organizations themselves the terms 'group' and 'team' are often interchangeable. Guzzo and Dickson argue that it is sometimes impossible to make a distinction between the two and thus it is pointless to attempt to do so.[34] But is there a difference between the two or is this a simple matter of wording? Whilst we have seen a group is made of individuals who see themselves and are seen as a social entity, a **team** is a small number of people with complementary skills, who are committed to a common purpose, performance goals and approach for which they hold them themselves mutually accountable.[35] Work groups can also be teams but they do not become a team just because that is what someone calls them. The essence of a team is *shared commitment*. Without it groups perform as individuals; with it they become a powerful unit of *collective performance*. Another important distinction is that whereas a group relies on its members to contribute to group performance and sometimes achieves synergy, an effective team is always worth more than the sum of its parts. Some suggest that groups and teams form a continuum. Groups, at one end, are collections of people whose individual efforts combine 'additively' towards the achievement of a goal. Teams, at the other end, are collections of people whose efforts combine synergetically towards the achievement of the team's particular goals as well as the goals of the organization.[36] Teams can be extremely powerful when they work well, but transforming a group of individuals into a team that can function well in any of the following settings can be hard work.[37]

Types of teams

First, there are *teams that recommend things*. Established to study specific problems and recommend solutions to them, these teams typically work with a target completion date and disband once their purpose has been fulfilled. They are temporary groups including working parties, ad hoc committees, project teams and the like. Members of these teams must be able to learn quickly how to work well together, accomplish the assigned task and make good action recommendations for follow-up work by other people. Second, *there are teams that run things*. Such management teams consist of people with the formal responsibility for leading other groups. These teams may exist at all levels of responsibility from the individual work unit composed of a team leader and team members to the top-management team composed of a CEO and other senior executives. Teams can add value to work processes at any level and offer special opportunities for dealing with complex problems and uncertain situations. Key issues addressed by top-management teams include, for example, identifying overall organizational purposes, goals and values; formulating strategies; and persuading others to support them.[38] Third there are *teams that make or do things*. These are functional groups and work units that perform ongoing tasks, such as marketing or manufacturing. Members of these teams must have good long-term working relationships with one another, solid operating systems and the external support needed to achieve effectiveness over a sustained period of time. They also need energy to keep up the pace and meet the day-to-day challenges of sustained high performance.

The nature of teamwork

All teams need members who believe in team goals and are motivated to work actively with others to accomplish important tasks, whether those tasks involve recommending things, making/doing things or running things. Indeed, an essential criterion of a true team is that the members feel 'collectively accountable' for what they accomplish.[39] This sense of collective accountability sets the stage for real teamwork, with team members actively working together in such a way that all their respective skills are well utilized to achieve a common purpose.[40] A commitment to teamwork is found in the willingness of every member to 'listen and respond constructively to views expressed by others, give others the benefit of the doubt, provide support and recognize the interests and achievements of others.'[41] Although such teamwork is essential for any high-performance team, developing and sustaining it are challenging leadership tasks (see Effective Manager 8.2). The fact is that it takes a lot more work to build a well-functioning team than simply assigning members to the same group and then expecting them to do a great job.[42]

High-performance teams have special characteristics that allow them to excel at teamwork and achieve special performance advantages:

High-performance teams excel in teamwork while achieving performance advantages.

- High-performance teams have strong core values that help guide their attitudes and behaviours in directions consistent with the team's purpose. Such values act as an internal control system for a group or team that can substitute for outside direction and supervisory attention.

- High-performance teams turn a general sense of purpose into specific performance objectives. Whereas a shared sense of purpose gives general direction to a team, commitment to specific performance results makes this purpose truly meaningful. Specific objectives, such as reducing the time of getting the product to market by half, provide a clear focus for solving problems and resolving conflicts. They also set standards for measuring results and obtaining performance feedback. And they help group members understand the need for collective versus purely individual efforts.

- Members of high-performance teams have the right mix of skills, including technical skills, problem-solving and decision-making skills and interpersonal skills.

- High-performance teams possess creativity. In the new workplace, teams must use their creativity to assist organizations in continuous improvement of operations and in continuous development of new products, services and markets.

A high performance work organization focuses on increasing people's influence on business as well as the processes, methods, the physical environment and the technology and tools that enhance their work.

The challenge for companies nowadays is to deliver, quickly and flexibly, new quality products and services in order to be able to respond to greater and changing demands from clients. One way of achieving this goal is to create not just high-performance teams but **high-performance work organizations** (HPWO). A view that is endorsed by the European Union as part of the European Union's Lisbon Strategy which aims to make the EU economy the most competitive and dynamic knowledge-based economy in the world.

An HPWO focuses on increasing people's influence on business as well as the processes, methods, the physical environment and the technology and tools that enhance their work.[43] An HPWO also implements a so-called holistic organizational approach which features flat hierarchical structures, job rotation, self-responsible teams, multi-tasking and a greater involvement of lower-level employees in decision making.

So how does teamwork contribute to achieving an HPWO? Research across the EU member states suggests that teamwork can help improve company performance.[44] People working in teams function more efficiently, are less prone to stress, make a greater effort in their work, come up with new ideas and try to improve their work. A number of European studies have shown that teamwork can also contribute to an HPWO by improving creativity and innovation, reducing turnover, increasing autonomy and increasing job satisfaction.[45] Some examples include a study of Ireland's top companies that confirmed a link between improved bottom line and HPWO;[46] in Portugal, teamwork in service sector companies contributed to increased creativity;[47] a Spanish survey of two plants in the steel sector found higher productivity in the plant that had adopted a team-based structure;[48] and in Finland, workers themselves believe that productivity improves when work is completed in groups.[49] But the evidence isn't just restricted to Europe, with study evidence from research in Egypt,[50] Nigeria[51] and Brazil[52] all suggesting that teamwork is important in creating an HPWO. It seems that organizations everywhere in the new workplace are finding creative ways of using teams to solve problems and make changes to improve performance.

OB IN ACTION

Acrobatic teamwork at Cirque du Soleil

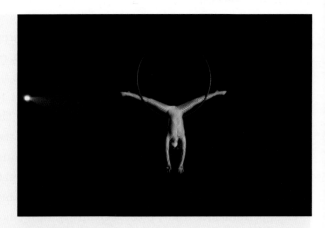

Lyn Heward is the former ambassador, creative director and executive producer of special projects for Cirque du Soleil. She speaks of how trust and creativity is so important in the diverse Cirque du Soleil team. With performers from all around the world who are experts in fields such as acrobatics, singing, diving or playing musical instruments, the circus has a lot of people with complementary skills who have to work together to make a show. Not only is a circus show artistic, but it can be very physical in that people trust in others to hold them up in a human pyramid. The people at the bottom contribute to the security and performance of the people on top. This teamwork contributes significantly to the act and, according to Heward, 'requires belief and trust in other people. It's essential.' Teamwork is also essential in creating ideas, no one individual makes the Cirque. 'Creativity is fostered in work groups where people first get to know each other and then learn to trust one another. And, in this playground, we recognize that a good idea can emerge from anywhere in the organization or from within a team. We make our shows from this collective creativity.'[53]

Teambuilding

Teamwork doesn't always happen naturally in a group. It must be nurtured and supported; it is something that team members and leaders must continuously work hard to achieve. In sports teams, for example, coaches and managers focus on teamwork when building new teams at the start of each season, but even experienced teams often run into problems as a season progresses. Members slack off or become disgruntled; some have performance 'slumps'; some are sold to other teams. Even world-champion teams have losing streaks, and the most talented players can lose motivation at times, quibble among themselves and end up contributing little to team success. When these things happen, the owners, managers and players are apt to examine their problems, take corrective action to rebuild the team and restore the teamwork needed to achieve high-performance results.[54]

Workgroups and teams have similar difficulties. When newly formed, they must master challenges as members come together and begin the process of growing and working together as they pass through the various stages of group development. Even when they are mature, most work teams encounter problems of insufficient teamwork at different points in time. This is why the process known as **teambuilding** is so important. This is a sequence of planned activities designed to gather and analyse data on the functioning of a group and to initiate changes designed to improve teamwork and increase group effectiveness.[55] When done well and at the right times, teambuilding is a good way to deal with teamwork difficulties when they occur or to help prevent them from developing in the first place.

The action steps and process of continuous improvement highlighted in Figure 8.4 are typical of most teambuilding approaches. The process begins when someone notices that a problem exists or may develop with team effectiveness. Members then work together to gather data relating to the problem, analyse these data, plan for improvements and implement the action plans. The entire teambuilding process is highly collaborative. Everyone is expected to participate actively as group operations are evaluated and decisions are made on what needs to be done to improve the team's functioning in the future. This process can

Teambuilding *is a sequence of planned action steps designed to gather and analyse data on the functioning of a group, and to implement changes to increase its operating effectiveness.*

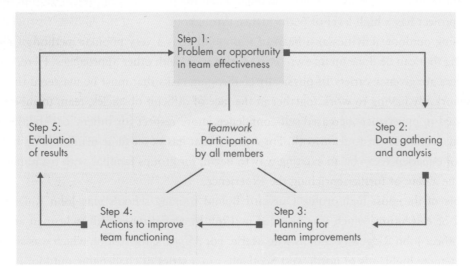

Figure 8.4: The teambuilding process.

and should become an ongoing part of any team's work agenda. It is an approach to continuous improvement that can be very beneficial to long-term effectiveness.

Teambuilding is participatory and it is data based. Whether the data are gathered by questionnaire, interview, nominal group meeting or other creative methods, the goal is to get good answers to such questions as: 'How well are we doing in terms of task accomplishment?' 'How satisfied are we as individual members with the group and the way it operates?' There are a variety of ways for such questions to be asked and answered in a collaborative and motivating manner.

Approaches to teambuilding

For most teams, teambuilding will take place as part of continuous improvement in the workplace. Managers, team leaders and group members take responsibility for regularly engaging in the teambuilding process. This may be as simple as having regular meetings that implement the teambuilding steps or having a formal review of team progress. In all cases team members commit themselves to continuously monitoring group development and accomplishments and making the day-to-day changes needed to ensure team effectiveness. Such continuous improvement of teamwork is essential to the themes of total quality and total service management so important to organizations today.

However, not all teambuilding is done at work, it may involve (particularly where there are problems, or at the formation stage) taking the team away from the work environment. This could result in structured 'away day/s' involving a formal review of the team's operation and performance, or may involve some form of 'outward bound' or fun experience such as 'paintballing' in order to improve team cohesion and effectiveness. Formal away days are often facilitated by consultants and involve group members working intensively on a variety of assessment and planning tasks that have been initiated by a review of team functioning, using data gathered through surveys, interviews and other means. One advantage of formal teambuilding interventions is that it allows companies to accelerate a process where a team can work in a cohesive manner when the pressure is on, thus ensuring that a work project has a high level of performance throughout.

Using outdoor activities as a basis of teambuilding is a very popular method of teambuilding that can be done on its own or in combination with other approaches. Here, group members are given a variety of physically challenging tasks that must be mastered through teamwork. By having to work together in the face of difficult obstacles, team members are supposed to experience increased self-confidence, more respect for others' capabilities and a greater commitment to teamwork. For a group that has never done teambuilding before, outdoor experience can be an exciting way to begin; for groups familiar with teambuilding, it can be a way of further enriching the experience.

One of the most high-profile Outward Bound training schools was John Ridgeway's School of Adventure, which was founded in 1969 by round-the-world yachtsman and ex-army officer John Ridgeway and his wife Marie. For 35 years, the school, which was situated in the remote highlands of north-west Scotland, ran a series of challenging outdoor courses encapsulating three principles: 'self-reliance', 'positive thinking' and 'leave people and places better than you find them', which over 12 000 people attended. However, his extreme methods led many to question the value and the ethics of such training programmes.[56]

Today, outdoor teambuilding encompasses a whole range of experiences including treasure hunts, paintballing in a forest, sailing adventures, high-wire courses and circus performances. Undoubtedly, taking part in these types of events can be hugely enjoyable and promote a temporary sense of wellbeing and camaraderie among team members, but this type of event should not be confused with properly thought-through and objective-based teambuilding. The key to successful teambuilding is to have clear objectives that are tied in with business strategies and performance management systems that have structured review sessions linking the experience back to the realities of the workplace.[57]

One newer approach to teambuilding in an economic downturn is that of volunteering, as shown in the following 'OB in Action'. However, as already mentioned, we must be cautious in evaluating the real effectiveness of these types of initiatives back in the workplace.

OB IN ACTION

Teambuilding in turbulent times

With training budgets being cut in what has been a difficult time for the Australian property market, Rilla Moore, like many other Human Resources Directors, has turned away from the annual conferences, weekend retreats and paintballing activities that are typical of teambuilding events. Instead she has found a far more effective way to boost staff morale, cement relationships and improve communications by getting staff at Stockland property group to take part in teambuilding experiences linked to the company's established volunteering programmes.

Stockland staff are entitled to two paid personal volunteering days each year and projects include renovating accommodation for parents of seriously ill children and mentoring and literacy work with underprivileged students across the country. This enthusiasm and commitment to the volunteer projects sees high levels of discretionary effort. The tasks strengthen teams, making people want to work together and get the job done. This attitude then flows into Stockland workplaces 'The feedback from staff is incredible,' says Moore, 'we know it works, our people want to do it and it helps people get things into perspective. We get so much out of it.'[58]

In addition to its general emphasis on improving teamwork and group effectiveness, teambuilding is useful for:

- clarifying core values to guide and direct the behaviour of members;
- transforming a broad sense of purpose into specific performance objectives;
- developing the right mix of skills to accomplish high-performance results;
- enhancing creativity in task performance.

Improving team working

Team working is a key feature of many contemporary workplaces, but multiple and shifting membership can cause complications. Team leaders and members alike must be prepared to deal positively with issues such as introducing new members, handling disagreements on goals and responsibilities, resolving delays and disputes when making decisions and reducing friction and interpersonal conflicts. Given the complex nature of group dynamics, teambuilding in a sense is never complete. Something is always happening that creates the need for further leadership effort to help improve team processes.

Entry of new members

Difficulties are likely to occur when members first get together in a new group or work team, or when new members join an existing one. Problems arise as new members try to understand what is expected of them while dealing with the anxiety and discomfort of a new social setting. New members, for example, may worry about:

Participation – 'will I be allowed to participate?'
Goals – 'do I share the same goals as others?'
Control – 'will I be able to influence what takes place?'
Relationships – 'how close do people get?'
Processes – 'are conflicts likely to be upsetting?'

Edgar Schein points out that people may try to cope with individual entry problems in self-serving ways that may hinder group operations.[59] He identifies three behaviour profiles that are common in such situations. The *tough battler* is frustrated by a lack of identity in the new group and may act aggressively or reject authority. These individuals want to understand their role in the group. The *friendly helper* is insecure, suffering uncertainties of intimacy and control. This person may show extraordinary support for others, behave in a dependent way and seek alliances in subgroups or cliques. The friendly helper needs to know whether he or she will be liked. The *objective thinker* is anxious about how personal needs will be met in the group. This person may act in a passive, reflective and even single-minded manner while struggling with the fit between individual goals and group directions. The problems of integrating new members into existing teams can pose significant problems as the 'OB in Action' section on expectation and newcomer performance in groups shows.

OB IN ACTION

Expectation and newcomer performance in groups

As the importance of teams in organizations is increasing, and as more of these teams are temporary and cross-functional types, the problem of

managing newcomer entry and integration into groups becomes increasingly important as well. Gilad Chen and Richard J. Klimoski tested a model of newcomer effectiveness in work teams with a special focus on the performance of knowledge workers. They studied the effects of leaders' expectations on newcomer performance, the effect of newcomers' personal expectations on their performance and related influences of self-efficacy, work characteristics and empowerment. Through survey research of some 70 work teams in three IT organizations in the US, Chen and Klimoski found that:

- newcomers' problems often develop within an organization and have mixed consequences;

- self-efficacy was positively related to their performance expectations;
- these expectations were positively related to newcomer empowerment; and
- this empowerment was positively related to newcomer role performance.

They concluded that work characteristics, social exchanges and newcomer empowerment help to explain the effectiveness of newcomers in groups. They suggest that this research should be extended to other types of teams, including management teams and production teams.[60]

TASK AND MAINTENANCE LEADERSHIP

Research suggests that the key to high-performance team working is the successful balancing of the needs of the task with the needs of the team (team maintenance).[61] Whilst the formally appointed group leader should help fulfil these needs, all members should also contribute helpful activities. This sharing of responsibilities for contributions that move a group forward, called **distributed leadership**, is an important characteristic of any high-performance team. Figure 8.5 describes group task activities as the various things members do that directly contribute to the performance of important group tasks. They include initiating discussion, sharing information, asking others for information, clarifying something that has been said and summarizing the status of a deliberation.[62] A group will have difficulty accomplishing its objectives when task activities are not well performed. In an effective team, by contrast, members each pitch in to contribute important task leadership as needed.

Distributed leadership *is the sharing of responsibility for fulfilling group task and maintenance needs.*

Figure 8.5: Task and maintenance leadership in group team dynamics.

Maintenance activities *are activities that support the emotional life of the group as an ongoing social system.*

Maintenance activities support the social and interpersonal relationships among group members. A team member can contribute maintenance leadership by encouraging the participation of others, trying to harmonize differences of opinion, praising the contributions of others and agreeing to go along with a popular course of action. When maintenance leadership is poor, members become dissatisfied with one another, the value of their group membership diminishes and emotional conflicts may drain energies otherwise needed for task performance. In an effective group, by contrast, maintenance activities help to sustain the relationships needed for team members to work well together over time.

In addition to helping meet a group's task and maintenance needs, group members share the additional responsibility of avoiding *disruptive behaviours* that harm the group process. Full participation in shared leadership of a team means taking individual responsibility for avoiding the following types of behaviour and helping others do the same:

- being overly aggressive toward other members;
- withdrawing and refusing to cooperate with others;
- horsing around when there is work to be done;
- using the group as a forum for self-confession;
- talking too much about irrelevant matters;
- trying to compete for attention and recognition.

ROLES AND ROLE DYNAMICS

*A **role** is a set of expectations for the behaviour of a person holding a particular office or position.*

In groups and teams, new and old members alike need to know what others expect of them and what they can expect from others. A **role** is a set of expectations associated with a job or position on a team. The roles that individuals perform in a group have an important effect on its development and cohesiveness. Within a typical group activity, such as a team meeting, members will show a consistent preference for certain behaviours and not for others. Research into the nature of team roles suggests that these roles can be categorized into those that support the task, such as problem solving, and those that support the team, such as resolving conflict. Early research by Benne and Sheats suggests that the roles performed in high-performing teams could be classified into three broad headings: group task roles, group building and maintenance roles, and individual roles. They argue that individual roles, such as dominating or avoiding need to be replaced with maintenance, building or task roles before the group can become a truly effective team.[63]

Belbin's team roles

Whilst there are many other models for identifying group roles, one of the most popular and influential is that developed by Meredith Belbin.[64] After many years of research effort, Belbin concluded that groups made up of, for example, similar personalities or entirely of creative people were less successful than those comprised of a range of roles undertaken by various members. Belbin argues that people contribute to teams in two ways:

they perform functional and team roles. Functional roles relate to technical or specialist expertise, whereas team roles relate to the type of contribution that they make to the internal workings of teams. Belbin initially identified eight team roles, which, upon further development, were expanded to nine. A team role is described by Belbin as a pattern of behaviour, characteristic of the way in which one team member interacts with another, whose performance serves to facilitate the progress of the team as a whole. He argues that it is these nine roles that team members need to fulfil if the team is to be effective and successful. For each team role Belbin identifies the strengths of the contribution but also its particular weaknesses (see Table 8.1). Clearly not all teams consist of nine people taking on one role but, regardless of team size, Belbin argues that members are able to perform two or three roles depending on the circumstances. Belbin calls these 'back up team roles', which individuals can perform if needed. For example, if the most junior team members cannot take on their preferred role of leaders, then they may look to contribute as team workers; however, as they become more senior in the organization their natural preference for a leadership role will become more dominant in group working situations.

Belbin's model has proved to be popular with HR professionals, is widely used internationally and has featured extensively in research on teams at work. This is partly because he developed a practical questionnaire, the 'Self-Perception Inventory', which he designed to help individuals assess their best team roles, and which training professionals have used to aid teambuilding in a variety of settings;[65] but also because research broadly supports his perception that the most effective teams have balance and diversity.[66] In fact, one of Belbin's key principles is that 'no one's perfect but a team can be'. Thus, Belbin stresses the benefits of diversity in teams and argues that his questionnaire is purely the starting point for teambuilding and development. There are varying views of how to build an effective team, the following Effective Manager section gives some suggestions.

EFFECTIVE MANAGER 8.2

How to build an effective team

1. Instil a sense of purpose – make sure all team members know why they are there and how their role fits into the organization's strategy.
2. Ensure that all organizational processes and procedures support team working – for example, the sharing of good practice.
3. Recruit people into teams not only for their specific skills, but also because they complement and challenge those already there.
4. Get the right leaders – team leaders have a vital role to play in the creation of high-performing teams so choose those who will guide rather than dominate the team.
5. Ensure teams have succession plans in place so that team members can develop into team leaders and can see the wider organizational picture.
6. Let them have fun! Spend time and effort maintaining the team including socializing and time away from the task in order to improve morale and strengthen relationships.
7. Involve everyone in target setting.
8. Review team performance regularly.[67]

Team role	Descriptors	Strengths	Allowed weaknesses
Completer-Finisher (CF)	Anxious, conscientious, introvert, self-controlled, self-disciplined, submissive and worrisome.	Painstaking, conscientious, searches out errors and omissions, delivers on time.	Inclined to worry unduly. Reluctant to delegate.
Implementer (IMP)	Conservative, controlled, disciplined, efficient, inflexible, methodical, sincere, stable and systematic.	Disciplined, reliable, conservative and efficient, turns ideas into practical actions.	Somewhat inflexible. Slow to respond to new possibilities.
Team Worker (TW)	Extrovert, likeable, loyal, stable, submissive, supportive, unassertive, and uncompetitive.	Cooperative, mild, perceptive and diplomatic, listens, builds, averts friction, calms the waters.	Indecisive in crunch situations.
Specialist (SP)	Expert, defendant, not interested in others, serious, self-disciplined, efficient.	Single-minded, self-starting, dedicated; provides knowledge and skills in rare supply.	Contributes on a narrow front only. Dwells on technicalities.
Monitor Evaluator (ME)	Dependable, fair-minded, introvert, low drive, open to change, serious, stable and unambitious.	Sober, strategic and discerning, sees all options, judges accurately.	Lacks drive and ability to inspire others.
Coordinator (CO)	Dominant, trusting, extrovert, mature, positive, self-controlled, self-disciplined and stable.	Mature, confident, a good chairperson, clarifies goals, promotes decision making, delegates well.	Can be seen as manipulative. Offloads personal work.
Plant (PL)	Dominant, imaginative, introvert, original, radical-minded, trustful and uninhibited.	Creative, unorthodox, solves difficult problems.	Too preoccupied to communicate effectively.
Shaper (SH)	Abrasive, anxious, arrogant, competitive, dominant, edgy, emotional, extrovert, impatient, impulsive, outgoing and self-confident.	Challenging, dynamic, thrives on pressure, has drive and courage to overcome obstacles.	Prone to provocation. Offends people's feelings.
Resource Investigator (RI)	Diplomatic, dominant, enthusiastic, extrovert, flexible, inquisitive, optimistic, persuasive, positive, relaxed, social and stable.	Extrovert, communicative, explores opportunities, develops contacts.	Over-optimistic. Loses interest after initial enthusiasm.

Table 8.1: Team role descriptors, strengths and allowed weaknesses.

Source: Belbin, R. M. (1993), *Team Roles at Work*, Butterworth Heinemann, p. 22. Reproduced by permission of Belbin Associates.

Role ambiguity, role conflict and role overload/underload

When team members are unclear about their roles or experience conflicting role demands, performance problems can occur. Unfortunately, this is a common problem in groups but it is also one that can be managed when leaders and members are able to identify role ambiguities and conflicts and to take action to clarify role expectations. **Role ambiguity** occurs when a person is uncertain about his or her role. To do any job well, people need to know what is expected of them. In new group or team situations, role ambiguities may create problems as members find that their work efforts are wasted or unappreciated by others. Even in mature groups and teams, the failure of members to share expectations and listen to one another may, at times, create a similar lack of understanding. Being asked to do too much or too little as a team member can also create problems. **Role overload** occurs when too much is expected and the individual feels overwhelmed with work; role underload occurs when too little is expected and the individual feels underutilized. Members of any group typically benefit from having clear and realistic expectations regarding their expected tasks and responsibilities.

Role conflict occurs when a person is unable to meet the expectations of others. The individual understands what needs to be done but for some reason cannot comply. The resulting tension can reduce satisfaction and affect both an individual's performance and relationships with other group members. There are four common forms of role conflict:

1. *Intra-sender role conflict* occurs when the same person sends conflicting expectations.
2. *Inter-sender role conflict* occurs when different people signal conflicting and mutually exclusive expectations.
3. *Person-role conflict* occurs when one's personal values and needs come into conflict with role expectations.
4. *Inter-role conflict* occurs when the expectations of two or more roles held by the same individual become incompatible, such as the conflict between work and family demands.

It is not only the job of the team leader but of team members to help clarify team roles and expectations in order to ensure that the team is performing effectively. This may involve negotiation of these expectations between team members. The starting point may be to agree group norms and terms of reference.

Role ambiguity *is uncertainty about what other group members expect of a person.*

Role overload *occurs when too much is expected of individuals within their role designation.*

Role conflict *occurs when a person is unable to respond to the expectations of one or more group members.*

GROUP NORMS

The norms of a group or team represent ideas or beliefs about how members are expected to behave. They can be considered 'rules' or 'standards' of conduct.[68] Norms help clarify the expectations associated with a person's membership in a group. They allow members to structure their own behaviour and to predict what others will do. They help members gain a common sense of direction and they reinforce a desired group or team culture. When someone violates a group norm, other members typically respond in ways that are aimed at enforcing the norm. These responses may include direct criticisms, reprimands, expulsion and social ostracism.

Managers and team leaders should help their groups adopt positive norms that support organizational goals. A key norm in any setting is the performance norm, which conveys expectations about how hard group members should work. Other norms are important too – for example, norms regarding attendance at meetings, punctuality, preparedness, criticism and behaviour are needed. Groups also commonly have norms regarding how to deal with supervisors, colleagues and customers, as well as norms establishing guidelines for honesty and ethical behaviour. Norms are often evident in the everyday conversations of people at work. The following examples show the types of norms that operate with positive and negative implications for groups and organizations:[69]

- *Ethics norms* – 'we try to make ethical decisions and we expect others to do the same' (positive); 'don't worry about inflating your expenses, everyone does it here' (negative).
- *Organizational and personal pride norms* – 'it's a tradition around here for people to stand up for the company when others criticize it unfairly' (positive); 'in our company, they are always trying to take advantage of us' (negative).
- *High-achievement norms* – 'on our team, people always try to work hard' (positive); 'there's no point in trying harder on our team, nobody else does' (negative).
- *Support and helpfulness norms* – 'people on this committee are good listeners and actively seek out the ideas and opinions of others' (positive); 'on this committee it's dog-eat-dog and save your own skin' (negative).
- *Improvement and change norms* – 'in our department people are always looking for better ways of doing things' (positive); 'around here, people hang on to the old ways even after they have outlived their usefulness' (negative).

TEAM COHESIVENESS

Cohesiveness *is the degree to which members are attracted to and motivated to remain part of the group.*

The **cohesiveness** of a group or team is the degree to which members are attracted to and motivated to remain part of it.[70] People in a highly cohesive group value their membership and strive to maintain positive relationships with other group members. In this sense, cohesive groups and teams are good for their members. In contrast to less cohesive groups, members of highly cohesive ones tend to be more energetic when working on group activities, less likely to be absent and more likely to be happy about performance success and sad about failures. Cohesive groups generally have low turnover and satisfy a broad range of individual needs, often providing a source of loyalty, security and esteem for their members.

Cohesiveness tends to be high when group members are similar in age, attitudes, needs and backgrounds. It also tends to be high in groups of small size, where members respect one another's competencies, agree on common goals and work on interdependent tasks. Cohesiveness tends to increase when groups are physically isolated from others and when they experience performance success or crisis.

Cohesive teams are good for their members. Members of highly cohesive teams are concerned about their teams' activities and achievements. In contrast to members of less cohesive teams, they tend to be more energetic when working on team activities, they are less likely to be absent and they tend to be happy about performance success and sad about failures. Cohesive teams generally have stable memberships and foster feelings of loyalty, security and high self-esteem among their members; they satisfy a full range of individual needs.

Cohesive groups or teams may or may not necessarily be good for an organization. The critical question is: 'how does cohesiveness influence performance?' Figure 8.6 helps answer this question by showing the relationship between team cohesiveness and team performance. Typically, the more cohesive the team, the greater the conformity of members to team norms. As you would expect, the performance norm is critical for any team. Thus, when the performance norm is positive, high conformity to it in a cohesive team should have a beneficial effect on task performance; when the performance norm is negative in a highly cohesive team, undesirable results may be experienced.

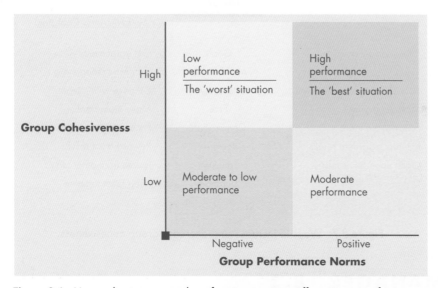

Figure 8.6: How cohesiveness and conformity to norms affect group performance.

Notice in Figure 8.6 the performance implications for various combinations of cohesiveness and norms. Performance is highest in a very cohesive team with positive performance norms. In this situation, members encourage one another to work hard on behalf of the team. The worst situation for a manager is a highly cohesive team with negative performance norms. Again, members will be highly motivated to support one another but the organization will suffer as the team restricts its performance consistent with the negative norm. Between these two extremes are mixed situations, in which a lack of cohesion fails to ensure member conformity to the guiding norm. The strength of the norm is reduced and the outcome is somewhat unpredictable but is most likely to be on the moderate or low side.

Influencing team cohesiveness

Look again at Figure 8.6. How would you feel with a team that falls into any cell other than the high-performance one? To deal with these possibilities a manager must recognize that there will be times when steps should be taken to build cohesiveness in a team, such as when the team has positive norms but low cohesiveness. There may be other times when steps must be taken to reduce cohesiveness, such as when the members of a highly cohesive team are operating with negative performance norms and when previous efforts to change these norms have failed. Managers must be prepared to deal with both situations. As shown in Figure 8.7, managers can take steps to increase or decrease team cohesiveness. These include making changes in team goals, membership composition, interactions, size, rewards, competition, location and duration. Trust is a very important ingredient for team cohesiveness and performance. The higher the level of trust in a team, the greater the cohesiveness, satisfaction and effectiveness. The genuine sharing of information can also greatly contribute to the building of trust; this simple act can demonstrate a strong commitment to the team.

How to Decrease Cohesion	TARGETS	How to Increase Cohesion
Create disagreement	Goals	Get agreement
Increase heterogeneity	Membership	Increase homogeneity
Restrict within team	Interactions	Enhance within team
Make team bigger	Size	Make team smaller
Focus within team	Competition	Focus on other teams
Reward individual results	Rewards	Reward team results
Open up to other teams	Location	Isolate from other teams
Disband the team	Duration	Keep team together

Figure 8.7: Ways to increase and decrease group cohesiveness.

EFFECTIVE MANAGER 8.3

Managing conflict in team situations[71]

- Give ample recognition to each member of the team.
- Focus on a win–win situation, in which both the individual and the team benefit.
- Establish a team charter that states the responsibilities of each team member.
- Mediate personal differences, allowing all team members an opportunity to express their views.
- Find areas of agreement to allow team members to focus on team goals rather than areas of conflict.
- Help team members to address personal behaviours that will facilitate change.

Conflict is frequently an unavoidable part of teamwork. It is not necessarily detrimental and can lead to creative solutions. However, if not managed, it can destroy team cohesiveness. Effective Manager 8.3 gives some guidance on how to manage conflict in team situations.

TYPES OF WORKPLACE TEAMS

There is no easy formula to tell us exactly what category a particular team may fit into, or for giving a precise picture of the types of teams that operate in organizations and how successful they are. However, we do know that managers in contemporary organizations are adopting many innovative ways of better using teams as effective components of organizations. The watchwords of these approaches are empowerment, participation and involvement. More recently, technology has enabled physically remote membership of teams. The following 'OB in Action' illustrates some aspects of these approaches.

OB IN ACTION

Some time ago, Mahmood Mohajer, a production supervisor at a Digital plant, realized that his work team was two weeks behind in an important production run. In the past, Mahmood would have immediately put everyone on an overtime schedule. This time, he did things differently. He first met with the production teams and outlined the problem. He then asked them to come up with a solution. 'It was a real risk', he says of the approach, 'I was so nervous I had to trust them.'

Mahmood got the team's response the following Monday. Everyone decided to work the entire weekend to catch up on the production schedule.

They had accepted responsibility for meeting the production goals and came up with a way of doing so that would meet their needs as well as those of the firm. It was still an overtime schedule but somewhat different from the one Mahmood might have set. Yet, theirs would also work…perhaps even better than his. Because it was their idea, team members were highly motivated to make their solution a real success.

Mahmood says that his new team approach requires a 'coaching' rather than a 'policing' role. One of his workers told him, 'We wanted to tell you how to fix some problems before, but you wouldn't listen to us.'[72]

The four most common types of teams are outlined in the following section: employee involvement teams, problem-solving teams, self-managing teams and virtual teams. Despite classifying them into types, it must be accepted that every team is different and may have features that overlap the types discussed here. For instance, it is possible to have a problem-solving team that is also an employee involvement team, or a self-managing team that is also a virtual team. You will come across many other terms to describe teams and/or types of teams, such as cross-functional teams and world-class teams.

Employee involvement teams

Employee involvement teams *are teams of workers who meet regularly outside their normal work units for the purpose of collectively addressing important workplace issues.*

Many of the creative developments applied to the use of teams in organizations fall into the category of **employee involvement teams**. This term applies to a wide variety of settings in which teams of workers meet regularly outside their normal work units for the purpose of collectively addressing important workplace issues. The goals of an employee involvement team often relate to total quality concepts and the quest for continuous improvement in all operations. Typically consisting of five to 10 members, these teams regularly spend time discussing ways to enhance quality, better satisfy customers, raise productivity and improve the quality of work–life.

Employee involvement teams are mechanisms for participation. They allow workers to gain influence over matters affecting them and their work. They also allow the full advantages of team decision making to become a part of everyday organizational affairs. These advantages include bringing the full extent of worker knowhow to bear on problems and gaining the commitment of these workers to implement fully any problem-solving approaches that may be selected.

For employee involvement to succeed, traditional managers like Mahmood Mohajer must commit to participation and empowerment. The opportunities for the workers to have an influence on what happens to them must be real. When accomplished, true employee involvement offers the potential for contributing positively to performance accomplishments in the new workplace. It also offers employees the advantages of filling higher-order needs such as achievement, recognition and growth (see Chapter 4).

Problem-solving teams

Quality circles *are groups of workers who meet periodically to discuss and develop solutions for problems relating to quality, productivity or cost.*

Some teams are created for the specific purpose of generating solutions to problems, for example, quality circles, taskforces and autonomous work teams. Developed as a means of generating ideas that would raise product quality by reducing defects and error rates, quality circles were a precursor to the total quality movement.[73] A **quality circle** is a small group of people who meet periodically (for example, for an hour or so once per week) to discuss and develop solutions for problems relating to quality, productivity or cost.

For the circles to be successful, members should receive special training in information-gathering and problem-analysis techniques. Quality circle leaders should emphasize democratic participation in identifying and analysing problems and choosing action alternatives. After proposed solutions are presented to management, implementation should be a joint effort between the quality circle and management.

Quality circles cannot be looked on as panaceas for all of an organization's ills, however. Indeed, a number of conditions must be met to keep quality circles from becoming just another management 'gimmick'. These include the following:

- an informed and knowledgeable workforce;
- managerial willingness to trust workers with necessary information;
- the presence of a 'team spirit' in the quality circle group;

- a clear emphasis on quality in the organization's goals;
- an organizational culture (see Chapter 7) that encourages participation.

The taskforce is another kind of team created to solve problems. **Taskforces** are temporary, created with a relatively well-defined task to fulfil. They have a more limited time horizon than that of quality circles; once the task is accomplished the taskforce is disbanded.

Teams may be formed to solve important problems or to develop new ideas. The intention is to remove these teams from the pressures and demands of day-to-day work. However, it is important to acknowledge that some teams are so intensely involved in their task that individual needs and group maintenance activities are neglected. In this sense, they would fail to live up to the criteria of being high performing and trusting over a long period.

> **Taskforces** *are temporary teams created to fulfil a well-defined task within a fairly short period of time.*

Virtual teams

Alongside the changing trends towards teamwork in organizations, other important developments have resulted in the emergence of virtual teams. A **virtual team** is one whose members work interdependently towards the achievement of a common goal across space and time.[74] Such teams can also work across organizational boundaries. They have developed in the context of new forms of organizational structures, the rapid and ongoing advances in information and communication technologies (ICT) and globalization. Virtual teams rely particularly on ICT to enable communication and team activity because they are physically separate. The degree of separation may range from being on separate floors of a large building to being located in different countries around the world. While those in the same building might get together more often, their dislocation from each other and the availability of technology allow them to work together remotely. The following example from TeleTech shows how virtual team working is becoming more prevalent.

> A **virtual team** *is one whose members work interdependently towards the achievement of a common goal across space and time.*

OB IN ACTION

A trend for companies to recruit, train and manage staff via the Internet has led to HR professionals servicing virtual teams of employees they have never met. When global outsourcing firm TeleTech set up its newly established virtual customer services branch in the UK a couple of years ago, around 700 staff were recruited online to work from home and never meet their manager face to face.

Once recruited, employees join intranet chat rooms to keep them up to date with business news and become part of a virtual community. Online operational managers regularly phone or e-mail their staff during the day. 'We were conscious that individuals working from home could feel disengaged,' said Cormac Twomey, TeleTech's managing director, 'but we use web-based seminars, self-learning modules, phone updates and virtual training rooms with online trainers, so there is always human contact amid the online environment.'[75]

There is a range of such virtual teams, including network teams, parallel teams, project or product-development teams, work or production teams, service teams, management teams and action teams. The most typical technologies used by such teams are direct e-mail, e-mail via list servers, specialized group software or 'groupware', videoconferencing and audio-conferencing.[76] Duarte and Tennant Snyder explain seven critical success factors for such teams:[77]

- Supportive human resource policies including career development, rewards for cross-boundary work and results and provision of resources for virtual work.
- Training and on-the-job education and development, especially in the use of the communication technology.
- Standard organizational and team processes including clarification of goals, costing, planning, reporting and controlling.
- Provision and maintenance of necessary electronic collaboration and communication technology.
- Organizational culture that allows free flow of information, shared leadership and collaboration.
- Leadership support that values teamwork, communication, learning and capitalizing on diversity.
- Team-leader and team-member competencies for operating in a virtual and cross-cultural environment.

In some ways virtual teams are no different from other teams, and many teams may have elements of the 'virtual team' present. However, virtual teams do face particular risks because of the context in which they operate. When people work together in the same place, they often have the same social systems and there are lots of opportunities for them to communicate face-to-face, in meetings or informal chats so that problems and misunderstandings can be easily rectified. By contrast, people who work remotely may not have this shared social system or opportunities for informal exchanges, so it is much harder for them to pick up on misunderstandings or other problems, as the 'OB in Action' from Eli Lily demonstrates.

Virtual teams also differ from other teams in the following crucial areas:

- *Dependence on technology*. Participation may be inhibited if a team member is uncertain of the technology or if equipment is inadequate.
- *Absence of nonverbal cues in communication*. Misunderstandings in communication may occur as words are read or heard in the absence of facial expressions and body gestures, for example.
- *Place of interaction*. Outside the context of a particular place and often a particular culture or subculture, there may be fewer initial shared assumptions and values among team members.
- *Timing of interaction*. Communication may be synchronous (real time) or asynchronous as members respond in their own time.
- *Degrees of public and private communication*. In a team that physically meets there is more chance that conflict, domination and other aspects of human interaction are

visible and unavoidable, whereas in virtual teams it is possible that private communications between some team members, in addition to full team shared communications, may influence behaviour.

- *Recording of the group process.* The electronic media used tend to record the group process automatically, whether or not the participants desire it, which may sometimes lead to team members exhibiting extra caution about what they are willing to 'say' in writing.[78]

OB IN ACTION

Team working at a distance

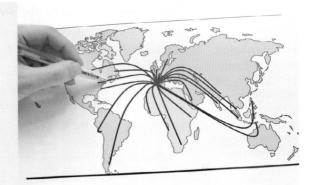

It's hard enough for people to work as a team when they are based in the same building, but for a virtual team of IT developers at pharmaceuticals manufacturer Eli Lily the challenges were far greater. The 15-strong team was split between the main site in Giessen, Germany and two smaller satellites in Berlin and London. An added complication was that members of this mixed nationality team communicated with each other in English, which for many was a second language.

Small wonder, then, that despite the team's shared professional background, there were misunderstandings – especially when the software developers used e-mail to convey complex information. Task coordination also became problematic as new members arrived. With role boundaries not always clearly defined and the added problem of distance, uncertainty arose about who was supposed to carry out activities such as updating the project database. Some tasks fell in the cracks because team members assumed someone else was dealing with them. There were also problems with dealing with customers across Europe and the server team based in the UK, because the sole use of virtual media led to misunderstanding and a lack of appreciation of each other's problems.

The team responded by clarifying and modifying individuals' roles. Teambuilding events also helped cement working relations between colleagues based at the different locations and over time led to improved communications between team members. Telephone conversations between those who had met several times began to include the social chat that goes on between people who really are part of the same team. Face-to-face meetings with customers and the server team helped resolve communication difficulties and the experience prompted team members to clarify procedures and roles for dealing effectively with them.

Although some of the lessons about managing virtual teams were learnt the hard way, the software development manager and his team were responsive to the problems they faced and dealt with them decisively. They agreed that the human and organizational aspects of virtual team working hampered effectiveness more than any inadequacies with the technology used to connect remote workers. In other words, if team roles and processes are not well structured and if diversity and relationships are ignored, no amount of technology is going to help. The principles of teambuilding still apply whether the team is virtual or co-located.[79]

Virtual teams can bring together a range of members with diverse contributions without requiring that those members be located in the same place. They have the ability to transcend borders and organizational structures. However, as for any other team, there are many other requirements for team success. Hackman[80] argues that virtual teams have the same needs and potential problems as any other team (as discussed throughout this chapter) but that it is even harder to create the right conditions for success in virtual teams.

Self-managing teams

Many organizations across the world have moved towards the concept of self-managed work teams in which employees work together as equals to solve problems and improve operations. Every **self-managing team** needs members with three different strengths:

Self-managing teams are small groups of people empowered to manage themselves and the work they do on a day-to-day basis.

* technical or functional expertise;
* problem-solving and decision-making skills;
* interpersonal skills.[81]

Self-managing teams are small groups of people empowered to manage themselves and the work they do on a day-to-day basis. They are also referred to as 'self-directed teams' or 'autonomous'. Typically, a self-managing work team is one in which the members themselves:

* make decisions on how to divide up tasks within the team;
* make decisions on scheduling work within the team;
* are able to perform more than one job for the team;
* train one another in jobs performed by the team;
* evaluate one another's job performance on the team;
* are collectively held accountable for the team's performance results.

What differentiates self-managing teams from more traditional work groups is the fact that their members have substantial responsibility for a wide variety of decisions involved in the accomplishment of assigned tasks. Indeed, the very purpose of the self-managing work team is to take on duties previously performed by traditional supervisors; that is, such things as quality control, work scheduling and even performance evaluation. The example of BDM in the following 'OB in Action' illustrates these features.

OB IN ACTION

Becton Dickinson Medical (BDM), based in Singapore, manufactures hypodermic syringes, needles, cannulas and other similar supplies for pharmaceutical industries. It prides itself on achieving its goals through mutual trust and respect and, accordingly, manages its 300-plus employees in teams. These are self-managing teams, though subdivided

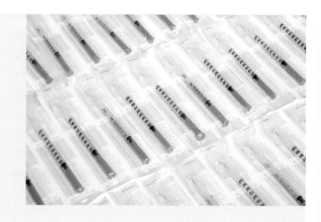

into a steering team, resource teams and process teams. As their name suggests, resource teams provide resources and are focused on achieving technical improvements, better quality, cost reduction and improvements in waste management and efficiency. Their members come from across the organization, offering a range of skills and expertise. The process teams directly produce the products and their members include technicians, programmers, auditors, storemen, clerks and administrative assistants. Team leaders encourage participation, decision making and focus on performance, targets and evaluation of results. They have authority and responsibility to prioritize their activities, change methods and procedures to meet standards, safety and customer requirements, to schedule their own activities and maintenance and many other aspects of their work.[82]

Well-designed, step-by-step methods of developing self-managed work teams can move authority and responsibility to all levels, allow employees to manage their own activities and help managers feel more comfortable with the process of empowering employees. This typically assumes that the proper foundations have been laid and the proper culture exists to allow an organization to begin this process.[83]

The establishment and implementation of the concept require a number of steps. These may include:

- learning about the self-managing work team concept;
- conducting a readiness assessment to determine if teams are right for the culture;
- communicating to employees the organization's vision and values as they relate to empowerment and teams;
- taking the organization through the workplace redesign process;
- implementing the redesign;
- evaluating the progress of self-managing work teams.

Organizing into self-directed work teams requires planning, selecting the right team members and leaders, designing teams for success, training continually and carefully managing the shift of power and responsibilities from leaders to team members.

Self-managing teams operate with fewer layers of management than do traditional organizational structures (see also Chapter 6). Research shows that, in comparison with individuals with no participation in a team, members of self-directed teams are significantly more likely (than nonmembers) to report that teams have increased profits, improved customer service and boosted the morale of both employees and management.[84]

When self-managing teams are embedded within an organization, a number of benefits are expected. Among the advantages that may be realized are:[85]

- improved productivity and production quality, and greater production flexibility;
- faster response to technological change;

- fewer job classifications and fewer management levels;
- lower employee absenteeism and turnover;
- improved work attitudes.

Because a self-managing team really does manage itself in many ways, there is no real need for the former position of supervisor. Instead, a team leader usually represents the team when dealing with higher-level management. The possible extent of this change is shown in Figure 8.8, where the first level of supervisory management has been eliminated and replaced by self-managing teams. Note also that many traditional tasks of the supervisor have been reallocated to the team. Thus, for people learning to work in such teams for the first time, and for those managers learning to deal with self-managing teams rather than individual workers, the implications can be quite substantial. Perhaps the most important prerequisite is for team members' jobs to be interdependent. Administrative systems must be able to record performance based on team accomplishments. At the same time, these systems should also enable rewards to be given to team members over time periods that may vary depending on the nature of team assignments. Self-managed work teams differ from traditional work groups in that the team, rather than the first-line supervisor, controls the critical management processes that typically include:

- planning
- organizing

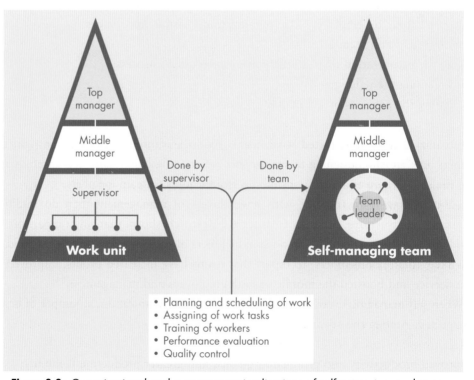

Figure 8.8: Organizational and management implications of self-managing work teams.

- directing
- staffing.

Typically these teams move through five stages of development as they grow from new creations to mature, fully functioning groups over a period. To reach a fully functioning stage teams may need to undergo training that includes communication, administrative and technical skills. Progressive levels of training in these areas through each of the stages of development become the driving force for team growth and development

TEAM LEADERSHIP

Contemporary research recommends moving beyond self-managed teams to self-leading teams. Self-leading team members should have more freedom and authority to make decisions, independent of external supervision. Leaders should not compromise team membership processes by imposing control, but rather encourage and facilitate the team's self-managing capacity.[86] This capacity for self-leading is not just anchored in the joint actions of team members but also rests on the development of individuals within the team who are better equipped to self-manage and self-lead. Such an approach appreciates that team members are competent individuals who may be willing and interested in playing a role in the strategic direction of the organization as well as influencing their own specific work performance. If self-leading teams are also oriented towards the organization's strategy, they will be able to operate effectively on the organization's behalf without constant referral to higher-level leaders.

A distinguishing feature of self-leading teams is that workers perform work more for the natural (intrinsic) rewards that are built into the task than to receive externally administered rewards. However, self-leading, team-based work systems can only work under two fundamental conditions:

- a significant involvement of the workforce in determining the direction of the organization as well as pursuing that direction;
- an opportunity for the work teams to influence that direction, especially as it relates to their specific work performance.

CONCLUSION

The study of groups and teams is pivotal within OB. If we believe that people have social needs for affiliation then we must pay close attention to academic work in this subject area, both to explain attitudes and behaviour at work and as a means to enhance worker performance and achievement of organizational goals or, more accurately, the goals of the dominant coalition within organizations. We have set out the distinctions between groups and teams and examined different types of both categories and the ways in which groups and teams develop. Groups and teams have both potential advantages and dangers within the workplace. Managers need to have an understanding of groups and teams in order to deploy them effectively.

SUMMARY

LEARNING OBJECTIVE 1
Groups and teams

A group is a number of people who interact with one another for a common goal whereas a team is a group of people who function as a unit. Groups can be either formal ('official groups' that are created by the organization) or informal ('unofficial' groups which emerge spontaneously). A team is a small group of people with complementary skills who work together as a unit to achieve a common purpose for which they hold themselves collectively accountable

LEARNING OBJECTIVE 2
Effective group and team working

Group effectiveness occurs when groups are able to achieve high levels of both task performance and human resource maintenance. Within groups, synergy occurs when a group is able to accomplish more than its members would accomplish individually. However, disruptive or negative behaviours such as social loafing (when individual members do not work as hard as they might otherwise) sometimes occur. Groups can be viewed as open systems interacting with their environments. Group effectiveness involves success in transforming a variety of inputs to the group (such as organizational setting, nature of the task, group membership characteristics and size) into group outputs (task performance and human resource maintenance) through the group process. The group processes or group dynamics represent the internal processes of the group.

Teams operate on three levels so that members engaged in team tasks are also concerned with individual needs and the maintenance of the team. Teams can operate to make or do things, or to run things in an organization. The most effective teams have members with a balance of complementary skills and strengths so that they can achieve synergy.

LEARNING OBJECTIVE 3
Group process and dynamics

Group dynamics are the forces operating within groups that affect task performance and human resource maintenance. They are the internal processes through which members work together to accomplish the transformation of group inputs into group outputs. The terms 'group dynamics' and 'group processes' are often used interchangeably. The behaviours within groups may be required or they may be emergent, additional behaviours. All groups pass through various stages in their lifecycles. Five different stages of group development pose somewhat distinct management problems. Groups in the forming stage have problems managing individual entry. The storming stage introduces problems of managing expectations and status. Groups in the norming stage have problems managing member relations and task efforts. Groups in the performing stage encounter problems managing continual improvement and self-renewal. Groups in the adjourning stage have problems managing task completion and the process of disbanding. Group norms or standards of behaviour will impact upon the behaviour of all group members. Group roles relating to particular positions in the group describe the expected behaviours for individuals in those roles. Emotions and patterns of communication and decision making are also elements of group dynamics.

LEARNING OBJECTIVE 4
Intergroup dynamics

Intergroup dynamics are the forces that operate between two or more groups. Although groups are supposed to cooperate in organizations, things do not always work this way. Groups can become involved in dysfunctional conflicts and competition. Sometimes, the origins of these conflicts lie in work flow interdependencies; at other times, the origins can be traced to differing group characteristics. Such things as status, time and goal orientations, reward systems and resource availabilities can all make a difference in the way in which groups work together. Managers must be aware of the potential for problems in intergroup relations and know how to deal with them, even as they recognize that some competition can be good. The disadvantages of intergroup competition can be reduced through management strategies to direct, train and reinforce groups to pursue cooperative actions instead of purely competitive actions.

LEARNING OBJECTIVE 5
Team performance and cohesiveness

An important aspect of any team is the set of norms within which it operates. Norms are rules or standards of member behaviour; they are ideas or beliefs about what is appropriate behaviour for team members. Norms identify the way in which 'loyal' members are supposed to behave. As such, they can exert a major influence on teams when members adhere to them. The clarification of roles is important for all members of work teams. Individuals have a preferred team role as well as backup roles that they can perform in order to contribute to team effectiveness. Role ambiguities and conflicts create anxieties and stress, and can detract from performance and personal satisfaction. Cohesiveness is a measure of the attractiveness of a team for its members. In a highly cohesive team, members value their place in the team and are very loyal to it. Thus, an important rule of thumb is that members of highly cohesive teams conform to team norms. Consequently, the combination of the team performance norms and level of cohesiveness can reveal a lot about its performance potential. The most favourable situation for any manager or team leader is to be in charge of a highly cohesive team with positive performance norms; the positive norms point behaviour in desired directions and the high cohesiveness creates desires to live up to the expectations set by these norms. Good managers are able to influence team cohesiveness in ways that support the accomplishment of long-term team effectiveness.

LEARNING OBJECTIVE 6
Teambuilding approaches

Teambuilding is a series of planned action steps designed to gather and analyse data on the functioning of a team. It is also about implementing changes to increase the team's operating effectiveness. Teamwork occurs when members of a team work together in a way that represents certain core values, all of which promote the use of skills to accomplish common goals. Teambuilding is thus a way of building the capacity for teamwork and high performance. The teambuilding process is participative and engages all team members in identifying problems and opportunities, planning appropriate actions, making individual commitments to implement these actions and conducting appropriate evaluation and feedback activities. Teambuilding can involve brainstorming to generate uninhibited ideas, facilitators to raise self-awareness and group awareness and training to develop team skills. Some specific teambuilding processes are away days, continual improvement and outdoor experiences.

LEARNING OBJECTIVE 7
Types of teams

An employee involvement team is any team whose members meet regularly outside of their formal task assignments to address important work-related problems and concerns. Most typically, these teams deal with issues involving total quality management and the quest for continual improvement in operations. Popular types of problem-solving teams are the quality circle, the taskforce and the autonomous work team. The latter was the precursor to the self-managed work team. A self-managing team is a work group whose members collectively take responsibility for performing the group task and making many of the 'supervisory' decisions relating to task performance on a day-to-day basis. The team members, in the full sense of the word, 'manage' themselves. The traditional level of supervisory management is eliminated and in its place the work team agrees to accept responsibility for self-management. Members of this team will plan, complete and evaluate their own work; they will collectively train and evaluate one another in task performance; they will share tasks and responsibilities and they may even determine one another's pay grades. Such teams are based on the concept of empowerment and offer another creative way to allow people to become more involved in important decisions affecting their work. Under the right circumstances, self-managing teams can contribute to improved productivity for organizations and improved quality of working life for their members. Virtual teams have members who work interdependently towards common goals even though they are not together in the same place at the same time.

CHAPTER 8 STUDY GUIDE

Now that you have read this chapter, you should be able to apply and further develop your knowledge by undertaking the following activities set out over the next few pages: test your knowledge questions, an individual activity and an end-of-chapter case study..

Please also go to this book's website: **www.wileyeurope.com/college/french** to find further material which will enhance your understanding and enable you to assess your knowledge.

TEST YOURSELF

1. Outline the different types of groups that can exist in organizations and provide your own example of each.
2. Explain the key differences between teams and groups and the reasons organizations might wish to instigate teams.
3. Explain how the size of a group or team might affect group processes and effectiveness.
4. Explain the difference between forming and performing in the group development stages.
5. What are the likely performance outcomes for a highly cohesive team and how can team cohesion be increased or decreased?
6. Compare and contrast employee involvement teams and self-managed teams.
7. If groups are to create positive synergy in the accomplishment of organizational tasks, what must managers do to overcome disruptive behaviours?
8. Until recently your group of seven members has been operating successfully and you felt that it was achieving high levels of effectiveness. However, since two members left your team (and the organization) to go to other jobs and you replaced them with two new members (one from outside the organization and one from another organizational section), there has been less group cohesion and more conflict. Discuss the reasons why these changes might have occurred and use theories and concepts about groups to explain them.
9. Your organization operates with four key groups: corporate services, sales, finance and production. Recently there have been problems with achieving its production targets because there is a shortage of workers; the corporate services group has been unable to replace departing employees rapidly enough. Sales are unhappy because they are unable to meet orders for stock, and finance is becoming increasingly stressed about the lack of cash flow in the business. What are the likely work flow relationships between each group and why might they cause problems?

10. Your team leader is always pushing your work group to work harder, to be more productive and to be the most successful production team in the company. You and your fellow team members just laugh at him and get on with your work. You feel you are all productive and there's no need to work any harder. You get your weekly pay and working harder won't change that. What is the likelihood that the team could be more productive and what could the manager do to improve productivity?

11. Your organization produces linen household goods. In the production of these goods, groups of 15–20 employees typically work in a production unit with a supervisor who gives them frequent directions about what is required. The organization has decided to go towards a model of self-managing teams after trialling it successfully in the finance and human resources departments. What are the likely changes that employees will face in changing to this way of working and how should management introduce the changes?

12. Your team is very close and members of the team will do anything to help each other out, including covering up for each other if there is a crisis or poor performance. What issues are there for the performance of the group?

13. You have a team of seven that operates in several different cities in your country. Your country is ethnically diverse and the level of knowledge of technological advances in communication and information technology is uneven across different ethnic groups owing to their socioeconomic position in society. Since the success of the team depends on using new technology to communicate, what can you do to encourage full and equal participation by team members and what will you do to build them into a team?

INDIVIDUAL ACTIVITY

Identifying norms that influence teams

Objectives
1. To help you determine the norms operating in an organization.
2. To assess the strength of response to particular norms.
3. To help clarify the importance of norms as influences on team behaviour.

Total time: 60 minutes.

Procedure
1. Choose an organization that you have worked for or of which you are closely aware.
2. Insert each of the statements below into the following question:

If an employee in your organization were to [insert statement here], most other employees would, too.

Statements

(a) show genuine concern for the problems that face the organization and make suggestions about solving them (organizational/personal pride)

(b) set very high personal standards of performance (performance/excellence)

(c) try to make the work group operate more like a team when dealing with issues or problems (teamwork/communication)

(d) think of going to a supervisor with a problem (leadership/supervision)

(e) evaluate expenditure in terms of the benefits it will provide for the organization (profitability/cost effectiveness)

(f) express concern for the wellbeing of other members of the organization (colleague/associate relations)

(g) keep a customer or client waiting while looking after matters of personal convenience (customer/client relations)

(h) criticize another employee who is trying to improve things in the work situation (innovativeness/creativity)

(i) actively look to expand their knowledge to be able to do a better job (training/development)

(j) be perfectly honest in answering this questionnaire (candor/openness).

3. For each statement in point 2 above, indicate your response in terms of A, B, C, D or E.

A Strongly agree or encourage it.

B Agree with it or encourage it.

C Consider it unimportant.

D Disagree with or discourage it.

E Strongly disagree with or discourage it.

Evaluation

Review your results to decide whether the organization is likely to provide a suitable environment for effective teams.

INTRODUCING TEAMS AT FLETCHER ALUMINIUM

English is a second language for 85% of the 150 manufacturing staff at the New Zealand based company Fletcher Aluminium. Whilst most have basic English skills, much of the time staff used to speak their own languages on the job which, while helpful in keeping the workforce engaged with one another, also meant management was often unaware of issues. At team meetings where employees

were encouraged to give their ideas on how work practices could be improved, most staff members were either too shy or lacked confidence to speak up. This lack of confidence and understanding became a potential barrier to be overcome when the company decided to introduce a new philosophy and build self-managed teams. It wanted teams to make their own decisions rather than being told what to do, but how do you achieve this when a large percentage of the workforce can't communicate with each other?

The answer lay in providing literacy support for its staff, and the company linked up with an external education provider 'Workbase' to provide this communications training. 'We decided we could handle 20 participants at one time,' explains HR manager Warwick Milbank, 'we asked for 20 volunteers and got 40.' Graduates of the programme are presented with a certificate in a special morning tea celebration and whilst Milbank is reluctant to quantify any figures, he says that the programme has definitely improved productivity. Health and safety has improved too. 'We have had two years now without a lost time accident,' he says.

Each course lasts 48 weeks and employees must do some of the learning in their own time, but there are no complaints as the benefits flow through to their life outside work. The training has meant that they can now help their children with their homework, use the family computer or talk to their bank manager – things they did not have the confidence to do before.

Each course starts with setting goals explains Marisa Maclachlan, Workbase's tutor. 'I give people an idea of what to expect and let them know the company goals – why we are here – so they understand within the context of what the company wants to achieve.' Any English language teaching is in the context of other topics such as health and safety and hazard identification. For example, participants are encouraged to identify potential hazards at work and then are shown how to fill out hazard reporting forms. These are then fed back to the company health and safety manager, who is very clear that he wants to hear about any hazard however small.

'Smart' (specific, measurable, achievable, realistic and timely) goals are introduced. Communication styles are discussed and participants are encouraged to be assertive. Listening skills including good questioning technique, clarifying and paraphrasing are also taught.

Maclachlan says she has found that many participants have a fear of computers. 'In the three years I have been here we have gone from having only a couple of people in the team working with the computer to everyone on the factory floor being able to process orders in their area. Some participants now take minutes at their team meeting and type them for distribution – something they would not have been able to do previously.'

Sione Ika is one success story from the Workbase training. 'It has encouraged me to talk as much as I can and to listen properly whilst others are talking to me.' When he first joined Fletcher Aluminium he used to listen to other staff members and watch what they were doing; now he can follow written instructions. 'When I first came here it was a new environment with new people and not enough friends. A lot of the time I kept my mouth shut and listened. Now I argue with everybody. I have more friends,' Ika says. Those arguments are not a sign of a bad attitude; on the contrary, it shows that Ika is getting much more involved in how the workplace is run, actively participating in the team and contributing his own ideas. As a result of the course Ika is continuing his studies and hopes to go on to university to study commerce at the end of his university access course.[87]

Questions

1. Why did Fletcher Aluminium introduce the communication skills course prior to introducing a self-managing teams programme?
2. If team members are actively contributing to team meetings, how might this help improve teamwork and productivity?
3. In the communications skills course, what skills are taught that help establish desired team norms?
4. What outcomes are attributed to the course in terms of benefits for individual workers, the team and the organization?

SUGGESTED READING

West, M. A., Tjosvold, T. & Smith K. G. (eds) (2005), *The Essentials of Teamworking: International Perspectives*, John Wiley & Sons, Ltd: Chichester. This text provides further discussion and analysis of team working in an international context. It has a good chapter on social loafing.

Nijstad, B. A. (2009), *Group Performance*, 2nd edn, Psychology Press: New York. This text examines group working from a psychological perspective.

Fineman, S., Sims, D. & Gabriel, Y. (2005), Us and Them, in *Organizing and Organizations*, 3rd edn, Sage: London. This provides a distinctive take on the topic, including some illuminating first-hand accounts of working in groups.

END NOTES

1. Source: www.raf.mod.uk/careers (accessed 4 January 2010).

2. Information from Kirkpatrick, D. (1998), The Second Coming of Apple, *Fortune*, 9 November. See also Linzmeyer, O. and Linzmeyer, O. W. (2004), *Apple Confidential 2.0: The Definitive History of the World's Most Colourful Company*, No Starch Press: San Francisco; Cruikshank, J. L. (2005), *The Apple Way*, McGraw-Hill: New York.

3. Schein, E. H. (1988), *Organizational Psychology*, 3rd edn, Prentice Hall: Englewood Cliffs, p. 145.

4. Handy, C. (1993), *Understanding Organizations*, Penguin Books: Harmondsworth.

5. For a good discussion of groups and teams in the workplace, see Katzenbach, J. R. & Smith, D. K. (1993), The discipline of teams. *Harvard Business Review*, March/April, 111–120; see also Stewart, G. L., Manz, C. C. & Sims, H. P. (1999), *Team Work and Group Dynamics*, John Wiley & Sons, Inc.: New York.

6. Leavitt, H. J. & Lipman-Blumen, J. (1995), Hot groups. *Harvard Business Review*, July/August, 109–116.

7. See, for example, Lawler, E. E. III (1986), *High-Involvement Management*, Jossey-Bass: San Francisco.

8. Shaw, M. E. (1976), *Group Dynamics: The Psychology of Small Group Behaviour*, 2nd edn, McGraw-Hill: New York.

9. Latané, B., Williams, K. & Harkins, S. (1978), Many hands make light the work: the causes and consequences of social loafing. *Journal of Personality and Social Psychology*, 37, 822–832; Weldon, E. & Gargano, G. M. (1985), Effort in additive task groups: the effects of shared responsibility on the quality of multi-attribute judgments. *Organizational Behaviour and Human Decision Processes*, 36, 348–361; George, J. M. (1992), Extrinsic and intrinsic origins of perceived social loafing in organizations. *Academy of Management Journal*, March, 191–202; Duncan, W. J. (1994), Why some people loaf in groups while others loaf alone. *Academy of Management Executive*, 8, 79–80.

10. Kravitz, D. A. & Martin, B. (1986), Ringelmann rediscovered. *Journal of Personality and Social Psychology*, 50, 936–941.

11. Likert, R. (1961), *New Patterns of Management*, McGraw-Hill: New York.

12. For a good discussion of taskforces see Ware, J. (1977), Managing a task force. Note 478–002, Harvard Business School.

13. See, for example, Bradford, L. P. (1997), *Group Development*, 2nd edn. Jossey-Bass: San Francisco.

14. Heinen, J. S. & Jacobson, E. (1976), A model of task group development in complex organization and a strategy of implementation. *Academy of Management Review*, 1, October, 98–111; Tuckman, B. W. (1965), Developmental sequence in small groups. *Psychological Bulletin*, 63, 384–399; Tuckman, B. W. & Jensen, M. A. C. (1977), Stages of small group development revisited. *Group and Organization Studies*, 2, 419–427.

15. Herold, D. M. (1979), The effectiveness of work groups, in *Organizational Behaviour* (ed. S. Kerr), John Wiley & Sons, Inc.: New York, p. 95; see also the discussion of group tasks in Manz, C. C. & Sims, H. P. (1999), op. cit., pp. 142–143.

16. CIPD (2009) Factsheet on Team Reward www.cipd.co.uk/subjects/pay/general/tmreward.htm (accessed 21 December 2009), CIPD: London

17. Carty, M. (2009), Case study: Making team bonuses pay at Fenner Dunlop. *IRS employment review* Issue 914, 23 January 2009.

18. CIPD (2009), *Reward Management Annual Survey Report 2009*, CIPD: London.

19. Carty op. cit.

20. Ilgen, D. R., LePine, J. A. & Hollenbeck, J. R. (1997), Effective decision making in multinational teams, in *New Perspectives on International Industrial/Organizational Psychology* (eds P. C. Earley & M. Erez), New Lexington Press: San Francisco; Watson, W. (1993), Cultural diversity's impact on interaction process and performance. *Academy of Management Journal*, 16.

21. Behfar, K. (2008), *Conflict in Organizational Groups: New Directions in Theory and Practice*, Kogan-Page: London.

22. Higgs, M., Plewnia, U. & Ploch, J. (2005), Influence of team composition and task complexity on team performance. *Team Performance Management,* **11** (7/8), 227–250.

23. Argote, L. & McGrath, J. E. (1993), Group processes in organizations: continuity and change, in *International Review of Industrial and Organizational Psychology* (eds C. L. Cooper & I. T. Robertson), John Wiley & Sons, Inc.: New York, pp. 333–389.

24. See Ilgen, D. R., LePine, J. A. & Hollenbeck, J. R. (1997), op. cit., pp. 377–409.

25. Katzenbach, J. R. & Smith, D. K. (1993), op. cit.

26. Shaw, M. E. (1976), op. cit.

27. Thomas, E. J. & Fink, C. F. (1969), Effects of group size, in *Readings in Organizational and Human Performance* (eds L. L. Cummings & W. E. Scott), Irwin: Homewood, IL, pp. 394–408.

28. Davis, P. (2005), Mix to match. *HR Monthly,* September, 42–43.

29. Ibid.

30. Homans, G. C. (1950), *The Human Group,* Harcourt Brace: New York.

31. Producer power. *The Economist,* 4 March 1995, p. 70.

32. Butler, M. (2007), Work is a team sport – but beware of group think that ignores the needs of the organization. *People Management Magazine,* 29 November, p. 43.

33. Purtill, T. (2007), Extract from 'Meeting alternatives'. *Management Today,* April, p. 36.

34. Guzzo, R. A. & Dickson, M. J. (1996), Teams in organisations: recent research on performance and effectiveness. *Annual Review of Psychology,* **47**, 307–338.

35. Katzenbach, J. R. & Smith, D. K. (1999), *The Wisdom of Teams: Creating the High Performance Organisation,* HarperCollins: New York.

36. Senior, B. & Swailes, S. (2004), The dimensions of management team performance: a repertory grid study. *Journal of Productivity and Performance Management,* **53** (4), 317–333.

37. Katzenbach, J. R. & Smith, D. K. (1993a), The discipline of teams. *Harvard Business Review,* March/April, 111–120; Katzenbach, J. R. & Smith, D. K. (1993b), *The Wisdom of Teams: Creating the High-Performance Organization,* Harvard Business School Press: Boston, MA.

38. See also Katzenbach, J. R. (1997), The myth of the top management team. *Harvard Business Review,* **75** (November/December), 83–91.

39. Katzenbach, J. R. & Smith, D. K. (1993a) op. cit. and (1993b) op. cit.

40. For a good overview, see Stewart, G. L., Manz, C. C. & Sims, H. P. (1999), *Team Work and Group Dynamics,* John Wiley & Sons, Inc.: New York.

41. Katzenbach, J. R. & Smith, D. K. (1993a), op. cit., p. 112.

42. Developed from ibid (1993a), pp. 118–119.

43. Burton, B. *et al.* (2005), High performance workplace defined, Gartner 2005, available from: www.microsoft.com/business/peopleready/innovation/insight/hpworkplace.mspx (accessed 22 December 2009).

44. Kyzlinkova, R., Dokulilova, L. & Kroupa, A. (2007), *Teamwork and High Performance Work.* European Working Conditions Observatory, Czech Republic, available from www.eurofound.europa.eu (accessed 22 December 2009).

45. Kyzlinkova *et al.* op. cit.

46. Dobbins, T. (2008), High-performance work systems can boost working conditions and productivity, www.eurofound.europa.eu/ewco/2008/02/IE0802029I.htm (accessed 22 December 2009).

47. Curral, L. A. & Chambel, M. J. (1999), Group processes in innovation teams. *Psicologia,* **13** (1–2), 153–192.

48. Galve Gorriz, C. & Ortega Lapiedra, R. (2000), *Team work and business performance: An empirical analysis at production plant level,* Faculty of Economics and Business Science, University of Zaragoza, Spain.

49. Tilastokeskus (Statistics Finland) (2003), *Quality of working life survey 2003.*

50. El-Kot, G. & Leat, M. (2005), Investigating Team Work in the Egyptian Context. *Personnel Review,* **34** (2), 246–261.

51. Afolabi, O. A. & Ehigie, B. O. (2005), Psychological diversity and team interaction processes: A study of oil-drilling work teams in Nigeria. *Team Performance Management,* **11** (7/8), 280–301.

52. Robson, S. R. (2010), Changing the imbalance of power: high performance work systems in Brazil. *Employee Relations,* **32** (1), 74–88.

53. Adapted from M. Stanton interviewing L. Heward, 'High Flying'. *HR Monthly*, May 2008, pp. 38–43 and Irupa Tessolin (2008), *Igniting the Creative Spark*, www.selfgrowth.com/articles (accessed 22 December 2009).

54. Johnson, R. (2000), The Beverage Report. *People Management*, 30 March.

55. For an interesting discussion of sports teams see Fagenson-Eland, E. (2001), The National Football League's Bill Parcells on winning, leading, and turning around teams. *Academy of Management Executive*, **15** (August), 48–57; Katz, N. (2002), Sports teams as a model for workplace teams: lessons and liabilities. *Academy of Management Executive*, **15**, 56–69. For a good discussion of teambuilding, see Dyer, W. D. (1995), *Teambuilding*, 3rd edn. Addison-Wesley: Reading, MA.

56. See Channel 4 programme, *Cutting Edge: Exposure*, 1993, http://www.ftvdb.bfi.org.uk/title/484281 (accessed 5 January 2010).

57. See Simon Hollingsworth in *Personnel Today*, 29 June 2007.

58. Ross, E. (2009), Team building in turbulent times. *People Management Magazine*, 11 June, CIPD: London.

59. Developed from a discussion by Schein, E. H. (1969), *Process Consultation*, Addison-Wesley: Reading, MA, pp. 32–37; Schein, E. H. (1988), *Process Consultation*, Vol. I, Addison-Wesley: Reading, MA, pp. 40–49.

60. Chen, G. & Klimoski, R. J. (2003), The impact of expectations on newcomer performance in teams as mediated by work characteristics, social exchanges and empowerment. *Academy of Management Journal*, **46**, 591–607.

61. The classic work is Bales, R. F. (1958), Task roles and social roles in problem-solving groups, in *Readings in Social Psychology* (eds E. E. Maccoby, T. M. Newcomb & E. L. Hartley), Holt, Rinehart & Winston: New York.

62. For a good description of task and maintenance functions, see Gabarro, J. J. & Harlan, A. (1976), *Note on Process Observation*, Note 9-477-029, Harvard Business School.

63. Benne, K. D. & Sheats, P. (1948), Functional roles of group members. *Journal of Social Issues*, **4**, 41–49.

64. Belbin, R. M. (1981), *Management Teams: Why they Succeed or Fail*, Butterworth-Heinemann: Oxford; Belbin, R. M. (1993), *Team Roles at Work*, Butterworth-Heinemann: Oxford.

65. Manning, T., Parker, R. & Progson, T. (2006), A revised model of team roles and some research findings. *Journal of Industrial and Commercial Training*, **38** (6), 287–296.

66. See Fisher, S. G., Hunter, T. A. & Macrosson, W. D. K. (2000), The distribution of Belbin team roles among UK managers. *Personnel Review*, **29** (2), 124–140; Belbin, R. M., op. cit. p. 22.

67. Hollington, S. (2007), How to build an effective team. *People Management*, 28 June, 11–12.

68. See Feldman, D. C. (1984), The development and enforcement of group norms. *Academy of Management Review*, **9**, 47–53.

69. See Allen, R. F. & Pilnick, S. (1973), Confronting the shadow organization: how to select and defeat negative norms. *Organizational Dynamics*, Spring, 13–17; Zander, A. (1982), Making Groups Effective, Jossey-Bass: San Francisco, Ch. 4; Feldman, D. C. (1984), op. cit.

70. For a summary of research on group cohesiveness, see Shaw, M. E. (1971), *Group Dynamics*, McGraw-Hill: New York, pp. 110–112, 192.

71. Guzzo, R. A. & Salas, E. (eds) (1995), *Team Effectiveness and Decision Making in Organizations*, Jossey-Bass: San Francisco.

72. Example from (1989) Time to toss tradition? *Enterprise*, Autumn, 35–39.

73. See Ohmae, K. (1982), Quality control circles: they work and don't work. *Wall Street Journal*, 29 March, p. 16; Steel, R. P., Mento, A. J., Dilla, B. L. *et al.* (1985), Factors influencing the success and failure of two quality circles programs. *Journal of Management*, **11** (1), 99–119; Lawler, E. E. III & Mohrman, S. A. (1987), Quality circles: after the honeymoon. *Organizational Dynamics*, **15** (4), 42–54.

74. Lipnack, J. & Stamps, J. (2000), *Virtual Teams*, 2nd edn, John Wiley & Sons Inc.: New York, p. 18.

75. Peacock, L. (2007), Cyber Office's growth increases virtual HR. *Personnel Today*, 11 September 2007.

76. Elwyn, G., Greenhalgh, T. & Macfarlane, F. (2001), *Groups: A Guide to Small Group Work in Healthcare, Management, Education and Research*, Radcliffe Medical Press: Abingdon, pp. 203–206.

77. Duarte, D. & Tennant Snyder, N. (2001), *Mastering Virtual Teams*, revised edition, Jossey-Bass: San Francisco, pp. 4–23.

78. Elwyn, G., Greenhalgh, T. & Macfarlane, F. op. cit., pp. 206–214.

79. Axtell, C., Wheeler, J., Patterson, M. & Leach, A. (2004), From a distance. *People Management*, CIPD: London.

80. Hackman, J. R. (2002), *Leading Teams: Setting the Stage for Great Performances*, Harvard Business School Press: Boston, MA, pp. 130–132.

81. Katzenbach, J. R. & Smith, D. K. (1993), The discipline of teams. *Harvard Business Review*, March/April, p. 112.

82. Spring Singapore (2000), Self-managing teams in Becton Dickinson Medical (Singapore), *Productivity Digest*, December, www.spring.gov.sg/portal/newsroom/epublications/pd/2000_12/index_IP.html, (accessed 27 November 2007).

83. Lacy, L. (1992), Self-managed work groups step-by-step. *Journal for Quality and Participation*, **15** (3), 68–73.

84. Gordon, J. (1992), Work teams – how far have they come? *Training*, **29** (10), 59–65.

85. Developed in part from Wellins, R. S., Byham, W. C. & Wilson, J. M. (1992), Proactive teams achieve inspiring results. *World Executive's Digest*, October, 18–24.

86. Stewart, G. L. & Barrick, M. R. (2000), Team structure and performance: assessing the mediating role of intrateam process and the moderating role of task type. *Academy of Management Journal*, April, 135–148.

87. Adapted from Tatham, H. (2008), Releasing Fletcher Aluminium's invisible handbrake. *Management Today*, July, 44–48.

CHAPTER 9

Leadership

LEARNING OBJECTIVES

After studying this chapter you should be able to:

- explain the difference between leadership and management
- understand and evaluate trait and characteristic theories of leadership
- describe and critique the behavioural theories of leadership
- understand and evaluate situational contingency theories of leadership
- discuss transformational and transactional leadership approaches
- outline some of the current issues in diversity in leadership.

BEHIND THE BATTLE FOR CHANGE IN THE NHS

As the NHS faces troubled times, there are increasing calls for a change in leadership style and strategy. With a culture of 'command-and-control', current leaders are being asked to think again and encourage middle managers to take stronger leadership roles to lead change at their local level. In an article for the *Health Services Journal*, Steve Onyett, an independent consultant and coach, suggests that allowing middle managers more freedom to lead change in their domains is the best way forward.

His argument is that those working in the NHS came into the organization to serve and help those with health problems. Middle managers would also have strong knowledge of issues as they are closest to the technology and systems around any particular problem. Couple this with their strong commitment to public service in health, and he sees middle managers as an untapped resource which could contribute significantly to the broadening agenda for change in the NHS.

Source: Adapted from NHS in troubled times, *Health Services Journal*, 5 July 2010.

INTRODUCTION

As the chapter opening shows, regardless of their rank, most managers can play a leadership role. As leaders, they are expected to foster work environments conducive to self-renewal, thus engaging in change programmes that can be radical. They need to develop a capability to create an appetite and agility amongst employees at all levels for continuous change. They must encourage relationships and be able to build trust across the organization. In fact, for most organizations to prosper and perform nationally and internationally, strong leadership skills are needed throughout the management hierarchy. While the importance of leadership is indisputable, there is no singular type or style of leadership that works in all situations. Yet the kind of leadership that is vital for organizational success is not a phenomenon that develops magically on its own, but is a challenge that needs to be tackled in every work environment.[1]

This chapter focuses on the topic of leadership – a form of influence and the subject of enduring interest at every level in the organizational behaviour field. Most attention has been focused on answering the central question – 'what makes a good leader?' Different approaches have been taken, which have included personality and 'personal' traits and characteristics, definitive sets of behaviours or the ability to adapt leadership style to different followers and situations. How far do we learn to lead, and through studying leadership can we understand how we interpret situations and other people to lead better?

When things are going well, we rarely hold back from giving some credit to the leader. But how far should we hold leaders accountable for failures or lack of achievement of their group or organization? Consider the soccer teams which failed to qualify or advance in the 2010 World Cup in South Africa. What is the likelihood of the senior coach taking the blame for the bad performance? Should the blame be shouldered by the on-pitch captain? Similarly in the financial crisis which began to show in 2008, do we blame the managers of employees who invented spurious financial products, the managers who supervised those who sold them or the leaders of the organizations which bought them? The arguments for and against who shoulders the responsibility apply to all aspects of work.

In this chapter we first differentiate between notions of leadership and management and summarize and evaluate the major threads of leadership theories. We will also discuss the issue of diversity as it poses a challenge to leadership.

THE DISTINCTION BETWEEN LEADERSHIP AND MANAGEMENT

In earlier chapters of this book we have often referred to 'managers' and to 'management functions'. A fundamental question is whether leadership and management are (or can be) separated. Is there a clear divide between leadership and management? If so, do all leaders also manage and do all managers also lead? What is the difference between management and leadership?

The **management** *process involves planning, organizing, leading and controlling the use of organizational resources.*

A simple distinction would be to suggest that **management** is more concerned with promoting stability and enabling the organization to run smoothly, while the role of **leadership** is to inspire, promote and oversee initiatives to do with long-term change. We might think of managers as 'minding the shop' whereas leaders are working out where the next shop is going to be and what it will sell. The managerial role sees and solves problems, while the leadership role goes beyond them and works in a broader and longer-term way.[2]

The role of leader is distinguishable from that of manager:

Leadership *is a special case of interpersonal influence that gets an individual or group to do what the leader wants done.*

- Managers are concerned with problem solving and making things happen within a stable context. They keep work on schedule and have routine interactions to fulfil planned actions.
- Leaders provide inspiration, create opportunities and coach and motivate people to gain (and then use) their support on fundamental long-term choices.

We would all agree that the person at the top of an organization is a 'leader'. However, as our understanding of leadership has grown, we have also realized that most people who are 'managers' are expected to play leadership roles as well as their day-to-day management remit. Although top leaders may spend most of their time concerned with long-term strategic leadership of the whole organization, all managers need to be able to influence and inspire the people in their organization to work willingly towards change and improvement, which is at the heart of the leadership role. Many would argue that all 'managers' need to undertake a leadership role as change is an embedded part of organizational life. While top leaders may be in a position to craft the overall direction and strategy of the organization, this has to be achieved by other managers throughout the hierarchy. Middle and junior managers may have less choice over the direction they are taking their subordinates, but make change happen they must, and their choices for how to lead their group are many and varied.[3]

Given that leadership is a case of interpersonal influence that gets an individual or group to achieve what the leader wants done, it is about using appropriate interpersonal styles and methods in guiding individuals and groups towards task accomplishment.

Formal leadership *is the process of exercising influence from a position of formal authority in an organization.*

OB IN ACTION

Mark Hurd, President, CEO and Chairman of HP comments:

> 'The definition of managers in my mind is "I have a hand. I'm going to optimize the hand I've been given." Leaders actively change the hand to drive the business ... Leading is not just about managing people. To lead, you have to help people understand where we're trying to take the company and what their role is in getting there.'[4]

This quote helps us see the close link between forward-looking strategy and the leadership role. Leaders at all levels of the hierarchy need to translate the strategic vision for the future and get their staff involved in shaping the reality that will result from strategic action.

Leadership may take two forms:

- **formal leadership** is exerted by those who have positions of formal authority in organizations;
- **informal leadership** is exerted by those who become influential because they have special skills or resources that meet the needs of others.

Both types of leadership are important in organizations.

DEVELOPMENT OF THEORIES OF LEADERSHIP

Academic interest in leadership has been going on for many years. The leadership literature is by now vast and consists of numerous approaches.[5] In Figure 9.1 these approaches are shown schematically to help you understand and use them.

We have divided the theories into two categories. The first is trait and characteristic theories, which try to identify what makes a good leader in most situations. The very early studies into 'traits of great leadership' (such as intellect and family background) have been replaced by more subtle recent studies which seek characteristics of effective leaders (such as charisma and authenticity). The trait and characteristic behaviour approaches conceptualize leadership as central to the achievement of tasks and human resource maintenance

Informal leadership *is the process of exercising influence through special skills or resources that meet the needs of other people.*

Figure 9.1: Representative traditional and new leadership perspectives.

outputs emphasized in our individual performance equation (see p. 108). However, history has shown that someone might be a terrific leader at one time but their effectiveness appears to wane, such as Winston Churchill, who saw Britain through the second World War but was then voted out of office. The second theoretical group is that of situational or contingency approaches which consider leadership as central but must be examined with the environment external to the leader, or 'situational contingencies'. The last of these approaches – Kerr and Jermier's substitutes for leadership theory – considers where hierarchical leadership is not needed, suggesting that experienced employees together with well-developed organizational policies and procedures may provide so much structure as to act as leadership substitutes. For example, think of how little leadership guidance you need to do something at which you are experienced and where you know the boundaries and limits of your work.

Reading this chapter will demonstrate that the search for that holy grail of 'What makes a good leader?' remains unanswered, but our understanding has undoubtedly improved, as has our appreciation that this is a complex task and hard to achieve in a sustained way.

OB IN ACTION

On 20 April 2010 an explosion at a deep-water terminal owned (but not operated) by BP caused an oil spill which continued for months. It affected wildlife, the sea shore and those who make a living from the Gulf of Mexico. BP's boss, Tony Hayward, spent most of the spring months in the USA, away from his British home. He undertook a vast number of press conferences for all audiences as well as keeping a personal involvement in the actions of the engineers to stop the leaks. He attended a Senate hearing in Washington where he absorbed complaints and anger from politicians.

Tony Hayward's leadership capability has been challenged by another leader – President Obama – even though Hayward has admitted BP's responsibility. After many months of activity and exposure, Mr Hayward handed over operational leadership for capping the leak to a senior BP executive in June. On 19 June 2010 he took his first day off since the spill. He was spotted at a yachting

'Round The Island Race' competition event near Portsmouth. He was with his son watching the race. The US President's Chief of Staff suggested this was the latest in a 'long line of PR gaffes and mistakes'.

Questions

1. How do you think managers within BP reacted to these events and Mr Hayward's actions?
2. How do you think Gulf fishermen affected by the spill reacted to these events and Mr Hayward's actions?
3. How far do you think Mr Hayward was right in keeping himself as the target for press and public focus in the disaster?

LEADERSHIP THEORIES BASED ON TRAIT AND LEADER CHARACTERISTICS

The trait and characteristic approaches assume that the effectiveness of individuals in their leadership roles depends on their traits, or characteristics, that have a major impact on leadership outputs; that is, according to these theories, leadership is central and other variables are relatively less important. They differ in how they explain leadership results.

Trait theory

Trait theory is the earliest approach used to study leadership and dates back to the turn of the 20th century. The early studies attempted to identify those traits that differentiated the 'great person' in history from the masses (for example, how did Napoleon, Margaret Thatcher or Henry Ford differ from their followers?). This approach tried to separate leaders from nonleaders, or more effective leaders from less effective leaders. The argument was that certain traits are related to success and that these traits, once identified, could be used to select leaders. This argument follows that made in Chapter 2 concerning individual attributes. Early research concentrated on leaders who were usually at the top of highly successful organizations or were remarkable in their ability to influence others to make dramatic change. They looked for general traits, cutting across all circumstances and organizations, and considered traits such as height, integrity and intelligence. Proof of this theory lies in predicting and finding a set of traits (charisma, intelligence and so on) that differentiate effective leaders from ineffective ones.[6]

For various reasons, including inadequate theorizing, inadequate measurement of many traits and failure to recognize possible differences in organizations and situations, the studies were not successful enough to provide a general trait theory. One can see the appeal of this approach, as if one could explain the success of great leaders in this way, then one could potentially identify people early in their lives or careers and coach them into greatness, or be far more effective at searching for and hiring really great leaders.

In many contemporary biographies of leaders, one can still observe writers attempting to encapsulate the traits of their subject. However, as a generalized predictive tool, the theory was not effective. Whatever trait one might take to indicate effectiveness, there are always many 'exceptions to the rule' which then invalidate the value of the 'rule'. But the trait theorists laid the groundwork for considering certain personal aspects (such as characteristic beliefs and attitudes) that form the basis for some of the more current theories.

Research in the modern era has identified individual characteristics which, it is argued, are important for very many leaders and successful managers. Good energy levels and a tolerance of stress[7] enable sustained working in our modern pressured environments. Self-confidence or 'self-efficacy' is necessary for the leader to initiate their influence attempts and is therefore necessary for them to do their job[8] and be sustained in those attempts.[9] There is a danger of over confidence which might lead to an unwillingness to take advice from others or arrogance leading to ineffectiveness. Connected, but distinct, is the issue of locus of control – to what extent do we think we are in control of the world (internal locus of control) or do we think the world controls us (external locus of control)? Effective leaders are more likely to be the former, and with self-confidence will assert their influence over others rather than being passive and reactive.

Motivation also has a role to play in the characteristics of effective leaders. Those who have reasonable needs for power and achievement (see Chapter 4) are often effective, but findings are complex and suggest that very high needs in either category can mean a risk of derailment.[10] What is more logical is that those who have a high need for affiliation (being liked by others) are less likely to be effective leaders as their desire to maintain relationships overrides difficult decisions where they might need to give negative messages to colleagues and subordinates, thus affecting how they are liked. But very low affiliation might also be dangerous in a leader, who may 'stamp on others' through the hierarchy, which is unlikely to be positive.[11] The 'big five' personality approach has been used to study leader effectiveness, but with inconclusive results.

After almost a century of study there is clearly no 'magic bullet' for leader effectiveness in aspects relating to traits or various aspects of personality and attitudes. As scholars of leadership we should pause and think about what this means. It would appear that leaders are probably not 'born' but they are shaped by their environment, including upbringing and career. The few areas where positive association has been found with leader effectiveness (internal locus of control and self-confidence for example) can be developed, but even though they might be important, effective leadership is about something more. Hence, the good news is that many of us can be effective leaders. The bad news is that effective leadership is clearly complex.

Leadership theories of attribution

One area of development in more recent years is the notion of bundles of attitudes and priorities which together make identifiable leadership approaches through an identifiable set of leader attributes. Attributes can include not only what someone does, but also how they do it. Also included in these modern ideas is the interaction between the manager and their followers.

Charismatic approaches

Charismatic leadership uses attribution theory to suggest that we make attributions of heroic leadership competencies or personal characteristics when we see good leaders in action. Conger and Kanungo thought that charismatic leaders were self-confident, displayed an articulate vision and had strong conviction of their vision.[12] Robert House sees **charismatic leaders** as those 'who by force of their personalities are capable of having a profound and extraordinary effect on followers'. Essentially, these leaders are quite high in need for power and have high feelings of self-efficacy and conviction in the moral rightness of their beliefs; that is, the need for power motivates these people to want to be leaders and this need is then reinforced by their conviction of their moral rightness. The feeling of self-efficacy, in turn, makes people feel that they are capable of being leaders. These traits then influence such charismatic behaviours as role modelling, image building, articulating goals (focusing on simple and dramatic goals), emphasizing high expectations, showing confidence and arousing others' motives to follow them.

> **Charismatic leaders** are those leaders who, by force of their personal characteristics, are capable of having a profound and extraordinary effect on followers.

House and his colleagues show us that one might be an excellent leader, but lead people in a very negative direction. Some interesting related work has shown that negative, or 'dark-side', charismatic leaders emphasize personalized power (focus on themselves), whereas positive or 'bright-side' charismatics emphasize socialized power, which tends to empower their followers. This helps explain differences between such dark-side leaders as Adolf Hitler, David Koresh and Reverend Jim Jones and bright-side leaders such as Martin Luther King Junior[13] and Gandhi.

Jay Conger has developed a four-stage charismatic leadership theory based on his work with Rabindra Kanungo.[14] In the first stage, the leader develops a vision of idealized change that moves beyond the status quo; for example, US President John F. Kennedy had a vision of putting a man on the moon by the end of the 1960s. In the second stage, the leader communicates the vision and motivates the followers to go beyond the status quo. In stage three, the leader builds trust by exhibiting qualities such as expertise, success, risk taking and unconventional actions. In the final stage, the leader demonstrates ways to achieve the vision by means of empowerment, behaviour modelling for followers and so forth. Conger and Kanungo have argued that if leaders use behaviours such as vision and articulation, environmental sensitivity and unconventional behaviour, rather than maintaining the status quo, followers will attribute charismatic leadership to them. Such leaders are also seen as behaving quite differently from those labelled 'noncharismatic'.[15]

Research on leadership involving three countries in Asia (Singapore, New Zealand and India) showed that charisma and vision were made up of two charismatic factors (social sensitivity and persuasive personality traits) and two visionary factors ('expert and analytical' and 'visionary and futuristic'). Tests across the three countries showed that the two visionary factors influenced reported performance and the two charismatic factors influenced employee commitment. Only social sensitivity predicted both performance and commitment of employees.[16]

Top leaders who have charisma are very impressive. Deconstructing their power to influence is useful. But how far can we all be charismatic? An important leadership scholar, Gary Yukl, suggests 'The essence of charisma is being perceived as extraordinary by followers who are dependent on the leader for guidance and inspiration'.[17] Can most of us be 'perceived as extraordinary'? If we did, probably the base line for judging 'extraordinary' would then move to be more elusive. How far (inevitable) failures dent charisma is not well known, but it is likely, hence the issue of sustainability must be raised. We might therefore suggest that although useful, true charismatic leadership is probably only accessible to a few leaders in some situations. That said, some level of charisma is used in the most up-to-date areas of leadership thinking which we present towards the end of the chapter under transformational leadership.[18]

A related but different set of constructs appears with the idea of authentic leadership[19] where the leader has great consistency with their presentation of self. They appear to followers to have a strong self-awareness and self-acceptance. Within this they hold values that are positive such as honesty, altruism, optimism, accountability and fairness. They will have strong ethical clarity and have moral courage. These attributes engender trust from others as well as respect. The theory lacks thorough testing as it relies on the self-awareness of the leader, which is always difficult to measure. This approach is not prescriptive, and does not specify a set of behaviours that a leader should engage in, other than being true to oneself and positive principles.

The area of ethical leadership is attracting considerable attention at this time.[20] Our understanding of this attribute has developed such that we know an ethical leader has to not only promote positive directions and engage in them, but also erect effective sanctions and barriers to those thinking of being unethical.[21] This is an area of leadership in which managers and supervisors at all levels need to be engaged with and potentially 'blow the whistle' on practices. But whistleblowing can only happen when the organization has ears to hear the alarm – and here everyone shares responsibility for the organization. The recent organizational crashes and accompanying misdemeanors provide useful evidence with which to warn others to take deviant behaviour seriously. However, it requires leadership traits and attributes such as moral courage and authenticity to intervene effectively.[22] An interesting and recent study by Linda Trevino and colleagues found that senior managers had a more 'rosy' picture of the organization's ethical standing than those further down the hierarchy, which underlines the importance of leaders keeping in touch with the attitudes and beliefs of those in other positions in the organization. This leads us to consider a final type of leadership – servant leadership. At the other extreme to charismatic leadership, servant leadership places followers at the centre of one's approach.

▶ COUNTERPOINT

Servant leadership

In recent times, some researchers have attempted to rejuvenate a relatively old concept of leadership: 'servant leadership'. Servant leaders are those who make a deliberate choice to serve others and to put other people's needs, aspirations and interests above their own.[23] The servant leader operates on the assumption that 'I am the leader, therefore I serve' rather than 'I am the leader, therefore I lead', which could be seen as more characteristic of most of the other perspectives on leadership.[24]

People follow servant leaders freely because they trust them. One of the tests of servant leadership is how those served (led) benefit.

Spears[25] identified ten critical characteristics of the servant leader. Many are similar to the characteristics identified in other models but with a very strong focus on the followers:

- servant leaders must reinforce their communication skills by listening to others;
- servant leaders strive to understand and empathize with others;
- learning to heal oneself and others is a unique characteristic;
- self-awareness strengthens the servant leader – as it does all leaders;

- servant leaders rely on persuasion rather than positional authority;
- servant leaders are able to conceptualize, to see beyond the day-to-day and to dream great dreams;
- foresight is the characteristic that enables servant leaders to understand the lessons of the past, the realities of the present and the likely consequences of a decision for the future;
- in these days of corporate distrust, stewardship is a most attractive element of servant leadership, particularly if it can be combined with foresight;
- servant leaders are committed to the personal, professional and spiritual growth of each individual in the organization;
- servant leaders seek to identify means for building community among those who work within any given institution.

Questions

1. Have you experienced servant leadership?
2. What do you think are the strengths and weaknesses of the servant leadership perspective on leadership?
3. Discuss the differences between servant leadership and charismatic leadership.

BEHAVIOURAL THEORIES

Two classic research programmes at the University of Michigan and Ohio State University provided the groundwork for behavioural leadership theory to develop. These were run at similar times and both revealed some key parameters that dominate our understanding of leadership, including whether leaders are focused on the task and/or focused on people. It is of note that while the trait theorists tended to examine the top leaders, research after this took a broader approach, extending the notion and possession of leadership throughout the organization hierarchy, as is reflected in how we approach the topic today.

The Michigan studies

In the late 1940s researchers at the University of Michigan wanted to identify the leadership pattern that results in effective performance. From interviews of high- and low-performing groups in different organizations, the researchers derived two basic forms of leader behaviour: employee centred and production centred. Employee-centred supervisors are those who place strong emphasis on the welfare of their employees. In contrast, production-centred supervisors tend to place a stronger emphasis on getting the work done than on the welfare of the employees. In general, employee-centred supervisors were found to have more productive work groups than those of the production-centred supervisors.[26]

These behaviours may be viewed on a continuum, with employee-centred supervisors at one end and production-centred supervisors at the other. Sometimes, the more general terms 'human relations-oriented' and 'task-oriented' are used to describe these alternative leader behaviours.

The Ohio State studies

An important leadership research programme was started at Ohio State University at about the same time as the Michigan studies. A questionnaire was administered in both industrial and military settings to measure subordinates' perceptions of their superiors' leadership behaviour. The researchers identified two dimensions similar to those found in the Michigan studies: 'consideration' and 'initiating structure'.[27] Highly considerate leaders are sensitive to people's feelings and are like the employee-centred leaders found by the Michigan team. In contrast, leaders high in initiating structure are more concerned with spelling out task requirements and clarifying other aspects of the work agenda; they may be seen as similar to production-centred managers. They relate to group maintenance and task activities as discussed in Chapter 8.

At first, the Ohio State researchers thought that a leader high on consideration, or socio-emotional warmth, would have more highly satisfied and/or better-performing employees. Later results indicated that leaders should be high on both consideration and initiating structure behaviours. Their conceptualization was not the single line of the Michigan group, but instead treated 'people' and 'task' orientation as different axes on a grid. The dual emphasis was developed by Blake and Mouton and became the Leadership Grid® approach.

The Leadership Grid®

Robert Blake and Jane Mouton developed the Leadership Grid® perspective.[28] It measures a manager's:

- concern for people and
- concern for production.

The results are then plotted on a nine-position grid that places these concerns on the vertical axis and horizontal axis, respectively (Figure 9.2). The ideal position is asserted to be a 9/9 position where a leader achieves the task through people. Blake and Mouton did not suggest that behaviours should be done at the same time or interchangeably but rather that every decision a manager/leader makes involves weighing these two facets of people and task and understanding how both demands can be met at the same time. Someone who only thinks of their employees (a 9/1 score) is termed a 'country-club manager' as it

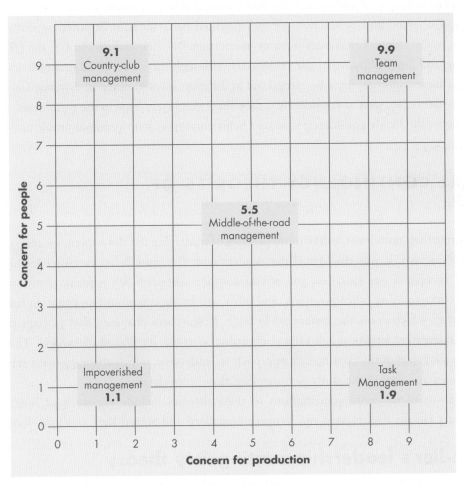

Figure 9.2: Leadership grid.

Source: Blake, R. and McCanse, A. (1995), *Leadership Dilemmas – grid solutions*, Gulf Publishing Company, Texas. © Elsevier.

is expected that little task achievement can be expected, as inferred by the hobbyist title. It is unlikely that in the 21st century any country-club managers survive in our highly target-driven and evaluated workplaces. The task management style (scoring 1/9) is more likely to have survived where, although tasks might be achieved, their lack of consideration for people would point to high grievance and turnover rates,[29] which would add to the actual cost of production. Other positions identified are 1/1 – the impoverished management style – where the manager appears to do very little. This has been termed laissez-faire leadership in other work (as will be found later in this chapter) and is reviewed negatively.[30] A 5/5 style, in the middle of the grid, is a middle-of-the-road management style. This probably describes a manager who we don't hate, but who fails to inspire us to go the extra mile!

Research evidence points to the importance of task- and people-focus being important. General 'rules' have been difficult to establish in both field studies and laboratory simulations. While a high task focus will get things done, there are costs in the form of staff leaving and hence recruitment and retraining issues.

The behavioural approaches discussed share a common emphasis on the importance of people-oriented and production- or task-oriented behaviours in determining outputs. But how well do these behaviours transfer internationally? Research in the US, the UK, Hong Kong and Japan shows that the behaviours, although they seem to be generally important in all these countries, must be carried out in different ways in different cultures. UK leaders, for instance, are seen as considerate if they show employees how to use equipment, whereas in Japan the highly considerate manager helps employees with personal problems.[31]

SITUATIONAL CONTINGENCY THEORIES OF LEADERSHIP

Despite their usefulness, behavioural theories of leadership did not explain success or failure on their own. It was discovered that leaders with the same behavioural tendencies could find success in one situation and not in another. Although 9/9 is ideal, many managers are effective using other positions, and most will be successful in one situation but not in another, which raises the sustainability issue. Researchers proposed that perhaps the leader's contextual situation is a critical contributor to the likelihood of success. This led to the emergence of the contingency approach to leadership, which encompasses a number of theories and moved the study of leadership along considerably.

Some of the main contributions to these theories include the work of Fred Fiedler, Robert House, Paul Hersey and Kenneth Blanchard and Steven Kerr and John Jermier.

Fiedler's leadership contingency theory

The first situational contingency approach we consider is that of Fred Fiedler, whose work essentially started the situational contingency era in the mid-1960s.[32] Fiedler's approach predicts work group effectiveness, again seeing leadership as an aspect of all managers' work. His theory holds that group effectiveness depends on an appropriate match between a leader's style and the demands of the situation. Specifically, Fiedler considers the amount of control the situation allows the leader. **Situational control** is the extent to which leaders can determine what their group is going to do and what will be the outcomes of the group's actions and decisions. Where control is high, leaders can predict with a good deal of certainty what will happen when they want something done.

Fiedler uses an instrument called the **least preferred co-worker** (LPC) scale to measure a person's leadership style. Respondents are asked to describe the person with whom they are able to work least well (their least preferred co-worker, or LPC), using a series of adjectives such as these:

Unfriendly	.....	.....	.....	.....	.....	.....	.....	.....	Friendly
	1	2	3	4	5	6	7	8	
Pleasant	.....	.....	.....	.....	.....	.....	.....	.....	Unpleasant
	1	2	3	4	5	6	7	8	

Fiedler argues that high LPC leaders (those describing their LPC very positively) have a relationship-motivated style whereas low LPC leaders have a task-oriented style. In other words, relationship-oriented leaders describe more favourably the person with whom they are least able to work than do task-oriented leaders.

Fiedler considers this task or relationship motivation to be a trait that leads to either directive or nondirective behaviour, depending on whether the leader has high, moderate or low situational control (as already described).

Let us now elaborate on Fiedler's situational control concept and its match with task- and relationship-oriented styles. Figure 9.3 shows the task-oriented leader as having greater group effectiveness under high and low situational control, while the relationship-oriented leader has a more effective group under a moderate-control situation.

Situational control is the extent to which leaders can determine what their group is going to do and what the outcomes of their actions and decisions are going to be.

The **least preferred co-worker** (LPC) scale is a measure of a person's leadership style based on a description of the person with whom respondents have been able to work least well.

Task-motivated leader							
High-control situations			**Moderate-control situations**			**Low-control situations**	
Leader–member relations	Good			Good	Poor		Poor	
Task structure	High		Low	Low	High		Low	
Position power	Strong	Weak	Strong	Weak	Strong	Weak	Strong	Weak
	I	II	III	IV	V	VI	VII	VIII

Relationship-motivated leader

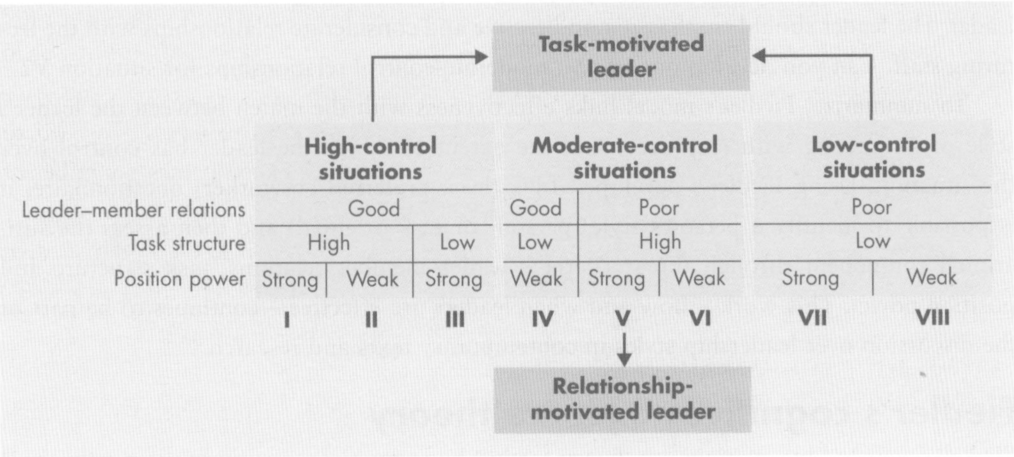

Figure 9.3: Predictions from Fiedler's contingency theory of leadership.

The figure also shows that Fiedler measures high, moderate and low control with the following three variables arranged in the situational combinations indicated:

- leader–member relations (good/poor) – member support for the leader;
- task structure (high/low) – spelling out the leader's task goals, procedures and guidelines in the group;
- position power (strong/weak) – the leader's task expertise and reward/punishment authority.

Let us examine some examples to show how different combinations of these variables provide differing amounts of situational control. First, consider the experienced and well-trained manager of a large local supermarket, which is part of a national chain of stores. The local leader is highly supported by his or her department supervisors and can hire/fire and promote and distribute bonuses. This leader would have high situational control and would be operating in situation I in Figure 9.3. Likewise, those leaders operating in situations II and III would have high situational control, although not as high as that of our store manager. In any of these three high-control situations, a task-oriented leader behaving nondirectively would have the most effective group.

Contrast the previous example with the chair of an internal organizational committee, which is tasked with making suggestions for the improvement of the work–life balance of employees. The chair has been 'volunteered' by their own manager, as have other committee members who do not see the chair as necessarily the best person to do the job and are of the same pay grade as the chair. Here we have a low-structured task in a low-control situation (situation VIII). According to the theory the appropriate leadership style would be task-motivation and for the leader to behave directively. In other words, Fiedler argues that the leader's decision on how to act is determined by the situation – in this circumstance he or she must act directively to keep the group together and focus on the ambiguous task.

Finally, let us consider a well-liked academic department head with a tenured lecturing staff. Fiedler argues that this is a moderate-control situation (IV) with good leader–member relations, low task structure and weak position power, calling for a relationship-motivated leader. The leader should emphasize nondirective and considerate relationships with the lecturing staff. Can you develop one or two moderate-control relationships for situation V?

To summarize, Fiedler's model links effectiveness with the match between the leader's style of interacting with employees and the extent to which the leader has control over the situation. Using Fiedler's developed LPC (least preferred co-worker) questionnaire, it is possible to identify a person's style (person- or task-oriented) and then assess the situational component through three criteria – leader–member relations, task structure and position power. This work – how and when leaders are effective – continues to be part of the discussion over leadership styles in contemporary texts and research.[33]

Fiedler's cognitive resource theory

Fiedler developed his contingency theory further by suggesting cognitive resource theory.[34] Cognitive resources are abilities or competencies. According to this approach, whether a leader should use directive or nondirective behaviour depends on the following situational contingencies:

- the leader's or subordinate group member's ability/competency;
- stress;
- experience, and
- group support of the leader.

A distinguishing feature of cognitive resource theory is that it incorporates both leader and subordinate group member ability, which other leadership approaches typically do not consider.

The theory views directiveness as most helpful for performance when the leader is competent, relaxed and supported. In this case, the group is ready and directiveness is the clearest means of communication. When the leader feels stressed, they are diverted. If group support is low, then the group is less receptive and the leader has less impact. Group member ability becomes most important when the leader is nondirective and there is strong support from group members. If group support is weak, then task difficulty or other factors have more impact than do either the leader or the followers.

More recent studies have verified and extended Fiedler's contingency model of leadership effectiveness to followers' behaviour. For instance, a recent study of personnel serving with the US army in Europe re-examined the relationship between followers' motivational disposition, situational favourability and followers' performance. That study found that, in accordance with Fiedler, relations-oriented followers performed better in moderately favourable situations while task-oriented followers performed better in highly unfavourable situations.[35]

Although there are still unanswered questions concerning Fiedler's contingency theory (especially concerning the meaning of LPC), the theory continues to receive relatively strong support both in academia and in practice.[36]

House's path–goal theory of leadership

Another well-known approach to situational contingencies is one developed by Robert House based on the early traditional studies.[37] This theory has its roots in the expectancy model of motivation (Chapter 4). The term 'path–goal' is used because it emphasizes how a leader influences employees' perceptions of both work goals and personal goals and the links or paths found between these two sets of goals.

The theory assumes that a leader's key function is to adjust his or her behaviour to complement situational contingencies, such as those found in the work setting. House argues that when the leader is able to compensate for things lacking in the setting, employees are likely to be satisfied with the leader. The leader could, for example, help remove job ambiguity or show how good performance could lead to more pay. Performance should improve as leaders clarify the paths by which effort leads to performance (expectancy) and performance leads to valued rewards (instrumentality). Redundant behaviour by the leader will not help and may even hinder performance. People do not need a boss telling them how to do something that they already know how to do!

House's model represents a process approach to leadership that takes into account three interrelated variables. The overall process in sequential order is:

leadership factors → context factors → employee motivation

Taking these three aspects together, they can lead to outputs that enhance the organization, the employee and the leader.

Details of House's approach are summarized in Figure 9.4. The figure shows four types of leader behaviour – directive, supportive, achievement-oriented and participative – and two categories of situational contingency variables – employee attributes and work-setting attributes. The leader behaviour is adjusted to complement the situational contingency variables to influence employee satisfaction, acceptance of the leader and motivation for task performance.

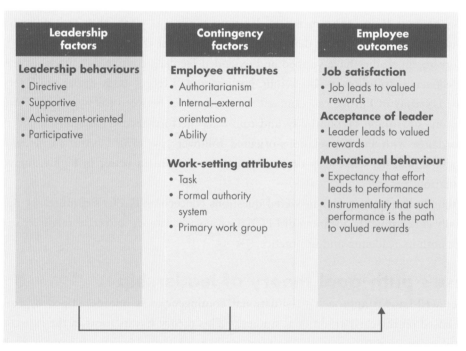

Figure 9.4: Summary of major path–goal relationships in House's leadership approach.
Source: Adapted from Osborn, R. N., Hunt, J. G. and Jauch, L. R. (1980), *Organizational Theory: an integrated approach*, John Wiley & Sons, Inc.: New York, p. 464. Reproduced by permission of John Wiley & Sons, Inc.

Directive leadership *is leadership behaviour that spells out the what and how of employees' tasks.*

Supportive leadership *is a leadership style that focuses on employee needs and wellbeing and promotes a friendly work climate; it is similar to consideration.*

- **Directive leadership** has to do with spelling out the what and how of employees' tasks; it is much like the initiating structure mentioned earlier.
- **Supportive leadership** focuses on employee needs and wellbeing, and promotes a friendly work climate; it is similar to consideration.

- **Achievement-oriented leadership** emphasizes setting challenging goals, stressing excellence in performance and showing confidence in the group members' abilities to achieve high standards of performance.
- **Participative leadership** focuses on consulting with employees and seeking and accounting for their suggestions before making decisions.

The contingency variables include employee attributes and work-setting or environmental attributes. Important employee characteristics are authoritarianism (closed-mindedness, rigidity), internal–external orientation (locus of control) and ability. The key work-setting factors are the nature of the employees' tasks (task structure), the formal authority system and the primary work group.

House's path–goal approach has attracted considerable research, and there is support for the theory in general as well as for the particular predictions discussed earlier.[38]

Not all aspects shown in Figure 9.4 have been tested and few applications have been reported in the literature. The path–goal approach lends itself to at least a couple of possibilities, however. First, training could be used to change leadership behaviour to fit the situational contingencies. Second, the leader could be taught to diagnose the situation and to learn how to change the contingencies (employee attributes and work-setting attributes).

Implicit in the situational theories is the notion that the leader can change their approach as the situation changes. This might mean changes in how their followers perceive them or the nature of the task or the favourability of the external environment which always exerts pressure to a greater or lesser extent on our workplaces. As these models developed so did our appreciation of the role of training, so that at last the manager/leader was seen as someone with potential to adopt many styles and approaches, rather than being steeped in one way of behaving. It is another step on our evolutionary road in how we have learned to conceptualize leadership.

Hersey and Blanchard's Situational Leadership® model

The Situational Leadership® model developed by Paul Hersey and Kenneth Blanchard is similar to the other situational approaches in its view that there is no single best way to lead.[39] Like the approaches discussed earlier, Situational Leadership® emphasizes situational contingencies, and this is a very popular model used in basic management training around the world. Hersey and Blanchard focus on the readiness of followers in particular. Readiness is the extent to which people have the ability and willingness to accomplish a specific task. Hersey and Blanchard argue that 'situational' leadership requires adjusting the leader's emphasis on task behaviours (for example, giving guidance and direction) and relationship behaviours (for example, providing socioemotional support) according to the readiness of followers to perform their tasks. As such it has extreme closeness to the Michigan and Ohio studies but, as will be seen, has a far less complex take on what this means for a manager in terms of their leadership role than House or Fielder.

Achievement-oriented leadership *is leadership behaviour that emphasizes setting challenging goals, stressing excellence in performance and showing confidence in the group members' abilities to achieve high standards of performance.*

Participative leadership *is a leadership style that focuses on consulting with employees and seeking and accounting for their suggestions before making decisions.*

The model identifies four leadership styles:

- delegating
- participating
- selling
- telling.

Each emphasizes a different combination of task and relationship behaviours by the leader. The model suggests a particular leadership style for followers at each of four readiness levels.

A telling style is best for low follower readiness. The direction provided by this style defines roles for people who are unable and unwilling to take responsibility themselves; it eliminates any insecurity about the task that must be done.

A selling style is best for low to moderate follower readiness. This style offers both task direction and support for people who are unable but willing to take task responsibility; it involves combining a directive approach with explanation and reinforcement to maintain enthusiasm.

A participating style is best for moderate to high follower readiness. Able but unwilling followers require supportive behaviour to increase their motivation; by allowing followers to share in decision making, this style helps enhance the desire to perform a task.

A delegating style is best for high readiness. This style provides little in terms of direction and support for the task at hand; it allows able and willing followers to take responsibility for what needs to be done.

This Situational Leadership® approach requires the leader to develop the capability to diagnose the demands of situations and then to choose and implement the appropriate leadership response. The theory gives specific attention to followers and their feelings about the task at hand. It also suggests that effective leaders reassess situations over time, giving special attention to emerging changes in the level of readiness of the people involved in the work. Again, Hersey and Blanchard advise that leadership style should be adjusted as necessary to remain consistent with actual levels of follower readiness. They further suggest that effectiveness should improve as a result.[40]

The Situational Leadership® approach has a great deal of intuitive appeal for managers but unfortunately little systematic research support. What support is available is not very strong and the theory still needs systematic empirical evaluation.[41] It could be argued that Hersey and Blanchard have considered the impact of the role of subordinates to the point where other situational factors are not given sufficient importance.

The approach does include an elaborate training programme that has been developed to train leaders to diagnose and emphasize appropriate behaviours. Internationally, this programme is particularly popular in Europe, where an organization headquartered in Amsterdam provides Situational Leadership® training for leaders in many countries. Hersey and Blanchard took theory and made it accessible to a very wide audience. Their model provides a straightforward introduction to the leadership aspects of a job for new and developing managers and has the accompanying training worked through for achievability. Their model is clearly less sophisticated than others, but given that most new managers are promoted after a period of task effectiveness at a lower level, being given a framework which enables them to come to terms with hitherto unexplored areas – leading those in their team – helps to explain the popularity of the model.

SUBSTITUTES FOR LEADERSHIP

In contrast to the previous approaches listed in Figure 9.1, the 'substitutes for leadership' perspective argues that sometimes hierarchical leadership makes essentially no difference. John Jermier and others contend that certain individual, job and organizational variables can either serve as **substitutes for leadership** or neutralize a leader's impact on employees.[42] Examples of these variables are shown in Figure 9.5. Experience, ability and training, for example, can serve as individual characteristics; a highly structured or routine job can serve as a job characteristic; and a cohesive work group can serve as an organizational characteristic.

Substitutes for leadership *are organization, individual or task-situational variables that substitute for leadership in causing performance/ human resource maintenance.*

Characteristics of individuals	Impact on leadership
Experience, ability, training	Substitutes for task-oriented leadership
Professional orientation	Substitutes for task-oriented and supportive leadership
Indifference towards organizational rewards	Neutralizes task-oriented and supportive leadership

Characteristics of job	
Highly structured/routine	Substitutes for task-oriented leadership
Intrinsically satisfying	Substitutes for supportive leadership

Characteristics of organization	
Coheive work group	Substitutes for task-oriented and supportive leadership
Low leader position power	Neutralizes task-oriented and supportive leadership
Leader physically separated	Neutralizes task-oriented and supportive leadership

Figure 9.5: Example leadership substitutes and neutralizers.

Source: Based on Kerr, S. and Jermier, J. (1992), Substitutes for leadership: their meaning and measurement. *Organizational Behaviour and Human Performance,* **22**, 387 and Luthans, F. (1992), *Organizational Behaviour,* 6th edn, McGraw Hill, New York.

Substitutes for leadership, it is argued, make a leader's influence both impossible and unnecessary. Neutralizers make a leader's influence impossible but not unnecessary; substitutes replace a leader's influence. As you can see in Figure 9.5 it will be difficult, if not impossible, for a leader to provide the kind of task-oriented direction already available to an experienced, talented and well-trained employee. This would apply to, for example the individual managing an actuaries department where all the staff are trained to a professional level, keep updated and have discussions about the future of their work and the profession as well as their specific case loads. Further, such direction will be unnecessary, given the employee's characteristics. The figure shows a similar argument for a highly structured task. In this instance one might think of the McDonald's fast-food approach to defining workers' roles where every role and task is minutely specified.

Now let us look at a couple of neutralizing examples. If leaders have low position power or formal authority, their leadership may be negated, even though task structuring and supportiveness are still needed. If leaders are physically separated from employees, their task-oriented and supportive leadership may be negated but still necessary.

The 'substitutes for leadership' perspective is a more generalized version of the situational contingency approaches mentioned earlier, particularly House's path–goal theory. However, the substitutes perspective goes further by assuming that leadership in some cases has no impact on outputs because it is replaced by other factors. The earlier situational approaches argued that both leadership and other factors are needed.

Research on the substitutes theory has shown mixed results. Some work comparing Mexican and US workers suggests both similarities and differences between various substitutes in the two countries.[43] Within the US, some early work appeared to support the theory but two later, comprehensive studies (covering 13 different organizations) provided little support.[44]

Despite this last finding, given the emerging importance and popularity of work teams, leadership substitutes are likely to be important and need to be tailored to the team-oriented workplace. Thus, in place of a leader specifying standards and ways of achieving goals (task-oriented behaviours), the team will set its own standards and substitute these for those set previously by a leader. Those occupying formal leadership roles are usually well paid, thus finding circumstances where specific individuals are not required can have an impact on the bottom line. The argument here is not that leadership is not required but rather that the leadership role can be distributed throughout the team (hence substituted).

► COUNTERPOINT

Stale Einarsen and his team in Bergen have been developing the idea of destructive leadership. In a provocative article they challenge the idea that managers are at worst scoring '0' on a grid. They suggest that our thinking about managers and leaders needs to extend into the negative and that leaders can act against their organization and against their staff. Their model needs further development, but their article is provocative to those presenting theories – leaders are not just working from the neutral to the wonderful – at times they should be able to be seen as destructive.[45]

EMERGING LEADERSHIP PERSPECTIVES

The more recent approaches to leadership have tended to endorse charisma, vision and transformation as catalysts to effective leadership.

OB IN ACTION

In his introduction to *Hitler and Churchill: secrets of leadership*,[46] Andrew Roberts suggests Adolf Hitler was a 'charismatic' leader whereas Winston Churchill was an 'inspirational' leader. Hitler rose to power by recognizing and capitalizing on the German resentment towards the Treaty of Versailles. He sustained his power using the convenient scapegoat of the Jewish people. He promoted a vision of a new and glorious German empire. Churchill's vision was to create a powerful alliance to defend freedom. He created a popular mood and sustained it demonstrating his personal courage, publicly valuing it in others and inspiring courage and persistence nationally. In the light of history, the inspirational leader prevailed over the charismatic one. Roberts suggests that leaders, be they like Churchill or Hitler, create a common goal with which people can wholeheartedly identify, but that managers lack that guiding vision.[47] One must caution that any leader's success also depends on issues other than leadership style – in this example, military resources would be fundamental. No leader is omnipotent, but has to work within the real world.

Transactional and transformational approaches

Transformational leadership usually involves empowering followers and making them partners in the change process, whereas charismatic leadership is more likely to require followers to place their trust in the leader's special expertise to achieve radical change. Building on notions originated by James MacGregor Burns, as well as ideas from House's work, Bernard Bass has developed an approach that focuses on both transformational and transactional leadership. The high points are summarized in Figure 9.6.

Let us start by discussing Bass's transactional category. **Transactional leadership** involves daily exchanges between leaders and employees, and is necessary for achieving routine performance on which leaders and employees agree. It is based on transactions that occur between leaders and followers. These transactions may include agreements, contingent rewards, communications or exchanges between leaders and followers. There are many dimensions of transactional leadership.

- **Contingent rewards** involve providing various kinds of reward in exchange for accomplishing mutually agreed goals (for example, your boss pays you a £500 bonus for completing an acceptable article by a certain date). Conversely, you could be subject to disciplinary action for failing to achieve the goals.

Transactional leadership *involves daily exchanges between leaders and followers, and is necessary for achieving routine performance on which leaders and followers agree.*

Contingent rewards *are rewards that are given in exchange for mutually agreed goal accomplishments.*

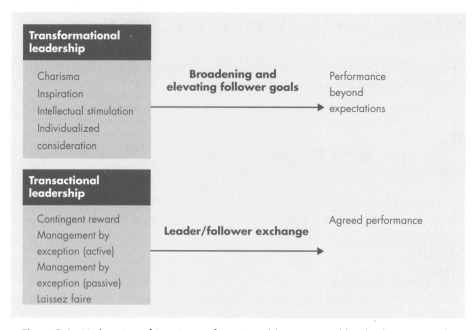

Figure 9.6: High points of Bass's transformational/transactional leadership approach.

Active management by exception *involves watching for deviations from rules and standards and taking corrective action.*

Passive management by exception *involves intervening with employees only if standards are not met.*

Laissez faire leadership *involves abdicating responsibilities and avoiding decisions.*

- **Active management by exception** involves concentrating on occurrences that deviate from expected norms, such as irregularities, mistakes, exceptions and failure to meet standards. This means watching for deviations from rules and standards and taking corrective action (for example, your boss notices that you have a number of defects in a new aspect of your work and helps you adjust by giving you further training).
- **Passive management by exception** involves intervening only if standards are not met (for example, your boss comes to see you after noticing the high percentage of defects in your work).
- **Laissez faire leadership** involves abdicating responsibilities and avoiding decisions (for example, your boss is seldom around and does not follow through on decisions that need action). This is not a neutral act, but instead has been shown to be destructive in its outcome.[48]

Transformational leadership might go beyond this routine accomplishment, as shown in Figure 9.6.

For Bass, transformational leadership occurs when leaders broaden and elevate the interests of their followers, when they generate awareness and acceptance of the purposes and mission of the group and when they stir their followers to look beyond their own self-interest for the good of others.

Transformational leadership is a leadership style by which the followers' goals are broadened and elevated, and confidence is gained to go beyond expectations. This approach to leadership is based on motivating followers to do more than they originally intended, and often more than they thought possible. It involves guiding, influencing and inspiring people to excel and to contribute towards the achievement of organizational goals.

OB IN ACTION

When Ralph Norris took over as head of Air New Zealand he set out to replace the company's earlier dictatorial leadership model with a model that emphasizes the power of the people working for the company. In his words, 'Companies can no longer get away with telling staff to check in their brain in the morning and then proceed to tell them what to do.'[49]

In recent times, the ethical nature of transformational leadership has been the subject of much debate and controversy. Parry and Proctor-Thomson[50] argued that such debate has been demonstrated through the ways transformational leaders have been described. Labels and descriptors have included 'narcissistic', 'manipulative' and 'self-centred', but also 'ethical', 'just' and 'effective'. Using the Perceived Leader Integrity Scale (PLIS) and the Multi-Factor Leadership Questionnaire (MLQ) in a national sample of 1354 managers, they found a moderate to strong positive relationship between perceived integrity and the demonstration of transformational leadership behaviour.

The more recent research has focused on training requirements for transformational leadership. In particular, Parry and Sinha tested the effectiveness of transformational leadership training, using the Full Range Leadership Development (FRLD) programme. Their research revealed an increase in the display of transformational leadership factors by the participants.[51]

Transformational leadership tends to have four dimensions: charisma, inspiration, intellectual stimulation and individualized consideration:[52]

- **Charisma** provides vision, a sense of mission and instils pride, along with follower respect and trust (for example, Steve Jobs, head of Apple Computer, showed charisma by emphasizing the importance of creating the Macintosh as a radical new computer and showed it again when he focused on the iMac, another radical departure from computer standards).[53]
- **Inspiration** communicates high expectations, uses symbols to focus efforts and expresses important purposes in simple ways (for example, Richard Branson, chief executive officer of Virgin Airlines, has been known to personally greet passengers on flights that have experienced difficulties or been delayed).[54]
- **Intellectual stimulation** promotes intelligence, rationality and careful problem solving (for example, your boss challenges you to look at a difficult problem in a new way rather than walking away from it).
- **Individualized consideration** provides personal attention, treats each employee individually and coaches and advises (for example, your boss drops by and makes remarks reinforcing your worth as a person).

Together, charisma and inspiration transform follower expectations, but intellectual stimulation and individualized consideration are also needed to provide the necessary follow-through.

OB IN ACTION

Mothercare is a retailer of parenting and children's products which operates on mainland Britain and through franchises all over the world. It has two distinct brand names within its portfolio – Mothercare and The Early Learning Centre. In Britain the high street retail operation is conventional in structure, operating through Area Managers, each in control of a geographic 'patch' within which are individual stores. Seeking to ensure sustainability of its growth, the company has invested in rethinking the role of the 21 Area Managers and re-skilling them to be able to provide excellent support to store managers during the recession. The investment laid a heavy emphasis on leadership training through a three-day course followed by individual coaching. Senior management listened to the needs of the Area Managers and emphasized dealing with staff performance and embedding a culture of accountability.

This has resulted in Area Managers setting their stores BHAGs – Big Hairy Audacious Goals.

One reported benefit is a rekindling of enthusiasm amongst the managerial teams, where improving customer service and loyalty are seen as central to increasing and sustaining store performance. Coaching of local store managers has also been undertaken. Although the results are not yet fully analysed, Mothercare expects that sales and spend-per-visit will rise.

_____

Source: Adapted from Morrell, L. (2010), The vital role of the area manager. *Retail Week*, 28 May.

Charisma is a dimension of leadership, based on personal qualities, which provides vision and a sense of mission, and instils pride, respect and trust.

Bass concludes that transformational leadership is likely to be strongest at the top management level, where there is the greatest opportunity for proposing and communicating a vision. But it is by no means restricted to the top level; it is found throughout the organization. Further, transformational leadership operates in combination with transactional leadership. Transactional leadership is similar to most of the traditional leadership approaches. Proponents of this view suggest that those in a position of power need both transactional and transformational leadership to be successful, just as they need to use both leadership and management.[55]

EFFECTIVE MANAGER 9.1

The 'four Is' of transformational leadership

The following useful pointers about transformational leadership are given by Bruce Avolio and his associates:[56]

- Individualized consideration – pay attention to individual employees.

- Intellectual stimulation – be concerned with helping people to think through new ways.
- Inspirational motivation – inspire people to give their best.

- Idealized influence – engender respect and trust that gives power and influence over people.

A trend in current business research considers emotional intelligence (EI), and one can easily see how such skills and aptitudes would apply to the 'four Is' to enable someone to become an effective transformational leader. It is always hard for a manager to balance 'task' and 'people' needs – 'the four Is' provide focus points for managers to enable maximum outputs from their staff. But none are easy! Without doubt the field of EI will contribute in future years to our understanding of manager effectiveness.[57]

To summarize, transactional leaders guide employees in their tasks towards the achievement of pre-stated goals, whereas transformational leaders inspire their employees to challenge and transcend their view of their contribution to the organization.

Bryman has summarized a large number of studies using Bass's approach, ranging from six studies on the extra effort of followers to 16 studies on performance or effectiveness, to nearly a dozen covering various aspects of satisfaction. Still other studies cover such outcomes as burnout and stress and the predisposition to act as innovation champions. The strongest relationships tend to be associated with charisma or inspirational leadership, although in most cases the other dimensions are also important. These findings are impressive and broaden leadership outcomes beyond those used in the traditional leadership studies.[58] Researchers continue to investigate Bass's model and contribute to the generalizability of the model.[59]

Bernard Bass has also recently reviewed the two decades of research into transformational leadership. Recent findings in the field include evidence about why transformational leadership is more effective than transactional leadership and about why female leaders may be more transformational than their male counterparts. Bass concluded, despite an abundance of applied research, that more basic research and theory development is needed. More work needs to be done, for example, on how context affects transactional and transformational leadership and on how transformational leadership moves followers from compliance to the identification and internalization of values and beliefs beyond their own self-interest.[60]

Inspiration *is the communication of high expectations, the use of symbols to focus efforts and the expression of important purposes in simple ways.*

Intellectual stimulation *promotes intelligence, rationality and careful problem solving.*

Individualized consideration *is a leadership dimension by which the leader provides personal attention, treats each employee individually and coaches and advises employees.*

OB IN ACTION

Lessons from Jack Welch

Jack Welch's goal was to make General Electric (GE) 'the world's most competitive enterprise'. He knew that it would take nothing less than a 'revolution' to transform that dream into a reality. 'The

model of business in corporate America in 1980 had not changed in decades. Workers worked, managers managed and everyone knew their place. Forms and approvals and bureaucracy ruled the day.' Welch's self-proclaimed revolution meant waging war on GE's old ways of doing things and reinventing the company from top to bottom.

Jack Welch is all about leadership not management. Actually, he wanted to discard the term 'manager' altogether because it had come to mean someone who 'controls rather than facilitates, complicates rather than simplifies, acts more like a governor than an accelerator.' Welch has given a great deal of thought to how to manage employees effectively so that they are as produc-

tive as possible. And he has come to a seemingly paradoxical view. The less managing you do, the better off your company. Manage less to manage more.

Welch decided that GE's leaders, who did too much controlling and monitoring, had to change their management styles. Managers slow things down. Leaders spark the business to run smoothly and quickly. Managers talk to one another, write memos to one another. Leaders talk to their employees and talk with their employees, filling them with vision, getting them to perform at levels the employees themselves didn't think possible. Then (and to Welch this is a critical ingredient) they simply get out of the way.[61]

CAN LEADERSHIP BE TAUGHT?

Can people be trained in leadership? Through reading this book, one would suspect you do think this – and certainly the authors would agree. Research in this area agrees that training in leadership is possible. Bass and his colleagues have put a lot of work into such training efforts. They have created one workshop that lasts from three to five days, with later follow-up. Initially, leaders are given feedback on their scores on Bass's measures. Then the leaders devise improvement programmes to strengthen their weaknesses and work with the trainers to develop their leadership skills. Bass and Avolio report findings that demonstrate beneficial effects from this training. They also report on team training and programmes tailored to individual organizations' needs.[62]

Similarly, Conger and Kanungo propose training to develop the kinds of behaviour summarized in their model.[63]

▶ COUNTERPOINT

Roger Eglin, senior columnist for the *Sunday Times*, has collected an array of evidence that questions whether leadership can be taught in conventional courses. He refers to a review by

the firm of business psychologists Kaisen that has revealed many courses are seen as 'valueless'. Their work reflects a similar study by David Feeney at Said Business School in Oxford University. The argument is that in a conventional setting only the theory and cognitive understanding are transmitted. Leaders also need to learn how to implement. Eglin suggests that coaching is a useful tool for such one-to-one attention-giving.[64]

Questions

1. Why do you think coaching is a good tool for helping managers learn?
2. Think of two nonclassroom methods for teaching leadership.

Kouzes and Posner reported the results of a week-long training programme. The programme involved training of leaders on five dimensions oriented around developing, communicating and reinforcing a shared vision. According to Kouzes and Posner, leaders showed an average 15% increase in these visionary behaviours ten months after participating in the programme. Many of the new leadership training programmes involve a heavy, hands-on workshop emphasis, so leaders do more than just read about vision.[65]

- Is charismatic leadership always good? Not necessarily. Khurana suggests that charismatic leaders can destabilize the organization with their radical leadership and lead them to inappropriate paths – consider the leadership that saw the collapse of Enron.[66]
- Is leadership always needed? No. Sometimes emphasis on a vision diverts energy from more important day-to-day activities. Thus, what the vision contains is always fundamental.[67]
- Is leadership important only at the top? Considered essential at the top levels, leadership applies at all organizational levels.

GENDER, AGE AND CULTURAL DIVERSITY – CURRENT ISSUES IN LEADERSHIP

Much leadership theory and research originates from a North American context and has focused primarily on masculine models of leadership. Given the globalization of business, the increasing cultural diversity of domestic societies, the ageing of the workforce and the importance of women in the workforce and the community, this is a significant gap in leadership studies.

Considerable research has been undertaken over many years concerning the 'glass ceiling' and the advancement of women as leaders.[68] It is clear that attitudes vary greatly between cultures such that, in public service for example, many senior leaders in New Zealand and Sweden are women. The issue of women in management and leadership is more prevalent in some cultures than others. In addition, as antidiscrimination laws extend into race, religion, age, disability and sexuality as well as gender, patterns for all 'disadvantaged' groups are being explored.[69]

Alice Eagley has recently reviewed the literature connected to women in positions of leadership in the US.[70] She has found that attitudes are changing in a positive way toward women as managers and leaders. She discovered that women continue to do best in female-dominated workplaces. Although there are fewer women in male-gendered occupational areas, when women are leaders in these situations, they tend to out-perform their male counterparts. Eagley's review provides encouraging reading as an example of how attitudes can change for those who can be considered at a disadvantage. Gary Yukl has reviewed the research on leadership and gender differences and argues that it is 'inconclusive', all reviewers pointing out that the differences *within* men and women on how they behave and perform are far wider than differences *between* the sexes. Others argue that leadership models need a fundamental re-examination. For example, Sinclair argues that we need to review the relationship between heroic masculinity and corporate leadership, and that if this is not done, leadership will remain the privilege of a homogeneous elite. Such homogeneity in leadership, in the face of dramatic changes in workforce and customer diversity, is a potential liability.

The difficulties that disadvantaged demographic groups still face in progressing up the corporate hierarchy lead to diverse paths to leadership positions. Some transfer into leadership positions from other fields (rather than rising within a corporate structure); others become leaders of organizations through succession in family business. Still others start their own small businesses, which may then grow into substantial corporations.

On a wider international scale, a recent study on Arab women's conceptions of leadership compared women's leadership authority values in Oman, the United Arab Emirates and Lebanon. It found evidence of common leadership authority values in the Gulf countries (Oman and the UAE). Lebanon, meanwhile, was distinguished by relatively low levels of 'traditional' authority and very high levels of 'charismatic' authority. The findings demonstrate important regional similarities and differences in leadership authority values in the 'Arab world'.[71]

COUNTERPOINT

Convincing the traditionalists

ComCo is a privately owned software company based in Dublin, Eire. Since its inception in the mid-1970s, ComCo has prided itself on successful staff retention strategies and employee loyalty. Because of this, ComCo has been the focus of many business press reports. ComCo's distribution channels are worldwide and the company continues to enjoy growth built on leading-edge development. Frank Barker is the founder and CEO of

the company and is highly respected among his peers. A charismatic man, Frank likes to lead from the front in highly visible ways. Frank's senior management team are long-time employees and very experienced in their roles.

Recently Frank has become concerned about the future and succession strategy of ComCo, as most of the senior managers are approaching the last years of their working lives. No one has raised retirement and, typical of many baby boomers, the senior managers are not thinking about the issue of being replaced or succeeded by someone else. However, Frank is aware of potential health issues associated with age and the way these might affect ComCo's managers over the next few years.

A senior management team meeting is scheduled for the end of the week. Frank has been surprised at the results of his informal soundings in the firm, hearing enthusiasm from more junior staff for the top team to give way! On the other hand his suggestion of promoting existing deputies into their boss's jobs has been met with less enthusiasm. He thinks the firm needs consistency and all the knowledge the longer tenured staff hold – why would he get new blood in, or try to alter the profile of a well-tested solution for leading a firm in a tough market? His current staff know ComCo's customers, suppliers and other important stakeholders, so any succession planning must be carried out carefully and slowly. Nonetheless Frank knows it is his responsibility as head of the company to develop a new generation of leadership at ComCo but he doesn't want to throw away years of achievement in the process.

Questions

1. How can Frank be enabled to broaden his thinking?
2. There are many 'Franks' in the world – what arguments can be made for taking a fresh look at his plans?

Leadership and culture

Using a similar approach to that of Geert Hofstede, Robert House and his colleagues[72] embarked on an ambitious research project involving 62 countries. The GLOBE project investigated how cultural values are related to organizational practices, conceptions of leadership, the economic competitiveness of societies and the human condition of an organization's members.[73] More than 17 000 managers participated worldwide. Some of the main results of the project indicated that cultural values contributed either positively or negatively to the leadership profiles. For example, power-distance values were found to be a negative predictor of charismatic/value-based and participative leadership, but gender egalitarianism proved to be a positive predictor of the same. One of the key recommendations of the project was that leaders need to be aware of the links between cultural values and leadership practices. Other recent cross-national comparative studies have also reinforced the relevance of culture in leadership.[74] The GLOBE project is ongoing and results from it continue to be published.

CONCLUSION

Leadership can be distinguished from management and all managers have an opportunity to practise leadership. As one progresses up the organizational hierarchy, so leadership becomes more important, hence considerable research has been undertaken with top leaders. The development of our understanding of leadership began with somewhat crude trait theories, which, although appealing, failed to stand up to scientific scrutiny. However, studying effective individual leaders has informed our theory development in a positive way. Recent years have seen development towards a far more sophisticated view of leaders and their interface with followers. It has also become apparent that situational and other contingencies are important for effective leadership, hence theory has developed to investigate these aspects to form a broader and more realistic picture.

Training in leadership continues to be a challenge for most organizations. Looking to the future, our appreciation of difference (such as national culture and aspects connected with diversity) and ability to lead within such variations is a challenge as geographic boundaries dissolve. The GLOBE project and other initiatives are broadening our understanding of leadership from its North American theory development roots. This is an engaging area of study, inexorably linked to practice, which no doubt will continue to evolve.

SUMMARY

LEARNING OBJECTIVE 1
Differences between leadership and management

Leadership and management differ in that management is designed to promote stability or to make the organization run smoothly, while the role of leadership is to promote adaptive change. Traditional and new leadership differ.

LEARNING OBJECTIVE 2
Trait and characteristic theories of leadership

Trait and characteristic leadership approaches centre on the qualities that are held by the leader. Early studies failed to locate straightforward traits held by the 'great' leaders. Recent work, operating at a more sophisticated level, argues that leader traits and characteristics should be taken more seriously. Traits and aspects of personality are more innate and harder to change than behaviours which we associate with leader characteristics such as charisma, authenticity and ethical or servant leadership. Many organizations invest time and money in training managers to enhance their capability in leadership characteristics.

LEARNING OBJECTIVE 3
Behavioural theories of leadership

Behavioural theories centre on how a manager behaves in his or her leadership role. Developed in the 1960s, these ideas centre around two aspects of leadership: where the focus lies with task or people and relationships respectively. Many studies subsequent to this period have found these two parameters can describe leader behaviour well, but that few leaders will be excellent at both, hence our scope needs to extend to those leaders who do less of one or both. In general, passive leadership (where neither task nor people are considered) is negative for an organization. These parameters do not predict performance success very well. Hence people/task focus might provide an accurate description of one aspect of leadership, but the real context is wider than these constructs.

LEARNING OBJECTIVE 4
Situational contingency theories of leadership

Leader situational contingency approaches argue that leadership, in combination with various situational variables, has a major impact on outcomes. Sometimes, as in the case of the substitutes for leadership approach, the role of the situational variables replaces that of leadership to the point that leadership has little or no impact in itself. Fiedler's contingency theory, House's path–goal theory and Hersey and Blanchard's Situational Leadership® theory are other approaches that consider the impact not just of leadership but of various situational contingencies.

LEARNING OBJECTIVE 5
Transformational and transactional leadership

Transactional leadership is about day-to-day routine tasks and has a level of achievement which is set and predictable. Transformational leadership approaches are typically broader, more enabling and support employees to stretch themselves and their capabilities outside their usual scope – they are hence 'transforming'. Although most research concerns the benefits of transformational leadership, there is a role for transactional leadership in day-to-day tasks. Bass and associates' transformational approach is a particularly well-known theory that includes charisma as one of its dimensions. It separates vision-oriented transformational leadership from day-to-day transactional leadership, and argues that the two work in combination. Transformational leadership is important because it facilitates change in our increasingly fast-moving world.

LEARNING OBJECTIVE 6
Diversity in leadership

Western, masculine models have dominated leadership theory and research. Such a limitation is significant given the increasing diversity of the workforce and society in general. In Australia the progress of women's representation in organizational leadership positions at executive and board level has been slow but recently women have gained a greater presence in leadership roles across many industries, some of which were traditionally male dominated. We are also seeing much younger company leaders, both male and female, who are excelling in their field. Recent research has explored the need to recognize the impact of culture on leadership styles and the appropriateness of approaches across different cultures.

CHAPTER 9 STUDY GUIDE

Now that you have read this chapter, you should be able to apply and further develop your knowledge by undertaking the following activities set out over the next few pages: test your knowledge questions, an individual activity and an end-of-chapter case study.

Please also go to this book's website: **www.wileyeurope.com/college/french** to find further material which will enhance your understanding and enable you to assess your knowledge.

TEST YOUR KNOWLEDGE

1. Review and discuss the advantages and disadvantages of the trait and behavioural approaches to leadership.

2. Discuss the reasons for the popularity of the contingency approach to leadership.

3. Explain how leadership and trust may be related.

4. What can managers do to help develop some of the new leadership characteristics?

5. You will recall that we discussed that there are two kinds of leadership: formal and informal. Think of a situation in which you have been part of a group or a team, maybe at work or in your recreational time. Reflect on that situation – its actual dynamics and the outcome. Identify the formal and informal leadership roles and how they played out in your example. How did each of the leaders contribute to the outcome? Who was the most effective? What did you learn from that?

6. You have recently formed a new consulting business with three colleagues whom you met while studying at university. Explain the process you will go through to establish the leadership role for the business. For example, would the role of leader automatically be given to the person who initiated the consulting idea or would you consider another method of selection?

7. Using an example of a situation you are familiar with, ideally in the workplace, identify and explain the different dynamics between leadership and management.

8. Your company has offered you a promotion as head of a division in a country that has a very different culture from that of your native country. You are excited by the new challenge but you are also aware that you need to consider whether your leadership style will be effective or appropriate for the new location. Using two countries of your choice (your native country and one with a different culture), outline four of the most important factors relating to the style of leadership you should adopt when considering the offer of promotion into the new culture.

9. In this chapter we discussed the concept of new leadership training. Prepare a two-page case either for or against the following statement: 'People can be trained in new leadership'. This exercise could provide an opportunity for an interesting debate among several groups in your organizational behaviour class.

10. Imagine you have been asked to address a class of school students who are in their final year and looking forward to leaving. Their teacher did not provide you with much information other than that she wanted you to deliver a ten-minute speech on how the students can develop their leadership potential. Prepare a list of the things you would include in your speech. Be sure to make the content relevant for the group you are speaking to – that is, young adults who are about to embark on their individual career journeys. Rather than past or current leaders, you may want to consider what the future might demand of leaders and what attributes they will need to cater to that demand. You should consider issues at a macro as well as micro level. This exercise will be interesting as a class discussion, and your lecturer may want to expand the topic into an assignment.

11. Some scholars have argued that the new leadership style in its various forms involves mystical qualities that few people possess. Others have argued that it can be readily identified and that people can be trained to display it. You are required to prepare two scripts. The first is a script for the CEO of a major hotel chain to present to a small group of junior managers who show great leadership potential. In this case, the CEO is emphasizing the need for new leadership approaches to be adopted by the junior managers. The second is a script for a leader supporting the case for a more traditional leadership approach to a particular situation. This might be a one-off situation in which a more directive leadership style is appropriate. Several questions now follow that you may want to consider, but you may prepare your own topics if you wish.

(a) How mystical is the new leadership? How desirable is it?

(b) How successful do you think leaders who use your new leadership script might be in convincing followers that they are charismatic or transformational?

(c) Do you think one particular leadership style is more appropriate than another when considering the gender of a particular group – for example, men leading women or women leading men?

(d) Do you think leadership approaches should change depending on the circumstances, the industry or the current environment?

12. Leadership is a topical and controversial subject in the global business arena. Using the Internet, search through leadership sites around the world and find out how different cultures emphasize different aspects of leadership. Compose a list of three common characteristics that successful leaders are currently perceived to display around the world and also find three that are unique in a particular country.

INDIVIDUAL ACTIVITY

Survey of leadership[75]

Objective

To develop your ability to assess leadership styles. Total time: 15 minutes. The following ten questions ask about your supervisor's leadership behaviour and practices. Try to respond on the basis of your actual observations of your supervisor's actions. Choose a response from the following five and place the score alongside it in the box beside each question.

To a great extent	5
To a considerable extent	4
To a moderate extent	3
To a slight extent	2
To almost no extent	1

To what extent:

1. Is your supervisor easy to approach? ☐
2. Does your supervisor encourage people to give their best effort? ☐
3. Does your supervisor show you how to improve your performance? ☐
4. Does your supervisor encourage people to work as a team? ☐
5. Does your supervisor pay attention to what you say? ☐
6. Does your supervisor maintain high standards of performance? ☐
7. Does your supervisor provide the help you need so you can schedule work ahead of time? ☐
8. Does your supervisor encourage people to exchange opinions and ideas? ☐
9. Is your supervisor willing to listen to your problems? ☐
10. Does your supervisor offer new ideas for solving job-related problems? ☐

Interpretation

Support (S) and interaction facilitation (IF) are the two dimensions that define interpersonal or relationship-centred leadership behaviour. Support refers to the leader's personal concern for employees, while interaction facilitation measures how the leader encourages teamwork among employees. The two scores, S and IF, can be added to yield an overall interpersonal relationship score.

Goal emphasis (GE) and work facilitation (WF) both centre on task-oriented leader behaviour. Goal emphasis simply refers to the degree to which the leader emphasizes the importance of achieving high goals, while work facilitation measures the degree to which the leader engages in behaviour that helps employees to do their jobs effectively. The two scores, GE and WF, can be added to yield an overall task orientation score.

LEADERSHIP CHALLENGE

ABC Accounting Associates is a small organization with a total of eight employees, including management. The organization has been in operation for 15 years and most of the employees have been there since the beginning. It has a traditional management structure – a managing director, Harry, and two other directors, Stephen and Margaret. The three senior managers – Lou, Mark and Maria – are responsible for most of the clients' basic accounting and bookkeeping needs. Two administration staff – Franco and Betty – are responsible for ABC's day-to-day office duties.

ABC has very few clients; however, they are profitable for the organization and very loyal. Most have been with ABC for more than ten years and it is highly unlikely that they will move to another accounting firm, as they are completely satisfied.

Internally, however, things are not so good. For many years, ABC functioned well under the leadership of Harry. Harry is now in his late 60s and is getting a little tired and bored with the day-to-day operations. He also suffers from poor health but without ABC his health would probably decline even more. Harry's boredom is reflected in his attitude to work and his motivation to expand the business. Stephen and Margaret are much younger and keen to expand ABC, although Stephen tends to let his outside interests get in the way of work and often disappears for several hours at a time. Over the past 18 months there has been a large inequity of commitment and productivity between the three directors. Harry shows no interest in the business at all. Stephen is keen to build the business but spends only half the amount of time at the office that Margaret spends. Margaret has the most experience and works extremely long hours, so does not have much time to socialize with the other employees.

More than 80% of the clients on ABC's books are there because of Margaret. If Margaret decided to leave ABC, the business would probably not survive, as the client would no doubt ultimately follow her. The employees at ABC are not aware of this think that it is Harry's efforts and experience that keep the clients loyal to the o tion. Margaret has so far tolerated the situation in the hope that one day she v Harry as managing director – she is, after all, Harry's daughter!

Margaret is getting to the point where her frustrations can no lon Although she gets some degree of support from the other employees a' Stephen and Harry are taking advantage of her. Margaret is a very ' are quickly coming to a head.

There is a directors' meeting this afternoon at 4 p.m., a. to prepare the agenda – the other two directors are out to lunch.

Source: From Wood, J. *et al.* (2006), *Organizational Behaviour: Core Concep* John Wiley & Sons Australia, Ltd: Milton, Qld.

Case Study

Margaret so she decides to prepare an agenda but not with the usual topics that Stephen and Harry expect. This time Margaret challenges the leadership issue at ABC.

Questions

1. Briefly explain how Margaret should approach the leadership issue with Harry and Stephen during the meeting.
2. What leadership style do you think would be appropriate for ABC Accounting?
3. Given that the employees are quite satisfied under Harry's directorship, how should they be approached regarding a potential leadership change at ABC?

SUGGESTED READING

Shelton, C. D., McKenna, M. K. & Darling, J. R. (2002), Leading in the age of paradox: optimizing behavioural style, job fit and cultural cohesion. *Leadership and Organization Development Journal*, **23** (7), 372–379. This article is unusual in that it attempts to bridge some of the apparent paradoxes within leadership in a practical manner.

Yukl, G. (2010), *Leadership in Organizations*, global edition, Prentice Hall: Thousand Oaks, CA. This is a book that both reviews the literature and provides critical commentary. It is excellent for the student interested in pursuing leadership to a greater depth and provides signposting for specialized work.

END NOTES

1. Pink, D. H. (2010), *Drive: The surprising truth about what motivates us*, Canongate Books: Edinburgh.

2. Kotter, J. (1990), *A Force for Change: How Leadership Differs from Management*, Harvard Business School Press: Boston MA.

3. Potter, J. & Hooper, A. (2005), *Developing Strategic Leadership Skills: Developing a Strategic Approach at All Levels*, CIPD: London.

4. Hurd, M. (2006), Questions and answers with Mark Hurd. *Baylor Business Review*, **25** (1), 26–29, quotation is on p. 26.

5. Yukl, G. (2010), *Leadership in Organizations*, global edition, Prentice Hall: Thousand Oaks, CA.

Stogdill, R. M. (1974), *Handbook of Leadership*, The Free Press: New York.

7. Bass, B. M. (1990), *Bass and Stogdill's Handbook of Leadership*, The Free Press: New York.

8. Paglis, L. L. & Green, S. G. (2002), Leadership self-efficacy and managers' motivation for leading change. *Journal of Organizational Studies*, **23**, 215–235.

9. Kipnis, D. & Lane, W. P. (1962), Self confidence and leadership. *Journal of Applied Psychology*, **46**, 291–295.

10. Aasland, M. S., Skogstad, A., Notelaers, G., Neilsen, M. B. & Einarsen, S. (2010), The prevalence of destructive leadership behavior. *British Journal of Management*, **21** (2), 438–452.

11. Yukl, G. (2010) op. cit. and Bass, B. M. (1990) op. cit. Chapter 12.

12. Conger, J. A. & Kanungo, R. N. (1988), *Charismatic Leadership, the Elusive Factor in*

Organizational Effectiveness, Jossey-Bass: San Francisco.

13. See Howell, J. M. & Avolio, B. J. (1992), The ethics of charismatic leadership: submission or liberation. *The Academy of Management Executive*, 6 (2), May, 43–54.

14. Conger & Kanungo, op. cit.

15. Ibid. Halpert, J. A. (1990), The dimensionality of charisma. *Journal of Business and Psychology*, 4 (4).

16. See Hwang, A., Khatri, N. & Srinivas, E. S. (2005), Organizational charisma and vision across three countries. *Management Decision*, 43 (7/8), 960–974.

17. Yukl, G. (2010) op. cit., p. 287.

18. Yukl, G. (1999), An evaluation of conceptual weaknesses in transformational and charismatic leadership theories. *Leadership Quarterly*, 10 (2), 285–305.

19. Gardner, W. L., Avolio, B. J., Luthans, F., May, D. R. & Walumba, F. O. (2005), Can you see the real me? A self-based model of authentic leadership and follower development. *Leadership Quarterly*, 16 (3), 343–372.

20. Brown, M. E. & Trevino, L. K. (2006), Ethical Leadership: A review and future directions. *Leadership Quarterly*, 10, 531–539.

21. Dineer, B. R., Lewicki, R. J. & Tomlinson, E. C. (2006), Supervisory guidance and behavioural integrity. *Journal of Applied Psychology*, 91 (3), 622–635.

22. Detert, J. R., Trevino, L. K. & Sweitzer, V. L. (2008), Moral disengagement and ethical decision making: A study of antecedents and outcomes. *Journal of Applied Psychology*, 93 (2), 374–391.

23. Greenleaf, R. K. (1977), *Servant Leadership: A Journey into the Nature of Legitimate Power and Greatness*, Paulist Press: New York.

24. Sendjaya, S. & Sarros, J. C. (2002), Servant leadership: its origin, development, and application in organizations. *Journal of Leadership and Organizational Studies*, 9 (2), 57.

25. Spears, L. C. (ed.) (1997), *Reflections on Leadership*, John Wiley & Sons, Inc.: New York.

26. Likert, R. (1961), *New Patterns of Management*, McGraw-Hill: New York.

27. Bass, op. cit., Chapter 24.

28. Blake, R. R. & Mouton, J. S. (1978), *The New Managerial Grid*, Gulf: Houston, TX.

29. For example, Fleishman, E. & Harris, E. F. (1962), Patterns of leadership behaviour related to employee grievances and turnover. *Personnel Psychology*, 15, 43–56.

30. Hinkin, T. R. & Schresheim, C. A. (2008), An examination on Nonleadership: From laissez-faire leadership to leader reward omission and punishment omission. *Journal of Applied Psychology*, 93 (6), 1234–1248.

31. See Peterson, M. F. (1988), PM theory in Japan and China: what's in it for the United States? *Organizational Dynamics*, Spring, 22–39; Misumi, J. & Peterson, M. F. (1985), The performance-maintenance theory of leadership: review of a Japanese research program. *Administrative Science Quarterly*, 30, 98–223; Smith, P. B., Misumi, J., Tayeb, M. *et al.* (1986), On the generality of leadership style measures across cultures. Paper presented at the International Congress of Applied Psychology, Jerusalem, July.

32. This section is based on Fiedler, F. E. & Chemers, M. M. (1984), *The Leader Match Concept*, 2nd edn. John Wiley & Sons, Inc.: New York.

33. For example Vroom, V. H. & Jago, A. G. (2007), The role of the situation in leadership. *American Psychologist*, 62 (1), 17–24.

34. This section is based on Fiedler, F. E. & Garcia, J. E. (1987), *New Approaches to Effective Leadership,* John Wiley & Sons, Inc.: New York.

35. Miller, R. L., Butler, J. & Cosentino, C. C. (2004), Followership effectiveness: an extension of Fiedler's contingency model. *Leadership and Organization Development Journal*, 25 (4), 362–368.

36. For example Hanbury, G. L., Sapat, A. & Washington, C. W. (2004), Know yourself and take charge of your own destiny: The 'fit model' of leadership. *Public Administration Review*, 64 (5), 566–576.

37. This section is based on House, R. J. & Mitchell, T. R. (1977), Path–goal theory of leadership. *Journal of Contemporary Business*, Autumn, 81–97.

38. House & Mitchell, op. cit.

39. See the discussion of this approach in Hersey, P. & Blanchard, K. H. (1988), *Management of Organizational Behaviour*, Prentice Hall: Englewood Cliffs, NJ.

40. Ibid.

41. For some criticisms, see Graeff, C. L. (1983), The situational leadership theory: a critical view. *Academy of Management Review*, 8, 285–291.

42. The discussion in this section is based on Kerr, S. & Jermier, J. (1978), Substitutes for leadership: their meaning and measurement. *Organizational Behaviour and Human Performance*, **22**, 375–403; Howell, J. P., Bowen, D. E., Dorfman, P. W. *et al.* (1990), Substitutes for leadership: effective alternatives to ineffective leadership. *Organizational Dynamics*, Summer, 21–38.

43. Posakoff, P. M., Dorfman, P. W., Howell, J. P. & Todor, W. D. (1989), Leader reward and punishment behaviours: a preliminary test of a culture-free style of leadership effectiveness. *Advances in Comparative Management*, **2**, 95–138; Peng, T. K. (1990), *Substitutes for Leadership in an International Setting*, unpublished manuscript, College of Business Administration, Texas Tech University: Lubbock, TX.

44. Based on *The Columbus Effect: unexpected findings and new directions in leadership research*. Presentation made at annual meeting, Academy of Management, Las Vegas, August 1992.

45. Einarsen, S. E., Aasland, M. S. & Skogstad, A. (2007), Destructive leadership behavior: a definition and conceptual model. *Leadership Quarterly*, **18** (3), 207–216.

46. Roberts, A. (2003), *Hitler and Churchill: Secrets of Leadership*, Weidenfeld & Nicolson: London.

47. Why good leaders are hard to find. *The Age*, 2 August 2003, www.theage.com. au/articles/2003/08/01/1059480538838. html?oneclick=true (accessed 28 September 2010).

48. Skogstad, A., Einarsen, S., Torsheim, T., Aasland, M. S. & Hetland, H. (2007), The destructiveness of laissez-faire leadership behavior. *Journal of Occupational Health Psychology*, **12** (1), 80–92.

49. See Huang, M., Cheng, B. & Chou, L. (2005), Fitting in organizational values: the mediating role of person-organization fit between CEO charismatic leadership and employee outcomes. *International Journal of Manpower*, **26** (1), 35–49.

50. Parry, K. W. & Proctor-Thomson, S. B. (2002), Perceived integrity of transformational leaders in organizational settings. *Journal of Business Ethics*, **35** (2), 75–96.

51. Parry, K. W. & Sinha, P. (2005), Researching the trainability of transformational organizational leadership. *Human Resource Development International*, **8** (2), 165–183.

52. See Bass, M. (1985), *Leadership and Performance beyond Expectations*. The Free Press: New York; Bryman, A. (1992), *Charisma and Leadership in Organizations*, Sage: London, pp. 98–99.

53. See Bryman, A. (1992), *Charisma and Leadership in Organizations*, Sage: London, Chapter 5.

54. De Vries, K. (1998), Charisma in action: the transformational abilities of Virgin's Richard Branson and AAB's Percy Barnevik. *Organizational Dynamics*, Winter, 18.

55. Bass, M. (1985), op. cit.

56. Avolio, B., Waldman, D. & Yammarino, F. (1991), Leading in the 1990s: the four Is of transformational leadership. *Journal of European Industrial Training*, **15** (4), 9–16.

57. See Ashkanasy, N. M. & Dasborough, M. T. (2003), Emotional awareness and emotional intelligence in leadership teaching. *Journal of Education for Business*, **79** (1), 18–22.

58. Bryman, A. (1992) op. cit., Chapter 6; Inkson, K. & Moss, A. T. (1993), Transformational leadership – is it universally applicable? *Leadership and Organizational Development*, **14** (4), 1–11.

59. For example, Sanders, K. & Schyns, B. (2006), Trust conflict and cooperative behaviour – considering reciprocity within organizations. *Personnel Review*, **35** (5), 538–556.

60. Bass, B. M. (1999), Two decades of research and development in transformational leadership. *European Journal of Work and Organizational Psychology*, **8** (1), 9–32.

61. Kotelnikov, V. (2007), 25 lessons from Jack Welch, www.1000ventures.com/business_guide/mgmt_new-model_25lessons-welch.html, (accessed 24 August 2007).

62. See Bass, B. M. & Avolio, B. J. (1990), The implications of transactional and transformational leadership for individual, team and organizational development. *Research in Organizational Change and Development*, 4, 231–272.

63. See Conger, J. A. & Kanungo, R. N. (1988) Training charismatic leadership: a risky and critical task, in Conger & Kanungo, op. cit., Chapter 11.

64. *Sunday Times*, Appointments, 21 January 2007, p. 9.

65. See Kouzes, J. R. & Posner, B. F. (1991), *The Leadership Challenge: How to Get Extraordinary Things Done in Organizations*, Jossey-Bass: San Francisco.

66. Khurana, R. (2002), The curse of the superstar CEO. *Harvard Business Review*, 80 (9), 60–66.

67. For a discussion of this see Spreier, S. W., Fountaine, M. H. & Malloy, R. L. (2006), Leadership run amok. *Harvard Business Review*, 84 (6), 72–82.

68. Ryan, M. & Alexander, S. (2005), The glass cliff: Evidence that women are over-represented in precarious leadership positions. *British Journal of Management*, 16 (2), 81–90.

69. Sinclair, A. (1998), *Doing Leadership Differently*, Melbourne University Press: Melbourne, p. 13.

70. Eagly, A. H. (2007), Female leadership advantage and disadvantage: resolving the contradictions. *Psychology of Women Quarterly*, 31 (1), 1–12.

71. See Hofstede, G. (1980), *Culture's Consequences: International Differences in Work-related Values*, Sage: Beverly Hills, CA.

72. House, R., Javidan, M., Hanges, P. & Dorfman, P. (2002), Understanding cultures and implicit leadership theories across the globe: an introduction to project GLOBE (global leadership and organizational behaviour effectiveness). *Journal of World Business*, 37 (1), 3–10.

73. House, R. J., Hanges, P. J., Javidan, M. *et al.* (eds) (2004), *Culture, Leadership and Organizations: the GLOBE Study of 62 Societies*, Sage: Thousand Oaks, CA.

74. See, for example, Zagorsek, H., Jaklic, M. & Stough, S. J. (2004), Comparing leadership practices between the United States, Nigeria and Slovenia: does culture matter? *Cross Cultural Management: An International Journal*, 11 (2), 16–34.

75. Adapted from *The survey of organizations*, © 1980 by the University of Michigan and Rensis Likert Associates. Reprinted by permission of the Institute for Social Research.

CHAPTER 10

Power, politics and decision making in organizations

LEARNING OBJECTIVES

After studying this chapter you should be able to:

- discuss the sources of power for managers and employees
- explain the relationship between power, authority and obedience
- discuss the meaning and importance of empowerment in organizations
- describe various kinds of political behaviour in organizations
- discuss the ethical implications of politics in organizations
- define decision making and contrast the classical and behavioural decision-making models
- summarize the sequential steps in the decision-making process
- evaluate the contributions of intuition, judgement and risk analysis to quality decision making
- state the conditions under which individuals or groups are best placed to make decisions in organizations
- identify contemporary issues affecting the decision-making context.

MASSAGING THE FIGURES...

One early victim of the financial crisis in the UK was the bank Northern Rock, which had to be brought into public ownership in 2008 after confidence in the bank fell to such an extent that investors were queuing outside branches to retrieve their deposits. Confidence in a bank stems from investors believing that they can recover their money, so a bank must be careful how much money it lends out in mortgages and other loans so that in the end it can 'balance the books'. Banks in the UK are controlled by the Financial Services Authority (FSA), which reported in 2010 on its

investigation of the decisions two senior Northern Rock employees made prior to the crisis. The FSA has fined the former deputy CEO (David Baker) and the former managing credit director (Richard Barclay). The FSA found both had deliberately misreported mortgage arrears. At the time Northern Rock sold mortgage products which enabled borrowers to borrow more money than their house was worth. In a rising housing market it might be argued that as the house price would be increasing and if the borrower sold, the sale of the house would bring in sufficient funds to cover the loan. However, when householders fail to pay their mortgage (becoming in arrears) this is a first signal that the loan may not be repaid. Although all mortgage lenders have some borrowers in arrears, when many borrowers are in arrears, investors start to wonder if the bank is lending prudently. As an expanding bank, Northern Rock needed investors, and used its huge success in the mortgage market to attract investors. The FSA found that staff in the debt management unit were under pressure to report arrears less than the industry average, and had been targeted as such. Staff apparently hid the number of arrears, effectively 'massaging the figures' over a period of time and this was only discovered after Barclay went off sick. The manager temporarily replacing Barclay discovered around 2000 loans in arrears not being reported, and let Baker (deputy CEO) know. Baker then failed to report this to the CEO, the Board or the Risk Committee for 'compassionate' reasons, allowing the unit six months to recover their positions. This led to false reporting to investors. Baker has been banned from working in the industry for life.

The deception involved clerical staff, managers and senior managers.

Questions

1. What pressures might there be on employees deciding to go along with the deception? How might these pressures be framed as 'power' or 'political'?
2. Why do you think the temporary manager decided to 'blow the whistle'?
3. How do you think you would have reacted if you were a middle manager in the debt management unit?

See FSA fines and bans former Northern Rock deputy chief executive and credit director for misreporting mortgage arrears figures, Press Release Number 066, 13 April 2010 http://www.fsa.gov.uk/pages/Library/Communication/ PR/2010/066.shtml (accessed 15 April 2010).

INTRODUCTION

With fast-paced, complex and rapidly changing business environments, the demands on leaders and managers have multiplied. Decisions need to be made quickly otherwise opportunities are lost. The need for managers to maximize their influence by acquiring and using power effectively is central to effective working, decision making and delegation to enable work to be undertaken efficiently.

As students of organizations, we need to understand that power and politics are very much part of decision making both within and across organizational boundaries. Most employees find themselves in situations where they need to influence others. This might be at a peer group level, upwards into the management hierarchy or with subordinates. There are many ways to achieve power and influence and, as the Northern Rock case shows, the effects of power and politics extend throughout hierarchies. Money and resources are not the sole vehicles of power. The ability to network, build and retain relationships can also be an important generator of influence in the modern organization. The power of partnerships and alliances is indisputable.

In this chapter we will first examine the issue of power and politics and then progress to apply that knowledge within the area of decision making. Together these topics form key foundations for anyone wishing to enter management grades and progress through an organization, or deal effectively with stakeholders (such as suppliers and clients) over a period of time.

INTRODUCTION TO POWER AND POLITICS

No discussion of organizational behaviour would be complete without a study of power and politics. Every day, in every kind of situation, managers and employees alike use power and politics to do their jobs. A manager hires a personal assistant, a finance manager audits a department, a working group decides the priorities for an improvement programme and a board of directors discusses the strategic plan – all of these are instances of the use of power and they often entail politics. Power and politics may be the source of solutions as well as problems in organizations. They are important but remain quite elusive as academic concepts in organizational behaviour. To be effective, managers need to know how power is acquired and exercised. They also need to know about political behaviour in organizations and about organizational dynamics.

In this chapter we first examine the meaning of power and politics and their effects at the interpersonal and organizational levels. We outline and discuss theories within the field and apply them in practice.

What is affected by organizational power and politics? Is this only relevant to those who are directly involved? Unfortunately not. Allocation of resources such as money, equipment and staff numbers, changes to rules and procedures, reorganization, delegation of authority, personnel changes such as promotions and transfers, recruitment and selection, pay and work appraisals and interdepartmental coordination are most commonly affected by politics, power and influence – and of course these affect everyone.[1]

Power and politics represent the essence of what happens in organizations on a daily basis.[2] This is because organizations are not democracies composed of individuals with equal influence. At the extreme, some organizations are more akin to medieval feudal states in which managers believe they can rule through a divine right. In such circumstances any attempt to change can be seen as undermining others' roles and requires immense skill. In such organizations employees are highly political animals. Some organizations have become so political that organizational interests are completely subordinated to individual interests.

Clearly, power and politics are important organizational tools that managers use to get the job done, and their use does not have to be negative. In effective organizations, astute individuals delicately develop, nurture and manage power and politics. In other words, power and politics may be unsavoury notions to some but, when used with care, they can bring together individual desires for joint accomplishment.[3]

POWER AND INFLUENCE

Power may be defined as the potential ability to influence behaviour. As such it is usually crucial if one wants to change the course of events, overcome resistance or to convince people to do things.[4] Politics and influence are the processes, actions and behaviours through which this potential power is used and realized.[5] In simpler terms, power may be defined as the ability to get someone to do something you want done or the ability to make things happen in the way you want. The essence of power is control over the behaviour of others.[6] Power is the force that makes things happen in an intended way; influence is a behavioural response to the exercise of power – that is, **influence** is an outcome achieved through the use of power. Managers use power to achieve influence over subordinates and others in the work setting.

Figure 10.1 summarizes the link between power and influence. It also identifies the key bases of power that managers can use to influence the behaviour of other people at work. Managers derive power from the organization and other individuals. We call these sources position power and personal power, respectively.[7] French and Raven first raised

Power *is the ability to get someone else to do something you want done, or the ability to make things happen or get things done in the way you want.*

Influence *is a behavioural response to the exercise of power.*

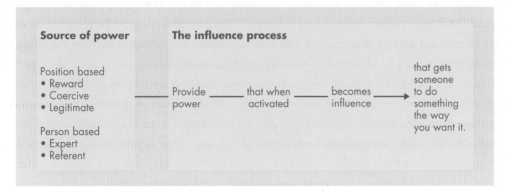

Figure 10.1: Power sources and the influence process.

this distinction in their landmark study and it underpins our discussion on the subject. Much of the key research into this area was based in the 1980s, and it is a credit to French and Raven's ideas that they have endured so many decades.

Position power

Three bases of position power are available to managers solely as a result of their position in the organization: reward, coercive and legitimate power. These will now be discussed in turn.

Reward power

Reward power *is the extent to which a manager can use extrinsic and intrinsic rewards to control other people.*

Reward power is the extent to which a manager can use extrinsic and intrinsic rewards. Managers usually hold power in organizations by virtue of their ability to reward. The strength of the power differs depending on the rewards that the manager controls and the strength of the employee's desire for the rewards.

Examples of such rewards include money, promotions, compliments or enriched jobs. These types of rewards are discussed in detail in Chapter 4. One should not forget that rewards such as praise and positive interaction are some of the 'soft' rewards for which employees will often work very hard. Such types of reward are available to everyone to use.

Coercive power

Coercive power *is the extent to which a manager can deny desired rewards or administer punishment to control other people.*

Power can also be founded on punishment as well as reward. Managers can cause others to have unpleasant experiences. In such circumstances **coercive power** is thought of as a form of punishment for failing to comply with the wishes of the power holder. A manager may withhold a pay rise, allocate least desirable tasks or times of work to a person as a form of punishment or exclude someone from training or crucial information. The strength of coercive power is based on the extent to which a manager can administer punishments to control other people. Naturally there are 'soft' punishments as there are 'soft' rewards. Thus, not engaging in positive social interaction with one member of staff can be seen as a coercive and punishing act.[8]

The availability of formal reward and coercive power varies very much from one organization and manager to another. Given the possible negative effects of this power, they should be used carefully and most organizations devise rules and principles to guide rewards and punishment, formal and informal. Thus, employees may be required to treat each other with dignity and respect and this will apply to managers in their handling of subordinates as well as on a peer-to-peer basis. Organizations have complaints systems and a system of 'appeal' to protect employees against coercion and various illegitimate acts, such as harassment in the workplace. Such organizational policies on employee treatment and the presence of unions, for example, can weaken coercive power considerably. Unions point out that when unemployment is high and job insecurity is rampant, employees may feel less able to confront coercive power; further, employees may not seek the assistance of unions for fear of further unpleasant consequences such as being labelled a troublemaker, or they might think that any complaint will be career limiting.

Bullying as a coercive power

Workplace bullying is a major source of employee discontent and lost productivity. Around a quarter of people who are bullied leave their jobs, often quietly and without making a complaint. In addition, witnesses leave – we presume because they are worried that they will be next in the frame.[9] Cultural differences are apparent, with the Scandinavian countries experiencing higher rates of peer-to-peer bullying whereas in the UK, US, Canada and Australia it is managers who are most often identified as the source of bullying.[10] Regardless of who is the perpetrator of the experience it is very negative for employees who suffer stress[11] and it is thought this issue contributes significantly to absenteeism. Students wishing to explore the estimated costs of workplace bullying should visit their own country's central government website to do with safety and health. Both employers and employees are damaged by the presence of workplace bullying and have an equal interest in its eradication.[12]

Legitimate power and formal authority

Legitimate power relates to the right (rather than capacity) to command. As the third base of power, legitimate power stems from the extent to which a manager can use the internalized belief of employees that the 'boss' has a 'right of command'. These beliefs are called implicit leadership theories – not an easy phrase – but we each have an internalized idea of what a leader should, should not, can and cannot do.[13]

Legitimate power is based on a mutually accepted perception that the power holder (in this case the manager) has the right to influence the employee. In this context, managers are the bosses, their employees are the subordinates and many routine instructions and requests are accepted simply because everyone agrees that employees should do what managers say.

Legitimate power is often used interchangeably with the term 'formal authority', drawing direct lines between responsibility, power and authority, and one has to have commensurate power and authority to meet job responsibilities. Legitimate power confers an authority (at the extreme in a legal sense) to use organizational resources to accomplish goals. For example, the organization's board of directors grants the legitimate power of a chief executive officer, which gives him or her authority over all organizational resources. In turn, the chief executive officer has the right to confer legitimate power upon managers lower down in the organization's hierarchy. Supervisors, too, have legitimate power over their employees, which reflects the responsibilities in their job.

Process power is part of legitimate power and is found in individuals whose positions influence how inputs are transformed into outputs. For instance, an organization may nominate a financial controller to monitor the efficiency of a production process, or an organization may use business process re-engineering systems. Such systems are typically designed to empower workers and supervisory staff by giving them responsibility for specific processes. In such circumstances they can overturn the traditional management hierarchy where processes are managed from the top down. Thus, legitimate power does not always follow the direction of the traditional hierarchy.

Legitimate power is the extent to which a manager can use the internalized belief of an employee that the 'boss' has a 'right of command' to control other people.

Process power is the control over methods of production and analysis.

Information power *is the extent to which individuals have control over information needed by others.*

Information power is the final source of position power. Students reading this text may be seeking to improve their information power base. Managers need access to information and can become dependent on those who hold such information. Hence, when managers exercise their legitimate power, they need to secure information for day-to-day managerial activities. The need for information provides a source of power to those who hold it. If someone withholds the information, this can be termed 'restrictive control'.[14] In the knowledge economy, information power becomes very important. Other sorts of knowledge also fit into this category. Gossip, or being linked into the 'grapevine' of informal information, can be a form of knowledge with which a person may potentially influence the behaviour of others.

Personal power

Personal power resides in the individual independent of the position the individual holds. However, the management literature considers that, in essence, the two main bases of personal power are expertise and reference.

Expert power

Expert power *is the ability to control another's behaviour through the possession of knowledge, experience or judgement that the other person does not have but needs.*

Linked to information power, **expert power** is the ability to control another person's behaviour through the possession of knowledge, experience or judgement that the other person does not have but needs. Employees would obey someone with expert power because they feel they know more and are making a better decision. Computer specialists can influence nontechnical staff behaviour because they have special knowledge that may be critical to them.

Access to key organizational decision makers is another element in expert power. A person's ability to contact key people informally can allow for special participation in the definition of a problem or issue, affect the flow of information to decision makers and lobby for use of special criteria in decision making. Managers have to develop good working relationships with employees who hold expert power.

OB IN ACTION

Steve Jobs at Apple

The age-old rivalry between Microsoft and Apple has seen tough times for Microsoft in 2010. Steve Jobs, who leads new product development at Apple, is launching the iPad this year, and the company's shares on the stock market have overtaken those of Microsoft. Jobs's leadership is central

to the success at Apple. Reclusive and secretive, little information seeps out about either Mr Jobs or new Apple products before their launch. Jobs created the iPod generation, revolutionizing how we consume music, and he has designs on how we consume both videos and now books. Bill Gates is reputed to admire Steve Jobs's ability in design, and although judgement on the iPad will be made as its release rolls out during 2010, it may herald the introduction of touch computing in a way that is entirely different. Tim Bajarin[15] at PC Magazine reported that he showed the new iPad to a senior citizen who could neither understand that it was a computer nor wanted to give it back to him. Bajarin reports that Jobs understands that we want to use computing in many other ways and situations other than sitting at a desk with a keyboard. Apple's financial backing means Steve Jobs has extraordinary influence over the industry, and coupled with his leadership and inventive flair geared to consumers, he commands extraordinary power.

Referent power

Referent power comes from others wanting to be like you, to be associated with you or the networks and contacts you have, which they also value. Thus, you may have chosen a university because it has some high-profile academics to whom you can refer at job interviews. A boss who is thought of as a 'good role model' would be a typical way of thinking of referent power. A more subtle approach comes from sociology, where the notion of 'prototypes' is useful. A prototype is the 'ideal' – for example what is the ideal police officer? The sociological approach is helpful in that there can be several different prototypes depending on the stakeholder view.[16] For example, one person might see the prototypical police officer as someone who uses judgement and will occasionally let someone off speeding. Another person may think that the prototypical police officer will issue a sanction every single time. One person's prototype may not be another's.

> **Referent power** is the ability to control another's behaviour because the individual wants to identify with the power source due to his or her perceived attractive characteristics.

Another aspect is working out exactly what one is prototyping. Hence, one might be a referent for some aspects of employment and gain power, but not other aspects.[17] For example, Richard Branson (founder of the Virgin group) would be acknowledged by most as an excellent publicist and figure-head leader, however some people might find his style of organizing too loose and prefer stronger structures. This would be an example where one might have referent power in some areas perceived by some people, but not others. Referent power can be seen where people are respected as well as liked and admired – for example, the data input clerk who looks after elderly parents but has a spotless attendance record. Admiration and respect for one area of work can infect other areas and lead to an overall good impression, which is called the 'halo effect'.[18]

All individuals have one or more source of power, to varying degrees and in varying combinations. It is important that managers do not rely on a single source of power as this may limit their effectiveness – power is assigned by others and will always change with time. Managers who rely only on legitimate power may have very limited ability to influence the behaviour of others and their efforts may be undermined by the referent power of informal leaders.

POWER, AUTHORITY AND OBEDIENCE

Power is the potential to control the behaviour of others; formal authority is the potential to exert such control through the legitimacy of a managerial position. Yet we also know that people who seem to have power do not always get their way. This leads us to the subject of obedience. Why do some people obey directives while others do not? More specifically, why should employees respond to a manager's authority or 'right to command' in the first place? Further, given that employees are willing to obey, what determines the limits of obedience?

The Milgram experiments

These last questions point to Stanley Milgram's seminal research on obedience.[19] Milgram's experiment sought to determine the extent to which people obey the commands of an authority figure, even if they believe they are endangering the life of another person. His sample was 40 males, ranging in age from 20 to 50 years and representing a diverse set of occupations (engineers, salespeople, schoolteachers, labourers and others). They were paid a nominal fee for participation in the project, which was conducted in a laboratory in America.

Each participant was told (falsely) that the purpose of the study was to determine the effects of punishment on learning and participants were to be the 'teachers'. The 'learner' (an actor) could be seen by the participant through a screen, strapped to a chair in an adjoining room with an electrode on his wrist. The 'experimenter' (another actor) appeared impassive and somewhat stern, instructing the learner in a fairly simple task concerning pairs of words.

The teacher (the participant) was instructed to administer an electric shock to the learner each time a wrong answer was given. The shock was to be increased in intensity each time the learner made a mistake (and the actor delivered many mistakes). The teacher controlled switches that ostensibly administered shocks ranging from 15 to 450 volts (although, of course, in reality there was no electric current). The question was how far the teacher would progress in shocking the learner. A summary of the switch markings and the learner's fake responses to the various levels of shock is shown in Table 10.1.

Switch voltage marking	Switch description	'Learner's' responses
15–60	Slight	No sound
75–120	Moderate	Grunts and moans
135–180	Strong	Asks to leave
195–240	Very strong	Cannot stand the pain
255–300	Intense	Pounds on wall
315–360	Extreme intensity	No sound
375–420	Danger: severe shock	No sound
435–450	XXX	No sound

Table 10.1: Shock levels and set learner responses in the Milgram experiment.

If a teacher was unwilling to administer a shock, the experimenter would escalate instructions to the teacher up to 'You have no choice, you must go on.' as the fourth level. Only if the teacher refused to go on after the fourth level would the experiment be stopped. In all, 26 subjects (65%) continued to the end of the experiment and shocked the 'learner' to the XXX level! None stopped before 300 V – the point at which the learner pounds on the wall. The remaining 14 subjects refused to obey the experimenter at various intermediate points.

Most people are surprised by these results, as was Milgram. There were many criticisms of Milgram's method, which allowed the 'teachers' to leave thinking that they might have done someone harm without being debriefed. A valuable lesson was learned in that many people will obey and comply to a point we all find surprising.

Obedience and the acceptance of authority

Applying Milgram's experiment in the workplace suggests there are strong tendencies among individuals to follow the instructions of the boss. Direct defiance within organizational settings is quite rare. If the tendency to follow instructions is great and defiance is rare then why do so many organizations apparently drift into chaos? The answer to this question lies at the heart of the contribution made by the well-known management writer Chester Barnard.[20] Essentially, Barnard's argument focused on the 'consent of the governed' rather than on the rights derived from ownership. He argued that employees will accept or follow a directive from the boss only under special circumstances and all four must be met:

- the employee can and must understand the directive;
- the employee must feel mentally and physically capable of carrying out the directive;
- the employee must believe the directive is not inconsistent with the purpose of the organization;
- the employee must believe the directive is not inconsistent with his or her personal interests.

These four conditions are carefully stated. To accept and follow an order, employees do not need, for instance, to understand how the proposed action will help the organization; they only need to believe the requested action is not inconsistent with the purpose of the organization. The astute manager will recognize that the acceptance of any request is not assured. If the directive is routine, then it is not surprising that the employee may merely comply without enthusiasm. If the request is unusual, it will be made by a manager giving assurances on the last two rules, which touches on Barnard's valuable concept of the 'zone of indifference'.

The zone of indifference

Most people seek a balance between what they put into an organization (contribution) and what they get from an organization in return (inducement). Within the psychological

*The **zone of indifference** is the range of authoritative requests to which an employee is willing to respond without subjecting the directives to critical evaluation or judgement – that is, the requests to which the employee is indifferent.*

contract (Chapter 1), employees agree to do many things for the organization because they think they should. That is, in exchange for inducements (such as wages), employees recognize the authority of the organization and its managers to direct their behaviour in certain ways. Based on his acceptance view of authority, Chester Barnard calls this area in which directions are obeyed the **zone of indifference**.

A zone of indifference is the range of authoritative requests to which employees are willing to respond without subjecting the directives to critical evaluation or judgement; that is, the range in which they are indifferent. Directives falling within the zone are obeyed; other directives may or may not be obeyed. This link between the zone of indifference and the psychological contract is shown in Figure 10.2.

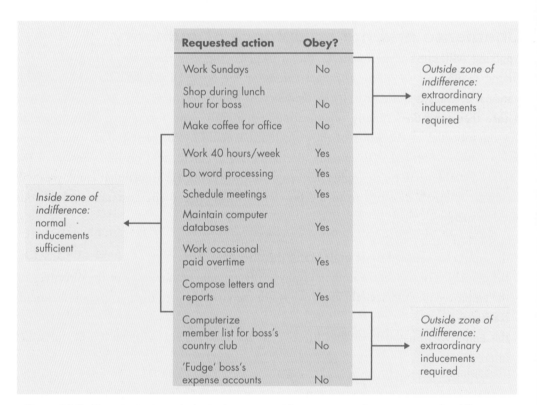

Figure 10.2: Hypothetical psychological contract with a secretary showing zone of indifference.

The secretary whose psychological contract is shown in Figure 10.2 expects to perform a number of activities falling within the zone of indifference (with no questions asked). Examples include scheduling meetings and maintaining computer databases. There may be times when the boss would like the secretary to do things falling outside the zone, such as running personal errands for the boss on the secretary's lunch hour. This requires efforts to enlarge the zone to accommodate additional behaviours. In these attempts, the boss will most likely have to use more incentives than pure position power. In some instances, such as Sunday work and 'fudging' of expense accounts, no legitimate power base may be arguable.

There is another side to power, authority and obedience with which you should be familiar as a manager: your own zone of indifference and tendency to obey. When will you say 'no' to your boss? When should you be willing to say 'no'? At times, work may involve ethical dilemmas, where you may be asked to do things that are illegal, unethical or both. Most of us will face ethical dilemmas during our careers. Saying 'no' or 'refusing to keep quiet' can be difficult and potentially costly, as many whistleblowers discover. Whistle-blowing may be the right thing to do, but contesting the power of a manager is not easy.

Consider employees in the last days of the Enron collapse when qualified accountants (who were all signed up to professional codes of conduct) spent time shredding documents that would implicate a cover-up.[21] While all those employees had the power and the ethical grounds to refuse to do this, for so many of them to have complied is reminiscent of the pressures of the Milgram experiments – how much power and what 'rights' did those employees really think they had?

EFFECTIVE MANAGER 10.1

Insubordinate employees

All managers need to hone the skill of dealing with insubordinate employees. Sometimes employees are unaware their behaviour is unacceptable and it is important to make sure it gets addressed.

The guidelines below are useful as a checklist when approaching an interview. It is important to make a note of your discussion in case the employee engages in the behaviour again, at which point you might need to invoke the relevant policies.

1. Explore the reasons for the unacceptable behaviour.
2. Inform the employee that he or she has engaged in unacceptable conduct and that certain conduct is strongly expected of all employees. Refer to the specific rules or policies in that respect.
3. Discuss the negative consequences that will occur if the employee fails to change unacceptable behaviour.
4. Clearly outline the positive consequences of changing the improper behaviour.
5. Develop an action plan that you and the employee agree on to change the unacceptable behaviour.
6. If further transgressions occur, deal with them swiftly, fairly and in line with what you have warned them about in point 3.

MANAGING WITH POWER AND INFLUENCE

Managing with power means recognizing that there are varying interests in almost every organization and that different stakeholder groups perceive issues differently. Young managers sometimes find the notion of power distasteful and attempt to manage through consensus and discussion. It is possible to manage in this way but one should never forget that power is sometimes given (such as that which comes with the authority of 'manager') thus, even if as a manager you dislike power, your staff may have already invested it in you!

Power is needed to get things done and anyone who is ambitious will want to get a lot done, hence sources of power must be developed. By learning to manage with power, managers are able to achieve both their own goals and the goals of their organization as well as enhancing others' careers through being associated with success.

Power and influence do not just work within the organization; customers also have the opportunity to exert influence over various processes and decisions in the organization. They do so through increasing consumer demands, creating consumer feedback and responding to the increasing availability of information online. Shareholders, and people in wider society, may also have some potential to influence decisions and behaviours in organizations. Such influence is not necessarily intentional and typically not as strong as power sources inside the organization. This would be reflected in any external analysis of the forces affecting an organization.

 **IN ACTION**

Yukl's review of influence tactics

Gary Yukl has reviewed research around influence tactics for many years. Practically speaking, there are many useful ways of exercising influence.[22] The tactics are:

* rational persuasion – using logical arguments and factual evidence;

* consultation – seeking support through asking for suggestions;

* collaboration – where each provides different components for the solution;

* inspirational appeals – appealing to a person's values, ideals or aspirations;

● apprising – explaining why agreement will benefit the collaborator personally;

● personal appeals – the request is directed to a person's feelings;

● ingratiation – using flattery;

● exchange – offering an exchange of favours/ benefits;

+ pressure – using demands, threats, frequent checking or constant reminders;

+ legitimating tactics – showing links with organizational policies, practices etc.;

+ coalition tactics – involving others as part of the argument.

+ = low effectiveness
● = moderate effectiveness
* = high effectiveness

In his overview of research in the area Yukl suggests that consultation, collaboration, inspirational appeals and strong rational persuasion are the most effective tactics. However, variation could be expected based on the context, the direction of the influence attempt and the objectives of the influence attempt. Managers need to diagnose their power relationships carefully in order to be able to use the tactics effectively.

EMPOWERMENT

How far should power be shared, and under what circumstances? It will be seen from Chapter 4 that control over work is a component of motivation and it is also a major factor in reducing stress.[23]

When all goes well, everyone can gain from empowerment. To keep the organization competitive, top management must attend to a variety of challenging and strategic forces in the external environment. While top management tends to concentrate on decisions about strategy and dynamic change, others throughout the organization must be ready and willing to make critical operating decisions. By providing these opportunities, empowerment increases the total power available in an organization. In other words, the top levels do not have to give up power for the lower levels to gain it. The same basic argument holds true in any manager–employee relationship.

EFFECTIVE MANAGER 10.2

Guidelines for implementing empowerment

- Encourage creativity by allowing employees ample flexibility in how they achieve organizational objectives.
- Provide all the necessary information to assist employees to make informed decisions.
- Communicate openly with employees on the organization's activities, performance and long-term goals. Let them know how the organization is doing and how their roles and actions affect the bottom line.
- Train on problem solving, time management and decision making to enhance key skills for increased responsibility.

- Run regular meetings between employees and management.
- Be sure to respond swiftly to input and suggestions from employees because lengthy silence can lead to discouragement and demotivation.
- Allow room for error; encouraging employees to be more creative means some risk taking – errors will occur, and one needs systems to pick these up quickly.

Empowerment is the process by which managers help others acquire and use the power needed to make decisions affecting themselves and their work. More than ever before, managers in progressive organizations are expected to be good at empowering the people with whom they work. Empowerment is a key foundation of the increasingly popular self-managing work teams and other creative worker involvement groups. Despite this, there are limits to the process of empowerment, which we discuss as a concept in some detail in Chapter 4.

Empowerment *is the process by which managers delegate power to employees who therefore have an enhanced view of their work and role within the organization.*

Power keys to empowerment

Empowerment gives a radically different view of power. Our discussion so far has focused on power exerted over other individuals. In contrast to this, the concept of empowerment emphasizes the ability to make things happen. Cutting through all the corporate rhetoric on empowerment is difficult because the term has become fashionable in management circles. However, each individual empowerment attempt needs to be examined in the light of how power in the organization will be changed. In this way, Honda has engendered a process of constant improvement by giving teams the power to make decisions for improvement in processes. Naturally this has changed the nature of the power of senior managers. However, they have made it a remarkable source of competitive advantage.[24]

Expanding the zone of indifference

When embarking on an empowerment programme, management needs to recognize the current zone of indifference and systematically move to decrease it. All too often, management assumes that its directive for empowerment will be followed; however, managers often fail to show precisely how empowerment will benefit the individuals involved.

Power as an expanding pie

Along with empowerment, employees need to be trained to expand their power and their new influence potential. This is the most difficult task for managers and a difficult challenge for employees, because it often changes the dynamic between supervisors and employees. The key is to change the concept of power within the organization – from a view that stresses power over others to one that emphasizes the use of power to get things done. Under the new definition of power, all employees can be more powerful.

In practical terms, empowerment means that all managers will need to emphasize different ways of exercising influence. Appeals to higher authority and sanctions will need to be replaced by appeals to reason, friendliness and bargaining. This will need a manager to draw on sources of power other than legitimate authority and use influence tactics (see above).

▶ ## COUNTERPOINT

When an organization attempts to move power down the hierarchy it also needs to alter the existing pattern of position power. Changing this pattern raises important questions. Can 'empowered' individuals give rewards and sanctions? Has their new right to act been legitimized with formal authority? All too often, attempts at empowerment disrupt well-established patterns of position power and threaten middle and lower level managers.[25]

Empowerment varies in the degree to which it is applied and accepted. It can range from small tasks to full responsibility for important decision making or project completion. Clearly, quantifying the degree of empowerment is a difficult and complex task. To meet this challenge in the UK an empowerment audit (EA) was developed to try to measure the degree of empowerment, resulting in a matrix of 15 major indicators, each with a five-point scale of traditional, participative, involved, early self-directed and mature self-directed.[26]

Empowerment involves the development of all employees, including managers. There is a significant risk that trying to introduce the highest degrees of empowerment too quickly will fail to give people time to develop and adjust to new demands. The result may be that they conclude that empowerment cannot or did not work, when a slower, steadier programme of introduction may have allowed individuals to adapt to empowerment over time. We also tend to assume that people want to be empowered and it is quite possible that some people want to just come to work and be told what to do. In the end empowerment means adding factors to employees' jobs, and some may resent and resist this.[27]

The limits of empowering others

Empowerment programmes can transform a stagnant organization into a vital one by creating a shared purpose among employees, encouraging greater cooperation and, most importantly, delivering enhanced value to customers. Despite that potential, empowerment programmes often fall victim to the same structural and cultural problems that made them desirable in the first place. On the one hand, many managers may view empowerment as a threat and may continue to measure their personal status and value in terms of the hierarchical authority they wield. These managers perceive the shift of responsibility for work assignments and output evaluation to employees as a loss of authority and a change to a less satisfying role. As a result, they may resist empowerment efforts.

On the other hand, some employees mistake empowerment for discretionary authority – that is, the power to decide things unilaterally – when a high level of communication and consultation is needed in even the most empowered situation. In addition, managers may neglect to train employees in new skills.

ORGANIZATIONAL POLITICS

Any study of power and influence inevitably leads to the subject of 'politics'. Political processes form the dynamic that enables the formal organization to function. In a sense, power and politics act as the lubricant that enables the interdependent parts of the organization to operate smoothly together. Organizations that engage in empowerment open up the area of politics to more employees as they have spread the power base.

The word 'politics' may conjure up thoughts of illicit deals, favours and special personal relationships. This image of organizational politics whereby shrewd, often dishonest, practices are used to obtain influence is reflected in Machiavelli's classic 16th-century work,

The Prince, which outlines how to obtain and hold power via political action. For that reason, political actions are also referred to in terms of 'Machiavellianism'.

Organizational politics may also be described in more positive terms as the art of using influence, authority and power to achieve goals.[28] These goals may be self-interested for an individual, group or department, or have an emphasis geared toward organizational goals. Ideally both are aligned so that personal interests also benefit the organization. Political skills, like technical skills, are a tool for getting things done. Managers should discuss the political ramifications of all decisions confronting a department, frequently and openly. They can use this to illustrate political realities and to explain the many nuances of good political planning.

Political activity is usually stronger where there are no prescribed routine answers or no stated policy. It also centres around the interpretation of existing policies and those situations involving value judgements.[29] Any organization that attempted to reduce these arenas of political activity totally by instituting rules, regulations and policies from the top would quickly be strangled in its own red tape.[30]

The two traditions of organizational politics

To survive in a highly political environment requires particular skills, including the ability to recognize those who are working through agendas despite surface appearances of openness and cooperation. It also requires the ability to identify the power sources of the key players and to build your own alliances and connections. There are two quite different traditions in the analysis of organizational politics.

Politics as unsanctioned and self-interested

This first tradition builds on Machiavelli's philosophy and defines politics in terms of self-interest and the use of unsanctioned means. In this tradition, **organizational politics** may be formally defined as the management of influence to obtain ends not sanctioned by the organization, or to obtain sanctioned ends through unsanctioned means of influence. Managers are often considered political when they seek their own goals or use means not currently authorized by the organization.[31] It is also important to recognize that where there is uncertainty or ambiguity, it is often extremely difficult to tell whether a manager is being political in this self-serving sense.

Organizational politics *is the management of influence to obtain ends not sanctioned by the organization, or to obtain sanctioned ends through nonsanctioned means of influence.*

Organizationally sanctioned politics

The second tradition treats politics as a necessary function resulting from differences in the perceived self-interest of individuals or groups. Sanctioned organizational politics is viewed as the art of compromise among competing interests. In a heterogeneous society, individuals will disagree on whose interest is most valuable and whose concerns should be bounded by collective interests, this applies at the personal level but also at the functional level. For example, should a potential customer be put through a credit check before or after a sale is closed? The sales team would suggest after; the finance team before. Politics arise because there is a need to develop compromises, avoid confrontation and live together. Thus, organizational politics is about the use of power to develop socially acceptable ends and means that balance individual and collective interests.

The perception of political behaviour

The study of power and political behaviour has been described as consistent, logical and finite in many books over many years. However, there are some arguments to suggest that this approach is limiting us in our understanding of how power and politics might actually work in organizations. Power is usually studied in terms of 'sources' of power, as in this chapter. However, there are arguments against a 'sources-of-power' approach, with power being defined instead as a force created by differences. Power can be seen as a far more social and cultural phenomenon where differences are perceived within a socially constructed reality developed through the shared meanings of culture. Thus, you may have power in relation to another person because that person perceives that you have something that he or she does not. This approach is useful in helping to explain not just individual power relations but also power and politics that occur in groups and organizational structures.[32] These perceived differences emerge, in part, from the wider social distinctions in society such as class, gender, law and education.[33]

The cultural approach to power and politics widens our understanding of political behaviour as being about social change. Different male and female management styles, as well as a range of different ethnic origins and other aspects of diversity, may increase differences, or perceived differences, in organizations and challenge the existing way that problems are framed there.[34] Earlier we mentioned the idea of 'prototypes' and that prototypes can be the ideal of any group. We used this to think of great managers and leaders. However, the cultural approach validates other uses for the prototype, for example: a wonderful woman manager; an excellent black architect. Political behaviour is not necessarily about self-interest, with people stepping outside the accepted rules. Political behaviour does not have to be about advancing self-interest, although it may be about advancing specific interests within organizations. While we understand position power as being linked to authority, rewards and coercion, in this alternative understanding, political behaviour provides a wider view of social order.[35]

ORGANIZATIONAL POLITICS IN ACTION

Political action is a part of organizational life; it is best to view organizational politics for its potential to contribute to managerial and organizational effectiveness. It is in this spirit that we now examine political action in organizations from the perspectives of managers, subunits and chief executives. Organizational politics occurs in different ways and across different levels in the organization.

Office politics and the informal network

An organizational chart can show who is the boss and who reports to whom. But this formal chart will not reveal which people confer on technical matters or enter into discussions over lunch; which people shape attitudes and beliefs on who has and who has not got power and influence. Much of the real work of an organization is achieved through this informal organization with its complex network of relationships that cross between functions and divisions.

As organizations continue to flatten their structures and rely on teams (see Chapter 8), managers need to understand these informal networks. To thrive in the political landscape of the workplace, it is a good idea to be aware of the 'prototypes' and become allied with these admired people (with referent power) but to focus your concern on your tasks rather than engaging in politics for the sake of it, as unless one is very skilled or powerful, this can backfire.

Political action and the manager

Managers will gain a better understanding of political behaviour by placing themselves in the positions of the other people involved in critical decisions or events. Each action and decision can be seen as having benefits and costs to all parties concerned. Where the costs exceed the benefits, people may act to protect themselves. Being prepared for such reactions can take some time and might also involve some research, especially if you are new to an organization. However, it is well worth doing as then you can at least work out some scenarios and think through the various tactics that might be used to influence others, choosing the one most likely to have the desired effect given others' circumstances.

The use of political power requires two sets of attributes: competence and political intelligence. The first (and probably most important) strategy for improving an individual's political intelligence is to be able to read the work climate, preferably before beginning work.

COUNTERPOINT

Consider the Steve Jobs case on pages 488–489

- If you were his personal assistant for a year, what types of power would you have after this time?
- What potential influence would you have and with whom?

- What might be the ethical dilemmas you would face?
- How *might* you engage in political activity?
- How *would* you engage in political activity?

Political action and subunit power

Political action links managers more formally to one another as representatives of their work units. In Chapter 8 we examined the group dynamics associated with such intergroup relationships. Table 10.2 highlights five typical lateral and intergroup relationships in which managers may engage: work flow, service, advisory, auditing and approval relationships.[36] The table also shows how lateral relationships further challenge the political skills of a manager; each example requires the manager to achieve influence through some means other than formal authority.

Type of relationship	Sample influence requirements
Work flow – contacts with units that precede or follow in a sequential production chain	An assembly-line manager informs another line manager responsible for a later stage in the production process about a delay.
Service – contacts with units established to help with problems	An assembly-line manager asks the maintenance manager to fix an important piece of equipment as a priority.
Advisory – contacts with formal staff units that have special expertise	A marketing manager consults with the personnel manager to obtain special assistance in recruiting a new salesperson.
Auditing – contacts with units that have the right to evaluate the actions of others	A marketing manager tries to get the credit manager to retract a report criticizing marketing's tendency to open bad-credit accounts.
Approval – contacts with units whose approval must be obtained before action may be taken	A marketing manager submits a job description to the company affirmative action officer for approval before recruiting for a new salesperson can begin.

Table 10.2: Relationships of managers and associated influence requirements.

To be effective in political action, managers should understand the politics of subunit relations. In general, units gain power as more of their relations with others are of the approval and auditing types. Workflow relations are more powerful than advisory associations, and both are more powerful than service relations. Units can increase their power by undertaking new actions that tackle and resolve difficult problems. Certain strategic contingencies can often govern the relative power of subunits. For a subunit to gain power, it must increase its control over:

- *access to scarce resources* – subunits gain in power when they obtain access to, or control, scarce resources needed by others;
- *the ability to cope with uncertainty* – subunits gain in power when they are able to cope with uncertainty and help solve problems that uncertainty causes for others;
- *centrality in the flow of work* – subunits gain in power when their position in the work flow allows them to influence the work of others;
- *substitutability of activities* – subunits gain in power when they perform tasks or activities that are nonsubstitutable (that is, when they perform essential functions that others cannot complete).[37]

Political action and resource dependencies

Executive behaviour can sometimes be explained in terms of resource dependencies; that is, the organization's need for resources that others control. Essentially, the resource dependence of an organization increases as:

- needed resources become more scarce;
- outsiders have more control over needed resources;
- there are fewer substitutes for a particular type of resource controlled by a limited number of outsiders.[38]

Thus, one political role of chief executives is to develop workable compromises among the competing resource dependencies facing the organization – compromises that enhance the executive's power. To create such compromises, executives need to diagnose the relative power of outsiders and to craft strategies that respond differently to various external resource suppliers.

ORGANIZATIONAL GOVERNANCE

Organizational governance *is the pattern of authority, influence and acceptable managerial behaviour established at the top of the organization.*

Organizational governance refers to the pattern of authority, influence and acceptable managerial behaviour established at the top of the organization. This system establishes what is important, how issues will be defined, who should and should not be involved in key choices and the boundaries for acceptable implementation. Those studying organizational governance suggest that a 'dominant coalition' comprising powerful organizational actors is a key to its understanding.[39]

We need organizational governance to set the boundaries for power and decision making. It provides the frame within which power and decisions can happen. For example, chief executives cannot set their own pay in publicly quoted companies; equally local council chief officers' pay is determined not by them but by a committee. Organizational governance provides the checks and balances that all senior staff have to comply with and submit to. It is in everyone's best interests to adhere to solid governance. Sometimes the rules of governance are set by external regulating bodies (such as the FSA in our opening case), sometimes pressure from stakeholders means governance 'better practice' becomes adopted. Analysis of organizational governance builds on the resource dependence perspective by highlighting the effective control of key resources by members of a dominant coalition. Hence, while you might expect top officers within the organization to be members of this coalition, the dominant coalition occasionally includes outsiders with access to key resources such as shareholders or regulating bodies which grant licences to do business.

The issue of the governance and accountability of both public and private sector organizations has recently come to the fore following a wave of high-profile corporate scandals and collapses. At Enron and WorldCom, a very large number of employees were left without jobs and pensions, and stakeholders (including stockholders) were taken by surprise when the collapses occurred. These two events made many employees and stockholders revisit their levels of knowledge and their trust in top management teams.[40] In both instances senior executives were allowed to drift into poor practice for some time without being discovered or challenged.

OB IN ACTION

The recent Icelandic parliamentary report into the country's financial collapse reveals governance failures at many levels. There were instances where the bank owners had borrowed money themselves and executive directors felt pressured to approve loans in fear of losing their jobs. Mr Arnason, the former CEO of Landsbanki, says, 'Resisting the requests from the owners of the banks would have equalled quitting from my position.' The report suggested that the island's three main banks, Kaupthing, Glitnir and Landsbanki, were controlled by a web of board directors and investors – five people who had 'unlimited influence.' The report found the prime minister at the time acted with 'gross negligence' as the crisis grew and ineffective action was taken.[41]

A strong governance system will ensure that the dominant coalition defines a reality which is accurate. The idea of groupthink has already been considered (see Chapter 8) and a recent review in the US suggests that selection onto boards continues to favour prototypical members.[42] Nonexecutive directors are experienced people from outside the organization who have a position on the board and, not being involved with the day-to-day management, can help ensure that the executive directors take an independent view, as far as possible.[43] Similar motives to balance opinion are an aspect behind the German work councils and EC directives to ensure workers have a voice within their organizations.

THE CONSEQUENCES OF POWER AND POLITICS

Whether or not organizational politics is good or bad may be a matter of perspective and depend on each situation and the outputs. It may be good for an individual but not for the organization, or individuals might suffer but the organization might be better off.

On the positive side it can serve a number of important functions, including helping managers to:

- *Overcome personnel inadequacies.* As a manager, you should expect some mismatches between people and positions in organizations. Even in the best managed organizations, some managers will be learning and others burned out or lacking the resources needed to accomplish their assigned duties. Organizational politics provides a mechanism for circumventing these inadequacies and getting the job done.
- *Cope with change.* Changes in the environment and technology of an organization often come more quickly than an organization can restructure formally. All organizations encounter unanticipated events and to rise to such challenges, people and resources must be moved into place quickly before small headaches become major problems. Organizational politics can help to bring effective decision making to bear and move appropriate, problem-solving managers into the breach.

- *Substitute for formal authority.* When a person's formal authority breaks down or fails to apply to a particular situation, political actions can be used to prevent a loss of influence. Managers may use political behaviour to maintain operations and to achieve task continuity in circumstances in which the failure of formal authority may otherwise cause problems.

There are negatives, however. Politics can pervade organizations and act against necessary changes. Chapter 12, on change management, emphasizes how important political issues are in achieving successful change. Where a dominant group is against moves that are needed, change initiatives can be stopped in their tracks.

Some individuals view political tactics to be highly counterproductive because they may be used to discredit and disable often more able colleagues.[44]

There may be cases in which politics dominates organizational activity to an extent that the activity is dysfunctional. Alternatively, it is unlikely that political behaviour never occurs, and if such a case existed it might be equally dysfunctional. The following sections on ethics and trust give further insight into political behaviour.

THE ETHICS OF POWER AND POLITICS

All managers use power and politics to get their work done but every employee also bears a responsibility to work in an ethical and socially responsible fashion. By recognizing and confronting ethical considerations, each of us should be better prepared to meet this important challenge. No treatment of power and politics in organizations is complete without considering the related ethical issues. We can begin this task by clarifying the distinction between the nonpolitical and political uses of power.[45]

Power is nonpolitical when it remains within the boundaries of usually formal authority, organizational policies and procedures and job descriptions, and when it is directed towards ends sanctioned by the organization. When the use of power moves outside the realm of authority, policies, procedures and job descriptions, or when it is directed towards ends not sanctioned by the organization, that use of power is said to be political.

▶ COUNTERPOINT

On 5 February 2007, *PR Week* reported that Todd Thomson, chief of Citigroup's wealth management unit, was removed partly for his dealings with CNBC reporter Maria Bartiromo. Maria apparently took trips on the Citigroup jet,

actions which were considered improper by Citigroup officials. However, CNBC defended the issue, stating that they have a system whereby such trips were pre-approved within the journalists' ethics code.

It is often the case that reporters buy their interviewees a drink or lunch and vice versa. But where should one draw the line?

Questions

1. If you worked for Citigroup, where would you draw the line?

2. If you worked for a newspaper where would you draw the line?

3. If you were a reporter and had accepted a good lunch or a flight on a jet, would you feel obliged to file a positive report on the hosting organization?

It is in this context that a manager must stop and consider more than a pure 'ends justify the means' logic. These issues are broader and involve distinctly ethical questions. Work in the area of ethical issues in power and politics suggests the usefulness of the integrated structure for analysing political behaviour depicted in Figure 10.3. This structure suggests that a person's behaviour must satisfy the following criteria to be considered ethical:[46]

- *Utilitarian outcomes.* The behaviour results in optimization of satisfaction of people both inside and outside the organization; that is, it produces the greatest good for the greatest number of people.
- *Individual rights.* The behaviour respects the rights of all affected parties; that is, it respects basic human rights of free consent, free speech, freedom of conscience, privacy and due process.
- *Distributive justice.* The behaviour respects the rules of justice; that is, it treats people equitably and fairly, as opposed to arbitrarily.

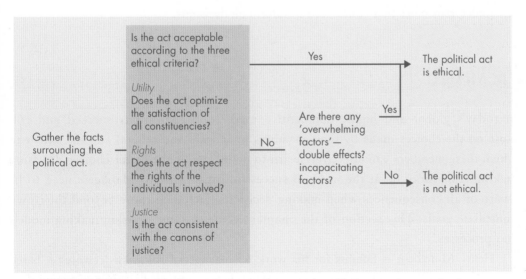

Figure 10.3: An integrated structure for analysing political behaviour in organizations.

Source: Velasquez, M., Moberg, D. J. and Cavanagh, G. F. (1983), Organizational statesmanship and dirty politics: ethical guidelines for the organizational politician. *Organizational Dynamics*, **11**, 73.

The figure also indicates that there may be times when a behaviour is unable to pass these criteria but can still be considered ethical in the given situation. This special case must satisfy the criterion of overwhelming factors, in which the special nature of the situation results in:

- conflicts among criteria (for example, a behaviour results in some good and some bad);
- conflicts within criteria (for example, a behaviour uses questionable means to achieve a positive end);
- an incapacity to employ the criteria (for example, a person's behaviour is based on inaccurate or incomplete information).

Choosing to be ethical often involves considerable personal sacrifice. Four rationalizations are often used to justify unethical choices:

- individuals feel the behaviour is not really illegal and thus could be moral;
- the action appears to be in the organization's best interests;
- it is unlikely the action will ever be detected;
- the action appears to demonstrate loyalty to the boss or the organization.

While these rationalizations may appear compelling at the moment of action, each deserves close scrutiny. The individual must ask: 'How far is too far?' 'What are the long-term interests of the organization?' 'What will happen when (not if) the action is discovered?' 'Do individuals, groups or organizations that ask for unethical behaviour deserve my loyalty?'[47]

Our chapter now moves its focus to that of decision making. When reading the remainder, remember that ethics need to inform all decisions.

DECISION MAKING

In today's global and highly competitive markets, organizations succeed and collapse on the choices made by their members (managers and others) and the extent to which these members can effectively learn to define and make better choices. Decision making really does lie at the heart of successful organizations. Managers need to be aware of all consequences when making decisions, including those beyond their own immediate goals. This section of the chapter evaluates some decision-making models and processes.

Henry Mintzberg is famous for his work on managerial roles. His research – based on following CEOs around during their working days – suggests that, in performing their tasks, they fulfil ten distinct roles broadly classified into interpersonal roles, informational roles and decision roles. In the latter category he defined decision making as the process of choosing a course of action for solving a problem or seizing an opportunity.[48] The choice usually involves two or more possible alternatives.

Types of managerial decisions

Two basic types of managerial decisions are distinguished by the presence of routine and nonroutine problems in the work situation. **Routine problems** are those that arise regularly and can be addressed through standard responses, called programmed decisions. These responses implement solutions that have already been determined by past experience as appropriate for the problem at hand. Examples of programmed decisions are the automatic reordering of inventory when stock falls below a predetermined level and issuing a written reprimand to someone who violates a personnel procedure. The decisions are often the focus of quality improvement initiatives, which seek to find optimal solutions for all situations.

Routine problems *are problems that arise routinely and that can be addressed through standard responses.*

Nonroutine problems are unique and new. When standard responses are not available, creative problem solving is called for. These crafted decisions are specifically tailored to a situation and take more time, sometimes involving many people. Senior managers will spend a greater proportion of their decision-making time on nonroutine problems. An example is the marketing manager who must counter a competitor's introduction of a new product from abroad. Although past experience may help, the immediate decision requires a solution based on the unique characteristics of the present situation.

Nonroutine problems *are unique and new problems that call for creative problem solving.*

Decision environments

When making routine or nonroutine decisions, managers do so in environments that can be thought of as certain, uncertain and risky (which is neither certain nor uncertain). These will now be discussed in turn.

Certain environments exist when information is sufficient to predict the results of each alternative in advance of implementation. When a person invests money in a savings account, for example, absolute certainty exists about the interest that the money will earn in a given period of time. Certainty is an ideal condition for managerial problem decision making where one locates the most satisfactory solution and represents areas where empowerment of junior staff can be appropriate. In such circumstances 'management by exception' can be used where the manager only gets involved if something unusual occurs.

Certain environments *are decision environments in which information is sufficient to predict the results of each alternative in advance of implementation.*

Uncertain environments are the most difficult and exist when managers are unable to assign probabilities to the outcomes of various problem-solving alternatives. It requires unique, novel and often totally innovative alternatives to existing patterns of behaviour. Responses to uncertainty are often heavily influenced by intuition, educated guesses and hunches, which in turn are heavily influenced by perception. Some people work in environments that are full of uncertainty, such as those who are developing new products or scientists. Others work in environments which have far more routine and certainty. People in the latter situation often find it difficult to label their circumstance, as they are so used to routine – as the following 'OB in Action' box illustrates.

Uncertain environments *are decision environments in which managers are unable to assign probabilities to the possible outcomes of various courses of action.*

OB IN ACTION

The 9/11 Commission report is an extraordinary document.[49] It charts, minute by minute, the events leading up to the hijackings and subsequent chaos. Aircraft controllers know about hijacking although fortunately very few have needed to handle such situations. What had not occurred before was multiple simultaneous hijackings. As such, command systems were in place but the speed of events overtook the decision-making process. Hence military aircraft were scrambled to follow the first plane into New York but were not given coordinates and were absent when the first plane hit the World Trade Center. The following exchange was recorded after the second plane had hit in New York, and relates to another (United 93) working its way to Washington:

FAA Headquarters: They're pulling Jeff away to go talk about United 93.
Command Centre: Uh, do we want to think, uh, about scrambling aircraft?

FAA Headquarters: Oh, God, I don't know.
Command Centre: Uh, that's a decision somebody's gonna have to make, probably in the next ten minutes.
FAA Headquarters: Uh, ya know, everybody just left the room.[50]

This aircraft was subsequently lost from radar but was then spotted by other planes and eventually crashed after passengers counterattacked. No one from the FAA had passed on information about United 93 to the military and no one had requested military assistance. It crashed before any decisions were made.

Risk analysis

Risk environments *are decision environments that involve a lack of complete certainty but that include an awareness of probabilities associated with the possible outcomes of various courses of action.*

Risk environments involve a lack of complete certainty regarding the outcomes of various courses of action but some awareness of the probabilities associated with their occurrence. Undertaking risk analysis uses two steps: assigning a probability to the likelihood that an event will occur and then assessing the impact of the event if it did occur. Assessments are usually made with a mixture of evidence and intuition and scores are usually simplified into high/med/low or other short scale. The two scores (probability and likelihood) are then multiplied together. Risk analysis prioritizes risks in terms of importance based on the scores. Articulating the actual risks (to whom and what) enables one to analyse who and what might be affected by the decision and work through who might be involved in the decision-making process.[51]

These risk analyses enable desk-based evaluation to identify areas of high risk. Action can then be taken to eliminate or moderate the risk. Action is guided by examining how to lessen the likelihood of the risk occurring or lessen its impact.

Steps in the decision-making process

Managers make decisions throughout their working day and the four basic steps in systematic decision making are shown in Figure 10.4. The first step is to recognize that a problem or opportunity exists and that something must be done about it. But, more than this, the real nature of the problem or opportunity has to be defined and assessed. A human resource manager investigating the low levels of job satisfaction indicated in an employee survey must first determine the root cause of the problem (low wages, poor physical conditions and so on) before making any attempt to solve the problem. The key is accurate information that is carefully evaluated.

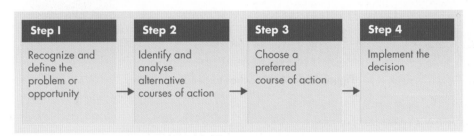

Figure 10.4: The decision-making process.

The next step is to pose alternative courses of action to remedy the situation and select the criteria to be used when assessing the relative merits of alternatives. Criteria might include ceilings on costs, industry specifications, work experience, ease of use, maintenance requirements and so on. Usually, two or more alternatives are available and they measure up against the assessment criteria in different ways. If poor physical conditions are found to be the root cause of the HR problem just mentioned, then the alternative solutions might include moving to a new factory site or refitting the existing facility. Minimizing the cost and production time lost are among the criteria important to management in their search for a solution.

The choice is made during step three, after analysing the various alternatives and implementation of the decision choice occurs during step four.[52]

Approaches to decision making

Organizational behaviour theorists maintain that there are two alternative approaches to decision making (Figure 10.5) – classical and behavioural.[53]

Classical decision theory views the manager as acting in a world of complete certainty. The manager faces a clearly defined problem, knows all possible action alternatives and their consequences, then chooses the alternative that offers the best or 'optimum' resolution of the problem. Classical theory is often used as a model for how managers should make decisions.

Classical decision theory views the manager as acting in a world of complete certainty.

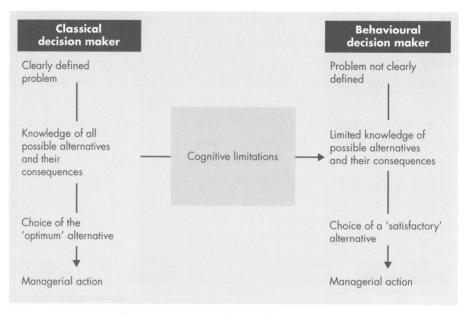

Figure 10.5: Approaches to decision making.

Behavioural scientists are more cautious, recognizing the human mind is a wonderful creation, capable of infinite achievements but also with limitations that mean nonoptimal solutions are achieved. Behaviourists suggest the human mind is limited in its information-processing capabilities, which can overload and thus compromise the ability of managers to make decisions according to the classical model. **Behavioural decision theory** states that people act only in terms of what they perceive about a given situation where the decision maker is seen as acting under uncertainty and with limited information.

Managers make decisions about problems that are often ambiguous; they have only a partial knowledge about the available action alternatives and their consequences; they choose the first alternative that appears to give a satisfactory resolution of the problem. This model is referred to by Herbert Simon as a satisficing style of decision making.[54] Simon and his colleagues suggest that in actuality we seek the discovery and selection of *satisfactory* alternatives; only in exceptional cases are we concerned with the discovery and selection of *optimal* decisions.

The key difference between a manager's ability to make an optimum decision in the classical style and the tendency to make a satisficing (or good enough) decision in the behavioural style is the presence of cognitive limitations and their impact on our perceptions. Cognitive limitations impair our abilities to define problems, identify action alternatives and choose alternatives – the key steps in the decision-making process.

Behavioural decision theory *refers to the idea that people act only in terms of what they perceive about a given situation.*

OB IN ACTION

The precautionary principle

The precautionary principle works on the basis that it is better to be safe than sorry. In a way, the principle limits personal perception of scientific data, and directs decision makers to err on the side of caution if the consequences of making the wrong decision are serious or irreversible.[55] For example, what level of scientific certainty on global warming is needed before organizations rethink their policies? According to many scientists, one of the causes of global warming is the destruction of rainforests. In particular, the clearing of South American rainforests is controversial; while governments allow communities to destroy the forests in order to survive, industrialized nations are condemning these practices as being dangerous to the global environment. In response, and based on the precautionary principle, the US pharmaceutical giant Merck & Company Inc. has found a creative solution to the commercialization of the rainforest much desired by locals – a solution that does not include the destruction of trees. Merck has an agreement worth US$1 million with the Costa Rican government for the right to search for usable species

within the rainforest. In addition, the company will share 5% of future royalties on any drug it develops from a species obtained in the Costa Rican rainforests. The Merck venture is significantly boosting the Costa Rican national budget of just over US$1 billion. Further, Costa Rica has preserved 25% of its natural environment with the help of Merck and other corporate venturers who have made the areas productive. As any royalties begin to filter into the Costa Rican government they will allow it to preserve even more of the natural environment.[56]

Intuition and decision making

A key element in successfully making nonroutine decisions is **intuition**. Intuition is the ability to know or recognize quickly and readily the possibilities of a given situation.[57] Intuition offers the potential for greater creativity and innovation, which are needed in risky and uncertain environments. A debate among scholars regarding how managers really plan highlights the importance of intuition for the practising manager. On one side of the issue are those who believe that planning can be taught and carried out in a systematic step-by-step fashion. On the other side are those who believe that the nature of managerial work is far more 'fuzzy', cannot be taught in this systematic way and that intuition has a fundamental role to play.

Intuition is the ability to know or recognize quickly and readily the possibilities of a given situation.

The ideas of Henry Mintzberg illustrate this:[58]

- Managers favour relational or interactive communications. Hence they prefer to obtain others' impressions and feelings about decisions, options and probabilities, rather than just a set of facts, in a way that would be hard to systematize on paper.
- Managers often deal with impressions. They are more likely to synthesize than analyse data as they search for the 'big picture' to make decisions.
- Managers work fast, do a variety of things and are frequently interrupted. Hence they do not have a lot of quiet time alone to think, plan or make decisions systematically.

One might suggest that managers should systematically plan in a step-by-step manner, but the realities of modern working life and its demands generally preclude such opportunities; hence they hone their intuitive skills. However, there can be drawbacks. Some commentators think mistakes are often a result of overreliance on intuition rather than objective facts. This can occur because experience combined with intuition can lead to snap judgements that are made before all objective evidence is available for evaluation.[59] In addition, conclusions made by different individuals on the same evidence can vary greatly, as decision makers are largely seeking confirmation of their initial hunches or suspicions and do not view information objectively.[60]

On the other hand, it would be naïve to suggest that decisions are best made by ignoring your intuition. In fact there are some individuals who are routinely required to make intuitive decisions, especially those who work in the emergency services (police, paramedics, hospital staff and firefighters). Intuition is said to be an instantaneous, emotional and often irrational reaction to a situation that can be risky. However, it is also said to be fast analytical reasoning that is clearly based on experience and practice drills, where judgement is simply analysis 'frozen into habit'. Confident decision makers will generally use a combination of logic and intuition to arrive at a sound decision.[61]

The use of judgement heuristics

Judgement, or the use of the intellect, is important in all aspects of decision making. Analysing alternative courses of action and choosing one course (steps 2 and 3 in the decision-making process) involve making judgements.

Heuristics
are simplifying strategies or 'rules of thumb' that people use when making decisions.

Research shows that managers and others use **heuristics** – simplifying strategies or 'rules of thumb' – when making decisions. Our 'Counterpoint' uses one such heuristic when budget setting. Heuristics are useful if they deal with uncertainty and limited information, but they can also lead to systematic errors.[62]

Making a choice and implementing a decision

Now we turn our attention to steps 3 and 4 in our model. Look back again at Figure 10.5. Once alternative solutions to a problem or opportunity have been developed, a preferred course of action must be chosen and that decision needs to be implemented, because management is about action! The overall aim is to achieve the best result using the least resources, and creating the least amount of risk and uncertainty (if that is possible).

COUNTERPOINT

Setting budgets for expenditure in many organizations, especially those in the public sector, revolves around 'last year and a bit more'. At the end of the financial year while some departments might struggle to contain their expenditure, others spend very freely because otherwise next year they will have their budget cut in a 'use it or lose it' mentality. In such circumstances optimal and logical decision making does not prevail.[63]

Take a few minutes to consider this from the following stakeholder positions:

- As a finance director, why might you use this heuristic?

- As the CEO, what might concern you about this heuristic?
- As the manager of a department, what would you do – save to show you are good at budgeting or spend so that you receive more next year?
- As a staff member, what would you want you department boss to do?

When it comes to managing the decision-making process, we can say that an effective manager is one who is able to pick precisely which problems are amenable to managerial decision making. Managers are too busy and have too many things to do with their valuable time to respond personally by making decisions on every problem or opportunity that comes their way. The effective manager knows when to delegate decisions to others, how to set priorities and when to empower others.

When confronted with a problem, therefore, managers ask themselves the following questions:[64]

- Is the problem easy to deal with? Small and less significant problems should not get as much time and attention as bigger ones. Even if a mistake is made, the cost of decision error is also small.
- Might the problem resolve itself? Putting problems in rank order leaves the less significant for last. Surprisingly, many of these less important problems will resolve themselves as they will be related to other issues anyway.
- Is this my decision to make? Routine problems can and should be delegated. Other problems can and should be referred to higher levels. This is especially true for decisions that have consequences for a larger part of the organization – more so than for those under a manager's immediate control.

To these three questions we add one of our own:

- Given the power and politics within the organization, who is best suited to be involved with and take this decision?

Strategies for involvement – who decides?

One mistake made by many new managers is to presume that they must solve the problems and make the decisions themselves. In practice, decisions are made in the following ways:

- *Individual decisions.* Managers make the final choice alone based on information that they possess and without the participation of others. Sometimes called an authority decision, this approach often reflects the manager's position of formal authority in the organization.
- *Consultative decisions.* The manager solicits input on the problem from other people. Based on this information and its interpretation, the manager then makes a final choice.
- *Group decisions.* The manager asks others to participate in discussions and in the decision choice. Although sometimes difficult, the group decision is the most participative of the three methods of final choice and the one that seeks true group consensus.

Good decisions can be made by each method – individual, consultative or group – if the method fits the needs of the situation.

EFFECTIVE MANAGER 10.3

Improving organizational problem-solving skills

Effective managers often focus on the process of problem solving and pay great attention to who is involved and that the interactions are positive. They:

- Believe that most problems can be solved.
- Ensure there is organizational commitment to solving problems. If top management is committed to continual improvement then a strong message is sent to the rest of the organization.
- Let people know that solving problems is part of their jobs and that they are accountable for solving their day-to-day problems.
- Ensure employees receive training in problem solving.
- Recognize when problems have been solved and praise successful problem solving.
- Ensure teams communicate their successful problem solving so other teams benefit from their experience.
- Work towards problem solving becoming a habit of every employee.[65]

Managing participation in decision making

Victor Vroom, Philip Yetton and Arthur Jago have developed a framework for helping managers to choose which of the three decision-making methods is most appropriate for the various problem situations encountered in their daily work efforts.[66] Their framework begins by expanding the three basic decision-making methods just discussed into the following five forms:

- AI (first variant on the authority decision). The manager solves the problem or makes the decision alone, using information available at that time.
- AII (second variant on the authority decision). The manager obtains the necessary information from employees or other group members, then decides on the solution to the problem. The manager may or may not tell employees what the problem is before obtaining the information from them. The employees provide the necessary information but do not generate or evaluate alternatives.
- CI (first variant on the consultative decision). The manager shares the problem with relevant employees or other group members individually, collecting their ideas and suggestions without bringing them together as a group. The manager then makes a decision that may or may not reflect the employees' inputs.
- CII (second variant on the consultative decision). The manager shares the problem with employees or other group members, collectively obtaining their ideas and suggestions. The manager then makes a decision that may or may not reflect the employees' inputs.
- G (the group or consensus decision). The manager shares the problem with the employees as a total group and engages the group in consensus seeking to arrive at a final decision.

The central proposition in this model is that the decision-making method used should always be appropriate to the problem being solved. The challenge is to know when and how to implement each of the possible decision methods as the situation requires.

Vroom and Jago use a flow chart to help managers analyse the unique attributes of a situation and use the most appropriate decision method for the problem at hand. Key issues involve the quality requirements of a decision, the availability and location of the relevant information, the commitments needed for follow-through and the amount of time available.

Vroom and Yetton outline a number of issues which help managers analyse the unique attributes of a situation and use the most appropriate decision method for the problem at hand. Key issues involve:

- quality requirements of a decision;
- availability and location of relevant information;
- commitment needed for follow-through;
- amount of time available.

How groups make decisions

Edgar Schein, a noted scholar and consultant, has worked extensively with groups to analyse and improve their decision-making processes. He observes that groups may make decisions through any of the following six methods:[67]

- *Decision by lack of response.* A course of action is chosen by default or lack of interest.
- *Decision by authority rule.* One person dominates and determines the course of action.

- *Decision by minority rule.* A small subgroup dominates and determines the course of action.
- *Decision by majority rule.* A vote is taken to choose among alternative courses of action.
- *Decision by consensus.* Not everyone wants to pursue the same course of action but everyone agrees to try it.
- *Decision by unanimity.* Everyone in the group wants to pursue the same course of action.

Consider the role power and politics might play in Schein's six methods.

Groupthink

Groupthink *is the tendency of members in highly cohesive groups to lose their critical, evaluative capabilities.*

Social psychologist Irving Janis defines **groupthink** as the tendency of members in highly cohesive groups to lose their critical, evaluative capabilities.[68] Groupthink is a rationalization process that develops when group members begin to think alike. It can be encouraged by leaders who do not tolerate dissent. It can develop when employees underestimate potential problems.

Groupthink is also a mode of thinking that people engage in when they are deeply involved in a cohesive ingroup and when the quest for unanimity overrides their motivation to realistically appraise alternative courses of action.

OB IN ACTION

Seventy-three seconds after its launch on 28 January 1986, the *Challenger* space shuttle exploded, killing the seven astronauts aboard. The cause of the explosion was found to be the failure of the O-ring seals on the solid rocket booster joints on the space shuttle. In the year prior to the *Challenger* launch, test launches and numerous investigations had shown that in low temperatures the O-ring seals failed to seal the joints, leaving them vulnerable to the high temperatures created at launch and thus increasing the possibility of explosion.

The day before the *Challenger* launch, managers were made aware of the low temperature forecast for the launch date and a meeting was called between managers and senior engineers. The engineers presented compelling data that a

launch with an outside temperature of −7.8°C was dangerous and strongly recommended against launching *Challenger*. NASA managers, burdened by the economic consequences of the delayed launch, argued for continuation of the mission.

Eventually the engineers' concerns were dismissed as the head of the management team, Jerry Mason, turned to Bob Lund, vice-president of engineering, and asked him to 'take off his engineering hat and put on his management hat'.

After some discussion, it was unanimously recommended that the *Challenger* mission go ahead as scheduled.[69]

Further information and an analysis of groupthink symptoms in this case can be obtained by watching the video *A Major Malfunction*.[70]

During groupthink, small groups develop shared illusions and related norms that interfere with critical thinking and reality testing. Some symptoms of groupthink are arrogance, overcommitment and excessive loyalty to the group. Other symptoms of groupthink are found in Effective Manager 10.4. They can be used to help spot this phenomenon in practice.

EFFECTIVE MANAGER 10.4

Groupthink

Janis suggests the following action guidelines for best dealing with groupthink:[71]

- Assign the role of critical evaluator to each group member; encourage a sharing of objections.
- The leader should avoid seeming partial to one course of action.
- Create subgroups operating under different leaders and working on the same problem.
- Have group members discuss issues with employees and report back on their reactions.
- Invite outside experts to observe group activities and to react to group processes and decisions.
- Assign one member of the group to play a 'devil's advocate' role at each meeting.
- Write alternative scenarios for the intentions of competing groups.
- Hold a 'second-chance' meeting after consensus is apparently achieved on key issues.

- Spot the symptoms of 'groupthink':
  - *Illusions of group invulnerability. Members believe the group is beyond criticism or attack.*
  - *Rationalizing unpleasant data. Members refuse to accept or thoroughly consider contradictory data or new information.*
  - *Belief in inherent group morality. Members believe the group is 'right' and above reproach by outsiders.*
  - *Negative stereotyping of outsiders. Members refuse to look realistically at other groups; they may view competitors as weak, evil or stupid.*
  - *Applying pressure to deviants. Members refuse to tolerate anyone who suggests that the group might be wrong; every attempt is made to obtain conformity to group wishes.*
  - *Self-censorship by members. Members are unwilling to communicate personal concerns*

or alternative points of view to the group as a whole.
- *Illusions of unanimity.* Members are quick to accept consensus; they do so prematurely and without testing its completeness.

- *Mind guarding.* Members of the group keep outsiders away and try to protect the group from hearing disturbing ideas or viewpoints.

Techniques for improving decision making in groups

As you can see, the process of making decisions in any group is a complex and delicate one. Group dynamics must be well managed to balance individual contributions and group operations. The following equation helps keep this point in mind:[72]

$$\frac{\text{Group decision}}{\text{effectiveness}} = \frac{\text{individual}}{\text{contributions}} + \frac{\text{group}}{\text{process gains}} - \frac{\text{group}}{\text{process losses}}$$

When do you back down?

We mentioned at the beginning of this section that effective managers should be making good decisions, and that they should be prepared to override previous commitments and discontinue courses of action that are just not working. Often this means being bold and decisive! However, many managers fall into the trap of escalating commitment. Recognized by social psychologists as common and potentially dysfunctional, it is the tendency to continue with a previously chosen course of action even though feedback indicates that it is not working.

Escalating commitment is encouraged by the popular adage: 'If at first you don't succeed, try, try again.' Current wisdom in organizational behaviour supports an alternative view: good decision makers know when to call it quits. They are willing to reverse previous decisions and commitments, and thereby avoid further investments in unsuccessful courses of action. However, the confidence and self-discipline required to admit mistakes and change courses of action is sometimes difficult to achieve. Often the tendency to escalate commitments to previously chosen courses of action outweighs the willingness to disengage from them. This occurs as decision makers:

- rationalize negative feedback as simply a temporary condition;
- protect their egos and avoid admitting the original decision was a mistake;
- use the decision as a way of managing the impressions of others, such as a boss or peers;
- view the negative results as a 'learning experience' that can be overcome with added future effort.

Escalating commitment is a form of decision entrapment that leads people to do things that are not justified by the facts of the situation. Managers should be proactive in spotting 'failures' and open to reversing decisions or dropping plans that do not appear to be working.[73]

Current issues in organizational decision making

In today's environments, the problems facing organizational decision makers seem to be harder and more complex. Prominent among the current issues relating to decision making in today's workplace are those dealing with culture, technology and the development of risk analysis.

Culture and decision making

The forces of globalization and workforce diversity have brought increased attention to how culture may influence decision making. The cultural dimensions of power-distance and individualism–collectivism have special implications for decision making. Workers from high power-distance cultures may expect their supervisors to make the decisions and may be less inclined than individualists to expect or wish to be involved in decision-making processes.

Values relating to individualism–collectivism also affect cultural tendencies towards participation in decision making. Decision making in collectivist cultures tends to be time consuming, with every effort being made to gain consensus. The results are slower decisions but smooth implementation. Decision making in individualist cultures (such as the Germanic countries), by contrast, is oriented more towards being decisive, saving time and using voting to resolve disagreements. The results are often faster decisions with implementation problems and delays.[74]

Culture may even play a role in determining whether a decision is necessary at all – in other words, whether the situation should be changed. North Americans tend to perceive situations as problems to be solved and want to do something about them. Other cultures, such as Thai and Indonesian societies, are more prone to accept the status quo.[75]

Technology and decision making

There is no doubt that today's organizations are becoming more sophisticated in applying computer technologies to facilitate decision making. Developments in the field of artificial intelligence – the study of how computers can be programmed to think like the human brain – are many and growing. Simple expert systems reason like a human expert and follow 'either/or' rules or heuristics to make deductions; fuzzy logic reasons beyond either/or choices in more imprecise territory and neural networks reason inductively by simulating the brain's parallel processing capabilities. Uses for such systems may be found everywhere from banks, where they help screen loan applications, and hospitals, where they check laboratory results and possible drug interactions, to the factory floor, where they schedule machines and people for maximum production efficiencies.[76] We have gradually learned to trust computers – we are willing to let them 'drive' planes, trains and automobiles! Medical technology brings computing into intimate contact with us, gradually building perceptions of trust.

Computer support for group decision making, as well as enhancing decisions can enable work to be restructured. People working in geographically dispersed locations can define problems and make decisions together and simultaneously by audio or video link. Research confirms that group decision software can be especially useful for generating ideas, as in electronic brainstorming, and improving the time efficiency of decision making.[77] People working under electronically mediated conditions tend to stay focused on tasks and avoid the interpersonal conflicts and other problems common in face-to-face deliberations. On the negative side, decisions made by 'electronic groups' carry some risk of being impersonal and perhaps less compelling in terms of commitment to implementation and follow through, not in keeping with the softer information Mintzberg's original work with CEOs found so essential (see p. 506–507). There is evidence that the use of computer technology for decision making is better accepted by today's university or college students than by people who are already advanced in their organizational careers.[78]

EFFECTIVE MANAGER 10.5

Ask yourself the following questions to 'road test' your decisions:

- If the decision goes on the public record, how will I feel? If you would not be happy then that is your inner self telling you that you are about to break your own moral code.
- How would you vindicate the decision to your close family members?
- What will this proposed course of action do to your character or the character of your organization? Reputation is a key business asset; making a decision that will irreparably damage that reputation is not a sound decision.
- Will everyone around you respond to the decision in the same way? If they cannot, then why should you be able to respond in that way?
- How would you like it if someone did this to you? If you would feel bad, then clearly others would probably not like it either.

- Will the proposed course of action bring about a good result for all involved? If the result is not good for all, then why are you doing it?
- Is the proposed course of action consistent with your espoused values and principles? Individuals make up an organization. In business life or personal life, individuals should always be true to their own values.

Now consider the following to further help you in your decision making:

- Define decision making and the sequential steps in the decision-making process.
- Summarize and contrast the classical and behavioural decision-making models.
- Evaluate the contributions of intuition, judgement and risk analysis to quality decision making.
- State the conditions under which individuals or groups are best placed to make decisions in organizations.

SUMMARY

LEARNING OBJECTIVE 1
Power and its sources

Power is an essential managerial resource. It is demonstrated by the ability to get others to do what you want them to do. Power vested in managerial positions derives from three sources: rewards, punishments and legitimacy. Legitimacy, which is the same as formal authority, is based on managers' position in the hierarchy of authority and the information to which they have access. Personal power is based on a person's expertise and reference; it allows managers to extend their power beyond that which is available in their position alone.

LEARNING OBJECTIVE 2
The relationship between power, authority and obedience

Power, authority and obedience are interrelated. Obedience occurs when one individual responds to the request or directive of another person. In the Milgram experiments, it was shown that people may have a tendency to obey directives coming from others who appear powerful and authoritative, even if these directives seem contrary to what the individual would normally consider to be 'right'. A zone of indifference defines the boundaries within which people in organizations will let others influence their behaviour without questioning it. Ultimately, power and authority work only if the individual 'accepts' them.

LEARNING OBJECTIVE 3
Empowerment

Empowerment is the process through which managers help others acquire and use the power needed to make decisions that affect them and their work. Clear delegation of authority, integrated planning and the involvement of senior management are all important to implementing empowerment. However, the key to success lies in redefining power so everyone can gain. The redefinition emphasizes power as the ability to get things done rather than to get others to do what you want.

LEARNING OBJECTIVE 4
Political behaviour

Organizational politics is use of power to find ways of balancing individual and collective interests in otherwise difficult circumstances. Machiavellian politics involves the use of power to obtain ends not officially sanctioned, or to achieve sanctioned ends through unsanctioned means. Political action in organizations can be examined at the managerial, subunit and chief executive levels. It may also occur formally and informally. For the manager, politics often occur in decision situations in which the interests of another manager or individual must be reconciled with their own. Politics also involve subunits that jockey for power and advantageous positions.

LEARNING OBJECTIVE 5
The ethics of power and politics in an organization

The ethics of power and politics are common to those found in any decision situation. Managers can easily slip into questionable territory unless they keep their behaviour limited to the task in hand. All behaviour can be 'rationalized' as acceptable, however it must meet the personal test of ethical behaviour established in Chapter 1. When political behaviour is ethical, it will satisfy the criteria of utilitarian outcomes, individual rights, distributive justice and/or overwhelming factors.

LEARNING OBJECTIVE 6
Types of decision making and models

Decision making in organizations is a continuing process of identifying problems and opportunities and choosing from alternative options. According to classical decision theory, managers seek 'optimum' solutions, whereas behavioural decision theory recognizes that managers 'satisfice' and accept the first available satisfactory alternative.

Routine problems arise on a regular basis and can be resolved through standard responses called programmed decisions. Nonroutine problems require tailored responses referred to as crafted decisions. Managers make decisions in three different environments: certain, uncertain and risky. Under certainty, everything about the alternative solutions is known and a choice will lead to an outcome that is highly predictable. Under risk, the manager can estimate the likelihood and impact from situations using risk analysis. In uncertain environments the choice is made with little real knowledge of what might happen.

LEARNING OBJECTIVE 7
Steps in the decision-making process

The decision-making process involves four sequential steps: recognize and define a problem; identify and analyse alternative courses of action; choose a preferred course of action and implement the decision.

LEARNING OBJECTIVE 8
Intuition, judgement and risk analysis

Intuition, judgement and risk analysis are all critical in effective managerial decision making. Intuition – the ability to recognize the possibilities of a situation quickly – is increasingly considered an important managerial asset. Judgement is the use of cognitive skills to make choices among alternatives, but heuristics (or simplifying rules of thumb) can potentially bias decision making. Risk analysis is a technique to both evaluate the risk and option outcomes as well as identifying who might be involved in decisions.

LEARNING OBJECTIVE 9
Conditions for decision making

Managers must know how to involve others in decision making and how to choose among individual, consultative and group decision methods. This is often a complex process. The Vroom–Jago model identifies how decision methods can be varied to meet the unique needs of each problem situation, which will also involve the power and political climate. Typically, a group decision is based on more information and results in better member understanding and commitment. The liabilities include greater time requirement and the dangers of groupthink.

LEARNING OBJECTIVE 10
Contemporary issues facing today's managers

Globalization and workforce diversity have brought into play the significance of national culture in managerial decision making. Culture can affect, for example, who should make the decision and the speed of the decision-making process within the organization.

Computers are being used more and more to facilitate decision making, but it is important to recognize both the benefits and the limitations of these sophisticated artificial intelligence initiatives.

Risk analysis is one response to the drive for more decisions to be simulated and thus rehearsed before they are required. In this way the potential for making a poor decision is theoretically reduced through 'uncertain' situations being addressed and hence increasing decision quality overall.

CHAPTER 10 STUDY GUIDE

Now that you have read this chapter, you should be able to apply and further develop your knowledge by undertaking the following activities set out over the next few pages: test your knowledge questions, individual activities and an end-of-chapter case study.

Please also go to this book's website: **www.wileyeurope.com/college/french** to find further material which will enhance your understanding and enable you to assess your knowledge

TEST YOURSELF

1. Explain how power is acquired.
2. Explain some of the ethical implications of power and politics.
3. How might personal power differ from authority?
4. How would you know if you were making an ethical decision?
5. Explain the meaning and importance of empowerment in an organizational context.
6. How might risk analysis have improved a difficult decision situation you know about?
7. Often students at university are required to work in groups with people they have never met before. When choosing potential group members how do you decide who you are going to work with? In your answer please explain the decision-making environments.

8. A member of your staff has put together a business plan to produce and market a new product. The plan is very comprehensive and conservative figures estimate that the new product would be highly profitable for your organization. However, your previous experience with this particular staff member has caused you to not trust him fully. Despite having no tangible reason for your lack of trust, you decide not to go ahead with the project. Your board of directors now wants an explanation for your decision. How do you justify and explain your behaviour? In your answer comment on rational, intuitive, heuristic and ethical considerations.

9. Why would organizations wish to empower their employees? Describe some of the risks associated with excessive empowerment.

10. Why are organizations unethical? Use the decision sequence to describe the influence of political and organizational power on individuals that might make them behave unethically.

11. Describe some of the political tactics and tricks that an employee may use to gain influence and some power advantage over his or her manager.

12. Identify two situations where you have come across cultural differences in decision-making processes. Undertake an analysis to see if and how these cultural differences affected the power balances within the situation.

INDIVIDUAL ACTIVITY

Think about a job you have held:

1. What are the sources of power theoretically available to the post holder?
2. To what extent did you feel able to use the power you could have?
3. Give examples of using your power sources.
4. Why did you choose to use the power sources you did?
5. Why did you choose to not draw on some power sources?
6. To what extent does politics come into play when choosing and using power sources in your examples?
7. Identify two contrasting decision scenarios: one demonstrating optimal decision making; another for satisficing decision making.

INDIVIDUAL ACTIVITY

Influence tactics

Objective

To check your understanding of influence tactics and when they may be most useful.

Procedure

Read each of the following 11 statements made by Jackie to Lee and, by applying them to the given scenario:

(a) Decide which influence tactic is being used and briefly explain your reasoning.

(b) Rank each statement from 1 to 11 in terms of how effective it might be in influencing Lee (although you have limited information, consider how you might feel and react if you were Lee).

(c) Decide whether and why you think the approach is ethical and briefly explain your reasoning.

Scenario

The senior management of the organization is developing a new proposal to introduce performance pay into the organization. Jackie and Lee are managers at the same level in the organization but in different sections. Jackie is seeking Lee's support to fight the proposal:

1. Come on, Lee. You've got to accept that this is the worst thing the company can do – look at the figures and how they show it won't work.

2. Lee, you've got to join me in fighting this proposal. I have to have your help.

3. I know you've always believed that performance pay will only ever advantage senior management while the rest of us are left carrying the workload. This is the only way our department is going to get ahead, and you're so good at speaking in public.

4. Lee, you need to help me fight this. If you don't, I'll have to reconsider the special arrangements I have for your staff when they want something from my department.

5. We need to get together to fight this proposal before it gets approved and ruins our operations.

6. Come on, Lee. The manager of Finance agrees with me that this proposal won't work.

7. I'd like you to help me fight this proposal. I'd help you out in the same situation, just as I did last year when you needed help with your upgrading application.

8. An intelligent person like you will immediately see that this proposal won't work.

9. Hi, Lee, you're looking great today. That was a great job you did on last month's report.

10. If you support me on fighting this, I'll support you in your promotion application.

11. Lee, would you look at this memo I've prepared to present a counter-argument to the performance pay proposal? I'd value your opinion.

Evaluation

Once you have ranked your responses, compare them to the information in the chapter that explains which influence tactics are likely to be most effective.

TOUGH DECISIONS AT FINANCECO

FinanceCo operates in the banking sector providing savings accounts and mortgages to individuals and couples. Not a big player in the market, it avoids direct competition with the large national banks. It has 12 branches in market towns across a geographic territory of 50 km. The small branches have a counter for customers to make payments and withdraw money. All branches have a private room for in-depth discussions such as arranging a mortgage or when  someone gets into difficulty repaying their mortgage. FinanceCo competes by treating its customers as individuals. Counter staff often know the people who come into their branches.

A recent change in strategy saw the establishment of a call centre. FinanceCo's sales director made the argument that the branches could not cope with the number of telephone calls coming in from customers, and the poor time-response they had to telephone enquiries was damaging their reputation and otherwise high levels of service. A large room in a building adjacent to Head Office was taken on a short-term rental (one year) to try out the idea. Fitting out the office cost € 200 000, took two months and provided seats for 50 staff. It was decided to begin with only 20 staff to enable FinanceCo to understand how to manage the operation. Of this first tranche of staff, six came from the branches. Others were recruited and trained as they had no finance background. The training for new staff took place in parallel to the office refurbishment. All call centre staff arrived on the same morning to start work at the new facility.

The first week had been a nightmare for Georgina and Fred, the two team leaders. The software had worked perfectly, but the staff had been problematic. The trainers had created two groups from the start, to provide the basis for the two teams Georgina and Fred would manage. On the first day the 'ex-branch' staff were unhappy with the rowdy atmosphere between the two teams of new staff, seeing their banter as unprofessional. Georgina observed that while there was joking around by the new staff, none of this happened while they were talking to customers. She put it down to the ex-branch staff being used to a quiet environment. The 'old' staff had been split between the teams equally but by the end of day two, Georgina could see them becoming physically exhausted by the pressure of answering call after call – perhaps FinanceCo had underestimated the nature of this job – it needed more than just knowledge of finance.

At the end of the first week Georgina, Fred and the Sales Director reviewed operations. The Sales Director had received several complaints (via branches) of poor advice given to customers. All complaints were about new staff members, but otherwise there were no patterns. Fred said that he had received a delegation of 'old' staff on Friday lunchtime.

They were struggling to cope with the new staff, saying that these employees lacked the correct FinanceCo attitude to customers, but Fred thought there was more to it than that.

At the same time as the management meeting, Mark was on the bus on his way home. He had worked for FinanceCo for many years and was horrified by his first week in the new call centre. The new staff had given all the 'ex-branchers' names, and most were nasty. None of the new staff had asked for his help with queries. He had heard several people give bad advice. When he went to Fred, Fred had said not to worry, it would all work out, but he urged Mark to tell the branches to complain to Head Office if they heard anything bad about the new staff. Mark had sent a quiet message to the branches, away from management 'radar'. Mark had seen Fred telephoning branch managers, but hadn't heard what was going on. His team called Fred 'Boiler', probably because Fred was prone to perspiring. They were making jokes, such as 'Ohh, the Boiler's blowing …' when Fred got upset at lunchtime because half the new staff went for a cafe lunch. Mark had eaten lunch on his own in the local park all week, pleased to get away from the abuse.

The Sales Director was worried by the level of gossip around FinanceCo, which was not used to such disturbances. He wondered if he needed to spend a few days working in the new office himself. He wasn't sure what the problem was and how to solve it. He didn't want to undermine Georgina or Fred, but they were clearly not up to the task of managing this group. Only one week had gone by and the call centre seemed quite out of control. His instinct told him that the problem was wider than the call centre, but where to look for clues?

Questions

1. Use concepts covered in this chapter to identify the problems at FinanceCo and the power dynamics that might be at play.
2. What are the questions the Sales Director needs to be asking, and of whom?
3. What decisions do you think should be given to Georgina and Fred – why do you think this?
4. What ethical issues does the chapter raise?
5. How would you redress the balance of power at the call centre?

SUGGESTED READING

Bazerman, M. & Moore, D. A. (2009), *Judgment in Managerial Decision-making*, 7th edn, John Wiley & Sons, Inc.: New York. This text provides a critical view of the realities of management decision making. It strays into the areas of power and politics, in which the authors are well versed.

Buchanan, D. & Badham, R. J. (2008), *Power, Politics and Organizational Change: Winning the Turf Game*, Sage: London. Aimed more at the regular manager, this text complements Bazerman and Moore through providing a non-US perspective and plenty of academic references.

END NOTES

1. Zanko, M., Badham, R., Couchman, P. & Schubert, M. (2008), Innovation and HRM: Absences and politics. *International Journal of Human Resource Management,* **19**(4), 562–581.

2. Buchanan, D. & Badham, R. J. (2008), *Power, Politics and Organizational Change: Winning the Turf Game,* Sage: London.

3. Kanter, R. M. (1979), Power failure in management circuit. *Harvard Business Review,* July/August, 65–75.

4. Pfeffer, J. (1992), Understanding power in organizations. *California Management Review,* **34** (2), 29–50.

5. Pfeffer, J. (1994), *Managing with Power: Politics and Influence in Organizations,* Harvard Business School Press: Boston, MA.

6. French, J. R. P. & Raven, B. (1962), The Bases of Social Power, in *Group Dynamics: Research and Theory* (ed. D. Cartwright), Peterson: Evanston, IL, pp. 607–623.

7. Ibid.

8. Ibid.

9. Rayner, C. (1998), Workplace bullying: do something! *Journal of Occupational Health and Safety – Australia and New Zealand,* **14**(6), 581–585.

10. Rayner, C. & Keashly, L. (2005), Bullying at work: a perspective from Britain and North America, in *Counterproductive Work Behaviour: Investigations of Actors and Targets* (eds S. Fox & P. E. Spector), American Psychological Association Publishers: Washington DC, pp. 271–296.

11. Hoel, H., Faragher, B. & Cooper, C. L. (2004), Bullying is detrimental to health, but all bullying behaviours are not necessarily equally damaging. *British Journal of Guidance and Counselling,* **32**(3), 367–387.

12. Rayner, C., Hoel, H. & Cooper, C. L. (2002), *Bullying at Work: What we Know, Who is to Blame and What Can We Do?* Taylor & Francis: London.

13. Schyns, B. & Sanders, K. (2004), Implicit leadership theories and the perception of leadership in the Netherlands. *International Journal of Psychology,* **39**(5/6), 129–159.

14. Scholl, W. (1999), Restrictive control and information pathologies in organizations. Social influence and social power: using theory for understanding social issues. *Journal of Social Issues,* **55**(1), 118.

15. See Tim Bajarin, *PC Magazine,* 26 April 2010.

16. Turner, J. C. (1987), *Rediscovering the Social Group – Self Categorization Theory,* Basil Blackwell: Oxford.

17. Chattopadhyay, P., Tluchowska, M. & George, E. (2004), Identifying the ingroup: a closer look at the influence of demographic dissimilarity on employee social identity. *Academy of Management Review,* **29**(2), 180–202.

18. O'Donnell, E. & Schultz, J. J. (2005), The Halo effect in business risk audits: can strategic risk assessment bias auditor judgement about accounting details? *Accounting Review,* **80**(3), 921–939.

19. Milgram, S. (1978), Behavioural study of obedience, in *The Applied Psychology of Work Behaviour* (ed. D. W. Organ), Business Publications: Dallas, TX, pp. 384–398. Also see: Milgram, S. (1963), Behavioural study of obedience. *Journal of Abnormal and Social Psychology,* **67**, 371–378; Milgram, S. (1964), Group pressure and action against a person. *Journal of Abnormal and Social Psychology,* **69**, 137–143; Milgram, S. (1965), Some conditions of obedience and disobedience to authority. *Human Relations,* **1**, 57–76; Milgram, S. (1974), *Obedience to Authority,* Harper & Row: New York.

20. Barnard, C. (1938), *The Functions of the Executive,* Harvard University Press: Cambridge, MA.

21. Morris, M. G. (2006), The executive role in culturing export control compliance, *Michigan Law Review,* **104**(7), 1785–2010.

22. Yukl, G. (2009), *Leadership in Organizations,* 7th edn, Prentice Hall: Thousand Oaks, CA.

23. Mackay, R., Cousins, J., Kelly, P. *et al.* (2004), Management standards and work-related stress in the UK: policy and background science. *Work and Stress,* **18**(2), 91–112.

24. Pascale, R. T. (1990), *Managing on the Edge*, Penguin: Harmondsworth.

25. Buchanan & Badham, op. cit.

26. Dufficy, M. (1998), The empowerment audit-measured improvement. *Industrial and Commercial Training*, 30(4), 142–146.

27. Pierce, J. L., Jussila, I. & Cummings, A. (2009), Psychological ownership within the job design context : revision of the job characteristics model. *Journal of Organizational Behavior*, 30(4), 477–496.

28. Pfeffer, J. (1993), *Managing with Power: Politics and Influence in Organizations*, Harvard Business School Publications: Boston, MA.

29. Buchanan & Badham, op. cit.

30. Greiner, L. E. (1982), Evolution and revolution as organizations grow. *Harvard Business Review*, 50(4), 37–41.

31. Pfeffer, J. (1993), op. cit.

32. Waters-Marsh, T. F. (2001), Exploiting differences: the exercise of power and politics in organizations, in *Management and Organizational Behaviour* (eds R. Wiesner & B. Millett), John Wiley & Sons: Brisbane, pp. 153–160.

33. Morgan, G. (2006), *Images of Organization*, updated edn, Sage: London, pp. 141–198.

34. Czechowicz, J. (2001), The winning ways of men and women. *Management Today*, January/February, 14–19.

35. Morgan, op. cit.

36. Developed from Hall, J. L. & Leldecker, J. L. (1982), A review of vertical and lateral relations: a new perspective for managers, in *Dimensions in Modern Management* (ed. P. Connor), 3rd edn, Houghton Mifflin: Boston, MA, pp. 138–146, which was based in part on Sayles, L. (1964), *Managerial Behaviour*, McGraw-Hill: New York.

37. See Pfeffer, op. cit. and Buchannan & Badham, op. cit.

38. Ibid.

39. Thompson, J. D. (1967), *Organizations in Action*, McGraw-Hill: New York.

40. Satava, D., Caldwell, C. & Richards, L. (2006), Ethics and the auditing culture: rethinking the foundation of accounting and auditing. *Journal of Business Ethics*, 64(3), 271–284.

41. At the time of writing, The Truth Report is yet to be translated in full into English, but commentary can be found from Rowena Mason who writes in the *Daily Telegraph* (London) 13 April 2010, and 'Iceland Banks' loans "excessive" report says', *National Posts Financial Post and FP Investing* (Canada), 14 April 2010.

42. Westphal, J. D. & Stern, I. (2007), Flattery will get you everywhere (especially if you are a male caucasian): how ingratiation, boardroom behaviour, and demographic minority status affect additional board appointments at US companies. *Academy of Management Journal*, 50(2), 267–288.

43. Edwards, J. & Wolfe, S. (2007), Ethical and compliance-competence evaluation: a key element of sound corporate governance. *Corporate Governance: An International Review*, 15(2), 359–369.

44. Buchanan, D. & Badham, R. (1999), op. cit.

45. Useem, M. (2006), How well-run boards make decisions. *Harvard Business Review*, 84(11), 130–145.

46. Adapted from Cavanagh, G., Moberg, D. & Velasquez, M. (1981), The ethics of organizational politics. *Academy of Management Review*, 6, 363–374.

47. Gellerman, S. W. (1986), Why 'good' managers make bad ethical choices. *Harvard Business Review*, 64 (July/August), 85–97.

48. Mintzberg, H. (1989), *Mintzberg on Management: Inside our Strange World of Organizations*, Free Press: New York.

49. National Commission on Terrorist Attacks upon the United States (2004), *The 9/11 Commission Report: Final Report of the National Commission on Terrorist Attacks Upon the United States*, WW Norton & Co.: New York.

50. Ibid., p. 31.

51. Borodzicz, E. (2005), *Risk, Crisis and Security Management*, John Wiley & Sons, Ltd: Chichester.

52. Doyle, T. C. & Lang, S. (2005), The leadership issue: managing your way to the top – insights from top executives and experts on management, decision-making and risk-taking. *VARbusiness*, issue 2116, 25 July, p. 30.

53. This discussion is based on March, J. G. & Simon, H. A. (1958), *Organizations*, John Wiley & Sons, Inc.: New York, pp. 137–142.

54. Ibid.

55. Ashford, N. (2005), Incorporating science, technology, fairness, and accountability in environmental, health, and safety decisions. *Human and Ecological Risk Assessment*, **11**(1), 85–96.

56. De George, R. T. (2006), *Business Ethics*, 6th edn, Prentice Hall: Englewood Cliffs, NJ.

57. Agor, W. H. (1989), *Intuition in Organizations*, Sage: Newbury Park, CA.

58. Mintzberg, H. (2001), Decision making: it's not what you think. *MIT Sloan Management Review*, **42**(3), 89–93.

59. Pipoli, R. (2005), CEOs and mistakes: study, discussion looks at management miscues. *Credit Union Journal*, **9**(7), 1.

60. Pipoli, op. cit., p. 1.

61. Patton, J. R. (2003), Intuition in decisions. *Management Decision*, **41** (10), 989.

62. The classic work in this area is found in a series of articles: Kahneman, D. & Tversky, A. (1972), Subjective probability: a judgement of representativeness. *Cognitive Psychology*, **3**, 430–454; Kahneman, D. & Tversky, A. (1973), On the psychology of prediction. *Psychological Review*, **80**, 237–251; Kahneman, D. & Tversky, A. (1979), Prospect theory: an analysis of decision under risk. *Econometrica*, **47**, 263–291; Kahneman, D. & Tversky, A. (1982), Psychology of preferences. *Scientific American*, **1**, 161–173; Kahneman, D. & Tversky, A. (1984), Choices, values, frames. *American Psychologist*, **39**, 341–350.

63. Bazerman, M. (2009), *Judgement in Managerial Decision-making*, 7th edn, John Wiley & Sons, Inc.: New York.

64. Stoner, J. A. F. (1982), *Management*, 2nd edn, Prentice Hall: Englewood Cliffs, NJ, pp. 167–168.

65. Harwood, C. C. (1999), Solving problems. *Executive Excellence*, **16**, 9 September, p. 17.

66. See Vroom, V. H. & Yetton, P. W. (1973), *Leadership and Decision Making*, University of Pittsburgh Press: Pittsburgh, PA; Vroom, V. H. & Jago, A. G. (1988), *The New Leadership*, Prentice Hall: Englewood Cliffs, NJ.

67. This discussion is developed from Schein, E. H. (1988), *Process Consultation*, Vol. I, 2nd edn, Addison-Wesley: New York, pp. 69–75.

68. Janis, I. L. (1971), Groupthink. *Psychology Today*, November, 43–46; Janis, I. L. (1982), *Groupthink*, 2nd edn, Houghton Mifflin: Boston, MA. See also Longley, J. & Pruitt, D. G. (1980), Groupthink: a critique of Janis's theory, in *Review of Personality and Social Psychology* (ed. L. Wheeler), Sage: Beverly Hills, CA; Leana, C. R. (1985), A partial test of Janis's groupthink model: the effects of group cohesiveness and leader behaviour on decision processes. *Journal of Management*, **11**(1), 5–18.

69. Boisjoly, R., Curtis, E. & Mellican, E. (1998), Roger Boisjoly and the Challenger disaster: the ethical dimensions, cited in Beauchamp, T. & Bowie, N. (eds) (2004), *Ethical Theory and Business*, 7th edn, Prentice Hall: Englewood Cliffs, NJ, pp. 123–136 quotation at p. 128; BBC (1998) *A Major Malfunction*, BBC Education and Training videorecording.

70. BBC (1998) *A Major Malfunction*, BBC Education and Training videorecording.

71. Developed from Janis, I. (1972), *Victims of Groupthink*, 2nd edn, Houghton Mifflin: Boston, MA.

72. See Hill, G. W. (1982), Group versus individual performance: are N + 1 heads better than one? *Psychological Bulletin*, **91**, 517–539.

73. Bazerman, op. cit., pp. 79–83.

74. See Trompenaars, F. & Hampden Turner, C. (2003), *Managing people across cultures*, Nicholas Brealey: London.

75. Adler, N. J. & Gundersen, A. (2007), *International Dimensions of Organizational Behaviour*, Thomson: Mason, OH.

76. Min, H. (2010) Artificial intelligence in supply chain management: theory and applications. *International Journal Of Logistics-Research And Applications*, **13**(1), 13–39.

77. Carrera, D. A. (2008), Supply chain management: a modular Fuzzy Inference System approach in supplier selection for new product development. *Journal of Intelligent Manufacturing*, **19**(1), 1–12.

78. Kabanoff, B. & Rossiter, J. R. (1994), Recent developments in applied creativity. *International Review of Industrial and Organizational Psychology*, **9**, 283–324 is an interesting article, given its age. This can be compared to recent press articles suggesting that our brains are being 're-wired' given sufficient hours on screen and text.

Communication, conflict and negotiation in organizations

LEARNING OBJECTIVES

After studying this chapter you should be able to:

- define communication and discuss its role in organizations
- define conflict and explain how it may affect organizational effectiveness
- explain how managers may deal with conflict effectively
- explain the role of negotiation in organizations
- discuss managerial issues in negotiation.

STRANDED IN THE TUNNEL!

On Friday 18 December 2009, five Eurostar trains running between Paris and London ground to a halt inside the tunnel which runs between France and England. It stranded over 2000 passengers who claimed they had insufficient food, water and clear information. Electrical failure meant no heating and crowded, uncomfortable conditions for most passengers on the stranded trains. Angry passengers eventually emerged, later 'twittering' their fury onto the web; a discussion which Eurostar did not enter for several days. Animosity towards Eurostar increased and fuelled demands for compensation.

Those waiting for trains (estimated to be over 30000 in France, Britain and Belgium on Saturday and over 25000 on Sunday) were also stranded, having to cancel or rearrange their travel plans for the seasonal holidays. Eurostar had staff on station platforms to talk to customers, but customers said staff could offer no direct help or connections to alternative transport such as flights.

For Saturday and most of Sunday Eurostar engineers said they could not locate the problem.

Questions

1. What effect did Eurostar's lack of communication have on passengers?
2. What communication strategies could Eurostar have used to lessen the conflict?

INTRODUCTION

Differences, misunderstandings and disagreements are a part of the daily life of individuals and organizations alike. If not dealt with constructively, such problems can be destructive for both the individual and the organization. Poor communication, or an absence of communication, is often the cause of conflict. Leaving conflict unresolved exposes organizations to greater risk of losing customers, employees and loss of confidence from stakeholders.

Communication problems and unresolved conflict cannot be expected simply to disappear of their own accord. While it may seem daunting, it is possible to take constructive steps to improve communication and resolve conflict in organizations. Managers need to strive to improve communication, address conflict and engage in appropriate negotiation processes.

The study of communication uses the topics basic to understanding human behaviour and at the collective level reflects how the organization works. Communication and organizational success are directly related. Good communication can have a positive and mobilizing effect on employees. Poor communication can produce powerful negative consequences, such as distortion of goals and objectives, conflict, misuse of resources and inefficiency in performance of duties.

The ability to manage good communication and handle conflict effectively is a necessary skill in all management roles. In any situation where people interact, there is potential for disagreement, challenge and conflict. No area of an organization is devoid of conflict, and in some cases conflict can be a good and healthy thing. Constructive conflict can promote creativity and make people reassess situations, identify problems and find new solutions. In some instances it can indicate that members of an organization are seeking more effective means of communication that will help resolve the conflict. In other instances, members could be challenging normal processes and procedures in an effort to improve productivity or introduce innovative systems. However, when conflict in the workplace becomes chronic or disproportionate, or leads to lost productivity and stress, then there is dysfunction. In order to resolve conflict, managers are increasingly required to possess negotiating skills. Such skills may also be used as a vehicle to create change or develop new opportunities.

In this chapter we will cover the basic process of communication and related issues in organizations. Also, because the daily work of people in organizations is based on communication and interpersonal relationships, conflict situations often arise and managers need to identify and understand them as well as know how to deal with them. Hence, the chapter will also introduce you to conflict management and negotiation as key processes of organizational behaviour.

COMMUNICATION IN ORGANIZATIONS

We can think of interpersonal communication as a process of sending symbols with attached meanings from one person to another. These interpersonal foundations form the basis for discussing the larger issue of communication within the organization.

Organizational communication is the process by which members exchange information and establish a common understanding.

When we communicate with others, we are usually trying to influence other people's understanding, behaviour or attitudes. We are trying to share meaning in some way. As Henry Mintzberg stresses,[1] we are communicating with others to inform, instruct, motivate or seek information. For example, you may wish to inform your chief executive that staff turnover is up 5% this month, or tell your staff about a new policy for sickness absence. Perhaps you want to have an informal chat with Harry to let him 'get things off his chest' in the hope that he will be happier and thus be more motivated to work effectively. Or perhaps you are going to call a staff meeting to gather feedback after hearing 'moans and groans' about the new computer system. Each of these communication tasks will have different aims and involve different skills.

While the function of interpersonal communication is really to share meaning, effective organizational communication can (and should) provide substantial benefits to the

Organizational communication is the process by which entities exchange information and establish a common understanding.

organization's members. Four functions are particularly important: achieving coordinated action, developing information, expressing feelings and emotions and communicating roles.[2]

From a top management perspective, a primary function of organizational communication is to achieve coordinated action. The collection of individuals that make up an organization remains an unfocused group until its members are in effective communication with one another. It is important that managers and individuals are aware of techniques in communication that are appropriate for their organization's structure.

Interpersonal communication

The key elements in the interpersonal communication process are illustrated in Figure 11.1. They include a source (a person who is responsible for encoding an intended meaning into a message) and a receiver (a person who decodes the message into a perceived meaning). The process may appear to be elementary but it is not quite as simple as it looks. Let us examine the model in some detail to identify the main elements in the process, the sequencing of these elements and weaknesses in the process that can lead to communication problems or distortions. The conventional communication process is made up of the following essential components: the information source, the encoding of a message, the selection of a channel, the transmission of the message, the decoding of the message, feedback from the receiver of the message and any 'noise' (or interference) that may have affected accurate decoding (or interpretation of the message).

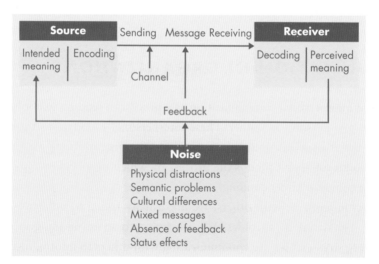

Figure 11.1: The communication process and possible sources of 'noise'.

*An **information source** is a person or group of people with a reason to communicate with some other person(s), the receiver(s).*

The **information source** is a person or group of persons with a reason to communicate with some other person(s), the receiver(s). The reasons for the source to communicate can vary enormously and include changing the attitudes, knowledge or behaviour of the receiver. A manager, for example, may want to communicate with the boss to make him or her understand why more time is needed to finish an assigned project. Of course, the manager will want to do so in such a way that indicates respect for the receiver and an understanding that the job is important, among other factors.

The next step in the process is **encoding** – the process of translating an idea or thought into meaningful symbols. This translation (encoding) process takes into account how the message is to be sent as the medium for transmission affects how the message is framed. For example, a personal interaction is a channel that includes verbal, written and/or nonverbal signals and symbols, whereas an e-mail transmission is restricted to written communication.

Encoding is part of the process of communication and involves translating an idea or thought into meaningful symbols.

The message is what is communicated. A **channel** is the medium through which the message is delivered. The choice of channels may alter the nature and effectiveness of the intended message. For many people it is easier to communicate face-to-face than in a memo or by e-mail. On the other hand, perhaps our manager would prefer to construct a formal memo carefully to his or her boss to set out the reasons why the work unit needs more time. Our manager should consider whether the boss might interpret the choice of a memo rather than a face-to-face meeting as avoidance. Alternatively, the boss might give the matter more weight if a letter arrives in an envelope in the in-tray than if the issue is briefly mentioned in an e-mail. The manager's message is simple: 'Our work unit needs more time to complete this task' but there are many ways to try to communicate that message.

Channels are the media through which the message may be delivered.

The process of communication does not stop with the sender. The **receiver** is the individual who hears (or reads or sees) the message. The receiver may or may not attempt to decode the message. **Decoding** involves interpreting or translating the symbols sent. Deleting e-mails before you have read them is an example of refusal to decode a message.

The **receiver** is the individual or group of individuals that hear or read or see the message within the communication process.

This decoding translation may or may not result in the assignment of the meaning intended by the source. Frequently, the intended meaning of the source and the meaning perceived by the receiver differ, or the receiver may have difficulty interpreting the message. Our manager wants the boss to understand that the work unit needs more time to complete a task. Will the boss get the correct message and what interpretation will he or she put on it? Alternative interpretations could be that the work unit is underperforming, that the manager is underperforming or something about the task has changed beyond the control of the work unit. The sender can influence how a message is interpreted.

Decoding is the interpretation of the symbols sent from the sender to the receiver.

Everyone knows the potential gap between an intended (sent) message and the message that is received. Feedback is the process by which receivers acknowledge the communication and return a message concerning how they feel about the original message. Throughout the process, there may be any number of disturbances. **Noise** is the term used to indicate any disturbance within the communication process that disrupts the matching process between sender and receiver.

Noise is anything that interferes with the effectiveness of the communication attempt.

Consider a simple example of noise. A lecturer is delivering a lecture in a lecture theatre filled with students who need to be there for their attendance score. The fact that only the lecturer speaks should create a 'silent' channel that allows the sound of the professor's voice and spoken words to flow freely to the ears of the students. However, if, in the midst of an uninteresting lecture topic, some students begin to text, whisper among themselves or giggle, their sounds will creep into the 'silent' channel, making the lecture 'noisy' to students who do wish to listen to the lecturer. Noise can effectively damage an otherwise well-planned communication. In this instance one would look for the reason for noise:

OB *IN ACTION*

Communication failure in New Orleans

Hurricane Katrina hit New Orleans in 2006, causing widespread destruction and stranding thousands. The practical aftermath is still being coped with more than five years later, as building projects continue. The event is now seen as a natural disaster compounded by human ineptitude. It has been analysed by several authors, most finding that poor communication was one underlying cause. The healthcare agencies (such as the various hospitals in New Orleans) each had individual emergency plans, which had been practised, but there was a lack of coordination between them (for example, not all staff knew their 'equivalent' in other facilities in the city) and none of them were in effective contact with the local National Guard, who themselves faced confusion.[3] While some IT solutions are being developed, for example a common portal held nationally to enable decision makers access to pollutant information,[4] lack of power to computers and mobile batteries failing would have paralysing effects in similar circumstances. Here the channels of communication were severely limited, not only by practical issues, but by lack of local knowledge of employees.

possibly the lecturer being poor at engaging the students and prompting them to engage in disruptive behaviour; possibly rude students.

Effective and efficient communication

Effective communication *is communication in which the intended meaning of the source and the perceived meaning of the receiver are one and the same.*

Effective communication occurs when the intended meaning of the source and the perceived meaning of the receiver are the same. This should be the manager's goal in any communication attempt. However, it is not always achieved. Even now, we worry whether you are interpreting our written words as we intend. Our confidence would be higher if we were face-to-face in class together and you could ask clarifying questions. The opportunity to offer feedback and ask questions is one way of increasing the effectiveness of communication.

Efficient communication has a minimum cost in terms of resources expended. Time is an important resource in the communication process. We continually create channels to enable communication; telephone conversations and texts, memos, posted bulletins, group meetings, e-mail, teleconferencing or videos. One needs to balance resource efficiency with effectiveness to ensure real communication occurs.

Resource-efficient communications are not always effective. A low-cost communication, such as e-mail, may save time for the sender but it does not always achieve the desired results, and receivers might understand anything other than the simplest of messages differently. Similarly, an effective communication may not be efficient. For a manager to visit each employee and explain a new change in procedures may guarantee that everyone truly understands the change but it may also be prohibitively expensive in terms of the required time.

Managers are busy people who depend on their communication skills to remain successful in their work. You need to learn how to maximize the effectiveness of your communications with others and to achieve reasonable efficiency in the process. These goals require the ability to overcome a number of communication barriers that commonly operate in the workplace. Such barriers may include cultural differences, defensiveness, misreading of nonverbal communication and stereotyping.[5]

Communication channels

In a very important sense the organization is a network of information and communication channels. Traditionally, there were formal and informal channels but the electronic age has added a third category – quasiformal channels. Using intranets and web-based technologies, managers are increasingly in a position to establish organization-wide communication channels; all managers should understand and be able to use each of the multiple channels for communication within their organization.

Formal communication channels follow the chain of command established by an organization's hierarchy of authority. An organization chart, for example, indicates the proper routing for official messages passing from one level or part of the hierarchy to another. As formal communication channels are recognized as official and authoritative, written communication in the form of letters, memos, policy statements and other announcements typically adheres to these channels.

> **Formal communication channels** *are communication channels that follow the chain of command established by the organization's hierarchy.*

Although necessary and important, formal channels constitute only one part of a manager's overall communication responsibilities. Interpersonal networks represent the use of a wide variety of **informal communication channels** that do not adhere to the organization's hierarchy of authority. These informal channels coexist with the formal channels but frequently diverge from them by skipping levels in the hierarchy and/or cutting across vertical chains of command. 'Water-cooler conversations' are a very good way to pick up 'grapevine' or informal communication. Here one might be including gossip, which is a very important type of informal communication and one which reflects and feeds the types of informal power groups discussed in Chapter 10.

> **Informal communication channels** *are communication channels that do not adhere to the organization's hierarchy.*

There are many instances of chief executive officers of contemporary organizations who go to great lengths to improve communication with the entire staff when communicating organizational messages. In some organizations managers may prefer to walk around to meet with and talk to floor employees as they do their jobs. 'Management by wandering around' (MBWA)[6] can help develop trust in working relationships with employees which, in turn, can affect commitment and lead to better productivity. Managers who spend time walking around can greatly reduce the perceived 'distance' between themselves and their employees and engage in far more meaningful communication. Management by wandering around can also reduce selective perception biases by reducing the gap between what individuals want to hear and see and what is actually occurring for both the senior executive or manager as well as employees. As a result, more and better information is available for decision making and the relevance of decisions to the needs of lower level personnel increases. Of course, the wandering around must be a genuine attempt to communicate; it should not be perceived as just another way to 'check up' on employees.

Quasiformal channels
are planned communication connections between holders of the various positions within the organization.

Formal channels conform to the organization's chain of command and informal channels emerge from day-to-day activities, but a set of **quasiformal channels** also exists in most organizations today. Quasiformal channels are planned communication connections between holders of various positions within the organization. For example, if the City of New Orleans had held meetings between all people who might be involved in a disaster recovery situation, the response to Hurricane Katrina might have been better.

An organization exists and must be managed as a system of interdependent parts performing distinct but coordinated functions. When workflow interdependence is such that a person or group must rely on task contributions from one or more others to achieve its goals, the circumstances are ripe for developing a quasiformal communication link.

▶ COUNTERPOINT

Social networking sites that are based on the web provide an extra communication channel for employees. Social capital is increased by managing social-professional networks based on websites such as LinkedIn.[7]

Questions

1. Do you think employees should be allowed to use sites such as LinkedIn in work time?
2. How is Facebook any different from LinkedIn?
3. What policies should an organization adopt concerning the use of such sites by employees in and out of work time?

How much information to share?

If knowledge is power, it is reasonable to propose that knowledge should be continually channelled to employees to give them the power to develop the organization. In fact, many modern managers no longer believe in the old concept that there is power in senior management holding onto information. Managers need to share information with employees to stimulate feedback from them on what is working, what isn't and why. Information can be an important part of motivation (see Chapter 4) and an integral part of the leadership process (see Chapter 9). It can, however, be difficult to know how much information and what sort of information to share. For example, employees need to be kept well informed about a company's strategic direction so they are able to make the right decisions in their individual and team capacities, yet there are many cases in which information is considered commercially confidential or private to certain individuals.[8]

Could this lead to an ethical dilemma for senior managers over what information to share and what to protect? The decision often remains at the discretion of the senior manager, who should be well informed on what the organization's leaders consider to be classified information and what information is to be shared with their employees. For example, how the organization is performing and what changes are planned are issues that should be discussed openly with everyone who is likely to be involved throughout the process. On the other hand, the early stages of potential takeovers or sensitive issues involving individual staff members are better kept confidential.[9] The increasing tendency for employees to regularly change employers must also be taken into account. Managers should consider the possibility that an employee will be working for a competitor in the future when considering the release of strategic information.

Managers at all levels must impress on their team what is important to employees and what should remain confidential.[10] Depending on the culture of the organization, some managers may encourage open communication and share information that would typically be considered confidential, even to the point of discussing one another's salary levels and other employment incentives.[11]

Senior managers who have open, ongoing discussions with their staff are probably better placed to judge how much information to communicate. Regular two-way conversations with employees will not only encourage valuable input from all levels of the organization but also tap into the internal grapevine, which can be a risky form of communication if left unchecked. The internal grapevine will always operate in organizations, so it is important that issues raised on this grapevine are identified and reframed to reflect an accurate picture.

Employees can complain of 'mushroom management' where they feel treated like mushrooms which are grown in the dark. So, while there can be commercial sensitivities in releasing information, it has to be balanced with the need to engage and motivate employees (see Chapters 4 and 5), where providing information is a factor. The other issue is that of trust. If employees feel uninformed, they may think that management perceive them as untrustworthy, which can undermine the psychological contract.[12] Or worse – that there is no plan and that their management is incompetent.[13]

An area which holds greater conflict is that of communicating to customers. This is a key feature of corporate ethics, typically involving how far organizations let customers know when a tangible product is less than perfect.[14] There are numerous examples of organizations handling their communication poorly in this context, leading to exacerbation of a problem; a recent example being the selective recall of baby carriers.[15] Service products are more tricky to both assure and quality control. Arguably much of the recent 'credit crunch' was caused by a combination of ambiguous communication and poor levels of responsibility. At the micro level, many householders took out mortgages about which they were poorly informed and, one might argue, did not care to understand.[16] At the macro level, the derivatives market provided products which were complex in nature such that many institutions were in a similar position to the mortgage buyers.[17] Whether the fault lies with the sender (the seller of financial products) or the receiver (the home owner or investing institution), these events provide a graphic example of poor communication.

Barriers to communication

Look back now to Figure 11.1. Communication is not always perfect. Interference of some sort in the telecommunication process is called 'noise'. Given the rapid developments in telecommunications over the past 30 years, 'noise' due to technical faults is diminishing. Less tangible barriers to communication relate directly to those people in the communication channel. For example, you will remember that earlier in the chapter we referred to the ever-increasing number of incoming and outgoing e-mails a manager is subjected to each day. Large volumes of e-mails might mean that they are only part-read, skim-read or posted in folders (without being read) only to be forgotten. While the development of technology can enhance the opportunity to communicate more frequently and faster, it still needs management.

Therefore, managers should select the most appropriate channel of communication to get each message across to the recipient without distortion. For example, a survey found that few managers from the sample researched agreed that e-mail was more persuasive than a face-to-face meeting, yet two-thirds of the same group researched reported that face-to-face communication skills had decreased as a result of e-mail use.[18] Face-to-face communication allows the transmission of body language, which can be up to 55% of the message received, with the oral communication (i.e. the words) perhaps as little as 7%. E-conferencing with webcams is thus a far richer environment than e-mail, but it is still very difficult to replace face-to-face interaction, which is favoured by all staff at all levels.[19]

OB IN ACTION

Mehrabian's rule

Mehrabian studied the relative influence of body language, tone of voice and words in laboratory settings almost 40 years ago (1971). He found the following formula for their influence on the message received:

7% for words
38% for tone of voice
55% for body language.

Known as 'Mehrabian's rule' this formula was, of course, a very surprising finding. But Mehrabian had never expected it to be generalized to all settings, which is unfortunately what has occurred! Every situation varies and so it is impossible to generalize, but the overall findings should not be ignored.

The results help us see how we must pay attention to nonverbal signs such as eye contact and body language. They also help to highlight the huge importance of tone of voice. None of these are to be found in e-mail contact. This means that care over use of words is crucial in e-mails. Writing in clear and simple language helps get the message across. Unfortunately, you don't know how your e-mail receiver is decoding, and so for e-mails you do not have the ability to obtain feedback and correct the signalled message if it is being understood in the wrong way.

Although retired, Albert Mehrabian continues to research and publish, publishing his most recent book in 2007.[20]

Noise still occurs in interpersonal communication in today's organization; so to improve communications, it is important to understand the sources of noise. The most common sources of noise are physical distractions and cultural differences.[21] Physical distractions include such things as a competing conversation being held in the office while you are trying to concentrate on an important telephone call, or the disturbance caused by someone fixing the road outside when you need to listen to someone who has come to see you. Environmental factors such as too much noise in open-plan offices or uncomfortable temperatures can fall into this category.

Cultural differences can present a number of complications or obstructions to effective communication between individuals. The problems that these blocks pose to managers are usually compounded by managers' deeply rooted orientations to life according to the pattern of their own society, as shown in Chapter 7 on culture. The acceptability of touching and 'personal space' varies greatly, with greater acceptance in most European countries than, for example, in China. While employees may recognize that people from other cultures are different, they may find it hard to understand and adjust to the great variety of ways in which this difference manifests itself.[22]

We need to recognize these sources of noise and to subject them to special managerial control. They are included in Figure 11.1 as potential threats to any communication process.

Effective communicators not only understand and deal with communication barriers – they are also exceptionally good at active listening. Effective communicators recognize that being a good receiver is just as important, and often even more important, than being an accurate sender. Poor communication can eventually lead to conflict, to which the chapter now turns.

The habits of good communicators

For good communication to occur, people need to:

- speak clearly
- write clearly
- be aware of cultural differences
- listen attentively
- question precisely
- answer honestly
- pause for feedback signals.

CONFLICT

Conflict is a universal phenomenon. It can facilitate learning, creativity and change but for some people it makes their workday less enjoyable. For others, the frequency and intensity of workplace conflict makes them uncomfortable and impedes their effectiveness.

Workplace conflict may reach such levels that people consider leaving the organization. Few people welcome conflict and many managers do not know how to manage it effectively. Yet successful conflict management is at the root of organizational effectiveness. It exists at all levels in the hierarchy to a greater or lesser degree. Much of the focus is on how to resolve conflict among employees at the lower levels of the hierarchy, but just as many conflict situations can erupt in the boardroom. It is common to read in mainstream media about disputes and conflict among top managers in major organizations. But not all conflict is negative.[23]

What is conflict?

Conflict occurs whenever disagreements exist in a social situation over issues of substance, or whenever emotional antagonisms create friction between individuals or groups.[24] Managers are known to spend up to 20% of their time dealing with conflict, including conflicts in which managers are themselves directly involved.[25] In other situations managers may act as mediators or third parties and try to resolve conflicts between other people. In all cases, managers must be skilled participants in the dynamics of interpersonal conflict. They must also be able to recognize situations that have the potential for conflict and deal with these situations to best serve the needs of both the organization and the people involved.

Petty disputes are common occurrences in all workplaces. Full-scale discord can always occur, often emerging after small incidents go unchecked.[26] Both levels cause stress to most involved,[27] and can overwhelm those involved to the detriment of other tasks and issues. Not all conflicts can be predicted, nor can they be prevented, but they can be managed. Among the common reasons for conflict are personal styles and differences in values and job perspectives. Differing needs for personal success and variations in skill level can also cause conflict.

It is important to listen to individuals in a conflict because their anger or frustration is frequently rooted in a desire to see change effected, often a positive motivation. A manager needs to know how to resolve such interpersonal conflicts. Where tension develops between managers or different management functions, the conflict can have a dramatic impact on organizational performance. Managers who understand the fundamentals of conflict and negotiation will be better prepared to deal with such situations.

If you listen in on some workplace conversations, you might hear the following:

- 'I don't care what you say, I don't have time and that's that!'
- 'I no longer want to open my e-mails when I first get to the office. I get too many, and most I don't need to see.'
- 'Why didn't I know about that? This has been going on for ages!'

The very words used in these statements are important. They all link to communication and convey a sense of discord in the workplace and 'frame' the thinking of the people making them in a negative or adversarial way. This way of thinking is bound to affect the speaker's working relationships with the other people involved. It is also likely to affect their attitudes and work behaviours. At issue in each case is conflict. The ability to deal with such conflict successfully is a key aspect of a manager's interpersonal skills.

Conflict must be managed effectively for an organization to achieve its goals. Before it can be managed, conflict must be acknowledged and defined by the disputants. However, it may be difficult for the parties involved to agree on what is in dispute in a shared conflict because they may experience, or frame, the same conflict in different ways.[28]

Substantive and emotional conflicts

Conflict in organizations can be as diverse as the people working there. Interpersonal conflict is natural and can actually spur creativity but the objective for managers is to manage it, often by preventing interpersonal differences from affecting productivity. As rational adults, we tend to expect that when we present an idea we will achieve consensus. We believe that others will see the logic of our views and support them, even when different cultures and backgrounds are apparent. However, because each of us has a different perspective it can be easier to support only those ideas and views that align with our own. To deal with conflict effectively, both objective and subjective elements contributing to the conflict need to be examined and addressed.

Two common examples of workplace conflict are a disagreement with your boss over a plan of action to be followed (for example, a marketing strategy for a new product) and a dislike for a co-worker (for example, someone who is always belittling the members of an ethnic or identity group). The first example is a traditional one of **substantive conflict** – that is, a conflict that usually occurs in the form of a fundamental disagreement over ends or goals to be pursued and the means for their accomplishment.[29] When people work together day in and day out, it is only normal that different viewpoints on a variety of substantive workplace issues will arise. It is common for people to disagree at times over such things as group and organizational goals, the allocation of resources, the distribution of rewards, policies and procedures and task assignments. Dealing successfully with such conflicts is an everyday challenge for most managers. The second example is one of **emotional conflict** – that is, a conflict that involves interpersonal difficulties that arise over feelings of anger, mistrust, dislike, fear, resentment and the like.[30] It is commonly known as a 'clash of personalities'. Emotional conflicts can drain people's energies and distract them from other important work priorities. They can emerge from a wide variety of settings and are common among co-workers as well as in superior–employee relationships. The latter is perhaps the most upsetting emotional conflict for any person to experience. Unfortunately, competitive pressures in today's business environment and the resulting emphasis on downsizing and restructuring have created more situations in which the decisions of a 'tough' boss can create emotional conflict.[31]

Both types of conflict can have a positive influence on management performance. However, substantive (or task-oriented) conflict is likely to have the most positive effect, depending on how it is managed.[32] Performance is what we typically think about when we consider effectiveness; it constitutes the decisions or solutions that affect productive output. Conflict can force managers to address some of their assumptions and override

Substantive conflict *is conflict that occurs in the form of a fundamental disagreement over ends or goals to be pursued and the means for their accomplishment.*

Emotional conflict *is conflict that involves interpersonal difficulties that arise over feelings of anger, mistrust, dislike, fear, resentment and the like.*

their attempts to achieve premature unanimity, thus leading to better performance. Managers engaged in substantive (task-oriented) conflict tend to direct their actions to their work because the conflict forces them to concern themselves with task functions and related issues. By contrast, emotional conflict is inward looking and positive outcomes can be harder to achieve and take energy away from the tasks at hand.

EFFECTIVE MANAGER 11.1

Communication that can lead to conflict

The conflict 911.com 'conflict help centre' warns that there are five types of communication that can lead to conflict. Managers should avoid:

- *Negative communication.* We all know a 'negative Nigel/Nancy' in every team – they exist and we find it near impossible to remove them. But constant negativity drains the other team members of enthusiasm, energy and self-esteem.

- *Blaming communication.* Blamers spray blame around, effectively stopping reflection and scrutiny of their performance and behaviour. However, their impact can be reduced by fostering a learning environment, as well as the use of 'I' messages, peer pressure and individual feedback.

- *Superior communication.* 'Superiors' frequently order people about, direct, advise and moralize. They are also very skilled at withholding information.

- *Dishonest communication.* Dishonest communicators frequently fail to practise listening to understand and fail to display empathy. They also display circumlocutory communication – also known as 'talking around the issue, not addressing it'.

- *Selective communication.* Selective communicators only tell what they think others need to know, hence keeping themselves in a position of power over the other team members. Such behaviour can be effectively addressed through assertive requests for having access to all the information.

Source: http://www.conflict911.com/guestconflict/minimzingconflict.htm (accessed 22 December 2009).

Levels of conflict

It is possible to examine conflict from a number of different communication levels. In particular, people at work may encounter conflict at four levels:

- intrapersonal, or conflict within the individual;
- interpersonal, or individual-to-individual conflict;
- intergroup conflict;
- interorganizational conflict.

When it comes to dealing personally with conflicts in the workplace, how well prepared are you to encounter and deal with various types of conflict?

Intrapersonal conflict

Among the significant conflicts that affect behaviour in organizations are those that involve the individual alone. These intrapersonal conflicts often involve actual or perceived pressures from incompatible goals or expectations of the following types. Approach conflict occurs when a person must choose between two positive and equally attractive alternatives. An example is having to choose between a valued promotion in the organization or a desirable new job with another organization. Avoidance conflict occurs when a person must choose between two negative and equally unattractive alternatives. An example is being asked either to accept a job transfer to another town in an undesirable location or to have your employment with an organization terminated. Approach-avoidance conflict occurs when a person must decide to do something that has both positive and negative consequences. An example is being offered a higher paying job but one with responsibilities that will make unwanted demands on your time.

Interpersonal conflict

Interpersonal conflict occurs between two or more individuals who are in opposition to one another; the conflict may be substantive or emotional in nature, or both. Two people debating aggressively over each other's views on the merits of hiring a job applicant is an example of a substantive interpersonal conflict. Two people continually in disagreement over each other's choice of work attire is an example of an emotional interpersonal conflict. To be in conflict over management style may contain both aspects of conflict. All managers will face conflict situations given the interpersonal nature of the managerial role. We will address this form of conflict in more detail when we discuss conflict management strategies later in the chapter.

Interpersonal conflict *is conflict that occurs between two or more individuals.*

Intergroup conflict

Another level of conflict in organizations occurs between groups, and can also have substantive and/or emotional underpinnings. Intergroup conflict makes the coordination and integration of task activities very difficult. Consider a mail-order company where the relationship between the sales department and the stock-ordering inventory department breaks down. Sales staff, often rewarded on the level of sales they are able to invoice, may be greatly affected if there is not enough stock to send once an order has been received. Customers may cancel late orders. The stock department wants to make sure that it does not keep too much stock, as this risks having redundant items which will never sell, and money tied up in stock on shelves is not welcome by senior management who want to optimize cash flow. It is a natural tension, and one which occurs in all organizations selling goods. These differences become apparent in terms of how group goals and the handling of information affects decision making in each setting where antagonistic relationships can mean that the whole organization suffers, and positive relationships mean the wheels turn smoothly.

Interorganizational conflict

Conflict may also occur between entire organizations or independent units in large organizations.[33] Such interorganizational conflict most commonly reflects the competition and rivalry that characterizes organizations operating in the same markets. However, interorganizational conflict is really a much broader issue than that represented by market competition alone. Consider, for example, disagreements between unions and the organizations employing their members; between government regulatory agencies and the organizations subject to their surveillance; between organizations and those who supply them with raw materials; and between units within an organization competing for organizational resources. If conflict between divisions in a company is ignored, the organization will often be more concerned with internal competition than with external competition.[34]

New organizational structures such as joint ventures, strategic alliances and networks have the potential to release conflicts both between the new partners and also within the participating organizations. These latter conflicts were contained within the old structure or resolved by rules. The changes inherent in restructuring bring them to the surface, and such conflicts within the organization and between organizations may result in the dissolution of partnerships.

When organizations are faced with big decisions such as restructuring or forming strategic alliances, it is the CEO or head of the company who is the focal point of the decision-making process and who is ultimately responsible for the outcome. In difficult, sensitive or hostile environments, when tough decisions are to be made, who does the CEO turn to for advice or to act as a sounding board? His or her immediate staff or a consultant may be obvious choices, yet some CEOs are finding the backup support they need in syndicates: formal groups that meet outside the office.

Take, for example, a situation in which a decision will ultimately result in conflict with one or more parties. The CEO is responsible for making the best decision for all parties but in cases such as staff cutbacks or plant relocation the decision is never an easy one to make because people are hurt, so the potential for conflict can be huge. In such delicate situations, discussions with internal staff may not always be appropriate, whereas discussions in confidence with external peers who may have experienced or are likely to experience a similar situation may provide a good source of advice, and even comfort.

Conflict and culture

Most developed countries are by now culturally diverse because of economic migrants and skills shortages. As such our employees come from diverse backgrounds, which are characterized by a wide range of traditions, languages, beliefs, values, ideas and practices.[35] In addition many graduates do not spend the whole of their working lives in the country in which they received their degree. In this world, where our borders are becoming more porous for crossnational work, any graduate has good opportunities to work abroad. One of the key reasons for the early return of expatriates is the uncertainty and frustration resulting from poor cross-cultural adaptation. The result of this is an increase in the interpersonal conflict expatriates experience in the workplace abroad, caused by cultural differences.[36] These should not be underestimated by anyone seeking to relocate to another country.

Constructive and destructive conflict

Conflict in organizations can be dangerous. It is often upsetting both to the individuals directly involved and to others who may observe it or be affected by it. On an emotional level, at least, many of us are more aware of its perils than its possibilities. A common byproduct of conflict is stress. It can be uncomfortable, for example, to work in an environment in which two co-workers are continually hostile towards each other. But conflict is not always negative. Organizational behaviour recognizes two sides to conflict – the constructive side and the destructive side (Figure 11.2).

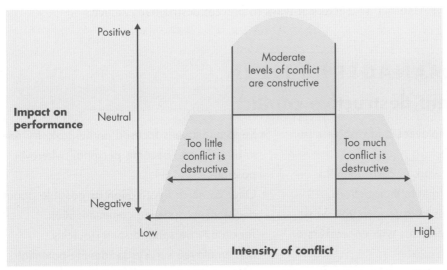

Figure 11.2: The two faces of conflict: functional conflict and dysfunctional conflict.

Constructive conflict results in benefits to the group or organization. It offers the people involved a chance to identify otherwise neglected problems and opportunities; performance and creativity can improve as a result. Indeed, an effective manager is able to stimulate constructive conflict in situations in which satisfaction with the status quo inhibits necessary change and development. Such a manager is comfortable dealing with both the constructive and the destructive sides of the conflict dynamic. Another value of conflict is that it can prevent stagnation, stimulate interest and curiosity and foster creativity. This is at the heart of the argument to promote diversity in working groups.

When conflict arises, most people's first reaction is to become angry or distressed and to seek to eliminate the problem. However, managers need to realize that if they can understand the issues that are causing the disagreement they will be in a better position to minimize the anger and distress and to use the conflict to the organization's advantage within the resolution.

Innovation can occur when different ideas, perceptions and ways of processing and judging information collide. Positive conflict can help organizations become more innovative. Creative thinking can be a powerful tool in managing conflicts that result from personal disagreements and cognitive differences. Such conflict nurtures creativity. Various organizational members who see the world differently need to cooperate. Even when the parties have different viewpoints, managing those differences can be productive.[37]

Destructive conflict works to the group's or organization's disadvantage. It occurs, for example, when two employees are unable to work together as a result of interpersonal hostility (a destructive emotional conflict), or when the members of a committee fail to act because they cannot agree on group goals (a destructive substantive conflict). Destructive conflict of these types can decrease work productivity and job satisfaction and contribute to absenteeism and job turnover. Managers must be alert to destructive conflicts, quickly acting to prevent or eliminate them, or at least minimize their resulting disadvantages. Effective Manager 11.2 looks at ways to prevent destructive conflict.

EFFECTIVE MANAGER 11.2

How to prevent destructive conflict

- Listen carefully to employees and resolve misunderstandings quickly.
- Monitor employees' work to assist them to understand and coordinate their actions.
- Encourage employees to approach you when they cannot solve difficulties with co-workers on their own.
- Clear the air with regular meetings that give employees a chance to discuss their grievances.
- Keep employees focused on the task, try not to let disputes 'become personal' wherever possible.
- Offer as much information as possible about decisions to optimize communication.
- Tackle interpersonal disputes quickly.
- Use employee surveys to identify potential conflicts that have not yet surfaced.

Conflict situations faced by managers

The manager's ability to deal with conflict situations may, in large part, determine whether they have constructive or destructive impacts on the work situation. More specifically, an effective manager is able to recognize and deal with each of the following conflict situations:[38]

- Vertical conflict occurs between hierarchical levels, and commonly involves supervisor–employee disagreements over resources, goals, deadlines or performance results.
- Horizontal conflict occurs between people or groups at the same hierarchical level and commonly involves goal incompatibilities, resource scarcities or purely interpersonal factors.
- Line–staff conflict occurs between line and staff representatives and commonly involves disagreements over who has authority and control over certain matters, such as personnel selection and termination practices.

- Role conflict occurs when the communication of task expectations proves inadequate or upsetting, and commonly involves uncertainties of expectations, overloads or underloads in expectations and/or incompatibilities among expectations.

Conflict becomes more likely in each of these situations when certain conditions exist. In general, managers should be aware that work situations with one or more of the following characteristics may be predisposed to conflict:[39]

- workflow interdependence;
- power and/or value asymmetry;
- role ambiguity or domain ambiguity;
- resource scarcity (actual or perceived).

As discussed in Chapter 6, the various parts of a complex organization must be well integrated for it to function well. However, interdependencies among components can breed conflict. When work flow interdependence is high – that is, when a person or group must rely on task contributions from one or more others to achieve its goals – conflicts often occur. You will notice this, for example, in a fast-food restaurant when the people serving the food have to wait too long for it to be delivered from the cooks. Good managers understand that the performance expectations and other aspects of such links must be handled carefully to ensure smooth working relationships. Indeed, one of the central precepts of total quality management is that 'internal customers' – other people or groups inside the organization – should receive the same dedicated attention and service that external customers receive.

Power or value asymmetries in work relationships exist when interdependent people or groups differ substantially from one another in status and influence, or in values. Conflict due to asymmetry is prone to occur, for example, when a low-power person needs the help of a high-power person who will not respond; when people who hold dramatically different values are forced to work together on a task; or when a high-status person is required to interact with – and perhaps depend on – someone of lower status. A common example of the latter case occurs when a manager is forced to deal with another manager through his or her deputy.

When individuals or groups operate with a lack of adequate task direction or clarity of goals, a stressful and conflict-prone situation exists. In Chapter 8 we discussed how role ambiguities might cause problems for people at work. At the group or department level, similar effects in terms of domain ambiguities can occur. These ambiguities involve misunderstandings over such matters as customer jurisdiction or scope of authority. Conflict is likely when individuals and/or groups are placed in situations in which it is difficult for them to understand just who is responsible for what. It may also occur where people resent the fact that their 'territory' is being trespassed upon.

A common managerial responsibility is the allocation of resources among different groups. Actual or perceived resource scarcity is a conflict-prone situation. When people sense the need to compete for scarce resources, working relationships are likely to suffer. This is especially true in organizations experiencing the financial difficulties associated with a period of decline. As cutbacks occur, various individuals or groups will try to position themselves to gain or retain maximum shares of the shrinking resource pool; they are also likely to try to resist or employ countermeasures to defend their resources from redistribution to others.

Most conflicts develop in stages, as shown in Figure 11.3. These stages include antecedent conditions, perceived and felt conflict, manifest conflict, conflict resolution or suppression and conflict aftermath.[40] The conditions that create conflict, as discussed, are examples of conflict antecedents; that is, they establish the conditions from which conflicts are likely to develop. In addition, managers should recognize that unresolved prior conflicts help set the stage for future conflicts of the same or related sort. Rather than try to deny the existence of conflict or settle on a temporary resolution, it is always best to deal with important conflicts so they are completely resolved.

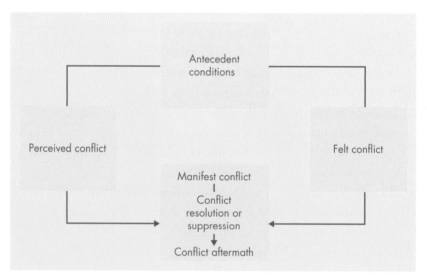

Figure 11.3: The stages of conflict.

When the antecedent conditions actually become the basis for substantive or emotional differences between people and/or groups, such as those situations already described, the stage of perceived conflict exists. Of course, only one of the conflicting parties may hold this perception. There is also a difference between perceived conflict and the stage of felt conflict. When people feel conflict, they experience it as tension that motivates them to take action to reduce feelings of discomfort. For conflict to be resolved, all parties should both perceive it and feel the need to do something about it.

Manifest conflict *occurs when conflict is openly expressed in behaviour.*

When conflict is openly expressed in behaviour it is said to be **manifest**. A state of manifest conflict can be resolved by removing or correcting its antecedents. It can also be suppressed by controlling the behaviour (although no change in antecedent conditions occurs); for example, one or both parties may choose to ignore the conflict in their dealings with each other. This is a superficial and often temporary form of conflict resolution. Indeed, we have already noted that unresolved conflicts – and a suppressed conflict falls into this category – may continue to fester and cause future conflicts over similar issues.

Unresolved conflicts of any type can result in sustained emotional discomfort and stress and escalate into dysfunctional relationships between individuals and work units. In contrast, truly resolved conflicts may establish conditions that reduce the potential for future conflicts and/or make it easier to deal with them. Thus, any manager should be sensitive to the influence of conflict aftermath on future conflict episodes.

Conflict management approaches

Conflict in organizations is inevitable. The process of managing conflict to achieve constructive rather than destructive results is clearly essential to organizational success. This process of conflict management can be pursued in a variety of ways. An important goal should always be to achieve or set the stage for true conflict resolution; that is, a situation in which the underlying reasons for a given conflict are eliminated.

EFFECTIVE MANAGER 11.3

What can be done to better manage workplace conflict?[41]

- Reinforce to managers their responsibility for managing conflict.
- Develop conflict management strategies.
- Ensure that employees are familiar with the organization's policy on interpersonal conflict.
- Facilitate discussion sessions to express workplace relationships and interpersonal tensions appropriately.
- Coach employees to effectively communicate to support the resolution of conflict.
- Appoint conflict contact officers to listen to concerns and help staff find ways to resolve them.
- Provide support services such as employee assistance programmes that can be accessed on a confidential, self-referral basis.

Conflict resolution styles

Research on the management of conflict shows that it depends to a great extent on the personality characteristics of individual managers. Blake and Mouton were the first to classify personality strategies or styles of conflict resolution into five basic types: forcing, withdrawing, soothing, compromising and problem solving.[42] Afzalur Rahim also points to five different personality styles, or strategies, in conflict resolution, which he analyses according to the orientation towards self or others. His five styles are: integrating, obliging, compromising, dominating and avoiding.[43]

Rahim draws attention to the fact that there is no one best style, because each has its advantages and disadvantages. The effectiveness of applying a particular style depends on the situation. In everyday life people tend to show a preference for a certain conflict resolution style; for example, a person with high affiliation needs will generally choose an obliging style and avoid a dominating style. It appears that in organizational life, the status of an organizational member could well influence the choice of conflict resolution style;[44] for example, people may choose different strategies when dealing with a boss, an employee or a peer.

Most researchers share the view that an integrating style is best for managing conflict in organizations, because this style is aimed at solving the problem, it respects the needs and interests of both sides and is based on achieving a satisfactory outcome for each side.[45] However, choice of style needs to be contingent on the situation. A manager may choose a dominating style where the goals of the conflicting parties are incompatible, there has been a previous failure to reach agreement and a quick decision needs to be made.[46] In contrast, an integrating style would probably work best in a conflict caused by communication problems or in solving strategic problems linked to goals, policies and long-term planning in organizations. Research shows that managers believe that the frequent use of a compromising style hampers performance and the attainment of goals but that they may endorse such a style in certain situations where mutual concessions are the only possible solution.[47] Research by Krum Krumov showed that the integrating style is used more often by women than men and that its use increases gradually with age. In contrast, the compromising style is used equally by women and men and its use tends to increase with age. However, the use of this style is more typical of employees than managers.[48]

Wayne Pace suggests that preferred ways of handling conflict occur because when two people come together expecting to claim their share of scarce resources, they think somewhat habitually about themselves and the other person. Thus, conflict resolution styles appear to be a combination of the amount of concern you have about accomplishing your own goals and the amount of concern you have about others accomplishing their goals. These concerns can be portrayed as two axes running from low concern to high concern. This paradigm results in a two-dimensional conceptualization of personal conflict resolution styles, as depicted in Figure 11.4 and briefly described here. Unfortunately, when conflict occurs people have the tendency to do and say things that perpetuate the conflict.[49]

- *Cell 1 – competitor or tough battler.* People who employ this style pursue their own concerns somewhat ruthlessly and generally at the expense of other members of the group. The tough battler views losing as an indication of weakness, reduced status and a crumbling self-image. Winning is the only worthwhile goal and results in accomplishment and exhilaration.
- *Cell 2 – collaborator or problem solver.* People who employ this style seek to create a situation in which the goals of all parties involved can be accomplished. Problem solvers work at finding mutually acceptable solutions. Winning and losing are not part of their way of looking at conflict.
- *Cell 3 – compromiser or manoeuvring conciliator.* The person who employs this style assumes that everyone involved in a disagreement stands to lose and works to help find a workable position. A pattern of 'giving in' often develops.

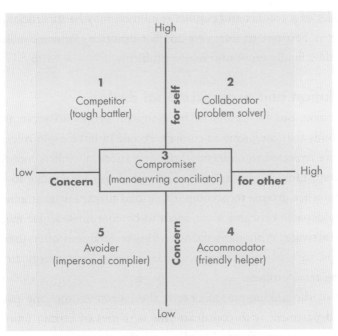

Figure 11.4: Personal conflict resolution styles.

Source: Wayne, R. and Faules, D. F. (1994), *Organizational Communication*, 3rd edn, Allyn & Bacon: Boston, MA, p. 250.

- *Cell 4 – accommodator or friendly helper.* People who employ this style are somewhat nonassertive and quite cooperative, neglecting their own concerns in favour of those of others. The friendly helper feels that harmony should prevail and that anger and confrontation are bad. When a decision is reached, accommodators may go along with it and wish later that they had expressed some reservations.
- *Cell 5 – avoider or impersonal complier.* The person who employs this style tends to view conflict as unproductive and somewhat punishing. Thus, the avoider sidesteps an uncomfortable situation by refusing to be concerned. The result is usually an impersonal reaction to the decision and little commitment to future actions.

Conflict resolution through hierarchical referral

Hierarchical referral makes use of the chain of command for conflict resolution; problems are simply referred up the hierarchy for more senior managers to reconcile. The managers involved will typically be those to whom the conflicting parties mutually report; they will be managers who ultimately have the formal authority to resolve such disputes by directive if necessary.

Hierarchical referral *uses the chain of command for conflict resolution; problems are referred up the hierarchy for more senior managers to reconcile.*

Hierarchical referral can be definitive in a given case but it also has limitations. If conflict is severe and recurring, the continual use of hierarchical referral may not result in true conflict resolution. For instance, managers may have the tendency to consider most conflicts a result of poor interpersonal relations. They may consequently seek outward signs of harmony as evidence of their conflict management skills, or they may act quickly to replace a person with a perceived 'personality' problem. In so doing, they may actually fail to delve into the real causes of a conflict and conflict resolution may be superficial. Employees may also learn that it is best not to refer any conflict upwards. Future conflicts may be kept from view until they finally erupt into major problems.

Conflict resolution and organizational design

Conflict management can be facilitated by assigning people to serve as formal linking pins between groups that are prone to conflict. People in linking-pin roles, such as project liaison officers, are expected to understand the operations, members' needs and the norms of their host group. Linking pins are supposed to use this knowledge to help their group work better with other groups to accomplish mutual tasks. For example where there are conflicts between departments and work needs to be coordinated, one might create a new post of resource manager. Although expensive, this technique is often used when different specialized groups, such as engineering and sales, must closely coordinate their efforts on complex and long-term projects.

A variation of the linking-pin concept is the liaison group. The purpose of such a group, team or department is to coordinate the activities of certain units and to prevent destructive clashes between them. Members of the department may be given formal authority to resolve disputes on everything from technical matters to resource claims or work assignments.

Stakeholder engagement and conflict resolution

In order to minimize conflict and community objections to mining projects, some multinational mining corporations involve key external stakeholders. Community involvement means working in conjunction with communities to create acceptable processes for improving communication, managing conflict and making appropriate decisions.

OB IN ACTION

Saving jobs on the Isle of Wight

The Isle of Wight is a small island just off the south coast of England. Its lovely climate and beaches make it a centre for retirement as well as the sailing and music festivals for which it is world renowned. Care homes and tourism are key employment sectors, both low paid and low skilled, creating a need for high-skilled employment to balance the economy. Vestas saw the opportunity to use local skills in boat building for production of blades for their wind turbines as both require production of

shaped surfaces from similar materials. In 2008 Vestas decided to close the Isle of Wight plant, claiming lower demand for wind turbines than they had forecast. The loss of 400 skilled and well-paid jobs and the ripple effect into the small island caused enormous concern. However, after local workers protested at the job losses and gained sufficient publicity, more stakeholders got involved to rescue the situation. Local politicians and funders worked together to provide an incentive plan for Vestas to build a research and development plant. Planning for new roads and new buildings was agreed quickly. Although many workers did leave the island for other jobs in the meantime, many were also recruited into the new operation.[50]

Question

Imagine you were the leader of the local council on the Isle of Wight in the situation described above. Your stakeholder group comprises the local Vestas CEO and HR Director, worker representatives and some family members, trade unions, the central government department concerned with the economy and enterprise, local councillors and a key regional funder. Imagine a private meeting between yourself, the central and regional representatives. Here you learn that the central government department will provide money for a grant to Vestas which will be administered by the local regional office. But you are warned that this money (representing around a half of all annual funding to the island) cannot be 'extra'. You know that only having half the usual money to give to local businesses will mean the loss of several struggling small local firms, and that no money will be available for small start-ups for more than a year. The Vestas workers and their families are a significant group of voters and are in a marginal constituency.

Would you take the government's offer?

NEGOTIATION

Conflict between individuals, groups and organizations is common. When parties are involved in conflict, negotiation is frequently used to resolve differences. This section introduces you to negotiation as an important process in managing people and organizations.

Managers need to understand some of the key areas of **negotiation** in order to improve workplace effectiveness and performance. Negotiation is the process of making joint decisions when the parties involved have different preferences. In other words, negotiation can be considered a way of finding the best solution with others in the process of making decisions.

Negotiation is the process of making joint decisions when the parties involved have different preferences.

Negotiation is especially significant in today's work settings, where more people are being offered opportunities to be involved in decisions affecting them and their work. As more people get involved in any decision-making process, so more disagreements are likely to arise over such diverse matters as wage rates, task objectives, performance evaluations, job assignments, work schedules, work locations and special privileges. Given that organizations are becoming increasingly participative, a manager's familiarity with basic negotiation concepts and processes is increasingly important for dealing with such day-to-day affairs.

Four types of negotiation situation

In the course of their work, managers may be faced with different types of negotiation situations. As shown in Figure 11.5, there are four main types of situations with which managers should be familiar. These are:

- *Two-party negotiation.* The manager negotiates directly with one other person, for example a manager and an employee negotiating a salary increase during an annual performance appraisal.
- *Group negotiation.* The manager is part of a team or group whose members are negotiating to arrive at a common decision; for example, a committee that must reach agreement on recommending a new sexual harassment policy.
- *Intergroup negotiation.* The manager is part of a group that is negotiating with another group to arrive at a decision regarding a problem or situation affecting both; for example, negotiation between management groups from two organizations to form a joint venture or strategic alliance.

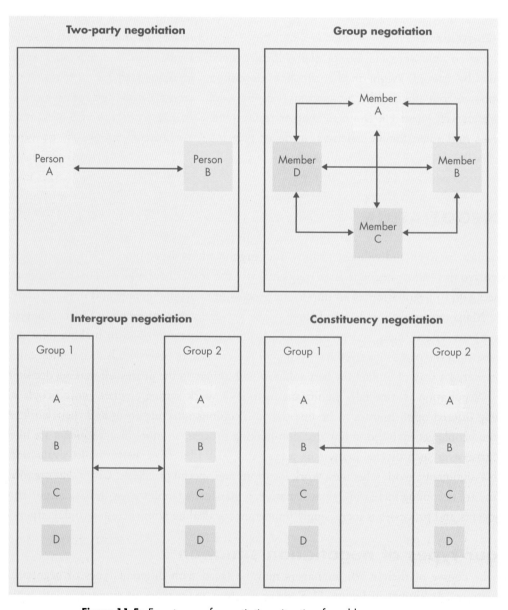

Figure 11.5: Four types of negotiation situation faced by managers.

- *Constituency negotiation.* The manager is involved in negotiation with other people and each individual party represents a broad constituency. A common example is a team representing 'management' negotiating with a team representing 'labour' to arrive at an agreement.

Negotiation goals and outcomes

Two goals are at stake in any negotiation. **Substance goals** are concerned with outcomes of the 'content' issues at hand, such as the dollar amount of a wage agreement in a collective bargaining situation. **Relationship goals** are concerned with outcomes relating to how well people involved in the negotiation and any constituencies they may represent are able to work with one another once the process is concluded. An example is the ability of union members and management representatives to work together effectively after a contract dispute has been settled.

Unfortunately, many negotiations result in a sacrifice of relationships, as parties become preoccupied with substance goals and self-interest. In contrast, effective negotiation occurs when substance issues are resolved and working relationships are maintained or even improved. The parties involved in negotiation may find themselves at an impasse when there are no overlapping interests and the parties fail to find common points of agreement. But agreement in negotiation can mean different things. The agreement may be 'for the better' or 'for the worse' for either or both parties involved. Effective negotiation results in making joint decisions that are 'for the better' for all parties. The trick is knowing how to get there.

Most people and organizations want to resolve workplace disputes quickly and fairly. Most governments fund an agency that is enabled to provide balanced advice to all employers and act as an arbitrator in case of unresolved conflict.

> **Substance goals** *are concerned with outcomes tied to the 'content' issues at hand in a negotiation.*
>
> **Relationship goals** *are concerned with how well people involved in a negotiation, and their constituencies, are able to work with one another once the process is concluded.*

OB IN ACTION

Most governments fund a national service that helps employers undertake negotiations and other forms of conflict resolution. In the UK this is called ACAS (Advisory, Conciliation and Arbitration Service). It was originally put into place to help employers cope with the large number of trade union strikes occurring in Britain in the 1970s. Its role was to help all parties on their case (advice), help undertake mediation services so that voluntary agreements could be reached (reconciliation) and, in the final stage, decide for the parties as a binding arbitrator.

It has seen a dramatic shift in its activities since the reduction of strike activity during the late 1980s and is now a valuable source of information for employers and employees for conflict avoidance and early conflict resolution. It has local offices and can provide staff who will be available for discussion or to undertake training. It also has a website full of helpful guidance and template policies for organizations to download free. It operates a helpline that provides information about terms and conditions of employment and helps to resolve conflicts. It does all of this because it has built a reputation as an 'honest broker' and both employers and employees respect the opinion of its staff and go to them for confidential help in all matters to do with conflict resolution.

Different approaches to negotiation

Consider the following scenario. It illustrates an important point. Two employees want to book their holidays in the same period (during school holidays). However, the boss can only allow one of them to take holidays in that period. They begin to negotiate over who should take the holiday in that period. For our purposes, the 'holiday' represents a valued outcome for both employees. The approach taken to the negotiation can have a major influence on its outcomes. It is useful to discuss two alternative approaches: distributive negotiation and integrative negotiation.

Distributive negotiation

Distributive negotiation *is negotiation in which the focus is on 'positions' staked out or declared by the parties involved, who are each trying to claim certain portions of the available 'pie'.*

In **distributive negotiation**, the focus is on 'positions' that conflicting parties stake out or declare. Each party is trying to 'claim' certain portions of the available 'pie'. Distributive negotiation is sometimes referred to as competitive or positional negotiation. Returning to the holiday scenario, if the two workers adopted distributive bargaining approaches they would each ask the question: 'Who is going to get the holiday at the requested time?' This question and the way in which it frames subsequent behaviour will have a major impact on the negotiation process and outcomes.

A case of distributive negotiation usually unfolds in one of two directions, neither of which yields optimal results. 'Hard' distributive negotiation takes place when each party holds out to get its own way. This leads to competition, whereby each party seeks dominance over the other and tries to maximize self-interests. 'Soft' distributive negotiation takes place when one party is willing to make concessions to the other to get things over with. In this case, one party tries to find ways to meet the other's desires. A soft approach leads to accommodation (one party gives in to the other) or compromise (each party gives up something of value in order to reach agreement).

In the case of the two employees wanting the same holiday period, the hard approach may lead to a win–lose outcome, in which one employee will dominate (perhaps by putting forth a stronger and more convincing case to the boss) and therefore wins the round. Or it may lead to an impasse, in which case neither employee will get the holiday. A soft approach (or compromise) may result in the holiday period being split equally between the two employees, where one employee gets half of the period and the second takes the other half. But here, too, dissatisfaction may exist because both employees are still deprived of what they originally wanted – the entire holiday period at the preferred time.

Integrative negotiation

In **integrative negotiation**, sometimes called principled negotiation, the focus is on the 'merits' of the issues. Everyone involved tries to enlarge the available 'pie' rather than stake claims to certain portions of it. For this reason, integrative negotiation is also sometimes referred to as problem-solving or interest-based negotiation. In the case of the employees, the integrative approach to negotiation would be prompted by asking the question: 'How can the available leave best be used?' Notice that this is a very different question from the one described for distributive negotiation. It is much less confrontational and allows for a broader range of alternatives.

Integrative negotiation is negotiation in which the focus is on the merits of the issues and the parties involved try to enlarge the available 'pie' rather than stake claims to certain portions of it.

The integrative approach to negotiation has much more of a 'win–win' orientation than does the distributive approach; it seeks ways of satisfying the needs and interests of all parties. At one extreme, this might involve selective avoidance, wherein both parties simply realize that there are more important things on which to focus their time and attention. In the holiday scenario, the two workers may mutually decide to forget about the holiday and to attend work. Compromise can also play a role in the integrative approach but it must have an enduring basis. This is most likely to occur when the compromise involves each party giving up something of perceived lesser personal value to gain something of greater value. In the case of the workers, one may get the holiday this time in return for the other getting one during the next school holidays.

Finally, integrative negotiation may involve true cooperation. In this case, the negotiating parties engage in problem solving to arrive at a mutual agreement that truly maximizes benefit to each. In the case of the holidays, this ideal approach could lead to both workers getting half the time off and spending the other half working but from home so they can still attend to their children. As you can see, this solution would be almost impossible to realize using the distributive approach because each worker would be preoccupied with getting the holiday. Only under the direction provided by the integrative approach – 'How can the available leave best be used?' – is such a mutually optimal solution possible. However, it is important to appreciate that the most effective negotiators will have a wide array of negotiation skills and will be able to use both approaches, mixing and matching them, depending on what they think works best for a specific issue or situation.

Managerial issues in negotiation

Given the distinctions between distributive and integrative negotiation, it is appropriate to identify some negotiation issues of special relevance to managers – specifically, the foundations for gaining integrative agreements, classic two-party negotiation and communication problems in negotiation.

Gaining integrative agreements

Underlying the concept of 'principled' negotiation is negotiation based on the 'merits' of the situation. The foundations for gaining truly integrative agreements cover three main areas: attitudes, behaviours and information. To begin with, there are three attitudinal foundations of integrative agreements:

- each party must approach the negotiation with a willingness to trust the other party;
- each party must be willing to share information with the other party;
- each party must be willing to ask concrete questions of the other party.

BATNA is the 'best alternative to a negotiated agreement', or each party's position on what they must do if an agreement cannot be reached.

As implied, the information foundations of integrative agreements are substantial; they involve each party becoming familiar with the **BATNA**, or 'best alternative to a negotiated agreement'. That is, both parties must know what they will do if an agreement cannot be reached. This requires that both negotiating parties identify and understand their personal interests in the situation. They must know what is really important to them in the case at hand and they must come to understand the relative importance of the other party's interests. As difficult as it may seem, each party must achieve an understanding of what the other party values, even to the point of determining its BATNA.

Reaching this point of understanding is certainly not easy. In the complex social setting of a negotiation things may happen that lead parties astray. An unpleasant comment uttered during a stressful situation, for example, may cause the other party to terminate direct communication for a time. Even when they return, the memory of this comment may overshadow any future overtures made by the offending party. In negotiation, all behaviour is important, both for its actual impact and for the impression it leaves. Accordingly, the following behavioural foundations of integrative agreements must be carefully considered and included in any negotiator's repertoire of skills and capabilities:

- the ability to separate the people from the problem and to avoid letting emotional considerations affect the negotiation;
- the ability to focus on interests rather than positions;
- the ability to avoid making premature judgements;
- the ability to judge possible agreements according to an objective set of criteria or standards.

Classic two-party negotiation

Figure 11.6 introduces the case of the new graduate. In this case, a graduate is negotiating a job offer with a corporate recruiter. The example illustrates the basic elements of classic two-party negotiation in many contexts.

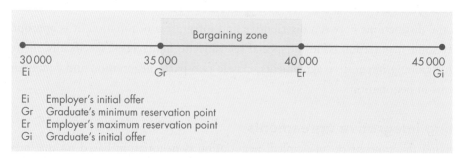

Bargaining zone

| 30 000 | 35 000 | 40 000 | 45 000 |
| Ei | Gr | Er | Gi |

Ei Employer's initial offer
Gr Graduate's minimum reservation point
Er Employer's maximum reservation point
Gi Graduate's initial offer

Figure 11.6: An example of the bargaining zone in classic two-party negotiation.

To begin with, look at the situation from the graduate's perspective. She has told the recruiter that she would like a salary of €45 000; this is her initial offer. But she also has in mind a minimum reservation point of €35 000 – the lowest salary that she will accept for this job. Thus, she communicates a salary request of €45 000 but is willing to accept one as low as €35 000. The situation is somewhat reversed from the recruiter's perspective. The recruiter's initial offer to the graduate is €30 000 and the maximum reservation point is €40 000; this is the most the recruiter is prepared to pay.

The bargaining zone is defined as the range between one party's minimum reservation point and the other party's maximum reservation point. In Figure 11.6, the bargaining zone is 35 000–40 000; it is a positive bargaining zone because the reservation points of the two parties overlap. Whenever a positive bargaining zone exists, bargaining has room to unfold. Had the graduate's minimum reservation point been greater than the recruiter's maximum reservation point (for example, €42 000), there would have been no room for bargaining. Classic two-party bargaining always involves the delicate tasks of first discovering the respective reservation points (your own and the other's) and then working towards an agreement that lies somewhere within the resulting bargaining zone and that is acceptable to each party.

▶ **COUNTERPOINT**

Underlying conflict

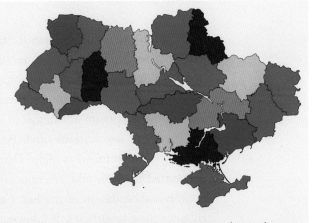

Olivia is a senior sales manager for VLC Software, a company that customizes telephone answering systems. She has been employed there for five years. VLC Software is a small software development company with 12 employees, but with a share of 25% of the national market. Olivia was initially employed by VLC as a junior IT account support officer and has worked her way through the company hierarchy to the senior position she is in today. Olivia has a very good relationship with all the other employees, horizontal and vertical. Six people – five salespeople and one administration person – report to her as senior manager. All employees at VLC have a lot of respect for Olivia because of her background with the company. They feel she 'knows the ropes' and often consult her about professional and personal problems.

Unfortunately, over the past six months VLC has been losing market share. Industry trends suggest that software sales are consistent, so there do not appear to be any macro issues to account for the downturn in sales. Nelson, the CEO of VLC, is very concerned and feels that if VLC is falling below the industry average then there is a chance the problem could be a human resource issue, either with his own staff or with the distributors. Because of Olivia's strong relationship with the other employees at VLC, and because it is easier to audit VLC than the external distributors, Nelson has asked her to prepare a confidential written report on the entire operation of VLC, identifying any weaknesses in systems and people. Olivia is concerned about the outcome, as over a period of time she has tried to deal with several operational and human resource problems but has ultimately failed. Olivia is aware of an underlying conflict between the five salespeople that is mainly due to the fact that sales territories are not clearly defined and there are no firm incentive or reward schemes in place. As a result of this some of the more experienced salespeople have been quietly operating outside their geographical areas, creating motivation problems among those who are staying within their boundaries.

Olivia is uncomfortable about how to conduct the audit because she is sensing something of an ethical dilemma. On one hand she feels it is her duty as senior manager to improve the operations and sales for VLC; on the other hand she wants to remain loyal to her team. However, to prevent the underlying conflict from erupting, Olivia realizes the time has come to conduct a complete audit and formally report her findings.

Questions

1. Should Olivia make it known to the employees at VLC that she is carrying out an audit? Explain why or why not.
2. If Olivia's findings suggest that the issue of underlying conflict among the salespeople is the reason for the downturn in sales, outline the process she should go through to counter that conflict. Bear in mind that Olivia's loyalty to all of the staff means she may need to draw on her negotiating skills to achieve a win–win outcome among the team.

It is too easy in negotiation to stake out your position based on the assumption that to gain your way something must be 'subtracted' from the other party's way. This myth of the 'fixed pie' is a purely distributive approach to negotiation. The whole concept of integrative negotiation is based on the premise that the 'pie' can sometimes be expanded and/or used to the maximum advantage of all parties, not just one.

Parties to negotiations often begin by stating extreme demands, so the possibility of escalating commitment is high. That is, once 'demands' have been stated, people become committed to them and are reluctant to back down. As a result, they may be prone to nonrational escalation of conflict. Concerns for 'protecting your ego' and 'saving face' may enhance these tendencies. It takes self-discipline to spot this tendency in your own behaviour as well as that of others.

It is also common for negotiators to develop the belief that their positions are the only 'correct' ones. This is characterized by overconfidence and ignoring others' needs. In some cases, negotiators completely fail to see merits in the other party's position – merits that an outside observer would be sure to spot. Such overconfidence makes it harder to reach a positive common agreement. It may even set the stage for disappointment if the negotiation is turned over to a neutral third party for resolution.

In arbitration, this third party acts as the 'judge' and issues a binding decision after listening to the positions advanced by the parties involved in a dispute. Sometimes, a manager may be asked to serve as an arbitrator of disputes between employees, from matters as important as the distribution of task assignments to those as seemingly trivial as access to a photocopy machine.

CONCLUSION

Communication is a deceptively easy topic to study but fraught with dangers and challenges, which reflect how hard it is to get a match between the message sent and the message received. Many elements have to be in place, such as effective channels and little noise, as well as senders who are good encoders and receivers who are able and willing to be effective.

It is no coincidence that this chapter is shared by the two topics of communication and conflict. Many conflicts begin with poor communication and are almost certainly exacerbated by weaknesses in communication. All managers need to understand their own communication weaknesses in order to minimize the conflict they cause and to help them mediate and negotiate a solution when conflicts arise from any source. Expertise in conflict negotiation and resolution is a sought-after skill within the workplace and allows for all employees to focus on positive value-creating activities without distraction.

SUMMARY

LEARNING OBJECTIVE 1
Communication and its role in organizations

Communication in an organization is a process by which organizational members share meanings by exchanging information. We communicate to inform, instruct, motivate or seek information, to achieve coordinated action throughout the organization, to develop information for the benefit of the organization, to express our feelings and emotions and to explain respective job responsibilities, roles and expectations. The interpersonal communication process involves an intricate matching of information that is encoded, sent, received and decoded, sometimes with and sometimes without feedback, but always affected by noise. Communication is effective when both sender and receiver interpret a message in the same way. It is efficient when messages are transferred at a low cost.

Communication channels include formal, informal and quasiformal relationships among members of the organization. The organization is a network of information and communication channels. The electronic age has provided organizations with new opportunities to link managers effectively. Barriers to communication include special sources of noise common to most interpersonal exchanges: physical distractions, cultural differences, the absence of feedback and status effects. Each of these sources of noise should be recognized and subjected to special managerial control. Managers can eliminate or reduce barriers through such techniques as wandering around, developing active listening skills, providing effective feedback to the sender of the communication and articulating job roles and responsibilities.

LEARNING OBJECTIVE 2
Conflict and its effect on organizations

Conflict can be either emotional (based on personal feelings) or substantive (based on work goals). Both forms can be harmful in organizations if, as a result, individuals and/or groups are unable to work constructively with one another. Conflict situations in organizations occur in vertical and lateral working relations and in line–staff relations. Often, they result from workflow interdependencies and resource scarcities. Most typically, conflict develops through a series of stages, beginning with antecedent conditions and progressing into manifest conflict. The conflict may or may not be entirely 'resolved' in the sense that the underlying reasons for the emotional and/or substantive conflict are eliminated. Unresolved conflicts set the stage for future conflicts of a similar nature. When kept within tolerable limits, conflict can be a source of creativity and performance enhancement. Even when managers have different viewpoints, ongoing questioning and discussion about their differences may unleash more creative approaches to a situation as they are further probed. On the other hand, such situations can become destructive when these limits are exceeded and the hostility between individuals or groups continues. In this case, managers must be made aware of such conflicts and take appropriate action to resolve them.

LEARNING OBJECTIVE 3
Managing conflict

Conflict management should always proceed with the goal of true conflict resolution. Indirect forms of conflict management include appeals to common goals, hierarchical referral and organizational redesign. Direct conflict management proceeds with different combinations of assertiveness and cooperativeness on the part of conflicting parties. Win–win outcomes are achieved through cooperation and problem solving most often associated with high assertiveness and high cooperation. Win–lose outcomes usually occur through direct competition or authoritative command. Lose–lose outcomes are typically found as a result of avoidance, smoothing and compromise approaches.

LEARNING OBJECTIVE 4
Negotiation and its role in organizations

Negotiation in organizations occurs whenever two or more people with different preferences must make joint decisions. Managers may find themselves involved in various types of negotiation situations, including two-party, group, intergroup and constituency negotiation. Both substance goals and relationship goals are at stake. Effective negotiation occurs when issues of substance are resolved and human relationships are maintained, or even improved, in the process. To achieve such results, ethical conduct must be carefully maintained even as negotiating parties represent viewpoints and preferences that differ greatly from one another.

LEARNING OBJECTIVE 5
Managers' issues in negotiation

Different approaches to negotiation can have very different results. In distributive negotiation, the focus of each party is on staking out positions in the attempt to claim desired portions of a 'fixed pie'. In integrative negotiation, sometimes called principled negotiation, the focus is on determining the merits of the issues and finding ways to satisfy one another's needs. The distributive approach is often associated with individual styles of competition (the 'hard' approach) or accommodation (the 'soft' approach). The integrative approach ideally leads to some form of cooperation or problem solving to achieve a mutually desirable solution.

CHAPTER 11 STUDY GUIDE

Now that you have read this chapter, you should be able to apply and further develop your knowledge by undertaking the following activities set out over the next few pages: test your knowledge questions, an individual activity and an end-of-chapter case study.

Please also go to this book's website: **www.wileyeurope.com/college/french** to find further material which will enhance your understanding and enable you to assess your knowledge.

TEST YOURSELF

1. Describe the main sources of noise and disturbance in communication. Give examples.

2. Under what circumstances would conflict be accepted and considered to be positive? Give examples.

3. What are some of the most common strategies used in resolving conflict? Briefly explain why conflict in the workplace can be positive.

4. Describe some of the most common managerial issues in negotiations.

5. Imagine you are a French national running the European HQ of an American-owned multinational drinks company. Your HQ is based in Paris, and you have just taken over five factories in Spain employing a total of 5000 people. What are some of the ways you would select to communicate your company's vision throughout the new acquisition?

6. If, as a manager, you felt it necessary to criticize the productivity of one of your employees, what would be some of the important factors you would consider before approaching that person?

7. As you read earlier, 'when conflict arises, most people's first reaction is to become angry or distressed, and to seek to eliminate the problem.' Provide an example in which you have been an observer of a conflict situation. The example you describe could be from your workplace or a different environment, such as a bank or an airport. Write down how the reaction of the parties involved in the conflict appeared to an onlooker – in this case, yourself. Then explain how you would have handled the situation if you had been one of the parties in conflict, remembering to take into consideration the emotional aspect that can escalate conflict.

8. Research indicates that managers are known to spend up to 20% of their time dealing with conflict, including conflicts in which managers are themselves directly involved. What implications does this have for business school educators and new managers?

9. Using an example, explain how destructive conflict can have a negative impact on performance. How would you remedy the conflict situation you have discussed?

10. Design a half-day awareness workshop aimed at teaching administrative staff the meaning of conflict and the various approaches to conflict resolution.

INDIVIDUAL ACTIVITY

Disagreeing with your boss

Objective

To develop your understanding and application of different approaches to conflict resolution.

Total time: 45–60 minutes.

Procedure

First think about the following scenario, then provide a solution or approach to the problem. Write down the approach you favour.

Scenario

You work in the sales area of a software distribution company operating in the Scandinavian market. You have been working for the company for seven years and your income depends on the sales figures achieved by the company because you are given a very generous bonus based on these figures.

You and your supervisor, Johansen, have not been getting along well for the past year or so. Johansen is a domineering individual and does not seem to want your input on any major activities being undertaken in your sales unit. However, a major project has been assigned to your unit and Johansen has instructed you to take responsibility for the project. The aim of the project is to develop a strategy for an effective market entry into a new geographical area in the region.

Johansen gives directions for completing the project. You examine the situation and after some thought tell Johansen that you have some ideas about how the project might be undertaken effectively. Johansen responds, 'I am not interested in hearing your ideas. I get paid for having ideas and you get paid for following my directions.'

Against your better judgement you follow Johansen's directions but, as you suspected, Johansen's ideas for the project are not sound and everything goes badly. The organization loses a lot of money on the project and you predict that things are likely to get much worse if the project continues in the way being directed by Johansen.

You are about to go to the regular Monday morning staff meeting, where you will be called on to report on the progress of the project. At this point, no one is aware of how badly the project is going. You have mentioned it several times to Johansen, who does not want to talk about it and says you are making excuses for your own incompetence. You are concerned about disagreeing with Johansen. At the same time you do not want to be embarrassed in front of your colleagues, who are also social acquaintances. Johansen has the ability to greatly influence your career and basically controls your pay, promotional opportunities and other incentive rewards within the company for at least the next three years. Because of family obligations, you do not feel ready to leave the company.

Case Study

CONFLICT OVER NEW BUSINESS STRATEGIES

Carrie recently joined Executive Improvement Strategies (EIS), a small consulting firm specializing in training and development programmes for senior managers. It is based in Prague, with a small client base that takes in several of the foreign multinationals in the city. There are three other consultants working for EIS and one managing partner, John, who started the firm five years ago.

Carrie is highly experienced and well known in the corporate training arena; in fact, her credentials far exceed those of the other consultants, including John, the managing partner. One of Carrie's strengths is successfully targeting new business. Part of this can be attributed to her outgoing, gregarious personality, along with her rather nontraditional, informal approach to obtaining new business; however, it fits Carrie's personality and it works.

As managing partner, John has implemented a very rigid culture at EIS, particularly in relation to seeking new business. Since Carrie has been with EIS, John has not been particularly impressed with her approach to potential clients and on several occasions has had discussions with her about this. These discussions have often resulted in conflict around the need for administration and proper records of conversations as John is worried about what Carrie might be promising to potential clients in terms of fees per day, discounts and products.

Carrie has just learned of an excellent opportunity to move into the public sector in the city. A new government policy has suggested that training for senior public-sector managers should, in the future, be sourced from the private sector to engender change and the uptake of contemporary management practices. Carrie has heard about this before it is public knowledge through someone she used to train with many years ago and still sees at professional networking events. Of course, Carrie will be following through the public sector lead for EIS, so she is keen to meet with John to brief him on her intentions.

Unfortunately, although the public sector opportunity is a good breakthrough for EIS, Carrie's enthusiasm is dampened knowing that John will have very set ideas about how to approach this market, and that those ideas will be completely contrary to Carrie's strategy. So what should be a positive meeting may ultimately turn into a disaster if it isn't handled correctly.

Source: From Wood, J. M. *et al.* (2006), *Organizational Behaviour: Core Concepts and Applications*, John Wiley & Sons Australia, Ltd: Milton, Qld.

Questions

1. If you were to advise Carrie about how to approach the meeting with John in order to avoid initial conflict, what would you say?

2. In order to please John, should Carrie attempt to change her approach to potential new clients? Why or why not?

3. Given that Carrie and John have very different approaches to obtaining new business, what processes can they put in place to ensure they can continue in a productive working relationship? Remember that John is head of EIS, yet Carrie has more experience and success.

SUGGESTED READING

Jones, A. (2007), More than 'managing across borders': the complex role of face-to-face interaction in globalizing law firms face-time. *Journal of Economic Geography*, 7 (3), 223–246. This article provides application of theory into real-life multi-site situations that uncover deep preferences for specific types of communication. It raises some interesting questions for the management of globally based organizations.

Mehrabian, A. (2007), *Nonverbal Communication*, Transaction Publishers: Piscataway, NJ. This is an aspect of communication that is extremely important to understand and Mehrabian has been the subject leader since its inception.

END NOTES

1. Mintzberg, H. (1990), *Mintzberg on Management: Inside our Strange World of Organizations*, Free Press, Macmillan: London.

2. Dahle, T. (1954), An objective and comparative study of five methods of transmitting information from management to business and industrial employees. *Speech Monographs*, **21** (March).

3. Kirkpatrick, D. V. & Bryan, M. (2007), Hurricane emergency planning by home health providers serving the poor. *Journal of Health Care for the Poor*, **18** (2), 299–314.

4. Pezzoli, K., Tukey, R., Sarabia, H. *et al.* (2007), The NIEHS environmental health sciences data resource portal: placing advanced technology in service to vulnerable communities. *Environmental Health Perspectives*, **115**(4), 564–571.

5. Wertheim, E. G. (2007), 'The importance of effective communication', Northeastern University College of Business Administration, web.cba.neu.edu/ewertheim/interper/commun.htm (accessed 4 January 2007).

6. Peters, T. J. & Waterman, R. H. (1984), *In Search of Excellence: Lessons from America's Best Run Companies*, Harper & Row: New York.

7. Garguilo, M., Ertug, G. & Galunic, C. (2009), The two faces of control: Network closure and individual performance among knowledge workers. *Administrative Science Quarterly*, **54**, 299–333.

8. Tarrant, D. (2002), Talking heads. *Australian Financial Review BOSS Magazine*, July, p. 58.

9. Olson, B. J. (2007), Strategic decision making: the effects of cognitive diversity, conflict, and

trust on decision outcomes. *Journal of Management*, 33(2), 196–222.

10. Tarrant, op. cit.

11. Case, J. (2001), When salaries aren't secret. *Harvard Business Review*, May, 37–39, 42–49.

12. Rousseau, D. M. & Schalk, R. (2000), *Psychological Contracts in Employment: Cross-national perspectives*, Sage: Thousand Oaks, CA.

13. Skogstad, A., Einarsen, S., Torsheim, T., Aasland, M. S. & Hetland, H. (2008), The destructiveness of laissez faire leadership behaviour. *Journal of Occupational Health Psychology*, 12(1), 80–92.

14. The *Journal of Business Ethics* is an excellent source of analysis for corporate and individual communication and dilemmas, with timely analysis of newsworthy events.

15. Terrisse, S. (2009), Opinion: Recalls aren't just for the Americans anymore. *Brandweek. com*, 2 December.

16. Gardner, N. & Campbell, J. (2008), Avoid the worst sorts. *Sunday Telegraph Australia*, State edition, p. 118.

17. Ferguson, N. (2008), *The ascent of money: A financial history of the world*, Penguin Books: New York.

18. Tarrant, op. cit.

19. Jones, A. (2007), More than 'managing across borders' the complex role of face-to-face interaction in globalizing law firms face-time. *Journal of Economic Geography*, 7(3), 223–246.

20. Mehrabian, A. (2007), *Nonverbal Communication*, Transaction Publishers: Piscataway, NJ.

21. DeChurch, L. A., Hamilton, K. L. & Haas, C. (2007), Effects of conflict management strategies on perceptions of intergroup conflict. *Group Dynamics Theory Research and Practice*, 1(1), 66–78.

22. Ibid.

23. Tjosvold, D. (2006), Defining conflict and making choices about its management. Lighting the dark side of organizational life. *International Journal of Conflict Management*, 17(2), 87–95.

24. Walton, R. E. (1969), *Interpersonal Peacemaking: Confrontations and Third-party Consultation*, Addison-Wesley: Reading, MA.

25. *Managing Conflict at Work: Survey Report* (2004), available from Chartered Institute of Personnel and Development, www.cipd.co.uk.

26. Kennedy, K. A. & Pronin, E. (2008), When disagreements get ugly: Perceptions of bias and the escalation of conflict. *Personality and Social Psychology Bulletin*, 34(6), 833–848.

27. Mackay, C. J., Cousins, R., Kelly, P. J., Lee, S. & McCaig, R. H. (2004), Management Standards and Work-related Stress in the UK: Policy background and science. *Work and Stress*, 18 (2), 91–112.

28. Ayub, N. & Jehn, K. (2006), National diversity and conflict in multinational workgroups – the moderating effect of nationalism. *International Journal of Conflict Management*, 17(3), 181–202.

29. Walton, R. E. (1969), *Interpersonal Peacemaking: Confrontations and Third-party Consultation*, Addison-Wesley: Reading, MA.

30. Ibid.

31. Salin, D. (2003), Ways of explaining workplace bullying: A review of enabling, motivating and precipitating structures and processes in the work environment. *Human Relations*, 56(10), 1213–1232.

32. Ibid.

33. Crook, T. R. & Combs, J. G. (2007), Sources and consequences of bargaining power in supply chains. *Journal of Operations Management*, 25 (2), 546–555.

34. Ibid.

35. Posthuma, R. A, White, G. O., Dworkin, J. B., Yanez, O. & Swift, M. S. (2006), Conflict resolution styles between coworkers in US and Mexican cultures. *International Journal of Conflict Management*, 17 (3), 242–260.

36. See Jassawalla, A., Truglia, C. & Garvey, J. (2004), Cross-cultural conflict and expatriate manager adjustment: an exploratory study. *Management Decision*, 42 (7), 837–849.

37. Leonard, D. & Straus, S. (1997), Putting your company's whole brain to work. *Harvard Business Review*, 75 (4), 111.

38. Developed from Hellriegel, D., Slocum, J. W. Jr & Woodman, R. W. (1983), *Organizational Behaviour*, 3rd edn, West: St Paul, pp. 471–474.

39. Developed from Johns, G. (1983), *Organizational Behaviour*, Forsman: Glenview, IL,

pp. 415–417; Walton, R. E. & Dutton, J. M. (1969), The management of interdepartmental conflict: a model and review. *Administrative Science Quarterly*, **14**, 73–84.

40. These stages are consistent with the conflict models described by Filley, A. C. (1975), *Interpersonal Conflict Resolution*, Foresman: Glenview, IL; Pondy, L. R. (1967), Organizational conflict: concepts and models. *Administrative Science Quarterly*, **12** (September), 269–320.

41. Adapted from Gaskell, R. (2003), *How effectively is your organization managing conflict?* http://www.hrconnection.net/hr_search.html (accessed 28 September 2010).

42. Blake, R. R. & Mouton, J. S. (1964), The *Managerial Grid*, Gulf: Houston, TX.

43. Rahim, M. A. (1985), A strategy for managing conflict in complex organizations. *Human Relations*, **38**(1), 83–85.

44. Jones, R. E. & Melcher, B. H. (1982), Personality and preference for modes of conflict resolution. *Human Relations*, **35**(8), 649–658.

45. Lawrence, P. R. & Lorsch, J. W. (1967), Differentiation and integration in complex organizations. *Administrative Science Quarterly*, **12**(1), 1–47.

46. Robbins, S. P. (1978), 'Conflict management' and 'conflict resolution' are not synonymous terms. *California Management Review*, **21**(2), 67–75.

47. Lawrence, P. R. & Lorsch, J. W. (1967), *Organization and Environment*, Harvard University Press: Cambridge, MA.

48. Krumov, K., Ilieva, S., Karabeliova, S. & Alexieva, L. (2007), Conflict resolution strategies in the transition to market economy. *Annals of the American Academy of Political and Social Science*, **552**(10), 65.

49. Lusseir, R. N. (1993), *Human Relations in Organizations: a skill building approach*, 2nd edn, Richard D. Irwin: Homewood, IL. © The McGraw-Hill Companies, Inc. Reproduced by permission.

50. Findon, R. (2010), *The legacy of Vestas*. County Press online, http://www.iwcp.co.uk/news/wight-living/the-legacy-of-vestas-34180.aspx (accessed 28 September 2010).

CHAPTER 12

Organizational change

LEARNING OBJECTIVES

After studying this chapter you should be able to:

- identify the nature and scope of change
- identify who initiates and leads the change
- identify the process of change and change strategies used by managers
- explain why people resist change and describe strategies to overcome resistance
- explain the role of the change agent.

GUASTALLA HOSPITAL, ITALY: FOSTERING EMPLOYABILITY THROUGH CHANGE

In February 2000, Guastalla hospital set up an organizational improvement project in association with the trade unions representing the healthcare sector. The project focused on redesigning the work organization and integration of diverse professional profiles around the same working process, improving cooperation and mutual learning, minimizing vertical hierarchy and segmentation, improving the quality of care and service and eliminating lead times and inefficiency.

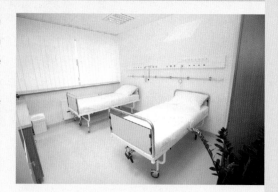

Organizational background

The hospital of Guastalla is a part of the Local Area Health Company (AUSL; Azienda Unità Sanitaria Locale). Since 1994, the Local Health Units in the province of Reggio Emilia have been a single-care structure. The company is situated in the centre of the Emilia-Romagna region and runs five hospitals: in Correggio, Scandiano, Castelnovo Monti, Montecchio and Guastalla. The total workforce of AUSL is about 3700 employees. Guastalla hospital has 504 employees: 104 senior doctors (of whom 38 are women) and 400 nurses, technicians and other job profiles (of whom 335 are women) and covers a population of 65000 inhabitants. About 50% of the employees are aged between 30 and 50. In the hospital of Guastalla, the union structure is made up of six representatives (of whom three are women). Union density is about 50%. The interaction between the management and the employee representatives is a constant factor, as they have a meeting almost weekly to discuss any new developments.

Description of the initiative

In February 2000, the public health agency (AUSL) of Reggio Emilia and the health care workers' and doctors' unions joined together to start an organizational improvement project in the Guastalla hospital, as Guastalla represents a strategically important context for the services provided by AUSL. To turn this improvement venture into reality, the social partners decided to seek the collaboration of a research institute specializing in labour. The intervention was organized into three closely interconnected main steps. The first stage – long-term scenario development – involved the identification of a goal(s) strategic for the organization at that exact moment, the imagination of a scenario and a back-casting process where the actors were committed to identifying and creating the right premises and conditions for achieving the planned goal.

In the short-term scenario, through communication and consensus research tools (such as work groups, information and actor involvement) the actors were asked to design a feasibility plan and an action plan.

Finally, the implementation phase was carried out by a partnership of actors willing to implement actions and changes in order to achieve the agreed scenario.

Particular attention was paid to experimentation in order to define the type of change intervention on work organization processes and to promote greater integration and collaboration among the vertical sectors. Collaboration between vertical sectors was established in the initial phases by setting up a working group comprising professionals, management representatives and unions, all coordinated by the research institute. Work then began with the aim of valuing the professionals better, listening to them, developing their ideas and making them participants in an organization that depends on each individual's potential. The study of the dynamics and characteristics of a health services organization are indeed indispensable for proceeding with the identification of problems, the adoption of actions for improvement and successful quality management. The project focused on:

- redesigning work organization and the integration of diverse professional profiles around the same working process;
- improvement in cooperation and mutual learning;
- redesigning the work organization and reducing vertical hierarchy and segmentation;
- organization of activities according to work flows;
- improvement in the quality of care and services;
- reduction in lead times and inefficiency.

The partnership created between management, trade unions and the workforce is formalized in an agreement between the hospital management and the union representatives around the premises and scope of the project, methodology and activities. In this specific case, two agreements were signed: one by the physicians' union and the other by the public employees' union. The agreements focused on the reorganization of productive and working processes; an increase in process efficiency; improvement in the quality of services and working conditions; and participation in the dialogue, negotiations and change processes. The involvement of the union representatives was particularly relevant in order to legitimize the process and guarantee the operative management of the project.

Some difficulties occurred due to tense relationships between partners, political elections, change in the hospital management, etc. However, the tense relations between the social partners, especially between management and unions, were managed through meetings, often promoted by the consultants.

Finally, a four-month period was devoted to developing many different projects in work organization change. The work was managed by groups of employees, self-organized and coordinated by an internal leader. Specific projects were planned to improve relations between the hospital and external organizations devoted to administrative and policy management, e.g. Direzione AUSL Reggio Emilia, territorial medicine and other services. The proposals gathered were aimed at creating a coordinating body to study and assess the performance levels and services of the health structures at a regional/local level. Furthermore, communication and integration between different departments had to be formalized.

AUSL has always paid much attention to training measures. In 2005, it delivered 501 training courses for a total of 88 000 training hours. The annual courses cost about €1 million, of which €260 000 is for the external courses (€34 000 for Guastalla hospital alone). The internal courses are mainly focused on new procedures or guidelines (evidence-based medicine). In order to map all the skills, AUSL created a specific database through which to find qualified employees (mainly doctors) to be used as internal trainers.

Questions

1. What approach to change was adopted here?
2. To what extent would you consider this to be a successful change intervention?

Source: http://www.eurofound.europa.eu/areas/qualityofwork/betterjobs/cases/it01guastalla.htm (accessed 3 January 2010).

INTRODUCTION

Change is not a recent phenomenon in organizations but certain aspects of change, for example, technological change, may be more distinguishable since the late 1980s because of the rate of change within that particular area. The rate of change within information technology has been dramatic. In the early 1980s global customers may have been using machines that loaded 56K of data, whereas, post 2010 customers use devices that contain terabytes of memory (10 to the power of 12) and dramatically enhanced processing speeds. This chapter will address the various types of change, as well as providing an understanding of the process of change, and how to address resistance to change.

WHAT IS ORGANIZATIONAL CHANGE?

It could be argued that a common sense definition of change is simply 'making things different'. Two important aspects of organizational change relate to the actual *change itself*, such as changing a manufacturing process in an organization, and the *perceived extent* of change in an organization, for example, in an organization that has not experienced much change, any change may be perceived as radical change, and possibly resisted on perceptual grounds only.

In OB, 'organizational change' refers to organization-wide change rather than to small changes such as adding a new role or making minor modifications to a process. Examples of organization-wide change might include a change of mission, restructuring operations, the adoption of major technologies and mergers and acquisitions.

THE SCALE OF CHANGE

Dunphy and Stace[1] provide a useful framework to analyse the scale of organizational change.

Scale type 1: fine tuning

Organizational change is an ongoing process characterized by fine tuning of the 'fit' or match between the organization's strategy, structure, people and processes, typically manifested at departmental/divisional levels, with one or more of the following:

- refining policies, methods and procedures;
- creating specialist units and linking mechanisms to permit increased volume and increased attention to the unit quality and cost;
- developing personnel especially suited to the present strategy (improved training and development or tailoring reward systems to match strategic thrusts);
- fostering individual and group commitment to the company mission and the excellence of one's own department;
- promoting confidence in the accepted norms, beliefs and myths;
- clarifying established roles (with their associated authorities and posers) and the mechanisms for allocating resources.

Scale type 2: incremental adjustment

This is organizational change characterized by incremental adjustments to the changing environment. Such change involves distinct modifications (but not radical change) to corporate business strategies, structures and managerial processes, for example:

- expanding sales territory;
- shifting the emphasis among products;
- improved production process technology;
- articulating a modified statement of mission to employees;
- adjustments to organizational structures within and across divisional boundaries to achieve better links in product/service delivery.

Scale type 3: modular transformation

Organizational change characterized by major realignment of one or more departments/divisions. The process of radical change is focused on these subparts rather than the organization as a whole, for example:

- major restructuring of particular departments/divisions;
- changes in key executives and managerial appointments in these areas;
- work and productivity studies resulting in significantly reduced or increased workforce numbers;

- reformed departmental/divisional goals;
- introduction of significantly new process technologies affecting key departments or divisions.

Scale type 4: corporate transformation

Organizational change that is corporate-wide, characterized by radical shifts in business strategy and revolutionary change throughout the whole organization involving many of the following features:

- reformed organization mission and core values;
- altered power and status affecting the distribution of power in the organization;
- reorganization – major changes in structures, systems and procedures across the organization;
- revised interaction patterns – new procedures, work flows, communication networks and decision-making patterns across the organization;
- new executives in key managerial positions from outside the organization.

Radical change *is change that results in a major makeover of the organization and/or its component systems.*

Some experts use organizational transformation to designate a fundamental and radical reorientation of the way the organization operates. Some of this change may be described as radical change.[2] This is change that results in a major makeover of the organization and/or of its component systems. In today's business environments, radical changes are often initiated by a critical event such as the arrival of a new chief executive officer, a new ownership brought about by a merger or takeover or a dramatic failure in operating results. Radical change occurs infrequently in the lifecycle of an organization. However, when it does occur, this change is intense and all-encompassing. There may be times in an organization's life when its survival depends on an ability to undergo successfully the rigours and demands of radical change. Radical change occurs when an industry's core assets and activities are both threatened with obsolescence, and knowledge and brand capital erode along with the customer and supplier relationships. It is most commonly caused by the introduction of new technologies or regulations, or by changing consumer preferences.

Incremental change *is change that occurs more frequently and less traumatically as part of an organization's natural evolution.*

Another, more common, form of organizational change is incremental change. This is change that occurs more frequently and less traumatically, as part of an organization's natural evolution. Typical changes of this type include new products, new technologies and new systems. Although the nature of the organization remains relatively unaltered, incremental change builds on the existing ways of operating and seeks to enhance them or extend them in new directions. The ability to improve continually through incremental change is an important asset to organizations in today's demanding environments. Although the nature and size of change is important, the next issue concerns the question of whether change is planned or unplanned.

PLANNED AND UNPLANNED CHANGE

Changes in organizations can be planned or unplanned. Planned change occurs when an organization deliberately attempts to make internal changes to meet specified goals or to pursue a set of strategies. For example, organizations often change their structures to meet given objectives or to pursue cost-cutting strategies. An organization might also engage in major updating of its operational systems, which would entail some form of technological change.

Unplanned change is usually prompted by some external driver, such as market forces, economic crises, economic opportunities or social changes. Typically, organizations engage in organization-wide change to respond to these forces and thereby evolve to a different level in their lifecycle; for example, going from a highly reactive to a more proactive and planned development. However, not all change in organizations happens as a result of an intended (or change agent's) direction. **Unplanned change** occurs spontaneously or randomly, and without a change agent's attention. The appropriate goal in managing unplanned change is to act immediately once the change is recognized, to minimize any negative consequences and maximize any possible benefits.

Unplanned change is change that occurs at random or spontaneously and without a change agent's direction.

In this chapter we are particularly interested in **planned change** – that is, change that comes about as a result of specific efforts on the part of a change agent. Planned change is a direct response to someone's perception of a **performance gap**. This is a discrepancy between the desired and actual state of affairs. Performance gaps may represent problems to be resolved or opportunities to be explored. It is useful to think of most planned changes as efforts initiated by managers to resolve performance gaps to the benefit of the organization and its members.

Planned change is change that happens as a result of specific efforts on the part of a change agent.

Rationality and change may not necessarily go hand-in-hand. Do employees always obey the rules and do exactly what they are told to do? Can everything always be described in task terms? If every employee did what was expected of them, then there would not be any cases of industrial sabotage, no working to rule, no cases of employees stealing from their employer, no fraudulent expense claims, etc. etc.

The performance gap is the discrepancy between an actual and a desired state of affairs.

Sometimes a rational approach may take a lot longer than a more ad hoc approach. Take the example of a senior manager that wants to bring about rapid change to a business unit. A metaphorical 'hand-grenade' could be delivered by this senior manager, whereby all employees are told that a complete organizational restructuring is taking place, and that all employees will have to make a case for the relevance and contribution that their job/role contributes towards business success and that they have to reapply for their jobs. Whilst this approach may prove to be chaotic and result in some employees who contribute strongly to business performance leaving the organization, it may have the effect of bringing about some change in a relatively short period of time and lead to a culture change. The problem for management here is one of control and responsibility.

Planned change often assumes that the future is predictable and there is an end state to be reached. In other words, managers tend to regard change as a once-only, major alteration to the organization. In reality, in the vast majority of cases change occurs in an incremental way, reflecting the assumption that what worked in the past will also work in the future. However, with contextual dynamism and complexity being the new rule, any linear extrapolation is at best misleading. The line representing the link between past and future is at best dotted and sometimes even discontinuous, with twists and thresholds everywhere.[3]

OB IN ACTION

Think about any organization that you have read about or researched. What made the organization change – internal or an external pressure or both? Who started the change agenda? Why was this change agenda initiated? Are there sometimes contradictions between what organizations report their reasons for change are as opposed to the actual reasons for organizational change? If this is the case, then why are organizations dishonest?

The metaphor for change could be described as a series of parallel DVD recordings, rather than a single photograph, as it may be rare for an organization to have a single change process in place running from beginning to end without any other change intervention happening at the same time (Figure 12.1).

Figure 12.1: Multiple change interventions running concurrently.

Unplanned change is a change that occurs at random or spontaneously and without a change agent's direction. Planned change is change that happens as a result of specific efforts on the part of a change agent. The performance gap is the discrepancy between an actual and desired state of affairs.

Child[4] discusses the concept of 'emergent change' and links this to the size/range of change (Figure 12.2). Change may also be defined in terms of the scale of change in relation to the extent to which the change is planned or emergent.

Planned	Emergent
BPR whole org.	Organic development (e.g. start-up company).
Radical --------------------------------	
Merger of departments	Changes to selection of new members made by part org. teams
Annual targeted improvements	Organizational Learning whole org.
Incremental -------------------------	
Changes agreed in staff performance plans	Continuous improvement part org. through project teams

Figure 12.2: Planned and emergent change.

Source: Child, J. (2005) *Organization: Contemporary Principles and Practice*, p. 288. Reproduced by permission of Blackwell Publishing.

LEADING CHANGE

Most change initiatives, especially radical change, require effective leadership, not just on the part of the chief executive and other senior managers but from leaders at all levels in the organization.

So what does the leadership of change involve? It encompasses many dimensions that need to be adapted to each situation. Initially, leadership involves preparing people for the change by challenging the status quo and communicating a vision of what the organization can aspire to become. Next, it involves building the commitment of employees and change agents throughout the organization, and enabling them to act by providing resources and training, delegating power, building change teams and putting appropriate systems and structures in place. Leaders then maintain the momentum of change through symbolic and substantive actions that reward progress and recognize reaching milestones, with the leaders acting as effective role models.[5]

Robert Miles, a successful change management consultant and writer, has summarized the leadership of change in the following terms.[6] First and foremost, according to

Miles, radical change is vision led; that is, it involves the creation of goals that stretch the organization beyond its current horizons and capacities. Secondly, it is based on a total-system perspective, wherein all major elements of the organization are carried forward. And thirdly, it requires a sustained process of organizational learning so that people and processes develop synergetically. Figure 12.3 provides a picture of the four essential ingredients of a successful change process.

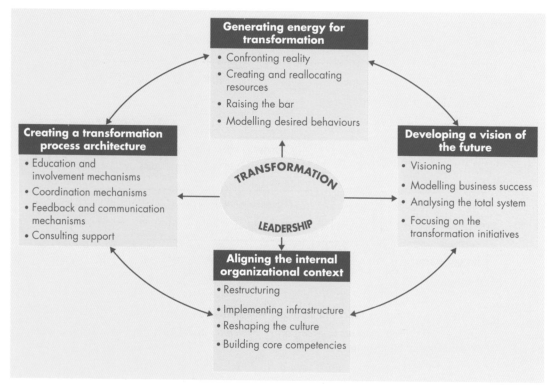

Figure 12.3: A framework for planned organizational change leadership.
Source: Miles, R. H. (1997), Corporate Comeback: The story of renewal and transformation at National Semiconductor, Jossey-Bass: San Francisco, p. 6. Reproduced by permission of John Wiley & Sons, Inc.

As Figure 12.3 suggests, the process depends on 'generating energy for transformation'. A key to this is in revealing to employees the shortfalls in current organizational performance – in essence, providing a reality check. One way to do this is by benchmarking the organization against customer expectations, industry leaders or competitors. Another method is to diagnose internal strengths and weaknesses, for example, by conducting a skills profile of employees to gauge their capacity to work cross culturally.

Based on such assessments, resources are released or reallocated to prepare the organization and its staff for the next ingredient – 'developing a vision'. While 'generating energy' puts people into a frame of mind that supports change, the vision provides them with a sense of what the future organization could be like and where they will be heading. A thorough organizational analysis is also needed as a basis for detailed planning of the change, which Miles describes as 'aligning the internal context'. The internal context consists of all the components that make an organization what it is – its structure, culture, technology and so on. Any or all of these components can become targets for change. The final ingredient is 'creating a transformation process architecture'. Key words that express what this is about are education, involvement and communication.

These ideas were specifically developed with radical change in mind, but you will see from reading this chapter that they generally apply to incremental change as well. All planned changes require careful preparation to ensure that they achieve the results hoped for and to reduce the likelihood that employees will resist change. You will also learn that there are several stages in the process of planned change, that there are at least four options of change strategy (the employee involvement strategy recommended by Miles is just one of these) and that managers must make careful choices about which aspects of the organization to target for change.[7]

FORCES OF CHANGE

In any change process, certain forces tend to encourage or favour the process whereas others militate against it. Change demands that organization members examine big-picture questions such as 'Who are we?' 'Where are we going?' and 'What do we want?' The major forces favouring organizational change are:

- A sufficient dissatisfaction with the existing situation, or state A.
- A strong attraction to moving towards a more desirable position, or state B. (This position can frequently be described in a vision statement, or in an analysis of the company's goals and performance in comparison to those of competitors.)
- A desire to formulate a well-thought-out strategy that will realize the vision – that is, how the company can move from A to B.[8]

All three of these forces must usually be present for managers to feel compelled to seek change. In the absence of any one of the three, there is little or no motivation to galvanize managers into action. Associated with these factors are other elements such as strong leadership, effective communication, a tight alignment of people and organizational goals and a clear definition of the compelling reasons to change.

Change may be triggered by internal or external forces. External forces include politics (for example a change in government or government policy), laws (for example anti-spam legislation), markets (for example competition from foreign companies entering the home market) and technology (for example the convergence of communications devices). Internal triggers include changes of ownership, products, services, process and measures of effectiveness that can happen in an organizational setting. Today's organizations must be able to react quickly and correctly to external change, while managing internal change effectively. External change is usually obvious and has immediate impact. In contrast, the need for internal change is often less obvious.

OB IN ACTION

Marris[9] equates change with bereavement. Organizations that go through change need to allow employees time to 'digest' the changes, as they would if they endured family bereavement. Carrying out continuous changes is stressful and may be harmful to an employee's health and wellbeing. Stuart[10] refers to organizational change as 'trauma'.

If we accept Marris's terminology of loss, then we might question whether, and to what extent, organizations have an ethical responsibility to ensure that their employees do not experience high and constant levels of stress   during change intervention programmes in organizations. Consider your own views about whether employers have a duty of care in the way that change is managed.

CULTURAL CHANGE

As we saw in Chapter 7, organizational culture is the pattern of an organization's shared beliefs, values, expectations and assumptions. Culture is a strong influence on people's thoughts and behaviour and affects all aspects of organizational life. It can significantly influence – positively and negatively – the outcomes of change, so it cannot be ignored when considering a change initiative. Even the most rigid of organizational cultures can be subject to significant change under the right circumstances.

It is a massive task to achieve a major culture change – one in which new values are antagonistic to the old ones. Successful culture change, in which there is a change in the underlying values that drive behaviour, can take a long time, even years.

In terms of how to effect culture change, Williams, Dobson and Walters[11] suggest that the following should be considered when attempting to change organizational culture:

- changing the people in the organization;
- changing people's positions in the organization;
- changing beliefs, attitudes and values directly;
- changing behaviour;
- changing systems and structures;
- changing the corporate image.

Organizational growth will engender change and new companies tend to see a rapid evolution of organizational culture as they undergo consistent change. Established companies tend to be more structured and thus slower to undertake change. A long-established company might not seek change until change is forced upon it as the result of a merger or acquisition, adverse media attention or undeniable changes in the environment. When a merger occurs, the question of which partner's organizational culture will become dominant inevitably arises. Both companies may be able to allow a new organizational culture to emerge. Cultural change may also occur internally in an unplanned fashion as the result of a labour dispute, a scandal or an accident.[12]

EFFECTIVE MANAGER 12.1

Pathways to effective cultural change

Gagliardi[13] recommends the following approach to culture change:

- educate stakeholders as to why change is necessary;
- communicate the new culture that is desired;
- use value statements to embed the new cultural requirements;

- give people the skills, knowledge and capabilities they will need to work differently;
- create processes, systems and ways of working that enable people to put the new values into practice;
- use performance management and rewards to enforce desired behaviours.

▶ COUNTERPOINT

Resistance to change

The idea that people will naturally resist change and that management must plan ways to overcome this is firmly entrenched in the management literature. However, it was not always so. The term was coined by Kurt Lewin as recently as 1948 and its meaning has shifted since then. Dent and Goldberg[14] argue that current conceptualizations present resistance to change as the unproductive or inappropriate actions that people take to thwart the change efforts of management. It suggests an 'us and them' mentality and a tendency to blame employees for the failure of changes that would otherwise have been good for the organization. In combating resistance, the focus is firmly on individuals and groups of employees. Managers are

advised to be proactive in preventing or countering resistance – through education, communication, training and support, negotiation, cooptation and so on. Thus, the suggestion in the contemporary literature is that resistance can be prevented by anticipating employee-related reactions followed by early intervention to deal with them.

So what is the alternative to this conceptualization of resistance? There are two points to consider here. First, people rarely resist change simply for the sake of doing so and few are so entrenched in their habits and certainties that they will not contemplate another way of doing things. On the contrary, we normally resist things that are unpleasant or against our best interests – the possible loss of a job, loss of status, less favourable working conditions, new reporting arrangements or being railroaded into something we don't understand, for example. Even then, we will often accept short-term discomfort for longer-term advantages. The second point is that resistance to change is not simply a characteristic of individuals; it can come from any component of an organizational system, of which individuals are only one part. While it is certainly true that planned change is often less than successful, many factors could explain this. It seems unreasonable, therefore, to place undue emphasis on the individual employee.

To better understand this alternative view of resistance to change, we will examine Kurt Lewin's work. For Lewin, nothing much could change in an organization as long as there was an equilibrium between the forces favouring change and the forces against change. To set off an unfreezing effect, the relative strengths of these two sets of opposing forces needed to change, either to weaken the barriers or to strengthen the drivers. Organizations were dynamic entities with many complex interconnections and effects. In short, resistance to change was 'a systems phenomenon, not a psychological one'.[15] If we take Lewin's original conceptualization, the role of employees in moving change forward is through their full collaboration in planning and implementation processes. On the other hand, contemporary conceptualizations of resistance to change often imply that people are 'part of the problem' and that their education and participation is primarily for the purpose of securing cooperation in a process that rests firmly in the hands of management.[16]

Questions

1. How do you normally respond to changes in your life and work? Do you think that resistance to change is a normal response for yourself and others?

2. Explain the two different management rationales for employee participation in the change process that are implied in the last paragraph above.

TECHNOLOGICAL CHANGE

The increased complexity of the business environment and of competition is due to a number of factors but technology is a key driving force for change. Companies are generally receptive to technological change and are ready to accommodate further technological change in the future (but resource and cost considerations remain important factors here). Companies use sophisticated networks and information systems that have unprecedented capacity for meeting customer and other business needs. Business transactions take place nearly instantaneously via e-mail and the Internet. These changes have increased the pace of business. This pace is another force of change with which managers must contend.[17]

Technological change that occurred slowly over centuries (such as the invention of the wheel) accelerated to change measured in decades (the impact of the car, for instance), which has now been transformed into continuous and pervasive change brought about by the computer chip and its successors.

Prahalad[18] argues that technological change will become more prominent in differentiating organizations in the future, thereby enabling some organizations to become more innovative and competitive in their change strategies. Prahalad asserts that the four key drivers for change are: connectivity to the Internet and communication sources, cost reduction through digitization, the convergence of technologies and industry boundaries and social networking. All of these drivers are linked to technological changes.

OB IN ACTION

The University of Wessex* is introducing its 20th major Information Technology change in three years. The project plan for introduction is looking at a single change intervention for communicating with students and has bespoke software that has not been tested against other potentially conflicting software, servers or platforms. The principal of the university is keen for a quick introduction and has asked the IT director to have the software introduced within three months. When it comes to change at this university, traditionally 12 to 18 months would be expected for the introduction of new systems. Eighteen months ago, two significant technology interventions were abandoned, with no communication to employees as to why this specific decision was taken.

Whilst staff training has been made available in the past, it has often been arranged when staff are busy or unavailable. There is no record or audit taken of which staff have had what training.

The IT director is known for her lack of interest in having a communications strategy and prefers to send long and unwieldy e-mails through her IT managers.

Questions

1. What advice would you give to the IT director with regards to planning for the new change?
2. What are the likely sources of resistance to change, and what practical suggestions can you make to help alleviate these sources?

* This is a fictitious university name.

THE PROCESS OF CHANGE AND CHANGE STRATEGIES

Phases of planned change

Earlier in the chapter we referred to the work of Kurt Lewin, a famous psychologist who developed a model of the process of change. We will now examine his work in greater detail. Lewin recommended that any change effort should be viewed as a process that includes the phases shown in Figure 12.4. Managers using Lewin's ideas will be sensitive to the need to ensure that any change effort properly addresses each of these three phases of change.[19]

- *unfreezing* – getting people and things ready for change;
- *changing* – implementing the change;
- *refreezing* – making sure the change 'sticks' as part of new routines.

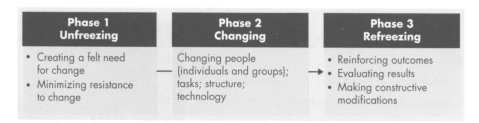

Figure 12.4: Lewin's three phases of planned change.

Source: Adapted from Tichy, N. (1983), *Managing Strategic Change: Technical, political and cultural dynamics*, John Wiley & Sons, Inc.: New York. Reproduced by permission.

Unfreezing *is the first stage of the planned change process in which a situation is prepared for change.*

Unfreezing is the managerial responsibility of preparing a situation for change. It involves disconfirming existing attitudes and behaviours to create a felt need for something new. Unfreezing is facilitated by environmental pressures, declining performance, the recognition of a problem or awareness that someone else has found a better way, among other factors. Many changes are never tried or fail simply because situations are not properly unfrozen to begin with. As a concept, unfreezing is very similar in meaning to 'generating energy for transformation', which was discussed in relation to Figure 12.3. 'Force-field analysis' is a useful tool for identifying the forces for and against change during the unfreezing stage. Force-field analysis is a management technique to diagnose and encourage change. It is based on the idea that in any situation there are both driving and restraining forces that influence any change that may occur. Driving forces push in a particular direction; they tend to initiate a change and keep it going. In terms of improving productivity in a work group, pressure from a supervisor, incentive earnings and competition may be examples of driving forces. Restraining forces restrain or decrease the driving forces. Apathy, hostility and poor maintenance of equipment may be examples of restraining forces against increased production. Changes occur when the driving and restraining forces are shifted out of equilibrium.[20] The basic steps are to identify the driving forces, identify the restraining forces, identify which forces can be changed and weight those forces based on the degree to which they can be influenced and the likely effects of that influence.[21]

Large systems seem particularly susceptible to the so-called 'boiled frog phenomenon'.[22] This refers to a classic physiological proposition that a live frog will immediately jump out when placed in a pan of hot water; but when placed in cold water that is then heated very slowly, the frog will stay in the water until it boils to death. Organizations can fall victim to similar circumstances. When managers fail to monitor their environments, recognize the important trends or sense the need to change, their organizations may slowly suffer and lose their competitive edge. The best organizations, by contrast, have managers who are always on the alert for 'unfreezing' opportunities.

The **changing** stage involves a managerial responsibility to modify a situation; that is, to change people, tasks, structure and/or technology. Lewin feels that many change agents enter this stage prematurely or are too quick to change things. As a result, they often end up creating resistance to change in a situation that is not adequately unfrozen. Changing something is hard enough, let alone having to do it without the proper foundations. Successful change requires sustained energy and clear goals to maintain the process.

> **Changing** involves a managerial responsibility to modify a situation; that is, to change people, tasks, structure and/or technology.

Successful change also depends on the degree of readiness to change, which suggests that two distinct forces act on people.[23] First, there are the forces within the individual. Second, there are the forces within the system, which (as we have discussed) include the type of leadership, the culture, the climate of the organization and the perceived consequences of success or failure within the organization. The combination of these factors affects the individual's degree of felt security. That is, if the degree of felt security is either high or low, then the efforts to introduce change will most likely be rejected. If people feel secure in their current work situation, then what need is there for them to change? If an individual's degree of felt security is very low, then anything you do to disturb that low state of security will be seen to be highly threatening. Thus, only in the middle ranges of felt security is the response to change most likely to be positive. Such a positive response will be expressed through behaviours such as listening, clarifying, negotiating and a willingness to explore alternatives.

Refreezing is the final stage of managerial responsibility in the planned change process. Designed to maintain the momentum of a change, refreezing positively reinforces desired outcomes and provides extra support when difficulties are encountered. Evaluation is a key element in this final step of the change process. It provides data on the costs and benefits of a change and offers opportunities to make constructive modifications in the change over time. Improper refreezing results in changes that are abandoned or incompletely implemented.

> **Refreezing** is the final stage of the planned change process in which changes are positively reinforced.

CHANGE LEVERS AND CHANGE CYCLES

Managers may limit their capacity to manage change by focusing on a restricted set of organizational change levers. In other words, regardless of the nature of the problem that the change is meant to solve, they reach for the same levers every time. This means that the change process is viewed from only one perspective. It may be viewed as a technical problem, a political problem or a cultural problem that needs resolving. Noel Tichy argues that those who design, manage and change organizations face the following three fundamental sets of problems, and effective change managers can recognize all three:

- *Technical design problem.* The organization faces a production or operational problem. Social and technical resources must be allocated to solve the problem and achieve a desired outcome.
- *Political allocation problem.* The organization faces an allocation of power and resources problem. It must determine how it will use its resources, as well as which parts of the organization will benefit.
- *Culture/ideological mix problem.* An organization is held together by shared beliefs. The organization must determine which values need to be held by which people.[24]

All of these problems tend to occur simultaneously in organizations. They therefore constitute the fundamental levers that prompt managers to contemplate strategic change. They form the basic parts of what could be described as the engine of change, as shown in Figure 12.5. When these areas are considered over time, you can identify cycles in their relative importance. Attempts to resolve each set of problems give rise to new situations and hence new problems, which in turn require new solutions.[25]

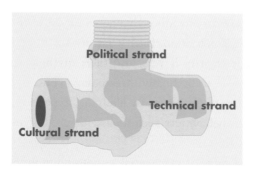

Figure 12.5: The engine of change – a metaphor.
Source: Adapted from Tichy, N. (1983), *Managing Strategic Change: Technical, political and cultural dynamics*, John Wiley & Sons, Inc.: New York. Reproduced by permission.

Seeing the change process as an engine allows us to understand some of the practical aspects of change. Managers may experience all of the problems outlined by Tichy but to a varying degree. At some stage of organizational development, technical problems may be the most pressing. At another stage, cultural problems may need the most urgent attention. As with the oil or water that feeds an engine, none of these issues can be ignored if the engine of change is to run. All components of the engine need attention to ensure high performance. Change agents and participants often fail to understand this. Too often during a change process, one group becomes frustrated because its problems are not seen to be

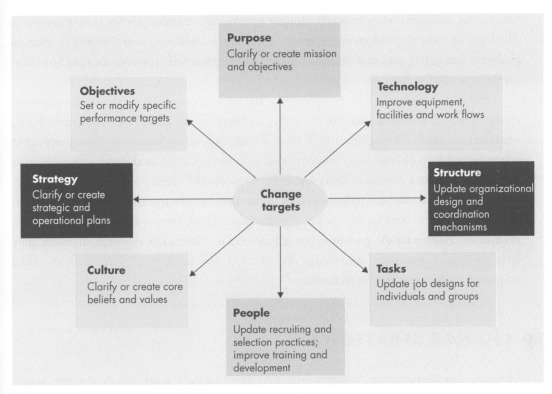

Figure 12.6: Organizational targets for planned change.

the most pressing. Managers need to understand that the different groups' problems are intertwined and that they must be dealt with simultaneously. In doing so, managers will find themselves addressing strategic change as shown in Figure 12.6.[26]

ORGANIZATIONAL TARGETS FOR CHANGE

The forces for change are ever present in today's dynamic work settings.[27] They are found in the relationship between an organization and its environment; mergers, strategic alliances and divestitures are examples of organizational attempts to redefine relationships with challenging environments. They are found in the lifecycle of the organization as it passes from birth through growth and towards maturity; changes in culture and structures are examples of organizational attempts to adjust to these patterns of growth. They are found in the political nature of organizational life; changes in internal control structures (including benefits and reward systems) are examples of organizational attempts to deal with shifting political currents. Planned change based on any of these forces can be directed towards a wide variety of organizational components or targets. As shown in Figure 12.6, these targets include organizational purpose, strategy, structure and people, as well as objectives, culture, tasks and technology. Sometimes, these targets for change are addressed mistakenly by management through 'fad' solutions that are offered by consultants and adopted by managers without much thought for the real situation and/or people involved. The logic of truly planned change requires a managerial willingness and ability to address problems concretely and systematically and to avoid tendencies towards an easy but questionable 'quick fix'.[28]

Further, the manager must recognize that the various targets of planned organizational change are highly intertwined. For example, a change in the basic tasks performed by an organization (that is, a modification in what it is the organization does) is almost inevitably accompanied by a change in technology (that is, a modification in the way in which tasks are accomplished). Changes in tasks and technology usually require alterations in the structure of the organization, including changes in the patterns of authority and communication as well as in the roles of members. These technological and structural changes can, in turn, necessitate changes on the part of the organization's members. For example, members may have to acquire additional knowledge and develop new skills to perform their modified roles and work with the new technology.[29]

PLANNED CHANGE STRATEGIES

Often the timeframe facing change agents is an unrealistically short one, so that the 'ready, fire, aim' technique is evidenced. Kotter (2007) argues that realizing that change takes time can improve the chances of success.[30]

Managers and other change agents use various means for mobilizing power, exerting influence over others and getting people to support planned change efforts. As described in Figure 12.7, each of these strategies builds from different foundations of social power (as discussed in Chapter 10) and each has somewhat different implications for the planned change process. Among the change strategies commonly used by managers to bring about planned organizational change are:[31]

* *top-down approach to change* – using centralized power to force compliance with change directives;
* *force-coercion* – using authority to force compliance with change directives;
* *rational persuasion* – using logic and information to persuade people to accept change directives;
* *shared power* – involving others in decisions identifying the need for change and desired change directions.

Top-down approach to change

In pursuing the top-down (or directional) approach to change, executives and managers believe that one-way communication backed by the formal authority of their position is enough to implement change. This approach to change is very akin to the military model in its style and assumes that members lower down in the hierarchy will understand what is intended and follow through exactly as requested.

Figure 12.7: Power bases, change strategies, management behaviours and predicted outcomes.

In many situations, this approach is problematic and ineffective, especially when the situation facing the organization is complex and difficult to interpret.[32] With complex problems requiring change, top managers do not have a monopoly on expertise, information and inputs. In such situations, having the additional perspectives of the lower level managers and employees would be an advantage.

Given that members at the lower levels are generally on the firing line (that is, closest to the machinery, the consumer and the community), they are in an excellent position to observe problems and to provide varied and valuable inputs to any required changes. When a directive approach to change pervades the organization, higher level managers are unlikely to listen. Thus, the lower levels become increasingly frustrated and may even refuse to lend their cooperation. Further, the extent to which the change process requires member commitment for successful implementation suggests that the lower level members may not comply automatically.[33] If members do not commit to the change process as intended, what is finally implemented may be a far cry from what top management had in mind.

Many eminent management scholars such as Tom Lupton have also indicated the idiosyncracies of authoritarian change. For instance, Lupton sees that change can be more successfully introduced from the bottom up than from the top down.[34] In general, individuals who are struggling to assert their autonomy tend to resist the efforts of people in authority to exercise control over them. By doing so, individuals do not necessarily reject the legitimacy of the authority but rather seek to extend their own autonomy by working to control their interactions with the authority.

However, the 'bottom-up' (participative) approach to change is often not possible. In the case of public sector organizations, for example, the change process may be imposed on them by drastic changes in government policies and legislation. In this situation, change may be more directive and less participative.

Force-coercion and planned change

A **force-coercion strategy** uses legitimacy, rewards and/or punishments as primary inducements to change. That is, the change agent acts unilaterally to try to 'command' change through the formal authority of their position, to induce change via an offer of special rewards or to

*A **force-coercion strategy** tries to 'command' change through the formal authority of legitimacy, rewards and punishments.*

bring about change via threats of punishment. People respond to this strategy mainly out of fear of being punished if they do not comply with a change directive, or out of desire to gain a reward if they do. Compliance is usually temporary and will continue only so long as the change agent remains visible in their legitimate authority, or so long as the opportunity for rewards and punishments remains obvious. If, as a change agent, you were to use the force-coercion strategy for bringing about planned change, the following profile might apply:[35]

> You believe that people who run things are basically motivated by self-interest and by what the situation offers in terms of potential personal gains or losses. As you feel that people change only in response to such motives, you try to find out where their vested interests lie and then put the pressure on. If you have formal authority, you use it. If not, you resort to whatever possible rewards and punishments you have access to and do not hesitate to threaten others with these weapons. Once you find a weakness, you exploit it and are always wise to work 'politically' by building supporting alliances wherever possible.

Rational persuasion and planned change

A rational persuasion strategy attempts to bring about change through persuasion based on empirical facts, special knowledge and rational argument.

Change agents using a **rational persuasion strategy** attempt to bring about change through the use of special knowledge, empirical support or rational arguments. This strategy assumes that rational people will be guided by reason and self-interest in deciding whether to support a change. Expert power is mobilized to convince others that the cost–benefit value of a proposed change is high; that is, that the change will leave them better off than before. When successful, this strategy results in a longer lasting, more internalized change than does the force-coercion strategy. If you use a rational persuasion strategy, the following profile may apply:

> You believe that people are inherently rational and are guided by reason in their actions and decision making. Once a specific course of action is demonstrated to be in a person's self-interest, you assume that reason and rationality will cause the person to adopt it. You approach change with the objective of communicating, through information and facts, the essential 'desirability' of change from the perspective of the person whose behaviour you seek to influence. If this logic is effectively communicated, you are sure that the person(s) will adopt the proposed change.

Shared power and planned change

A shared power strategy (or normative-re-educative strategy) attempts to bring about change by identifying or establishing values and assumptions so that support for the change emerges naturally.

In order to minimize the likelihood of resistance, some of the best approaches to change put strong emphasis on involving all parties affected by the change. For example, a leader might meet with all managers and employees to explain reasons for the change and generally how it will be carried out. A plan may be developed and communicated. Staff forums may be organized to give members the opportunity to express their ideas about the proposed change. They are also given the opportunity to express their concerns and frustrations. This approach to change coincides with what is commonly known as a **shared power strategy** to change. This strategy actively and sincerely involves other people who will be affected by a change in planning and making key decisions in respect to it. Sometimes called a normative-re-educative strategy, this approach seeks to establish directions and social support for change through the empowerment of others. It builds essential foundations, such as personal values, group norms and shared goals, so support for a proposed change emerges naturally. Managers using this approach emphasize personal preference and share power by allowing others to participate in planning and implementing the change. Given this high level of involvement, the strategy is likely to result in a longer-lasting and internalized change. If you use a shared power strategy for bringing about planned change, the following profile may apply:

> You believe that people have complex motivations. You feel that people behave as they do as a result of socio-cultural norms and commitments to these norms. You also recognize that changes in these orientations involve changes in attitudes, values, skills and significant relationships, not just changes in knowledge, information or intellectual rationales for action and practice. When seeking to change others you are sensitive to the supporting or inhibiting effects of any group pressures and norms that may be operating. You try to find out their side of things and to identify their feelings and expectations.

RESISTANCE TO CHANGE

Resistance towards change encompasses behaviours that are acted out by change recipients in order to slow down or terminate an intended organizational change.[36] Typically, change initiatives are met by some resistance. This is because employees are often afraid of the unknown. Many of them may think things are already just fine and do not understand the need for change. Many may also be cynical about change. Some may even think that the proposed change goes against the values held by members in the organization. That is why much

organizational change is often discussed in conjunction with needed changes in the culture of the organization, including changes in members' values and beliefs. In essence, resistance to change is often viewed by change agents as something that must be 'overcome' for change to be successful. This is not always the case. It is helpful to view resistance to change as feedback that can be used by the astute change agent to help accomplish his or her change objectives.[37] The essence of this notion is to recognize that when people resist change they are defending something important that appears to be threatened by the change attempt. **Resistance to change** is any attitude or behaviour that reflects a person's unwillingness to make or support a desired change.

Both passive and active resistance work against organizational change. Passive resistance can include the widespread cynicism often found among workers exposed to frequent

Resistance to change is any attitude or behaviour that reflects a person's unwillingness to make or support a desired change.

management change initiatives, where insufficient attention was paid to implementation and the effects on organizational members. Passive resistance can also occur where organizational members feel that the psychological cost of adjusting to new systems and processes is greater than any recommended or perceived benefits. Active resistance occurs where the redistribution of power threatens vested self-interest. This form of resistance can be dangerous for an organization and can undermine even well thought-out change programmes.[38]

Why people resist change

It could be argued that individuals, teams or the organization as a whole can show resistance to the process of change itself and/or the content of change, reflecting the way in which the change is brought about, or what is being changed in particular. This process versus content argument could also be presented as the perception of the process versus the perception of the content.

It could also be argued that change could constitute a breach of the psychological contract if it is brought about without sufficient consultation and negotiation.[39]

There are several reasons for possible resistance to the introduction of a new management practice. People who report directly to a manager, for example, may resist the introduction and use of e-commerce (electronic commerce) in their workplace because:

* they are not familiar with online business and Internet use and wonder whether they could become familiar with it successfully (*fear of the unknown*);
* they may wonder if the manager is introducing e-commerce just to 'get rid' of some of the workers eventually (*need for security*);
* they may feel they are doing their jobs well and do not need the new facility (*no felt need for change*);
* they may sense that the manager is forcing e-commerce on them without first discussing their feelings on the matter (*vested interests threatened*);
* they may have heard from workers in other departments that e-commerce is being introduced to get more work out of people with no increase in pay (*contrasting interpretations*);
* they are really busy at the present time and do not want to try something new until the work slackens a bit (*poor timing*);
* they may believe that they will be left on their own to learn how to operate the new systems (*lack of resources*).

These and other viewpoints often create resistance to even the best and most well-intended planned changes. To deal better with these forces, managers often find it useful to separate such responses into resistance to change directed towards the change itself, the change strategy and the change agent as a person.

Sometimes a manager may experience resistance to the change itself. A good manager understands that people may reject a change because they believe it is not worth their time, effort and/or attention. To minimize resistance in such cases, the change agent should make sure that the people affected by the change know specifically how it satisfies the following criteria:

- *Benefit*. The change should have a clear relative advantage for the individuals being asked to change; that is, it should be perceived as 'a better way'.
- *Compatibility*. The change should be as compatible as possible with the existing values and experiences of the people being asked to change.
- *Complexity*. The change should be no more complex than necessary. It must be as easy as possible to understand and use.
- *Triability*. The change should be something that people can try on a step-by-step basis and make adjustments as things progress.

Managers will always experience some resistance to their change strategy. Someone who attempts to bring about change via force-coercion, for example, may create resistance among individuals who resent management by 'command' or the threatened use of punishment. People may also resist an empirical-rational strategy in which the data are suspect or expertise is not clearly demonstrated, or a normative-re-educative strategy that appears manipulative and insincere.

Finally, managers may experience resistance to the change agent. In this case, resistance is directed at the person implementing the change and may reflect inadequacies in the personality and attributes of the manager as a change agent. Change agents who are isolated from other people in the change situation, who appear self-centred or who have a high emotional involvement in the changes are especially prone to such problems. Research also indicates that change agents who are different from other key people on such dimensions as age, education and socioeconomic factors are likely to experience greater resistance to change.[40]

How to deal with resistance to change

An informed change agent can do many things to deal constructively with resistance to change in any of its forms. In general, resistance will be managed best if it is recognized early in the change process. All things considered, the following general approaches for dealing with resistance to change have been identified:[41]

 RESEARCH IN OB

Look at the article by Kiefer on our website **www.wileyeurope.com/college/french**. In her research article Kiefer provides examples of how ongoing organizational change is experienced emotionally. Three antecedents of negative emotion are put forward: perceptions of an insecure future, perceptions of inadequate working conditions and perceptions of inadequate treatment by the organization. Two outcomes are also examined, namely: variations in trust towards the organization and withdrawal from that organization. The article is useful in highlighting that change – for all the rational models proposed in business and management literature – is ultimately *felt* as an emotional response.

- *Education and communication* – using one-on-one discussions, presentations to groups, memos, reports or demonstrations to educate people about a change before it is implemented and to help them see the logic of the change.
- *Participation and involvement* – allowing others to help design and implement the changes; asking individuals to contribute ideas and advice; forming taskforces or committees to work on the change.
- *Facilitation and support* – providing socio-emotional support for the hardships of change; actively listening to problems and complaints; providing training in the new ways; helping to overcome performance pressures.
- *Negotiation and agreement* – offering incentives to actual or potential resistors; working out tradeoffs to provide special benefits in exchange for assurance that the change will not be blocked.
- *Manipulation and cooptation* – using covert attempts to influence others; selectively providing information and consciously structuring events so the desired change receives maximum support; buying off leaders of resistance to gain their support.
- *Explicit or implicit coercion* – using force to get people to accept change; threatening resistors with a variety of undesirable consequences if they do not go along as planned.

Figure 12.8 summarizes additional insights into how and when each method may be used by managers when dealing with resistance to change. When such resistance seems to be based on a lack of information or the presence of inaccurate information, education and communication are good managerial responses. Once persuaded that the change is for the best, people will often help implement the change. The downside is that the process of education and communication can be time consuming if too many people are involved. Participation and involvement is a good approach when the manager or change agent does not have all the information needed to design the required change. This is especially true if other people have a lot of power to resist. People who are allowed to participate in designing a change tend to be highly committed to its implementation. But, again, this process can be time consuming.

In cases where people are resisting the change because there will be adjustment problems, facilitation and support are recommended responses. In such circumstances, people are probably trying hard to implement a change but they are frustrated by external constraints and difficulties. Here a manager must play the 'supportive' role and try to make it as easy as possible to continue with the planned change. Of course, the manager must be able to invest the time and energy needed to provide this support and to gain needed commitment from the organization. Negotiation and agreement tend to be most useful when a person or group will clearly lose something as a result of the planned change. When the person or group has considerable power, resistance can be particularly costly to the change effort. Direct negotiation can sometimes prove a relatively easy way of avoiding or eliminating this form of resistance. This response requires a foundation of trust and may involve extra 'costs' in terms of any agreements that may be reached.

There is no avoiding the fact that resistance to change can be – and is – managed at times through manipulation and cooptation. These responses may be used when other

METHOD ➝	USE WHEN ➝	ADVANTAGES ➝	DISADVANTAGES
Education and communication	People lack information or have inaccurate information	Creates willingness to help with the change	Can be very time consuming
Participation and involvement	Other people have important information and/or power to resist	Adds information to change planning; builds commitment to the change	Can be very time consuming
Facilitation and support	Resistance traces to resource or adjustment problems	Satisfies directly specific resource or adjustment needs	Can be time consuming; can be expensive
Negotiation and agreement	A person or group will 'lose' something due to the change	Helps avoid major resistance	Can be expensive; can cause others to seek similar 'deals'
Manipulation and cooptation	Other methods do not work or are too expensive	Can be quick and inexpensive	Can create future problems if people sense manipulation
Explicit and implicit coercion	Speed is important and change agent has power	Quick; overpowers resistance	Risky if people get angry

Figure 12.8: Methods for dealing with resistance to change.

tactics just do not work or are too expensive. They may also make up a 'style' that a manager or change agent uses on most occasions. In some cases, manipulation and co-optation can provide a relatively quick and inexpensive solution to resistance problems. But a good manager understands that these approaches can also lead to future problems if people feel manipulated. A more extreme approach is explicit or implicit coercion. Coercion is often used when speed is of the essence or when the manager or change agent possesses considerable power. It is a fast response and can overpower resistance. It also runs the risk of offending people, however. People who experience coercion may feel angry at the manager or change agent and be left without any true commitments to ensuring that the change is fully implemented. Coercion may unfreeze and change things but it does not do much to refreeze them.

Regardless of the chosen strategy, managers must understand that resistance to change is something to be recognized and constructively addressed instead of feared. The presence of resistance typically suggests that something can be done to achieve a better 'fit' between the change, the situation and the people affected. A manager should deal with resistance to change by 'listening' to such feedback and acting accordingly.

Whilst recognizing resistance to change is, in itself, important in overcoming the barriers to change, there may be other, more generic, issues that need to be addressed. Burnes[42] outlines the top ten barriers to change, namely competition for resources, functional boundaries, lack of management skills etc.

THE ROLE OF THE CHANGE AGENT

When we consider the complexities involved with change, the range of skills and expertise of the change agent could be considerable. Change agents are more readily associated with planned change but the degree to which planning is reliable and sequential will depend on the context and all the people and processes associated with it. Buchanan and Boddy[43] indicate that the context is vital to the role of the change agent and the extent to which the change agent has support from senior management. It could be argued that the more strategic the change, the more political it will become, and the more 'exposed' the change agent will be.

Buchanan and Boddy argue that there is a range of core competences that the change agent needs to exhibit, and these are set into five clusters:

Cluster	Core competence	Description
Goals	1. Sensitivity	to changes in personnel, top management perceptions, and market conditions, and to the way in which these impact upon the project in hand.
	2. Clarity	in specifying goals, in defining the achievable
	3. Flexibility	in responding to changes outside the control of the project manager, perhaps requiring major shifts in project goals and management style, and risk taking.
Roles	4. Teambuilding	bringing together key stakeholders and establish effective working groups, and clearly to define and delegate respective responsibilities.
	5. Networking	skills in establishing and maintaining appropriate contacts within and outside of the organization.
	6. Tolerance of ambiguity	to be able to function comfortably, patiently and effectively in a certain environment.
Communication	7. Communication	transmit effectively to colleagues and subordinates the need for changes in project goals and in individual tasks and responsibilities.
	8. Interpersonal skills	including selection, listening, collecting appropriate information, identifying the concerns of others and managing meetings.
	9. Personal enthusiasm	in expressing plans and ideas.
	10. Stimulating motivation	and commitment in others involved.
Negotiation	11. Selling	plans and ideas to others, by creating a desirable and challenging vision for the future.
	12. Negotiating	with key players for resources, or for changes in procedures, and to resolve conflict.
Managing up	13. Political awareness	in identifying potential coalitions, and in balancing conflicting goals and perceptions.
	14. Influencing	to gain commitment to project plans and ideas from potential sceptics and resistors.
	15. Helicopter perspective	to stand back from the immediate project and take a broader view of priorities.

Table 12.1: Skills and competencies for the change agent.

Internal versus external change agents

Whilst the political context together with resource capability (and competence as change agents) may shape the choice of whether to use internal or external change agents, internal change agents may be better equipped to carry out change because of their awareness of customer needs and expectations. Nisbet (2009)[44] argues that internal change agents need to carry out four change agent roles, namely: catalyst, solution giver, process helper and resource linker, with the process helper role cited as the most critical. In times of economic recession the choice of recruiting an external versus an internal change agent may come down to simple financial constraints, but ultimately, the change agent will need to be equipped with the necessary skills and competences in order to carry out their job effectively (see Table 12.1).

CONCLUSION

Rieley[45] questions whether organizations change for worthwhile reasons, or is it 'simply rearranging the deck chairs on the *Titanic*'? Change, like any other organizational intervention, must have material benefits, whether it is to the organization's bottom line, employee wellbeing or simply organizational survival. The ends may justify the means. Taking the counterargument of the means justifying the ends, we have to question and evaluate the process in a similar fashion. Some managers may revert to draconian measures like scaring people in order to effect change.[46] The balance of the two arguments may give us an overall idea of the change intervention.

SUMMARY

LEARNING OBJECTIVE 1
Radical versus incremental planned change
Planned change is directed by managers and others acting as change agents. Radical change involves a significant transformation of the organization and/or its objectives, systems and processes. It often occurs in response to a critical event such as the presence of a new chief executive officer, an emerging competitive threat or a merger with another company. Incremental change is more gradual and involves an adjustment to the way things are currently done in one or a limited number of organizational departments. It is less disruptive and generally more frequent than radical change.

LEARNING OBJECTIVE 2
Forces favouring change and the targets of change
Within organizations, change is more likely to take place successfully when there is sufficient dissatisfaction with the way things are currently done, a strong attraction towards a more desirable state and a

willingness to work towards a strategic approach to change. External factors in favour of change include increasing complexity in the business environment. Complexity is increased through globalization, technological change competition and the need to be more efficient, innovative and responsive to customer demands. Organizational targets for planned change include purpose, strategy, culture, structure, people, tasks and technology.

LEARNING OBJECTIVE 3
Change strategies

Planned change strategies are the means used by change agents to implement desired change. Force-coercion strategies of change use aspects of a manager's position power to try to 'command' that the change will take place as directed. Temporary compliance is a common response of people who are 'forced' to change in this manner. Rational persuasion strategies of change use logical arguments and appeal to knowledge and facts to convince people to support change. When successful, this method can lead to more commitment to change. Shared power strategies of change seek to involve other people in planning and implementing change. Of the three strategies, shared power creates the longest lasting and most internalized commitment to the change.

LEARNING OBJECTIVE 4
Resistance to change and what can be done about it

Resistance to change is to be expected. Dealing successfully with resistance begins with awareness that it represents 'feedback' that can be used by a change agent to increase the effectiveness of a change effort. People sometimes resist because they do not find value or believe in the change. They sometimes resist because they find the change strategy offensive or inappropriate. Sometimes they resist because they do not like or identify positively with the change agent as a person. Successful change agents are open to resistance and are capable of responding to it in ways that create a better 'fit' between the change, the situation and all the people involved.

LEARNING OBJECTIVE 5
The role of the change agent

The change agent needs to have a political awareness and a range of skills and abilities in both managing tasks and people. There is no general agreement about a definitive set of competences that a change agent requires but Buchanan and Boddy's 15 core competences provide a useful framework for analysis. No one person can manage all change, as change normally happens through people, and therefore change agents need to embody the spirit of change.

CHAPTER 12 STUDY GUIDE

Now that you have read this chapter, you should be able to apply and further develop your knowledge by undertaking the following activities set out over the next few pages: test your knowledge questions, an individual activity and an end-of-chapter case study.

Please also go to this book's website: **www.wileyeurope.com/college/french** to find further material which will enhance your understanding and enable you to assess your knowledge.

TEST YOURSELF

1. Explain the difference between planned and unplanned change. Give examples of situations where these occur.
2. Explain what managers can do to manage change and minimize resistance.
3. Design a one-day training course targeting the mid-level managers of a medium-size organization. There would be 20 participants coming from a diverse range of functions in the organization, including production, design, administration, marketing, sales and product development. The aims of the programme are to make participants aware of the meaning of 'cultural change', and also to gauge views on the current culture and potential required changes.
4. As a team leader in an organization facing increasing competition from new entrants to your industry, you have been tasked with implementing changes within your unit. These changes are likely to disrupt current schedules, rosters and work processes significantly. Prepare a strategy for the unfreezing stage of the change process for your team, with a view to minimizing resistance so that the changes can be implemented as smoothly as possible.
5. The best way to approach change is through the 'shared power' approach. Do you agree?

INDIVIDUAL ACTIVITY

Innovative attitude scale

Introduction

Change and innovation are important to organizations. The following assessment surveys your readiness to accept and participate in innovation.

Instructions

Indicate the extent to which each of the following statements is true of either your actual behaviour or your intentions at work. That is, describe the way you are, or the way you intend to be, on the job. Use the following scale for your responses.

Almost always true	5
Often true	4
Not applicable	3
Seldom true	2
Almost never true	1

1. I openly discuss with my boss how to get ahead.
2. I try new ideas and approaches to problems.
3. I take things or situations apart to find out how they work.
4. I welcome uncertainty and unusual circumstances related to my tasks.
5. I negotiate my salary openly with my supervisor.
6. I can be counted on to find a new use for existing methods or equipment.
7. Among my colleagues and co-workers, I will be the first or nearly the first to try out a new idea or method.
8. I take the opportunity to translate communications from other departments for my work group.
9. I demonstrate originality.
10. I will work on a problem that has caused others great difficulty.
11. I provide critical input towards a new solution.
12. I provide written evaluations of proposed ideas.
13. I develop contacts with experts outside my firm.
14. I use personal contacts to manoeuvre myself into choice work assignments.
15. I make time to pursue my own pet ideas or projects.
16. I set aside resources for the pursuit of a risky project.
17. I tolerate people who depart from organizational routine.
18. I speak out in staff meetings.
19. I work in teams to try to solve complex problems.
20. If my co-workers are asked, they will say I am a wit.

Interpretation

To determine your score on the 'Innovative attitude scale', simply add the numbers associated with your responses to the 20 statements. The higher your score, the more receptive to innovation you are. You can compare your score with that of others to see if you seem to be more or less receptive to innovation than a comparable group of business students.

Score	Percentile*
39	5
53	16
62	33
71	50
80	68
89	86
97	95

*Percentile indicates the percentage who are expected to score below you.

OTICON — A DANISH HEARING AID MANUFACTURER — THE TRANSFORMATIONAL ORGANIZATION

Introduction

Oticon, the first hearing aid manufacturing company, was founded in 1904 and specialized in 'behind-the-ear' hearing aids. The situation changed in the 1980s and 1990s and the company suffered both financially and in terms of loss of market share. Whilst the likes of companies like 3M, Panasonic, Sony, Philips and Siemens were specializing in digital technology, Oticon was still using analogue technology. Oticon was strong in subsidized markets in Scandinavia and northern Europe but it was less strong in buoyant markets in America and the Far East.

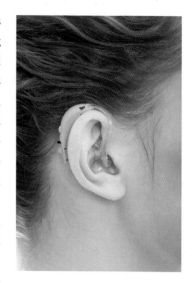

The appointment of a new CEO, Lars Kolind, in 1988, was the start of the company transformation. He described the organization as having 'slept for the last ten years'. Within two years he attempted to transform the organization through cost-cutting measures: paring the company down, cutting staff, increasing efficiency and reducing the price of a hearing aid by 20%. Kolind managed to change the traditional company culture by making it more responsive, speedy and customer focused. By 1990 Oticon made a $16 million profit on a $400 million turnover. However, this was within a market that was growing at 6% per annum. The major difficulty that Kolind now faced was economy of scale – how could a small Danish manufacturer compete with the world's largest electronic companies?

The vision

Kolind came up with a vision by 'thinking the unthinkable'. Technology was not the only factor to consider and Kolind argued that the business that they were in was to 'make people smile'. The new company mission statement embellished this concept – 'to help people with hearing difficulties to live life as they wish, with the hearing they have'. A new holistic approach to customer care was adopted, investigating customer needs, lifestyle and so forth. Married to this was a new mix of expertise in micro-mechanics, microchip design, audiology, psychology, marketing, manufacturing, logistics and all-round service capability. This shift can best be described as moving towards a knowledge-based business, from its previous technology-based business. Kolind saw his role as a naval architect rather than the ship's captain, creating the spaghetti organization – a chaotic tangle of relationships and interactions that would force the abandonment of preconceived ideas and barriers to innovation and competitiveness.

Adapted from Burnes, B. (2000), *Managing Change*, FT Prentice Hall: Harlow, pp. 319–327.

The strategy

The formation of four key principles helped to reinforce the concept of the 'disorganized organization'. The head office was the first line of attack.

- Departments and job titles disappeared, and all activities became project based, pursued informally by groupings of interested people.
- Jobs were redesigned into fluid and unique combinations of functions to suit employees' needs and capabilities.
- The formal office was eradicated and replaced by open space filled with workstations usable by anyone.
- Informal face-to-face dialogue replaced memos as the acceptable mode of communication.

Departments, department heads and other managerial/supervisory roles were eliminated. In liberating staff, the organization nonetheless needed to retain some measure of control and did this through direction and highlighting human values. Direction involved lengthy discussions about where the company was going (strategy) and attempts were also made to establish the fundamental values, summed up in their company statement – 'We build this company on the assumption that we only employ adults, and everything we do will rest on that assumption, so we will not treat our staff as children – we will treat them as responsible adults.'

Implementing the strategy

Kolind's vision relied upon communication. Computers supported employees' work. Oticon attempted to operate a 'paperless office' where any important information was scanned and available to other users. Information access was therefore fluid and available.

Resistance to change

Not all staff welcomed the changes. Some managers' loss of power, information monopoly and status symbols proved problematic. Managers also had to compete with everyone for project leader status and lacked subordinates. The project team role did not suit all staff.

Kolind pre-empted some of these concerns by implementing a range of measures, including providing employees with their own home PC, and encouragement to identify their own training needs. Kolind also offered an ultimatum – 'accept the new arrangements or leave'!

Conclusion

Oticon's market share rose from 8% in 1990 to 12% in 1993. By 1994, sales were growing at 10% per annum, after a period of ten years without any real growth. Lead time had halved, and 15 new products had been launched.

Burnes identifies seven factors critical to Oticon's success:

- changing the rules of the game;
- moving to a project-type structure which fits the strategy and vision of the business;

- creating a whole-hearted commitment from everyone to working cooperatively and proactively;
- creating a learning organization;
- visionary leadership;
- consistent vision, with passion;
- societal values – industrial and social democracy.

Questions

1. To what extent was Kolind's approach to resistance to change (take it or leave it) a high-risk approach? Could it have turned out to be the wrong approach?
2. What incentives were there for former managers to stay at Oticon?

SUGGESTED READING

Child, J. (2005), *Organization: Contemporary Principles and Practice*, Blackwell: Oxford. This author provides a useful summary of issues related to change within a context of new organizational forms such as strategic alliances and virtual organizations.

END NOTES

1. Dunphy, D. & Stace, D. (1993), The Strategic Management of Corporate Change. *Human Relations*, **46** (8), 917–918.
2. For more on the concepts of frame-breaking and frame-bending change, see Nadler, D. & Tushman, M. (1988), *Strategic Organizational Design*, Scott, Foresman: Glenview, IL.
3. Tichy, N. M. (1983), *Managing Strategic Change: Technical, Political and Cultural Dynamics*, John Wiley & Sons, Inc.: New York.
4. Child, J. (2005), *Organization*, Blackwell Publishing: Oxford.
5. Graetz, F. (2000), Strategic change leadership. *Management Decision*, **38** (8), 550–562.
6. Miles, R. (1997), *Corporate Comeback; the Story of Renewal and Transformation at National Semiconductor*, Jossey-Bass: San Francisco.
7. Graetz, F. op. cit.; Miles, R. op. cit.

8. Deming, W. E. (1986), *Out of the Crisis*, MIT Center for Advanced Engineering Study: Cambridge, MA.
9. Marris, P. (1986), *Loss and Change*, Routledge & Kegan Paul: London.
10. Stuart, R. (1996), The trauma of organizational change. *Journal of European Industrial Training*, **20** (2), 11–16.
11. Williams, A. P. O., Dobson, P. & Walters, M. (1993), *Changing Culture*, 2nd edn, Institute of Personnel Management: London.
12. Silvester, J., Anderson, N. R. & Patterson, F. (1999), Organizational culture change: an intergroup attributional analysis. *Journal of Occupational and Organizational Psychology*, **72** (1), 1.
13. Gagliardi, P. (1986), The creation and change of organizational cultures: a conceptual

framework. *Organization Studies*, **7** (2), 117–134, cited in Parker, S. (2004), Tactical change, www2.agsm.edu.au/agsm/web.nsf/Content/AGSMMagazine-Tacticalchange, (accessed 5 January 2006).

14. Dent, E. & Goldberg, S. (1999), Challenging 'resistance to change'. *Journal of Applied Behavioural Science*, **35** (1), 25–41.

15. Ibid., p. 31.

16. Ibid., pp. 25–41.

17. Weston, S. & Harper, J. (1998), The challenge of change. *Ivey Business Quarterly*, **63** (2), 78.

18. Prahalad, C. K. in Allio, R. J. (2008) *Journal of Strategy and Leadership*, **36** (6), 11–14.

19. Lewin, K. (1952), Group decision and social change, in *Readings in Social Psychology* (eds G. E. Swanson, T. M. Newcomb & E. L. Hartley), Holt, Rinehart & Winston: New York, p. 4.

20. Accel Team, *Team building*, www.accel-team.com/techniques/force_field_analysis.html, (accessed 5 January 2006).

21. Charles Sturt University, *Managing Change*, NSW.HSConline, http://hsc.csu.edu.au/business_studies/mgt_changemanaging_change/Manage-change.html#top, (accessed 27 September 2005).

22. Tichy, N. M. & Devanna, M. A. (1986), *The Transformational Leader*, John Wiley & Sons, Inc.: New York, p. 44.

23. Zeffane, R. (1996), Dynamics of strategic change: critical issues in fostering positive organizational change. *Leadership and Organization Development Journal*, **17** (7), 36–43.

24. Tichy, op. cit.

25. See Tichy, N. M. (1983), *Managing Strategic Change: Technical, Political and Cultural Dynamics*, John Wiley & Sons, Inc.: New York.

26. Op. cit.

27. Kanter, R. M., Stein, B. A. & Jick, T. D. (1993), Meeting the challenges of change. *World Executive's Digest*, May, pp. 22–27.

28. See, for example, Kilmann, R. H. (1984), *Beyond the Quick Fix*, Jossey-Bass: San Francisco; Tichy, N. M. & Devanna, M. A., op. cit.

29. Cooke, R. A. (1979), Managing change in organizations, in *Management Principles for Non-profit Organizations* (ed. G. Zaltman) American Management Association: New York. See also

30. Nadler, D. A. (1987), The effective management of organizational change, in *Handbook of Organizational Behaviour* (ed. J. W. Lorsch), Prentice Hall: Englewood Cliffs, NJ, pp. 358–369.

30. Kotter, J. (2007), Leading Change. *Havard Business Review*, **85** (1), 96–103.

31. Chin, R. & Benne, K. D. (1969), General strategies for effecting changes in human systems, in *The Planning of Change*, (eds W. G. Bennis, K. D. Benne, R. Chin & K. E. Corey), 3rd edn. Holt, Rinehart & Winston: New York, pp. 22–45.

32. Zeffane, R. M. (1995), The downsizing paradox: problems in the quest for leaner organizations. *Journal of Industrial Affairs*, **4** (1), 45–48.

33. Zeffane, R. M. (1994), Patterns of organizational commitment and perceived management styles: a comparison of public and private sector employees. *Tavistock Institute Journal of Human Relations*, **47** (8), 13–27; Emery, M. & Emery, M. (1992), Participative design: work and community life, in *Participative Design for Participative Democracy* (ed. M. Emery). Australian National University, Centre for Continuing Education: Canberra.

34. Lupton, T. (1991), Organizational change: 'top-down' or 'bottom-up' management? *Personnel Review*, **20** (3), 4–10.

35. The change strategy examples in this part are developed from an exercise reported in Pfeiffer, J. W. & Jones, J. E. (1973), *A Handbook of Structured Experiences for Human Relations Training*, vol. II, University Associates: La Jolla, CA.

36. Lines, R. (2004), Influence of participation in strategic change: resistance, organizational commitment and change goal achievement. *Journal of Change Management*, **4** (3), 193–215.

37. Klein, D. (1969), Some notes on the dynamics of resistance to change: the defender role in Bennis, Benne, Chin & Corey, op. cit., pp. 117–124.

38. Dervitsiotis, K. N. (1998), The challenge of managing organizational change: exploring the relationship of re-engineering, developing learning organizations and total quality management. *Total Quality Management*, **9** (1), 109.

39. Chew, M. M. M., Cheng, J. S. L. & Petrovic-Lazarevic, S. (2006), Manager's role in implementing organizational change: case of the restaurant industry in Melbourne. *Journal of Global Business and Technology*, **2** (1), Spring, 58–67.

40. See Rogers, E. M. & Shoemaker, F. F. (1971), *Communication of Innovations*, 2nd edn. The Free Press: New York.

41. Kotter, J. P. & Schlesinger, L. A. (1979), Choosing strategies for change. *Harvard Business Review*, **57** (March/April), 109–112.

42. Burnes, B. (2003), Managing change and changing managers from ABC to XYZ. *Journal of Management Development*, **22** (7), 627–642.

43. Buchanan, D. & Boddy, D. (1992), *The Expertise of the Change Agent: Public Performance and Backstage Activity*, Prentice-Hall: Englewood Cliffs, NJ.

44. Nisbet, S. (2009), The role of employees in encouraging customer adoption of new gaming machine payment technologies. *International Journal of Hospitality Management*, **21** (4), 422–436.

45. Rieley, J. (2005) Is it change, or the past preserved? *Telegraph*, 28 January.

46. Diefenbach, T. (2007), The managerialistic ideology of organizational change management. *Journal of Organizational Change Management*, **20** (1), 126–144.

Journal Article

POLITICAL SKILL, SUPERVISOR–SUBORDINATE *GUANXI* AND CAREER PROSPECTS IN CHINESE FIRMS

Li-Qun Wei, Jun Liu, Yuan-Yi Chen and Long-Zeng Wu

Hong Kong Baptist University; Renmin University of China; Hong Kong Baptist University; Hong Kong Baptist University

ABSTRACT The role of political skill was examined in the dynamics of supervisor–subordinate relationship in Chinese firms. Data from a survey of 343 employees, their 343 direct supervisors, and 662 of their peers were applied to test a model proposing that Chinese subordinates employ political skill to influence their *guanxi* with their supervisors, and so promote their career development. We found that supervisor–subordinate *guanxi* mediated the relationship between political skill and career development of the subordinates. Implications of the findings were discussed.

INTRODUCTION

The past decade has seen the growth of a body of research on political skill in business. Political skill refers to '... the ability to effectively understand others at work and to use such knowledge to influence others to act in ways that enhance one's personal and/or organizational objectives' (Ferris *et al.*, 2005b, p. 127). Research has addressed the direct relationship between political skill and its outcomes, including human resource decisions (Wayne *et al.*, 1997), job/team performance (Ahearn *et al.*, 2004; Ferris *et al.*, 2001), and influence effectiveness (Kolodinsky *et al.*, 2007), but there is very little on the process by which political skill functions.

Additionally, most studies of political skill have taken the supervisor's perspective, investigating supervisors' political skill and its effect on subordinate outcomes (e.g. Treadway *et al.*, 2004), subordinates' ratings of their supervisors' effectiveness (e.g. Douglas and Ammeter, 2004), and team performance (Ahearn *et al.*, 2004). However, until recently there have been very few studies examining the role of the subordinate's political skill, especially its effect on career success. Breland *et al.* (2007) tested a model linking subordinates' political skill to their career success and including the moderating effect of leader–member exchange (LMX) (Dienesch and Liden, 1986; Graen and Ulh-Bien, 1995). Yet, the conclusions of that study are difficult to interpret, since both political skill and career success were self-reported by the subordinates. The process linking political skill and career success was also not properly treated. The present study

---

Address for reprints: Jun Liu, Department of OB & HR, School of Business, Renmin University of China, Beijing 100872, China (junliu@ruc.edu.cn).

Taken from: *Journal of Management Studies*, 47:3, May 2010. © 2010 Blackwell Publishing Ltd and Society for the Advancement of Management Studies reproduced with permission.

therefore was designed to take the subordinate's perspective and examine how a subordinate employs political skill to promote his or her career development by establishing what, in China, is termed *guanxi*.

Guanxi is an indigenous Chinese construct describing an informal connection between two or more individuals or groups involving shared social experience, the exchange of favours and trust (Bian, 1997; Hwang, 1987; Luo, 1997). *Guanxi* is often translated in English as 'relationships', but the concepts differ in that relationships can be positive or negative, while *guanxi* can be only strong or weak. The concept goes beyond the friendly cooperation often found in Western business relationships because it has deep Chinese historical and cultural roots. King (1991) has described the five cardinal relationships (*wu-lun*) of Confucian ethics: between ruler and subject, father and son, husband and wife, elder brother and younger brother, and between friends. These were seen as underpinning the order and hierarchy of ancient Chinese societies, and are still considered important today. Although the structure and nature of *guanxi* have been evolving, modern Chinese societies remain very much *guanxi*-oriented (Chen and Chen, 2004). Supervisor–subordinate *guanxi* (s-s *guanxi*) in a Chinese organization is still seen as corresponding to the 'ruler–subject *guanxi*' of old, and it is the most critical interpersonal relationship in various Chinese organizational settings.

S-s *guanxi* is similar to the concept of LMX in the west, which reflects the quality of exchange between the supervisor and the subordinate. But unlike LMX, which is usually restricted to the workplace only, the cultivation of s-s *guanxi* involves more after-work activities (Law *et al.*, 2000). Chinese subordinates work through informal channels such as various after-work social activities to establish *guanxi* with their supervisors. Such activities give Chinese subordinates more scope to apply any political skills they may have. Subordinates who are more politically skilful are thus better able to cultivate *guanxi* with their supervisors through both formal (in-work) and informal (after-work) activities. Building on the prior work in this area (e.g. Breland *et al.*, 2007; Ferris *et al.*, 1989, 1996, 2005b), this study focused on the role of a subordinate's political skill in establishing s-s *guanxi* so as to benefit the career success of the subordinate. Recent research in China has shown that *guanxi* is an important variable accounting for individual outcomes in Chinese firms (Bruton and Lau, 2008; Chen and Tjosvold, 2007; Law *et al.*, 2000). This should make s-s *guanxi* a mediator in the relationship between a subordinate's political skill and his/her career development in Chinese organizations. The research framework of this study is illustrated in Figure 1.

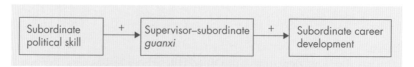

Figure 1: Conceptual model of the study.

THEORETICAL BACKGROUND AND HYPOTHESES

Supervisor–Subordinate *Guanxi* in China

Guanxi refers to the connection between parties and an extended network of interpersonal relationships which involve the exchange of favours (Bian, 1997; Hwang, 1987). It is pervasive in Chinese social groups (Chow and Ng, 2004; Fan, 2002; Tung, 1996), and its importance is deeply rooted in the mindset of Chinese people, many of whom are strongly influenced by Confucian cultural values (Zhou *et al.*, 2007). Even after the modernization of China's economy since the 1980s, *guanxi* remains intricately entwined with Chinese people's ethics, despite the introduction of advanced management philosophies and practices into Chinese businesses (Peng, 2003; Wei, 2000). Apart from formal network relationships, *guanxi* works more as a private channel by which people communicate and exchange favours based on a high level of trust, obligation, and respect (Chen and Chen, 2004).

Unlike the clear distinction between workplace and after-work relationships in the West, Chinese employees tend to mix both realms when building *guanxi* (Trompenaars, 1993). In general, s-s *guanxi* in Chinese organizations is very important due to the high power-distance typical of China's hierarchical culture. Unlike LMX, s-s *guanxi* can be accumulated through non-work activities such as dinners, gift-giving, and doing favours (Law *et al.*, 2000). It contains more group cognition and social emotional elements which go beyond the job relationship.

There have been many prior studies of the relationships between subordinates and supervisors in the workplace. They have looked at LMX and subordinate competence, time spent with the supervisor, expectations of the supervisor, and organizational support (e.g. Colella and Varma, 2001; Varma and Stroh, 2001; Wayne *et al.*, 1997). Their conclusions, however, may not apply to Chinese firms due to the different nature of the relationship between subordinates and their supervisors.

Political Skill and Supervisor–Subordinate *Guanxi*

Political skill is an interpersonal effectiveness construct that combines social understanding with the ability to adjust behaviour to the demands of the situation in ways that appear sincere, inspire trust and support, and effectively influence others (Ferris *et al.*, 2005a). Political skill has been described as '. . . social skill and networking ability people need to successfully navigate their organizations' (Douglas and Ammeter, 2004, p. 538). If one is more politically skilful, he/she tends to have better networking abilities. Since such social and networking ability are helpful in accumulating ties and building up networks, and these are essentials of *guanxi* capital, one who is more politically skilful is more likely to be able to establish good *guanxi*, including s-s *guanxi*.

First, politically skilled individuals tend to emphasize interpersonal interactions, which should be a significant factor in establishing *guanxi*. Skilled subordinates will tend to view interpersonal interactions, and interactions with their supervisors in particular, as opportunities rather than threats (Perrewé *et al.*, 2000). Biberman (1985) has shown that people with stronger political tendencies score somewhat higher in self-esteem. Politically skilled individuals also tend to be more convinced that they can control the processes and outcomes of their interactions with others (Perrewé *et al.*, 2000). Higgins (2000) found that applicants' political skill influenced recruitment interviewers' ratings and their overall evaluations. The politically skilled are at their best in interpersonal interactions (Perrewé *et al.*, 2000), especially in interactions with their supervisors.

Ferris has proposed that the concept of political skill can be described in terms of four dimensions: social astuteness, interpersonal influence, networking ability, and apparent sincerity (Ferris *et al.*, 2005a). Each dimension describes a different aspect of a person's political skills – the ability to read and understand people, the ability to act on that knowledge in influential ways, the ability to interconnect and cooperate with others, and the ability to do all these in a seemingly genuine and sincere manner. These four aspects of political skill should also apply to the process by which a subordinate establishes and maintains *guanxi* with his/her supervisor.

Politically skilled individuals are keenly attuned to diverse social situations (Ferris *et al.*, 2005b), and have an engaging personal style that facilitates their ability to influence others (Blass and Ferris, 2007). According to Ferris *et al.* (2005b), these two dimensions of political skill, i.e. social astuteness and interpersonal influence, involve adapting one's behaviour to the situation and to different targets of influence in different contexts in order to achieve one's goals. In developing s-s *guanxi*, a politically skilled subordinate is likely to rely on upward influence techniques such as reasoning, bargaining, assertiveness, appeals to higher authority, coalition building, and/or friendliness (Kipnis and Schmidt, 1982), depending on the leadership style of the supervisor. For instance, when the supervisor values competence, a politically skilled subordinate may influence him/her through reasoning; with a supervisor who values loyalty, coalition building may be emphasized by the subordinate.

Politically skilled individuals are adept at developing and using social networks (Ferris *et al.*, 2005a). People with good networking abilities have been shown to be more calculating and shrewd about the social connections needed to achieve their goals (Ferris *et al.*, 2007). Individuals who are more politically skilful find it easier to develop friendships and build stronger beneficial alliances and coalitions. Both describe quality s-s *guanxi*. Politically skilled individuals have the social astuteness to disguise any ulterior motives for their actions, and accordingly are not perceived as manipulative or coercive (Blass and Ferris, 2007). Politically skilled subordinates appear to others as having greater integrity, sincerity, and genuineness; and they are appreciated by their supervisors (Ferris *et al.*, 2005a). Political skill can also enhance trust and reputation (Ferris *et al.*, 2000), both of which are key preconditions for personal *guanxi* formation, especially *guanxi* with a supervisor. Finally, politically skilled subordinates tend to inspire confidence and believability, and are more likely to be able to influence or even control the responses of others (Ferris *et al.*, 2002). All of these traits are beneficial to establishing quality s-s *guanxi*.

In sum, politically skilled subordinates not only value interaction with their supervisors, but are also able to use such interactions to build quality s-s *guanxi*. A subordinate's political skill should thus influence s-s *guanxi* in Chinese firms.

Hypothesis 1: In the Chinese organizational context, a subordinate's political skill is positively associated with the strength of his or her supervisor–subordinate *guanxi*.

Supervisor–Subordinate *Guanxi* and the Subordinate's Career Development

That employees' interpersonal ties contribute to their career success has been amply demonstrated (Bozionelos, 2003, 2006; Chen and Tjosvold, 2006; Ng *et al.*, 2005; Wong and Slater, 2002). In a Chinese workplace, good *guanxi* with a supervisor is an important factor influencing promotion and other rewards because, just as in the West, positive affection is usually linked to favourable treatment (Law *et al.*, 2000). Indeed, this is especially true under Chinese leadership, which emphasizes people and relationships more than job tasks (Warren *et al.*, 2004).

In China, it has been noted that decision making and resource allocation are strongly influenced by the extent of *guanxi* between the person who makes the decision or performs the allocation and the individuals about whom the decisions are made or to whom the resources are allocated (Bond and Hwang, 1986). Foreign managers complain that rules and regulations in Chinese firms can often be bypassed by invoking *guanxi* (Wall, 1990). Better s-s *guanxi* can provide the subordinate more opportunities to acquire valuable resources and gain him/her distinct competitive advantages (Braendle *et al.*, 2005). In addition to decision making and resource allocation, supervisors may also use their personal and positional power to stimulate better performance from a subordinate if there is better *guanxi* between them.

Moreover, supervisors want to be assured that subordinates have the competence to complete the task when making job allocations and promotions (Bae and Lawler, 2000; Ramus and Steger, 2000). They will be unlikely to promote those whose ability they do not appreciate, even when they are actually more competent. It is to some extent through the *guanxi* developed between a subordinate and his/her supervisor that this appreciation is established. As a result, those with better *guanxi* are granted a higher level of trust, respect, and loyalty. Accordingly, the better *guanxi* a subordinate has with his/her supervisor, the more likely that any missteps will be overlooked or, indeed, even misdeeds will be forgiven (Kiong and Kee, 1998). It is argued that Chinese employers value loyalty more than competence, which makes *guanxi* highly important to individual career development (Daniels *et al.*, 1985).

Scholars have previously examined the positive influence of social capital such as *guanxi* on promotion decisions (Cannings and Montmarquette, 1991; Lin, 1999). Bian (1994, 1997) found that under the former state-controlled system of employment allocation in China, the only way individual subordinates could influence their job placement and mobility was through *guanxi*. Although this system is changing, institutional inertia ensures that the influence of s-s *guanxi* is still important in Chinese firms (Chen and Chen, 2004).

Hypothesis 2: In the Chinese organizational context, supervisor–subordinate *guanxi* is positively associated with the career advancement of the subordinate.

Combining the above two predictions suggests that s-s *guanxi* should mediate the relationship between a subordinate's political skill and his/her career development. Recall that politically skilled subordinates possess social savvy that enables them to influence the supervisor and develop quality s-s *guanxi* in a manner that casts their motives in a favourable light. Better *guanxi* provides an opportunity for politically skilled subordinates to manipulate these abilities to: (a) achieve control of resources that are beneficial for career development; (b) show the supervisor the competence and favourable personality traits necessary for career success; and thus (c) influence the supervisor's career-related decisions. No matter how politically skilful a subordinate is, without harmonious *guanxi* with his/her supervisor, he/she is less likely to be promoted. This is especially true in China, where *guanxi* can carry more weight than legal standards (Gabrenya and Hwang, 1996; Luo, 1997), and take precedence over justice (Li, 1993; Tsui and Farh, 1997).

> *Hypothesis 3:* In the Chinese organizational context, supervisor–subordinate *guanxi* mediates the relationship between political skill and career development.

METHODS
Sample and Procedure

Data for this study were collected from 16 large construction material manufacturing firms in southern China. The firms' total employment ranged from 780 to 3300. Each firm's HR professionals assisted in identifying survey respondents who had graduated from university two years previously. The purpose of this criterion was to control for education and age, as well as for the time available for learning political skills. Political skills are acquired through certain social learning processes, and new graduates experience a dramatic socialization, including political socialization in their organization's unique context (Blass and Ferris, 2007). Twenty to 38 subordinates were identified at each firm, giving 426 subordinates in total.

Each subordinate was surveyed along with two of his/her peer workers and his/her direct supervisor. One of the authors visited each firm and distributed the questionnaires to the selected respondents in person. The subordinates were asked to evaluate their own performance over the past two years, including task performance and contextual performance such as organizational citizenship behaviour (OCB). They were also asked to assess their *guanxi* with their supervisors as well as the organization's political climate. With the help of each firm's HR professionals, the subordinates' peers and supervisors were then asked to respond to another set of questionnaires. These questionnaires named the subordinates for the purpose of matching. The peers were asked to rate the subordinate's performance, his/her political skill, as well as the organization's political climate. The supervisors rated the subordinate's career development potential, and his/her own *guanxi* with the subordinate. Mutual evaluations were avoided in the design. All the respondents were told that the purpose of the study was general research on the firm's HRM practices, and each respondent received a gift to encourage completion of the questionnaire. The questionnaires were returned via either the HR professionals, who collected and mailed them, or the subordinates who mailed the completed instruments themselves.

A total of 368 usable questionnaires were received from subordinates, 755 from their peers, and 359 from their direct supervisors after three months (with two reminding mails during that period). The response rates were thus 86, 89, and 84 per cent, respectively. This yielded 343 matched sets of questionnaires (343 subordinates, 662 peers, and 343 direct supervisors). The response rate after matching was 80 per cent. The final sample was 59 per cent male with an average age of 25 (SD = 1.98), and the average number of years of working experience was 2.1 (SD = 0.45).

Measures

The major variables studied were political skill, s-s *guanxi*, and career development of the subordinate.

Political skill. The two peers of each subordinate were asked to rate his/her political skills using a translated version of 18 questions formulated by Ferris *et al.* (2005b). Previous studies have found that peer reports of political skill correlate significantly with self reports and supervisor reports (e.g. Liu, 2006; Semadar, 2004). Since the subordinates were asked to rate s-s *guanxi* (subordinates should be one of the best judges for this measure) and they also responded about the organization's climate, the peers were asked to evaluate their political skill so as to reduce common method variance problems. Sample items for the political skill assessment included: 'He/she spends a lot of time and effort networking with others'; 'He/she pays close attention to people's facial expressions'; 'It is important that people believe him/her to be sincere in what he/she says and does'; 'He/she tries to show a genuine interest in other people'; 'It is easy for him/her to develop good rapport with most people'; and 'He/she is able to communicate easily and effectively with others'.

Since most prior studies have employed a composite scale rather than analysing the four sub-dimensions of political skill (e.g. Hochwarter *et al.*, 2007; Liu *et al.*, 2007; Treadway *et al.*, 2007), the 18 items were aggregated into a single composite. The LISREL 8.30 software package (Jöreskog and Sörbom, 1993) was applied to perform a second-order confirmatory factor analysis (CFA) to assess the homogeneity of the four sub-dimensions. The 18 items were modelled to load to the corresponding sub-dimensions and all four sub-dimensions were loaded to an overall factor measuring political skill. Convergent validity was examined by investigating the item loadings and their significance. The second-order CFA model fitted the data well[1] (χ^2 = 513.31, d.f. = 131; TLI = 0.89, IFI = 0.90, CFI = 0.90, and RMSEA = 0.09), and all the factor loadings were significant. All 18 items converged to four dimensions which further converged to one construct. So these items were aggregated into a composite score for the subsequent analyses. Cronbach's alpha for this construct was 0.95, indicating acceptable construct reliability.

Supervisor–subordinate guanxi. The six items developed by Law *et al.* (2000) were employed to measure s-s *guanxi*. Both the subordinate and his/her direct supervisor were asked to make the evaluation. Sample items for the subordinate's ratings included:

'My boss invites me to meals'; 'I stand by my boss when there is any dispute'; 'I visit my boss and give him/her gifts during festivals'; and 'I take the initiative to talk to my boss, telling him/her my thoughts, worries, and needs'. The Cronbach's alpha values of the self and supervisor's ratings were 0.85 and 0.86, indicating acceptable reliability.

Career development. Two items developed by Bedeian *et al.* (1991) were used to measure the subordinate's potential for career development, rated by his/her direct supervisor. They were: 'He/she will attain his/her career goals in this organization'; and 'He/she is likely to gain growth and development in this organization'. Cronbach's alpha for this scale was 0.70, indicating acceptable reliability.

Control variables. As described previously, the survey's design has controlled for some other important demographics of the subordinates. We surveyed subordinates with two years' working experience, which yielded subjects similar in age, education, organizational tenure, and job position. However, in anticipation of 'glass ceilings' (e.g. Pang and Lau, 1998; Powell and Butterfield, 1994) and/or possible 'good soldier' effects (e.g. Organ, 1988), gender, task performance, and OCB were also controlled for so as to minimize confounding influences on estimates of the subordinates' career development potential. Gender was represented by a dummy, with male coded as '0' and female coded as '1'.

Task performance was controlled since job performance had been argued to positively relate to career advancement prospects (Igbaria and Baroudi, 1995). The five-item job performance scale was developed by Williams and Anderson (1991) and later used by Hui *et al.* (1999) in the Chinese context to capture the essential aspects of respondents' performance. Sample items included: 'Always completes the duties specified in his/her job description'; 'Fulfils all responsibilities required by his/her job'; and 'Never neglects aspects of the job that he/she is obligated to perform'. The Cronbach's alpha values for the self, peer, and supervisor ratings were 0.85, 0.91, and 0.89, respectively.

Previous studies have shown that OCB has an association with resource exchange and career growth opportunities in China (e.g. Kwan and Hui, 2008). Researchers have identified many different 'types' of OCB, but this study focused on five dimensions: altruism, courtesy, conscientiousness, sportsmanship, and civic virtue (Podsakoff *et al.*, 1990). Podsakoff's group devised a scale comprising 25 items, but most scholars have preferred a shortened form of their questionnaire with one or two questions for each dimension. In this study, since OCB was only a control variable, Podsakoff's questionnaire was abridged to six items covering the five dimensions. Each dimension was assessed by one item, except that two items assessed altruism. The Cronbach's alpha values for the self, peer, and supervisor ratings were 0.82, 0.77, and 0.84, respectively.

Finally, the organization's political climate was controlled due to its potential influence on the motivation of *guanxi* employment by the organizational members. Nine items developed by Drory (1993) were adopted to measure the political climate of the organization. The subordinates and their peers were asked to indicate how the decisions related to promotion, task assignments, allocation of personal benefits, and so forth are usually made in the organization. The Cronbach's alpha values of the subordinates' and peers' ratings were 0.89 and 0.91, respectively.

The respondents for multi-item variables and the methods for calculating the scores, together with the reliability alpha values are summarized in Table I.

		Political skill	Supervisor–subordinate guanxi	Career development	Task performance	OCB	Organization's political climate
				Variables			
Response source (reliability alpha)	Subordinate (n = 343)	–	X (0.85[a])	–	X (0.85)	X (0.82)	X (0.89)
	Supervisor (n = 343)	–	X (0.86)	X (0.70)	X (0.89)	X (0.84)	–
	Peers (n = 662)	X (0.95)	–	–	X (0.91)	X (0.77)	X (0.91)
Measure		Aggregation (0.95)	Aggregation (0.86)	Supervisor (0.70)	Aggregation (0.89)	Aggregation (0.80)	Aggregation (0.90)

Notes: [a]Numbers in parentheses are Cronbach's alpha values.

Table I: Data sources and the measurement of major variables.

Data Analysis

As shown in Table I, some individual level variables, including task performance, OCB and s-s *guanxi*, were rated by more than one source. The first step in the analysis was to combine the scores from different sources. In doing so, inter-rater reliability (R_{wg}) (James *et al.*, 1984) was evaluated for each construct. According to James (1988), agreement is achieved and the combination is proper if the R_{wg} value is above 0.70. The average R_{wg} coefficients for task performance, OCB, *guanxi*, and political climate were all between 0.72 and 0.79, providing enough justification for combining them.

At the individual level, the subordinates and their peers were asked to provide their perceptions of their organization's climate in terms of politics. However, political climate was an organization level variable. For further analyses, it was necessary to aggregate individual scores to the firm level. To justify the appropriateness of this aggregation, ICC (1), ICC (2), and R_{wg} were calculated and evaluated. The mean score on the multi-item scale was first calculated for each individual. An ANOVA then showed that the between-firm variance of the variable was larger than the within-firm variance (F (15, 986) = 19.98, p ≤ 0.01), which helped confirm within-firm agreement on the climate rating. ICC (1) and ICC (2) for the variable were 0.23 and 0.95, which were higher than the conventional cut-off values of 0.05 and 0.50 (James, 1982). The R_{wg} coefficients of all 16 firms exceeded the critical value of 0.70 suggested by James (1988). The scores provided by individuals were thus averaged to obtain scores at the firm level.

Hierarchical linear modelling (HLM) was employed to analyse the cross-level data. This method takes into account the individual-level error in estimating firm-level coefficients. It can simultaneously estimate two models: one identifying the relationships within each firm, the other representing how these within-firm relationships vary among firms (Bryk and Raudenbush, 1992). The relationships among political skill, s-s *guanxi* and career development were modelled at the individual level, while the firm-level control variable (organization's political climate) was modelled to explain inter-firm variation of s-s *guanxi* and career development.

RESULTS

Discriminant Validity

The conceptual distinction between s-s *guanxi* and political skill has already been discussed. The discriminant validity of the two variables was examined statistically before testing the hypotheses. Each subordinate's two colleague assessments of political skill were first aggregated. Each subordinate's s-s *guanxi* rating was also aggregated with that of his/her direct supervisor. This yielded matched cases for discriminant validity analysis of particular variables. LISREL 8.30 software was used to specify and compare two second-order factor models. In one model a second-order political skill factor (the same factor discussed in the 'Measures' section) and a first-order *guanxi* factor were specified. This allowed for correlating the two factors. In the other model the correlation between the two factors was constrained to 1.00. This constraint suggested a strong covariation of the two variables and no distinction between the concepts. Factorial analysis results showed that the former model fit the data well ($\chi^2 = 1442.25$, d.f. = 247; TLI = 0.90, IFI = 0.92, CFI = 0.93, and RMSEA = 0.07) while the latter did not ($\chi^2 = 1701.93$, d.f. = 248; TLI = 0.83, IFI = 0.84, CFI = 0.84, and RMSEA = 0.11). The distinction between the two models was statistically significant, suggesting the distinguishability of the two variables.

Hypothesis Testing

The means, standard deviations, and correlations among major variables are listed in Table II. Political skill, s-s *guanxi* and career development were positively correlated ($r = 0.23$, 0.18, and 0.34; $p \leq 0.01$). These three variables were also positively correlated with task performance ($r = 0.13$, 0.28, and 0.47; $p \leq 0.05$). OCB was positively correlated with both s-s *guanxi* and career development ($r = 0.38$ and 0.45; $p \leq 0.01$). Finally, there was a positive correlation between task performance and OCB ($r = 0.53$; $p \leq 0.01$).

The results of the HLM analyses are presented in Table III. Models 1 and 2 specified the effects of the control variables and then political skill on s-s *guanxi*. Models 3, 4, and 5 specified the effects of the control variables, political skill, and s-s *guanxi* on career development.

In Model 1, one individual-level control variable, OCB showed a positive relationship with s-s *guanxi* (the average slope was 0.48, $p \leq 0.01$); the organization-level control variable (political climate) showed a negative relationship with the average s-s *guanxi* within the firm (slope = −0.32, $p \leq 0.05$). In Model 2, political skill showed a positive relationship with s-s *guanxi* (the average slope was 0.15, $p \leq 0.05$). So Hypothesis 1 was supported. In Models 3–5, the outcome variable was the subordinate's career development. Model 3 showed that both task performance and OCB predict subordinate career development (average slopes of 0.45 and 0.46, $p \leq 0.01$). Model 4 suggested that political skill is also a significant predictor of career development (with an average slope of 0.11, $p \leq 0.05$), after controlling for task performance and OCB. In Model 5, where both s-s *guanxi* and political skill were included to predict the outcome variable (career development), the positive relationship between political skill and career development disappeared (with an average

	Mean	SD	1	2	3	4	5	6
1. Gender[a]	0.41	0.49						
2. Task performance	3.74	0.56	0.03					
3. OCB	3.51	0.50	0.01	0.53**				
4. Organization's political climate[b]	3.26	0.58	−0.01	−0.10*	−0.06			
5. Political skill	3.29	0.87	−0.03	0.13*	0.07	−0.08		
6. Supervisor–subordinate *guanxi*	3.62	0.72	−0.01	0.28**	0.38**	−0.21**	0.23**	
7. Career development	3.70	0.79	−0.02	0.47**	0.45**	−0.04	0.18**	0.34**

Notes: [a]Coding: 'male' = 0; 'female' =1.
[b]To calculate the correlation coefficient, the 'organization's political climate' score was disaggregated to each individual within the organization.
*Significant at the 0.05 level (2-tailed).
** Significant at the 0.01 level (2-tailed).

Table II: Means, standard deviations, and correlations

slope of 0.08, NS), while s-s *guanxi* still had a significant relationship with career development (with an average slope of 0.22, $p \leq 0.01$). According to the criteria suggested by Baron and Kenny (1986), s-s *guanxi* mediated the relationship between political skill and career development, so Hypothesis 2 and Hypothesis 3 received support. In addition, we conducted Sobel's test (1982) of mediation. Results also supported a significant mediating effect of *guanxi* in the political skill–career development linkage.

DISCUSSION

Previous studies of political skill have overlooked the role of subordinates. Despite the dominance of supervisors, subordinates also have a role in these dyadic relationships. Adopting the subordinate's perspective, this study tested and confirmed that the subordinates' political skill is positively related to the establishment of s-s *guanxi*, and that such s-s *guanxi* helps the career development of the subordinates. Since prior studies of influence behaviours and career success were based on self-reported measures (i.e. Breland *et al.*, 2007; Judge and Bretz, 1994), this study with the subordinates' career outcomes rated by the supervisor more validly confirms the role of subordinates' political skill in improving their career prospects, thus contributing to our understanding of political skill in employees' career success.

	Outcome = supervisor–subordinate guanxi		Outcome = career development		
	Model 1	Model 2	Model 3	Model 4	Model 5
Individual-level control variables					
Gender	−0.01 (0.06)	−0.01 (0.06)	−0.06 (0.06)	−0.06 (0.06)	−0.05 (0.05)
Task performance	0.07 (0.09)	0.04 (0.10)	0.45** (0.08)	0.43** (0.08)	0.42** (0.07)
OCB	0.48** (0.08)	0.48** (0.11)	0.46** (0.07)	0.46** (0.06)	0.35** (0.06)
Organization-level control variable					
Organization's political climate	−0.32* (0.13)	−0.32* (0.14)	−0.07 (0.05)	−0.07 (0.05)	−0.07 (0.05)
Predicting variable					
Political skill	–	0.15* (0.08)	–	0.11* (0.05)	0.08 (0.05)
Mediating variable					
Supervisor–subordinate guanxi	–	–	–	–	0.22** (0.06)
Individual level variance explained (%)	15.2%	18.8%	26.9%	28.2%	32.1%
Organization level variance explained (%)	28.2%	28.3%	1.5%	1.5%	1.5%
Total variance explained (%)	17.5%	20.4%	26.5%	27.7%	31.5%
Increase in individual level variance explained (%)	15.2%	3.6%	26.9%	1.3%	3.9%
Increase in organization level variance explained (%)	28.2%	0.1%	1.5%	–	–
Increase of total variance explained (%)	17.5%	2.9%	26.5%	1.2%	3.8%

Notes: *Significant at the 0.05 level (2-tailed).
**Significant at the 0.01 level (2-tailed).

Table III: HLM results for testing hypotheses

While the political perspective is helpful in predicting career success (Judge and Bretz, 1994; Pfeffer, 1992), very few published works on political influence behaviour and career success focused on the mechanism through which one's political skill affects his/her career development. Our study filled this gap and our data confirmed that subordinates could be able to apply their political skills to gain career advancement do so, at least in part, through establishing good *guanxi* with their supervisors. S-s *guanxi* is found to be a meaningful mediator in the political skill–career development linkage in the Chinese organizational context. This helps further our knowledge of *how* political skill facilitates one's career development.

The results of this study confirm that *guanxi* remains important in China (Chen and Chen, 2004). This type of social capital (Bian, 1994, 1997; Bian and Ang, 1997; Luo,

1997) could play a substantial role in various situations. In the work setting, if a subordinate wants to gain career prospect, he or she has to pay special attention to the *guanxi* establishment with significant others. For a fresh employee, his or her direct supervisor is such a significant other. Our study suggests a politically skilled employee is likely to achieve his or her career development through establishing *guanxi* with the supervisor in the organization. This, however, may minimize the importance of HRM policies to the extent that s-s *guanxi* dominates as a basis for managerial evaluation and employee promotion in Chinese firms. This finding further suggests the importance of HRM reform, especially evaluation reform, in Chinese businesses, and the necessity of educating Chinese managers to evaluate subordinates' performance and career potential as well based on more objective criteria rather than subjective bases such as personal *guanxi*.

Our results can also offer foreign investors and managers some help in doing business in China. For historical and cultural reasons, *guanxi* capital is fundamental to the smooth functioning of any Chinese society. Understanding *guanxi* and developing strategies to accumulate *guanxi* are critical to business success in China. Due to cultural differences, foreign managers find this a challenge when managing Chinese employees. For example, Chinese employees may engage in OCB primarily so as to make a better impression and foster their *guanxi* with the supervisor. It is hard for the supervisor to make a reasonable evaluation of such employees if they interpret OCB as unselfishly motivated. To change this, it is necessary to improve HRM systems, but this may involve changing the mindset of local managers. Such changes will probably happen gradually with the marketization of Chinese firms (Wei and Lau, 2008). On the other hand, *guanxi* is not entirely irrelevant in Western firms despite the difference between Western relationships and Chinese *guanxi*. Perhaps these findings may provoke more thought about the distinction between *guanxi* and Western business relationships and their formation and function in organizations.

There were, of course, some limitations inherent in this study. The first limitation related to our data collection. Our design specified collecting data from multiple sources, which helped control common source bias (Podsakoff *et al.*, 2003). Despite this merit, the cross-sectional nature of the study limits our inference of the causality. It is thus expected that future research with longitudinal data will better infer the causality. Secondly, most of our measurements were adapted and translated from the literature of the West, except that for s-s *guanxi*. Although a recent study (Luo, 2006) has found that the four dimensions of political skill are pertinent in Chinese business, more indigenous measures need to be developed in future research to better understand the unique political skills of Chinese employees as well as their career development. Thirdly, this study tested the role of political skill in building up s-s *guanxi*, but other factors that may work together with political skill to influence the quality of s-s *guanxi*, such as other personal traits of the subordinates or supervisors, need to be identified and tested empirically in the future. Finally, we sampled on the junior staff in 16 manufacturing firms only. Although this sampling strategy helps limit extraneous learning effects arising from political skill and the timing effect in *guanxi* formation, such design may limit the generalizability of the conclusions to other types of employees as well as firms. Future studies might profitably be designed with samples from other industries and employees with broader demographic characteristics.

To conclude, the findings of this study support the view that a Chinese subordinate is able to gain a career advantage by establishing better s-s *guanxi*, and this can be done through applying appropriate political skills. This should motivate subordinates to learn political skills for their career advancement. This study has contributed to our understanding of political skill by partially opening the 'black box' of the political process in Chinese firms. Our findings about s-s *guanxi* as a mediator in the relationship between political skill and career development could help elucidate the functioning of political skill, and uncover how political skill can benefit one's career prospect in the Chinese organizational context.

ACKNOWLEDGMENTS

This work was supported by grants from the Hong Kong Baptist University (FRG/06-07/II-17) to the first author and from China's National Natural Science Foundation (70802060) to the second author. We are grateful to the editor and the three anonymous reviewers for their constructive feedback and suggestions. Comments from Dr Emily Huang are also appreciated.

NOTE

[1] A first-order four-factor model, in which the four sub-dimensional factors were assumed to be inter-correlated instead of being loaded to a second-order factor, was also examined. This model also fitted the data well (χ^2 = 510.08, d.f. = 129; TLI = 0.89, IFI = 0.90, CFI = 0.90, and RMSEA = 0.09), and comparing the first-order to the second-order model indicated no significant difference in the degree of fit ($\Delta\chi^2$ = 3.23, Δd.f. = 2, NS). The results suggest that political skill can be examined at either the dimensional level or the construct level. In addition, in order to check whether common method variance constructed the convergence of items, a third factor analysis was performed. In this analysis, we used on the four-factor model as a basis to specify a fifth factor that 'represented' the independent common method bias. Besides loading to their corresponding dimensional factors, all items were also loaded to the common method factor. The five-factor model did not fit the data well (χ^2 = 760.91, d.f. = 111; TLI = 0.82, IFI = 0.85, CFI = 0.85, and RMSEA = 0.12). These analyses indicated that the common method factor did not hold, so there was no significant threat of common method biases to the validity of the results and conclusions.

REFERENCES

Ahearn, K. K., Ferris, G. R., Hochwarter, W. A., Douglas, C. and Ammeter, A. P. (2004). 'Leader political skill and team performance'. *Journal of Management*, **30**, 309–27.

Bae, J. and Lawler, J. J. (2000). 'Organizational and HRM strategies in Korea: impact on firm performance in an emerging economy'. *Academy of Management Journal*, **43**, 502–18.

Baron, R. M. and Kenny, D. A. (1986). 'The moderator-mediator variable distinction in social psychological research: conceptual, strategic, and statistical considerations'. *Journal of Personality and Social Psychology*, 51, 1173–82.

Bedeian, A. G., Kemery, E. R. and Pizzolatto, A. B. (1991). 'Career commitment and expected utility of present job as predictors of turnover intentions and turnover behavior'. *Journal of Vocational Behavior*, 39, 331–43.

Bian, Y. (1994). '*Guanxi* and the allocation of urban jobs in China'. *The China Quarterly*, 140, 971–99.

Bian, Y. (1997). 'Bringing strong ties back: indirect ties, network bridges, and job searches in China'. *American Sociological Review*, 62, 366–85.

Bian, Y. and Ang, S. (1997). '*Guanxi* networks and job mobility in China and Singapore'. *Social Forces*, 75, 981–1006.

Biberman, G. (1985). 'Personality and characteristic work attitudes of persons with high, moderate, and low political tendencies'. *Psychological Bulletin*, 88, 588–606.

Blass, F. R. and Ferris, G. R. (2007). 'Leader reputation: the role of mentoring, political skill, contextual learning, and adaptation'. *Human Resource Management*, 46, 5–19.

Bond, M. H. and Hwang, K. K. (1986). 'The social psychology of Chinese people'. In Bond, M. H. (Ed.), *The Psychology of the Chinese People*. New York: Oxford University Press, 231–66.

Bozionelos, N. (2003). 'Intra-organizational network resources: relation to career success and personality'. *International Journal of Organizational Analysis*, 11, 41–66.

Bozionelos, N. (2006). 'Intra-organizational network resources: how they relate to career success and organizational commitment'. Poster Paper presented at the 26th International Congress of Applied Psychology, Athens.

Braendle, U. C., Gasser, T. and Null, J. (2005). 'Corporate governance in China: is economic growth potential hindered by guanxi?'. *Business and Society Review*, 110, 389–405.

Breland, J. W., Treadway, D. C., Duke, A. B. and Adams, G. L. (2007). 'The interactive effect of leader-member exchange and political skill on subjective career success'. *Journal of Leadership and Organizational Studies*, 13, 1–14.

Bruton, G. D. and Lau, C-M. (2008). 'Asian management research: status today and future outlook'. *Journal of Management Studies*, 45, 636–59.

Bryk, A. S. and Raudenbush, S. W. (1992). *Hierarchical Linear Models: Applications and Data Analysis Methods*. Newbury Park, CA: Sage.

Cannings, K. and Montmarquette, C. (1991). 'Managerial momentum: a simultaneous model of the career progress of male and female managers'. *Industrial and Labor Relations Review*, 44, 212–28.

Chen, X. P. and Chen, C. C. (2004). 'On the intricacies of the Chinese *guanxi*: a process model of *guanxi* development'. *Asia Pacific Journal of Management*, 21, 305–24.

Chen, Y. F. and Tjosvold, D. (2006). 'Participative leadership by American and Chinese managers in China: the role of relationships'. *Journal of Management Studies*, 43, 1727–52.

Chen, Y. F. and Tjosvold, D. (2007). '*Guanxi* and leader member relationships between American managers and Chinese employees: open-minded dialogue as mediator'. *Asia Pacific Journal of Management*, **24**, 171–90.

Chow, I. H. S. and Ng, I. (2004). 'The characteristics of Chinese personal ties (*guanxi*): evidence from Hong Kong'. *Organization Studies*, **25**, 1075–93.

Colella, A. and Varma, A. (2001). 'The impact of subordinate disability on leader-member exchange relationships'. *Academy of Management Journal*, **44**, 304–16.

Daniels, J. D., Krug, K. and Neigh, D. (1985). 'US joint ventures in China: motivation and management of political risk'. *California Management Review*, **27**, 46–58.

Dienesch, R. M. and Liden, R. C. (1986). 'Leader-member exchange model of leadership: a critique and further development'. *Academy of Management Review*, **11**, 618–34.

Douglas, C. and Ammeter, A. P. (2004). 'An examination of leader political skill and its effect on ratings of leader effectiveness'. *Leadership Quarterly*, **15**, 537–50.

Drory, A. (1993). 'Perceived political climate and job attitudes'. *Organization Studies*, **14**, 59–71.

Fan, Y. (2002). '*Guanxi*'s consequences: personal gains at social cost'. *Journal of Business Ethics*, **38**, 371–80.

Ferris, G. R., Fedor, D. B., Chachere, J. G. and Pondy, L. R. (1989). 'Myths and politics in organizational contexts'. *Group and Organization Studies*, **14**, 83–104.

Ferris, G. R., Frink, D. D., Galang, M. C., Zhou, J., Kacmar, K. M. and Howard, J. L. (1996). 'Perceptions of organizational politics: predictors, stress-related implications, and outcomes'. *Human Relations*, **49**, 233–66.

Ferris, G. R., Perrewé, P. L., Anthony, W. P. and Gilmore, D. C. (2000). 'Political skill at work'. *Organizational Dynamics*, **28**, 25–37.

Ferris, G. R., Witt, L. A. and Hochwarter, W. A. (2001). 'Interaction of social skill and general mental ability on job performance and salary'. *Journal of Applied Psychology*, **86**, 1075–82.

Ferris, G. R., Anthony, W. P., Kolodinsky, R., Gilmore, D. C. and Harvey, M. G. (2002). 'Development of political skill'. In Wankel, C. and DeFillippi, R. (Eds), *Research in Management Education and Development, Rethinking Management Education for the 21st Century*. Greenwich, CT: Information Age Publishing, **3**, 3–25.

Ferris, G. R., Davidson, S. and Perrewé, P. (2005a). 'Developing political skill at work'. *Training*, **42**, 40–5.

Ferris, G. R., Treadway, D. A., Kolodinsky, R. W., Hochwarter, W. A., Kacmar, C. J., Douglas, C. and Frink, D. D. (2005b). 'Development and validation of the political skill inventory'. *Journal of Management*, **31**, 126–52.

Ferris, G. R., Treadway, D. C., Perrewé, P. L., Brouer, R. L., Douglas, C. and Lux, S. (2007). 'Political skill in organizations'. *Journal of Management*, **33**, 290–320.

Gabrenya, W. K. and Hwang, K. K. (1996). 'Chinese social interaction: harmony and hierarchy on the good earth'. In Bond, M. H. (Ed.), *The Handbook of Chinese Psychology*. New York: Oxford University Press, 309–21.

Graen, G. B. and Ulh-Bien, M. (1995). 'Relationship-based approach to leadership: development of leader-member exchange (LMX) theory of leadership over 25 years: applying a multi-level multi-domain perspective'. *Leadership Quarterly*, **6**, 219–47.

Higgins, C. A. (2000). *The Effect of Applicant Influence Tactics on Recruiter Perceptions of Fit*. Unpublished Doctoral Dissertation, Department of Management and Organizations, University of Iowa, Iowa City.

Hochwarter, W. A., Ferris, G. R., Gavin, M. B., Perrewé, P. L., Hall, A. T. and Frink, D. D. (2007). 'Political skill as neutralizer of felt accountability – job tension effects on job performance ratings: a longitudinal investigation'. *Organizational Behavior and Human Decision Processes*, **102**, 226–39.

Hui, C., Law, K. S. and Chen, Z. X. (1999). 'A structural equation model of the effects of negative affectivity, leader-member exchange and perceived job mobility on in-role and extra-role performance: a Chinese case'. *Organizational Behavior and Human Decision Processes*, **77**, 3–21.

Hwang, K. K. (1987). 'Face and favor: the Chinese power game'. *American Journal of Sociology*, **92**, 945–74.

Igbaria, M. and Baroudi, J. J. (1995). 'The impact of job performance evaluations on career advancement prospects: an examination of gender differences in the IS workplace'. *MIS Quarterly*, **19**, 107–23.

James, L. R. (1982). 'Aggregation bias in estimates of perceptual agreement'. *Journal of Applied Psychology*, **67**, 219–29.

James, L. R. (1988). 'Organizational climate: another look at a potentially important construct'. In Cole, S. G. and Demaree, R. G. (Eds), *Applications of Interactionist Psychology: Essays in Honor of Saul B. Sells*. Hillsdale, NJ: Lawrence Erlbaum, 253–82.

James, L. R., Demaree, R. G. and Wolf, G. (1984). 'Estimating within-group inter-rater reliability with and without response bias'. *Journal of Applied Psychology*, **69**, 85–98.

Judge, T. A. and Bretz, R. D. (1994). 'Political influence behavior and career success'. *Journal of Management*, **20**, 43–65.

Jöreskog, K. G. and Sörbom, D. (1993). *LISREL 8: Structural Equation Modeling with the SIMPLIS Command Language*. Hillsdale, NJ: Lawrence Erlbaum Associates.

King, A. Y. (1991). '*Kuan-Hsi* and network building: a sociological interpretation'. *Daedalus*, **120**, 63–84.

Kiong, T. C. and Kee, Y. P. (1998). '*Guanxi* bases, *xinyong* and Chinese business networks'. *The British Journal of Sociology*, **49**, 75–96.

Kipnis, D. and Schmidt, S. M. (1982). *Profile of Organizational Influence Strategies*. San Diego, CA: University Associates.

Kolodinsky, R. W., Treadway, D. C. and Ferris, G. R. (2007). 'Political skill and influence effectiveness: testing portions of an expanded Ferris and Judge (1991) model'. *Human Relations*, **60**, 1747–77.

Kwan, H. K. and Hui, C. (2008). *The Role of Organizational Citizenship Behavior in Resource Exchange and Career Growth Opportunities*. Paper presented at the third conference of the International Association for Chinese Management Research, Guangzhou, 19–22 June, Guangzhou, PRC.

Law, K. S., Wong, C. S., Wong, D. and Wong, L. (2000). 'Effect of supervisor–subordinate *guanxi* on supervisory decisions in China: an empirical investigation'. *International Journal of Human Resource Management*, **11**, 751–65.

Li, Q. (1993). *Dangdai Zhongguo de Shehui Fenceng yu Liudong (Social Stratification and Mobility in Contemporary China)* (in Chinese). Beijing: China Economics Publications.

Lin, N. (1999). 'Social networks and status attainment'. *Annual Review of Sociology*, **25**, 467–87.

Liu, Y. (2006). *The Antecedents and Consequences of Emotion Regulation at Work*. Unpublished Doctoral Dissertation, Florida State University.

Liu, Y., Ferris, G. R., Zinko, R., Perrewé, P. L., Weitz, B. and Xu, J. (2007). 'Dispositional antecedents and outcomes of political skill in organizations: a four-study investigation with convergence'. *Journal of Vocational Behavior*, **71**, 146–65.

Luo, S. M. (2006). *The Moderating Effect of Political Skill in the Integrative Model of Network Benefit and Social Capital* (in Chinese). Unpublished Master Thesis, National Chung Cheng University, Taiwan.

Luo, Y. (1997). '*Guanxi*: principles, philosophies and implications'. *Human Systems Management*, **16**, 43–51.

Ng, T. W. H., Eby, L. T., Sorensen, K. L. and Feldman, D. C. (2005). 'Predictors of objective and subjective career success: a meta-analysis'. *Personnel Psychology*, **25**, 367–408.

Organ, D. W. (1988). *Organizational Citizenship Behavior: The Good Soldier Syndrome*. Lexington, MA: Lexington.

Pang, M. and Lau, A. (1998). 'The Chinese in Britain: working towards success?'. *International Journal of Human Resource Management*, **9**, 862–74.

Peng, M. W. (2003). 'Institutional transitions and strategic choice'. *Academy of Management Review*, **28**, 275–96.

Perrewé, P. L., Ferris, G. R., Frink, D. D. and Anthony, W. P. (2000). 'Political skill: an antidote for workplace stressors'. *Academy of Management Executive*, **14**, 115–23.

Pfeffer, J. (1992). *Managing with Power: Politics and Influence in Organizations*. Boston, MA: Harvard Business School Press.

Podsakoff, P. M., MacKenzie, S. B., Moorman, R. and Fetter, R. (1990). 'Transformational leader behaviors and their effects on trust, satisfaction, and organizational citizenship behaviors'. *Leadership Quarterly*, **1**, 107–42.

Podsakoff, P. M., MacKenzie, S. B., Lee, J. Y. and Podsakoff, N. P. (2003). 'Common method biases in behavioral research: a critical review of the literature and recommended remedies'. *Journal of Applied Psychology*, **88**, 879–903.

Powell, G. N. and Butterfield, D. A. (1994). 'Investigating the "glass ceiling" phenomenon: an investigation of actual promotions to top management'. *Academy of Management Journal*, **37**, 68–86.

Ramus, C. A. and Steger, U. (2000). 'The roles of supervisory support behaviors and environmental policy in employee "ecoinitiatives" at leading-edge European companies'. *Academy of Management Journal*, **43**, 605–27.

Semadar, A. (2004). *Interpersonal Competencies and Managerial Performance: The Role of Emotional Intelligence, Leadership Self-efficacy, Self-monitoring, and Political Skill.* Unpublished Doctoral Dissertation, Department of Psychology, University of Melbourne, Melbourne, Australia.

Sobel, M. E. (1982). 'Asymptotic confidence intervals for indirect effects in structural equation models'. *Sociological Methodology*, **13**, 290–312.

Treadway, D. C., Hochwarter, W. A., Ferris, G. R., Kacmar, C. J., Douglas, C., Ammeter, A. P. and Buckley, M. R. (2004). 'Leader political skill and employee reactions'. *Leadership Quarterly*, **15**, 493–513.

Treadway, D. C., Ferris, G. R., Duke, A. B. and Adams, G. L. (2007). 'The moderating role of subordinate political skill on supervisors' impression of subordinate ingratiation and ratings of subordinate interpersonal facilitation'. *Journal of Applied Psychology*, **92**, 848–55.

Trompenaars, F. (1993). *Riding the Waves of Culture: Understanding Cultural Diversity in Business.* London: The Economist Books.

Tsui, A. S. and Farh, J. L. (1997). 'Where *guanxi* matters: relational demography and guanxi in the Chinese context'. *Work and Occupations*, **24**, 56–79.

Tung, R. L. (1996). 'Management in Asia: cross-cultural dimensions'. In Joynt, P. and Warner, M. (Eds), *Managing Across Cultures: Issues and Perspectives.* London: International Thomson Business Press, 233–45.

Varma, A. and Stroh, L. K. (2001). 'The impact of same-sex LMX dyads on performance evaluations'. *Human Resource Management*, **40**, 309–20.

Wall, J. A. (1990). 'Managers in the People's Republic of China'. *Academy of Management Executive*, **4**, 19–32.

Warren, D. E., Dunfee, T. W. and Li, N. (2004). 'Social exchange in China: the double-edged sword of guanxi'. *Journal of Business Ethics*, **55**, 353–70.

Wayne, S. J., Shore, L. M. and Linden, R. C. (1997). 'Perceived organizational support and leader-member exchange: a social exchange perspective'. *Academy of Management Journal*, **40**, 82–112.

Wei, L. Q. (2000). *A Three-Level Model of Guanxi in China's Transitional Economy.* Poster Paper presented at the Asia Academy of Management meeting, Singapore.

Wei, L. Q. and Lau, C. M. (2008). 'The impact of market orientation and strategic HRM on firm performance: the case of Chinese enterprises'. *Journal of International Business Studies*, **39**, 980–95.

Williams, L. J. and Anderson, S. E. (1991). 'Job satisfaction and organizational commitment as predictors of organizational citizenship and in-role task behaviors'. *Journal of Management*, **17**, 601–17.

Wong, L. Y. and Slater, J. R. (2002). 'Executive development in China: is there any in a Western sense?'. *International Journal of Human Resource Management*, **13**, 338–60.

Zhou, L. X., Wu, W. P. and Luo, X. M. (2007). 'Internationalization and the performance of born-global SMEs: the mediating role of social networks'. *Journal of International Business Studies*, 38, 673–91.

JOURNAL ARTICLE QUESTIONS

Journal Article 4

When you read this paper you may choose to do as much as you can with the detail of the numbers in the findings section and then skip straight to the discussion.

1. Summarise the findings of this study in three bullet points.
2. Do you think the findings here apply just to Chinese workers?
3. Discuss the impact on a workgroup if one or two members have strong *guanxi*, while others do not.
4. Should a manager let a subordinates' political skill influence their decisions?

PART 5

CASE STUDIES

Case Study 1

Eyes for East Africa: A communications challenge in Kenya

Fredrik Larsen sat on the edge of his desk, rather overwhelmed by the noise from the busy street market one storey below. Even though he had been prepared for heat differences between his native Oslo and Africa, it was the noise that had been the surprise – the effect of chaotic noises coming up from the street seemed to add to the heat. He reflected how smart it was to hold the main management meetings at 7 a.m. before the heat became difficult and also give everyone a proper day for work. He now had to get down to a special project that he had just been given.

Fredrik was on a sabbatical placement with a medical charity – Eyes for East Africa.[1] He had some background in advertising in Oslo, and so taking a year away from his regular job to get refreshed in a completely different culture had seemed very appealing, and it was working already. Here the beautiful lines of minimalism and cool Scandinavian design held no influence; instead bright colours and make-do seemed to dominate. But all was not bright for this charity. The recession had led to some large funders cutting donations, and at the meeting the Head of the Charity, Dr Helen Roberts, had presented the revised targets.

Blindness can be caused by many things, and in rural Africa the effect can be devastating; farmers unable to provide for their families, children unable to get to school or study. But most blindness in Africa is curable. When someone has cataracts, a straightforward operation will work in most cases, enabling previous sufferers to return to productive lives. Other conditions are also curable through medical intervention. Eyes for East Africa was set up in 1993 and Fredrik was based in the Kwale District Eye Centre (KDEC) run by Dr Roberts which, by 2010, covered the local area through a combination of patients either getting to clinics or temporary field clinics. A friend had put him onto the YouTube video (http://www.youtube.com/watch?v=IFeVafL6-u8) and he knew then that he wanted to help. Coming from the very visual world of advertising design, he was always stuck when someone said to him 'but suppose someone can't see this design, where is the message to give them?'

The charity still struggled to get across its messages to the local population though – traditionally local belief was that blindness cannot be cured. Preventative work to ensure all children get the necessary vitamins for sight development was also necessary. Hence visits to schools, midwives and tribal leaders have been prioritized to spread these new messages through people who have high legitimate power and whose advice is likely to be followed. Fredrik had mostly been 'mucking in' with the staff at the charity as an extra

---

1. Eyes for East Africa is a real charity. If you would like to raise money for them, you can contact them through their website. They do terrific work in a very poor area. Please do help.

pair of hands. But now Helen had asked him to use some of his communications management expertise to turn a problem into an opportunity.

In the period of cuts, it was essential that KDEC used all its money as effectively as possible and also held a very tight control over finances. Helen wanted him to do a task on communication between funders and the charity. Fundraising worked such that donor organizations funded specific things – it would never be money into an empty hole for the charity to fritter away. She wanted him to work out a system of giving feedback to funders about their project. She needed it to be lean and an efficient use of KDEC staff time. On the one hand she wanted to involve the funders, but on the other hand she wanted to ensure she had control over the field workers and their time. She wasn't sure how the communication might be interactive when she also wanted to keep operational control. And every moment spent for a field worker communicating with a donor meant time away from their 'real' work, so it was essential to set up something that was quick for her staff.

As Fredrik thought about this, he could see her logic. In the 'now' environment of social networking, interaction was extremely appropriate. Getting funders involved in the day-to-day life-changing events in which the charity was involved could make wonderful 'news'. But capturing the news would surely be too time-consuming? What channel should he suggest the updates use? How often might a funder want feedback? Might all funders get some feedback about the charity in general? The more he looked at the problem the more he realized this wasn't an easy assignment. In terms of internal management he could see it would need very clear guidelines for charity staff.

He looked around for an example on which to base some ideas. Every so often the charity would gather everything together and run a field clinic in a remote part of the district where they could reach patients who lived too far away to get to the charity offices. He had heard stories from a colleague who said it was amazing when so many people brought their relatives for treatment – just getting to the temporary hospital required huge organization for the patients' families, who often came along too. Then they all needed feeding, some shelter and water to get home. So this meant the host village also had to get very well organized to cope with a sudden influx of people for the clinic. Each clinic cost around £3000 ($5K) but it was incredibly effective for those at a distance (i.e. they were unlikely to ever get treatment without this local treatment) and very efficient for the charity as they could do so many operations in one session. Although it meant terrific organization on everyone's part (three months' preparation would be normal), the field clinics were very impactful.

Questions

1. Identify some of the individuals and groups who would wish Eyes for East Africa to be a high-performing organization.

2. In Chapter 1 of our book we state that effective managers need to seek two key results: *task performance* and *human resource performance*. How can the 'managers' of Eyes for East Africa achieve these twin aims?

3. How would you characterize Fredrik Larsen's psychological contract with Eyes for East Africa? What might he hope to give to, and receive from, this organization?

4. Look at the titles of Chapters 2 to 12 in our book. Before commencing your study of organizational behaviour, show how you anticipate that any *five* topics contained in these chapters might be relevant in the case of Eyes for East Africa.

Case Study 2

Sedlacek Software Spolecnost (SSS): Applying OB in practice

Karla Zelenka is General Manager of Sedlacek Software Spolecnost (SSS), a software company founded in 1983 which is based in Prague in the Czech Republic. Karla is relatively new to the company – she has only been with them for three months – and she is having a difficult day. On two separate occasions during the morning, two of her senior sales consultants, Ivona and Emil, have approached her asking for more flexible or, if possible, reduced working hours over the next few months. Karla thinks this is not a good time because, although sales have been steady and Ivona and Emil are performing well, she has been under pressure from the company's directors to win more clients. Competition in the industry is at an all-time high and SSS's market share is constantly under threat.

SSS already has one of its senior sales consultants, Jarmila, working flexible hours. Jarmila has been with the company for two years and has an excellent track record and good client base. She is a single parent with two children aged six and three and last year made an arrangement with Karla's predecessor to work more flexible hours in order to care for her children. While she still completes a full-time working week, Jarmila is able to start later in the morning after taking the children to school, then makes up her time by taking short lunch breaks and working occasional Saturdays.

SSS has always taken pride in being compassionate towards its employees and has adopted the philosophy that all employees should lead a balanced life between work and leisure. Families of employees are encouraged to take part in social activities, and management at SSS has been known to help out those employees who have suffered financial stress or experienced other personal setbacks.

Karla came to SSS after spending three years in the USA working for Hardware-Software, a Chicago-based company that had a very different organizational culture to SSS. The software industry in the USA is known to be tough and Hardware-Software would expect its employees to work long hours, take work home and be in the office at least one day during the weekend. Trying to take holidays (holiday entitlement in the US is typically less than in European countries) was always an issue, especially as staff were not allowed to accumulate leave entitlement from one year to the next. As a result, staff turnover was quite high and three years at Hardware-Software could be considered a long-term appointment. Karla began work in Chicago as junior sales support and after six months was promoted to senior consultant. A year later she became National Sales Manager. Karla had no problem with the long hours but always planned to move back to Prague, her home city, which she had loved since she was a little girl. It was a difficult decision to make at the time but when the opportunity to be general manager of a software company came up in Prague, how could she refuse? Hardware-Software was Karla's second job after she left university – she had been trained in a Danish software design company after obtaining her bachelors and masters degrees. Other than her jobs in Denmark and the US, her work experience had been limited to short-term casual jobs as a restaurant waitress in Prague during her years of study. Also, Karla was a later entry into university as she chose to travel overseas for 12 months after passing her school leaving certificate.

For Karla, the transition from Hardware-Software to the SSS organization has not been easy, and to some extent her difficulties have been exacerbated by moving across national boundaries. While she likes to consider herself a relatively easygoing, amiable type of person socially, her attitude to work is one of strict focus; achieving corporate goals is always her first priority. Karla has been single minded since adolescence, and even while studying at university she was very focused and devoted many long hours working to gain her degrees. After completing her undergraduate studies, Karla stayed on to undertake a masters degree; all the while keeping career prospects in longer-term view. Karla's single-minded attitude also resulted in her very quick progress up the corporate ladder at Hardware-Software. For a 28-year-old she has certainly achieved a lot and is in a very senior position compared to others of similar age. Possibly because Karla lives alone and has only a small circle of friends and relatives in Prague, she spends much of her supposed leisure time at the office. She does, however, intend joining a social club but hasn't decided exactly what that will be. Whatever interests she had when she was younger have become completely overtaken by her professional life. When Karla studied at university, she was introduced to the work of Geert Hofstede who categorized cultural differences between nations. When reading his work, Karla was attracted to the values of an individualist type of society and when in The United States, strongly identified with work practices there: in some curious way she felt that deep down she was 'more American than the Americans'.

Karla's appointment at SSS has not been particularly well received by some of its senior staff. Part of that is due to the reputation of Hardware-Software (which is internationally renowned), and the fact that Karla worked there for three years clearly suggests to some people that she is a workaholic with very few other priorities in her life. This perception was formed by the senior staff soon after Karla's arrival at SSS – very much a first impression – and, as she has only been with the company for a short time, there really has not been much opportunity for her to try to change that perception. As we know from our discussion of perception in Chapter 2, first impressions can, in any case, be difficult to change. Karla has been very preoccupied trying to orientate herself into her work role and hierarchical position as general manager and has not really spent much time developing the social aspect of the office environment.

Prior to Karla's appointment, Ivona had applied for the job as general manager with total support from Emil and Jarmila, as well as other members of staff at SSS. In addition to her role as senior sales consultant, Ivona is also supervisor of the entire sales department, which has a total of 14 employees. Ivona has been with SSS for nine years and is an excellent mentor for Emil and Jarmila. Ivona initiated a staff development programme several years ago and has put many hours of her own time into counselling some of the younger members of the sales team. She is fully aware of the need to develop staff with a view to retaining them in the company, as turnover in the software industry is very high due to the competitive nature of the industry.

When Ivona failed to get the position as general manager and Karla arrived from another country, morale among the senior sales consultants dropped and Ivona in particular began to question her role at SSS, using Emil and Jarmila as 'sounding blocks' on many occasions. This, of course, did not help the overall acceptance of Karla's appointment and tended to add to the negativity which was already developing. Now, three months later, the hitherto friendly atmosphere at SSS is not what it used to be, even among the senior sales consultants who are seriously considering other options as their loyalty and motivation diminish and priorities are reshuffled.

Since Karla's appointment, and with no other option for promotion in sight, Ivona now wants to work flexible hours as she feels she is suffering burnout and would like to prioritize her domestic life and health as she now plans to have children. She has consulted her doctor who told her that she works too many hours and should cut back. Ivona's boyfriend totally supports this and would really prefer that she gave up work altogether.

Emil has requested a more flexible, reduced workload so he can train for the Czech squash selection game in three months' time, as he wants to make the national team. He is a single man who is ranked in the top ten amateur squash players in the Czech Republic. Emil has been with the company for five years and has an excellent track record and good client base.

Both Emil and Ivona know of Jarmila's flexible working arrangement and, although they appreciate SSS's philosophy towards families, they think this should apply equally to all employees wanting to lead a balanced lifestyle, not just those with children.

Karla has told both Emil and Ivona that she will meet with them tomorrow to discuss their situations. Personally, Karla doesn't think either of them should be given more flexible hours, especially after her time spent with Hardware-Software and the sacrifices she has made in her career. Karla also doesn't think Jarmila should have been given preference merely because she had children, but that is something she inherited when she took over as general manager of SSS. Karla is concerned about the pressures placed on staffing issues by the company's directors. All staff issues have to be approved by them and, once they find out that their entire senior sales team is now seeking flexible working hours, she knows it will be difficult for them to support, especially as the pressure is on to increase the client base. However, Karla is also vaguely aware that, although there are only three senior sales consultants at SSS, there is a very good pool of second-tier salespeople who are currently being developed by Ivona and who could quite possibly be promoted should a vacancy suddenly become available. She makes a mental note to check this out before meeting with Emil and Ivona tomorrow, just in case things get a little heated and she has to offer an ultimatum. Hopefully, it won't come to that. She also realizes that she needs to consult with the company's Human Resource Manager to check out the legal position; as far as she knows, while the right to maternity leave is recognized within national and EU legislation, flexible work arrangements more generally are still within the discretion of individual companies in the Czech Republic.

Karla leaves the office that night knowing she will not sleep well. Tomorrow the situation has to be resolved. Fortunately, the meeting times with Emil and Ivona have yet to be scheduled, so Karla decides to meet with them both, separately, in the afternoon so she can spend the entire morning reviewing the staff situation at SSS and developing a sound strategy.

Questions

1. List and briefly analyse each issue that Karla faces. Consider those things that are directly related to Karla as a manager, linking each of the issues to organizational behaviour theories and concepts.

2. Assuming Karla has no confidante at SSS, if you were a close friend of hers and that evening she called you and asked for advice on how to approach the meetings with Emil and Ivona, what would you say? As a close friend it is expected that you will take into consideration Karla's personal and professional attributes when preparing your answer.

3. Assume that Karla has had harmonious discussions with both Emil and Ivona and they have agreed to consider a redesign of their existing roles to accommodate a flexible work arrangement. Bearing in mind that the outcome of this must be presented, by Karla, to SSS directors, how would you structure the redesign in order to benefit both SSS's corporate goals and the satisfaction of the employees concerned? Remember to consider all employees at SSS, not just Emil and Ivona.

4. Refer to Hofstede's model of cultural difference as applied to the USA and Czech Republic and consider the extent to which it can aid our understanding of the issues and events depicted in this case study.

This case is fictional. It has been adapted from 'Solutions Software Company' written by Val Morrison and featured in Wood, J., Zeffane, R., Fromholtz, M. and Fitzgerald, J. (2006), *Organizational Behaviour: Core Concepts and Applications*, John Wiley & Sons: Milton, Qld.

Case Study 3

Hermitage University: Perceiving opportunities and threats

Hermitage University is a large higher education establishment situated in the South of England. It is the thirteenth oldest institute of higher education in the world. It has, in the period since 1950, been recognized as amongst the top 20 universities in the United Kingdom, although its international profile is patchy. It is well-known in India, Hong Kong and the West Indies, but less so in mainland Europe and North America.

It is a very traditional university and relies largely on its academic reputation and social networking opportunities to attract students, staff and research funding. Its graduates have, for centuries, been successful in forging successful careers, with a particular concentration in the UK public sector and in administrative posts in British Commonwealth countries.

It benefits from substantial endowments from benefactors and, despite the funding and related issues addressed later in this case, is considered to be financially secure in the foreseeable future. Again, despite the issues addressed later in the case, it benefits from a formidable international reputation; albeit one which is clustered in certain areas of the world.

As with all universities, it prides itself on the range of academic subjects it embraces. Amongst these are Classics, Arts, Politics, Philosophy and Economics (PPE), Law and Pure Science. Although its reputation is formidable across the wide range of academic subjects, it has, for centuries, been seen as one of the market leaders in Science and Law. Its reputation in other areas, although impressive, is less high profile than other traditional universities in the United Kingdom. However, this secondary status is perceived only at the very highest levels of achievement and its reputation in these areas is still world class.

Although the university has a substantial administrative support team, its policies and procedures on teaching, learning and student assessment are limited. Furthermore, although it has never found a problem with student recruitment, again its policies and procedures in this area are somewhat under-developed. Its research record and success in attracting research funding is impressive, but once more its actual policies and procedures in terms of sustaining such funding are limited. University academic staff pride themselves on their world class status and are somewhat resistant to complying with formal procedures, considering administrative functions to be there to support their existence. In some respects the university can accurately be described as exhibiting characteristics of a person culture – see Chapter 7 for a fuller description. Professors and senior lecturers, in particular, benefit from a substantial degree of academic independence, which traditionally has been extended into freedom from both managerial and administrative interference.

Over the last few years the world of academia has experienced major change. Some specific initiatives and developments are set out below:

1. Universities are required to operate in a much more public and transparent environment. Government audits of academic procedures at Hermitage University have suggested a number of deficiencies:
   - Academic assessments (although favourably commented upon in the main) have been subject to occasional criticism – assessments have not been subject to peer appraisal (scrutiny by other lecturers), there is a lack of an audit trail in marking, criticisms have been made of the standards of assessments and marking and there is no second marking of any assessments.
   - Quality of teaching – this has been judged to be at best adequate and occasionally poor. The main criticisms have been lack of documentation in syllabus construction, lack of coherent syllabus development, lack of lesson planning and no peer observation of teaching. Students have complained of difficulties in making appointments with tutors in the Law and Philosophy departments.
   - Lack of a coherent strategy on student recruitment – criticisms have been made, particularly of failure to recruit from certain sections of the community, manifested in under-representation of some socio-economic groups, together with imbalances in terms of ethnic groupings, gender and age profiles.
   - Limited policies on providing access for the chronically sick and disabled.
   - Inadequate liaison with the world of employment.
   - Little exposure of students to outside speakers from other business sectors.
   - Poor employment advisory services for undergraduate students.
2. Worldwide competition for students.
   - Recruitment is still healthy across all academic disciplines but there is some (limited) evidence that students who previously entered Classics, Arts or PPE disciplines are beginning to seek places elsewhere on more work-related courses.
   - There has been a slight but growing difficulty in recruiting the highest calibre teaching staff in Classics, Arts and PPE. This tendency was first noted in the field of Applied Science and in 1999 the university took action in this area by establishing 'arms' length' companies where tutoring staff could supplement their income by providing consultancy services to client companies. These, as will be attested later in the case, have been very successful.
   - There has been a reduction in applications for some study areas, for example Pure Science, but this has been matched by a corresponding increase in others such as Applied Science.
3. The advent of a new student fee regime and, in particular, the introduction of so-called 'top-up' fees in 2006.
   - Overall this has not had an adverse impact on student recruitment but there is some evidence that potential students, other than those in Law and Applied Science, are beginning to look for more job-related courses.

- The reaction of the university is that top-up fees, predicted to rise after 2009, with some suggestion that a free market might be introduced, will place them in an even more favourable position in the student recruitment market. The consensus internally is that students will be more than willing to pay high fees to enter this prestigious institution. However, some academic commentators have suggested that such top-up fees will result in a significant leakage of potential UK students to overseas institutions. A prestigious East Coast American institution has recently established a student recruitment office in London.

- There is some suggestion that students will increasingly regard themselves as customers of higher education, resulting in an increasing concern with 'value for money'. This could be manifested in a number of ways. For example, the university has already received unwanted and embarrassing publicity when mobile phone camera footage of Professor Alexander Crustie apparently falling asleep during a seminar was shown on the YouTube website and subsequently featured in a British tabloid newspaper. Overall, it is felt that the consequences of an increasing customer orientation amongst students is far-reaching, unpredictable and will need managing.

4. Universities being obliged to supplement their Government-supported income with self-generated funds.

   - The general internal reaction to this change is that Hermitage University will find no difficulty in attracting such funds. Endowments are as healthy as ever, research funding will be secure in an academically prestigious institution, with private sector organizations 'queuing up' to sponsor university activity. Such sponsorship has been evidenced to a massive extent in the Applied Science area.

   - As has been mentioned previously, the Applied Science part of the university has been complemented with university-owned businesses – undertaking research and consultancy on behalf of private organizations under the knowledge transfer banner. This type of activity has involved Hermitage University entering into partnership with private organizations in developing new applications for scientific knowledge. University-owned establishments in this area have attracted significant levels of sponsorship from private sector organizations. These ventures have secured substantial and growing funds for the university. There has been disagreement regarding the distribution of surplus funds from these activities. Initially these funds were used to support university-wide initiatives but of late these funds have been used to support Applied Science activities exclusively. These developments have reversed the leakage of high-quality staff to overseas institutions. In 2005, however, there was extensive tabloid newspaper coverage of financial impropriety in one of the high-profile Applied Science Companies operated by the university.

In August 2007 Hermitage University created a new staff post of Strategic Developments Director (SDD), who would report directly to the Vice-Chancellor. The first SDD is Dr Christina Raglan, appointed in January 2008. Christina has a PhD in Earth Science, awarded by the University of Edinburgh in the field of Environmental Sustainability. Prior to her arrival at Hermitage University, she worked at Greenspace, a major environmental pressure group, well-known throughout Europe, rising to the post of Director of Communications and Fundraising. At the time of her appointment at Hermitage she was 29 years old. In March 2008 she was asked to set up a meeting of the university's Senate; a decision-making body comprising professors from across the university's academic schools. She was asked to make a Powerpoint presentation to the Senate outlining the challenges faced by the university and the opportunities thrown up by the new environment in which it was forced to operate.

Questions

1. With reference to concepts set out in Chapter 2, advise Christina on how she is likely to be perceived by members of the university Senate as she commences her presentation.
2. Suggest three ways in which she could create positive perceptions of herself personally and her new role during the upcoming presentation.

_____

Source: Case by Tony Dawson, adapted by Ray French. Reproduce by permission of Tony Dawson.

Case Study 4

It isn't fair!

Elina Karpinnen was in her final year at Niemi University, situated near Helsinki in Finland. As she approached the end of her course, she actively engaged in seeking work after graduation. Elina was in the top 1% of her class, active in numerous extracurricular activities (including a help group for visually impaired children across Finland) and highly respected by her professors. After going through several selection procedures, Elina was offered positions with every company to which she applied for employment. After much thought, she decided to take the offer from Casper Electric, a company formed in 1991, specializing in electronic component s. She felt that the salary was superb (40 000 Euros); there were also excellent benefits, plus she was told that there were good prospects for promotion.

Elina started work a few weeks after graduation and learned her job assignments and responsibilities thoroughly and quickly. Elina was asked on many occasions to work late because report deadlines were often moved forward. Without hesitation she said 'Of course!' even though she would receive no overtime within the terms of her contract.

Frequently she took work home with her and used her personal laptop to do further analyses. At other times she would come into the office on weekends to monitor the progress of her projects or just to catch up on the ever-growing mountain of correspondence.

On one occasion her manager asked her to take on a difficult assignment. It seemed that the company's Slovakian manufacturing facility was having production problems. The quality of one of the products was highly questionable, and the reports on the matter were confusing. Elina was asked to be part of a team sent to investigate the quality issues and to report back on problems. The team stayed in rather basic accommodation for the entire three weeks they were there. This was because of the plant's location in a remote part of the country. Within the three-week period the team had located the source of the quality problem, corrected it and altered the reporting documents and processes. The head of the team, a quality engineer, wrote a note to Elina's manager Matti stating the following:

> 'Just wanted to inform you of the superb job Elina Karpinnen did with us in Slovakia. Her suggestions and insights into the reporting system were invaluable. Without her help we would have been down there for another three weeks, and I was getting tired of the food! Thanks for sending her.'

Casper Electric, like most companies, has a performance review system; in this case conducted annually. Once Elina had been with the company for a little over one year, it was therefore time for her review. Elina entered her manager's office feeling a little nervous, since this was her first review ever and she didn't know what to expect. After closing the door and exchanging the usual pleasantries, her manager, Matti got straight to the point.

Matti: Well, Elina, as I told you last week this meeting would be for your annual review. As you are aware, your performance and compensation are tied together. Since the philosophy of the company is to reward those who perform, we take these reviews very sincerely. I have spent a great deal of time thinking about your performance over the past year, but before I begin I would like to know your impressions of the company, your assignments and me as a manager.

Elina: Honestly, Matti, I have no complaints. The company and my job are everything I was led to believe. I enjoy working here. My colleagues are all very helpful. I like the team atmosphere, and my job is very challenging. I really feel appreciated and that I'm making a contribution. You have been very helpful and patient with me. You got me involved right from the start and listened to my opinions. You taught me a lot and I'm very grateful. All in all I'm happy being here.

Matti: Great. Elina I was hoping that's the way you felt because from my vantage point, most of the people you worked with feel the same. But before I give you the qualitative side of the review, allow me to go through the quantitative appraisal first. As you know, the rankings go from 1 (lowest) to 5 (highest). Let's go down each category and I'll explain my reasoning for each.

Matti starts with category one (Quantity of Work) and ends with category ten (Teamwork). In each of the categories, he either gives Elina a 5 or a 4. Indeed, only two categories have a 4 and Matti explains these are normal areas for improvement for most new employees.

Matti: As you can see, Elina, I've been very happy with your performance. You have received the highest rating I have ever given any of my subordinates. Your attitude, desire and help are truly appreciated. The other people on the Slovakian team gave you glowing reports, and speaking with the plant manager, he felt that you helped him understand the reporting system better than anyone else. Since your performance has been stellar, I'm delighted to give you a 10% increase effective immediately!

Elina (mouth agape, and eyes wide): Matti, frankly I'm totally amazed! I don't know what to say, but just…well thank you very much. I really hope I can keep doing a great job for you again next year. Thanks once again.

After exchanging some parting remarks and some more thank-yous, Elina left Matti's office with a smile that stretched from ear to ear. She was floating on air! Not only did she feel the performance review process was itself uplifting, but her review was outstanding and so was her raise. She knew from other employees that the company was only giving out a 5% average increase. She had figured that if she got that, or perhaps six or seven, she would be happy. But to get 10%…wow, just imagine !!

Ahti: Hi, Elina! Lost in thought? My, you look great. Looks like you got some great news. What's up?

Ahti Seppa was a recent recruit; also working for Matti. He had graduated from Niemi University too, but a year after Elina. Ahti had performed well at Niemi, graduating in the top 8% of his class. He had qualified letters of recommendation from his professors and was well known as the captain of the university football team, which won the Finnish university trophy for three consecutive years.

Elina: Oh, hi Ahti! Sorry, but I was just thinking about this company and the opportunities here.

Ahti: Yeah it's promising isn't it?

Elina: Ahti, I'm just back from my performance review and let me tell you, the process isn't that bad. As a matter of fact I found it quite rewarding, if you get my drift. I got a wonderful review, and can't wait till next year's. Casper is a great company!

Ahti: You can say that again! I couldn't believe them hiring me right out of college at such a good salary. Between you and me, Elina, they started me at 45 000 Euros. Imagine that? Jeez, was I impressed? I just couldn't believe that they would…Where are you going, Elina? Elina? What's that you say, 'It isn't fair'? What are you talking about? Elina, Elina…

Source: Adapted by Ray French from a case study developed by Barry R. Armandi, SUNY-Old West-bury, in Schermerhorn, J. R., Hunt, J. G. and Osborn, R. N. (2010), *Organizational Behaviour,* 11th edition, John Wiley & Sons, Inc.: Hoboken, NJ.

Questions

1. To what extent do you think Adams's Equity Theory of motivation provides a good explanation of the events in this case? Give reasons for your conclusions.
2. In Adams's model what course of action could Elina now take?
3. Do you find Adams's Equity Theory to be a useful framework when applied to your own life, both inside and outside of work? Provide examples to illustrate your answer.

Case Study 5

The forgotten group member

The Organizational Behaviour course for the semester appeared to promise students an opportunity not just to learn, but also to apply some of the theories and principles contained in textbooks and discussed in class. Tim Brinkerhoff was a devoted, hard-working student who had performed well across all subjects in his Business Studies degree so far. Although the skills and knowledge he had acquired through his courses were important to him, he was also very concerned about his examination and coursework marks. He felt that the marks showing on his transcript would be key to giving him a competitive edge when looking for a job, and as a second-year student he realized that he'd soon be doing just that. Tim did not come from a wealthy or professional background. He would find it difficult financially to go into unpaid training or an internship after graduation and could not rely on family contacts. He foresaw that any future career achievements would be the result of his efforts alone.

Sunday afternoon. Two o'clock. Tim was working on an accounting assignment but didn't seem to be able to concentrate. His courses were working out very well this semester, with the exception of OB. A high proportion of the overall mark in that subject was to be based on the quality of group work. This had both positive and negative aspects. He thought back over the events of the past five weeks. The module leader, Dr Callum Blackhall, had divided the class into groups of five people and had given them a major group assignment worth 60% of the final grade. The task was to analyse a seven-page case study and to come up with a written analysis. In addition, Dr Blackhall had asked the groups to present the case in class, with the idea that the rest of the students in the class would regard themselves as members of the human resources (HR) department in the case study organization. As such, they would listen critically to how the team of presenting students dealt with the problem at hand.

Tim was elected 'Team Coordinator' at the first group meeting. The other members of the group were Amanda, Jane, Steve and Nico. Amanda was quiet and never volunteered suggestions; but when asked directly, she would come up with workable ideas. Nico was the clown. Tim remembered quite early on suggesting that the group should get together weekly before class to discuss progress; Nico had balked, saying 'No way man!! This is a

9:00 class, and I barely make it on time anyway! Besides, I'll miss my *Jeremy Kyle show*[1] on television!' The group couldn't help but laugh at his indignation. Steve was the business-like individual, always wanting to ensure that group meetings were guided by an agenda and noting the tangible results achieved or not achieved at the end of every meeting. Jane was a nurturing person who would always do more for the group than was expected of her. When they ran into problems she would invariably suggest a break for coffee or other recreation. Tim saw himself as meticulous and organized and a person who tried to give his best in whatever he did.

It was now week five of the semester, and Tim was deep in thought about the OB assignment. He had called everyone to arrange a meeting for a time that would suit them all, but he seemed to be running into a 'roadblock'. Nico couldn't make it, saying that he was working that night in the club where he had a part-time job as barman. In fact, he seemed to miss most meetings and would occasionally send in brief notes to Tim, which he was supposed to present on Nico's behalf at group meetings. Tim wondered how to deal with this. He also remembered an incident last week. Just before the class started, Amanda, Jane, Steve and he were joking with one another before class. They were laughing and enjoying themselves before Dr Blackhall came in. No one noticed that Nico had slipped in very quietly and had unobtrusively taken his seat, seemingly wishing to avoid his colleagues.

Tim also recalled the cafeteria incident. Two weeks ago, he had gone to the cafeteria to grab something to eat, as he had rushed to his accounting class and had skipped breakfast. When he got a club sandwich and headed to the tables, he saw his OB group and joined them. The discussion was light and enjoyable as it always was when they met informally. Nico had come in. He approached their table. 'You guys didn't say you were having a group meeting,' he blurted. Tim was taken aback.

'We just happened to run into each other. Why not join us?'

Nico had looked at them, with a noncommittal glance. 'Yeah…right,' he muttered, and walked away.

Callum Blackhall had frequently told all students that if there were problems in their coursework group, the members should make an effort to deal with them first internally. If the problems could not be resolved in that way, he had said that they should come to him as the responsible lecturer. Tim pondered on this as a solution to some concerns that were increasingly nagging at him. Nico now seemed quite disconnected, despite the apparent camaraderie of the first meeting.

---

1. The *Jeremy Kyle show* is a daytime programme airing on the UK's ITV network. It features real people discussing issues which are problematic to them, including sexual infidelity, family conflicts and alcohol abuse.

Source: Adapted by Ray French from a case study developed by Franklin Ramsoomair, Wilfred Laurier University. Included in Schermerhorn, J. R., Hunt, J. G. and Osborn, R. N. (2010), *Organizational Behavior,* 11th edition, John Wiley & Sons, Inc.: Hoboken, NJ.

An hour had passed, bringing the time to 3 p.m., and Tim found himself biting the tip of his pencil. The written case analysis was due next week. All the others had done their designated sections, but Nico had just handed in some rough handwritten notes. He had called Tim the week before, telling him that in addition to his course and his job, he was having serious arguments with Macarena, his girlfriend. Macarena was known to be an exuberant but erratic person and Tim empathized with him. Yet, this was a group project! Besides, the final mark would be peer evaluated. This meant that whatever mark Blackhall gave them could be lowered or raised, depending on the group's opinion about the value of the contribution of each member. He was definitely worried. He knew that Nico had creative ideas that would help to raise the overall mark. He was also concerned for him and the multiple pressures Nico seemed to be facing. As he listened to the music in the background, he wondered what he should do next.

Questions

1. How could an understanding of the stages of group development assist Tim in leadership situations such as this one?
2. Locate Tim, Amanda, Jane and Nico within Belbin's model of team roles.
3. Is Tim an effective group leader in this case? Why or why not?

Case Study 6

Novo Nordisk and Southwest Airlines

In the early years of the 21st century, it seemed no matter where we looked there was clear and shocking evidence of the erosion of business ethics and some even more basic concepts of right and wrong. Hitherto respected corporations and individuals, who had spent many years building their reputations for integrity, seemingly lost these overnight – perhaps forever. But some companies hold themselves to a higher set of standards and recognize that their business practices have lasting and worldwide effects. Let's look at one example from the United States – Southwest Airlines – and another – Novo Nordisk – from northern Europe.

Southwest Airlines has grown from a regional Texan carrier into one of the most profitable and well-known airlines in American history. Its success has often been attributed to its core values, developed by Herb Kelleher, co-founder and former CEO, and embraced daily by the company's 35 000 employees: namely humour, altruism and 'LUV' (the company's NYSE stock tickersymbol).[1]

At Southwest Airlines they believe that low costs are crucial; change is inevitable; innovation is necessary; and leadership is essential – particularly during troubling economic times. 'Our competitors take drastic/short-sighted measures to compete with us on the price level...they make draconian reductions in their employees' salaries, wages, benefits and pensions. In doing so, they ultimately sacrifice their most important assets – their employees and their employees' goodwill.'[2]

Southwest applies this philosophy in an organizational culture that respects employees and their ideas. As executive vice president, Colleen Barrett started a 'culture committee' made up of employees from different functional areas and levels. The committee meets quarterly to 'brainstorm' ideas for maintaining Southwest's corporate spirit and image. All managers, officers and directors are expected to 'get out in the field,' meeting and talking with employees to understand their jobs. Employees are encouraged to use their creativity and sense of humour to make their jobs – and the customers' experiences – more enjoyable. Gate agents are given books of games to play with passengers waiting for delayed flights. Flight agents might imitate Elvis or Mr. Rogers when making announcements.[3]

To encourage employees to treat one another as well as they treat their customers, departments examine linkages within Southwest to see what their 'internal customers' need. The provisioning department, for example, whose responsibility is to provide the snacks and drinks for each flight, selects a flight attendant as 'customer of the month.' The provisioning department's own board of directors makes the selection decision. Other departments have sent pizza and ice cream to their internal customers. Employees write letters commending the work of other employees or departments that are valued as much as letters from external customers. When problems occur between departments, employees work out solutions in supervised meetings.

Employees exhibit the same attitude of altruism and 'luv' (also Southwest's term for its relationship with its customers) toward other groups as well. A significant portion of Southwest employees volunteer at Ronald McDonald Houses throughout Southwest's service territory.[4] When the company purchased a small regional airline, employees sent cards and company T-shirts to their new colleagues to welcome them into the Southwest family.

Southwest Airlines is a low-cost operator. But, according to Harvard University professor John Kotter, setting the standard for low costs in the airline industry does not mean Southwest is *cheap*. 'Cheap is trying to get your prices down by nibbling costs off everything…[Firms such as Southwest Airlines] are thinking 'efficient,' which is very different. They recognize that you don't necessarily have to take a few pennies off of everything. Sometimes you might even spend more.'[5] By using only one type of plane in its fleet, Southwest saves on pilot training and aircraft maintenance costs.[6] The *cheap* paradigm would favour using second-hand planes, but Southwest's choice for high productivity over lower capital expenditure has given it the youngest fleet of aircraft in the industry.

By using each plane an average of 13 hours daily, Southwest is also able to make more trips with fewer planes than any other airline. It has won the monthly 'Triple Crown' distinction – Best On-Time Record, Best Baggage Handling and Fewest Customer Complaints – more than 30 times. The company has created employee satisfaction by focusing on its internal 'customers,' who are then positively motivated to show the same degree of concern for external customers.

When Herb Kelleher relinquished his role as Southwest's CEO, investors worried because so much of Southwest's success came from Kelleher's unique management and leadership. But events showed that Kelleher's successor, Colleen Barrett, was well prepared to handle the challenges of maintaining Southwest's culture and success.

Now, Barrett too has retired and 22-year employee of the firm Gary Kelly has taken the helm. Kelly is navigating Southwest Airlines through one of the industry's most turbulent periods by expanding into new markets, adding flights to heavily trafficked domestic airports and seeking cross-border alliances with foreign carriers. The airline remains steadfast against charging customers for checking suitcases and using pillows, as rivals have done. Some analysts question if management has made the right call by not charging for these services, which are generating hundreds of millions of dollars for rivals.[7] Even without the extra revenue Southwest Airlines continues to post profits; perhaps flyers continue to choose Southwest over the competition because they're not being charged for everything from pillows to packs of peanuts. In fact, Southwest recently earned the top spot in *Fortune* magazine's Most Admired Airline list and is the only airline to make the magazine's top 20 list in its annual survey assessing corporate reputations.[8]

Headquartered in Denmark, Novo Nordisk is another company whose concerns run beyond the financial bottom line. Novo Nordisk not only manufactures and markets pharmaceutical products and services; it also realizes that *responsible business is good business*.

One of the world's leading producers of insulin, Novo Nordisk also makes insulin analogues, injection devices and diabetes education materials. Its products include analogues Levemir and NovoRapid and the revolutionary FlexPen, a pre-filled insulin injection tool. In addition to its diabetes portfolio, the firm has products in the areas of haemostasis management (blood clotting), human growth hormone and hormone replacement therapy.[9]

Today, diabetes is recognized as a pandemic. Novo Nordisk rallies the attention of policy makers and influencers to improve the quality of life for those with diabetes, to find a cure for Type 1 diabetes and to prevent the onset of Type 2 diabetes. The company has framed a strategy for inclusive access to diabetes care. The ambition to ultimately defeat diabetes is at the core of Novo Nordisk's vision. Much like one finds at Southwest, this vision puts the company's objectives in perspective and inspires employees in their work. It is a beacon that keeps everyone's focus on creating long-term shareholder value and leveraging the company's unique qualities to gain competitive advantage.

In making decisions and managing its business, Novo Nordisk uses its Triple Bottom Line business principle to balance three considerations: Is it economically viable? Is it socially responsible? And is it environmentally sound? This ensures that decision-making balances financial growth with corporate responsibility, short-term gains with long-term profitability and shareholder return with other stakeholder interests. The Triple Bottom Line is built into the corporate governance structures, management tools, individual performance assessments and rewards.

Novo Nordisk strives to manage its business in a way that ensures corporate profitability and growth, while it seeks to leave a positive economic footprint in the community. The company's environmentally sound decisions address Novo Nordisk's impact on the world as well as the bioethical implications of its activities. As part of Novo Nordisk's ambitious nonfinancial targets, they aim to achieve a 10% reduction in their company's CO_2 emissions by 2014, compared with 2004 emission levels. In 2009 it was announced that the company had already reduced CO_2 emissions by 9% and water consumption by 17%, even as production and sales increased![10] Novo Nordisk considers the people who rely on the company's products and its employees, as well as the impact of their business on society.

Novo Nordisk adopted the Balanced Scorecard as the company-wide management tool for measuring progress. As part of their payment package, individuals are rewarded for performance that meets or exceeds the financial and nonfinancial targets in the Balanced Scorecard. Financial performance is guided by a set of four long-term targets focusing on growth, profitability, financial return and cash generation. Nonfinancial performance targets include job creation, the ability to manage environmental impacts and optimize resource efficiency, and social impacts related to employees, patients and communities.[11]

Corporate sustainability – the ability to sustain and develop a business in the long-term perspective, in harmony with society – has made a meaningful difference to Novo Nordisk's business, and they believe it is a driver of their business success. Surveys indicate that ethical behaviour in business today is the number one driver of reputation for pharmaceutical companies. Any company that is not perceived by the public as behaving in an ethical manner is likely to lose business, and it takes a long time to regain trust.

Southwest Airlines' perpetual profitability stems not from miserliness but from attention to customers, value and sensible cost savings. For Novo Nordisk, a business with integrity and innovation, their commitment to corporate sustainability has always been based on values. For both companies, doing the right thing is making a direct return on their bottom line.

References

1. Southwest Airlines Corporate Fact Sheet, at http://www.swamedia.com/swamedia/fact_sheet.pdf (accessed May 25, 2009. See also James Campbell Quick, Crafting and Organizational Culture: Herb's Hand at Southwest Airlines, *Organizational Dynamics*, 21 (August 1992), p. 47.

2. http://www.swamedia.com/swamedia/speeches/fred_taylor_speech.pdf (accessed July 22, 2009).

3. Colleen Barrett, Pampering Customers on a Budget, *Working Woman* (April 1993), pp. 19–22.

4. Southwest Airlines Corporate Fact Sheet.

5. Did We Say Cheap? *Inc.* (October 1997). p. 60.

6. Southwest Airlines Corporate Fact Sheet.

7. Adapted from Mike Esterl. Southwest Airlines CEO Flies Unchartered Skies. *The Wall Street Journal.* (March 25, 2009), p. B1.

8. *The World's Most Admired Companies. FORTUNE*, (March 16, 2009).
   Adapted from http://www.novonordisk.com/sustainability/default.asp.

9. http://www.hoovers.com (accessed July 22, 2009).

10. http://www.environmentalleader.com/2009/02/05/novo-nordisk-cuts-co2-emissions-9/ accessed July 12, 2009.

11. Ibid.

Questions

1. What leadership style dominates at Southwest and Novo Nordisk? What could each company learn from the other? Cite examples to support your opinion.

2. How does each company's leadership influence its organizational design and shape its competitive strategy?

3. What differences emerging between the two companies in this case study might be attributed to differences in the wider societies – of the USA and Denmark respectively? Refer to the work of Geert Hofstede when considering this question.

Case Study 7

Channel 6 TV: Power and politics in action

Channel 6 was formed in 1998 in Brighton, England as a bidder for a new UK terrestrial television franchise. It was awarded the franchise in 2001. In 2005 the franchise was due for renewal under the terms of the original agreement. The independent regulator and competition authority for the UK communications industry (Ofcom) had already advertised for bids for the franchise.

As a terrestrially available television station – also available via satellite and other digital packages – Channel 6's position is seen as most attractive. A terrestrial television station is regarded as having key advantages in terms of building audience loyalty in the run-up to the switch-off of analogue signals, prior to the advent of an all-digital platform. There are therefore certain to be a number of strong bids for this franchise from other consortia. It has been rumoured that a consortium including two of the largest global media players may be preparing a bid.

Channel 6 has succeeded in attracting its target audience share after a 'shaky' first two years, and advertising revenue is strong. However, there have been financial concerns as programmes have regularly run over budget and, furthermore, the station has attracted regular controversy regarding its programme output which has included a large proportion of downmarket late night 'shock shows', or so-called docu soaps such as:

- *I'm a Celebrity: I'm Locked in the Toilet*
- *Britain's Stupidest Bus Drivers*
- *Holiday Reps 'Go Mental'*.
- *Footballers' Private Parts*
- *Pregnant Grandmothers*

One programme which has attracted particular scrutiny is *Westminster Sleaze*, screened live late on Friday evenings in which politicians have been doused in porridge and had their clothing removed on air.

The Chair of Channel 6 has, in anticipation of the upcoming franchise renewal, brought in a new Chief Executive, Kamran Malik, who has a successful track record in high street retailing and, specifically, the home improvement or do-it-yourself (DIY) sector, where he was responsible for leading a series of mergers resulting in the creation of Brilliant Homes, which is now the second largest DIY chain in the UK. Kamran has been given the remit of giving the company 'more commercial sharpness' and to provide a new public face in dealing with the channel's various stakeholders, including regulatory bodies.

As a condition of his appointment Kamran Malik brought in an old confidante, Claire Holloway, as Human Resources Director. With a history of overseeing substantial staff restructuring in several previous companies while retaining her personal popularity, Claire Holloway's role is seen as crucial in the run-up to the franchise renewal in terms of dealing with potentially sensitive staffing and interpersonal issues.

The remaining senior management group members all have a long and successful history in the media area. They include: George Tyson the Finance Director, Ken Redfern as Marketing Director and Liam O'Kane the Director of Programmes. O'Kane is a tall flamboyant individual with over twenty years' experience of first making, and later commissioning, distinctive television programmes of various types which have always secured the requisite audience figures. A former Royal Shakespeare Company actor, he has taken on a more populist approach in recent years and has been quoted as saying that 'you should never underestimate the taste of the neanderthal British public,' although he insists this comment was taken out of context. Liam O'Kane has a very considerable reputation as a scheduler and commissioner of programmes. He is also said to be a highly proficient networker within the media world, with both formal and informal links to Ofcom. A Labour Party supporter, he is rumoured to cherish friendships with senior politicians.

The problem

Channel 6's turnover, although large by industry standards, formed only a small part of that of the parent company (Stellar Media) which underpins Channel 6's operations. Profits, which have been proportionately large, accrue to Stellar Media. Little has returned to Channel 6 in terms of investment but, on the other hand, not much has been demanded of it in terms of cost control or efficient management. Kamran Malik's appointment is intended to strengthen these areas. His new brief is to control costs and ensure that Channel 6 has an 'appropriate reputation' with its audience, employees, with 'The City' and, not least, the regulatory body Ofcom. However, the company is on line to make substantial profits, partly as a result of Liam O'Kane's far-sighted selection of admittedly downmarket, not to say outrageous, programmes, which have attracted lucrative advertising revenue.

The independent television industry has, in the past, had a reputation for high spending. Funds are often treated with little genuine concern. This culture is certainly true of Channel 6's Programmes Department which, under Liam O'Kane's leadership, regularly runs as much as

300% over budget. This is despite commissioning programmes such as *Cosmetic Surgery Close-ups* which are cheap to make and do not require extensive creative input. In fact, the culture of this department is such that attempts to control costs are resented as interference with 'core business'. A recent argument over the budget of *Pregnant Grandmothers* proved to be a particularly robust discussion, with O'Kane threatening to take his case directly to the Chairman of Ofcom while describing Malik as a 'jumped-up paint salesman'. Kamran Malik regards this approach to expenditure as cavalier and immoral. In the areas he has been able to control he has succeeded in streamlining operations. Claire Holloway succeeded in introducing a new flexible rewards system for studio staff while averting a threatened strike which would have shut down the station. Together they have introduced a new Joint Consultative Committee which, initially, has resulted in improved morale amongst staff.

Perspectives on the situation

The Head of Engineering, Terry Holbrook, recruited two years ago from the BBC, can see the complexity of the issues facing Kamran Malik. 'He is faced with getting things right very fast in order to secure the future. And he doesn't know the industry well. Sometimes he is a stranger to what really goes on here. Liam O'Kane is the best Programmes Director I have ever met. If he feels he must do something he will pursue it and pursue it and pursue it. He definitely does not lack drive or courage. Very much his own man though and if you put him alongside Kamran, who has a hell of a track-record elsewhere, then there is going to be one huge confrontation looming. The tragedy is we need both of them to stay.'

Liam O'Kane is also acutely aware of a changing climate at Channel 6. 'I've been told to do a job for this television station and if they don't like the way I operate they can get rid of me. I could walk into a job with the BBC tomorrow and even buy up the Shopping Channel if I want. Don't play daft games with me! What you do running DIY stores has nothing at all to do with television. I will not crawl in and out of Kamran's office telling him every little thing that happens in my department.'

Matters are brought to a head during a senior management meeting when recent newspaper reviews of *Westminster Sleaze* are discussed. Kamran Malik reads out part of a review from *The Daily Telegraph* describing the programme as 'mindless putrefying cack: moronic filth of the worst kind'. When he stops laughing, Liam O'Kane retorts by asking why his computer printer has not been fixed for five days; 'the really important issue for me, not your pathetic attempts to go all moralistic on a subject you know **** all about. None of the audience watching it was sober anyway. Why not talk about the ratings? You didn't' mention that the *Daily Sport* thought that the programme was "a laugh a minute riot" did you? Well next month I plan to do a nude *Songs of Praise* special – are you going to stop me Kamran?'

Source: This case study has been adapted by Dr Ray French from, 'TVN' by Iain Mangham, Chapter 7 in Clegg, C., Kemp, N. and Legge, K. (1985), *Case Studies in Organizational Behaviour*, Harper & Row: London. All names and dates contained in this case study are fictional. Channel 6 TV is a fictional organization. Quotes attributed to real-life organizations have been invented.

Questions

Please refer to Chapter 10 on power and politics before attempting the questions.

1. Identify possible sources of power which the following characters may have in Channel 6 TV: Kamran Malik; Liam O'Kane; Claire Holloway.

2. What are the possible options open to Kamran at this stage? What are the likely consequences of each? What would you do now if you were in his position? Explain your answer.

3. To what extent are the issues facing Kamran Malik affected by political behaviour in this particular workplace?

Case Study 8

Two decades of managerial resistance to change

Twenty-five-year-old Martin Johnson* was overjoyed when appointed to a new management post at one of the UK's most prestigious department stores, based in London. He succeeded a previous succession of male divisional managers, who, unlike him, were in their fifties and long service members of staff. The division that Martin was charged with running consisted of over 100, predominantly male, full-time members of staff. Having an office was a rarity (because the cost for space was several thousand pounds per square metre) and Martin found his windowless three-square-metre office highly claustrophobic. The office had a metal carpet divider separating it from a corridor which led to the shop floor.

Like many retail outlets, there was a clear management hierarchy, with supervisors, first line managers, second line managers (sales managers) and a divisional manager. Each level of management had a distinctive line of authority, and was reflected in the amount that each level of manager could sign for when a customer refund was provided. Symbolic of this hierarchy was the colour of employees' identity cards, from white to light green to dark green to orange (the highest colour available) – for divisional managers and directors.

The employees were differentiated in terms of which staff restaurant they were allowed to eat in, and even which door they were allowed to enter and leave by. White identity card employees had to travel under the basement and through a cordon of security guards, with light and dark green through one specific door on the ground level. Orange card users could leave through any of the dozen or so doors available.

During an opening speech, Martin introduced himself to staff and told them that he operated an 'open-door' policy and welcomed suggestions and discussions from all members of the division. Unbeknown to him, previous divisional managers had also made this comment, but had not followed through with meaningful actions. Within a couple of months of Martin's appointment, he had one of the sales managers transferred to another division. This particular sales manager was very popular with staff, but in Martin's opinion, he was too familiar with staff and was not fulfilling his management responsibilities to the required level. The staff was not notified of the reasons for this transfer.

After about three months in post, three salesmen approached Martin, who was sitting in his office. They filled the narrow doorway, but noticeably did not cross the carpet divider, holding their ground, and looking down on the divisional manager. They wanted to ask about changing the positioning and display (merchandising) of one part of the Man's Shop. One of the salesmen had 25 years' service and was a shop steward for Unison (the Retail Trade Union), the second salesman had over 30 years' service and was a 'senior' (given a light green identity card which entitled him to various privileges). The third salesman was the top-selling salesman, with over 20 years' service.

The three men outlined what they wanted to do, what the ramifications were and what the potential benefits were. Martin asked when they wanted to bring about the planned change. They responded that they would do this after store hours and would take two to three hours. After successfully answering a few questions around logistics, Martin told the salesmen 'OK, do it, tonight.' The three salesmen stood there, dumbstruck. After about twenty seconds, Martin repeated his response.

Working after hours had become a bone of contention following the department store changing its closing times from 5 p.m. to 6 p.m., with some staff refusing to sign the new employment contract. Ironically all three salesmen had refused to sign the new contract, and when offered overtime (working from 5 to 6 p.m.) would systematically refuse. Any other staff on the 'old contract' who undertook occasional requested overtime would get their overtime claim in and signed by the divisional manager in a speedy and ritualistic manner. On this occasion, for the merchandising change the three salesmen worked after hours and did not request overtime payment.

The salesmen were paid a basic salary and relied heavily on their commission on sales, which, for the top quartile of salesmen, resulted in a handsome final salary. Martin knew that the effectiveness and impact of the merchandising change would be most harshly judged by the three salesmen concerned, as their salary would be affected by it. What Martin didn't know was that the three salesmen had spent two decades trying to get the respective divisional managers to agree to this change.

After two days of trying the new merchandising layout, the shop steward approached Martin on the shop floor and asked if they could change the display back to its original layout. Without any questions whatsoever, Martin said 'sure, change it back.'

*The name provided is fictitious.

Questions

1. Why were the salesmen so wary of management?
2. Following the merchandising change episode, do you think that the sales staff would be more or less inclined to ask about making changes? Support your answer with practical reasons.
3. To what extent was Martin in control of this particular situation? Are there practical things that he could have also done in order to handle the situation more effectively?

GLOSSARY

Ability is the capacity to perform the various tasks needed for a given job. p.

Absenteeism is the failure of people to attend work on a given day. p.

Achievement-oriented leadership is leadership behaviour that emphasizes setting challenging goals, stressing excellence in performance and showing confidence in the group members' abilities to achieve high standards of performance. p.

Active management by exception involves watching for deviations from rules and standards and taking corrective action. p.

An adhocracy is an organizational structure that emphasizes shared, decentralized decision making, extreme horizontal specialization, few levels of management, the virtual absence of formal controls and few rules, policies and procedures. p.

The adjourning stage is the fifth stage of group development, in which members of the group disband when the job is done. p.

The affective components of an attitude are the specific feelings regarding the personal impact of the antecedents. p.

Annualization is a scheme whereby employees' working time and pay are scheduled and calculated over a period of a year. p.

Anthropology is the comparative study of different societies or tribes. p.

Aptitude is the capability to learn something. p.

Arbitration occurs when a neutral third party acts as judge and issues a binding decision affecting parties at a negotiation impasse. p.

Artificial intelligence, or AI, studies how computers can be made to think like the human brain. p.

An attitude is a predisposition to respond in a positive or negative way to someone or something in your environment. p.

Attribution errors occur within the process of perception and relate to the reasons we attribute to events and behaviour. A common attribution error is to overemphasize the contribution of our own efforts and abilities when explaining our successes and, contrastingly, to attribute negative occurrences to outside influences such as bad luck. p.

Authoritarianism is a personality trait that focuses on the rigidity of a person's beliefs. p.

Automation is a job design that allows machines to do work previously accomplished by human effort. p.

Autonomous work teams are teams given significant authority and responsibility over their work in contexts of highly related or interdependent jobs. p.

The **bargaining zone** is the zone between one party's minimum reservation point and the other party's maximum reservation point in a negotiating situation. p.

BATNA is the 'best alternative to a negotiated agreement', or each party's position on what they must do if an agreement cannot be reached. p.

The **behavioural components of an attitude** are the intentions to behave in a certain way based on a person's specific feelings or attitudes. p.

Behavioural decision theory refers to the idea that people act only in terms of what they perceive about a given situation. p.

Behaviourists study observable behaviours and consequences of behaviour, and reject subjective human psychological states as topics for study. p.

Beliefs represent ideas about someone or something and the conclusions people draw about them. p.

Bet-your-company culture refers to a type of organizational culture characterized by a long-term outlook in which significant levels of investment are made, the results of which may take many years to feed through. p.

Blended learning is an approach that blends, mixes or combines on-line learning with classroom instruction, coaching or mentoring. p.

Brain drain refers to a characteristic of today's skilled workforce whose members are now more mobile and prepared to take their knowledge with them to their new workplaces as they pursue opportunities across the globe. p.

Brainstorming is a technique by which team members generate as many ideas as possible, without being inhibited by other team members. p.

Buffering is a conflict management approach that sets up inventories to reduce conflicts when the inputs of one group are the outputs of another group. p.

Bullying refers to abusive and intimidating behaviour which leads to the recipient feeling upset, threatened and vulnerable. It is often the result of an abuse of power and can include such behaviour as ignoring employees or excluding people from a meeting. p.

A **bureaucracy** is an idealized form of organization whose characteristics include a clear division of labour, hierarchical control, promotion by merit with career opportunities for employees and administration by rule. p.

Burnout is a negative felt emotion relating to one's work. It is characterized by emotional exhaustion, cynicism and doubts regarding self-efficacy. p.

Casual work is work where the number and schedule of work hours vary and there is little or no security of ongoing employment. p.

Centralization is the degree to which the authority to make decisions is restricted to higher levels of management. p.

Certain environments are decision environments in which information is sufficient to predict the results of each alternative in advance of implementation. p.

Change agents are individuals or groups that take responsibility for changing the existing pattern of behaviour of a person or social system. p.

Changing involves a managerial responsibility to modify a situation; that is, to change people, tasks, structure and/or technology. p.

Channels are the media through which the message may be delivered. p.

Charisma is a dimension of leadership, based on personal qualities, which provides vision and a sense of mission, and instils pride, respect and trust. p.

Charismatic leaders are those leaders who, by force of their personal characteristics, are capable of having a profound and extraordinary effect on followers. p.

Classical conditioning is a form of learning through association that involves the manipulation of stimuli to influence behaviour. p.

Classical decision theory views the manager as acting in a world of complete certainty. p.

Coercive power is the extent to which a manager can deny desired rewards or administer punishment to control other people. p.

Cognitive abilities refer to our mental capacity to process information and solve problems. p.

The **cognitive components of an attitude** are the beliefs, opinions, knowledge or information a person possesses. p.

Cognitive dissonance is a state of perceived inconsistency between a person's expressed attitudes and actual behaviour. p.

Cognitive learning is a form of learning achieved by thinking about the perceived relationship between events and individual goals and expectations. p.

Cohesiveness is the degree to which members are attracted to and motivated to remain part of the group. p.

Common assumptions are the collection of truths that an organization's members share as a result of their joint experiences and that guide values and behaviour. p.

Commonsense thinking is apparently obvious or assumed analysis of OB topics, without reference to rigorous study or evidence, which can result in false conclusions. p.

Competency is the umbrella term for any task-related knowledge or skill possessed by an individual. Competencies could be technical or interpersonal. p.

A compressed work week is any scheduling of work that allows a full-time job to be completed in fewer than the standard five days. p.

Conflict occurs when two or more people disagree over issues of organizational substance and/or experience some emotional antagonism with one another. p.

Conflict resolution occurs when the reasons for a conflict are eliminated. p.

Conglomerates are organizations that own several unrelated businesses. p.

Constructive conflict is conflict that results in positive benefits to the group. p.

Consultative decisions are decisions made by an individual after seeking input from, or consulting with, members of a group. p.

Content theories of motivation offer ways to profile or analyse individuals to identify the needs that are assumed to motivate their behaviour. p.

A contingency approach within organizational behaviour identifies how situations can be understood and managed in ways that appropriately respond to their unique characteristics or circumstances. p.

Contingent rewards are rewards that are given in exchange for mutually agreed goal accomplishments. p.

Continuous reinforcement is a reinforcement schedule that administers a reward each time a desired behaviour occurs. p.

Contrast effects occur within the process of perception when an object or person is perceived due to it standing out from its surroundings or group. p.

Contributions are individual work efforts of value to the organization. p.

Control is the set of mechanisms used to keep actions and outputs within predetermined limits. p.

Controlled processing refers, within the topic of perception, to conscious decisions made to pay attention to certain stimuli while ignoring others. p.

Controlling is the process of monitoring performance, comparing results with objectives and taking corrective action as necessary. p.

Coordination is the set of mechanisms used in an organization to link the actions of its subunits into a consistent pattern. p.

A corporate culture is an attempt by managers to deliberately create and mould organizational culture to achieve specified results. p.

Corporate social responsibility refers to the notion that corporations have a responsibility to the society that sustains them; and the obligation of organizations to behave in ethical and moral ways. p.

Countercultures are the patterns of values and philosophies that outwardly reject those of the larger organization or social system. p.

Crafted decisions are decisions created to deal specifically with a situation at hand. p.

Creativity is the development of unique and novel responses to problems and opportunities. p.

A cultural symbol is any object, act or event that serves to transmit cultural meaning. p.

Culture shock describes a series of stages experienced by people when they encounter a new cultural setting. It is normally depicted as a U-curve with initial elation followed by negative feelings, succeeded in turn by recovery and adjustment. p.

Decentralization is the degree to which the authority to make decisions is given to workers at lower levels in an organization's hierarchy. p.

Decision making is the process of identifying a problem or opportunity and choosing among alternative courses of action. p.

Decoding is the interpretation of the symbols sent from the sender to the receiver. p.

Decoupling involves separating or reducing the contact between two conflicting groups. p.

Demographic characteristics are background variables (for example, age and gender) that help shape what a person becomes over time. p.

Departmentalization by customer is the grouping of individuals and resources by client. p.

Departmentalization by geography is the grouping of individuals and resources by geographical territory. p.

De-skilling refers to a diminution of the attributes and proficiency required to perform work tasks. In Braverman's view, de-skilling is a deliberate strategy by owners and managers of organizations in order to reassert control over work. p

Destructive conflict is conflict that works to the group's or organization's disadvantage. p.

The differentiation perspective views an organization's culture as a compilation of diverse and inconsistent beliefs that are shared at group level. p.

Directive leadership is leadership behaviour that spells out the what and how of employees' tasks. p.

Discourse involves ways of presenting and understanding any facet of the world via ideas, assumptions, vocabulary and actions. In this way reality is *framed*, thereby informing people's understanding and behaviour. p.

Disruptive behaviour is any behaviour that harms the group process. p.

Distributed leadership is the sharing of responsibility for fulfilling group task and maintenance needs. p.

Distributive justice refers to the perceived fairness of how rewards are allocated. p.

Distributive negotiation is negotiation in which the focus is on 'positions' staked out or declared by the parties involved, who are each trying to claim certain portions of the available 'pie'. p.

The diversity-consensus dilemma refers to a tendency for diversity in group membership to make it harder for people to work together even though diversity itself expands a group's problem-solving capacity. p.

Division of labour is the process of breaking the work to be done into specialized tasks that individuals or groups can perform. p.

Divisional departmentalization is the grouping of individuals and resources by product, service and/or client. p.

Divisionalized design is an organizational structure that establishes a separate structure for each business or division. p.

Dogmatism is a personality trait that regards legitimate authority as absolute. p.

A **dominant coalition** denotes the people who are in a strong position of power and influence within organizations at any one time. Dominant coalitions are shifting and can be replaced by others. p.

Double-loop learning is learning that involves innovation and creativity, by going beyond the basic line of questioning and thinking outside of the box. p.

Effective communication is communication in which the intended meaning of the source and the perceived meaning of the receiver are one and the same. p.

Effective groups are groups that achieve high levels of both task performance and human resource performance. p.

An **effective manager** is a manager whose work unit achieves high levels of task accomplishment and maintains itself as a capable workforce over time. p.

Effective negotiation occurs when issues of substance are resolved without any harm to the working relationships among the parties involved. p.

Efficient communication is communication at minimum cost in terms of resources expended. p.

E-learning is learning that is delivered, enabled or mediated using electronic technology for the explicit purpose of training in organizations. p.

Emergent behaviours are those things that group members do in addition to, or in place of, what is formally asked of them by the organization. p.

Emotion management is exercising emotional self-control and self-regulation influenced by the context in which individuals find themselves. p.

Emotional conflict is conflict that involves interpersonal difficulties that arise over feelings of anger, mistrust, dislike, fear, resentment and the like. p.

Emotional intelligence is a form of social intelligence that allows us to monitor and shape our emotions and those of others. p.

Employee involvement teams are teams of workers who meet regularly outside their normal work units for the purpose of collectively addressing important workplace issues. p.

Empowerment is the process by which managers delegate power to employees who therefore have an enhanced view of their work and role within the organization. p.

Encoding is part of the process of communication and involves translating an idea or thought into meaningful symbols. p.

Environmental complexity is the magnitude of the problems and opportunities in the organization's environment, as evidenced by the degree of richness, interdependence and uncertainty. p.

Equity theory is based on the phenomenon of social comparison and posits that because people gauge the fairness of their work outcomes compared with others, any felt inequity will result in an unpleasant feeling which the individual will be driven to remove through a variety of possible actions. p.

ERG theory categorizes needs into existence, relatedness and growth needs. p.

Ergonomics involves the application of scientific principles to the interaction between humans and their work environment including task and work areas, including physical layout, work systems and scheduling. p.

Escalating commitment is the tendency to continue with a previously chosen course of action even when feedback suggests that it is failing. p.

Ethical behaviour is behaviour that is morally accepted as 'good' and 'right' as opposed to 'bad' and 'wrong' in a particular social context. p.

The ethical climate is the shared set of understandings in an organization about what is correct behaviour and how ethical issues will be handled. p.

An ethical dilemma occurs when a person must make a decision that requires a choice among competing sets of principles. p.

Existence needs arise from a desire for physiological and material wellbeing. p.

Expectancy is the probability that the individual assigns to work effort being followed by a given level of achieved task performance. p.

Expectancy theory argues that work motivation is determined by individual beliefs about effort–performance relationships and the desirability of various work outcomes from different performance levels. p.

Expert power is the ability to control another's behaviour through the possession of knowledge, experience or judgement that the other person does not have but needs. p.

External adaptation is the process of reaching goals and dealing with outsiders. p.

Externals are people with an external locus of control, who believe what happens to them is beyond their control. p.

Extinction is the withdrawal of the reinforcing consequences for a given behaviour. p.

Extrinsic rewards are positively valued work outcomes that the individual receives from some other person in the work setting. p.

Feedback is the process of telling someone else how you feel about something the person did or said, or about the situation in general. p.

Felt negative inequity exists when individuals feel they have received relatively less than others have in proportion to work inputs. p.

Felt positive inequity exists when individuals feel they have received relatively more than others have. p.

The five key dimensions of personality are extroversion–introversion; conscientiousness; agreeableness; emotional stability; and openness to experience. p.

Flexible working hours (flexitime) is any work schedule that gives employees daily choice in the timing of work and nonwork activities. p.

Flexiyear or annual hours is a system whereby total agreed annual hours are allocated by workers as they see fit. p.

Focus groups are a form of qualitative research method in which a group of people are asked about their attitudes towards particular items or issues. p.

A force-coercion strategy tries to 'command' change through the formal authority of legitimacy, rewards and punishments. p.

Formal communication channels are communication channels that follow the chain of command established by the organization's hierarchy. p.

Formal groups are 'official' groups that are designated by formal authority to serve a specific purpose. p.

Formal leadership is the process of exercising influence from a position of formal authority in an organization. p.

The formal structure is the intended configuration of positions, job duties and lines of authority among the component parts of an organization. p.

Formalization is the written documentation of work rules, policies and procedures. p.

The forming stage is the first stage of group development, in which the primary concern is the initial entry of members to the group. p.

The founding story is the tale of the lessons learned and efforts of the founder of the organization. p.

The four basic drives of motivation are the drive to acquire, the drive to bond, the drive to comprehend and the drive to defend. p.

The fragmentation perspective views organizational culture as lacking any form of pattern as a result of differing meanings between individuals and within individuals over time. p.

Friendship groups consist of people with natural affinities for one another who may do things together inside or outside the workplace. p.

Functional departmentalization is the grouping of individuals and resources by skill, knowledge and action. p.

The glass ceiling refers to an invisible barrier that stops women from attaining senior positions within organizations. It can involve unstated or unofficial views of women and their roles at work. p.

Global management skills and competencies include understanding of international business strategy, cross-cultural management, international marketing, international finance, managing e-business and the Internet, risk management, managing sustainable organizations, re-engineering organizations, managing the virtual workplace, knowledge management, international economics and trade and Asian languages. p.

Globalization brings a greater sense of interconnectedness between people from diverse cultures. It has also been defined as the process of becoming more international in scope, influence or application. p.

Goal setting is the process of developing, negotiating and formalizing an employee's targets and objectives. p.

A **group** is a collection of two or more people who interact with each other regularly to achieve common goals. p.

Group decisions are decisions made by all members of the group, ideally with consensus being achieved. p.

Group dynamics are the forces operating in groups that affect group performance and member satisfaction. p.

Group inputs are the initial 'givens' in a group situation that set the stage for all group processes. p.

Group norms are the standards of behaviour that group members are expected to display. p.

Group outputs are the results of the transformation of group inputs through group processes. p.

Group roles are the sets of behaviours expected by the managers of the organization and the group members for the holder of a particular position. p.

Groupthink is the tendency of members in highly cohesive groups to lose their critical, evaluative capabilities. p.

Growth needs relate to the desire for continued personal growth and development. p.

The **halo effect** within interpersonal perception occurs when our perception of another person is framed on the basis of a single striking favourable characteristic (the rusty halo phenomenon occurs when the characteristic is perceived negatively). p.

Heterogeneous groups are groups whose members have diverse backgrounds, interests, values, attitudes and so on. p.

Heuristics are simplifying strategies or 'rules of thumb' that people use when making decisions. p.

Hierarchical referral uses the chain of command for conflict resolution; problems are referred up the hierarchy for more senior managers to reconcile. p.

High-performance teams excel in teamwork while achieving performance advantages. p.

A **high performance work organization** focuses on increasing people's influence on business as well as the processes, methods, the physical environment and the technology and tools that enhance their work. p.

Higher-order needs are esteem and self-actualization needs in Maslow's hierarchy. p.

Homogeneous groups are groups whose members have similar backgrounds, interests, values, attitudes and so on. p.

Horizontal loading involves increasing the breadth of a job by adding to the variety of tasks that the worker performs. p.

Horizontal specialization is the division of labour through the formation of work units or groups within an organization. p.

Hot desking occurs where an employer provides a work space or surface which is available to any worker rather than any one worker. p.

Human resource performance must be sustained if it is to have meaning; high performance should be sustainable. High levels of performance are affected by a manager's attention to a range of matters within the people management heading. p.

Human resources are the individuals and groups whose contributions enable the organization to serve a particular purpose. p.

Hygienes (hygiene factors) are dissatisfiers that are associated with aspects of a person's work setting. p.

The **idiographic** approach to understanding personality focuses on individual uniqueness. It regards personality as potentially shifting according to an individual's self-image and experiences. p.

Incremental change is change that occurs more frequently and less traumatically as part of an organization's natural evolution. p.

Individual decisions are decisions made by one individual on behalf of the group. p.

Individualized consideration is a leadership dimension by which the leader provides personal attention, treats each employee individually and coaches and advises employees. p.

Inducements are what the organization gives to the individual on behalf of the group. p.

Influence is a behavioural response to the exercise of power. p.

Informal communication channels are communication channels that do not adhere to the organization's hierarchy. p.

Informal groups are groups that emerge unofficially and are not formally designated as parts of the organization. p.

Informal leadership is the process of exercising influence through special skills or resources that meet the needs of other people. p.

Information power is the extent to which individuals have control over information needed by others. p.

An **information source** is a person or group of people with a reason to communicate with some other person(s), the receiver(s). p.

The **initial integration stage** is the third stage of group development, at which the group begins to come together as a coordinated unit; it is sometimes called the norming stage. p.

Innovation is the process of creating new ideas and putting them into practice. p.

Inspiration is the communication of high expectations, the use of symbols to focus efforts and the expression of important purposes in simple ways. p.

Instinct is made up of inherited patterns of unreasoned and unchangeable responses to particular actions and behaviours. p.

Instrumentality is the probability that the individual assigns to a level of achieved task performance leading to various work outcomes. p.

The **integration perspective** views organizational culture as a system of shared meanings, unity and harmony. p.

Integrative negotiation is negotiation in which the focus is on the merits of the issues and the parties involved try to enlarge the available 'pie' rather than stake claims to certain portions of it. p.

Intellectual stimulation promotes intelligence, rationality and careful problem solving. p.

Interest groups consist of people who share common interests, whether those interests are work or nonwork related. p.

Intergroup conflict is conflict that occurs between groups in an organization. p.

Intergroup dynamics are the dynamics that take place between groups, as opposed to within groups. p.

Intermittent reinforcement is a reinforcement schedule that rewards behaviour only periodically. p.

Internal integration is the creation of a collective identity and the means of matching methods of working and living together. p.

Internals are people with an internal locus of control, who believe they control their own fate or destiny. p.

Interorganizational conflict is conflict that occurs between organizations. p.

Interpersonal conflict is conflict that occurs between two or more individuals. p.

The **interpretivist** tradition within OB believes that research into human behaviour should incorporate the subject's understanding of their own and other people's behaviour and the meanings attached to actions. Research within this tradition typically uses qualitative methods specific to social sciences. p.

Intrapersonal conflict is conflict that occurs within the individual as a result of actual or perceived pressures from incompatible goals or expectations. p.

Intrinsic motivation is a desire to work hard solely for the pleasant experience of task accomplishment. p.

Intrinsic rewards are positively valued work outcomes that the individual receives directly as a result of task performance. p.

Intuition is the ability to know or recognize quickly and readily the possibilities of a given situation. p.

A **job** is one or more tasks that an individual performs in direct support of an organization's production purpose. p.

The job characteristics model identifies five core characteristics (skill variety, task identity, task significance, autonomy and job feedback) as having special importance to job designs. p.

Job content refers to what people do in their work. p.

Job context refers to a person's work setting. p.

Job design is the planning and specification of job tasks and the work setting in which they are to be accomplished. p.

A job diagnostic survey is a questionnaire used to examine each of the dimensions of the job characteristics model. p.

Job enlargement involves increasing task variety by combining into one job tasks of similar skill levels that were previously assigned to separate workers. p.

Job enrichment is the practice of building motivating factors into job content. p.

Job involvement is the degree to which a person is willing to work hard and apply effort beyond normal job expectations. p.

Job rotation involves increasing task variety by periodically shifting workers among jobs involving different tasks at similar levels of skill. p.

Job satisfaction is the degree to which individuals feel positively or negatively about their jobs. p.

Job sharing is the assignment of one full-time job to two or more people, who divide the work according to agreements made between themselves and the employer. p.

Job simplification involves standardizing work procedures and employing people in clearly defined and specialized tasks. p.

Judgement is the use of the intellect in making decisions. p.

Key performance indicators are standards against which individual and organizational performance can be measured. p.

A knowledge-based economy is an economy in which the production, distribution and use of knowledge is the main driver of growth, wealth creation and employment across all industries – not only those classified as high-tech or knowledge intensive. p.

Knowledge management focuses on processes designed to improve an organization's ability to capture, share and diffuse knowledge in a manner that will improve business performance. p.

Laissez faire leadership involves abdicating responsibilities and avoiding decisions. p.

The law of contingent reinforcement is the view that for a reward to have maximum reinforcing value, it must be delivered only if the desired behaviour is exhibited. p.

The law of effect refers to Thorndike's observation that behaviour that results in a pleasant outcome is likely to be repeated; behaviour that results in an unpleasant outcome is not likely to be repeated. p.

The law of immediate reinforcement states that the more immediate the delivery of a reward after the occurrence of a desirable behaviour, the greater the reinforcing effect on behaviour. p.

Leaders provide inspiration, create opportunities, coach and motivate people to gain their support on fundamental long-term choices. p.

Leadership is a special case of interpersonal influence that gets an individual or group to do what the leader wants done. p.

Leading is the process of directing and coordinating the work efforts of other people to help them to accomplish important tasks. p.

Learning is a relatively permanent change in behaviour that occurs as a result of experience. p.

The least preferred co-worker (LPC) scale is a measure of a person's leadership style based on a description of the person with whom respondents have been able to work least well. p.

Legitimate power is the extent to which a manager can use the internalized belief of an employee that the 'boss' has a 'right of command' to control other people. p.

Liaison groups are groups that coordinate the activities of certain units to prevent destructive conflicts between them. p.

Lifelong learning adopts the philosophy that we learn throughout our lives, and that learning does not cease when we reach a certain age. p.

Line personnel are work groups that are involved with the core business of an organization. p.

Linking pins are people who are assigned to manage conflict between groups that are prone to conflict. p.

Locus of control is the internal–external orientation – that is, the extent to which people feel able to affect their lives. p.

Lower-order needs are physiological, safety and social needs in Maslow's hierarchy. p.

Machiavellians are people who view and manipulate others purely for personal gain. p.

Maintenance activities are activities that support the emotional life of the group as an ongoing social system. p.

A management philosophy links key goal-related issues with key collaboration issues to come up with general ways by which the organization will manage its affairs. p.

The management process involves planning, organizing, leading and controlling the use of organizational resources. p.

A manager is responsible for work that is accomplished through the performance contributions of others. Managers are concerned with making things happen and keeping work on schedule, engaging in routine interactions to fulfil planned actions. p.

Manifest conflict occurs when conflict is openly expressed in behaviour. p.

Material resources are the technology, information, physical equipment and facilities, raw material and money that are necessary for an organization to produce some product or service. p.

A matrix structure is a combination of functional and divisional patterns in which an individual is assigned to more than one type of unit. p.

Mechanistic design emphasizes vertical specialization, hierarchical levels, tight control and coordination through rules, policies and other impersonal methods. p.

Merit pay is a compensation system that bases an individual's salary or wage increase on a measure of the person's performance accomplishments during a specified time period. p.

A motivating potential score is a summary of a job's overall potential for motivating those in the workplace. p.

Motivation to work refers to the forces within an individual that account for the level, direction and persistence of effort expended at work. p.

The motivator–hygiene theory distinguishes between sources of work dissatisfaction (hygiene factors) and satisfaction (motivators); it is also known as the two-factor theory. p.

Motivators (motivator factors) are satisfiers that are associated with what people do in their work. p.

Multi-skilling helps employees acquire an array of skills needed to perform the multiple tasks in an organizational production or customer service process. p.

The nature/nurture controversy is the argument over whether personality is determined by heredity or genetic endowment or by one's environment. p.

The need for achievement (nAch) is the desire to do something better, solve problems or master complex tasks. p.

The need for affiliation (nAff) is the desire to establish and maintain friendly and warm relations with others. p.

The need for power (nPower) is the desire to control others, influence their behaviour or to be responsible for others. p.

Negative reinforcement is the withdrawal of negative consequences, which tends to increase the likelihood of the behaviour being repeated in similar settings; it is also known as avoidance. p.

Negotiation is the process of making joint decisions when the parties involved have different preferences. p.

A network organization is a de-layered organization aligned around the complementary competencies of players in a value chain. p.

Noise is anything that interferes with the effectiveness of the communication attempt. p.

Nomothetic approaches to understanding personality locate individuals within types on the basis of their traits. There is also a belief that personality is stable and unchanging, possibly as a result of inherited characteristics. p.

Nonroutine problems are unique and new problems that call for creative problem solving. p.

The norming stage in group development refers to the point at which the group forms a coordinated unit. At this stage the group will strive for harmony and balance. p.

Norms are rules or standards about the behaviour that group members are expected to display. p.

Observable culture is behavioural patterns that a group displays and teaches to new members. p.

Open systems transform human and physical resources received from their environment into goods and services that are then returned to the environment. p.

Operant conditioning is the process of controlling behaviour by manipulating its consequences. p.

Organic design is an organizational structure that emphasizes horizontal specialization, an extensive use of personal coordination and loose rules, policies and procedures. p.

An organization is a collectivity with a relatively identifiable boundary, a normative order, ranks of authority, communications systems and membership coordinating systems; this collectivity exists on a relatively continuous basis in an environment and engages in activities that are usually related to a set of goals; the activities have outcomes for organizational members, the organization itself and society. p.

Organization charts are diagrams that depict the formal structures of organizations. p.

Organizational behaviour is the study of individuals and groups in organizations. p.

Organizational behaviour modification is the systematic reinforcement of desirable work behaviour and the nonreinforcement or punishment of unwanted work behaviour. p.

Organizational commitment is the degree to which a person strongly identifies with, and feels a part of, the organization. p.

Organizational communication is the process by which entities exchange information and establish a common understanding. p.

Organizational culture is a system of shared beliefs and values that guides behaviour. p.

Organizational design is the process of choosing and implementing a structural configuration for an organization. p.

Organizational governance is the pattern of authority, influence and acceptable managerial behaviour established at the top of the organization. p.

Organizational learning is the process of acquiring or developing new knowledge that modifies or changes behaviour and improves organizational performance. p.

Organizational politics is the management of influence to obtain ends not sanctioned by the organization, or to obtain sanctioned ends through nonsanctioned means of influence. p.

Organizational strategy is the process of positioning the organization in the competitive environment and implementing actions to compete successfully. p.

Organizing is the process of dividing the work to be done and coordinating the results to achieve a desired purpose. p.

Output controls are controls that focus on desired targets and allow managers to use their own methods for reaching defined targets. p.

Output goals are the goals that define the organization's type of business. p.

Outsourcing involves organizations obtaining aspects of their work, for example production systems, from external suppliers for reasons of cost and/or quality rather than carrying out the work themselves. p.

Participant observation is a method of study which involves the researcher becoming a member of the group – either overtly or via 'undercover' involvement – that they are studying. p.

Participative leadership is a leadership style that focuses on consulting with employees and seeking and accounting for their suggestions before making decisions. p.

Passive management by exception involves intervening with employees only if standards are not met. p.

Perception is the process through which people receive, organize and interpret information from their environment. p.

A **perceptual set** comprises those factors that predetermine an individual's ability to perceive particular stimuli and respond in characteristic ways. p.

Performance is a summary measure of the quantity and quality of task contributions made by an individual or group to the work unit and organization. p.

Performance equation: Job performance = attributes × work effort × organizational support. p.

The **performance gap** is the discrepancy between an actual and a desired state of affairs. p.

The **performing stage** in group development signifies the emergence of a mature well-functioning group able to deal with complex tasks and handle internal disagreements. p.

Permanent formal work groups perform a specific function on an ongoing basis. p.

Person culture is a type of organizational culture in which an organization exists for the benefits of members, particularly star performers. It has been located in barristers' chambers and other professional work settings. p.

Personality is the overall profile or combination of traits that characterize the unique nature of a person. p.

Physical abilities refer to our natural and developed motor capacities for speed, strength, flexibility and so on, as well as our use of the five senses. p.

Planned change is change that happens as a result of specific efforts on the part of a change agent. p.

Planning is the process of setting performance objectives and identifying the actions needed to accomplish them. p.

The pluralist view of organizations views them as being populated by individuals and groups that may have diverse aims and interests and which, as a result, can come into conflict with the dominant coalition and other groups. p.

A policy is a guideline for action that outlines important objectives and indicates how an activity is to be performed. p.

Positive reinforcement is the administration of positive consequences that tend to increase the likelihood of repeating the behaviour in similar settings. p.

Positivism is the view that social sciences such as OB can, and should, be studied in the same way as natural sciences like physics, using similar methods with a view to predicting and controlling behaviour and perform-ance. p.

Power is the ability to get someone else to do something you want done, or the ability to make things happen or get things done in the way you want. p.

Power culture is a type of organizational culture in which a central figure exercises power on a personalized basis, there being relatively few formal rules in place. p.

Primary beneficiaries are particular groups expected to benefit from the efforts of specific organizations. p.

Procedural justice refers to the perceived fairness of the process used to determine the distribution of rewards. p.

A procedure (or rule) is a more specific, rigid guideline that describes in detail how a task is to be performed. p.

Process controls are controls that attempt to specify the manner in which tasks will be accomplished. p.

Process culture is a type of organizational culture characterized by clear processes which need to be followed correctly: it can be found in highly regulated sectors such as healthcare. p.

Process innovation is innovation that results in a better way of doing things. p.

Process power is the control over methods of production and analysis. p.

Process re-engineering is the fundamental rethinking and radical redesign of business processes to achieve improvements in performance. p.

Process theories of motivation seek to understand the thought processes that take place in the minds of people and how these act to motivate their behaviour. p.

Product innovation is innovation that results in the creation of a new or improved good or service. p.

Productivity is a summary measure of the quantity and quality of work performance that also accounts for resource use. p.

Programmed decisions are decisions that implement specific solutions determined by past experience as appro-priate for the problems at hand. p.

Projection involves projecting our own emotions or motives on to another person. It is an example of a perceptual error. p.

A **prototype** is a perception of a person based on group characteristics, from which the individual person may diverge. p.

The **psychological contract** specifies what an individual expects to give to and receive from an organization. p.

Psychology is the study of mental life, with a particular focus on the individual's thought processes and behaviour. p.

Psychometric testing involves an attempt to extract an individual's key characteristics via controlled measures such as personality inventories. p.

Punishment is the administration of negative consequences or the withdrawal of positive consequences, which tends to reduce the likelihood of repeating the behaviour in similar settings. p.

Quality circles are groups of workers who meet periodically to discuss and develop solutions for problems relating to quality, productivity or cost. p.

Quality of work–life refers to the overall quality of human experience in the workplace. p.

Quasiformal channels are planned communication connections between holders of the various positions within the organization. p.

Radical change is change that results in a major makeover of the organization and/or its component systems. p.

A **rational persuasion strategy** attempts to bring about change through persuasion based on empirical facts, special knowledge and rational argument. p.

The **receiver** is the individual or group of individuals that hear or read or see the message within the communication process. p.

Referent power is the ability to control another's behaviour because the individual wants to identify with the power source due to his or her perceived attractive characteristics. p.

Refreezing is the final stage of the planned change process in which changes are positively reinforced. p.

Reinforcement is the administration of a consequence as a result of behaviour. p.

Relatedness needs are about the desire for satisfying interpersonal relationships. p.

Relationship goals are concerned with how well people involved in a negotiation, and their constituencies, are able to work with one another once the process is concluded. p.

Required behaviours are those contributions the organization formally requests from group members as a basis for continued affiliation and support. p.

Resistance to change is any attitude or behaviour that reflects a person's unwillingness to make or support a desired change. p.

Resource dependencies occur when the organization needs resources that others control. p.

Reward power is the extent to which a manager can use extrinsic and intrinsic rewards to control other people. p.

Risk environments are decision environments that involve a lack of complete certainty but that include an awareness of probabilities associated with the possible outcomes of various courses of action. p.

Rites are standardized and recurring activities used at special times to influence the behaviour and understanding of organizational members. p.

Rituals are systems of rites. p.

A role is a set of expectations for the behaviour of a person holding a particular office or position. p.

Role ambiguity is uncertainty about what other group members expect of a person. p.

Role conflict occurs when a person is unable to respond to the expectations of one or more group members. p.

Role culture is a type of organizational structure in which set rules, task procedures and job descriptions are particularly important. p.

Role overload occurs when too much is expected of individuals within their role designation. p.

Routine problems are problems that arise routinely and that can be addressed through standard responses. p.

A saga is an embellished heroic account of the story of the founding of an organization. p.

Satisficing means choosing the first satisfactory alternative rather than the optimal decision. p.

Schemas are cognitive frameworks developed through experience. p.

Screening is the umbrella term for the ways we selectively perceive objects and people. p.

Selective perception refers to the ways in which we categorize and organize stimuli leading us to perceive the world in a unique way. p.

Self-concept is the concept that individuals have of themselves as physical, social and spiritual or moral beings. p.

Self-efficacy refers to a person's belief that they can perform adequately in a situation. p.

A self-fulfilling prophecy occurs when a prophecy comes true simply because it has been made. For example, if we label people in a particular way, they will behave in the expected manner. p.

Self-managing teams are small groups of people empowered to manage themselves and the work they do on a day-to-day basis. p.

Shaping is the creation of a new behaviour by the positive reinforcement of successive approximations to the desired behaviour. p.

A shared power strategy (or normative-re-educative strategy) attempts to bring about change by identifying or establishing values and assumptions so that support for the change emerges naturally. p.

Shared values are the set of coherent values held by members of the organization that link them together. p.

A simple design is a configuration involving one or two ways of specializing individuals and units. p.

Single-loop learning is learning by rote, with an emphasis on memorization rather than comprehension. p.

Situational constraints are organizational factors that do not allow workers to perform adequately. p.

Situational control is the extent to which leaders can determine what their group is going to do and what the outcomes of their actions and decisions are going to be. p.

The social information-processing approach argues that individual needs, task perceptions and reactions are a result of socially constructed realities. p.

Social learning is learning that is achieved through the reciprocal interaction between people and their environments. p.

Social loafing is the tendency of people not to work as hard in groups as they would individually. p.

Sociology is the study of social structures and patterns, both in whole societies and subgroups. p.

Socio-technical job design is the design of jobs to optimize the relationship between the technology system and the social system. p.

The span of control is the number of individuals reporting to a supervisor. p.

Staff personnel are groups that assist the line units by performing specialized services for the organization. p.

Standardization is the degree to which the range of actions in a job or series of jobs is limited. p.

Status is the indication of a person's relative rank, worth or standing within a group. p.

Status incongruence occurs when a person's expressed status within a group is inconsistent with his or her standing in another context. p.

A stereotype is a view of an individual person or group which is derived from assumed wider characteristics, e.g. Italians are emotional. p.

Stereotyping describes the process by which we attribute characteristics to an individual based on our understanding of wider groups, e.g. she is Italian therefore she is an emotional person. p.

A stimulus is something that incites action. p.

The storming stage is the second stage of group development, which is marked by a period of high emotion and tension among group members. Hostility and infighting may occur while individual members begin to understand each other's interpersonal styles. p.

Strategic alliances are announced cooperative agreements or joint ventures between two independent organizations. p.

Stress is a state of tension experienced by individuals facing extraordinary demands, constraints or opportunities. p.

Stress prevention involves taking action to prevent the emergence of stress that becomes destructive. p.

Stressors are things that cause stress (for example, work, nonwork and personal factors). p.

Subcultures are unique patterns of values and philosophies within a group that are not inconsistent with the dominant culture of the larger organization or social system. p.

Sub-goal optimization occurs when a group achieves its goals at the expense of the goals of others. p.

Substance goals are concerned with outcomes tied to the 'content' issues at hand in a negotiation. p.

Substantive conflict is conflict that occurs in the form of a fundamental disagreement over ends or goals to be pursued and the means for their accomplishment. p.

Substitutes for leadership are organization, individual or task-situational variables that substitute for leadership in causing performance/human resource maintenance. p.

Supportive leadership is a leadership style that focuses on employee needs and wellbeing and promotes a friendly work climate; it is similar to consideration. p.

Synergy is the creation of a whole that is greater than the sum of its parts. p.

Systems goals are goals concerned with conditions within the organization that are expected to increase its survival potential. p.

Task activities are the various things members do that directly contribute to the performance of important group tasks. p.

Taskforces are temporary teams created to fulfil a well-defined task within a fairly short period of time. p.

Task performance is the quality and quantity of work produced. p.

A **teaching organization** aims to pass on learning experiences to others, thereby allowing the organization to achieve and maintain success. p.

Teambuilding is a sequence of planned action steps designed to gather and analyse data on the functioning of a group, and to implement changes to increase its operating effectiveness. p.

A **team role** is a pattern of behaviour characterizing the ways one team member interacts with others. p.

Teams are small groups of people with complementary skills, who work together as a unit to achieve a common purpose for which they hold themselves collectively accountable. p.

Teamwork is when members of a team work together in a way that represents certain core values that promote the use of skills to accomplish certain goals. p.

The **technological imperative** is the idea that if an organization does not adjust its internal structure to the requirements of technology, it will not be successful. p.

Technology is the combination of resources, knowledge and techniques that creates a product or service output for an organization. p.

Telework principles relate to work conducted remotely from the central organization using information technology. p.

Temporary formal work groups are created for a specific purpose and typically disband once that purpose has been accomplished. p.

The total integration stage is the fourth stage of group development, which sees the emergence of a mature, organized and well-functioning group; it is also referred to as the performing stage. p.

Tough guy culture is a type of organizational culture driven by a need to take quick decisions, leading to a preoccupation with risk taking and a competitive ethos. p.

Transactional leadership involves daily exchanges between leaders and followers, and is necessary for achieving routine performance on which leaders and followers agree. p.

Transformational leadership is a leadership style by which the followers' goals are broadened and elevated, and confidence is gained to go beyond expectations. p.

Transmission is the actual communication of a message from one person to another through a chosen channel. p.

Turnover is the churn of employees into and out of a work organization. p.

Uncertain environments are decision environments in which managers are unable to assign probabilities to the possible outcomes of various courses of action. p.

The term unconscious, within Freud's theory of personality, refers to basic desires below the conscious level, which drive our behaviour and potentially conflict with values learned through socialization. p.

Unfreezing is the first stage of the planned change process in which a situation is prepared for change. p.

Unity of command is the situation in an organization where each worker has a clear reporting relationship to only one supervisor. p.

Unplanned change is change that occurs at random or spontaneously and without a change agent's direction. p.

Valence represents the values that the individual attaches to various work outcomes. p.

Value-added managers are managers whose efforts clearly enable their work units to achieve high productivity and improve 'bottom-line' performance. p.

Value congruence occurs when individuals express positive feelings on encountering others who exhibit values similar to their own. p.

Values are global beliefs that guide actions and judgements across a variety of situations. p.

Vertical loading involves increasing job depth by adding responsibilities, like planning and controlling, previously held by supervisors. p.

Vertical specialization is a hierarchical division of labour that distributes formal authority and establishes how critical decisions will be made. p.

Virtual organizations comprise individuals, groups and businesses that work together across time and space. p.

A virtual team is one whose members work interdependently towards the achievement of a common goal across space and time. p.

Voluntary reduced work time (V-Time or time–income tradeoffs) is a scheme by which workers trade income for additional leisure time that is packaged to suit their needs. p.

Whistleblowers are employees, ex-employees or other people connected to an organization who report perceived misconduct on the part of that organization to a person or body who can take or initiate action. p.

Work flow interdependency is the way work flows in an organization from one group to the next. p.

Work hard/play hard culture is a type of organizational culture that stresses the twin roles of performance and fun at work. p.

Work–life balance refers to a concern which people have with balancing work hours with other responsibilities including caring for children or adults. It has become a key issue for employers with the advent of 24/7 societies and customers' expectations of where and when services should be provided for them. p.

Work teams or units are task-oriented groups that include a manager and his or her direct reports. p.

Workforce diversity means a workforce consisting of a broad mix of workers from different racial and ethnic backgrounds, of different ages and genders and of different domestic and national cultures. p.

Zero hours contracts are defined as arrangements where work is not guaranteed; rather a worker is expected to be available as and when an employer requires them. The worker is paid only for the hours in which they actually perform tasks. p.

The zone of indifference is the range of authoritative requests to which an employee is willing to respond without subjecting the directives to critical evaluation or judgement – that is, the requests to which the employee is indifferent. p.

INDEX